BAGENDON. Air view, from E.

The excavated areas of Monument (1) are in the valley at C. The Roman road (arrowed) from Cirencester to Gloucester passes behind S, the Romano-British settlement at Stancombe (DUNTISBOURNE ROUSE (4)).

ROYAL COMMISSION ON HISTORICAL MONUMENTS
ENGLAND

Ancient and Historical Monuments in the COUNTY OF GLOUCESTER

Volume One
Iron Age and Romano-British Monuments in the Gloucestershire Cotswolds

LONDON · HER MAJESTY'S STATIONERY OFFICE
MCMLXXVI

First published 1976

ISBN 0 11 700713 7* (red binding)

ISBN 0 11 700717 x* (grey binding)

TABLE OF CONTENTS

	PAGE
LIST OF ILLUSTRATIONS	iv
CHAIRMAN'S FOREWORD	xiii
THE ROYAL WARRANT	xv
LIST OF COMMISSIONERS	xviii
OFFICIAL REPORT	xix
SECTIONAL PREFACE	xxiii
The Iron Age	xxiv
Discredited 'Hill-forts' and 'Camps'	xxix
The Roman Period	xxxiv
Appendix A. Place-Names	lii
Appendix B. Ring-Ditches	lv
EDITORIAL NOTES	lvi
INVENTORY of Iron Age and Romano-British Monuments in the Gloucestershire Cotswolds	1
CHRONOLOGY etc.	136
GLOSSARY	137
ABBREVIATIONS and SHORTENED TITLES	139
INDEX	140
Large MAPS and PLANS	End pocket

LIST OF ILLUSTRATIONS

PLATE OR (p.) PAGE

GENERAL

Map showing distribution of Iron Age and Romano-British monuments . End pocket
Map showing parish boundaries, with list of parishes . . . . . End pocket

PREFACE

Geological map of area N.E. of Cirencester, showing distribution of Iron Age and Romano-British monuments . . . . opp. p. xxiii
Selected hill-forts, comparative plans . . . . opp. p. xxvi
Dyke systems at Bagendon and Minchinhampton, comparative plans . . . p. xxviii
Discredited 'hill-forts' and 'camps'
Dixton Hill, Alderton. Plan . . . . p. xxxi
Eubury, Condicote. Plan . . . . p. xxxii
,, Air view 68
Hawkesbury Knoll. Air view from N.W.† 68
Rendcomb Camp. Plan . . . . p. xxxiii
Upper Coscombe, Stanway. Air views† 67
,, ,, Plan . . . . p. xxxiii
Drakestone Point, Stinchcombe. Profile . . . . p. xxxiv
Langley Hill, Winchcombe. Plan . . . . p. xxxiv
Romano-British monuments near Cirencester. General plan . . . . opp. p. xxxvi
Rectilinear enclosures, probably Romano-British . . . . p. xxxix
Roman villas, comparative plans of selected examples . . . . . . opp. p. xl
Roman Roads and Tracks . . . . p. xlvi
Prehistoric and Romano-British monuments in the area of Upper Thames river gravels p. liv

PARISHES

ALDERTON
Natural ridges and hollows on Dixton Hill . . . . p. xxxi

ALDSWORTH
(1) 'Celtic' fields (also Eastleach) Plan . . . . p. 2
,, Detail . . . . p. 1

AMPNEY CRUCIS
(1) Probable settlement. Plan . . . . p. 3

AMPNEY ST. PETER
Map . . . . p. 3
(1) Ranbury Ring hill-fort. Plan and profiles . . . . p. 4

AVENING
(1) and (2) Romano-British settlements. Plan . . . . p. 5

BADGEWORTH
(1) Roman villa at Dryhill. Plan . . . . p. 5

BADMINTON
(1) 'Celtic' fields. Air photograph 42

BAGENDON
General air view from E. . . . . Frontispiece
Dyke systems at Bagendon and Minchinhampton. Comparative plans . . . p. xxviii
(1) Iron Age and Romano-British settlement. Plan . . . . . . opp. p. 7
,, ,, Profiles . . . . . . p. 7
,, ,, Crop-marks of Dyke 'a' etc., from N.E.† 46
,, ,, Crop-marks of Dyke 'a' and possible enclosure 'o', from W.† . . 46
,, ,, Dyke 'a', W. of Cutham Lane, looking S. 47
,, ,, Air view, looking S.W.† . . 47

Barnsley
(1) Roman villa. Plan . . . p. 10
(2) 'Celtic' fields . . . opp. p. 11
(4) Probable settlement. Air view from E. . . . 55

Barrington
Map . . . p. 11
(2) Romano-British settlement. Air view from N.W., before 1939 . . . 50

Batsford
(1) Romano-British settlement at Dorn. General plan of area . . . p. 12
" " Detailed plan . . . p. 12
" " Air view from S.W.† . . . 48

Bibury
Map . . . p. 14
(1) Ablington Camp. Plan . . . p. 14
(2) Roman villa. Plan of earthworks . . . p. 15

Bisley with Lypiatt
Map . . . p. 15
(1) Roman villa. Plan . . . p. 16

Blockley
(1) Probable Romano-British settlement at Upton. Plan . . . p. 17

Bourton-on-the-Water
Map . . . p. 18
(1) Salmonsbury. Plan and profile . . . opp. p. 19
(2a) Roman Buildings, Lansdown. 'Leadenwell' Villa. Plan . . . p. 20

Brockworth
Map . . . p. 41
(1) Cross-ridge dyke. Plan and profile . . . p. 22

Buckland
(1) Hill-fort on Burhill. Plan and profile . . . pp. 22–3

Charlton Kings
(2) Linear dyke. Plan and profile . . . p. 24

Chedworth
Map . . . p. 25
(1) Roman villa, Chedworth Woods. Plan . . . p. 26
" " Apses etc. . . . 25
" " Hypocaust . . . 25
" " Column bases . . . 26
" " Pillar . . . 26
" " Miscellaneous columns . . . 26
" " Corridor to room 14 . . . 6
" " Pavement of room 5 . . . 3
" " Pavement of room 5 . . . 4 and 5
" " Pavement of room 10 . . . 2
" " Pavement of room 11 . . . 6
" " Pavement of room 14 . . . 6
" " Fragments of mosaics in room 22 . . . 7
(6) Roman villa, Listercombe. Plan . . . p. 28

Cherington
(1) Roman building, Hailstone. Plan . . . p. 29

Cirencester
Geological map of area to N.E., showing distribution of Iron Age and Romano-British monuments . . . opp. p. xxiii
Romano-British monuments near Cirencester. General plan . . . opp. p. xxxvi
(1) Roman villa, The Barton. Mosaic pavement . . . 1
(3) Romano-British settlement. Plan . . . p. 30

CIRENCESTER (*cont.*)
(4) Enclosure. Plan . . . p. 30
,, Crop-marks† . . . 65
(5) Enclosures. Plan . . . p. 30
(6) Enclosures. Plan . . . p. 31

COATES
Map . . . p. 31
(1) Trewsbury hill-fort. Plan and profiles . . . p. 32
(6) Enclosure. Air view from S.E. . . . 58

COBERLEY
(1) Hill-fort on Crickley Hill. Plan and profile . . . p. 33
,, ,, During excavations . . . 40

COLESBOURNE
Map . . . p. 54
(1) Norbury hill-fort. Plan and profile . . . pp. 34–5
,, Air view from S.W.† . . . 37
(2) Roman villa. Plan by Lysons . . . p. 36
,, Plan as at present . . . p. 35
,, Pavement of corridor in Building A (Lysons) . . . 7
,, ,, Building B (Lysons) . . . 7
,, Column bases etc. probably from Colesbourne villa . . . 27

COLN ST. ALDWYNS
(1) Dean Camp hill-fort. Plan and profiles . . . pp. 36–7
(2) Romano-British settlement, The Chessels. Map (2½ inches to 1 mile) and plan p. 96

COLN ST. DENIS
(1) Enclosure and linear ditches. Plan . . . p. 37

COMPTON ABDALE
(1) Roman villa. General plan of area . . . p. 38
,, Plan made in 1931 . . . p. 38

CONDICOTE
Eubury. Discredited hill-fort. Plan . . . p. xxxii
,, ,, Air view . . . 68
(1) Pit-alignment, ditch and enclosure. Plan . . . p. 39
,, N. part, and ditch. Air view . . . 56

COWLEY
(6) Enclosure. Plan . . . p. 40
,, Air view from S.W.† . . . 57

CRANHAM
Map . . . p. 41

DAGLINGWORTH
Map . . . p. 42
(3) Enclosure. Plan . . . p. 42

DIDMARTON
(1) Probable settlement. Plan . . . p. 42

DOWDESWELL
(1) Hill-fort. Plan and profiles . . . pp. 43–4
,, Air view from N.W.† . . . 38

DOWN AMPNEY
(1) Enclosures and linear ditches. (2) Settlement and road. Plan . . . p. 44
(4) Rectilinear enclosure. Plan . . . p. 45

DOYNTON
Map . . . p. 45
(1) Royal Camp. Plan and profile . . . p. 46

DRIFFIELD
(1) Roman villa and enclosures. Plan . . . p. 47
,, ,, Air view from S.† . . . 49
(2), (3) Enclosures and linear ditches. Plan . . . p. 47

DUNTISBOURNE ABBOTS
Map . . . . . p. 48
Track N. of (1). Air view from S.E. 62
(2) Enclosure and broad track. Air view from S.E. 63

DUNTISBOURNE ROUSE
Maps. . . . . . p. 48
(1) Pinbury hill-fort. Plan . . . . . p. 49
(4) Romano-British settlement, Stancombe. Plan . . . . . p. 50
,, ,, From S.E. 50
,, ,, Building 'a' 51

DYRHAM AND HINTON
Map . . . . . p. 50
(1) Hill-fort on Hinton Hill. Plan and profile . . . . . p. 51
(2) Probable settlement. Plan . . . . . p. 51
,, Air view from N.† 64

EASTLEACH
(1) 'Celtic' fields and (2) Roman road. Plan . . . . . p. 52
,, ,, From S.E. 43
(2) Roman road. Profile . . . . . p. 52

EBRINGTON
Map . . . . . p. 53
(1) Roman villa. Plan . . . . . p. 53
,, Mosaic pavement 8

EDGEWORTH
(1) Cross-ridge dyke. Plan and profile . . . . . p. 53

ELKSTONE
Map . . . . . p. 54
(2) Enclosure. Air view from N. 59

FAIRFORD
(1) Track. Plan . . . . . p. 55
(2) Enclosures and linear ditches. Plan . . . . . p. 55
Enclosure 'a'. Air view from N.† 66
(3–6) Enclosures. Plan . . . . . opp. p. 55
(3) Enclosure and other crop-marks, from S.W.† 58
(4) Enclosures and tracks. Air view from S.E.† 66
(6) ,, Air view† 61

FARMINGTON
Map . . . . . p. 88
(1) Roman villa. Plan . . . . . p. 56
(2), (4) Romano-British settlements. (3) Enclosure. Plans. . . . . . p. 56

FROCESTER
Map . . . . . p. 57
(2) Roman villa. Plan . . . . . p. 58
,, Mosaics 8

GOTHERINGTON
(1) Nottingham Hill Camp. Plan and profile . . . . . opp. p. 59

GREAT RISSINGTON
Map . . . . . p. 59
(2) Probable settlement. (3) Pit-alignment. Plan . . . . . p. 60

GREAT WITCOMBE
(1) Roman villa. Plan . . . . . p. 60
,, From N.W. 24
,, Mosaic in room 5 12
,, Mosaic in room 6 11
,, Mosaic in room 10 10
,, Column base 28

GREAT WITCOMBE (*cont.*)
(1) Roman villa (*cont.*)
,, Column and balustrade fragments 28
,, Columns 29

HAMPNETT
(1) Enclosure. Plan . . . . p. 62

HARESFIELD
Map . . . . p. 62
(1) Hill-fort on Ring Hill. (2) 'The Bulwarks'. Plan . . . . . . p. 63
(2) 'The Bulwarks'. Profile . . . . p. 64

HATHEROP
(1) Probable settlement. Plan . . . . p. 64

HAWKESBURY
Hawkesbury Knoll from N.W. showing strip lynchets 68

HORSLEY
(3) Enclosure. Plan . . . . p. 65

HORTON
Map . . . . p. 66
(1) 'The Castles' hill-fort. Plan and profile . . . . p. 65
,, ,, Interior from S.W. 35
,, ,, Air view from N.† 35

ICOMB
Map . . . . p. 66
(1) Probable hill-fort. Plan . . . . p. 67
,, Air view from W. 36

KEMBLE
(1) Probable settlement . . . . p. 68
,, Air view from S.† 63

KEMPSFORD
Circular enclosure of Highworth type 64
(2) Enclosures, tracks and linear ditches. Plan . . . . p. 68
(3) Enclosures and linear ditches. Plan . . . . p. 69
(4–5) Enclosures etc. Plan . . . . opp. p. 55
(6) Enclosures. Plan . . . . p. 69
,, Air view from S.E.† 62
(7) Enclosures, tracks and linear ditches. Plan . . . . p. 69
,, ,, Air view of crop-marks 60

KING'S STANLEY
(1) Cross-ridge dyke. Plan and profile . . . . p. 70

KINGSCOTE
Map . . . . p. 71
(1) Romano-British settlement, The Chessalls. Plan . . . . . End pocket
(4–6) Enclosures, tracks and linear ditches. Plan . . . . p. 72

LECHLADE
Map . . . . opp. p. 73
(1–6) Pit, enclosures, ditches, tracks and settlement. Plan . . . . . p. 74
(2) Ring-ditches, enclosures and tracks. Air view from S.† 60
(5) Iron Age and Romano-British settlement. Plan . . . . . End pocket
,, ,, Soil marks to E. of modern road. Air view 52
(8) Enclosures and tracks. Air view† 61
,, ,, Plan . . . . opp. p. 55
(9) Enclosure and linear ditches. Plan . . . . p. 75
(10–13) Enclosures, tracks, linear ditches and settlement. Plan . . . . p. 76

LECKHAMPTON
Map . . . . p. 77
(1) Hill-fort. Plan and profile. (2) Barrow . . . . p. 77

LONGBOROUGH
(1) Probable settlement. Plan . . . . p. 78

LOWER SLAUGHTER
Map . . . . p. 18
(1) Romano-British settlement. Plan . . . . opp. p. 79
,, ,, Crop-marks and soil marks from S.E. 53
(2) Enclosure. From S. 55
(4) Circular enclosure. From W. 65

MINCHINHAMPTON
Map . . . . p. 81
Dyke systems at Bagendon and Minchinhampton, comparative plans . . p. xxviii
General air view of monuments (1–3), (7) and (8)† 44
(1) 'The Bulwarks', Iron Age bank and ditch. Looking S.W. 44
(1) 'The Bulwarks'. (3) Bank and ditch 45
(1–8) Banks and ditches. Plan . . . . opp. p. 82
,, Profiles . . . . p. 82
(7) Iron Age bank and ditch, facing S.W. 45

MORETON-IN-MARSH
(1) Probable settlement. Plan . . . . p. 84

NORTH CERNEY
(1) 'The Ditches'. Air view from W. 36
(2) Hill-fort. (3) Romano-British settlement. Plan . . . . p. 85

NORTH NIBLEY
Map . . . . p. 86
(1) Brackenbury Ditches hill-fort. Plan and profiles . . . . . . p. 87

NORTHLEACH WITH EASTINGTON
Map . . . . p. 88
(1) Norbury Camp hill-fort. Plan . . . . p. 89
,, ,, Profiles . . . . p. 88
(3) Linear ditches and enclosures. Plan . . . . p. 90

NOTGROVE
(1) Enclosures. Plan . . . . p. 88

OXENTON
(1) Iron Age settlement, 'The Knolls'. Plan and profile . . . . . . p. 92

PAINSWICK
Map . . . . p. 93
(1) Kimsbury Hill-fort. Plan and profile . . . . p. 93
,, Air view, from S.E.† 37
(2) Roman villa. Plan . . . . p. 94
,, Pavement 8

POOLE KEYNES
(1) Wide track and enclosure. Plan . . . . p. 94

PRESTON
(1) Enclosures and linear ditches. Plan . . . . p. 95
(2), (3) Enclosures and linear ditches. Plan . . . . p. 95

QUENINGTON
Map . . . . p. 96
(1) Probable settlement and linear ditches. Plan . . . . p. 96
(2) Roman road. (3) Probable settlement. (4) Track . . . . . . p. 96
(5) Enclosures and linear ditches. Plan . . . . p. 97

RANDWICK
(1) Cross-ridge dyke. Plan and profile . . . . p. 97

RENDCOMB
Natural ridges and pillow mounds. Plan . . . . p. xxxiii

RODMARTON
Crop-marks (ST 928987). Air view from S.W.† 66
(1) Roman villa, 'Hocberry'. Plan . . . . p. 98

SAPPERTON
(1) Roman settlement. Plan . . . . p. 99
,, Air view, from S.E.† 49

SEVENHAMPTON
(1) Rectangular enclosure. Air view from S. 54

SHERBORNE
Map . . . . p. 100
(1) Romano-British settlement. Plan . . . . p. 100

SHIPTON
(1) Romano-British settlement. (2) Enclosure. Plan . . . . . . p. 101

SIDDINGTON
(2) Enclosures. Plan . . . . p. 101
(3) Romano-British settlement. (4), (5) Enclosures and trackway. Plan . . p. 102
(6) Romano-British settlement. Plan . . . . p. 102

SODBURY
Map . . . . p. 66
Possible enclosure. Air view, from S.† 59
(1) Sodbury Camp hill-fort. Plan and profiles . . . . p. 104
,, ,, Air view, from N.† 34
,, ,, Interior, between N. ramparts looking S.E. . . 34

SOMERFORD KEYNES
(1) Probable settlement. Plan . . . . p. 105
(3) Enclosure associated with track and other crop-marks. Air view from N.W. 59
(4) Probable settlement. Plan . . . . p. 105

SOUTH CERNEY
(1–3) Enclosures etc., and possible trackways. Plan . . . . p. 106

SOUTHAM
Map . . . . p. 107
(1) Hill-fort, Cleeve Cloud. Plan and profile . . . . p. 108
,, ,, Air view, from N.W.† 40
(2–6) General air view from S.W. 41
(4), (5) 'The Ring' and Ringwork. Plan and profiles . . . . . . p. 108
,, ,, Air view from E.† 41
(6) Dyke. Profiles . . . . p. 109

SOUTHROP
(1) Enclosure. Plan . . . . p. 109
,, Air view, from W.† 54

STANTON
Map . . . . p. 109
(1) Hill-fort on Shenberrow Hill. Plan and profile . . . . p. 110
,, ,, Air view, from N. 39

STANWAY
Ridges and soil-marks, Upper Coscombe. Air view, from S.† 67
,, ,, ,, from W. 67
,, ,, Plan . . . . p. xxxiii
(1–6) Roman buildings etc., undated enclosures and tracks. Plan . . . . p. 110

STINCHCOMBE
Map . . . . p. 86
Natural ridges, Drakestone Point. Profile . . . . p. xxxiv

SUDELEY
Map . . . . p. 112
(1) Roel Camp, ?hill-fort. Plan and profile . . . . p. 113
,, ,, Air view, from W.† 32
(2) Roman villa, Wadfield. Plan . . . . p. 113
,, ,, Pavement, after Lysons 13
(4) Roman villa, Spoonley Wood. Plan . . . . p. 114
,, ,, Room 18 from N.W. 24
,, ,, Pavement, room 8 14

Roman villa, Spoonley Wood. Rooms 7 and 18 15
,, ,, ,, Man with rake 15
,, ,, ,, Column base 30

SWELL
Map . . . . p. 115
(2) Roman villa, Abbotswood. Plan . . . . p. 116

TEMPLE GUITING
(1) Beckbury Camp hill-fort. Plan and profile . . . . p. 117
(4) Pit-alignment. Air view, from N. 56
(5) Enclosures and ditches. Air view from S.E. 57
(4–9) Pit-alignment, enclosures and ditches. Plan . . . . p. 118
(10) Enclosure and ditch. Plan . . . . p. 119
(11) Enclosure. Plan . . . . p. 119
,, Air view from S.E.† 54

TORMARTON
(1) 'Celtic' fields. Air view, from S.E. 43
(2) Rectangular enclosure. Air view, from W.† 54
(1), (2) 'Celtic' fields and enclosure. Plan . . . . p. 120
(3) Enclosure. Plan . . . . p. 120

ULEY
Map . . . . p. 121
(1) Uley Bury hill-fort. Plan and profile . . . . p. 122
,, ,, Air view from N.E.† 33
,, ,, Crop-marks inside hill-fort. Air view 32

WESTON SUBEDGE
Map . . . . p. 124

WHITTINGTON
Map . . . . p. 124
(2) Romano-British settlement, Wycomb. Plans . . . . . . opp. p. 125
,, ,, Air view, from S.W.† 48
(3) Roman villa. Area plan . . . . p. 127
,, Plan of building . . . . p. 128
,, Pavements in rooms 3 and 5, and in corridor II 9
,, Impost 30
,, Unprovenanced column base 30

WILLERSEY
Map . . . . p. 128
(1) Hill-fort. Plan and profile . . . . p. 129

WINCHCOMBE
Natural ridges, Langley Hill. Plan . . . . p. xxxiv

WINDRUSH
Map . . . . p. 100
(1) Windrush Camp hill-fort. Plan and profile . . . . p. 130

WITHINGTON
Map . . . . p. 131
(2) Roman villa. Plan . . . . p. 132
,, Mosaic pavement in B.M. 15
,, ,, of corridor (Lysons) 13
,, ,, ,, ... 14
,, Mosaic pavements as drawn by Lysons 16
,, During excavation (Lysons) 51

WOODCHESTER
(1) Roman villa. Plan . . . . p. 133
,, Plan of churchyard and adjoining land (Lysons) 31
,, Mosaic pavement, room 1 17
,, ,, ,, Details 19–21
,, ,, rooms 3 and 6 18

Woodchester (*cont.*)
Roman villa. Mosaic pavement, room 10 19
,, ,, corridors 5 and 8. 22
,, ,, rooms 12, 15 and 18 22
,, ,, corridor 2 23
,, ,, room 13 23
Wotton-under-Edge
(1) Enclosures. Plan . . . . p. 134
Yanworth
(2) Ditches. Plan . . . . p. 135

In the foregoing list, † indicates a photograph supplied by the Committee for Aerial Photography in the University of Cambridge. Mrs. O'Neil has supplied the photograph of Ebrington villa on Plate 8 and all photographs on Plate 9; those of the Frocester villa on Plate 8 were provided by Captain Gracie, R.N. The photograph of the Withington mosaic on Plate 15 is the property of the British Museum. The North Cerney photograph on Plate 36 was taken by Mr. W. A. Baker as also was that of Stanway from W. on Plate 67. The Crickley Hill photograph on Plate 40 was supplied by the Committee for Research into the Iron Age in the North-west Cotswolds. Plate 42 was photographed by the R.A.F. The view of Tormarton on Plate 43, taken by Major W. G. Allen, is the property of the Ashmolean Museum. Maps and plans based on data hitherto unpublished, generously made available by private research workers, include that of the Roman villa at Barnsley (1) by Dr. Graham Webster; of the fields associated with this villa by Mr. P. J. Fowler; of Roughground Farm, Lechlade (5) by Mrs. M. U. Jones; and of Chessels in Lower Slaughter (1) by Mrs. H. E. O'Neil.

FOREWORD

By the Chairman, the Rt. Hon. the Lord Adeane, P.C., G.C.B., G.C.V.O.

The responsibility of the Royal Commission on Historical Monuments to record ancient Monuments which are threatened with obliteration by present-day development has prompted the compilation of this Inventory of Iron Age and Romano-British Monuments in the Cotswold area of Gloucestershire.

For convenience of reference we have continued our usual practice of arranging the Inventory under the names of the modern parishes in which the Monuments lie, even though these divisions are irrelevant to the subjects discussed. Our acceptance, for similar reasons, of the county boundary to delimit the area included in the volume results in the omission of the most south-westerly Cotswold parishes, which are in Somerset. Our investigators' notes on these parishes are lodged in the Field Monuments Section of the National Monuments Record and are open for consultation by interested students. Apart from this, the use of the county boundary entails no serious truncation of the Cotswold area, the bounds of which are largely a matter of choice. The Jurassic ridge of which the Cotswolds are part extends across England, from Lincolnshire to Dorset.

The use of the county boundary enables us to include in the volume some small but important areas not on the wolds limestone, notably the parishes of FAIRFORD, KEMPSFORD and LECHLADE, where abundant traces of Iron Age and Romano-British occupation occur on the river-gravels of the upper Thames.

The Inventory does not include Bronze Age and earlier Monuments since these consist predominantly of burial mounds, already extensively catalogued by H. E. O'Neil and L. V. Grinsell (*Transactions of the Bristol and Gloucestershire Archaeological Society*, vol. 79 (1960), part i). Roman Cirencester is discussed only summarily because a long-term programme of excavation and study by the Cirencester Excavation Committee is still in progress.

While air photographs were being examined for the purposes of the Inventory a large number of ring-ditches were discovered, most of them probably of the Bronze Age; these have been described elsewhere (I. F. Smith in *Archaeology and the Landscape* (ed. P. J. Fowler, 1972), chapter vi), but a brief note will be found on page lv. The discovery of several mediaeval earthworks has been another by-product of our investigators' work, and notes on these have been passed to the Deserted Mediaeval Villages Research Group. So-called 'pillow-mounds', mediaeval and later, occur in large numbers in the area and a brief note on them appears in the Inventory (*s.v.* MINCHINHAMPTON, where they are used to indicate the relative antiquity of other features); a further account will shortly be published elsewhere by our investigator, Mr. H. C. Bowen.

Any field survey subject to chronological limits must, on grounds of probability, admit items which may eventually be found to lie wholly or partly outside the period envisaged. Conversely it is sometimes possible to show that items which were formerly thought to lie within the scope of a survey do not in fact do so. Among the latter are a number of so-called 'hill-forts' and 'camps' in the Gloucestershire Cotswolds which now appear to have been identified wrongly. Because absolute certainty in the question cannot always be claimed and because some of the sites require further investigation, these 'monuments' are discussed in some detail in our Sectional Preface.

All accessible Monuments described in the Inventory have been inspected by one or more of our investigators and manv of them have been the subject of prolonged study. After compilation, the drafts of the text and preliminary versions of the maps and plans have been carefully scrutinised by my fellow Commissioners. As in other inventories we have thought best in the matter of place-names to adhere to the spelling used in the latest series of Ordnance Survey maps, without prejudice as to accuracy. Notes on the archaeological significance of certain place-names will be found on page lii.

In the Inventory the parishes are dealt with alphabetically, and a list of parishes together with a general map will be found at the end of the volume. Under each parish heading, generally, Iron Age Monuments are dealt with first, then Roman, and finally 'undated' Monuments. In many parish accounts an introductory paragraph serves to draw attention to important Monuments, to mention unprovenanced finds and sites which can no longer be precisely located, and to give general information relevant to the Iron Age and Romano-British periods.

Most of our hill-fort plans are based on Ordnance Survey drawings, checked by our investigators and amended where this appeared desirable. Our plans of Roman villas are based on those made by the excavators, willingly supplied in the case of modern discoveries. Some area plans, notably of 'Chessels' in LOWER SLAUGHTER, of Roughground Farm in LECHLADE and of the villa fields in BARNSLEY are also due to the generosity of modern archaeologists. To Samuel Lysons, whose rare talents are perpetuated in three splendid volumes, *Reliquiae Britannico-Romanae*, published in 1813 and 1817, the Commission's debt can hardly be exaggerated. Plans of sites revealed by crop-marks on air photographs should be regarded as carefully considered sketches rather than as measured drawings; we do not yet have facilities to make accurate transcripts from low-level oblique photographs. The sketches, however, are nearly always compiled from several photographs taken under differing conditions. Our most extensive and detailed crop-mark plan (FAIRFORD (3–6) with part of LECHLADE) was transcribed from vertical air photographs taken for us by Cambridge University Committee for Aerial Photography and is therefore accurate, though it may include modern features as well as ancient indications from outside our period. As the interpretation of crop-marks from air photographs is to some extent subjective, the volume includes reproductions of a large number of these photographs.

The compilation of so extensive a survey would be impossible without the help and sufferance of the many landowners within whose property the Monuments lie, and to them, too numerous for individual mention, I express the Commission's sincere thanks. The names of the directors of public institutions and those of private persons to whom we are indebted for help will be found in our Official Report, reprinted elsewhere in the volume. Special acknowledgement must, however, be made of the help and encouragement constantly afforded to our investigators by Mrs. H. E. O'Neil, and by Captain H. S. Gracie, R.N. (rtd.).

In an inventory such as this there must be some mistakes, but I believe they are neither numerous nor serious; my colleagues and I will, of course, welcome any corrections that may be proposed with a view to a future edition. Such corrections will be added to the Commission's files, which may be consulted by accredited persons on application to the Secretary. Copies of the photographs reproduced in the volume, and of many others taken while the volume was in preparation, are obtainable from the National Monuments Record.

ADEANE

THE ROYAL WARRANT

WHITEHALL,
2ND OCTOBER, 1963

The QUEEN has been pleased to issue a Commission under Her Majesty's Royal Sign Manual to the following effect:

ELIZABETH R.

ELIZABETH THE SECOND, by the Grace of God of the United Kingdom of Great Britain and Northern Ireland and of Our other Realms and Territories, QUEEN, Head of the Commonwealth, Defender of the Faith,

To

Our Right Trusty and Entirely-beloved Cousin and Counsellor Robert Arthur James, Marquess of Salisbury, Knight of Our Most Noble Order of the Garter;

Our Trusty and Well-beloved:

Sir Albert Edward Richardson, Knight Commander of the Royal Victorian Order;
Sir John Newenham Summerson, Knight, Commander of Our Most Excellent Order of the British Empire;
Nikolaus Pevsner, Esquire, Commander of Our Most Excellent Order of the British Empire;
Christopher Edward Clive Hussey, Esquire, Commander of Our Most Excellent Order of the British Empire;
Ian Archibald Richmond, Esquire, Commander of Our Most Excellent Order of the British Empire;
Henry Clifford Darby, Esquire, Officer of Our Most Excellent Order of the British Empire;
Donald Benjamin Harden, Esquire, Officer of Our Most Excellent Order of the British Empire;
John Grahame Douglas Clark, Esquire;
Howard Montagu Colvin, Esquire;
Vivian Hunter Galbraith, Esquire;
William Abel Pantin, Esquire;
Stuart Piggott, Esquire;
Courtenay Arthur Ralegh Radford, Esquire;
Arnold Joseph Taylor, Esquire;
Francis Wormald, Esquire,

GREETING!

Whereas We have deemed it expedient that the Commissioners appointed to the Royal Commission on the Ancient and Historical Monuments and Constructions of England shall serve for such periods as We by the hand of Our First Lord of the Treasury may specify and that the said Commissioners shall, if The National Buildings Record is liquidated, assume the control and management of such part of The National Buildings Record's collection as does not solely relate to Our Principality of Wales and to Monmouthshire, and that a new Commission should issue for these purposes:

Now Know Ye that We have revoked and determined, and do by these Presents revoke and determine, all the Warrants whereby Commissioners were appointed on the twenty-ninth day of March one thousand nine hundred and forty six and on any subsequent date:

And We do by these Presents authorize and appoint you, the said Robert Arthur James, Marquess of Salisbury (Chairman), Sir Albert Edward Richardson, Sir John Newenham Summerson, Nikolaus Pevsner, Christopher Edward Clive Hussey, Ian Archibald Richmond, Henry Clifford Darby, Donald Benjamin Harden, John Grahame Douglas Clark, Howard Montagu Colvin, Vivian Hunter Galbraith, William Abel Pantin, Stuart Piggott, Courtenay Arthur Ralegh Radford, Arnold Joseph Taylor and Francis Wormald, to be Our Commissioners for such periods as We may specify in respect of each of you, to make an inventory of the Ancient and Historical Monuments and Constructions connected with or illustrative of the contemporary culture, civilisation and conditions of life of the people in England, excluding Monmouthshire, from the earliest times to the year 1714, and such further Monuments and Constructions subsequent to that year as may seem in your discretion to be worthy of mention therein, and to specify those which seem most worthy of preservation.

And Whereas We have deemed it expedient that Our Lieutenants of Counties in England should be appointed ex-officio Members of the said Commission for the purposes of that part of the Commission's inquiry which relates to ancient and historical monuments and constructions within their respective counties:

Now Know Ye that We do by these Presents authorize and appoint Our Lieutenant for the time being of each and every County in England, other than Our County of Monmouth, to be a Member of the said Commission for the purposes of that part of the Commission's inquiry which relates to ancient and historical monuments and constructions within the area of his jurisdiction as Our Lieutenant of such County:

And for the better enabling you to carry out the purposes of this Our Commission, We do by these Presents authorize you to call in the aid and co-operation of owners of ancient monuments, inviting them to assist you in furthering the objects of the Commission; and to invite the possessors of such papers as you may deem it desirable to inspect to produce them before you:

And We do further authorize and empower you to confer with the Council of The National Buildings Record from time to time as may seem expedient to you in order that your deliberations may be assisted by the reports and records in the possession of the Council: and to make such arrangements for the furtherance of objectives of common interest to yourselves and the Council as may be mutually agreeable:

And We do further authorize and empower you to assume the general control and management (whether as Administering Trustees under a Scheme established under the Charities Act 1960 or otherwise) of that part of the collection of The National Buildings Record which does not solely relate to our Principality of Wales or to Monmouthshire and (subject, in relation to the said part of that collection, to the provisions of any such Scheme as may be established affecting the same) to make such arrangements for the continuance and furtherance of the work of The National Buildings Record as you may deem to be necessary both generally and for the creation of any wider record or collection containing or including architectural, archaeological and historical information concerning important sites and buildings throughout England:

And We do further give and grant unto you, or any three or more of you, full power to call before you such persons as you shall judge likely to afford you any information upon the subject of this Our Commission; and also to call for, have access to and examine all such books, documents, registers and records as may afford you the fullest information on the subject and to inquire of and concerning the premises by all other lawful ways and means whatsoever:

And We do by these Presents authorize and empower you, or any three or more of you, to visit and personally inspect such places as you may deem it expedient so to inspect for the more effectual carrying out of the purposes aforesaid:

And We do by these Presents will and ordain that this Our Commission shall continue in full force and virtue, and that you, Our said Commissioners, or any three or more of you, may from time to time proceed in the execution thereof, and of every matter and thing therein contained, although the same be not continued from time to time by adjournment:

And We do further ordain that you, or any three or more of you, have liberty to report your proceedings under this Our Commission from time to time if you shall judge it expedient so to do:

And Our further Will and Pleasure is that you do, with as little delay as possible, report to Us, under your hands and seals, or under the hands and seals of any three or more of you, your opinion upon the matters herein submitted for your consideration.

Given at Our Court at Saint James's the Twenty-eighth day of September, 1963, in the Twelfth year of Our Reign.

By Her Majesty's Command,

HENRY BROOKE

COMMISSIONERS

The Right Honourable the Lord Adeane, P.C., G.C.B., G.C.V.O. (*Chairman*)
Her Majesty's Lieutenant of the County of Gloucester (*ex officio*)
Henry Clifford Darby, Esq., O.B.E.
Courtenay Arthur Ralegh Radford, Esq.
Howard Montagu Colvin, Esq., C.B.E.
Arnold Joseph Taylor, Esq., C.B.E.
William Francis Grimes, Esq., C.B.E.
Maurice Willmore Barley, Esq.
Sheppard Sunderland Frere, Esq.
Richard John Copland Atkinson, Esq.
Sir John Betjeman, Kt., C.B.E.
Harold McCarter Taylor, Esq., C.B.E.
George Zarnecki, Esq., C.B.E.
John Kenneth Sinclair St. Joseph, Esq.
Paul Ashbee, Esq.
Arthur Richard Dufty, Esq., C.B.E.

Secretary

Robert William McDowall, Esq., O.B.E.

ROYAL COMMISSION ON THE ANCIENT AND HISTORICAL MONUMENTS AND CONSTRUCTIONS OF ENGLAND

REPORT to the Queen's Most Excellent Majesty

MAY IT PLEASE YOUR MAJESTY

We, the undersigned Commissioners, appointed to make an Inventory of the Ancient and Historical Monuments and Constructions connected with or illustrative of the contemporary culture, civilisation and conditions of life of the people of England, excluding Monmouthshire, from the earliest times to the year 1714, and of such further Monuments and Constructions subsequent to that year as may seem in our discretion to be worthy of mention therein, and to specify those which seem most worthy of preservation, do humbly submit to Your Majesty the following Report, being the thirty-third Report on the work of the Commission since its appointment.

2 With regret we have to record the retirement from the Commission upon expiry of term of office of Sir John Newenham Summerson, Knight, Commander of the Order of the British Empire, Fellow of the British Academy, Fellow of the Society of Antiquaries, Associate of the Royal Institute of British Architects, and John Nowell Linton Myres, Esquire, Commander of the Order of the British Empire, Fellow of the British Academy, past President of the Society of Antiquaries.

3 We have to thank your Majesty for the appointment to the Commission of Paul Ashbee, Esquire, Master of Arts, Fellow of the Society of Antiquaries, and Arthur Richard Dufty, Esquire, Commander of the Order of the British Empire, Fellow of the Society of Antiquaries, and for the reappointment of Courtenay Arthur Ralegh Radford, Esquire, Fellow of the British Academy, Fellow of the Society of Antiquaries, all under Your Majesty's Royal Warrant dated 5 March, 1975.

4 We have pleasure in reporting the completion of our recording of the Iron Age and Romano-British Monuments in the Cotswold area of the County of Gloucester (excluding Cirencester), an area of 182 civil parishes containing about 330 relevant Monuments, including 29 Hill-forts, 56 Romano-British Settlements and 40 Roman Villas. We believe that no relevant Monument known at the time of writing has been omitted from our survey.

5 Following our usual practice we have prepared an illustrated Inventory of these Monuments which will be issued as a non-Parliamentary publication entitled *Iron Age and Romano-British Monuments in the Gloucestershire Cotswolds*. This will be the first volume (*Glos.* I) of the general Survey of Monuments in Gloucestershire which we intend, in due course, to complete in obedience to Your Majesty's command.

6 Our thanks are due to many owners and occupiers of lands who have allowed us and members of our staff to investigate the Monuments in their charge or ownership. We are also grateful for ready assistance furnished by Directors, Curators and Officers of numerous Institutions: notably the Ordnance Survey; the Institute of Geological Sciences; the Committee for Research into the Iron Age in the North-west Cotswolds; the Committee for Aerial Photography in the University of Cambridge; Gloucester City Museum; Corinium Museum; Cheltenham Museum, and Stroud Museum.

7 Many persons have helped our staff in the execution of this survey, and we especially wish to thank Mrs. H. E. O'Neil, M.B.E., F.S.A. and Instructor Captain H. S. Gracie, C.B., M.A., F.S.A., R.N. (rtd.), whose

assistance has been of outstanding value. We are also glad to acknowledge information and other help generously provided by—Mr. W. A. Baker, Mr. B. Beveridge, Dr. R. Cave, Mr. Giles Clarke, Mr. Wilfred Cox, Dr. G. C. Dunning, Miss S. Evans-Lawrence, Mr. P. J. Fowler, Mrs. E. Gander, Mr. P. E. Gascoigne, Capt. P. Gibbs, Mr. R. Goodburn, Mr. A. N. Irvine, Mrs. M. U. Jones, Dr. G. A. Kellaway, Mr. C. E. Key, Mr. R. Knight, Dr. J. Liversidge, Dr. R. M. Reece, Mr. J. F. Rhodes, Mr. R. D. A. Savage, Mr. N. Spry, Miss M. Travell, Mr. D. J. Viner and Dr. Graham Webster: to all these, and others named in the Inventory, the Commissioners offer sincere thanks.

8 The rapid and widespread destruction of field monuments continues to be a cause of anxiety. All field monuments listed in the Inventory of Iron Age and Romano-British Monuments in the Gloucestershire Cotswolds should be treated with respect, not only on account of their rarity, but also because the visible remains need not by themselves indicate a monument's archaeological importance; this can be revealed only by excavation. Destruction should never be allowed until competent archaeological investigation has taken place. With this in mind, we humbly recommend to Your Majesty's notice the following Iron Age and Romano-British Monuments in the Cotswold area of Gloucestershire, as *Most Worthy of Preservation*:

ALDSWORTH

(1) 'CELTIC' FIELDS and associated ditches on Bibury old race-course, a remarkably well-preserved portion of a formerly more extensive field system.

AMPNEY ST. PETER OR EASTINGTON

(1) RANBURY RING hill-fort.

BAGENDON (extending into DAGLINGWORTH and NORTH CERNEY)

(1) IRON AGE AND EARLY ROMANO-BRITISH SETTLEMENT with DYKES, the site of a capital of the Dobunni.

BARNSLEY

(1) ROMAN VILLA with walled closes, the subject of recent excavations.
(2) 'CELTIC' FIELDS associated with (1); a very rare example to survive.

BATSFORD

(1) ROMANO-BRITISH SETTLEMENT, Dorn.
(3) ROMAN ROAD, The Foss Way, a rare survival, with road bank and side ditches.

BIBURY

(1) ABLINGTON CAMP hill-fort.
(2) ROMAN VILLA, near Bibury Mill, marked by exceptionally extensive earthworks.

BISLEY WITH LYPIATT

(1) ROMAN VILLA, Lillyhorn.*

BOURTON-ON-THE-WATER

(1) SALMONSBURY, an Iron Age settlement with bivallate defences enclosing some 56 acres.

BROCKWORTH

(1) CROSS-RIDGE DYKE in Brockworth Wood, a well-preserved rarity.

BUCKLAND

(1) HILL-FORT on Burhill.

CHARLTON KINGS

(2) LINEAR DYKE, a rarity in the Cotswolds.

CHEDWORTH

(1) ROMAN VILLA, Chedworth Woods, mainly of the 4th century, but including 2nd-century elements (National Trust).
(4) ROMAN TEMPLE (platform), in Chedworth Woods.

COATES

(1) TREWSBURY hill-fort.

COBERLEY

(1) HILL-FORT on Crickley Hill, shown by modern excavation to be of the early Iron Age, with important evidence of earlier occupation.

COLESBOURNE

(1) NORBURY hill-fort.
(2) ROMAN VILLA at Stockwood, of unusual form and with adjacent terraces.

COLN ST. ALDWYNS

(1) DEAN CAMP hill-fort.

DAGLINGWORTH see BAGENDON

DOWDESWELL

(1) THE CASTLES hill-fort.

DOYNTON

(1) LINEAR DYKE, unusually sited; formerly called 'Royal Camp'.

DUNTISBOURNE ROUSE

(4) ROMANO-BRITISH SETTLEMENT, Stancombe, with rare earthworks and terraces.

DYRHAM AND HINTON

(1) HILL-FORT on Hinton Hill.

EASTLEACH

(1) 'CELTIC' FIELDS, covering some 10 acres adjacent to a Roman road; a rare survival, albeit disturbed.
(2) ROMAN ROAD, Akeman Street, a terraceway (with adjacent 'Celtic' fields) leading to a crossing of the R. Leach.

EDGEWORTH

(1) CROSS-RIDGE DYKE on Juniper Hill.

FAIRFORD

(4–6) SETTLEMENTS, ENCLOSURES AND TRACKS,* indicated by crop-marks extending over some 50 acres.

GOTHERINGTON

(1) NOTTINGHAM HILL CAMP, a very large promontory hill-fort.

GREAT RISSINGTON

(2) PROBABLE IRON AGE AND ROMANO-BRITISH SETTLEMENT.*
(3) PIT-ALIGNMENT.*

GREAT WITCOMBE

(1) ROMAN VILLA, excavated and maintained by the Department of the Environment.

HARESFIELD

(2) THE BULWARKS, hill-fort.

HORTON

(1) THE CASTLES, hill-fort.

KEMPSFORD

(7) ENCLOSURES, TRACKS AND LINEAR DITCHES,* indicated by crop-marks over some 70 acres.

KING'S STANLEY

(1) CROSS-RIDGE DYKE.

KINGSCOTE

(1) ROMANO-BRITISH SETTLEMENT,* The Chessalls, especially notable for its size.

LECHLADE

(2) ENCLOSURES AND TRACKS,* revealed by crop-marks covering some 50 acres.

LECKHAMPTON

(1) HILL-FORT, Leckhampton Hill.

MINCHINHAMPTON

(1–8) 'THE BULWARKS' and other remarkably well-preserved dykes, banks and scarps.

NORTH CERNEY see BAGENDON

NORTH NIBLEY

(1) BRACKENBURY DITCHES, hill-fort.

NORTHLEACH WITH EASTINGTON

(1) NORBURY CAMP, a very large Iron Age hill-fort, subsequently occupied in the Roman period.

PAINSWICK

(1) KIMSBURY, a multivallate Iron Age hill-fort of a type very uncommon in the Cotswold area.

RANDWICK

(1) CROSS-RIDGE DYKE in Randwick Wood.

SAPPERTON (extending into COATES)

(1) ROMAN SETTLEMENT, 'Tunnel Mouth Camp', and associated buildings, a complex possibly centred on a temple.

SODBURY

(1) SODBURY CAMP, hill-fort.

SOUTHAM

(1) CLEEVE CLOUD, hill-fort.
(4) THE RING, an undated earthwork, possibly of the Iron Age.
(5) PLATFORMED RINGWORK, undated, possibly an Iron Age hut platform.
(6) DYKE, undated, but probably of the Iron Age.

STANTON

(1) HILL-FORT on Shenberrow Hill, a very small bivallate hill-fort.

SUDELEY

(1) HILL-FORT(?) W. of Roel Gate, probably of the Iron Age.
(2) ROMAN VILLA at Wadfield.
(4) ROMAN VILLA at Spoonley Wood.

SWELL

(2) ROMAN VILLA AND OTHER BUILDINGS at Abbotswood.

TEMPLE GUITING

(1) BECKBURY CAMP, hill-fort.
(4) PIT-ALIGNMENT.*
(5) ENCLOSURES AND DITCHES,* probably Iron Age and Romano-British.

---

* Monuments marked with an asterisk lie wholly below the surface. Those listed are representative of a large number of similar sites generally recognisable by crop-marks, any one of which may contain archaeological information of significance.

Uley

(1) Uley Bury hill-fort, on a prominent spur of the Cotswold escarpment.

Whittington

(2) Romano-British Settlement,* Wycomb, with temple and paved streets.

(3) Roman Villa, dating from the second century, with 4th-century mosaic pavements; also adjacent mediaeval earthworks partly overlying the villa, and other earthworks which may be contemporary.

Willersey

(1) Hill-fort on Willersey Hill.

Windrush

(1) Windrush Camp, hill-fort.

Woodchester

(1) Roman Villa,* of exceptional size and magnificence including the largest Roman mosaic pavement known in Britain.

9 The foregoing list has a purely scholarly basis. In compiling it we have considered the archaeological importance of each Monument, its rarity in the national as well as in the local field and the degree of cultural loss that would result from its destruction, always bearing in mind the extent to which the Monument is connected with or is illustrative of the contemporary culture etc. of the inhabitants of this land, as required in Your Majesty's Warrant. We have taken no account of attendant circumstances such as cost of maintenance or difficulty of preservation.

10 We desire to acknowledge the good work done by our executive staff in the production and preparation of the Inventory; especially by our Investigators, Mr. H. C. Bowen, O.B.E., M.A., F.S.A., Mr. B. N. Eagles, B.A. and Dr. I. F. Smith, B.A., F.S.A.; also Mr. J. N. Hampton, F.S.A. and Mrs. V. G. Swan, B.A. We commend the skilful work of our illustrator, Mr. A. L. Pope, A.R.C.A., A.R.E., and that of our photographers, Messrs. W. C. Light, R. E. W. Parsons, R. F. Braybrook and J. Parkinson. The index was compiled by Mrs. H. Green. The editor was Mr. G. U. S. Corbett, PH.D., F.S.A.

11 In conclusion we desire to commend our Secretary and General Editor, Mr. R. W. McDowall, O.B.E., M.A., F.S.A., who continues to afford unremitting assistance to us in the discharge of Your Majesty's Commission.

All of which we submit to Your Majesty with our humble duty.

Signed:

ADEANE (*Chairman*)
BEAUFORT
H. C. DARBY
C. A. RALEGH RADFORD
H. M. COLVIN
A. J. TAYLOR
W. F. GRIMES
M. W. BARLEY
S. S. FRERE
R. J. C. ATKINSON
JOHN BETJEMAN
H. M. TAYLOR
G. ZARNECKI
J. K. S. ST. JOSEPH
PAUL ASHBEE
A. R. DUFTY

R. W. McDOWALL (*Secretary*)

GLOUCESTERSHIRE I

SECTIONAL PREFACE

GEOLOGY, TOPOGRAPHY AND DISTRIBUTION

(see distribution map in end pocket)

THE GREATER PART of the area with which this volume is concerned is a plateau of Jurassic rocks, mostly Oolitic limestones, extending in a dip-slope E. and S.E. from a prominent escarpment overlooking the Severn Vale. The highest point on the scarp is Cleeve Cloud, Southam, at 1,083 ft. above O.D. River valleys penetrating the plateau from W. and S. produce a broken terrain; those from the W. are steep-sided combes. The use of county boundaries to delimit the area described in the volume causes the inclusion of a substantial area of River Gravels of the Upper Thames. On the N. and W. of the Cotswolds, individual parishes extend the area into the Severn Vale and cause the inclusion of certain upstanding outliers, such as Oxenton Knolls, eroded relics of an earlier escarpment. The characteristic soils of the dip-slope are calcareous, ranging from a fine loam to soil of a clayey texture. Where well drained and on suitable slopes the land is well suited to tillage, but in the Middle Ages it was extensively devoted to grazing. Some of the more clayey areas are by nature imperfectly drained, but this did not prevent their use for agriculture during the period considered in this survey. The Lias clays offer a sticky and unstable subsoil, but it is notable that the large Roman villa at Great Witcombe was built on the Middle Lias at its junction with the Oolite; presumably the situation was dictated by over-riding need for a plentiful water supply such as was afforded by an adjacent spring.

The *Iron Age* is represented most clearly by the earthworks of hill-forts and dykes which, unlike Roman remains, are usually clearly visible. The situation of almost all hill-forts is closely related to defence; they lie on relatively high ground and as near as possible to a water supply. Other Iron Age settlements are suggested by casual small finds, occasionally on Romano-British sites; some were immediately by streams (Whittington (1) and Bagendon). Doubtless some are related to those complexes of ditched enclosures, seen in large numbers on the gravels by the Upper Thames and so far known only as undated crop-marks, which are included in our distribution map as 'probable settlements'. On the other hand, Romano-British debris found in the area of crop-marks is not necessarily related directly to such features.

There must be many unknown *Romano-British* sites in the area; this can be demonstrated simply by reference to the list of former finds, such as mosaics, which can no longer be closely located. S.W. of Cirencester the evidence is notably sparse, partly because of the indented nature of the land and partly because its use (largely pastoral) since the destruction of the earthworks inhibits discovery either from the air or on the ground. Throughout the area it is clear that many sites, particularly off the gravels, are difficult to recognise from the air even when under plough, natural irregularities in soil distribution being to some extent responsible for obscuring spreads of debris. On the other hand, some blank areas may truly reflect the sparsity of former land-use. It is tempting to think that much of the comparatively waterless limestone plateau, notably that N.E. of Cirencester, was a sheep-run in Romano-British times.

As is to be expected, the discernible associations of settlement are predominantly with water. This applies particularly to villas, where plentiful supplies of water were needed for bathing arrangements. Romano-British conduits and drains were very complex and numbers of them still function. Roman roads attracted settlement (*e.g.* around Bourton-on-the-Water), but communication must have been largely by means of roads and tracks which are no longer certainly recognisable (see p. xlv). Pottery finds from sites such as Springhill in Lower Slaughter, near the junction of Buckle Street and the Foss Way, show a great variety of places of manufacture.

The subsoil allowed a wide variety of uses (map opp. p. xxiii). In almost all areas it is calcareous and suitable for corn crops (see 'Celtic' fields, p. xlviii), but it is also suitable for pasture, the occasional low water supply being tolerated better by sheep than by cattle.

It is difficult to discuss questions of grouping and pattern when the known distribution is so incomplete, but some points of interest emerge, notably the closeness of the large rural settlement of Chessells in Lower Slaughter to the exceptionally large Roman settlement on the site now occupied by Bourton-on-the-Water. For the situation around Corinium, see p. xxxvi. Whether there was a colonate distribution of settlements around villas, or of villas around community settlements, or what territory might be attached to any settlement are things that cannot be fully explored until the nature of each settlement has been determined in a totally exposed pattern of distribution.* There are certain suggestive clusterings in Chedworth and around Clearcupboard in Farmington, and in areas of this kind it may become possible to assemble enough material for such considerations.

THE IRON AGE

In contrast to the remains of the Roman period, discussed below, the evidence for Iron Age occupation of the Cotswolds lies chiefly in earthworks. These are the hill-forts and dykes, a high proportion of which seem to survive to the present day in forms still recognisable on the surface. Because Iron Age pottery seems rarely to survive protracted attrition, as from ploughing, information on the occupation of hill-forts is available only where the sites have been excavated. For the same reason our information on the presence of 'open' sites and on the dating of enclosures (whether surviving as earthworks or as crop-marks and soil-marks) is minimal and must be regarded as a very small part indeed of what remains to be recovered.

Chronology and Relationships

Information about the development and relationships of Iron Age culture in the Gloucestershire Cotswolds is severely limited by the restricted number of sites excavated and by the still smaller number of excavated sites for which definitive reports have been published. Casual finds attributable to this period are rare, with the exception of the coins which belong to its final phase. Pottery constitutes the bulk of potentially datable material, but while finds are known from about thirty localities a high proportion are small and often featureless sherds. Stratified sequences are attested only at Salmonsbury in Bourton-on-the-Water (as yet not fully published) and at Crickley Hill in Coberley, where excavations are still in progress.

Evidence from Crickley Hill indicates that coarse undecorated pottery was succeeded by a finer ware with incised decoration and white infill. Pottery with similar ornament from a pit at Lechlade (1) included haematite-coated sherds. The material from a second site at Lechlade (5), from Sandy Lane in Charlton Kings and from a ditch at Fairford appears to be comparable, and this fine ware may reflect the early Wessex ceramic influence noted in the Upper Thames region (D. W. Harding, *The Iron Age in the Upper Thames Basin* (1972), 79–83).

Sherds with stamped and linear-tooled decoration, all from the W. fringe of the area, are allied to the duck-stamped and linear-tooled pottery more abundantly represented further west. Examples from Beckbury Camp hill-fort in Temple Guiting, from settlements at The Knolls in Oxenton, at The Stables and King's Beeches in Southam, from a pit at Foxcote in Withington and from Ireley Farm in Stanway have been attributed on petrological grounds to a source on or near the Malvern Hills (*PPS*, XXXIV (1968), 414–27).

Belgic pottery is known only from Bagendon and Rodborough.

---

* Professor H. P. R. Finberg has indicated lines of enquiry in papers on Withington (*e.g. Lucerna* (1964), 21–65).

Hill-forts

The twenty-nine monuments classed as hill-forts are listed below in alphabetical order of the names commonly used. They include three recently recognised examples: Burhill, The Castles (Dowdeswell) and Woodmancote; and two, Ring Hill and Roel, which are provisionally placed in this category even though anomalous. As explained below (p. xxix), the Inventory omits thirty-seven sites formerly identified as 'hill-forts' or 'camps'.

Common Name	*Inventory No.*
Ablington Camp	Bibury (1)
Beckbury Camp	Temple Guiting (1)
Brackenbury Ditches	North Nibley (1)
Bulwarks, The	Haresfield (2)
Burhill	Buckland (1)
Castle Godwyn (see Kimsbury)	
Castles, The	Dowdeswell (1)
Castles, The	Horton (1)
Cleeve Cloud	Southam (1)
Crickley Hill	Coberley (1)
Dean Camp	Coln St. Aldwyns (1)
Drum, The (see Icomb Hill)	
Dyrham Camp (see Hinton Hill)	
Haresfield Beacon (see Ring Hill)	
Hinton Hill	Dyrham and Hinton (1)
Horton Camp (see Castles, Horton)	
Icomb Hill	Icomb (1)
Kimsbury	Painswick (1)
Leckhampton Hill	Leckhampton (1)
Little Sodbury Camp (see Sodbury Camp)	
Norbury	Colesbourne (1)
Norbury Camp	Northleach with Eastington (1)
Nottingham Hill Camp	Gotherington (1)
Painswick Beacon (see Kimsbury)	
Pinbury	Duntisbourne Rouse (1)
Ranbury Ring	Ampney St. Peter (1)
Ring Hill	Haresfield (1)
Roel	Sudeley (1)
Salmonsbury	Bourton-on-the-Water (1)
Shenberrow	Stanton (1)
Sodbury Camp	Sodbury (1)
Trewsbury	Coates (1)
Uley Bury	Uley (1)
Willersey Hill	Willersey (1)
Windrush Camp	Windrush (1)
Woodmancote	North Cerney (2)

Most of the monuments listed have defensive potential, though only four have been shown by excavation to be of the Iron Age. Small quantities of unstratified pottery recovered from the interiors of another five, though generally of indeterminate character, seem likely to denote occupation during the Iron Age. For the rest, classification depends on analogy.

Future research may cause some revision of the list. The enclosure on Ring Hill is atypical in respect of the character and plan of the rampart as well as in its proximity to The Bulwarks. The very small enclosure at Roel with its relatively slight and perhaps interrupted bank hardly qualifies as a defensive structure. Excavation may indicate a different date or purpose for these monuments and perhaps for others discussed in this section. On the other hand, further investigation may substantiate the existence of some monuments for which there is at the moment insufficient evidence; others may be recognised from air photographs or on the ground. Place-names can offer useful clues (see p. lii).

Preservation. Brackenbury Ditches, which lies in woodland, is the only hill-fort wholly untouched by ploughing or quarrying, yet most of the others have survived in comparatively good condition. The ramparts of three (Ablington Camp, Woodmancote, Pinbury) are nearly levelled by ploughing, but their main course can still be traced or inferred. Quarrying has removed rampart-ends at Nottingham Hill and Cleeve Cloud and has severely disturbed the interiors of Ring Hill and Kimsbury. At Burhill, Norbury (Colesbourne) and Dean Camp, fragmentary ramparts now stand at the edges of arable fields. The rampart at Icomb Hill cannot now be seen to form part of a circuit, but it is included in our list of hill-forts on the testimony of an early plan which purports to show an enclosure of some 25 acres. The relationship to this rampart of an interrupted ditch, seen to the S. on air photographs, is uncertain.

Siting. The distribution of hill-forts within the Cotswold area responds strongly to the obvious defensive advantages offered by the steep-sided spurs and edges of the escarpment; fifteen of the hill-forts are placed along its 50-mile length. These hill-forts may, however, have been related to the territory in the vale to the W. as well as to the Cotswold plateau on the E. Five other hill-forts are comparably situated at the edges of deeply incised river valleys. Of the other nine, five stand on hill-tops or ridge-tops partly surrounded by moderate slopes, three are in places that lack evident tactical advantages, and Salmonsbury, more accurately called a defended settlement, lies beside a river. Salmonsbury's situation, together with its double banks, its size and copious evidence of occupation, invites comparison with Dyke Hills, Dorchester-on-Thames, as yet unexcavated.

As remarked above, geology may have limited the extent of permanent occupation in waterless areas of Great Oolite. Windrush Camp, standing in such an area a mile from any source of surface water, is exceptional. No other hill-fort is more than half a mile from water and twenty-four are within 500 yds. of a spring, stream or river.

Defences and Scale. For purposes of comparison, small-scale plans of most of the hill-forts that have survived in relatively complete condition are shown opposite. Nineteen hill-forts are univallate (fifteen shown opposite), with ramparts generally of modest dimensions; only four rise more than 10 ft. above the silted surface of their ditches. Eleven, including some not shown opposite (among them the Haresfield Bulwarks), consist simply of a bank and an outer ditch terminating at each end on scarp edges. Norbury Camp is clearly defined by what can be regarded as a pair of cross-ridge dykes set at each end of a slight rise on a ridge. At Uley Bury and Ring Hill the banks follow the edges of spurs.

The defences of seven out of the ten bivallate hill-forts are also of relatively small size. Only at Brackenbury Ditches, Kimsbury and Sodbury Camp does the vertical interval between the crest of the rampart and the silted surface of the ditch exceed 20 ft.; Kimsbury alone attains dimensions comparable with those of most bivallate hill-forts in Wessex. Cleeve Cloud is curiously situated at a point on the escarpment where it is dominated by higher ground to the east.

Excavations have disclosed that timber was incorporated in the burnt ramparts at Crickley Hill and Leckhampton Hill, and that they were faced with dry-stone walls. Fire-reddened limestone is visible in the ramparts of The Castles at Horton, in the rampart of Beckbury Camp, and in the inner rampart at Sodbury Camp. Large blocks of limestone exist in the W. rampart of Norbury Camp. Similar blocks were found at Salmonsbury, where the gravel bank may have had a dry-stone revetment in addition.

Entrances are generally simple. At Kimsbury the inturned rampart-ends may be compared with those of Wapley hill-fort (R.C.H.M., *Herefordshire*, III, 184), where the plan, siting and scale of defences are similar; but disturbance makes it uncertain if the inner curve of the entrance at Kimsbury is an original feature. A hornwork at Crickley Hill was added when the entrance was remodelled. Guard-chambers were set within the enlarged rampart ends at Leckhampton.

Fourteen hill-forts enclose 10 acres or less; two univallate examples (Roel and Windrush Camp) cover $2\frac{1}{2}$ to $3\frac{1}{2}$ acres. The bivallate Shenberrow is of comparable size. An enclosure partly revealed by a crop-mark (*a*) at Fairford (2) may be comparable with Roel and Windrush. Exceptionally large areas are defined at Norbury Camp, Northleach (80 acres) and at Nottingham Hill Camp (120 acres).

Occupation and Dating. The plans of Iron Age houses inside hill-forts have been recovered by excavation at Crickley Hill (where a rectangular aisled type preceded a round type), and at Salmonsbury. Storage pits are recorded at Salmonsbury; one such pit together with areas of occupation is known at Shenberrow. Crop-marks suggest the presence of small enclosures in Uley Bury, and casual finds are indicative of settlement at this and other hill-forts.

Late Bronze Age metalwork from the interior of Nottingham Hill may suggest that the sites of some hill-forts were centres of significance before the Iron Age, as does the Neolithic camp within the hill-fort on Crickley Hill. The finds so far recovered in the excavations at Crickley Hill and Leckhampton Hill appear to indicate a very early Iron Age date for the construction of these hill-forts. At Shenberrow the more abundant pottery found in primary positions in the inner rampart and its ditch, and associated with occupation of the interior, seems also to be early. At Salmonsbury, 'saucepan' pots of the later pre-Roman Iron Age were associated with the bivallate defences.

Dykes and Linear Boundaries

Linear banks define annexes or areas of control outside the defences of two or perhaps three hill-forts; at Salmonsbury, on the S.E. side, towards a marshy area; at Sodbury Camp, on the N.E. corner. The parallel banks running downhill from Willersey Hill may be comparable although their physical connection with the main defences has been obliterated.

There are four cross-ridge dykes: Brockworth (1), King's Stanley (1), Randwick (1) and on Juniper Hill, Edgeworth (1). On Juniper Hill the dyke does not extend to the scarp edges and its situation near the tip of a sloping spur is anomalous. A dyke in Southam (6) is a very long cross-ridge boundary. Straight lengths of ditch seen as crop-marks at Yanworth (2) are interrupted by a re-entrant valley and a probable entrance. Dykes at Charlton Kings (2), Cranham (1) and Doynton (1) are variously sited in ways not readily explicable. Other dykes, conspicuously infrequent in the Cotswolds, occur in concentrated groups only in the three monuments discussed below.

The very unusual complex at Northleach with Eastington (3), known from crop-marks, is a linear setting of short, uniformly narrow lengths of ditch with attached enclosures; they can be traced on air photographs for a distance of 1¼ miles. Systems of dykes at Bagendon and Minchinhampton appear to demarcate large zones of control although the individual elements are not of massive proportions. The nine dykes at Bagendon, a Dobunnic capital, may represent control over an area of some 500 acres; in arrangement they are loosely comparable with concentrations of Belgic dykes in S.E. England or the contemporary Grim's Ditch of North Oxfordshire. Variations in size and form suggest that individually the Bagendon dykes served a variety of functions, but in combination they appear to represent a unified expression of political power. The dykes on Minchinhampton Common conform to a different arrangement and are in a different topographical situation, but they too suggest imposition of control over an area, here perhaps of 300 acres. A complex of very low scarps (Minchinhampton (8)), possibly of the Iron Age, may be related to the upstanding ramparts which they join and perhaps pre-date. The two systems are compared on p. xxviii.

Pit-alignments, constituting boundaries now defined only by a line of pits, have been revealed by crop-marks at Condicote (2), Great Rissington (3) and Temple Guiting (4). Such pits, usually about 6 ft. across, are spaced at intervals of 6 ft. or less. Most of the known examples occur on river gravels where, sometimes in conjunction with ditches, they bound large blocks of land (R.C.H.M., *A Matter of Time* (1960), 28–31; *Arch J*, CXXI (1964), 9). The situation of those at Condicote and Temple Guiting, high on the limestone, is very unusual. Excavation elsewhere suggests a late Iron Age or early Romano-British date (W. G. Simpson in C. Thomas (ed.), *Rural Settlement in Roman Britain*, C.B.A. Research Report No. 7 (1965), 18–19).

Open Settlements

The slight evidence as yet available for occupation within hill-forts has been mentioned above. Knowledge of unenclosed settlements is equally sparse (cf. p. xxiv). Pottery and other finds indicative of occupation, but unassociated with structures, are recorded at The Knolls in Oxenton (1), at Charlton Kings (1), Rodborough (1), Duntisbourne Abbots and Upper Slaughter. Shallow pits containing pottery lay under a rampart at Salmonsbury; others occur at Guiting Power, Lechlade (5) and Withington (1). Pottery was rescued from a ditch in a gravel-pit at Fairford. Post-holes and wattle-marked daub were observed at one of the two occupation sites at Southam (3). The Ring at Southam (4) and an adjacent ring-work (5) are undated, but it is possible that they enclosed Iron Age hut platforms. The plan of a circular timber house was recovered during excavations at Lechlade (5); two Iron Age pits were found in the vicinity of the house, and a third pit at Lechlade (1) was isolated. Some crop-marks at Whittington (2) could be of the Iron Age.

At Bagendon, the two occupation areas that have been excavated were originally used for industrial purposes; small circular houses were secondary and the main residential area has yet to be identified. Similar houses at Salmonsbury are attributed to later occupation and differed in construction from those contemporary with the building of the defences.

Iron Age settlements probably lie among some of the complexes of crop-marks which have been included in the Inventory.

Burials

Burials accompanied by grave-goods are known from a single grave in Badgeworth and from the small cemetery at Barrow Wake, Birdlip (Cowley (1)), where the decorated mirror and other metal objects

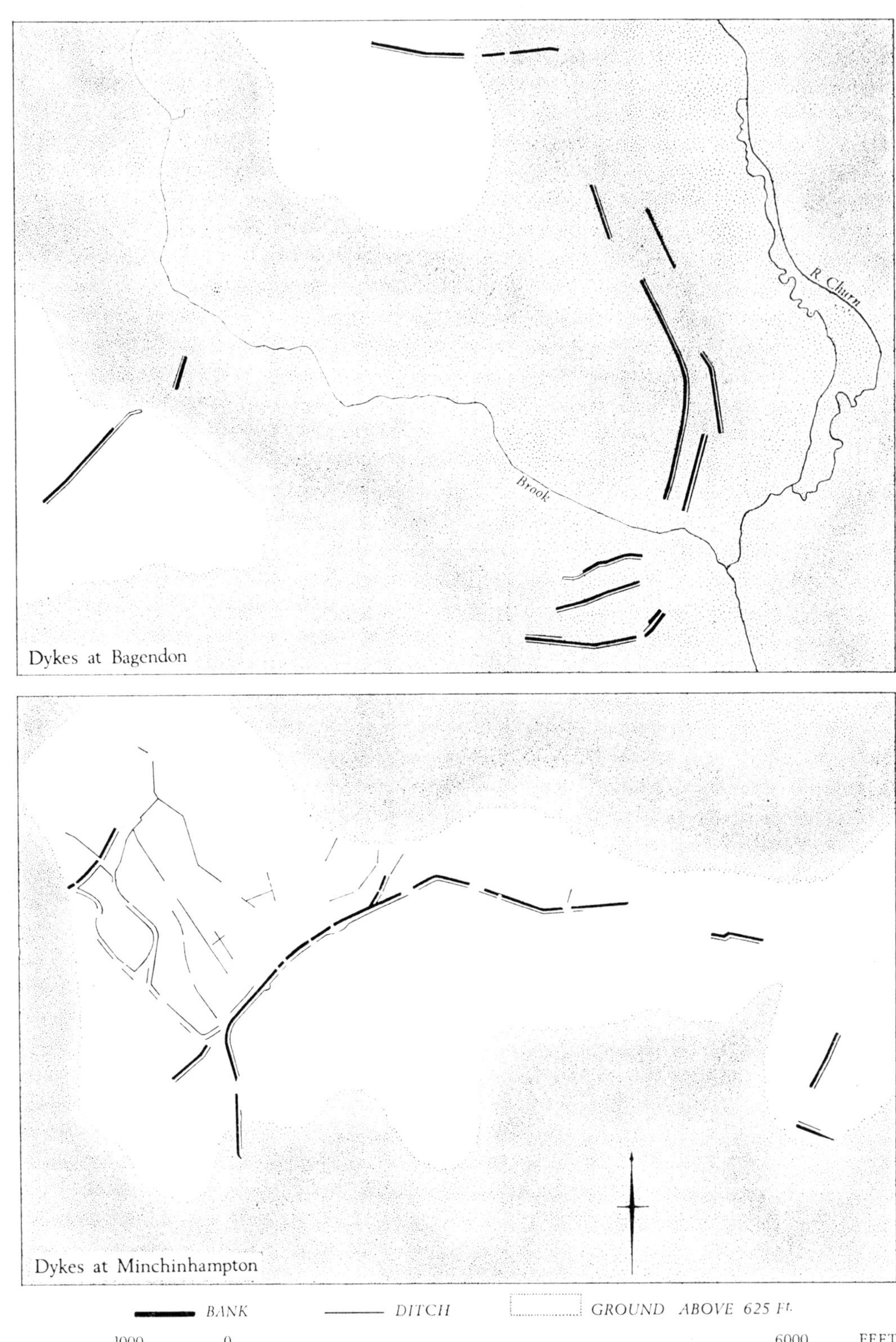

Dyke systems etc. at BAGENDON and MINCHINHAMPTON.

accompanying a female skeleton imply a princely caste whose existence could hardly be inferred from other small finds in the area. Six inurned cremations in 'Belgic' pots are known from Bagendon. A reputed cremation in a pot of earlier type at Cranham is less well documented. Casual interments found at Salmonsbury were in pits of the earlier Iron Age and in the bank of the enclosure. A possible Iron Age barrow within a square ditch stands near the entrance to Leckhampton hill-fort.

Continuity of Occupation

Direct evidence of uninterrupted occupation from the Iron Age into the Roman period has been found only at Bagendon and Bourton-on-the-Water. Pre-Roman antecedents seem to be implied for Roman settlements at Charlton Kings, Lechlade, Lower Slaughter, Stanway and Wycomb (Whittington); others are less certainly suggested, for example at Siddington (6). Indications of activity in the Roman period have been noted in the interiors of thirteen hill-forts. Roman settlements were established within Woodmancote, Norbury Camp (Northleach with Eastington) and Ring Hill, and indications of activity in the Roman period have been noted in the interiors of nine other hill-forts. Dobunnic coins found in Roman settlements at Kingscote, West Hill (Uley) and Wycomb are not securely related to continuity of occupation.

DISCREDITED 'HILL-FORTS' AND 'CAMPS'

Thirty-seven sites formerly classed as 'hill-forts' or 'camps' cannot, on present evidence, be included in the Inventory as defensive Iron Age enclosures. The sites have been put forward at various times, from the 18th century onwards, on the basis of a variety of categories of evidence, examined below. Some have always depended on illusory factors. Others may have suffered so much destruction that the significant remains are unrecognisable, but further investigation on the ground or from the air may enable them to be rediscovered or allowed new significance; for this reason all the sites are listed and some are described in detail to assist future reappraisal.

The list has three main parts: *a.* Monuments which are probably Iron Age earthworks, but not hill-forts. *b.* Sites with features visible on the ground, of uncertain origin and often natural. *c.* Sites where no visible traces remain and for which no convincing documentary evidence exists. Parts *b* and *c* are subdivided into (i) sites which have been presented in literature or on maps in such a way as to suggest that they are hill-forts, in the sense in which the term might be used today, and (ii) other 'camps'. Although an Iron Age date or a defensive purpose has not necessarily been attributed to every 'camp' included under *b* (ii) and *c* (ii) the term, unless qualified, is likely to be understood to imply such date and purpose; hence to remove potential ambiguity all 'camps' which cannot be accepted as Iron Age hill-forts are considered.

Parish and Monument No.	*Name*
a. Sites reclassified as dykes (probably Iron Age)	
Brockworth (1)	Cooper's Hill
Cranham (1)	High Brotheridge
Doynton (1)	Royal Camp
Edgeworth (1)	Juniper Hill
Minchinhampton (7)	Amberley Camp (cross-dyke only)
Randwick (1)	Randwick Wood
b. Visible remains of uncertain origin, often natural	
(i) *'Hill-forts'*	
Alderton	Dixton Hill*
Charlton Kings	Battledown*
Condicote	Eubury*
Cowley	Birdlip Camp
Dowdeswell	? Camp No. 3 (Burrow)*
King's Stanley	Selsley Hill Camp*
Nympsfield	Owlpen†
Oxenton (1)	The Knolls
Rendcomb	Rendcomb Camp*
Stanway	Upper Coscombe*
Do.	Hailes Wood*
Stinchcombe	Drakestone Point*
Winchcombe	Langley Hill*
(ii) *Other 'camps'*	
Aston Blank	Cold Aston Camp†
Avening	Hazel Wood Copse Camp†
Bitton	Bitton Camp
Cold Ashton	Tog Hill Camp

* Described below (pp. xxxi–xxxiv). † See introductory paragraph in parish inventory.

Parish and Monument No.	*Name*
Condicote	Condicote Camp†
Dowdeswell	Camp No. 2*
Horsley	Enoch's Hill Camp
Saintbury	Saintbury Camp†
Sevenhampton	Puckham Camp
Tormarton	Hebdown Camp†

c. NO VISIBLE REMAINS

(i) *'Hill-forts'*

Parish and Monument No.	*Name*
Condicote	Staites Brake, or Hinchwick Camp*
Hawkesbury	Hawkesbury Knoll*
Sapperton	Green Ditches†
Stow-on-the-Wold	'Hill-fort'†

(ii) *Other 'camps'*

Parish and Monument No.	*Name*
Cam	Cam Long Down Camp
Condicote	'Oval British Camp'†
Doynton	Doynton Camps†
Notgrove	Stainbarrow Camp†

a. Of the six monuments which cannot be seen to form enclosures and are reclassified as dykes, probably Iron Age, Cooper's Hill and Randwick Wood lie across ridges. Juniper Hill and High Brotheridge might each have been part of an enclosure, but their situation is not obviously good for defence. Different but related problems arise in the position of two other dykes. 'Royal Camp' has a bank and ditch of hill-fort proportions and lies on the brow of the main escarpment, but there is no sign of any continuation behind this forward position to complete an enclosure. Minchinhampton (7) is an almost straight length of Iron Age rampart on a plateau, unconnected with any obvious defensive advantage and misleadingly dividing a slight earthwork enclosure, 'Amberley Camp', which is of later date. It should also be noted that the disconnected dykes of Bagendon (1) define an area of control. It has sometimes been called an *oppidum*, but it must be distinguished from the *oppida* of the Continent which mostly comprise complete enclosures.

b. These twenty-three sites are of natural or uncertain origin; they include ten heterogeneous enclosures or other earthworks which diverge both in plan and in form from constructions demonstrably of the Iron Age. Some result from post-Roman activities: excavations at 'Bitton Camp' have established that it is mediaeval; the situation and form of 'Dowdeswell Camp No. 2' suggest manorial origins; much of the common to S. of 'Selsley Hill Camp', King's Stanley, was formerly sprinkled with pits and mounds, not unlike those on Rodborough and Minchinhampton Commons, with 13th-century 'hut' sites between them (*TBGAS*, 68 (1949), 22–44; see also p. 98).

The thirteen other sites in group *b* are either natural in origin or they are the incidental result of quarrying or of cultivation; some result from several such factors in combination. The nature of some of the artificial remains associated with four of the sites is uncertain.

The revised evaluation of these thirteen sites results from consideration over a long period. Upper Coscombe, Stanway, may be cited as an example. Air photographs indicate a multivallate enclosure of some 50 acres, overall, at the top of a high, domed hill. Initial ground inspection showed what were taken at first to be degraded and ploughed banks and ditches at least 240 ft. across; it seemed as if land hunger at some time had warranted the levelling of defences as big as those of Maiden Castle (*Dorset*, II, 493–501), the most massive in Britain. Further inspection aroused suspicion. No clear entrance could be identified; there were no archaeological finds in the wholly ploughed interior. As the survey of the Cotswolds progressed it became apparent that the archaeological context is anomalous. The massive multivallation is entirely out of character for the region. Moreover, the postulated land hunger is not attested by comparable destruction of other hill-forts whose defences, compared with those in many parts of the country, are slight. Advice was sought from the Institute of Geological Sciences. The geological explanation of this and other sites results from ensuing consultations and we wish to acknowledge valuable information and opinions from Dr. Richard Cave and Dr. G. A. Kellaway of the Institute.

Air photographs show other 'false enclosures', to be explained as in the examples given, but only sites which have been published as 'of the Iron Age' are considered here. The phenomena result from the erosion of Jurassic strata of varying composition and hardness. As in the example at Upper Coscombe, differential erosion can leave bands of harder rock standing along contours in plausible 'hill-fort' positions. Such bands may proliferate in complex patterns (Condicote), or appear as banks across ridges with corresponding

* Described below (pp. xxxi–xxxiv). † See introductory paragraph in parish inventory.

gulleys (Stinchcombe). Slumping may leave scars which look like scarps at the top or like banks at the bottom of slopes (Alderton and Rendcomb). Lias formations can be very confusing (Alderton and Charlton Kings). Differential leaching and soil-fill can produce patterns which blur the outlines of archaeological remains (cf. Plate 37).

On some sites the origin of features clearly artificial can only be guessed at. Quarrying may be responsible for certain massive banks, although when there is evidence of nearby Iron Age settlement in a likely hill-fort situation, as at Oxenton Knolls, such banks present a difficult problem. At Oxenton Knolls the banks have no external ditches, are discontinuous, and lie at the foot of a quarried hill-top where much Iron Age pottery has been found. The unditched remains on Langley Hill, Winchcombe, are probably similar in origin and perhaps represent the careful disposal of waste material along the sides of allocated zones. A massive bank, part of the complex taken to compose 'Eubury Camp', Condicote, lying in a valley bottom, likewise appears to have no ditches, but it is not obviously associated with quarrying and remains unexplained.

Description of Selected Sites

ALDERTON. *Dixton Hill* (SO 986305), an isolated outcrop of Middle Lias capped with Marlstone Rock Bed, is sometimes shown as a hill-fort (*IASB*) and sometimes as a motte and bailey (O.S., 1 inch). The features are partly geological and partly artificial, the latter possibly a consequence of quarrying. This activity, however, had been forgotten by the end of the 18th century when Bigland (1791, p. 27) recorded 'ancient entrenchments'.

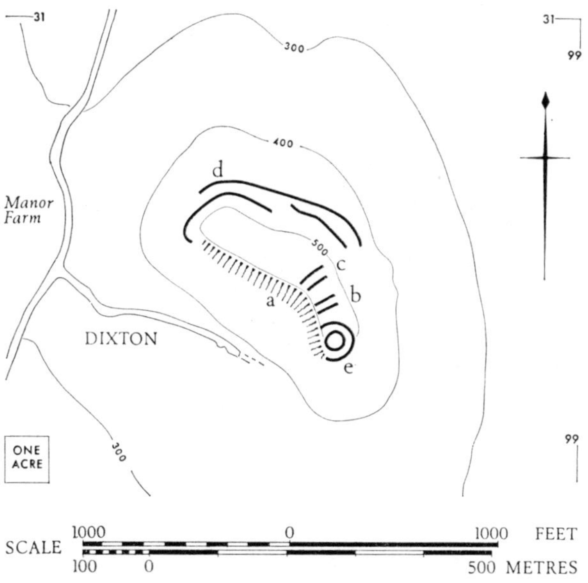

There is no record of a castle here. The Middle Lias is liable to slumping. The feature at 'a' on the plan is an arcuate slip scar with a prominent ledge of varying width at its foot. Slumping on the north slopes probably contributed to banks east of 'd' (not all shown), but uphill of them there are also discontinuous linear hollows which might be due to quarrying. Features 'b' and 'c' are cuts across the narrow spine of the hill with rough dumps east of each. Feature 'e' is an uneven, roughly circular mound, sloping gently south; it is 2 ft. high and 30 ft. across, with a shallow hollow of varying width on the north; it lies on the relatively low southern edge of a hill above a broken slumped slope.

Air photographs here can be misleading since they tend to emphasise the strongly suggestive plan without showing corrective details, such as the illogical levels at which the remains occur (R.A.F., VAP V 58 RAF 8390, 49–50).

CHARLTON KINGS. *Battledown* (or Hewlett's Camp?), (SO 970222). Early O.S. 6-inch maps show a 10-acre 'hill-fort' called 'Hewlett's Camp' on a hill-top adjacent to Battledown House and Battledown Manor. This is certainly the site described by J. Sawyer in 1895 (*PCNFC*, XII (1895/6), 86), but he says that Battledown is a short distance from Hewlett's Camp, indicating the possibility of two separate sites. Witts (1883, No. 52) defines Hewlett's Camp as an enclosure of $1\frac{1}{4}$ acres on a hill-top between The Hewletts and Northfield Farm. This suggests a location near SO 982225, but there is no hill-top there, and no earthwork is known to match Witts's description. It is just possible that he was referring to part of the scarps and ridges on Battledown itself, noted by Sawyer. Burrow (1924) lists Battledown Camp, No. 130, and Hewlett's Camp, No. 131.

No ditches can be seen and the remains are best interpreted as natural irregularities in the Middle Lias outcrop. The 'entrance' on the E. is a gully with a broad irregular mound on its N. side and a 10-ft. drop below it. The effects of ploughing probably contribute to the 'remains'; broad ridge-and-furrow sweeping up to the steep scarp is up to 5 ft. high on the S. side.

CONDICOTE. *Eubury* (SP 157288), deriving from an 'enclosure' noted by Playne (1876, No. 5) and by Witts (1883, No. 43), is composed in reality of four independent elements (a–d), drawn with thick lines on the accompanying plan. The first three are artificial, but of uncertain origin; the fourth is largely natural and similar to wholly natural features which are indicated with broken lines. (Plate 68.)

(a) A bank with limestone core, 570 ft. long, up to 40 ft. wide and 10 ft. high, with no visible ditch, lies on Inferior Oolite, on a flat valley floor.

(b) A sharply defined scarp about 3 ft. high and over $\frac{1}{4}$ mile long, on Fuller's Earth, formerly extended from the top of a spur along its N. side, descending to the valley floor. In 1937 large limestone blocks were seen revetting the W. parts of the scarp. They were photographed by Mrs. H. E. O'Neil, to whom we are indebted for this, as well as for other information on past investigation.

(c) A terrace on Fuller's Earth, about 900 ft. long, hollowed as if embodying a ditch with a counterscarp bank, lies athwart the contours on the S. side of the spur. Midway along its length the terrace is 22 ft. wide; above, a scarp 10 ft. high is capped by a slight bank 12 ft. across and 1 ft. high. Revetment stones were visible before 1939. A scarp drops 8 ft. from the terrace to elide with a natural slope of about 14°.

(d) Slight scarps and banks suggest an entrance, but they are continuous with natural ridges, scarps and hollows on the Great Oolite and are comparable with similar features in Upper Coscombe (cf. C.U.A.P., AMK 34). In 1937, Romano-British pottery was discovered W. of 'd'.

The 4-acre enclosure at X, defined by a ditch inside a bank and sometimes called Condicote Camp (Playne (1876), No. 6; Witts (1883), No. 31; *TBGAS*, 76 (1957), 141–6), is probably a henge monument.

CONDICOTE. *Staites Brake* (SP 150302), or 'Hinchwick Camp', is said by Witts (1883, No. 53) to have been a circular enclosure of about 1 acre in 'camp ground'. It was levelled *c.* 1803 and there is no sign today of any ancient earthwork.

COWLEY. *Birdlip Camp* (SO 924150), now in woodland, depends for its authenticity on a cross-ridge bank of uncertain origin, perhaps wholly or partly natural. The situation would, however, be very suitable for a promontory enclosure, cutting off some 3 acres at the tip of a steep-sided spur. Playne (1876, No. 15) found the 'camp' nearly levelled by cultivation; Witts (1883, No. 11) follows Playne. Both authorities allow the enclosure only 1 acre, but more before quarrying cut back the sides of the spur.

The bank is of very variable form along its length. At the N. end it is 50 ft. across with a fall of 1 ft. on the W. and of

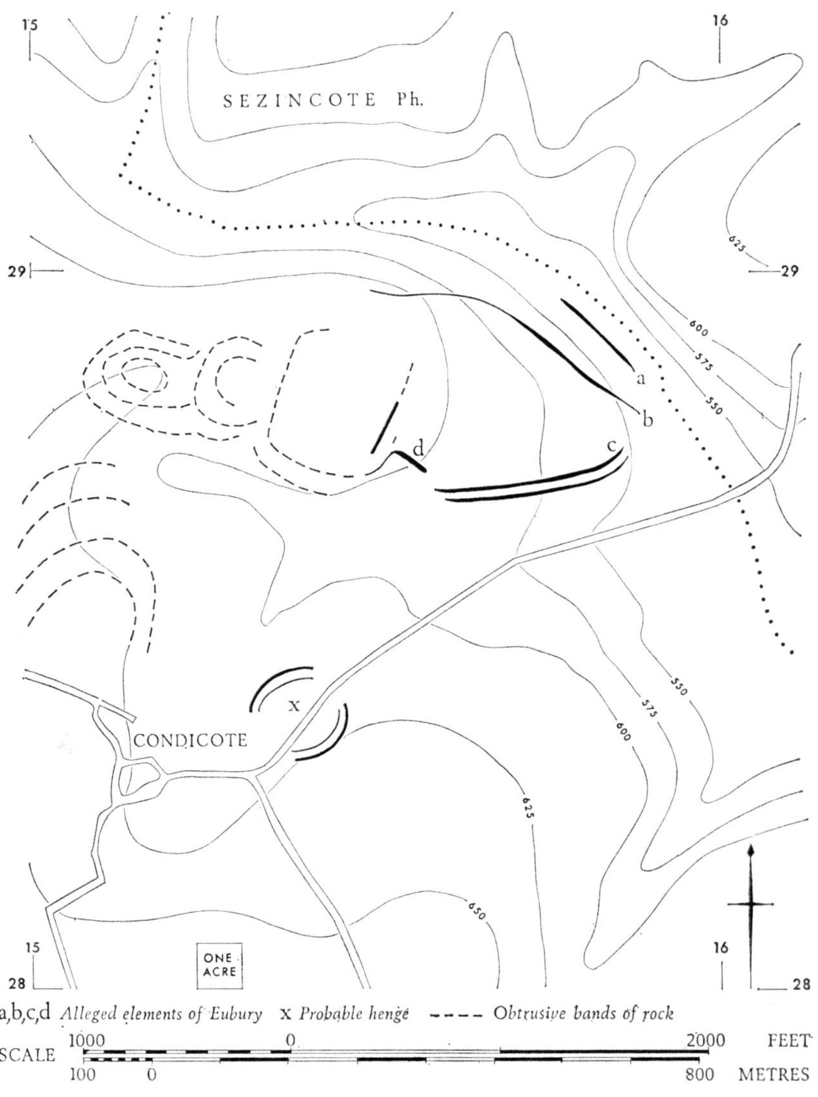

Eubury. Discredited hill-fort at CONDICOTE.

2 ft. on the E. Augering met rock at a depth of 1 ft. on the line of any possible ditch. Some 40 yds. from the N. end, the bank is 33 ft. across with a short steep fall of 2½ ft. on the E.; a broad shallow gully up to 45 ft. wide lies beside the bank on this side. The auger penetrated no further than 1 ft. 8 in. on the E. side of the S. angle in the bank.

Some 90 yds. to N.W. another broad, low and irregular bank spans most of the ridge. About 70 ft. across and 2 ft. high, it also is of uncertain origin and possibly natural. In the 19th century a number of flint arrowheads were found about 200 yds. N.W. of the first bank.

DOWDESWELL. *Dowdeswell Camp No. 2* (SP 003191), (Witts (1883), No. 37), immediately E. of the Manor House, is marked as an ancient earthwork on the 6-inch O.S. The site consists of two much disturbed, roughly parallel banks, up to 50 ft. across and in places 7 ft. high, each with a ditch on the E. side; they are undated. The site slopes gently N., with a steep fall N. of the road. To the S. the ground rises from the earthworks. The situation suggests manorial origins.

DOWDESWELL. '*Camp*' (area SP 003198), possibly identical with Burrow's 'Camp No. 3', is variously marked on old O.S. maps as E. and N. of St. Michael's Church, Lower Dowdeswell. The site is probably explained as degraded strip lynchets and natural scarping.

HAWKESBURY. *Hawkesbury Knoll* (ST 768872) has no trace of Iron Age defences. Strip lynchets, some showing signs of substantial alteration and including areas of 19th-century narrow plough ridges, curve around the domed spur of the knoll on the W. side (Plate 68). On the brow is a long barrow (Hawkesbury I, *TBGAS*, 79 (1961), 80).

An Iron Age pot is said to have been found here in 1910 (O.S. records), but it has not been traced.

Air photographs—C.U.A.P., AIO 90–4; AML 23–4. R.A.F., VAP 106 G/UK 1721: 3184–6.

KING'S STANLEY. *Selsley Hill Camp* (SO 83100347), (Witts (1883), No. 90), presumably the same as 'ancient earthwork' on O.S. 6-inch, consists of a scarp of variable form, up to 5 ft. high, extending in three sections over a total length of 100 yds. A 'ditch' or a long, narrow hollow lies along the foot of the central section. The situation is perhaps 50 ft. below the brow of an even slope of some 8°, facing N. The scarps roughly follow the contour, but do not span the ridge.

The central section is a scarp about 4½ ft. high with slight traces of an uneven bank above it; the 'ditch' at its foot is 10 ft. across and up to 2 ft. deep. The other sections are separated from the central section by a hollow-way and a quarry. That on the E. has parallel linear hollows with a medial 'bank' above a scarp some 5 ft. high. On the W. is a scarp 4 ft. high without any sign of an associated bank or ditch. There is no indication of date and nothing to indicate Iron Age origin.

RENDCOMB. *Rendcomb Camp* (SP 020103) appears on some O.S. maps. The situation is appropriate to a hill-fort, but the banks and scarps, some seen recently during mechanical stripping and grading, are mainly geological (assessment by Dr. Cave, Inst. Geol. Sc.). To N.W., a 6-ft. scarp (a) capped by a low bank, mostly humus, drops to a hollowed terrace with a scarp falling a further 6 ft. beyond. The scarps are slightly uptilted

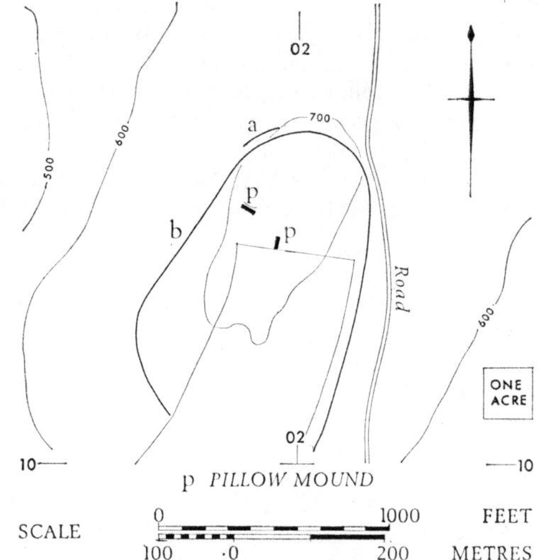

ridges of natural limestone. The hollowing is perhaps due to a track; there is no ditch. Another scarp (b), of variable height and generally lower down the E. side of the hill, following the contour, may be partly explained as the upper edge of land-slip zones. Pillow-mounds suggest former rabbit farming in the area.

STANWAY. *Upper Coscombe* (SP 074295). This so-called multivallate hill-fort is the product of a natural oval of soil-marks of alternating dark and light bands (corresponding with banks and linear hollows) encircling more than 35 acres of a prominent hill-top. They are most clearly seen on air photographs

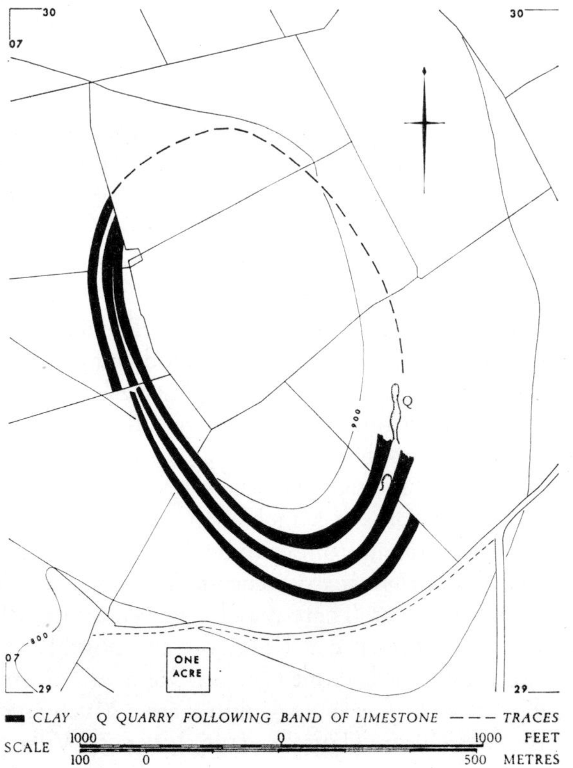

(Plate 67), especially at S. and S.E. where there are three dark and two light bands. The dark bands consist of clay of the Inferior Oolite series, embodying lines of limestone. The linear quarry at S.E. follows one of these limestone lines. On the ground the lines occur as broad banks, several feet high, between hollow lines of dark soil.

Air photographs—Meridian VAP 89 67, 163–6. C.U.A.P., OAP, AKV 10–12; AQJ 66. Geological data provided by Dr. Cave.

STANWAY. *Hailes Wood* (SP 056301), called a 'camp' by St. Clair Baddeley (*TBGAS*, LII (1930), 198, No. 4), lies on a slope 400 ft. below and 700 yds. W. of Beckbury hill-fort. Confused ridges and hollows over about 2 acres are probably attributable to geological causes and to wear along tracks.

STINCHCOMBE. *Drakestone Point* (ST 73639795), variously described as a camp (*Arch*, XIX (1821), 166–7), a signal station (Witts (1883), No. 39) and a motte and bailey (Playne (1876), No. 36; *PCNFC*, VIII (1883–4), 158), consists of natural ridges and gullies cutting off a very small part of the narrow, tapering tip of a ridge. The thirty-two 'pit-dwellings' described by Witts a little to the N. of Drakestone Point are also natural. Some of them were planned by Playne.

WINCHCOMBE. *Langley Hill* (SP 008290) is sometimes described as a camp (*e.g.* Burrow (1924), 131). The site, on Inferior Oolite and heavily quarried in more than one phase, is at the highest point of the hill. Irregular banks with hollowing immediately inside them define the limits of early quarrying on W. and S. Quarrying extends outside the line on the E. There is a gap of at least 100 yds. without any trace of bank or

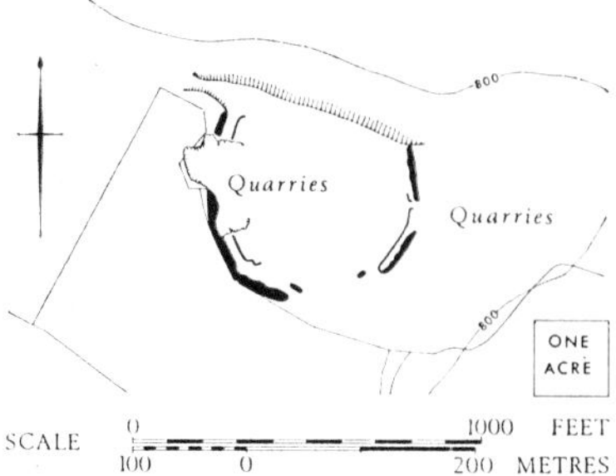

ditch on S., where the ground slopes gently away. To the N. the ground falls steeply from a scarp edge. The banks, none of which have external ditches, tend to have regular faces on the outside only. They are from 3 ft. to 7 ft. high and from 12 ft. to over 30 ft. across. The internal hollowing varies from very slight in the N.W. to over 30 ft. across and 7 ft. deep in the S.W. A relatively late and deep quarry cuts through the bank on the W.; to N. and S. the remains are fairly regular for stretches of some 20 yds.

These remains appear to be comparatively orderly lines of dumps on the edge of an early quarry (cf. Oxenton (1)). No Iron Age finds are known.

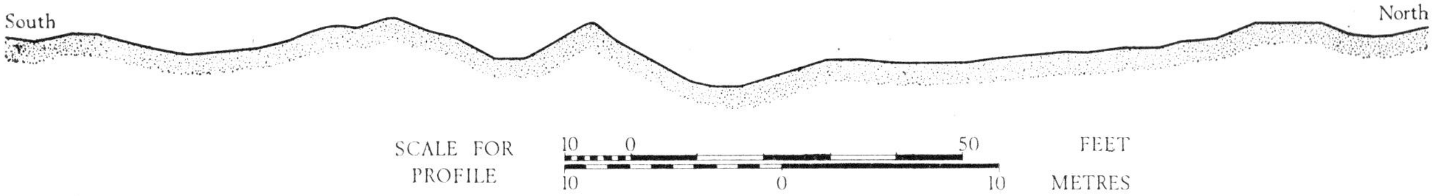

STINCHCOMBE. Profile of natural ridges and gullies, Drakestone Point.

THE ROMAN PERIOD

The Gloucestershire Cotswolds were part of the territory of the *Dobunni*. Numismatic evidence suggests that in the two decades preceding the Roman conquest there was dual power, coins inscribed ANTED and EISU from the earlier part of the period being succeeded by a different series, with CORIO and BODVOC. The romanised epigraphic style of the last perhaps reflects a significant political attitude. It is known that part of a tribe, probably to be identified with the Dobunni, surrendered to Aulus Plautius in A.D. 43. The Iron Age hill-forts of the Cotswolds area are generally slight compared, for instance, with those of Wessex W. of the R. Test, and they show no signs of added fortification, as though there were little care for any military threat. Earthworks at Minchinhampton include unfinished elements, but remain an enigma.

The first Roman frontier to be established (by about A.D. 47) was based upon the line of the Foss Way; it pivoted on *Corinium* (Cirencester) where the only positively identified early Roman forts in the area of this volume occur. There may have been a fort at Dorn (Batsford), but undated, and there are indications of a military presence at Kingscote and possibly at Rodborough.

Corinium was laid out very early as a large Roman town, once the garrison had moved on. The region had great virtues as an agricultural area. Much attention was paid to Mars, probably in his original role as god of agriculture (Toynbee (1964), 154–5). Villas were well established in the 2nd century, but it is in the

4th century that many are seen to expand to richness. The loss of authority by the central Roman power came officially here, as elsewhere, with the rescript of Honorius in 410, but was not abrupt. The ensuing change in the pattern of life is tentatively discussed below (pp. xxxvi and xliv).

Corinium Dobunnorum

Corinium, the administrative centre of the tribal territory of the Dobunni, lies 2½ miles S. of Bagendon, a capital of the tribe in the immediate pre-Roman period; it also marks the point where the R. Churn emerges from the limestone uplands (over 400 ft. above O.D.), the southern edge of which was chosen as the alignment of Roman roads to E. and S.W. (map opp. p. xxiii). Corinium became the second largest city in Britain and must in the later Roman period have been the capital of *Britannia Prima* (*RIB*, No. 103). Its walls enclosed over 240 acres.

The earliest known occupation is military. At least two successive 1st-century forts have been identified, but the evidence is too fragmentary for overall description; the north defences of one fort lay under the basilica. Other military works lie partly under later civilian defences at the S. end of the city. A garrison appears to have been maintained at Corinium until the early Flavian period. Both its attested units are of cavalry, the *ala Indiana* and the *ala Thracum* (*RIB*, Nos. 108–9).

The essential components of the still-discernible Roman road system are likely to have been constructed soon after military occupation started. The convergence of Ermin Street, Akeman Street, the Foss Way and the White Way made Corinium an important centre of control (see map on p. xlvi). None of these roads has been excavated as it approaches the town and precise alignments are in places uncertain. Kingshill Lane, to the E., may be of Roman origin; it lies between the Foss Way and Ermin Street and for most of its length is coincident with the parish boundary between Cirencester and Preston (map opp. p. xxxvi).

Excavations within the walled area, particularly since 1960, have provided many details of the town's development, although the 'rescue' nature of much of this work has not allowed the full examination of most buildings. Traces of Neronian timber buildings probably represent the first civilian settlement; they were part of a *vicus* outside the N. fort. A street grid was laid down later in the 1st century, not long after the withdrawal of troops and the levelling of the military defences. By its rigid pattern most of the new town was divided into fifteen rectangular insulae. The forum with its basilica (known since 1897, the largest in Roman Britain outside London), a smaller market adjacent to it, many houses and shops, and the amphitheatre outside the town to the S.W. originated in this period. The basilica was built across the soft fill of the underlying fort ditches; it subsequently collapsed and was rebuilt. Plausible evidence for a theatre has been traced near the N. gate of the city.

As in most Romano-British towns the private houses were at first built of timber, but as the 2nd century progressed they were rebuilt in stone and decorated with mosaics and painted wall plaster. The amphitheatre was strengthened by masonry. Limestone suitable for the purpose is easily accessible immediately W. of the town and part of the extensive quarrying in that area has now been shown by excavation to be of Roman origin. Through the vicissitudes of development the individual bounds of property seem often to have been maintained. Ultimately, the larger private houses as well as public buildings displayed notable luxury.

The defences can be dated from the later 2nd century when an earthen rampart and ditch were made around the city, with at least one stone watch-tower and with the monumental St. Albans (Verulamium) Gate on the N.E. The R. Churn, early canalised along the E. side of the city, was crossed by a stone bridge outside the gate. Floodwater on this side of the city remained a problem throughout the Roman period. The rampart was later cut back to receive a stone wall, itself in places subsequently rebuilt and widened. In the 4th century polygonal external bastions were added.

It is probable that a reorganisation of provincial administration by Diocletian involved the promotion of Corinium to capital of the new province of *Britannia Prima* around A.D. 300; if so, the residence of the provincial governor was here. Much rebuilding took place. The most notable projects known are the division and enlargement of the forum, and the reconstruction of the adjacent market building. There is evidence for the presence in the city of sculptors, mosaic workers and other craftsmen.

Cirencester provides much evidence for the worship of gods, both Roman and Celtic in origin. A temple to Mercury is implied by reliefs and a stone head. Minerva and Diana are represented by other sculptural fragments and Jupiter Optimus Maximus by a dedication. The Syrian Jupiter Dolichenus is portrayed in a small bronze statuette. Native deities include a river god, *genii* personifying the locality, *genii cucullati*, often in triad, and *deae matres*.

Evidence of Christianity in the city by the 2nd or 3rd century is probably shown by a word-square cryptogram scratched on wall-plaster; it was found in 1868 and apparently embodies Pater Noster, A(lpha) and O(mega). The Orpheus motif, the most notable characteristic of the Corinian school of mosaicists, is sometimes thought to have Christian connotations, but this is disputable.

The environs include native settlements of imprecise status and date (map opposite). Cemeteries are known on the W., E. and S. sides (see list with map key below). To the N., a single skeleton was recorded in 1842 at some unlocated point near Ermin Street. Most burials occur to the W., near the presumed course of the Foss Way, or between the city wall and the amphitheatre, or scattered in the large area known as 'the Querns' between the amphitheatre and the Foss. Cremation burials were recorded as early as the 16th century in a probable barrow of undetermined date, N. of the Tetbury Road (Foss Way), (b on map). Modern excavation of cemeteries has taken place only at d, S.E. of b and at m, N.E. of the amphitheatre. At site d cremation burials began in the 1st century A.D., and inhumation in the 3rd century. At site m inhumations continued into the 5th century, witness a worn coin of Honorius found sealed under one of the skeletons excavated in 1969. To the S., burials by Ermin Street include two 1st-century military tombstones (at v), also cremations and inhumations. Little information is available concerning burials along Akeman Street on the E. side of the town, and no cremations are yet recorded there.

At present only very limited evidence is available concerning the end of Roman Cirencester. It seems from the dearth of rubbish and coins on the worn floor of the forum that this public place was maintained and cleaned until well into the 5th century. The large inhumation cemetery (m) near the amphitheatre, currently under excavation, remained in use after A.D. 400, as noted above. Five bronze buckles decorated in a style characteristic of late Roman military dress are an indication that the city was garrisoned in the early part of the 5th century (*Med. Archaeol.*, V (1961), 43, 47, 50). The absence, however, of grass-tempered pottery and of fine wares imported from the Mediterranean suggests that it had become largely deserted by the later 5th century. A skeleton was found in the last ditch cut alongside Ermin Street—suggestive evidence of the breakdown of urban life.

Select bibliography: *PNG*, I (1960), 60–2. *Arch*, LXIX (1917–18), 161–209 (summary). *Ant J*, XXXVII (1957), 206–15 (excavations, 1952); XLI (1961), 63–71; XLII (1962), 1–14, 160–82 (excavations, 1959); XLIII (1963), 15–26; XLIV (1964), 9–18; XLV (1965), 97–110; XLVI (1966), 240–54; XLVII (1967), 185–97; XLIX (1969), 222–43 (interim reports on excavations, 1960–8). *TBGAS*, 76 (1957), 21–34 (cryptogram); 78 (1959), 44–85 (excavations, 1957). *Britannia*, I (1970), 227–39. *RIB*, Nos. 101–18. J. M. C. Toynbee, *Art in Roman Britain* (1962), 7; Toynbee (1964), *passim* (sculptors). Lewis (1966), *passim* (pagan religion). For data on Roman burials we owe much to a MS. kindly made available by Mr. D. J. Viner; Messrs. P. D. C. Brown and A. D. McWhirr have provided other details. We are grateful to Mr. J. S. Wacher for permission to use information contained in his chapter on Roman Cirencester in *The Towns of Roman Britain* (Batsford, 1974).

Key to map opposite.

- a Stone coffin, 1877
- b ? barrow: cremations reported 16th–18th centuries (Grismund's Tower)
- c Skeleton, 1896
- d At least 46 cremations and 8 inhumations, 1960. Stone coffin
- e Urns, 2 stone coffins, stone cist, 1867 (Cattle Market)
- f Stone coffins, 1760 and 1825; 'cremation stone' and stone coffin, 1969
- g Cremation, 1934
- h Stone coffin
- j Stone coffin, 1913
- k Skeletons, *c.* 1850
- l Stone coffin
- m A cremation and 267 inhumations (1972), N. and S. of a Roman road
- n Skull and bones, up to 1949
- p Human remains, 1971
- q Inhumation, 1967
- r Human remains, 1916
- s 4 tombstones, ? reused, 1971
- t 6 inhumations, 1954
- u 2 military tombstones (*RIB*, Nos. 108, 109), one other tombstone (*RIB*, No. 110), 8 inhumations, 1835–1955
- v 'Cremation stone', 1955

Other burials have been reported, but are less precisely located than those listed.

Rural Romano-British Sites

In considering the nature of the remains it must be noted that there are few earthworks to indicate with certainty the former existence of Roman buildings. Some are marked by mounds, others by levelled areas, and discovery has been largely a matter of chance. There are therefore substantial difficulties both in the assessment of the overall pattern of distribution and in the interpretation of individual sites. Even where earthworks exist there may be problems of interpretation; such may be expected when mediaeval and Roman remains are intermixed as, for instance, at Whittington (3), at Slutswell in Elkstone and at Upton in Blockley.

Even large and well-marked sites present difficulties. In their unexcavated state the earthworks near Bibury Mill, Bibury (2), are thought to show the site of a large house and an adjacent cluster of small buildings, but this is by no means certain; it could be a hamlet. At Stancombe in Duntisbourne Rouse (4) the interpretation of most of the earthworks is dubious. The terraces are almost certainly Roman, and Roman buildings stood close by (one occupying a prominent rectangular mound), but the terraces have no revetment and it is not certain that they supported buildings; similar terraces are known to be integral with rural settlements in certain unexcavated Wiltshire sites. The enigmatic Romano-British site at Baunton (1) may well result from the ploughing down of such a site. The remains of the major Romano-British settlement at Dorn in Batsford (1) have been much ploughed, but they suggest a very large ditch surrounding a rectangular area of 10 acres which was a focal point throughout the Roman period.

In some places the former presence of Roman buildings is indicated merely by debris in ploughed fields. In others, air photographs disclose crop-marks of enclosures etc., mostly undated by finds and assigned to the Iron Age or to the Romano-British period solely on the evidence of their shape and situation.

The discovery of the remains of Roman settlement is part of the history of land use. The earliest specific records are of the 17th century, when finds are reported from arable fields, but at a much earlier period people were certainly aware of their existence. Roman sites were robbed for building stone, rubble and material for lime-burning at a date early enough to be reflected in mediaeval place-names. It was natural to treat such sites as quarries; Lysons describes the avid exploitation in the 18th century of such easily procured stone. The villa at Stockwood in Colesbourne (2), on Fuller's Earth, suffered the loss of at least 200 cartloads, and some of the Roman column fragments now at Combend Manor in Elkstone (Plate 27) were removed probably at this time. The villa at Spoonley Wood, Sudeley (4), was exposed during a search for stone, but the presence of old walls must already have been known; no one would search for natural stone in so unpromising an area.

Before Victorian times, when there were noteworthy attempts to preserve and partly reconstruct the villas at Chedworth (1) and at Sudeley (2) and (4), nothing was done for the preservation of Roman villas. At Whittington (3) the Saxon and mediaeval village street cuts across the Roman site. At Swell (2) and at Chedworth (1) lime kilns are found, and moulded stones were among the pieces found gathered at Chedworth presumably in readiness for the kiln. A 19th-century farmyard at Abbotswood was paved with pottery fragments taken from the nearby Roman villa at Swell. Certain apparently destructive processes were less damaging than the surface remains might suggest; for example, ridge-and-furrow ploughing at Withington (2) and at Great Rissington (1) caused accumulations of ridge-soil actually to protect the mosaic pavements, but the plough-shares probably skidded on the hard surface of the tesserae in the furrows (Plate 51).

Subsequent land use has thus caused many villas or parts of villas to be removed and others to be built over, perhaps for the reuse of their foundations. The drawing facing p. xl shows graphically the incompleteness of even well-recorded remains. Often only foundations survive, and evidence for architectural ornament is sparse. The amount of debris is rarely indicative of original wall height. At Sudeley (4), however, the stone walls can be assessed as having stood at least 7 ft. high.

As with villas, the recognition of Romano-British settlements often depends on the discovery of datable debris in the course of farming or quarrying. Settlements identified through crop-marks are usually imprecise in area and date; it is often impossible to recognise the limits of clustering domestic closes, or the function of rural enclosures. In some cases, *e.g.* Siddington (7), the extent of recorded Romano-British debris does not tally with the crop-marks, and it must be accepted that spreads of debris are never a sure indication of the dates of crop-marks.

In certain places general clearance may shift the apparent site of a former settlement; this may have happened at Withington (3), and excavation has recently proved it at Charlton Kings (p. 23). Other crop-marks contain evidence of periods outside the scope of this work, notably Bronze Age ring-ditches (see Appendix B) and post-Roman drainage ditches (*e.g.* Fairford (4)–(6)).

Spreads of blackened earth are found in certain settlement areas, notably in a field called Black Close at Wycomb, Whittington (2). On other sites, such as the very large ones at Kingscote (1), blackening is totally absent. Apart from being obviously related to the survival of burnt material, the phenomenon is more easily noted than explained.

Romano-British Villas

To avoid ambiguity the term 'villa' is used in this work to denote a rural establishment of consequence, independent of a settlement, containing a building with heated rooms, or baths, or mosaic pavements, or sophisticated architectural features such as columns. In the absence of complete plans and adequate knowledge of local Roman systems of tenure and estate areas, our criteria may admit into the category of 'villa' such diverse things as the headquarters of an estate, an independent farm, or part of a religious establishment. It must be remembered, too, that analogous buildings occur in rural settlements and towns.

Most villas would have contained all the architectural features mentioned above. Twenty-five villas are known in the area, some comprising more than one building. Thirteen more are attested by debris representing at least one of the four diagnostic factors. There can be no doubt that our present record is incomplete and that it will be greatly augmented by future research.

As yet there are very few indications of Roman villas on sites that are known to have been used in the Iron Age (for hill-forts possibly so occupied, see p. xliv). An Iron Age ditch lies underneath the villa at Great Witcombe (1). Romano-British antecedents of unknown form, but certainly dating from the 1st century A.D., are known at Great Witcombe (1) and at Frocester (2). Samian ware suggests 2nd-century occupation in several places, and 2nd-century buildings occur at Chedworth (1) and at Whittington (3). Some small villas, Barnsley (1) and Farmington (1) for example, originated late in the 3rd or in the 4th century and despite additions remained obscure, never attaining any great size. The really grand villas were built in the 4th century.

According to the available evidence, villas both great and small suffered changes of use and deteriorating standards of living towards the end of the 4th century. At Barnsley (1) and Chedworth (1) the coin count drops dramatically in this period (*TBGAS*, 86 (1967), 79). But at both these places and also at Frocester (2) there is evidence of renewed activity in the 5th century. Para-military buckles of the late 4th or early 5th century have been found in the areas of Barnsley (1), Chedworth (1) and Sudeley (4).

Villas were usually sited near copious supplies of water, necessary to sustain the elaborate bathing arrangements. They may be by a river or a stream or, if uphill, near a springline such as occurs at the junction of Great Oolite and Fuller's Earth (map opposite p. xxiii). A situation on a shelf or shoulder above a valley is not obviously well watered, but on occasion, as at Farmington (1), excavation has shown it to be so. The water supply may be profuse and require elaborate channelling, as at Ebrington and Great Witcombe; the present wetness of the ground on the E. of the villa in Spoonley Wood (Sudeley (4)) probably results from long neglect of such channelling. At Chedworth (1) the water passed through a nymphaeum, but this is the only certain example to be recognised in the area. Some villas are served by wells; the villa at Barnsley also has ponds near by and these suggest other sources of supply, as does the pond at Woodchester. There is no clear indication that any particular subsoil or soil was avoided or favoured and the settings are very varied. Great Witcombe stands on a steep slope (Plate 24).

There is a tendency for villas to face S.E., and the orientation occasionally continues in adjacent closes and fields, as is particularly noticeable at Barnsley Park. If not derived merely from considerations of practical utility, the south-eastward orientation of villas could be a continuation of the practice found in Iron Age round houses. Of possible significance in this context are a number of sharply rectangular enclosures, most of them discrete and without any indication of date, which have entrances in their E. or S. sides. At Driffield (1) the mound of a collapsed Roman building is still seen within the crop-mark, itself undated in a strict sense, and at Temple Guiting (5) two comparable enclosures are connected with an axial system which includes pit-alignments of conventional late Iron Age or early Roman date.

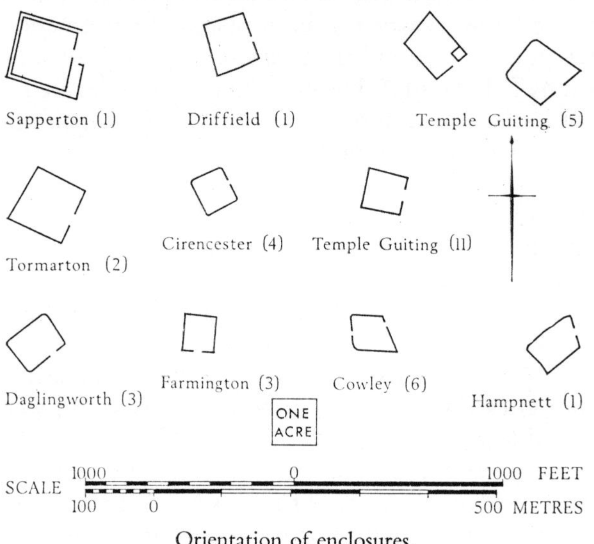

Orientation of enclosures.

The physical boundaries of villa land-holdings have not been recognised at any point in the Gloucestershire Cotswolds (but see footnote on p. xxiv). Our ignorance of tenurial relationships makes it difficult to establish the status and influence of different sites and prohibits the analysis of relative position. Groups of buildings around a villa are likely to be closely connected with it but, if a colonate system be allowed, buildings two or three miles distant, whether in a community settlement or not, might equally well be associated.

The list of villas given on p. xlii includes establishments of widely varying status, as is reflected in their size, arrangement and probable function of rooms and in the quality of the architectural detail. Such plans as can be determined are shown together in simplified form in the illustration facing p. xl. The simplest clearly recognisable forms, some of them originating no earlier than the mid 4th century, combine rural functionalism with the architectural features that justify calling the building a villa. At Farmington (1), Barnsley (1) and Frocester (2), oblong areas, divided by inset walls and by the treatment of their floors according to the different uses of the several parts, are set behind impressive façades, perhaps added, comprising porticos with wing-like end rooms. There is no certainty how the oblong areas were roofed. Rooms added to or built within the central area sometimes had mosaic floors and hypocausts. The portico or corridor was present in the simplest as also in the most complex villas and provided a characteristic Roman frontage. Signs of partitions within the corridor, as at Farmington (1), or of width greater than would be required by a mere passage, as at Great Witcombe, indicate that the corridors were something more than a mere means of communication between rooms or parts of the building; they gave architectural unity to the façade. Very infrequently there are traces of precinct enclosures contributing to the unity of the site, notably at Chedworth (1), at Frocester (2), where ditches mark the boundary, at Swell (2) and at Bisley (1). At Bisley, a very large and enigmatic site, the 19th-century excavator noted that the walls surrounding the area of building were 5 ft. thick, more than twice the breadth of the exterior walls in most Cotswold villas.

The significance of the ranges of rooms inside the villas is often controversial. At Chedworth the kitchens, the dining rooms and the baths are all duplicated and the baths are of different types, suggesting use by separate elements of the same household, or perhaps use in different seasons, as classical authors advised.

The position of the main entrance, and so of the room normally first entered, is sometimes made clear by approach paths or by gates; normally it leads directly to the central room of the main range. In contrast, the entrances to the inner court at Woodchester and Chedworth are not precisely opposite the probable entrances to the main block. At Sudeley (4), where the main court has an indication of subdivision, and at Frocester, paved tracks run symmetrically to the centre of the main blocks. The identity of kitchens, dining rooms and bath rooms is rarely in doubt. The mediaeval practise of placing a dais in a dining room suggests an explanation of the higher floor-level of a room (33) adjoining a kitchen at Chedworth. The differing levels of the floors noted by Lysons at Withington are curious and hardly divergent enough to be explained, as at Great Witcombe, by the inclination of the ground. Any interpretation of plan must take the possibility of upper storeys into account. Suggestive evidence has been put forward for these at Great Witcombe, Chedworth Woods, Whittington Court and Frocester Court. Colesbourne (2) is the only villa where the remains do not lie within roughly rectangular limits; there, long and broad terraces beside the buildings add to the difficulties of interpretation.

The importance of a villa in the social sense may be considered on the basis of its size and architectural quality. The large central room at Woodchester, in the position noted as suitable for a principal reception chamber, matches in its magnificence the richness of the inner court. The room in a comparable position at Great Witcombe is small by comparison, but it was curiously shaped in both phases of construction. The significance of the contrast between these elaborate focal rooms and the coarse-floored halls of some small villas, such as Farmington (1), has been discussed by J. T. Smith.* The position of rooms devoted to domestic economy is another indication of the status of a villa. No such rooms existed in the magnificent inner court at Woodchester, where heated rooms and mosaic floors are found in all ranges; by contrast the wide-set lateral ranges of the second court, invisible through the entrance from the inner court, had fewer signs of opulence (although there is a possibility of mosaics in the S.W. range and statuary was found in the N.E. range). While domestic industries in the great buildings may thus be relegated to separate ranges or to attendant buildings (Sudeley (4)), in the smaller villas like Barnsley, Farmington or Frocester (2) they may be in or near the main house. At Frocester the central area contained a forge, and there is evidence that fulling took place against the N.E. side of the villa. Kitchens may or may not be present in ranges of residential rooms; at Chedworth (1) rooms with ovens lay close to each dining room. Stone-built latrines have been found only at Chedworth (1), Ebrington and Great Witcombe and those at Chedworth were converted to another use in a later stage of the villa's existence.

The indications of economy are preponderantly compatible with a rural estate or farm, a diversity of attendant domestic services being indicated with different degrees of clarity. At Frocester (2), for instance, as well as fulling there are suggestions of lime-slaking and tanning together with builders' and craftsmens' debris. Walled paddocks around Barnsley (1) are integral both with the villa and with the extensive arable fields beyond, aptly illustrating the mixture of pasture and tillage which probably was practised over wide areas. Scythes of 'Great Chesterford' type found at Barnsley are highly developed harvesting implements. Unfortunately we have no statistical analysis of animal bones. Sheep-rearing on the downs is indicated by a sheep-bell found at Frocester. Cattle stalls have been proposed for the aisled structure in Sudeley (4) and also for a building without 'villa' characteristics at Cherington (Applebaum, *Agrarian History*, I, ii, 143–4). The same commentator would see a cow-byre at one end of Rodmarton (1). Money chests sunk in floors at Frocester (2) and probably at Chedworth (1) represent a practice found also in a settlement without clear signs of fine buildings, Chessels at Lower Slaughter (1). Large numbers of coins and *styli* at Barnsley are, however, a reminder that the villa may have been part of a large estate or some other commercially involved establishment. Possible indications of religious practices or attitudes are discussed below (p. l).

It is clear that professional builders, stone-masons, plasterers and tile-makers were present in the area, the last named being attested by the frequent occurrence of stamps bearing initials impressed on the wet clay, presumably to identify their source; one at least of these was municipally owned. Repairs were occasionally done by improvisation to lower standards than the original building; for example, stone *pilae* of baluster form are found reused in walls at Chedworth. The inferior patching of mosaics (Plates 2 and 4/5) is another instance of repairs done by craftsmen less skilful than the original ones. In hypocaust systems stone *pilae* are sometimes replaced by channels, a simpler if less efficient form.

Limestone rubble, perhaps reinforced with timber, appears to have been the normal material for the walls of villas. Red sandstone was sometimes used for flues, doubtless because it is more heat-resistant, but the limestone pillars in hypocausts seem to have been little affected by the underfloor heat. Barrel vaults over bath-house areas were sometimes of tufa, but hollow earthenware voussoirs were found at Chedworth. Roofs generally were covered with stone slates, frequently the very heavy 'Stonesfield' slates, but *tegulae* predominate at Great Witcombe (1); the ridges might terminate in stone finials such as were found at Chedworth (1).

Columns of whatever size were normally of local limestone, lathe-turned and with double-torus mouldings at the base (Plate 29). Wooden column shafts were probably used in the large room at Woodchester. It may be noted that some stone columns were used in exposed situations while others were protected from the weather; Great Witcombe has examples of both sorts, weathered and unweathered. One use was on

---

* Paper read to Society of Antiquaries of London, 15 March 1973.

dwarf walls along corridors. Fretted limestone panels with double-S motifs (Plate 28) at Chedworth (1) and Great Witcombe (1) probably formed balustrades, but they were not found *in situ*; details indicate that they were not free-standing. The exterior faces of walls, as at Chedworth, were sometimes and perhaps always rendered. Inside, the use of painted wall-plaster was commonplace, but only one villa (Colesbourne (2)) has evidence of a frieze with human figures. Window glass is frequently recorded. Statuary only occurs in the large villas, and from the remains found it appears generally to have been of small size. Imported marble emphasises the richness at Ebrington as well as at Woodchester.

Tessellated and Mosaic Pavements

The tesserae are usually set in patterns, but we include examples where the surviving evidence consists only of plain fragments. Such pavements are known in detail in twelve villas; their presence is certain in another five villas, but without details, and they are suspected as having been present in five more. In settlements other than villa complexes, tesserae have been noted in seven buildings and suspected on three more sites. This tally of thirty-two known or suspected rural sites with mosaics is certainly fewer than existed. Mosaics have been reported, but can no longer be precisely located, in Badminton Park, at Bitton, at Chedworth village and at Kingscote. The latter example was probably in or near The Chessalls, Kingscote (1).

The materials used for tesserae were various kinds of earthenware, oolitic limestone, sandstone and blue lias; hence the colours are predominantly red, white or cream, and blue, brown and black. A 19th-century report mentions glass at The Capitol, Chedworth (2).

The area covered by Gloucestershire, Somerset and Dorset is rich in Roman mosaic pavements, containing half the total number known in Britain (D. J. Smith, *RVB*, 74), and a high proportion of this wealth is found in the Gloucestershire Cotswolds. The villa at Woodchester has the largest Roman floor mosaic known in N.W. Europe (Plates 17, 19–21). The limited archaeological evidence (best at Frocester (2)) and stylistic affinities indicate that all the pavements are of the 4th century.

Regional schools of mosaicists are suggested by the recurrence of certain characteristic themes and motifs within particular areas. The largest as yet postulated in Britain, presumably based on workshops in Corinium, is called the Corinian school; its products are found from Dorset to Oxfordshire and perhaps even further afield. To assist in the analysis of pattern which is fundamental to such identifications the Inventory seeks wherever possible to present, at a constant scale, vertical photographs or drawings of every mosaic pavement known in the Cotswold area; some examples are presented in both vertical and oblique views to give a better idea of the setting.* Samuel Lysons's drawings, on which we have to rely for our knowledge of some pavements, have been proved accurate whenever comparison with the originals is possible.

The most obvious pointer to the existence of the Corinian school is the appearance, in three villas, of elaborate and closely comparable pavements showing Orpheus seated within a frame of concentric borders on which are depicted friezes of beasts, fishes and birds (Plates 1, 16, 17). Strong evidence of the school is seen in the recurrence of certain natural and geometric motifs, best illustrated in the great array of pavements at Woodchester (Plates 17–23). Some sort of pattern book was evidently used, although treatments rarely correspond in exact detail (cf. the stylistically similar tiger and tigress in the pavements at The Barton in Cirencester, and at Woodchester). Certain geometrical motifs such as the laurel wreaths in the Orpheus pavements of Woodchester and Cirencester have not been noted outside the area served by the Corinian school. Other motifs, known elsewhere, are devised in characteristic ways; for example the saltire in room 10 at Chedworth (1), (Plate 2). At Painswick (2) the remains of interlaced squares with a particular floral motif (Plate 8) can just be seen; this motif is characteristic of a certain design, which may be called 'saltire derivative', found in villas in the S.W. of the Cotswold area and on other sites with mosaics attributable to the Corinian school.† In the often-used pattern of intersecting circles, variety was achieved by varying the size, colour and minor details of the elements (Plates 6 and 7), the change in emphasis producing a marked variety of effect. Regrettably we have little information on the complementary effect of floor mosaics with painted wall-plaster.

---

* Two pavements, now inaccessible, are recorded only in oblique photographs.

† We are grateful to Dr. D. J. Smith for his comments on this and other points.

Not all mosaics in the Cotswold area were of the Corinian school. A pavement at Withington (2) is thought from the treatment of Neptune and aquatic creatures (Plate 15) to belong to a school postulated at Durnovaria (Dorchester). Other pavements were made by craftsmen of inferior competence; such could be the pavement of coarse tesserae, badly sunken over a flue, in building (a) at Duntisbourne Rouse (4).

Changes of taste, attitudes or resources are attested by the superimposition of one floor on another. At Cirencester (1) an earlier mosaic was thought to lie beneath the Orpheus pavement. At Chedworth (1), on the other hand, a mosaic was superseded by a pavement of stone slabs. In other rooms of the same villa there were ill-matched repairs (as in room 5, R on Plate 4/5), and similar repairs are seen in corridor 2 at Woodchester (Plate 23). Such examples complement other evidence of the eventual decline in technical ability, resources and taste.

Buildings other than Villas

In the Inventory, the word 'building' is used to denote Romano-British structures which have none of the attributes of villas. The surviving evidence consists generally of foundations and spreads of stone; little is known of wooden buildings. In size and complexity these monuments sometimes match the smaller villas, *e.g.* Cherington (1). Smaller buildings existed in relatively large numbers; the settlement at Kingscote (1) contains a notable concentration. Apart from some buildings at Chessels, Lower Slaughter (1), individual plans are unknown and size can usually be inferred only from the extent of debris or the area of a platform. The earthwork remains of a building 40 ft. long occur in the area of the Romano-British settlement at Avening (1), but these are not certainly Roman.

Most known buildings are rectangular. Circular examples include the drystone structures under the Barnsley villa, a walled structure near the villa at Swell (2) and wooden huts in the Chessels settlement at Lower Slaughter. Chedworth (2), apparently an elaborate stone building, may also have been round.

Of the fifteen known buildings outside settlements, three (Coates (2)–(4)) are grouped around an enigmatic compound which may have enclosed a temple, and two (Chedworth (3), Sudeley (3)) are so close to villas that they may have been directly associated.

List of Romano-British Buildings

The following list divides the known and firmly located Romano-British structures in the Gloucestershire Cotswolds into four classes: *i* Villas. *ii* Isolated buildings other than villas. *iii* Villa-like buildings in settlements. *iv* Other buildings in settlements.

Parish and Monument No.	*Local name*
i Villas	
Badgeworth (1)	Dryhill
Barnsley (1)	
Barrington (1)	
Bibury (2)	
Bisley (1)	Lillyhorn
Brookthorpe-with-Whaddon (1)	
Chedworth (1)	Chedworth Woods
Do. (2)	The Capitol
Do. (6)	Listercomb
Cirencester (1)	The Barton
Do. (7)	
Colesbourne (2)	
Compton Abdale (1)	
Cowley (3)	
Daglingworth (2)	
Ebrington (1)	
Farmington (1)	Clearcupboard
Frocester (1)	
Frocester (2)	Frocester Court
Great Rissington (1)	Chessels
Great Witcombe (1)	
Do. (2)	
Harescombe (1)	
Horsley (1)	
King's Stanley (2)	
Lechlade (7)	
Painswick (2)	Ifold
Rodmarton (1)	Hocberry
Stinchcombe (1)	
Sudeley (2)	Wadfield
Do. (4)	Spoonley Wood
Swell (2)	Abbotswood
Tetbury Upton (1)	
Weston Subedge (1)	
Whittington (3)	Cow Pasture
Withington (2)	
Woodchester (1)	

Parish and Monument No.	Local name
ii OTHER ISOLATED BUILDINGS	
Broadwell (1)	
Brockworth (2)	
Chedworth (3)	
Cherington (1)	Hailstone
Coaley (1)	
Coates (2)	
Do. (3)	
Do. (4)	
Cowley (4)	Barrow Wake
Duntisbourne Abbots (1)	Duntisbourne Leer
Dursley (1)	Chestals Farm
Haresfield (3)	Ring Hill
Marshfield (2)	The Hams
Stanway (3)	
Sudeley (3)	
Weston Subedge (2)	
Do. (3)	
iii VILLA-LIKE BUILDINGS IN SETTLEMENTS	
Barrington (2)	
Bourton-on-the-Water (2b)	
Do. (4)	
Coberley (3)	
Driffield (1)	
Duntisbourne Rouse (4)	Stancombe
Kingscote (1)	The Chessalls
Lechlade (5)	Roughground Farm
Long Newnton (1)	
Northleach (2)	Norbury Camp
Siddington (3)	
Uley (2)	
Willersey (4)	Badsey Lane
Withington (3)	Wall-Well

Parish and Monument No.	Local name
iv OTHER BUILDINGS IN SETTLEMENTS	
Ashley (1)	
Do. (2)	
Avening (1)	
Blockley (1)	Upton
Bourton-on-the-Water (1a)	Salmonsbury
Do. (2)	
Do. (2a)	'Leadenwell Villa'
Do. (2c)	Whiteshoots Hill
Chedworth (5)	
Cirencester (3)	Chesterton Farm
Coln St. Aldwyns (2)	Chessels
Elkstone (1)	Slutswell
Farmington (2)	Chestles
Do. (4)	Starvall
Great Witcombe (3)	
Do. (4)	
Haresfield (5)	The Lessons
Horsley (2)	
Kingscote (1)	The Chessalls
Lechlade (13)	
Lower Slaughter (1)	Chessels
Do. (3)	Springhill
North Cerney (3)	Woodmancote
Poulton (1)	
Quenington (3)	Coin Slade
Sapperton (1)	Tunnel Mouth Camp
Sherborne (1)	
Shipton (1)	
Siddington (6)	Worm's Farm
Stanway (1)	Millhampost
Do. (2)	
Temple Guiting (2)	Rook Pool Piece
Winson (1)	
Wyck Rissington (1)	
Yanworth (1)	

ROMANO-BRITISH SETTLEMENTS

The word 'settlement' is used of places where there are traces of Roman occupation not directly associated with a villa or a lone building. It embraces a great variety of entries and includes the identification of several structures over a wide area as well as the occurrence of scattered pottery over a small area. In some cases buildings are found as components of settlements, but we cannot always be sure they are contemporary with the evidence for settlement around them. This difficulty is particularly acute where crop-marks are concerned.

'Enclosures' (sometimes associated with linear ditches and tracks) are likely to mark the sites of former settlements, but in the absence of datable refuse cannot be so denominated; they are shown on the distribution map (end-pocket) with an open symbol, barred; other complexes regarded for other reasons as 'probable settlements' are similarly shown.

A few sites where buildings or refuse occur may not have been settlements in the sense of dwelling areas. Where their purpose is recognised, it is specified on the distribution map. In some instances the presence of substantial quantities of occupation refuse may be explained otherwise than as a former settlement; for example debris may have been moved because it formed an obstruction in its original position, or because it was needed elsewhere for, say, hard-core.

Classification of settlements has not been attempted. Apart from the fort-like defences of Dorn (Batsford (1)), Corinium (not included in the Inventory, but see p. xxxv) is the only walled settlement.

Four other settlements covered more than 25 acres: Kingscote (1), its size and importance only recently demonstrated; the Roman remains in and around Bourton-on-the-Water; Wycomb (Whittington (2)); and Chessels (Lower Slaughter (1)). Finds from all four span the period of Roman occupation, and Wycomb and Bourton have pre-Roman antecedents. Wycomb alone of the four large settlements had an internal system of metalled streets; elsewhere, metalled streets are known only in the 10-acre enclosure at Dorn. Metalled roads lead into Bourton and Kingscote, the latter bounded by side-ditches. There are pointers to the existence of villa-type buildings in all the large settlements except at Chessels, Lower Slaughter (1), which lies close to Bourton. At least forty other settlements or probable settlement areas covered 10 acres or more, some very much more. Few of them can be dated closely or defined precisely. Among the crop-mark sites, attention is drawn to recurrent nuclei consisting of clusters of circular or subrectangular features, distinguishable from 'ring-ditches'; Fairford has a number of clear examples. See also Religious Buildings, p. l.

Settlements may occur in any situation where the slope is not too steep and where water is not too far away. Three Iron Age hill-forts were partly occupied by Romano-British settlements and one of them contains evidence of villa-type structures. Settlements may occur on clay, whether in the Severn Vale or upland. In the area S.W. of Kingscote distribution is curiously sparse (except nearer Bath); also N. of Temple Guiting, except around Willersey. For the central part of our area the relationship of settlement to geological drift and water is shown on the map opp. p. xxiii; the overall situation in relation to land-relief is shown on the distribution map (end-pocket). The situation of Romano-British sites may have been more profoundly influenced by the Iron Age pattern of occupation than present evidence allows us to determine. The relative absence of surface pottery from the earlier period is probably due in a large measure to its destruction by ploughing and weathering. Gravels by river or stream, heavily developed in the Roman period, retain evidence of Iron Age occupation; examples occur in Bourton-on-the-Water, Stanway, Whittington, Lechlade and Fairford. A connection between Romano-British settlements and early Roman military activity may be suspected at Kingscote (1), Batsford (1), Rodborough and possibly other sites. Areas of settlement probably grew up along some Roman roads in a kind of ribbon development, as near Bourton-on-the-Water, Coln St. Aldwyns and Quenington.

The inter-relationship of various types of site is open to investigation and discussion. Factors affecting grouping include as yet unidentified religious foci, such as are suggested by finds in Bisley and Daglingworth. The road system, not yet fully established, and the possibilities of water transport must bear heavily on, for example, 'central place theories' of locational analysis. The identity of market centres can only be suggested; presumably they include the four settlements of over 25 acres noted above, as well as others yet undiscovered. Some may correspond with present towns and villages. The relationship of the walled city of Corinium to the areas of settlement, with 'villas', set close beside it on the W. remains problematical, as also its relationship with discrete settlement areas, mostly undated, set a little further away (map, opp. p. xxxvi). Corinium, however, offered services to a region vastly wider than its immediate environs, the most obvious being connected with building (cf. I. R. Hodder in D. L. Clarke, *Models in Archaeology* (1972), 887–909).

Continuity

That Roman sites were sometimes occupied by Saxons cannot be doubted, but continuity of settlement is not always demonstrable. Wycomb (Whittington (2)) and Kingscote (1) were abandoned, as well as many lesser places; it may be noted that Wycomb occupies the kind of situation favoured elsewhere for Saxon settlement. A mile W. of Wycomb the Roman villa at Whittington (3) illustrates how, despite use of the same site, local arrangements on the ground might be quite altered. The villa lies within the Saxon village of Whittington, yet on a different axis, and one of its rooms is crossed by the hollow-way marking the village street. Saxon burials were inserted through the mosaic pavement at The Barton, Cirencester (1). Romano-British walls occur under or near several churches (see p. li), although no religious connection is implied. At Winchcombe, Roman material has been found in the Saxon town rampart. It is reasonable to assume that the Roman road system was largely used in the later period, but there were notable exceptions.

Roman Roads and Tracks

Four major Roman roads traverse the area (map p. xlvi): the Foss Way (Exeter to Lincoln), Ermin Street* (Silchester to Gloucester), Akeman Street (St. Albans to Cirencester) and Ryknild Street (from the Foss Way, N. of Bourton-on-the-Water, to Templeborough). The first three, probably military in origin, are followed for most of their course by modern roads; they all meet at Cirencester. To the S.W. of Cirencester the Foss Way forms the county boundary for a distance of 7 miles. It survives as a green lane, except for the stretch now obliterated by Kemble airfield. Lengths of *agger* off the course of the modern road are visible at Stow-on-the-Wold and in the parishes of Moreton-in-Marsh and Batsford. Sections that have been examined, both N. and S. of Cirencester, do not indicate massive construction, and side-ditches where visible are close to the *agger*. Probable vestiges of the *agger* of Ermin Street exist at Birdlip, Cowley (2). Akeman Street appears as a crop-mark at the crossing of the R. Coln in the parishes of Quenington and Coln St. Aldwyns, and as both *agger* and terrace-way where it crosses the R. Leach in the parish of Eastleach.

Disuse of the Foss Way as a major through route in the pagan Saxon period is indicated by burials in the *agger* near Bourton. As a through route, the 12-mile stretch of Ryknild Street across the N. Cotswolds seems to have been permanently abandoned at an early post-Roman date; its junction with the Foss Way has been located N. of Slaughter Bridge (Bourton-on-the-Water (3)). The section of Ryknild Street that passes through Swell and Condicote, now called Condicote Lane, is mentioned in a Saxon charter as *Buggilde Street* (H. P. R. Finberg, *Early Charters of the W. Midlands* (1961), 74). To N.W. of Hinchwick the road reappears as a crop-mark and degraded *agger* traceable through the parishes of Cutsdean, Bourton-on-the-Hill and Snowshill; two sections have been excavated across the *agger* where it is followed by the parish and county boundaries (Chipping Campden (1)). After it crosses the road from Stow-on-the-Wold to Evesham (SP 124366) the line of Ryknild Street is followed for about $\frac{1}{8}$ mile by the boundary between Willersey and Chipping Campden; it constitutes the *stret* of a Willersey charter (Grundy (1935–6), 260) and the *Buggildestret* of two charters relating to Evesham (Grundy, 'Saxon Charters of Worcestershire', *Trans. Birmingham Archaeol. Soc.*, LII (1927), 95, 103). The probable course of Ryknild Street down the escarpment is marked by the parish boundary between Saintbury and Weston Subedge. A section has been excavated across the *agger* just S. of the point where the alignment is overlain by the modern road (Weston Subedge (4)). The name *Buggildstret* or *Bugghilde Straet* is recorded for the continuation of the road in Warwickshire (Grundy, *op. cit.* (1927), 92, 94, 101, 102), and this stretch has also the modern alternative name *Buckle Street.*

A number of secondary roads referred to as *straet* (or variation) in Saxon charters and surveys would seem from the name to have been metalled, at least in part. Surviving charters relate mainly to parishes in the N. part of the area. In the northern Cotswolds three routes known as *Sealt Straet* may have formed part of the distributional network from the salt springs of the Midlands, first exploited on a large scale in the Roman period.

The White Way may have linked Corinium with the *Sealt Straet* mentioned in a survey of the parish of Hawling. There are remains of a ridge which could be its *agger* in North Cerney parish; it is in two discontinuous sections, much disturbed by delvings and degraded by ploughing. The northern section is offset to the W. from the alignment of the southern, suggesting that the precise course of the road may be difficult to locate where there are no upstanding remains. The circumstance that the road does not appear as a landmark in a charter for the parish (bounds in Grundy (1935–6), 59), although the boundary crosses its course to N. and S. of the ridge, may indicate that the *agger* was never continuous. A test excavation across the traditional line in the area of Withington airfield (SP 0413) failed to disclose Roman metalling (W. F. Grimes, *Excavations on Defence Sites*, I (1958), 133). Before joining *Sealt Straet* the road appears to bifurcate at SP 039128. The W. branch passes through Withington, whence a modern road extends N.W. for nearly $2\frac{1}{2}$ miles in a straight line. In its present form this extent is ascribable to the Enclosure Commissioners in 1819 (H. P. R. Finberg, *Roman and Saxon Withington* (1955), 11), but it is shown on drawings

* The name has been transferred in recent times from the true Ermin Street of eastern Britain, named from the Earningas (*P.N. Beds. & Hunts.*, 1926, 3–4).

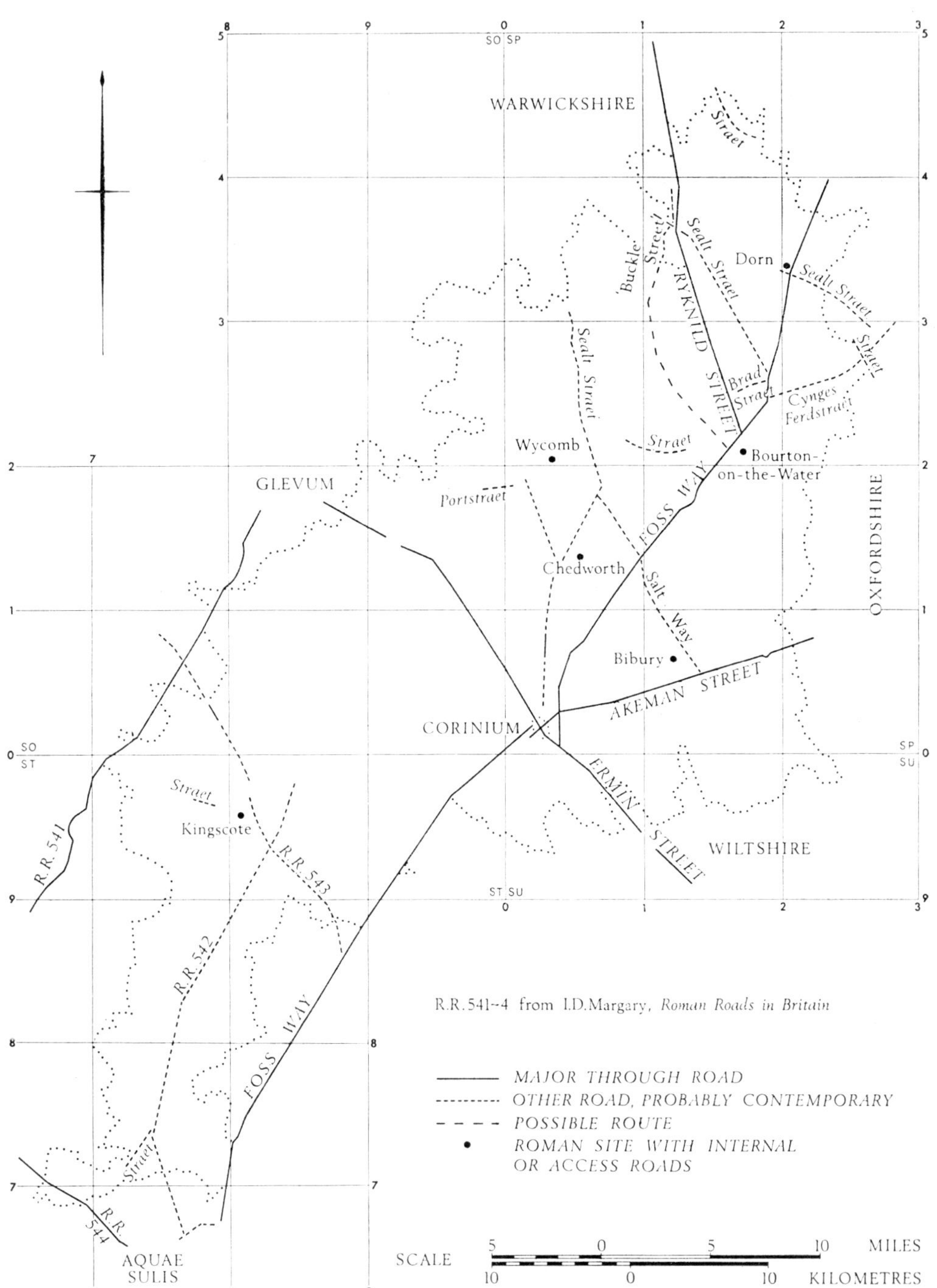

Roman Roads and Tracks in the Gloucestershire Cotswolds.

at a scale of 2 inches to the mile made for the first O.S. in 1815. Although inconclusive, the evidence might encourage consideration of a possible Roman origin for a straight stretch of terrace-way roughly continuing this line N. from the gates of Sandywell Park, just W. of the Roman villa at Whittington (3). This 18-ft. terrace-way is shown in use on estate maps of 1816 in the possession of Miss Evans-Lawrence; it was 'stopped up' as a footway in 1824 (Glos. Record Office, Q/SRL/1824 B/4).

At Frocester, metalling believed to belong to a Roman road has been observed in the vicinity of the villa (2); it appears to form part of a route leading from the Foss Way near Easton Grey (Wiltshire), by way of Kingscote to Frampton on Severn. To the E. of Kingscote parish boundaries follow this line for nearly 4 miles. It has been suggested that a Roman road skirts the complex around the villa at Barnsley (1).

Other secondary routes must have existed to serve settlements. The ridgeway W. of Ryknild Street, to which the name Buckle Street has been transferred in recent times, was probably one of these; there is no evidence that it was metalled.

Access or internal roads are recorded at Roman settlements at Bourton-on-the-Water, Dorn (Batsford (1)), Kingscote and Wycomb (Whittington (2)), and in the vicinity of the villa at Chedworth, where the field-names Streetfold and Street Acres in the adjoining part of Yanworth probably commemorate the former road. Another possible example approaches the Roman villa in Bibury. These sites, together with all roads attested by *agger* remains or suggested by Saxon *straet* names, appear in the map on p. xlvi. *Straet* names are listed below.

SECONDARY ROMAN ROADS DESIGNATED *STRAET* IN SAXON CHARTERS

Parish	N.G.R.	Modern road	Saxon name	Charter (Sawyer No.)	Identification
Adlestrop	SP 2326	A 436	Cynges Ferd-straet	1340 (Daylesford)	Grundy (1935–6), 105
Adlestrop	SP 2627	Minor road on county boundary	straet	550, 1340 (Daylesford)	Do. 21, 106
Broadwell	SP 1827	A 424	Sealt Straet	1550	Do. 55
Donnington		A 424	Sealt Straet	115	Do. 109
Dowdeswell	SP 0018	A 436	Portstraet	1556 (Withington)	Do. 268
Doynton	ST 7372	Minor road on Tog Hill	straet	553 (Pucklechurch)	Do. 204
Evenlode	SP 2332	A 44	Sealt Straet	1325	Do. 128
Hawling	SP 0522	Salt Way	Sealt Straet	179	Finberg (1961), 190, 191
Mickleton	SP 1643	No modern road	straet	911	Grundy (1935–6), 170
Notgrove	SP 1021	B 4068	straet	99	Do. 178
Swell	SP 1825	A 436	Brad Straet	935 (Maugersbury)	Finberg (1961), 67
Willersey	SP 1236	A 44	Sealt Straet	786 (Broadway, Worcs.)	Grundy (1927), 42
Wotton-under-Edge	ST 7795	B 4058	straet	467	Grundy (1935–6), 283

In addition to the roads listed, a substantial number of ditched tracks are seen as crop-marks on air photographs; many are related to 'native' settlements probably existing in the Roman period. The majority occur on the gravels of the upper Thames, notably in Fairford, Kempsford and Lechlade parishes, and on other gravel deposits. (For a relationship with a prehistoric mound, see Appendix B.) Less surely attributed, but probably Roman, are similar tracks such as those meeting Ermin Street in Duntisbourne Abbots parish, between monuments (1) and (2), or in the vicinity of probable Roman remains N.E. of Pinbury (Duntisbourne Rouse (2)). As the table on p. xlviii shows, most of the tracks are about 20 ft. wide. Tracks about 10 ft. between ditches occur within settlements at Fairford (4) and (6), Lechlade (8) and (11), and Stanway (4). A paved road 8 ft. to 10 ft. wide is known to have existed within the Roman settlement at Wycomb (Whittington (2)). Tracks with ditches more widely spaced, perhaps 30 ft. to 40 ft. apart, are found in several parishes; a few can be traced on air photographs for varying distances: South Cerney (3) for $\frac{1}{4}$ mile; Fairford (5) for $\frac{1}{3}$ mile; Siddington (4) for $\frac{1}{2}$ mile. The wide tracks are occasionally unassociated, but at Down Ampney (2) it appears that one such ran past the settlement on a course which at some time had been set a little to one side of the original alignment. At Kingscote a track 30 ft. wide, dated by excavation, is seen on air photographs to narrow by 10 ft. or so and then to disappear as it approaches the Chessalls settlement. This access track may be continuous with a *straet* further W. (map p. xlvi).

DITCHED TRACKS KNOWN FROM CROP-MARKS

Parish and Monument No.	Approximate width between ditches			
	Narrow (10 ft.)	Standard (20 ft.)	Wide (30–40 ft.)	Very wide (80–100 ft.)
Coates (5)	—	one	—	—
Down Ampney (2)	—	—	two	—
Duntisbourne Abbots between (1) and (2)	—	—	one	—
Duntisbourne Rouse (2)	—	two	—	—
Fairford (1)	—	one	—	—
Do. (2)	—	one	—	—
Do. (4)	one	one	—	—
Do. (5)	—	one	two	—
Do. (6)	one	two	—	—
Kempsford (2)	—	one	—	—
Do. (6)	—	one	—	—
Do. (7)	—	six	—	—
Kingscote (1)	—	—	two	—
Do. (4)	—	one	—	—
Lechlade (2)	—	one	—	—
Do. (3)	—	one	—	—
Do. (5)	—	—	one	one
Do. (8)	one	one	one	—
Do. (10)	—	two	—	—
Do. (11)	one	two	—	—
Do. (13)	—	six	—	—
Lower Slaughter (1)	—	—	—	one
Do. (3)	—	one	—	—
North Cerney (3)	—	—	two	—
Pool Keynes (1)	—	—	one	—
Quenington (4)	—	—	one	—
Siddington (4)	—	—	one	—
Do. (6)	—	—	—	one
South Cerney (3)	—	—	one	—
Southrop (2)	—	two	—	—
Stanway (4)	two	four	—	—

There are two examples of very wide-set parallel ditches (80 ft. to 100 ft. apart), perhaps comparable to the 'broad ways' of Romano-British settlements in Wessex (C. Thomas (ed.), *Rural Settlement in Roman Britain*, C.B.A. Research Report, 7 (1966), 51). They occur at the Chessels settlement in Lower Slaughter (1), and near the Roughground settlement in Lechlade (5).

Fields and Pasture

'Celtic' fields, small roughly rectangular arable fields found in certain parts of Britain, range in date from the middle of the second millennium B.C., at latest, to the 5th century A.D. Apart from a group on West Littleton Down, Tormarton (1), it was thought until recently that 'Celtic' fields were absent from the Gloucestershire Cotswolds. The supposed absence was sometimes associated with the well-known virtues of the land for sheep pasture and with the emphasis on sheep farming in the Roman period which the alleged presence of a fullery (now discredited) at the Chedworth villa seemed to warrant. It is now known that 'Celtic' fields do occur, but the evidence is still small compared with (*e.g.*) Wessex. Research at Barnsley has shown that over 100 acres of 'Celtic' fields (2) survive there in association with the Roman villa (1). Other large blocks, though undated, are recognisable in Badminton, Aldsworth and Eastleach. Faint traces, not absolutely certain, occur in five other parishes, and three of these examples (Stinchcombe,

Frocester and Compton Abdale) are near Roman villas. Certain natural ridges or terraces, which might be confused with or mask arable lynchets, introduce such a measure of doubt in certain areas (as N. of the discredited 'camp' at Rendcomb) that no other mention is made of them in this volume.

The full extent of the former 'Celtic' fields is impossible to determine; there are very few geological or topographical obstacles to the kind of agriculture from which they spring. Of the four major blocks to survive, two are in land which was emparked early (Badminton and Barnsley), one probably occupied a stretch of waste (Eastleach (3), by 'No Man's Land'), and one is on a racecourse (Aldsworth). It is certain that 'Celtic' fields can be totally eradicated. There is little doubt, for instance, that fields extended across the S. of Barrington, connecting the two groups last mentioned, but not the faintest sign of them appears either on air photographs or on the ground. On the other hand, 'Celtic' field lynchets are rarely seen in those marginal situations, such as steep slopes, where in other areas of formerly widespread 'Celtic' fields they frequently survive.

Of uncertain significance is the apparent absence of any widespread system of 'ranch-boundaries'. The curious line of ditches in Northleach (3) and 'pit-alignments' in other parishes may suggest stock control.

Field sides may be marked by lynchets up to 3 ft. high, but mostly less, or by earthen baulks as in Barnsley Park. In the latter case the fields were probably open, or only temporarily fenced, in contrast with the system of stone-walled enclosures on the same axial arrangement which covered at least 4 acres around the Barnsley villa. Stone walls probably bounded some of the fields in Aldsworth and Eastleach.

There is little to distinguish the plan of 'Celtic' fields in the Cotswolds from those elsewhere. Parallel pairs of double lines (boundaries with tracks?) seen in Aldsworth and Eastleach are matched on Wylye Down (Wilts.), in a context probably Roman. The Aldsworth group includes one of the most notably regular patterns of small fields so far recognised, but it must not be assumed for this reason that they are necessarily Roman.

Relationships, apart from those mentioned, are few. There is a round barrow at a field angle in Eastleach (3). The fields in Badminton extend eastwards into Luckington (Wilts.) where a lynchet of the system is aligned with the Giant's Cave long barrow.

It is not known if fields other than 'Celtic' fields existed in the Cotswolds in the Iron Age or in Romano-British times. The heavy iron plough-coulter, with a set to the blade, from the Great Witcombe villa perhaps belonged to a heavy plough, suggesting that larger or longer fields may have been developed, but none has been recognised. Adjacent ridge-and-furrow is later, as can be seen from its encroachment on a collapsed part of the villa.

Romano-British Burials

Burials by cremation and inhumation are recorded, in the rural areas, generally singly or in small groups although there is evidence to suggest that a few larger cemeteries existed. Inhumations may be extended or crouched, in earthen graves, in cists or in coffins; they are found as secondary burials in barrows, inserted into earthworks, in rubbish pits and, in one case, in a mound of rubbish. Many of the inhumations are without grave goods and undated, but apparently in a non-Christian context. In other instances the goods are not demonstrably or specifically Roman. Thus some of the burials included in the Inventory may be Iron Age or early Anglo-Saxon rather than Romano-British. Burials near Cirencester are noted on p. xxxvi.

Cremations have been noted at Ampney Crucis, Dodington, Lechlade (5), Minchinhampton, Notgrove, Temple Guiting (3) and Whittington (2). At Temple Guiting an unknown number of cremations occurred with inhumations. A cremation at Lechlade and another at Whittington were respectively in and immediately N. of settlements.

Contracted inhumations have been noted as follows: Upper Slaughter, in a circular stone-cut pit; Condicote (2), with a bronze pin and in a wooden container; Leckhampton, wearing a bronze crown; Withington (1), two or three, with double-sided bone combs (as likely to be Romano-British as Saxon), in pits.

Cist burials occur in the following places: Compton Abdale (5); Naunton, three, including one at monument (1); Stanway (6); Willersey (2); Chedworth, an infant immediately outside the villa (1); Lower Slaughter (1), with a coin of Magnentius.

Coffins, generally of local Oolite, have been found widely dispersed in the Gloucester Cotswolds area; many are no longer *in situ*. A wooden coffin was recorded in the cemetery at Kineton, Temple Guiting (3), and another was probably found at Cutsdean. Lead coffins, not substantiated as Roman, are mentioned at South Cerney and Upper Slaughter. Coffined burials without grave goods occur at Bitton, at Cold Ashton, at Dyrham, at Tormarton, and at Whittington; others were found at Bourton-on-the-Water (2d) and near Kingscote (1). Grave goods inside the coffin are recorded only at Down Ampney. A coffin at Lower Slaughter contained the skeleton of a man with hob-nailed boots.

Secondary burials in Neolithic and Bronze Age barrows are technically undated although (except at Miserden) there may be evidence of Romano-British, but not of Anglo-Saxon, disturbance in the mounds. Such burials have been found in long barrows at Miserden and Uley (Hetty Pegler's Tump) and in round barrows at King's Stanley and Withington (Foxcote Tumulus). At least four inhumations, one female, were inserted into a Roman rubbish mound at Bisley-with-Lypiatt (2).

Cemeteries are indicated in early accounts of Haresfield, Temple Guiting and at a place near 'Beggy Hill Way' in Upper Slaughter, but their size and significance are not recorded. In 1796 at least six burials were reported at Brownshill in Painswick. Excavations at Lechlade (5) revealed a group of seven graves in a rectangular enclosure; this is the only modern record of a rural Roman cemetery within the area covered by this volume. Hob-nails were recorded with two burials at this site.

Certain burials may be distinguished as probably of the 4th century or later. At Whittington (2), six skeletons were found lying on the Roman ground surface and are referable perhaps to the last phase of the settlement. At Frocester (2), a male interment immediately outside the villa belonged probably to the latest period of occupation. Finds associated with other burials may indicate late Roman or pagan Anglo-Saxon date or custom; examples are at Withington and at Broadwell where two contracted female burials in pits by the Foss Way were accompanied by a bronze spiral-headed pin and an iron knife.

Roman tombstones recorded at Beverstone, Horsley, Stinchcombe, Westonbirt with Lasborough, and probably at Winchcombe cannot be shown to have been found *in situ*.

Barrows containing Romano-British Material

Nine, possibly ten, long barrows and seven or eight round barrows have yielded Roman finds, mostly coins and pottery, in disturbed areas of the mounds or in their ditches. Another long barrow, Giant's Cave, Luckington, Wilts., just outside the area considered in this volume, contained over 500 Romano-British sherds (*WAM*, 65 (1970), 54–6); this barrow lies among the remains of 'Celtic' fields which are continuous with those in Badminton.

The finds are preponderantly of the 3rd or 4th century and they occur for various reasons. A number of secondary burials, probably Roman and accompanied by Romano-British material, occur in barrows. Coin hoards, on the other hand, are known to have been deposited in barrows and other pre-Roman earthworks, from which locations, presumably easily recognised, it may be assumed that recovery was intended (*WAM*, *loc. cit.*, 199). Some finds may result from casual loss or from the dumping of rubbish. Other material could have been left by people digging into the barrows (cf. 19th-century pottery recently found in areas of the Great Witcombe Roman villa which were dug in the early part of that century). None of these explanations is likely to account for the presence of a Roman tile in the apparently isolated Sales Lot long barrow at Withington. It is possible that some of the finds represent offerings made out of respect for an older culture, and a pointer to such respect may be seen in the protected situation of a round barrow at the corner of a 'Celtic' field in Eastleach (3); also in the preservation of a group of four barrows just outside the same field group.

Religious Buildings and Objects

The Inventory includes only two certainly identified temples: Chedworth (4) and Wycomb, Whittington (2). The latter was in a river valley near Iron Age occupation. The site of a probable shrine with a stone eagle is noted on the shoulder of a hill in Sudeley (5). An unusual enclosure at Sapperton (1) has approximately the same shape as the outer *temenos* of the temple at Gosbecks Farm, near the old Trinovantian capital by *Camulodunum* (Lewis (1966), *passim*); the enclosures are also similar in their multiple boundaries, size and orientation, and in having entrances on the E. The Sapperton site has not been excavated and no cult objects are recorded. The nearby canal runs past a traditional source of the R. Thames, noted on O.S. maps, a mile E.S.E. (For comment on the site of the source of the Thames, see *PCNFC*, XXXV, part iv (1970), 194.)

Elsewhere, altars, votive objects and various forms of sculpture suggest in different degrees the presence of temples or shrines, some possibly within villas. Such finds have been made in Baunton, Batsford, Bisley, Chalford, Chedworth (1) and (2), Colesbourne, Daglingworth, Hampnett, Kingscote, King's Stanley, Lechlade, Lower Slaughter, Sudeley and Woodchester. Cult objects from Wycomb, some not previously recorded, include crude decorated stone figurines as well as a miniature bronze statue of Mars, a god frequently noted in the Cotswold area. A full description of these objects will be published shortly in *TBGAS*. A miniature stone altar comparable in crudity to the figurines from Wycomb was found at Chedworth (1). An earthenware 'fir-cone' in the villa at Great Witcombe (1) suggests that certain other features in the villa may have had ritual use. Antecedent Iron Age influences are to be expected; *e.g.*, the carved limestone 'idol' from Salmonsbury.

Outside Corinium, the only certain sign of christianization occurs in the villa at Chedworth (1), but this was followed by a phase in which stones with *chi–rho* inscriptions were taken from the nymphaeum for reuse in a flight of steps. Roman structures are found beneath churches at Frocester and at Woodchester, but there is nothing to indicate continuity of religious use. Pagan altar fragments have been found under the church at Bisley-with-Lypiatt, and other Roman finds are noted under or near the churches at Bitton, King's Stanley and Swell; there are five more instances of Roman material found within 200 yds. of a church. A finger-ring found at Barnsley bore an intaglio probably representing the Good Shepherd. It has been suggested that the Orpheus pavement motif (above, p. xli) was favoured by Christians.

APPENDIX A

PLACE NAMES AND MONUMENTS

A critical examination of names on early as well as recent editions of O.S. maps and, particularly, of field-names on estate and tithe maps, enclosure awards etc., may yield information on the existence of hitherto unknown archaeological sites. Many significant names have been gathered together in *The Place Names of Gloucestershire*, but the coverage is by no means exhaustive. These sources of information have been utilised only sporadically in the compilation of the Inventory, but attention may be drawn to some possibilities. For example, the area containing the hill-fort at Woodmancote (North Cerney (2)) was named 'The Ditches' on an early O.S. map, yet the site escaped identification until it was seen from the air by Mr. W. A. Baker in the 1960s. The hill-fort on Burhill (Buckland (1)), also recorded on an early O.S. map as Burrell Hill, was discovered only in 1960 when Mr. L. V. Grinsell recognised the possible implication of the first element in the name (OE. *burh*, 'fortification'); Hinton Hill (Dyrham and Hinton (1)) was also once known as Burrill or Burrell. As the suffix 'bury', the element often appears in hill-fort names, both those in use (see list, p. xxv) and former designations. The Bulwarks (Haresfield (2)) was probably known as Eastbury until comparatively recently (*PNG*, II, 184) and the Saxon name for the hill-fort on Nottingham Hill (Gotherington (1)), *Cocca burh*, survives as Cockbury at three places near by. But 'bury' is also commonly incorporated in place and field-names where no hill-fort is known (*e.g.* Hawkesbury and Eubury). The occurrence in the Cotswolds of natural formations which resemble artificial constructions (see p. xxx) may account for the relative frequency of 'bury' names; it has been pointed out (*PNG*, IV, 191) that only about a quarter of those recorded refer to actual fortifications. In the same way the later names 'castle' and 'camp', many of them probably antiquarian inventions (*PNG*, IV, 23), have been applied both to genuine hill-forts and to supposed fortifications; the 'castle' names formerly used for Dixton Hill, Alderton and Cooper's Hill, Brockworth and the 'camp' names in Aston Blank and Tormarton are examples.

The name Chessells and its variants (OE. *ceastel*, 'heap of stones'), associated with the sites of six Roman settlements or buildings in the area, indicate that the remains of structures were visible there in the post-Roman period. The *caestello* of a Naunton charter, apparently referring to the structure at New Buildings, Upper Slaughter (1), would carry the same meaning (cf. *PNG*, I, 164). Since 'Chessells' names appear to have a particular significance, reference may be made to those, listed in *PNG*, IV, 22–3, which relate to places where Roman remains have not been identified: Westchestle at Aldsworth, Wet Chessells at Driffield (a field near the site of the building, Driffield (1)), Chestels or Chistles at Dyrham and Hinton (ST 718774) and Great and Little Chessels at Sodbury (centred ST 752823). The situation of the last named, on a brown earth subject to occasional waterlogging, but capable of drainage, is a likely one for Roman settlement.

Names derived from *ceaster*, often applied to Roman towns, are sometimes associated with villas, as in Frocester (*Frome ceaster*, 'settlement near the Frome') and Woodchester. Chesterton, S. of Cirencester, is usually taken to mean 'farmstead belonging to or near the town' (*PNG*, I, 64), but it might, for instance, relate to the extra-mural Roman settlement, Cirencester (3), or to the villa (1), or to the amphitheatre, as suggested by J. S. Wacher. 'Wycomb' (Whittington (2)) may come from *vicus*, a Roman settlement (*Med. Archaeol.* XI (1967), 87–104).

Dorn (Batsford (1)) probably means 'fort' or 'gate'. The name Stancombe (stony valley) often occurs in the Cotswolds; its association with two of the monuments listed below, and the record of Roman material from Stancombe Wood, Sudeley, suggests that the stoniness is not always of natural origin. The Roman villa at Frocester Court is in a field known as Big Stanborough; on this gravel soil clearly a reference to the remains of a building. On the other hand Stanborough Lane, between the parishes of Naunton and Notgrove, is believed to take its name from the nearby Neolithic long barrow (*PNG*, I, 176), while Stanborough Fields, containing the crop-marks of enclosures (Notgrove (1)), are presumably named from the lane. It seems probable that Roughground Farm, on which was situated the Roman settlement, Lechlade (5), was so called by reason of former unevenness of the ground resulting from the remains of structures on this otherwise flat gravel terrace.

Other local names which may point to undiscovered sites include Crockemede ('crock or pottery meadow') in Brockworth, 'The Brickbats' in Lechlade and 'Money Quarr', recorded in the vicinity of the Roman settlement on West Hill, Uley (2), (*PPS*, IV (1938), 193, No. 1). It is, however, uncertain if 'Coin Slade' (Quenington (3)) is to be taken literally in view of the alternative names 'Quoin Slade' and 'Cold Slad'. The survival until recently of 'Celtic' fields in Eastleach may be related to the occurrence of 'No Man's Land' as an adjacent place-name.

Roman site names	*Inventory No.*
Abbotswood	Swell (2)
Barton, The	Cirencester (1)
Chessalls	Kingscote (1)
Chessels, The	Coln St. Aldwyns (2)
Chessels	Great Rissington (1)
Chessels	Lower Slaughter (1)
Chestals	Dursley (1)
Chestles	Farmington (2)
Clearcupboard	Farmington (1)
Combend—see Stockwood	
Dorn	Batsford (1)
Dryhill	Badgeworth (1)
Great Lemhill	Lechlade (7)
Hailstone	Cherington (1)
Highfold—see Ifold	

Roman site names	*Inventory No.*
Hocberry	Rodmarton (1)
Ifold	Painswick (2)
Leadenwell	Bourton-on-the-Water (2a)
Lemhill—see Great Lemhill	
Lillyhorn	Bisley-with-Lypiatt (1)
Listercombe	Chedworth (6)
Millhampost	Stanway (1)
Roughground Farm	Lechlade (5)
Stancombe	Duntisbourne Rouse (4)
Stancombe	Stinchcombe (1)
Stockend	Harescombe (1)
Stockwood(s)	Colesbourne (2)
Wadfield	Sudeley (2)
Whiteshoots Hill	Bourton-on-the-Water (2c)
Wycomb	Whittington (2)

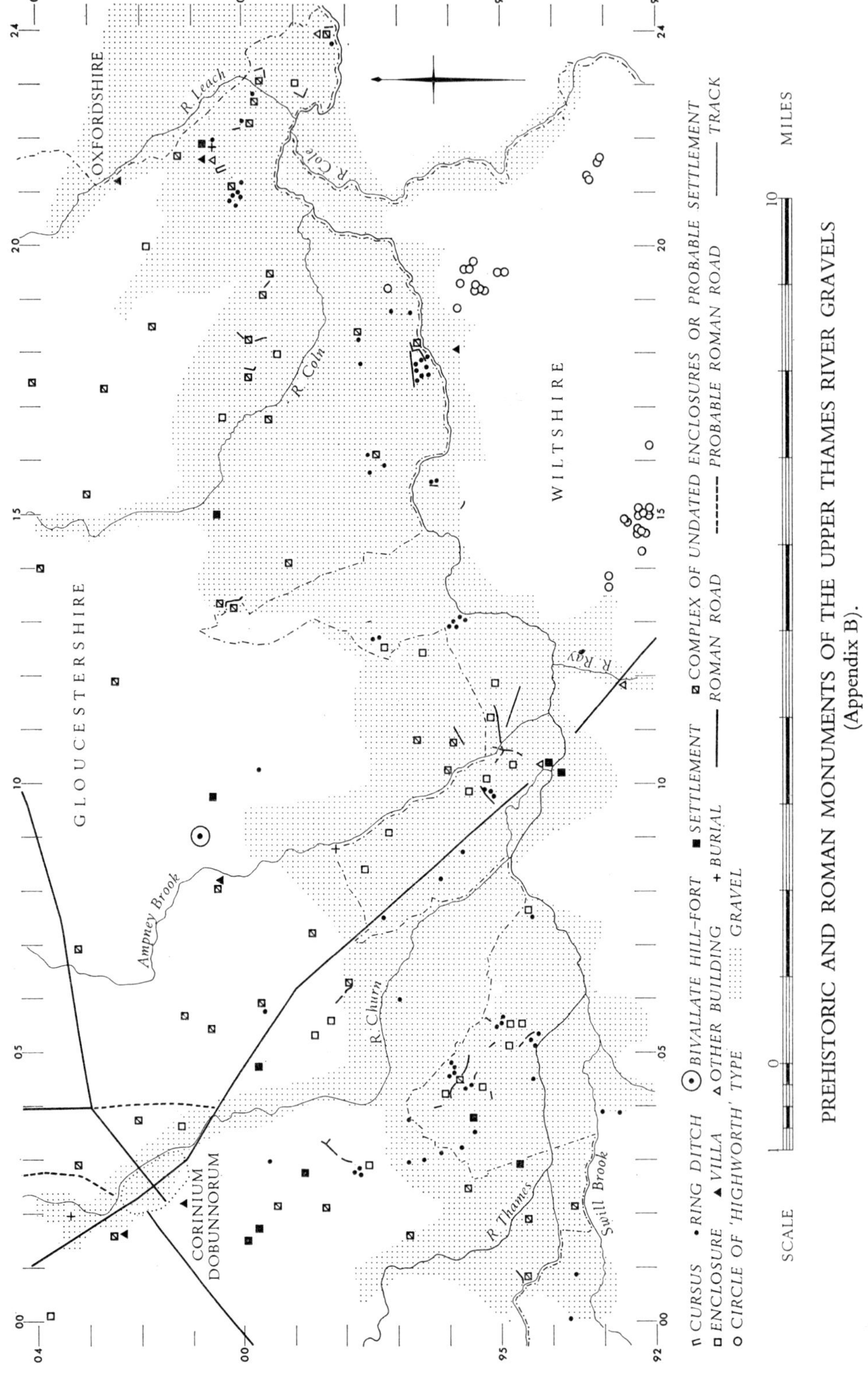

PREHISTORIC AND ROMAN MONUMENTS OF THE UPPER THAMES RIVER GRAVELS (Appendix B).

APPENDIX B

RING-DITCHES

Ring-ditches (*i.e.* ditches presenting more or less circular plans, sometimes interrupted by causeways) appear as crop-marks in many air photographs; they are difficult to interpret and have been referred to in the following Inventory only when they occur near an area of Iron Age or Romano-British settlement. The full range of such crop-marks appears on the accompanying plan, which shows the relationship of all known Prehistoric and Roman monuments in the area of Upper Thames river-gravels, extending from Gloucestershire into Wiltshire. For a summary discussion of the ring-ditches noted within the area described in the volume (approximately 150), and problems of their interpretation and dating, see I. F. Smith in *Archaeology and the Landscape* (ed. P. J. Fowler, 1972), chapter vi.

Some ring-ditches are likely to belong to ploughed-out Bronze Age round barrows, as shown by the excavation of examples in the area of the Chessels Romano-British settlement at Lower Slaughter (1). Intensive occupation in the gravel terraces (where most of the examples have been noted) seems frequently to have resulted in the obliteration or degradation of pre-existing earthworks; for instance, linear ditches are sometimes seen to cross ring-ditches without interruption, indicating that any former mound or bank was already flattened. The circumstances contrast markedly with those observed in upland situations on chalk or limestone, where earlier monuments were usually left unploughed in Iron Age and Roman times. But there is an occasional indication that certain ring-ditches still enclosed mounds in the Iron Age and Roman periods. At Lechlade (2), one of the ditches flanking a track shows faintly in comparison with the other where it intersects a ring-ditch, suggesting that the ditch was cut through a mound, subsequently flattened, leaving traces of only that part of the ditch which penetrated the subsoil. At Kempsford (7) a ring-ditch is seen in a space relatively free of ditched features and approached by apparent tracks (Plate 60). The suggestion here is very strong that a mound still stood at one side of the open space, although at some time the ditches of rectangular features impinged on its S.W. side.

Circular or penannular crop-marks with exceptionally broad ditches suggestive of recutting occur at Lechlade (6) and at Kempsford (6–7). A circular ditch of this kind in the area of another settlement at Lechlade (5) proved under excavation to be Roman in date and of uncertain purpose.

Small penannular or semicircular features, about 30 ft. in diameter and with very narrow ditches, dispersed among linear ditches at Fairford (5) and Lechlade (8), and clusters of similar crop-marks at Lechlade (2) and (6), Kempsford (6) and Great Rissington (2), may represent the sites of circular houses. The patterns are comparable with those of unploughed Iron Age hut-circles at Hod Hill in Dorset (*Dorset*, III, 263–5).

EDITORIAL NOTES

For convenience of identification the monuments in the Inventory are grouped (with minor exceptions explained as they occur) under the names of the Civil Parishes in which they now lie. The boundaries of the parishes, as defined on the provisional 6-inch Ordnance Surveys of 1954–61, are shown on a supplementary copy of the general distribution map of monuments, included in the pocket at the end of the volume. Thirty parishes in the Gloucestershire Cotswolds are without relevant monuments so far recognised.

In the text, monuments are located by means of the National Grid (explained inside the covers of O.S. 1-inch maps). Generally, six-figure references are used, permitting location within a square of 100 metres, but eight-figure references (10-metre squares) are given when greater precision is desirable. Altitudes above O.D. are not stated if the information is obtainable from maps or plans in the Inventory. The geology of sites is normally not specified if it is Oolite. A geological map of the area N. and E. of Cirencester appears opposite p. xxiii.

In many parish inventories an opening paragraph gives general information relevant to the Iron Age and Romano-British periods; it also mentions sites and finds which cannot be precisely located. After this the monuments and archaeological sites are listed, each entry being numbered and titled for convenience of reference. It may be that a few of the monuments listed will be shown at some future period to be neither Iron Age nor Romano-British, but they are all included in the present belief that they are one or the other, or both; the term 'undated' means only that there are no small finds to support the assumption. A select bibliography and a list of air photographs follows the entry where appropriate. The N.M.R. has, or has records of, air photographs embracing most of the sites mentioned in the volume.

All maps and plans are orientated with N. at the top of the page. In many parishes the location of sites is indicated by a map at 2½ inches to the mile. Sites revealed by crop-marks on air photographs are mostly illustrated by plans at 6 inches to the mile; a few from which the top-soil has been stripped demand presentation at 1: 1250 or 1: 2500. As the 6-inch scale hardly admits distinction in widths of ditches etc., certain plates have been included to illustrate the variations. Hill-forts, dykes etc. are presented at 1: 5000 and profiles of these earthworks at 32 ft. to the inch. In hill-fort plans, thick solid lines indicate banks; thin solid lines show edges of ditches or counterscarp banks; broken lines show the approximate position of former features, now gone; stippled areas are scarps; areas shaded with parallel lines are berms. Plans of most Roman buildings are drawn at 80 ft. to the inch; a few are drawn at 32 ft. to the inch, with an inset plan at 80 ft. to the inch to permit comparison of size. Conversion tables showing Imperial and Metric dimensions will be found on p. 136. While the plans have been redrawn to standard scales, conventions and orientation, the rooms etc. of villas normally retain the numbering or lettering given to them by their excavators. Stippled areas on villa plans denote rooms with mosaic pavements, even though these may be attested only by the presence of unpatterned tesserae; generally the stipple covers the whole area of the room in which mosaics are believed to have existed.

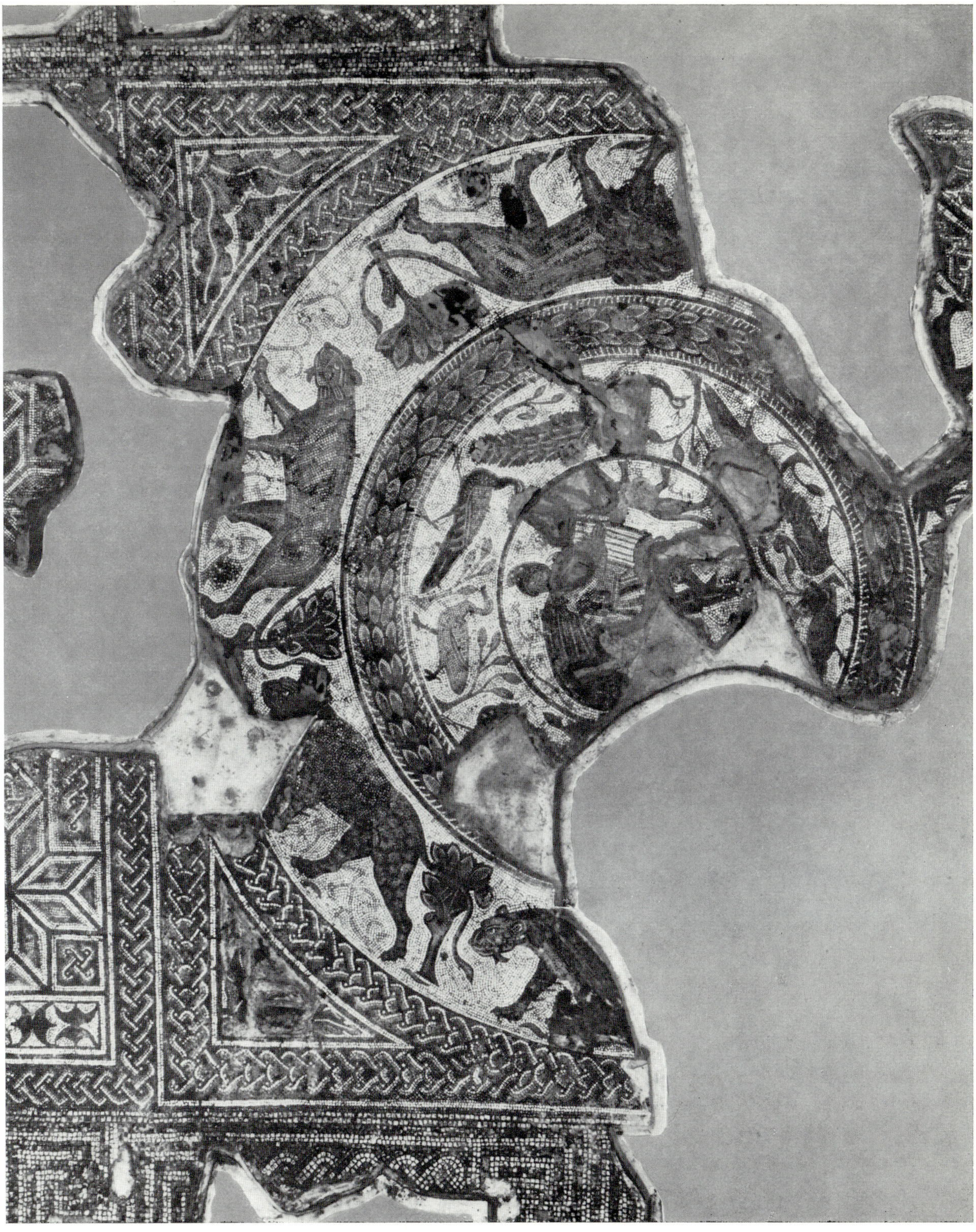

CIRENCESTER. (1) Villa at Barton Farm. Mosaic pavement now in Corinium Museum. Scale 1:25

Scale at centre 1:25

CHEDWORTH. (1) Villa. Pavement of Room 10, looking W.

CHEDWORTH. (1) Villa. Pavement of Room 5 (cf. Pl. 4–5). Scale in foreground 1:25

CHEDWORTH. (1) Villa. Pavement of Room 5. N. to right. R: repair.

Scale 1:25

Corridor leading to Room 14. From a drawing in the Fox Collection (Society of Antiquaries).

Pavement of Room 14.

Pavement of Room 11.

CHEDWORTH. (1) Villa.

Scale 1:25

COLESBOURNE. (2) Villa. Corridor in Building B (Lysons, *Reliquiae*, II, Pl. ii, Nos. 6 and 7). Scale 1:30

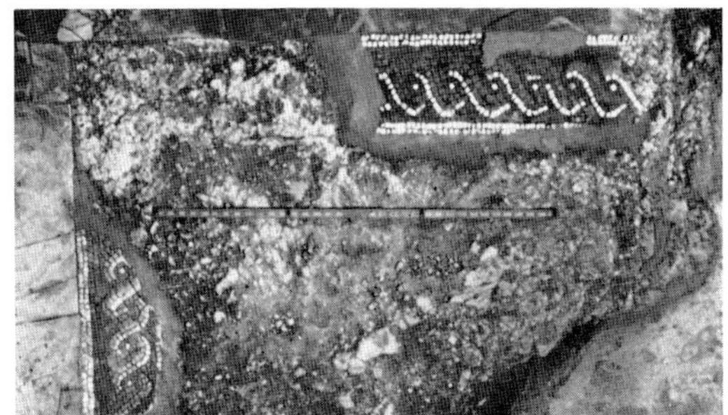

CHEDWORTH. (1) Villa. Mosaics in Room 22 (cf. Pl. 25). Scale 1:25

COLESBOURNE. (2) Villa. Corridor in Building A (Lysons, *Arch.* IX, pl. xx). Scale, fig. 1, 1:25

EBRINGTON. (1) Villa. Pavement of Room 1, looking N.

FROCESTER. (2) Villa. Pavement of corridor, W. end, from S.W.

FROCESTER. (2) Villa. Pavement of corridor.

PAINSWICK. (2) Villa at Ifold. Pavement of Room 10. (*TBGAS*, XXVII (1904), opp. p. 162.)

FROCESTER. (2) Villa. Pavement of corridor.

Corridor II, from W.

Corridor II, from E.

Room 5, from W.

Room 3, from S.E.

WHITTINGTON. (3) Villa.

Scales marked in inches.

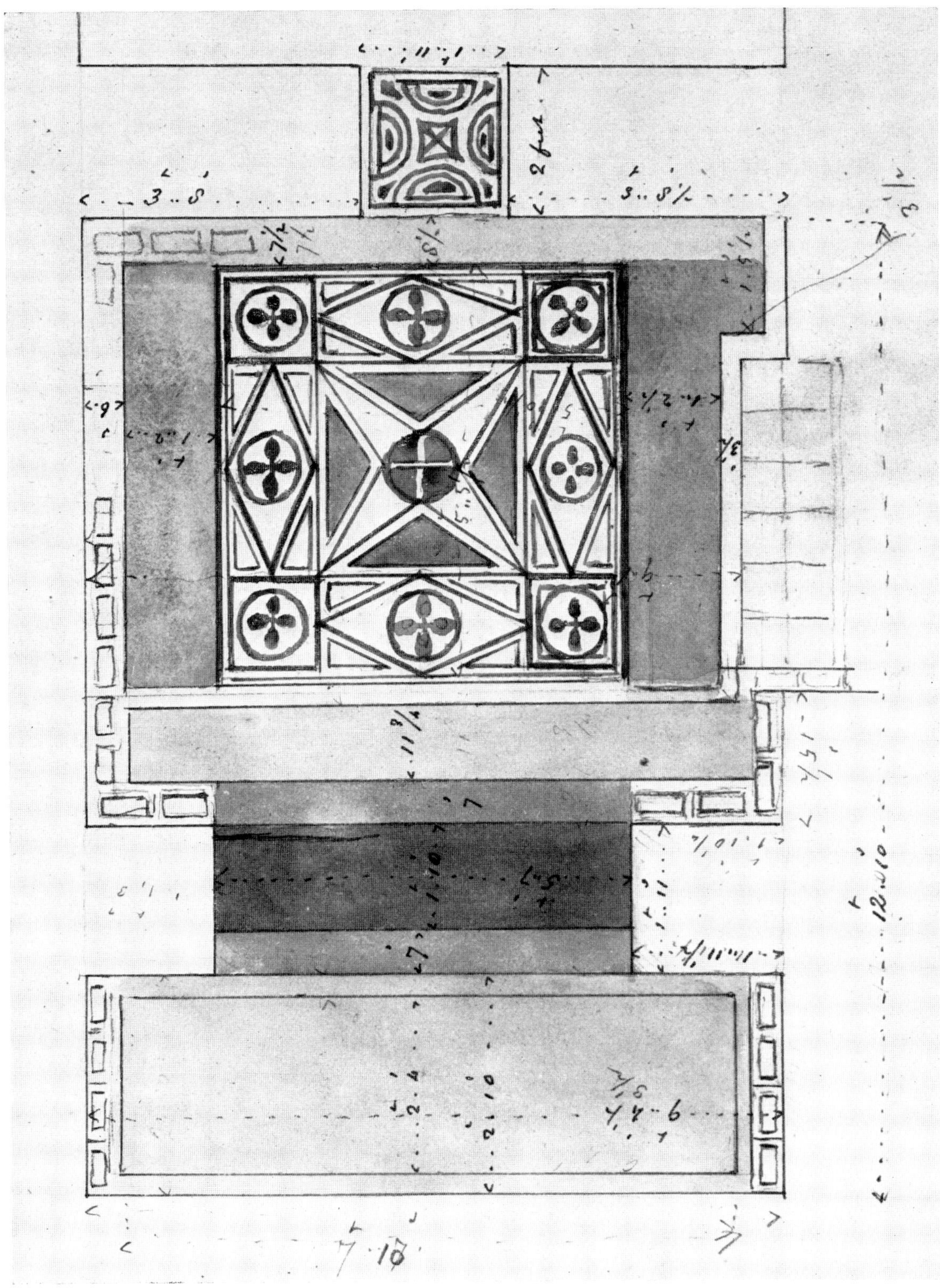

GREAT WITCOMBE. (1) Villa. Mosaics in Room 10. Drawing by S. Lysons in the Society of Antiquaries' Collection.

Scale 1:25

GREAT WITCOMBE. (1) Villa. Pavement in Room 6, after Lysons. Scale 1:27

GREAT WITCOMBE. (1) Villa. Pavement in Room 5, after Lysons. Scale 1:25

SUDELEY. (2) Villa at Wadfield. Pavement in Room 1 (*Annals of Winchcombe and Sudeley*). Scale 1:25

WITHINGTON. (2) Villa.
Pavement of corridor (Lysons).
Scale 1:25

SUDELEY. (4) Villa in Spoonley Wood. Pavement of Room 8 (*Annals of Winchcombe and Sudeley*).
Scale 1:25

WITHINGTON. (2) Villa. Pavement of corridor (Lysons). Scale 1:25

SUDELEY. (4) Villa in Spoonley Wood. Pavement of Room 18 (*Annals of Winchcombe and Sudeley*). Scale 1:25

SUDELEY. (4) Villa in Spoonley Wood. Man with rake. Scale unknown

SUDELEY. (4) Villa in Spoonley Wood. Pavement of Room 7 (*Annals of Winchcombe and Sudeley*). Scale 1:25

WITHINGTON. (2) Villa. Mosaic, now in B.M. (cf. Pl. 16). Scale 1:25

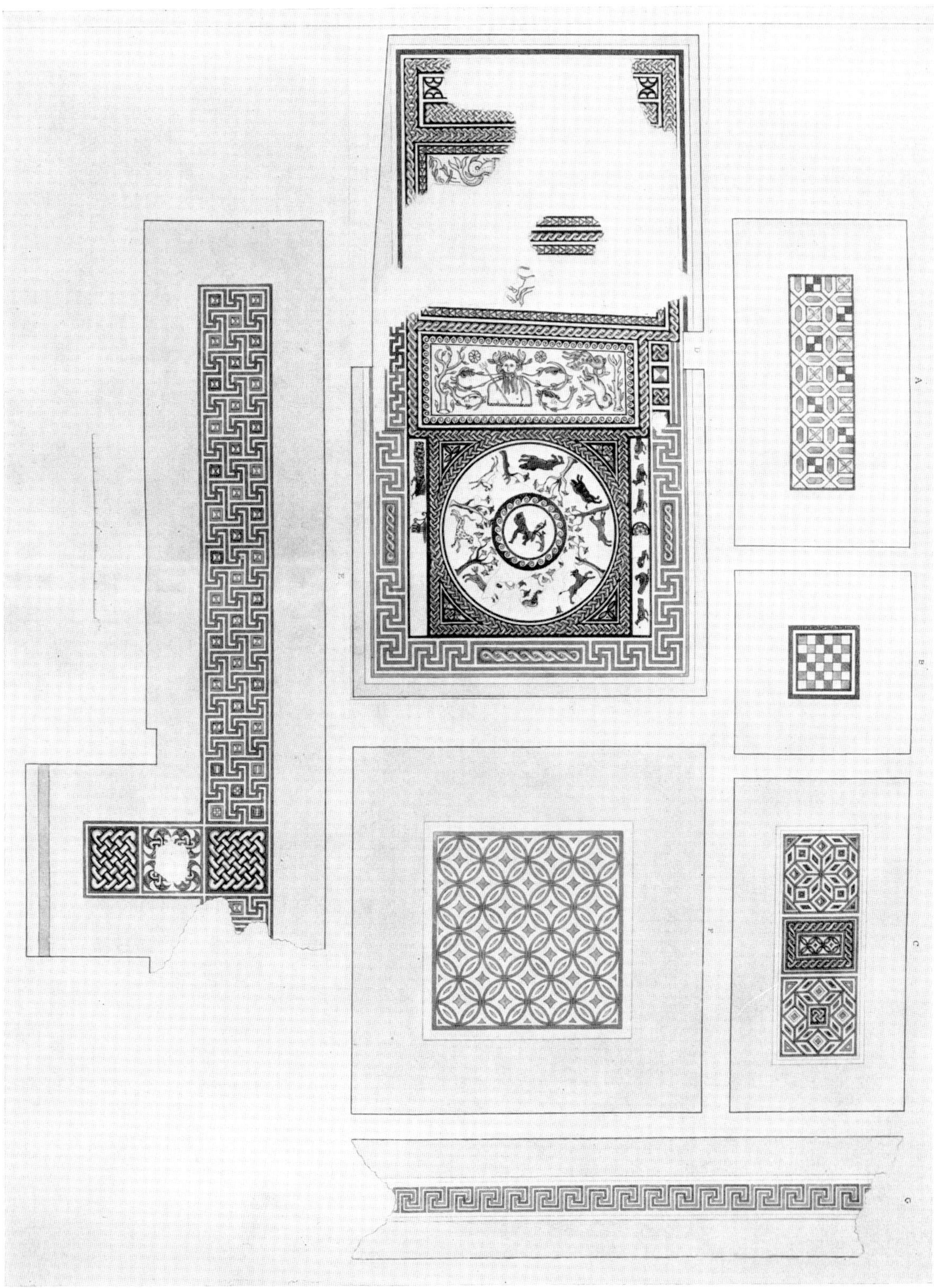

WITHINGTON. (2) Villa (Lysons (1817), Plate xix). Scale 1:100

WOODCHESTER. (1) Villa. Pavement of Room 1. N. at top. Scale 1:70

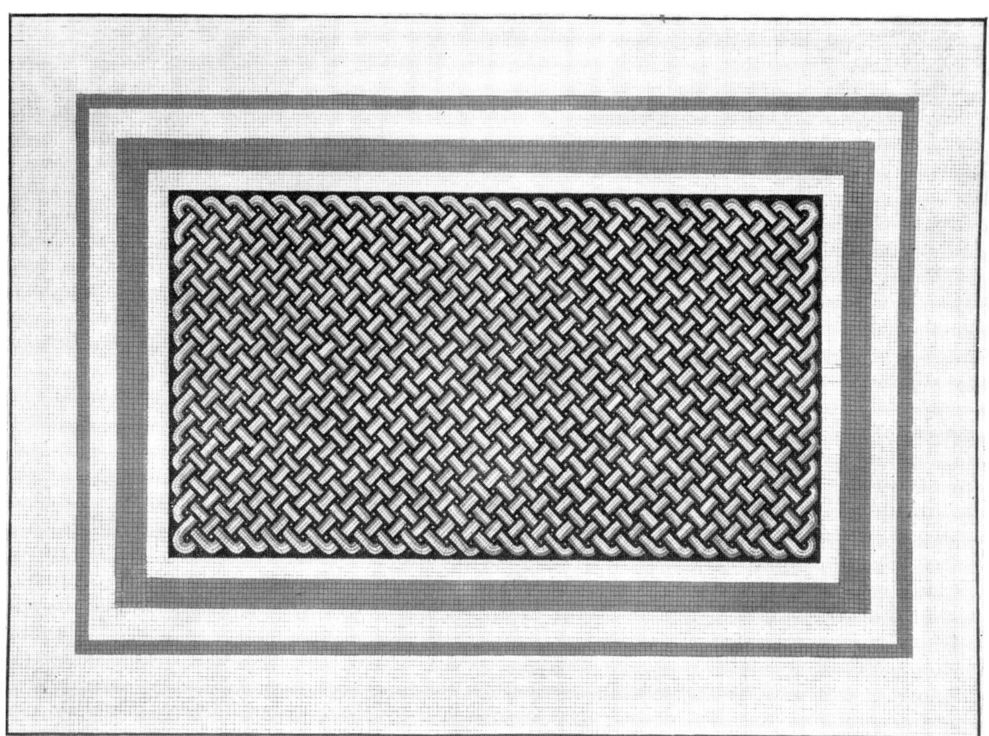

Pavement in Room 3.

Pavement in Room 6.

WOODCHESTER. (1) Villa. Pavements recorded by Lysons. Scale 1:45

Pavement in Room 10, recorded by Lysons.

Detail of Pavement in Room 1 (E. side).

WOODCHESTER. (1) Villa. Scale 1:45

Scale 1:12

Scale 1:12

Scale 1:24

WOODCHESTER. (1) Villa. Details of Pavement in Room 1 (cf. Plate 17).

Animals in outer zone.

Birds in inner zone.

WOODCHESTER. (1) Villa. Details of pavement in Room 1 (cf. Plate 17). Scale 1:24

WOODCHESTER. (1) Villa. Pavements recorded by Lysons.

Scale 1:60

Corridor 8.

Room 18.

Room 15.

Room 12.

Corridor 5.

Corridor 2. Scale 1:170

Corridor 2, W. part. Scale 1:60

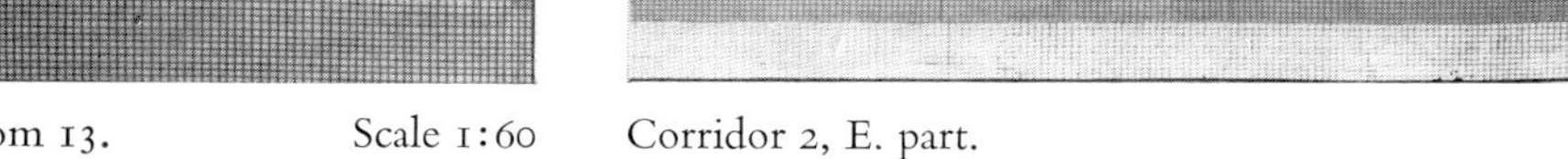

Room 13. Scale 1:60

Corridor 2, E. part. Scale 1:60

WOODCHESTER. (1) Villa. Pavements recorded by Lysons.

SUDELEY. (4) Villa in Spoonley Wood. Room 18, from N.W.

GREAT WITCOMBE. (1) Villa, from N.W., showing octagonal room overlying rectangular structure.

CHEDWORTH. (1) Villa. Apses and fragmentary mosaic in Room 22, from N.E. (cf. Pl. 7).

CHEDWORTH. (1) Villa. Hypocaust pillars under Room 26, from S.E.

Column base *in situ* outside Room 21.

Column base *in situ* outside Room 21.

Hypocaust pillar, Room 26.

Column shafts etc.

CHEDWORTH. (1) Villa.

Ranging rods scaled in feet.

Base (inverted).

Base (inverted).

Shaft.

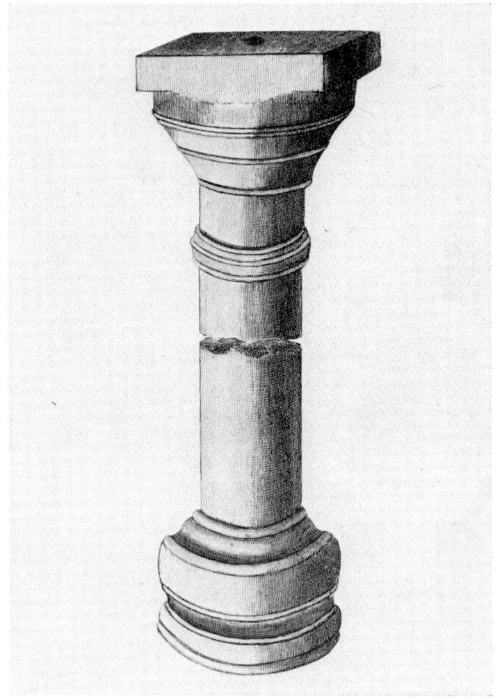

Column (Lysons, *Arch.* IX, Pl. xx).

Base (?).

Base (?).

COLESBOURNE. Column fragments at Combend Manor, probably from villa (2), compared with Lysons's illustration. Ranging rods scaled in feet.

Part of shaft. Scale 1:8

Column base. Scale 1:8

Base. Scale 1:8

Balustrade fragments. Scale 1:12

Scale 1:6

GREAT WITCOMBE. (1) Villa.

GREAT WITCOMBE. (1) Villa. Fragments of columns. Scale 2:15

SUDELEY. (4) Villa. Column base (inverted). 1:4

WHITTINGTON. (3) Villa. Carved impost. 1:4

WHITTINGTON. (3) Villa. Unprovenanced column base, now at Whittington Court.

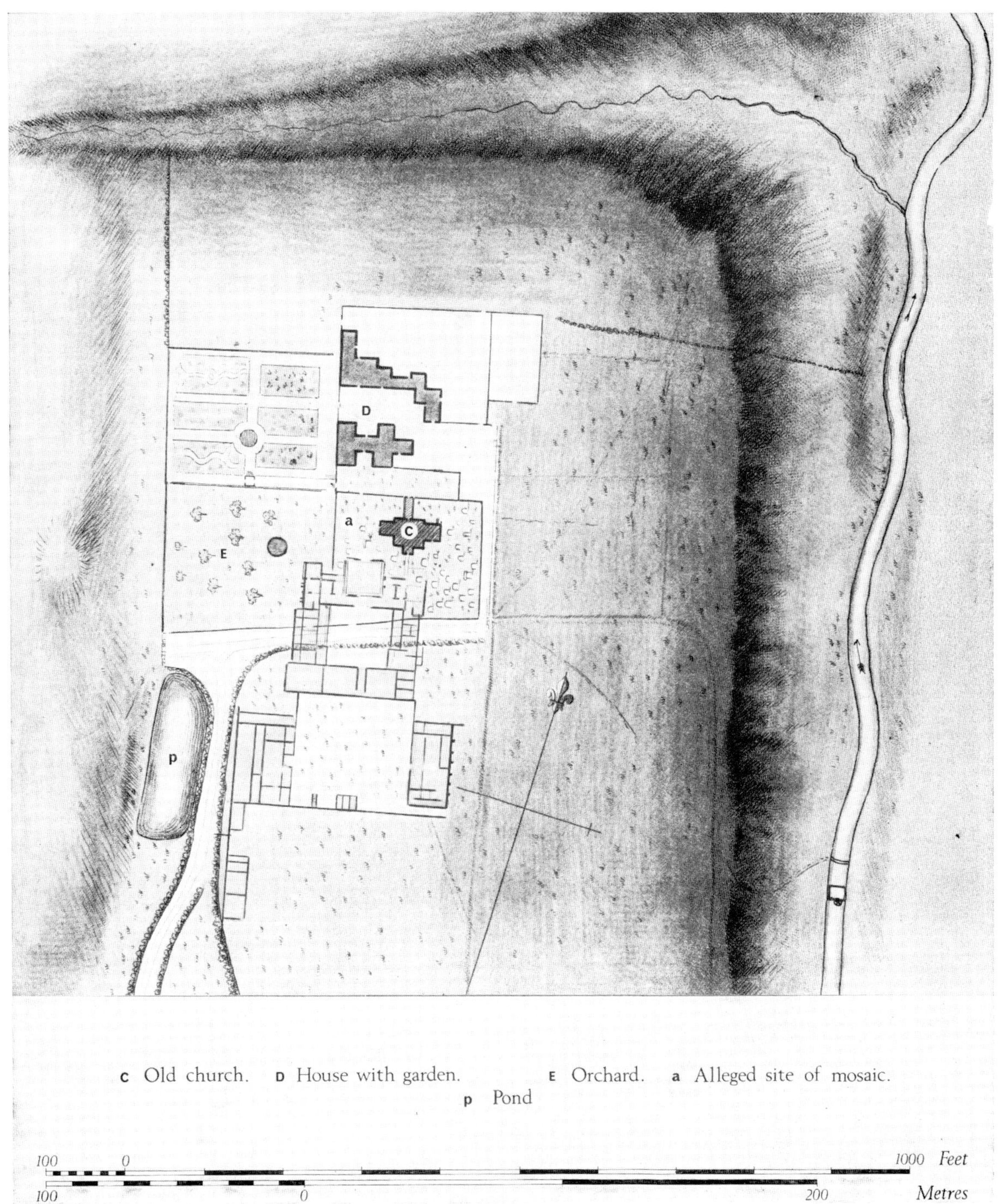

WOODCHESTER. (1) Villa. General plan by Lysons.

SUDELEY. (1) Roel Camp, from W.

ULEY. (1) Uley Bury. Crop-marks of enclosures inside hill-fort, from S.E.

ULEY. (1) Uley Bury, from N.E. Arrows point to area of crop-marks seen on Plate 32.

From N.

Interior, between N. ramparts, looking S.E.

SODBURY. (1) Sodbury Camp Hill-fort (cf. plan, p. 104).

From N.

Interior, looking N.E.

HORTON. (1) 'The Castles' Hill-fort.

ICOMB. (1) Probable hill-fort, from N.W. (cf. plan, p. 67). b-b, discontinuous ditches.

NORTH CERNEY. (2) 'The Ditches', from W.

COLESBOURNE. (1) Norbury Hill-fort, from S.W. Broken line indicates bank.

PAINSWICK. (1) Kimsbury Hill-fort, from E.

DOWDESWELL. (1) Hill-fort, from N.W. Remains of strip cultivation seen top left.

STANTON. (1) Shenberrow Hill-fort, from N.E. (cf. plan, p. 110).

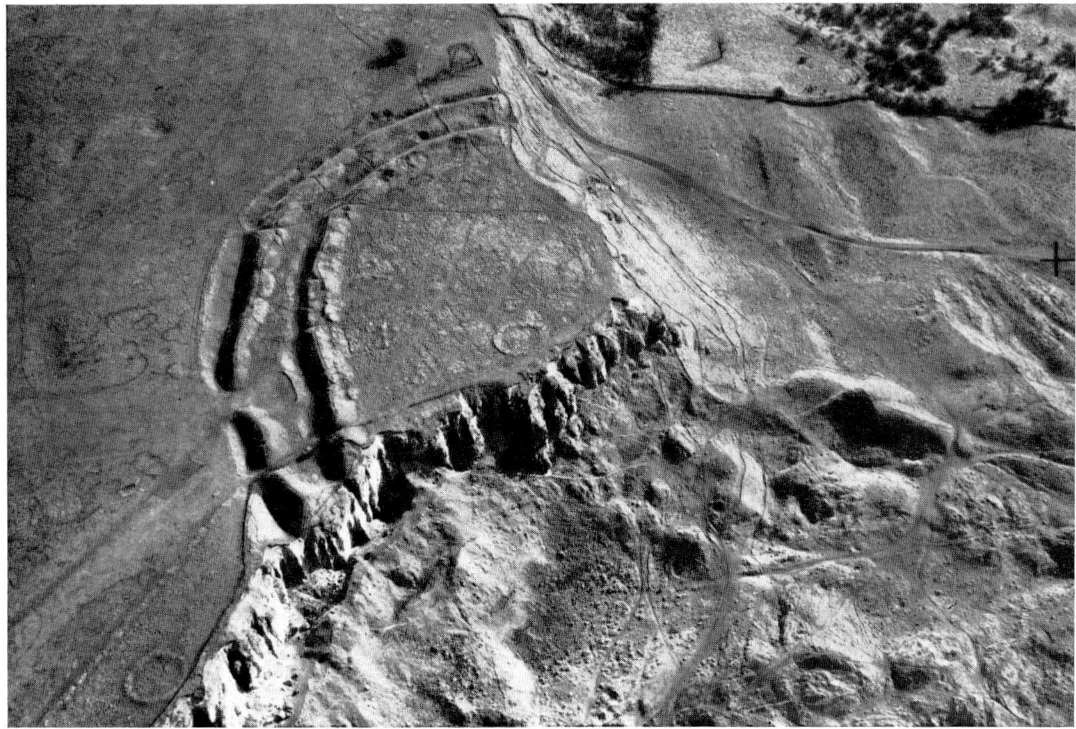

SOUTHAM. (1) Cleeve Cloud Hill-fort, from N.W. (See also introductory note, p. 106.)

COBERLEY. (1) Crickley Hill Hill-fort, from E., during excavation. To r., hornwork in front of entrance. Metric scales.

SOUTHAM. General view from S.W., showing monuments (2–6). The Ring (4) is r. from centre.

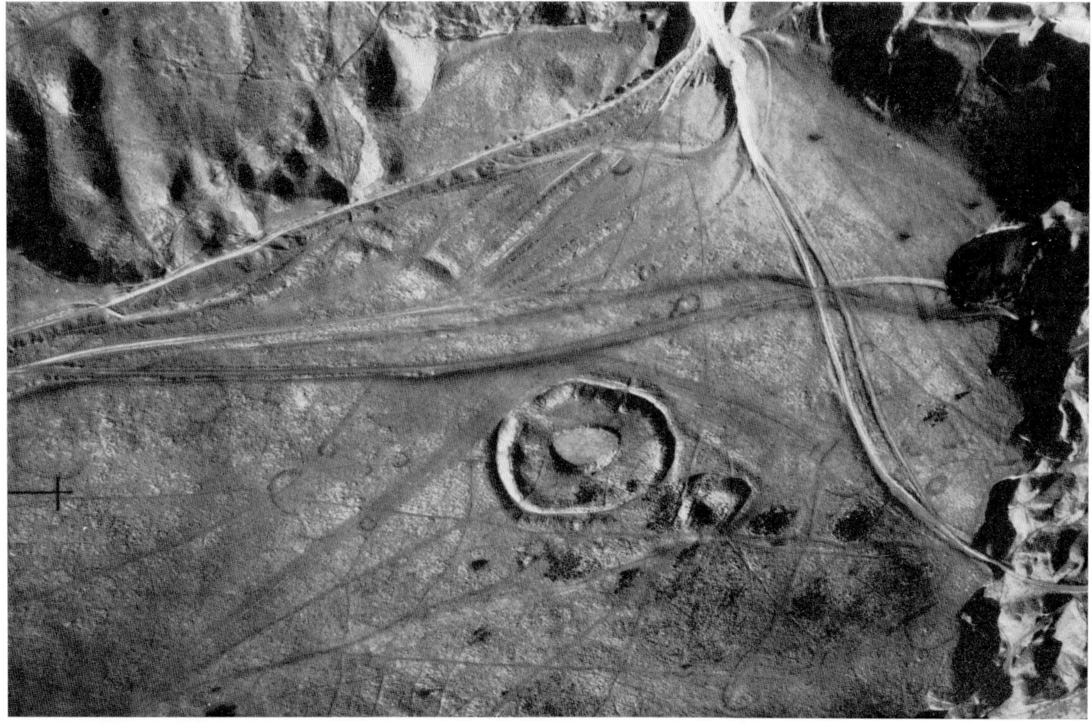

SOUTHAM. (4) The Ring and (5) Ringwork, from E.

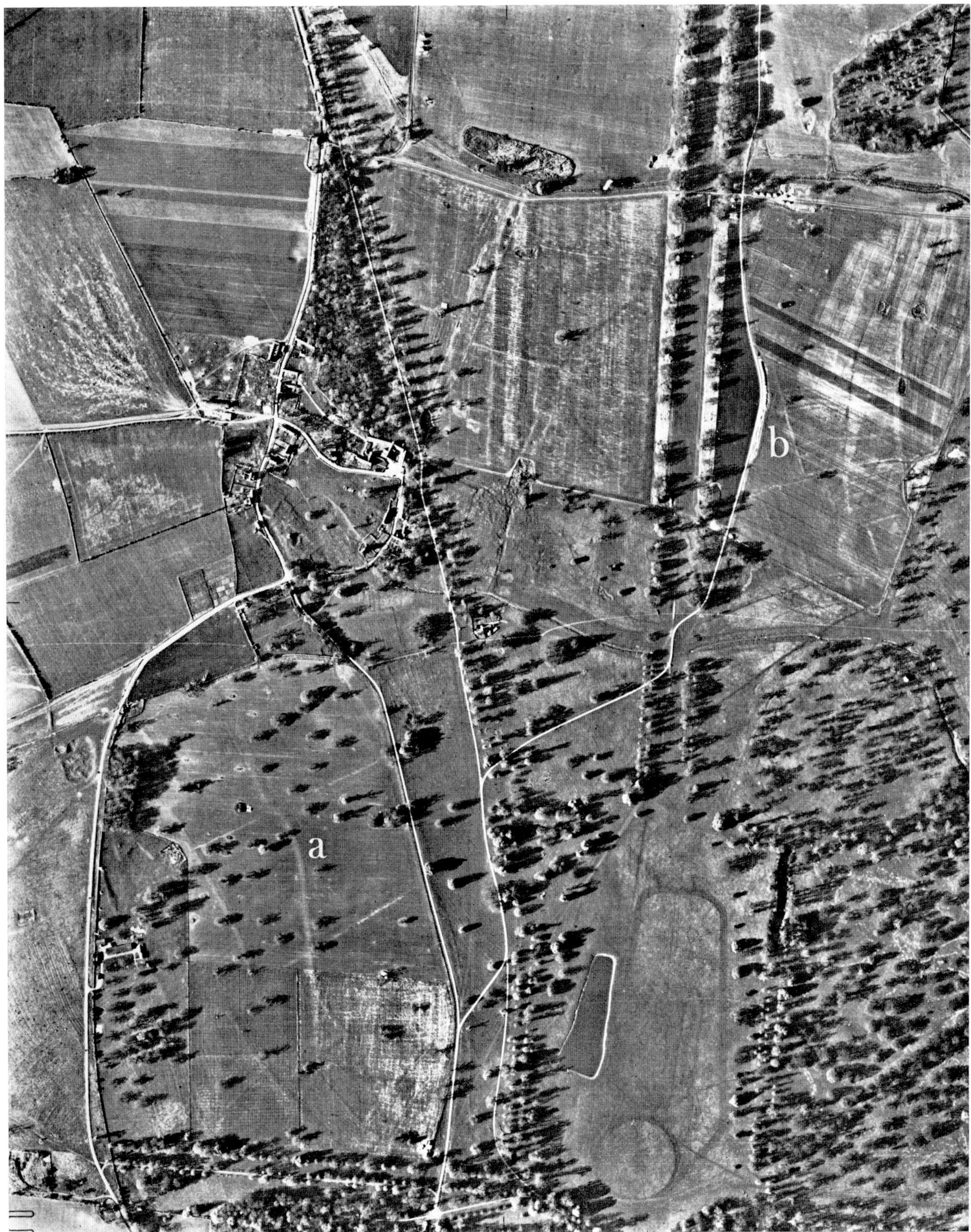

BADMINTON. (1) 'Celtic' Fields (a and b) in Badminton Park. N. at top. Scale approx. 6 ins. to 1 mile

EASTLEACH. (1) 'Celtic' Fields above (2) the Roman terraceway of Akeman Street as it approaches the R. Leach. Facing N.W.

TORMARTON. (1) 'Celtic' Fields partly overlain by later ridge-and-furrow. Facing N.W.

General view of monuments (1–3), (7) and (8), from N.W. (cf. plan opp. p. 82).

(1) The Bulwarks, looking S.W. near section E–F.

MINCHINHAMPTON.

(1) The Bulwarks and (3) Bank and Ditch. Ranging rod at centre marks intersection of (3) by hollow-way. Facing N.E.

Pits and mounds of uncertain origin W. of (7). Facing S.W.

MINCHINHAMPTON.

Dyke 'a' from W. Arrow points to crop-mark O.

Dyke 'a' from N.E.

BAGENDON. (1) Crop-marks of ditches and possible enclosures near N. part of Dyke 'a'. (Plan opp. p. 7.)

Dyke 'a', looking S., near section R–S.

General view, looking S.W. Dyke 'b' in foreground. Dyke 'a' masked by tree-belt.

BAGENDON. (1) Dykes 'a' and 'b'. (Cf. plan opp. p. 7, and frontispiece.)

BATSFORD. (1) Romano-British settlement at Dorn, from S.W. Arrows show Foss Way.

WHITTINGTON. (2) Romano-British settlement at Wycomb, from S.W.

DRIFFIELD. (1) Villa and enclosures, from S.W.

SAPPERTON. (1) Roman settlement, from S.E.

BARRINGTON. (2) Romano-British settlement, from N.W.; photograph taken before 1939. Probable track at 't'.

DUNTISBOURNE ROUSE. (4) Romano-British settlement at Stancombe, from S.E. Pile of stones marks position of building 'a'. Cf. plan, p. 50, and Plate 51.

WITHINGTON. (2) Villa under excavation, from S.E. (after Lysons).

DUNTISBOURNE ROUSE. (4) Romano-British building 'a' at Stancombe, looking E.

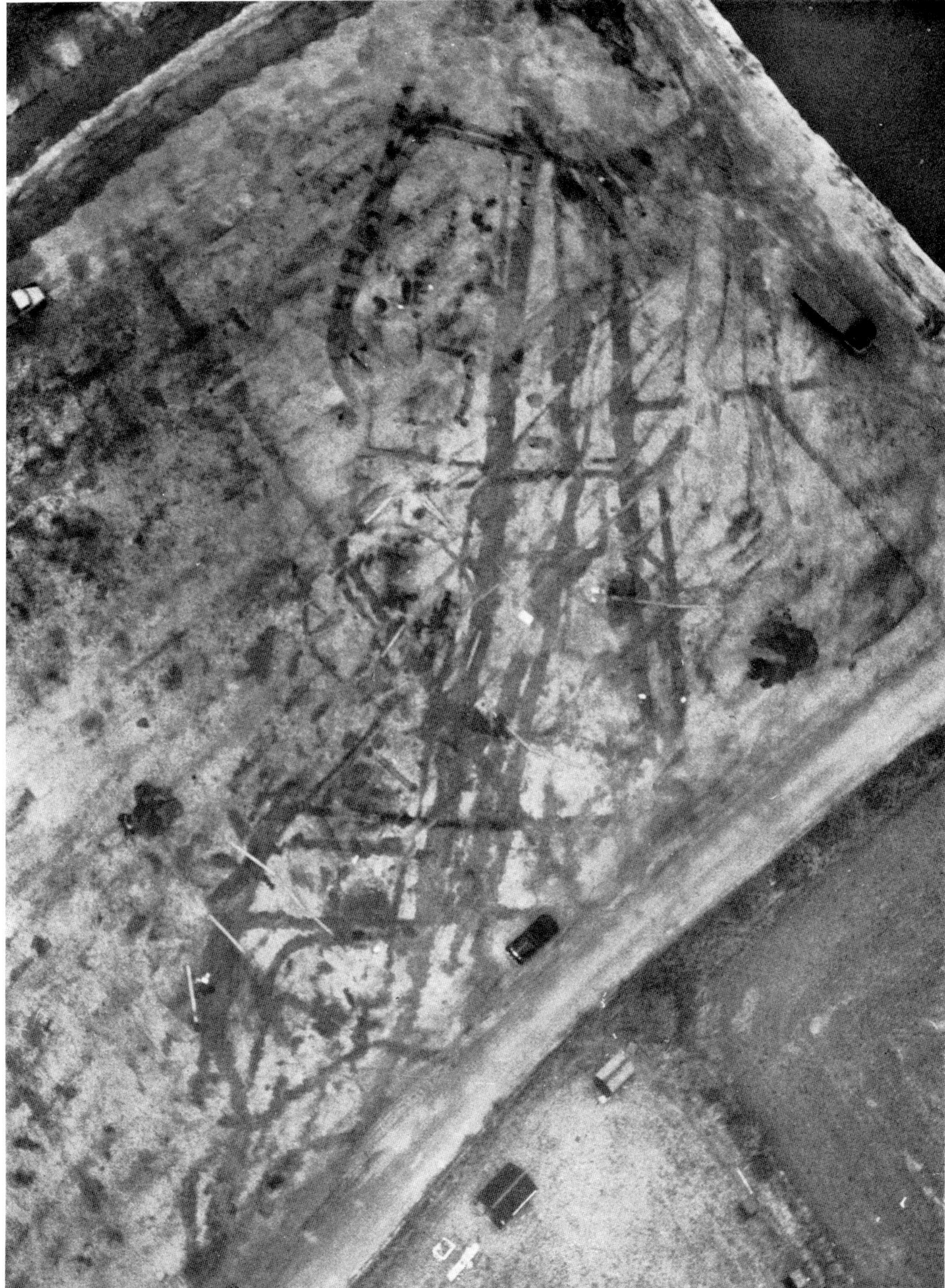

LECHLADE. (5) Iron Age and Romano-British settlement, Roughground Farm. Air view, looking N.W., of soil-marks E. of road (plan in end-pocket).

LOWER SLAUGHTER. Romano-British settlement, Chessels, from S.E., showing the position of structure '83' (plan opp. p. 79).

TEMPLE GUITING. (11) Enclosure, from S.E.

TORMARTON. (2) Rectangular enclosure, from W.

SEVENHAMPTON. (1) Rectangular enclosure, from S.

SOUTHROP. (1) Enclosure, from W.

LOWER SLAUGHTER. (2) Enclosure, from S.

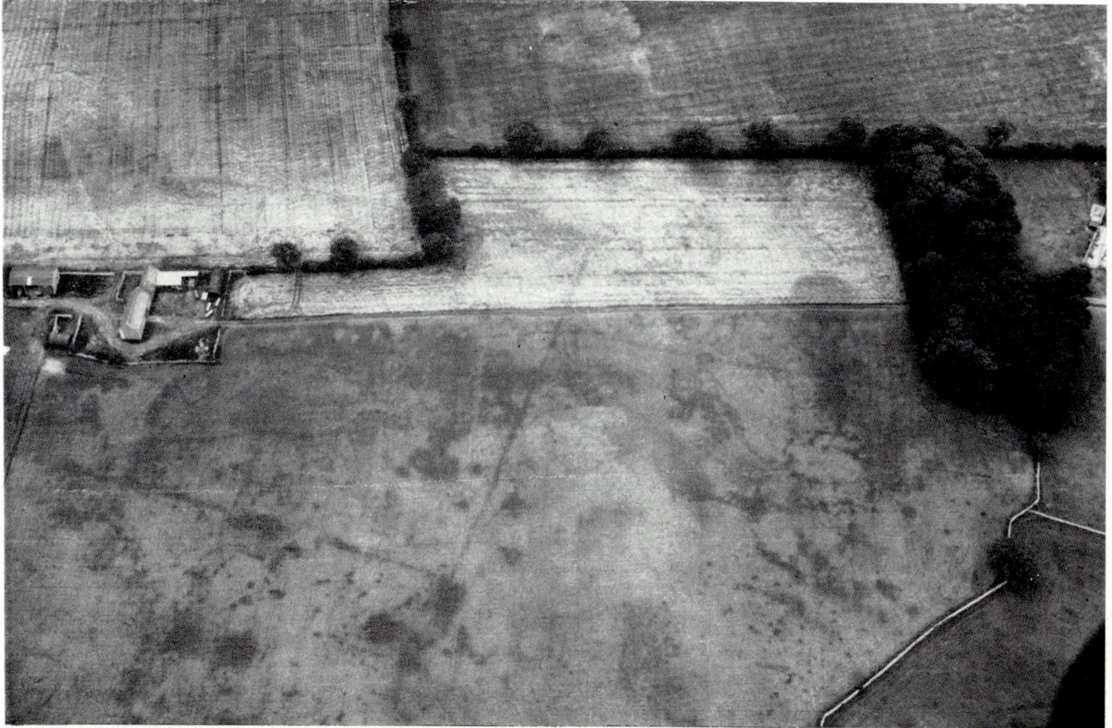

BARNSLEY. (4) Probable settlement, from E.

TEMPLE GUITING. (4) Pit-alignment, from N.

CONDICOTE. (1) Pit-alignment (N. part) and ditch, from E. Arrow points to the intersection of the two features.

(4)↘

TEMPLE GUITING. (5) Enclosures and ditches, from S.E.; (4) in background. Cf. Plate 56 and plan on p. 118.

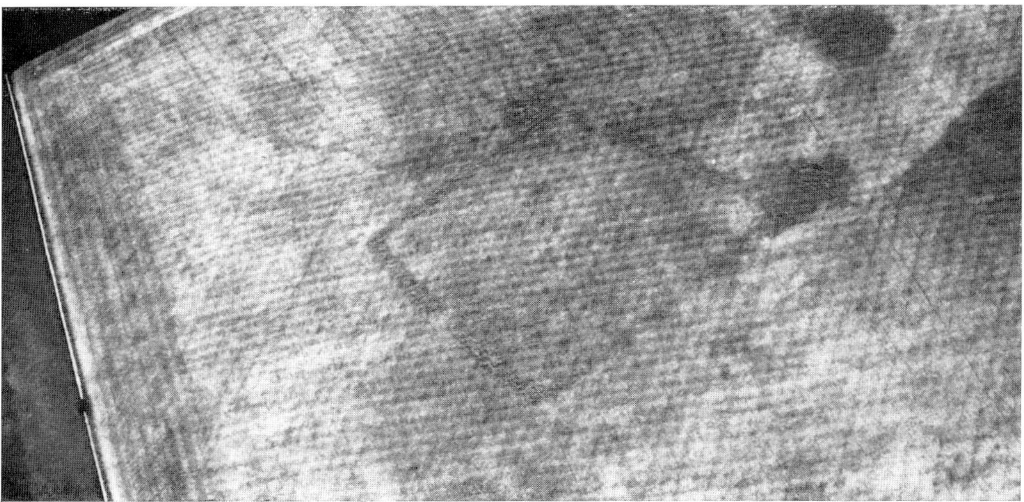

COWLEY. (6) Enclosure, from S.W.

COATES. (6) Enclosure, from S.E.

FAIRFORD. (3) Enclosure and other crop-marks, from W.

ELKSTONE. (2) Enclosure, from N.

SODBURY. Possible enclosure, from S. (ST 769805).

SOMERFORD KEYNES. (3) Rectangular enclosure, track (arrowed) and other crop-marks, from N.W.

LECHLADE. (2) Ring-ditches, enclosures and tracks, from S. Cf. plan, p. 74 and Appendix B, p. lv.

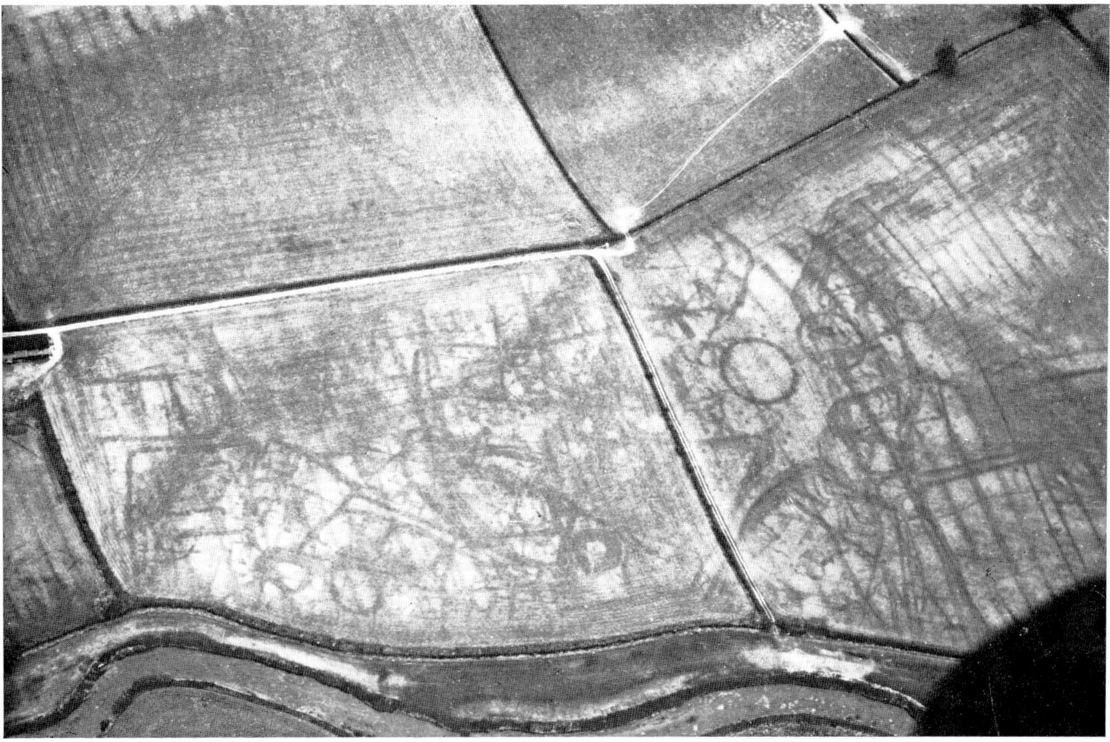

KEMPSFORD. (7) Crop-marks, from S.

Enclosures and tracks in FAIRFORD (6) and LECHLADE (8). N. at top.

KEMPSFORD. (6) Enclosures, from S.E.

DUNTISBOURNE ABBOTS. Ditched track (arrowed) N. of monument (1), from S.E. (Ermin Street, r.)

KEMBLE. (1) Probable settlement and other ditched features, from S.

DUNTISBOURNE ABBOTS. (2) Enclosure and broad track (arrowed), from S.E. (Map, p. 48)

DYRHAM AND HINTON. (2) Probable settlement, from N.

KEMPSFORD. Circular enclosure of 'Highworth' type.

LOWER SLAUGHTER. (4) Circular enclosure, from W.

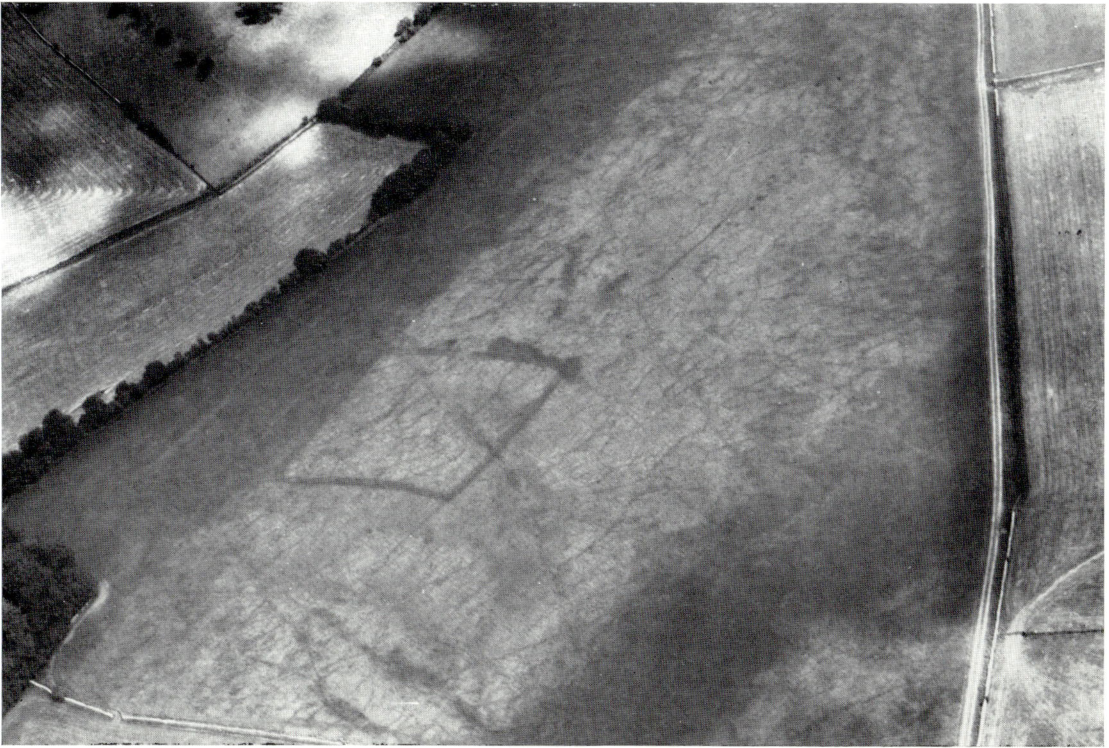

CIRENCESTER. (4) Enclosure, from W.

RODMARTON. Crop-marks (ST 928987), from S.W.

FAIRFORD. (4) Enclosures and tracks, from S.E.

FAIRFORD. (2) Enclosure 'a' from N.

From S.

From W.

STANWAY. Ridges and soil-marks at Upper Coscombe (p. xxxiii).

Natural features N. of Condicote, in area of 'Eubury' (p. xxxi).

Hawkesbury Knoll, from N.W., with strip-lynchets (p. xxxiii).

AN INVENTORY OF IRON-AGE AND ROMANO-BRITISH MONUMENTS IN THE GLOUCESTERSHIRE COTSWOLDS

Arranged by Parishes

ACTON TURVILLE

(19 miles S.W. of Cirencester)

Romano-British pottery was found and ditches were recorded (ST 810799)[1] during motorway construction. The site is on Forest Marble.

1. *MPBW Excavations*, 1969, 53.

ADLESTROP

(21 miles N.E. of Cirencester)

A coin of Allectus and Romano-British pottery came from a superficial position on the Adlestrop Hill long barrow (SP 25372829).[1]

1. H. E. Donovan in *TBGAS*, 60 (1938), 161. *Ibid.* 79 (1960), 69, Adlestrop (I). Finds in Stroud Museum.

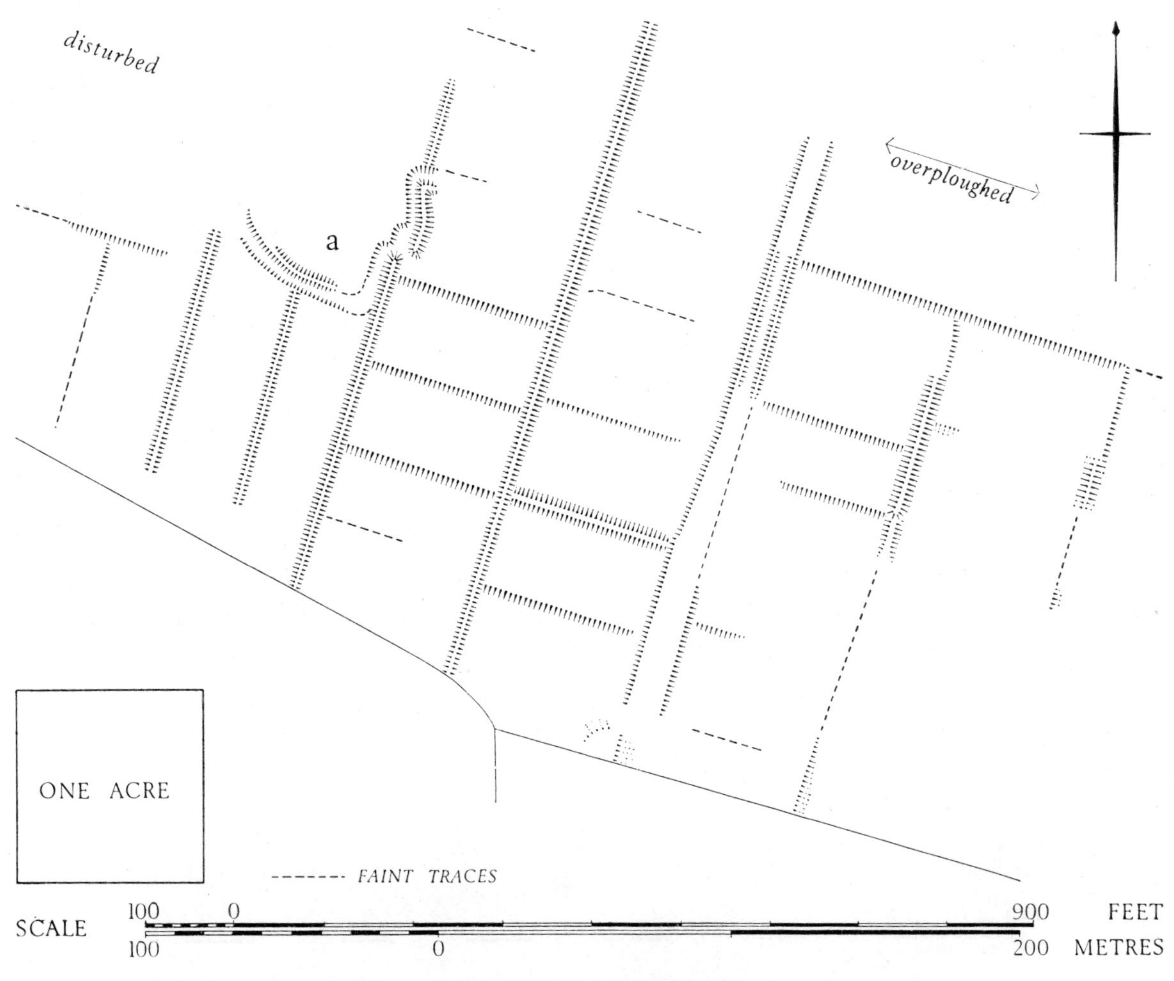

ALDSWORTH. (1) 'Celtic' fields.

ALDERLEY

No Iron Age or Romano-British monument is known in this parish.

ALDERTON

(19 miles N. of Cirencester)

The alleged hill-fort on Dixton Hill (SO 985305), formerly known as Castle Hill,[1] and the 'motte' associated with it cannot be accepted as such. The surface features are partly geological and partly due to later human disturbance (see p. xxxi).

1. *PNG*, II, 49.

ALDSWORTH

(10 miles N.E. of Cirencester)

(1) 'Celtic' Fields (SP 180093) covering some 70 acres are recognisable on the limestone pasture of Bibury old race-course and on the arable ground immediately to the S., the whole area being flat or gently sloping. In the W., the fields which lie S. and S.E. of earthworks 'a' (SP 178092), which appear to be contemporary, are remarkably well preserved although others have been broken or obliterated by ploughing, some of it marked by low plough-ridges 5 yds. wide. The fields formerly continued in all directions; they are similarly orientated

'Celtic' fields in ALDSWORTH and EASTLEACH.

and were probably continuous with the fields in Eastleach (3), 300 yds. to the S.E. (Plans, pp. 1 and 2.)

The fields are bounded by stony banks up to 20 ft. across and 1 ft. high, probably collapsed walls, and by lynchets $1\frac{1}{2}$ ft. to 3 ft. high. A double line of collapsed walls about 4 yds. apart, suggesting a track, runs for nearly $\frac{1}{2}$ mile N.N.E. through the fields, approximately parallel with and some $\frac{1}{2}$ mile away from a less well-defined but probably similar line in Eastleach. The banks are regularly arranged in parallel lines, resulting in individual fields between 58 yds. and 62 yds. long. Areas vary from about $\frac{1}{3}$ acre to $\frac{1}{2}$ acre. The fields S.S.E. of 'a' are not less than 80 yds. long and one of them is only 25 yds. wide. The earthworks at 'a', from which these fields extend, are undated and incomplete; their surviving stony banks are up to 15 ft. across and 2 ft. high above the accompanying silted ditches.

R.A.F., VAP 106G/UK 1721: 6262–3.

AMPNEY CRUCIS

(2 miles E. of Cirencester)

Akeman Street runs E.–W. across the parish. A cinerary urn and Roman coins, including a silver coin of Honorius, were found in a quarry beside the turnpike road to Oxford, *c.* 1777.[1]

1. Rudder (1779), 228.

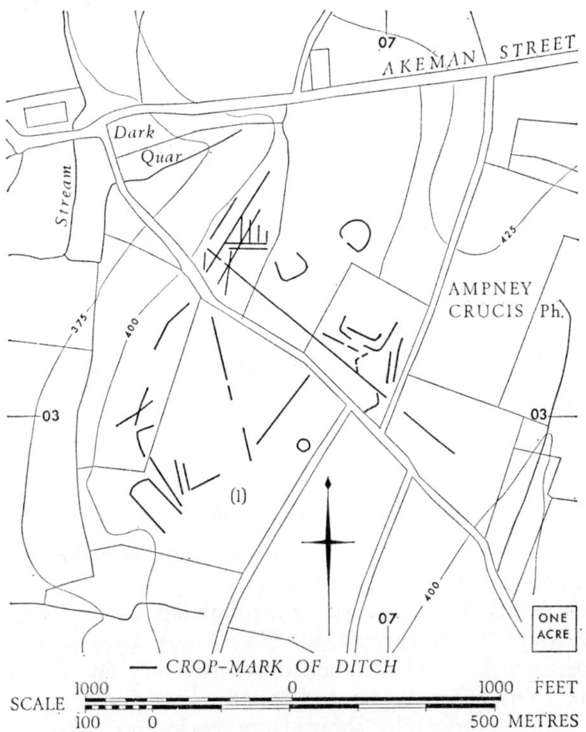

AMPNEY CRUCIS. (1) Probable Settlement.

(1) Probable Settlement (SP 069031), undated, S. of Akeman Street, is revealed by crop-marks covering about 30 acres of level ground on Forest Marble.

C.U.A.P., OAP AOS 22–3.

AMPNEY ST. MARY

No Iron Age or Romano-British monument is known in this parish.

AMPNEY ST. PETER or EASTINGTON

($3\frac{1}{2}$ miles E. of Cirencester)

A Romano-British building imprecisely located about $\frac{1}{4}$ mile N. of the village was partly excavated by J. Y. Akerman, *c.* 1860.[1] His account refers to an urn containing a hoard of Roman coins dug up in a garden 'not many hundred yards from Ranbury Ring'.

1. *PSA*, 2nd series, III (1864–7), 203–4. Finds lost.

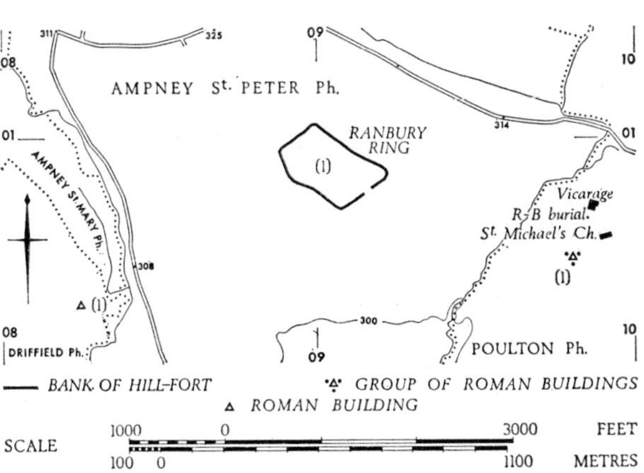

Monuments in AMPNEY ST. PETER and POULTON.

(1) Ranbury Ring Hill-fort (SP 090009), bivallate by reason of a feeble outer bank and ditch, its banks tree-covered, unexcavated, encloses $11\frac{1}{2}$ acres on the plain S.E. of the village, about 310 ft. above O.D. The perimeter of the enclosure generally follows the contours of a slight eminence, rising from the almost flat surrounding ground. The inner bank, about 35 ft. wide, stands 7 ft. above the interior and 12 ft. above the ditch, which is 30 ft. wide. Beyond this is a berm 10 ft. to 15 ft. wide. The generally denuded outer bank, about 15 ft. wide, survives in places to a height of 4 ft. The outer ditch can be traced only along the S. half of the S.W. side, where it is 6 in. deep and 12 ft. wide. The entrance, in the middle of the S.E. side, is now marked by a gap

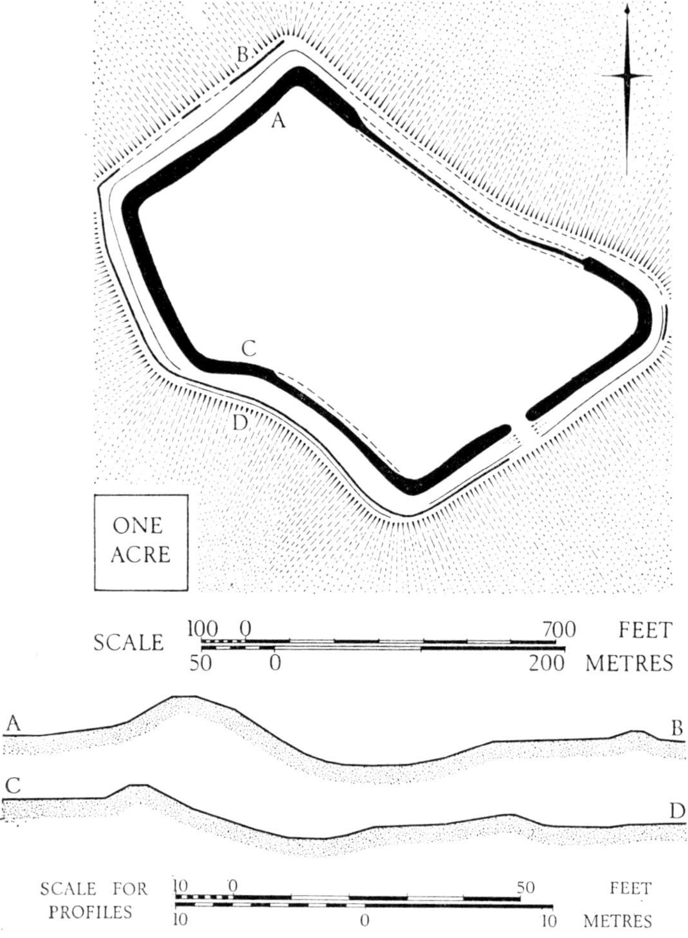

AMPNEY ST. PETER. (1) Hill-fort. Plan and profiles.

40 ft. wide in the inner bank. The outer bank has been destroyed on the N.E. of the entrance. The interior has been much ploughed.

Playne (1876), 216, No. 35. Witts (1883), 42, No. 84. *Bagendon*, 25, n. 4.

ANDOVERSFORD

(11½ miles N. of Cirencester)

For Romano-British settlement extending S. into this new civil parish at about SP 027198, see WHITTINGTON (1). For note on burials in Sandywell Park, probably Roman, see introductory note to Whittington, p. 124.

ASHLEY

(7 miles S.W. of Cirencester)

The E. boundary of the parish follows the Foss Way.

(1) ROMANO-BRITISH SETTLEMENT (around ST 92309350), E. of Addy's Firs, occupies level ground in the plain, about 440 ft. above sea-level and 1 mile S.E. of the village. The site is marked by a diffuse scatter of pottery, reddened limestone, slag and fragments of sandstone tiles in an arable field.

Finds (in a private collection) are said to include two 4th-century coins, pottery of 2nd to 4th-century types, and roof tiles.

TBGAS, 87 (1968), 203, No. 2.

(2) SETTLEMENT (around ST 93059315), Romano-British, N.E. of Ashley Marsh Covert, is on level ground at about 400 ft. above sea-level, 150 yds. W. of the Foss Way and 1 mile S. of the village. Fragments of sandstone tiles are scattered in ploughsoil.

Finds (in a private collection) are said to comprise pottery of 2nd to 4th-century types. The footings of a stone wall are recorded.

TBGAS, 87 (1968), 203, No. 1.

ASTON BLANK

(13 miles N.E. of Cirencester)

'Entrenchments', from which Camp Farm (SP 142206) presumably takes its name, are said to have existed in the area SP 143208.[1] Irregular but natural ridging[2] of the fairly steep S. side of the Windrush valley, immediately on the N., may have prompted the identification. Roman coins found in the same area may come from the long barrow a little E. of Camp Farm (SP 14342064).[3]

Roman finds beside the Foss Way on Whiteshoots Hill (SP 158207) are noted *s.v.* BOURTON-ON-THE-WATER (2c), p. 20.

1. Rudder (1779), 238. Witts (1883), 14, No. 29, 'Cold Aston Camp'.
2. *PCNFC*, XXXVI (1971–2), 97 (Aston Farm).
3. Fosbroke, *History of Gloucestershire* (1807), 421.

ASTON SUBEDGE

No Iron Age or Romano-British monument is known in this parish.

AVENING

(9 miles W.S.W. of Cirencester)

Earthworks extending over 10 acres in Hazel Wood, about ST 864987, were called 'Hazlewood Copse Camp' by Witts (1883, 25, No. 49), following an illustrated account by Playne (*PCNFC*, V (1870), 284–5). The earthworks survive, much disturbed; they are slight, make no coherent plan and are of unknown date.

Air photographs show large enclosures, possibly Iron Age, 530 yds. S.S.E. of Star Farm, at ST 891964.[1]

Casual Roman finds reported from imprecise locations are in private hands. For an altar possibly found in Hazel Wood, see KING'S STANLEY.

1. N.M.R., OAP ST 8996/1/282 (1969).

(1) ROMANO-BRITISH SETTLEMENT (ST 86909835), immediately S. of the old line of Shipton's Grave Lane, in a small area of arable on the ridge top above 550 ft. O.D., was indicated by a score of sherds, including samian, small fragments of brick or tile, some imported sandstone and a concentration of fire-reddened limestone. The sherds are in Gloucester City Museum.

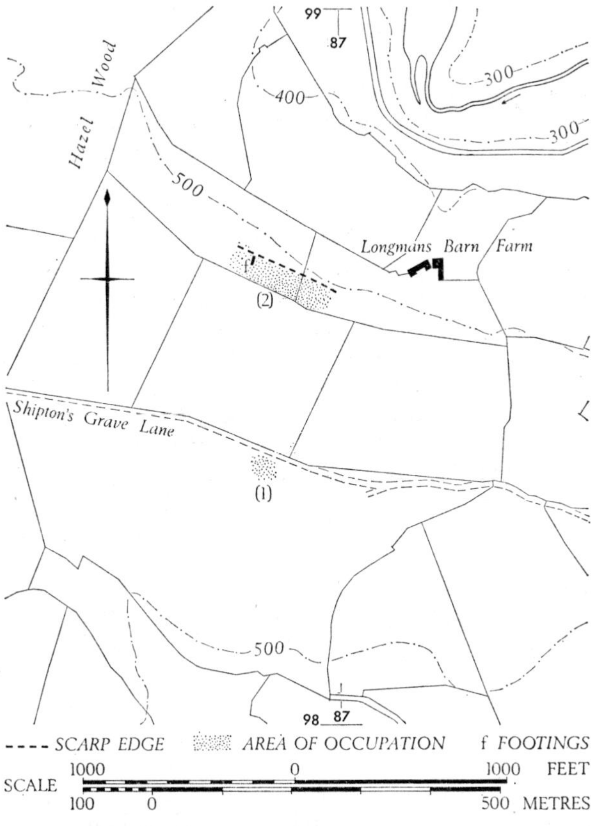

AVENING. (1), (2) Romano-British Settlements.

(2) ROMANO-BRITISH SETTLEMENT (ST 869986), near Longmans Barn Farm, 270 yds. N. of (1), (see foregoing map), occupies a terrace about 60 ft. wide, with traces of platforms, banks and depressions over at least ½ acre. The present spring-line is around the 400-ft. contour, more than 200 yds. to the north.

Footings, 3 ft. wide, of a building 14 ft. wide internally and at least 42 ft. long, possibly of Roman date, lie on the terrace some 70 yds. W. of the field wall at ST 86949860; the N. end has collapsed over the edge of the steep scarp. At the foot of the scarp is a partly buried block of dressed limestone, 2 ft. by 1½ ft., with a groove and a square socket cut into one face.

Above the terrace, on the S., scoops have been dug into the 30-ft. high scarp for a length of more than 100 yds. Most of them are small and irregular, and some have sloping bottoms.

Finds, now mostly in Stroud Museum, include twenty-four 3rd and 4th-century coins, samian and other pottery, the former with potters' stamps, and imported stone; most of these have been found over a number of years in the crumbling steep scarp on each side of the modern field wall below the terrace (ST 86969860). Occupation debris and blackened earth were exposed when post-holes were dug for the erection of a gate in the wall on the terrace.

TBGAS, 87 (1968), 203, No. 3.

BADGEWORTH

(13 miles N.W. of Cirencester)

A skeleton, probably Iron Age, found in gravel on the N. side of Crickley Hill (SO 926162) *c.* 1883,[1] was accompanied by iron articles which have recently come to light and comprise a pot-hook, a bracelet and two short pointed rods.[2]

Six 3rd and 4th-century Roman coins, found after ploughing in the Dryhill area, are in Gloucester City Museum.[3] A fragment of Romano-British pottery from Badgeworth churchyard (902192) is in Cheltenham Museum.

Romano-British pottery was noted in 1920 in a copse to W. of Barrow Wake (SO 92851523) (map, p. 40), on a steep slope near the foot of the escarpment (O.S. records).

1. *Cheltenham Examiner*, 7 Nov. 1883. A 'sandpit' is shown on O.S. maps.

2. Information from Mr. J. F. Rhodes; finds in Gloucester City Museum.

3. *TBGAS*, 83 (1964), 47.

(1) ROMAN VILLA (SO 93171689) at Dryhill (map, p. 40), in arable on a broad terrace near the foot of the escarpment, lies 150 yds. S. of a small brook and about the same distance N.E. of a spring. Excavation in 1849, following discovery during ploughing, revealed the Oolite walls, up to 3 ft. high, of a corridor building which

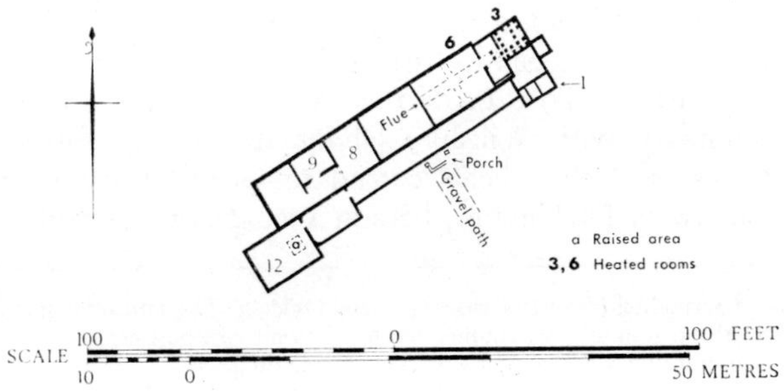

faced the escarpment. Alterations were noted in room 1, a 'bath' with stuccoed walls and a flagged floor, and also where the walls of room 9 had been built on the floor of room 8. Painted plaster was found on the inner faces of walls. The few surviving floors were of *opus signinum* or sandstone; the roof had been covered with rhomb-shaped stone tiles. A slightly raised area (a) in room 12 was plastered, like the surrounding floor, with *opus signinum*; a hole nearby, filled with bones and charcoal, contained a coin of Valentinian. A column base was found in the corridor area, and the plan suggests a pillared entrance. The villa is said to have been destroyed by fire.

Coins dating from Constantine I to Valens were found beneath the disturbed floor of room 9. The earliest reported coins, found elsewhere on the site, were of Tetricus. Other finds included a stylus, the handle of a glass jar, a millstone, a stone trough, Kimmeridge shale, coal in the arched flues under room 6, and a tile said to have been stamped 'PRC' (perhaps a misreading of RPG). All finds appear now to be lost.

W. H. Gomonde, *Notes on Cheltenham, Ancient and Mediaeval* (privately printed, 1849), 7–13. The text is reproduced without illustrations in *Norman's History of Cheltenham* (ed. J. Goding, 1863), 20–3. Witts (1883), 60, No. 10. *JRS*, XLV (1955), 72, No. 20 (tile).

BADMINTON

(17 miles S.W. of Cirencester)

A Roman mosaic pavement is said by John Aubrey to have been noted here *c.* 1686.[1] A Roman building in Badminton Park (ST 8083) was excavated by the Duchess of Beaufort and Lord Albert Conyngham, probably in 1846. There is no record of the structure, but finds included much pottery, coins of 'the Lower Empire', a bronze statuette and three intaglios.[2]

1. *TBGAS*, LII (1930), 163, note 28.
2. *JBAA*, II (1847), 90.

(1) 'CELTIC' FIELDS (ST 797832–ST 811845) in Badminton Park, extending into Hawkesbury parish, can be detected within some 70 acres of pasture and arable, above the 400-ft. contour, in two main areas centred respectively (a) ½ mile S. and (b) ½ mile E. of Little Badminton (Plate 42). To S.W. the traces continue outside the park. The remains survive in pasture as a skeleton of lynchets up to 3 ft. high; other field sides have been flattened by strip cultivation and by ridge-and-furrow. To S.E. of the park, across the county boundary with Wiltshire (about ST 819832), further traces of 'Celtic' fields extend to Giant's Cave long barrow in Luckington; here in 1960–2 copious 2nd to 4th-century Roman pottery was found, and also six 4th-century coins (*WAM*, 65 (1970), 39–63).

R.A.F., VAP 106G/UK 1416: 4372–5.

BAGENDON

(3 miles N. of Cirencester)

Monument (1) includes features in the adjoining parishes of NORTH CERNEY, DUNTISBOURNE ROUSE and DAGLINGWORTH.

(1) IRON AGE AND EARLY ROMANO-BRITISH SETTLEMENT with DYKES (frontispiece and Plates 46–7), the site of a Dobunnic capital and perhaps identifiable with Ptolemy's *Corinion* (A. L. F. Rivet in *Civitas Capitals of Roman Britain*, ed. Wacher (1966), 102), comprises two excavated areas of settlement, nine dykes (one of them known from excavation to be contemporary with the settlement), several lesser ditches, undated enclosures, and burials. Monument (2) may be associated. A 'British Camp' (G. E. Rees, *History of Bagendon*) once thought to lie in Black Grove (SP 011064) is composed of strip lynchets, and remains of other strip lynchets and ridge-and-furrow covering much of the parish testify to a long period of destructive activities. The full extent of settlement is yet to be discovered.

The excavated areas of settlement (B and C on the plan opp. p. 7), at first largely industrial and probably containing the environs of a mint, cover ⅖ acre near Bagendon Brook (SP 01750627), *Briting Broc* in a Saxon charter (Grundy (1935–6), 56). Dyke 'a', known from excavation to be contemporary with the settlement, extends uphill N. of the brook. Eight other dykes, 'b' and 'c' in North Cerney, 'd'–'f' in Bagendon, 'g' and 'h' in Daglingworth, and Scrubditch in North Cerney, lie in varied situations and are probably contemporary with dyke 'a'.* Lesser ditches associated with the N. end of dyke 'a' and a poorly marked dyke (x) in Duntisbourne Rouse may also be integral with the Monument. A linear scarp (j) in North Cerney, N.E. of dyke 'a' is not certainly a dyke. Undated enclosures S. of Scrubditch Farm, around SP 01220795, are of uncertain origin. Burials include six 'Belgic' inurned cremations from near SP 011068 (two of the urns are in Corinium Museum) and two Romano-British inhumations inserted in dyke 'a'.

All the dykes are on Great Oolite, and all except Scrubditch (NORTH CERNEY (1)) and dyke 'h' (DAGLINGWORTH (1)) have the ditches on the side away from the area of known settlement. It is difficult to detect any defensive siting, but a dyke occasionally lies on or near the brow of a secondary slope. Scrubditch partly

* Scrubditch(NORTH CERNEY (1)) and Dyke 'h' (DAGLINGWORTH (1)) are less positively associated with BAGENDON (1) than are the other dykes; for this reason they are enumerated in relation to the parishes in which they lie. Other dykes etc. are treated for convenience as though in Bagendon, notwithstanding their situation outside the parish.

crosses the spur above Bagendon, but towards the E. it is sited on the far side of a lateral re-entrant. Dyke 'h' partly spans the W.–E. ridge traversed by the Welsh Way, possibly being crossed by the present road. Dyke 'g' lies on the N. side of the same ridge, on the E. side of a shallow re-entrant. Dyke 'f' extends up the E. end of a ridge on the S. side of a re-entrant which penetrates it from the E. Dyke 'e' follows the other side of the same re-entrant.

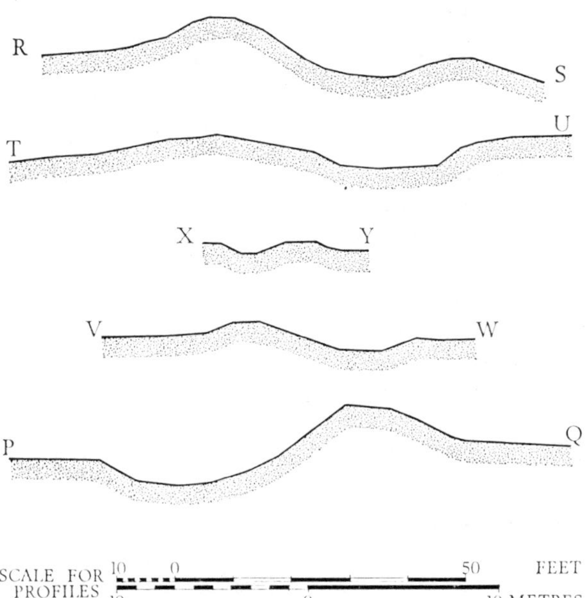

BAGENDON. Profiles of dykes (*see* plan opposite).

The earthworks vary in size. Banks are from 10 ft. to 52 ft. wide; ditches vary from 10 ft. to 28 ft. in width and from a few inches to 4 ft. in depth. The dykes together do not form an obvious enclosure and there is no evidence that any of them, except possibly Scrubditch and dyke 'g', extended beyond the limits shown on the accompanying plan. There is, however, a strong presumption that the dykes delimit an area of control, and if dyke 'h' and the brook on the N. of it are taken as the W. limit of that area, Scrubditch as the N. and dyke 'f' as the S., it amounts to some 500 acres. This area comprises the Great Oolite spur between the R. Churn and its Bagendon Brook tributary, together with the valley of the Bagendon Brook and the ridge to S. with its ancient Welsh Way.

The Areas of Settlement

Areas B and C (SP 017062), excavated by Mrs. E. M. Clifford in 1954–6, are on a limestone gravel terrace overlying Fuller's Earth, 30 to 40 yds. N. of the present course of the Bagendon Brook. North-west of area B a spring emerges from the junction of Fuller's Earth and Great Oolite and flows S. into the brook. The site is subject to overflow spring inundation.

Mrs. Clifford recognised four periods of occupation within the estimated date-range A.D. 10 to 60. (But *see* V. G. Swan, *Britannia*, VI (1975), for a reconsideration of the dating of the initial phases.) The two earlier periods were characterised in area B by round-bottomed clay-lined ditches, some of them intended to hold water, varying in depth from a few inches to 4 ft.; these ditches flanked an area about 100 ft. by 40 ft., paved in the second period. An iron-smelting furnace was thought to lie in one of the ditches and three other ditches were regarded as possible 'blowing pits' for metal working. Huts were suspected in the earlier, but they are demonstrable only in the later phases; among others thought to exist, two small stone-floored circular huts were seen to have been built over ditches when the metal-working features had been abandoned. A second stone floor, covering the area in the later phases, was partly pitched and consisted mainly of Oolite blocks over 2 ft. long; it is thought that it once extended 765 ft. from E. to W. Occupation of area C began later than in area B, but the pattern of development was comparable, the earliest features being a stone floor and ditches. Coin-moulds and many Dobunnic coins were found on the floor and, as in area B, a later floor of large stones partly covered the ditches. Both areas appear to have been quietly abandoned.

Finds were abundant and notable. There was more evidence of industry, particularly high-grade iron-working, than of domestic occupation. Close connection with S.E. Britain is suggested for the later phases. There were 35 silver and plated Dobunnic coins, one of them inscribed ANTED and another EISU, one silver Catuvellaunian coin inscribed EPATICCU, one bronze Durotrigian coin, two late 3rd-century and two 4th-century Roman bronze coins. A miniature currency bar was perhaps votive. Over 70 bronze or iron brooches included 13 Aucissa-related forms (now dubbed 'Bagendon type') and 9 of Colchester type; none of these was necessarily later than A.D. 50. Pottery included Arretine ware and S. Gaulish samian, almost all undecorated, also Gallo-Belgic *terra rubra* and *nigra* (some of the latter bearing potters' stamps) and in addition a variety of beakers and platters, jugs and flagons, fragments of amphorae (two probably of S. Spanish origin) and one or two pieces of mortaria (including a Claudian type) and of flanged bowls of late Roman form. With these, at all levels and more abundant than any other pottery, were storage jars, mostly of grey paste and wheel-made. There was also a variety of native pots, some copies of imports, others of traditional native form, all hand-made and sometimes heavily gritted.

Iron objects included the brooches noted above, carpenter's and hob nails, probable coin dies, spring tongs, steel wire, an ox goad, gouges, awls and other tools, a knife, a 'door-latch', and timber cramps. Bronze included the brooches noted above, pendants from a necklace, parts of mirrors (one square), ornamental fittings and a fish-hook with leaden attachments. Other lead objects included elongated pellets. There were clay slingstones, fragments of crucibles, coin-moulds and intensely heated daub. Stone objects included quern fragments of Old Red Sandstone, a lydite touchstone and a mica-schist polisher. Glass included fine but minute fragments akin to finds from Colchester, also beads and counters. Bones included fragments of a human skull and nine 'points' from sheep bones; also fragments of 'Celtic' ox, sheep, pig, and horse bones in that order of abundance; there was also evidence of dog, fowl and roebuck bones. Oyster shells were found, and various charcoals and coal. Numerous worked flints were thought not to be contemporary.

C.U.A.P., OAP TH 71 (showing the site under excavation).

Bagendon (*passim*). D. P. S. Peacock, 'Roman Amphorae in Pre-Roman Britain', in D. Hill and M. Jesson (eds.), *The Iron Age and its Hill-forts* (1971), 180–1.

The Dykes

Dyke 'a' extends uphill for 3,900 ft. northwards from a point N.E. of area C. An original interruption may have occurred in the length of 500 ft. now obliterated by Cutham Lane. The land falls E. from the ditch, or from points close to it.

West of Cutham Lane, where it marks the parish boundary, the dyke is generally preserved as a bank some 30 ft. across and up to 6 ft. high with a ditch on the E. side; the ditch, probably widened as a 'hollow-way', is about 26 ft. across and 4 ft. deep (Plate 47). The dyke has been truncated for an uncertain length at the S. end, but the parish boundary prolongs the alignment for a short distance. Two skeletons, probably Romano-British, are said to have been found in the bank in this region. North of Cutham Lane the bank is much spread in arable ground. Air photographs show that the N. end was joined (or almost joined) by a narrow ditch on the N.W., with other ditches adjacent on flat ground. Immediately W. of this area one set of air photographs (Plate 46) shows a crop-mark forming an unbroken circle about 30 ft. in diameter (SP 015072); it is marked 'o' on the plan. No datable objects have been found under plough in the area, nor is there evidence of any structure but the dyke.

A section cut by Mrs. Clifford, 450 yds. N. of the settlement area (SP 01900668), shows that the bank was of dump construction, 4½ ft. high and 20 ft. wide, with a berm 4 ft. wide separating it from a V-shaped rock-cut ditch, 14 ft. across and 5 ft. deep. Profile R–S is adjacent. Of six potsherds found, one, of Arretine ware, came from the rapid silting of the ditch.

C.U.A.P., OAP TH 69–75, VM 31, AJL 29.
Bagendon, 5, 8–10.

Dyke 'b' (in North Cerney) lies about 80 yds. E. of dyke 'a'; it is 70 ft. wide overall and extends N.–S. for 880 ft. on falling ground, in arable. The bank stands from 1 to 2½ ft. high above the ditch.

C.U.A.P., OAP TH 70, VM 32, ACQ 80, AJL 30–1. N.M.R., OAP SP 0204/3/357–8.

Dyke 'c' (in North Cerney), S. of dyke 'b', is some 80 ft. wide overall and extends N.–S. for 860 ft. Mostly in arable, it survives as a spread scarp, up to 6 ft. high, embracing both bank and ditch. At the S. end, in a very disturbed area of old pasture, there is no bank and the ditch line is deeper than elsewhere. It is possible that dyke 'c' was linked with other banks seen on an early air photograph (Crawford VAP 7026, Aug. 1931).

Dyke 'd', on Bear Ridge, extends E.–W. for some 900 ft., mostly in pasture. The bank stands on a prominent natural shoulder with a steep drop to the N. The overall width of the bank and ditch is about 70 ft. The W. extension is seen on an air photograph (N.M.R., OAP SP 0105/1/354), but is not visible from the ground.

Dyke 'e', over 1,000 ft. long, shows in arable as a low scarp; its ditch is seen only on air photographs (N.M.R., OAP SP 0105/1/352). Test excavations made on the S. of the dyke yielded no archaeological data (*MPBW Excavations, 1961*, 5).

Crawford VAP 7008, Aug. 1931.

Dyke 'f', 1,650 ft. long, is much disturbed, particularly at the E. end, and tree-covered. In places the bank is 52 ft. across and 4 ft. high, with a ditch 24 ft. across and 2 ft. deep (profile T–U).

Dyke 'g' (in Oysterwell Grove in Daglingworth parish) is 330 ft. long and lies 100 yds. E. of a re-entrant. The bank, about 12 ft. across, stands 2½ ft. high above a ditch of the same width (profile X–Y); it lies at right angles to the contours on a slope of 15° or less. To N., the parish boundary continues in the same alignment.

G. E. Rees, *History of Bagendon* (1932), 23.

Dyke 'h' (Daglingworth (1)) extends for 1,000 ft. on flat ground across a ridge-top. North of the Welsh Way air photographs indicate an extension of the dyke in an alignment slightly offset from that of the visible earthwork, which ends at the Welsh Way. The bank, some 18 ft. across, stands up to 4 ft. high above the ditch, which is about 10 ft. wide (profile V–W).

Crawford VAP 6987–8.

Scrubditch (North Cerney (1)) extends for 2,300 ft. across the ridge, its ditch on the downhill side. Towards the E. it lies on the N. shoulder of a narrow re-entrant, at the head of which stands Scrubditch Farm; the ground on the S. of the re-entrant, falling gently N.E., bears traces of undated enclosures. The earthworks of the dyke are disturbed; the ditch is partly filled in and its line is interrupted by farm buildings. On the W. the earthwork is truncated, but early air photographs indicate that it continued in a straight line as far as the parish boundary. Where best preserved the bank is 34 ft. across and 6 ft. high; the ditch is 28 ft. wide and 4 ft. deep (profile P–Q).

Crawford OAP 7019, Aug. 1931.

DYKE 'x', in Duntisbourne Rouse, extending N.W. from SP 00200745, has been almost flattened in arable. The ditch extends uphill from the Bagendon Brook on a slope of some 7°. At the top it enters an area of broken scarps, W. of Scott's Bushes and 200 yds. E. of a Romano-British Settlement (DUNTISBOURNE ROUSE (4)), where it becomes unrecognisable.

N.M.R., OAP SP 0007/1/270. Meridian VAP 89 67, 189.

EARTHWORK 'j', a low scarp, extends in a straight line for some 700 ft. directly below the alignment of a former road, shown on O.S. map drawings of 1817 and recognisable on air photographs.

C.U.A.P., OAP AJL 29, AWO 9.

(2) BANKS (SP 008062), possibly 'Celtic' fields with other enclosures, extend on Bagendon Downs, N. of the Welsh Way, in a place where the nearly level ridge has now become arable. The broken pattern of limestone banks covers at least 10 acres. The banks are up to 20 ft. wide and 1 ft. high. Some are straight and lie parallel with other banks 30 yds. to 40 yds. away; others are curved or meet at obtuse angles. Two oyster shells were found on the surface among a scatter of 19th-century debris.

N.M.R., OAP SP 0006/3/283.

BARNSLEY

(3 miles N.E. of Cirencester)

The area covered by monuments (1)–(4) is on Forest Marble, except for a strip of Great Oolite along the parish boundary with Winson. The buildings (1) and the fields (2) are clearly connected, but it is notable that the field lynchets contain grass-tempered pottery, of which no example has yet been found in the area of the house. Undated monuments (3) and (4) are almost certainly Romano-British and are possibly related to (1), as might also be the Romano-British settlement in WINSON, ¾ mile to N.W.

(1) ROMAN VILLA, Barnsley Park (SP 08100615), currently being excavated by Dr. Graham Webster (plan, p. 10), is sited on almost flat ground with ample water supplies near by. It consists of a building (a) with a winged 'veranda' facing S.E.; it is nearly 100 ft. long and concealed a 'yard', perhaps roofed, with a bath-house in one corner, a room or rooms at either end and other structures including a channelled hypocaust (h) on the N.W. A barn (b), 57 ft. long and 17 ft. wide internally, is set at right angles to (a) Occupation of the site originated in the 2nd century. Both (a) and (b) lie over gullies and post-holes associated with agricultural activity, and dry-stone walls. The circular walls, up to 3 ft. wide, are dated to *c.* 280–330. The earliest, but undated masonry building, originally an open shed, stands N.E. of (a). The main building and bath-house, associated with domestic occupation, were erected *c.* 350–60. Wells (W) 1 and 2, were both dug to a depth of about 25 ft. Within about 20 years of its construction building (a) was reduced to primarily agricultural use. The barn (b), partly coeval with the main building phase, continued in use after 380. Straight dry-stone walls packed with mud and debris, including coins, stand in the courtyard and under the barn, and have the same orientation as the buildings and the 4 acres or more of walled closes which surround them; this is also true of most of the associated fields (2). Some walls are older than the upper paving level of the courtyard. Occupation of the site continued into the 5th century.

The masonry of the building of *c.* 350–60 is generally of high quality. A wall stone was inscribed FIRMINI, and decorative stone roof finials were found in a well. Pilaster bases and column fragments suggest an elegant veranda. The bath-house had tufa voussoirs. The only certainly heated living room (5) had a channelled hypocaust, later blocked, and a concrete floor. Part of another channelled hypocaust was disclosed at (h) in 1971. Room 29 had a concrete floor coved at its junction with the walls. The barn (b) was built of fine herring-bone masonry. The paved courtyard between (a) and (b) was resurfaced in several places with high-quality pitched stone; the latest surface, dated after 380, shows parallel wheel ruts 4 ft. 8 in. apart. There were also carefully constructed stone paths about 5 ft. wide.

Finds: Over 700 coins have been found, ranging from the third quarter of the 3rd century to the end of the 4th century, the peak period being 330–75. Pottery includes samian, the earliest pieces being Trajanic. An intaglio had a Good Shepherd design, probably Christian. Twenty styli were found and large numbers of agricultural and domestic tools, including two very long scythes of 'Great Chesterford' type and a massive carpenter's chisel. Other finds include quern stones, stone troughs, widespread animal bones and, from the wells, worked wood and leather, and identifiable insects.

TBGAS, 86 (1967), 74–87. Additional information supplied by Dr. Webster.

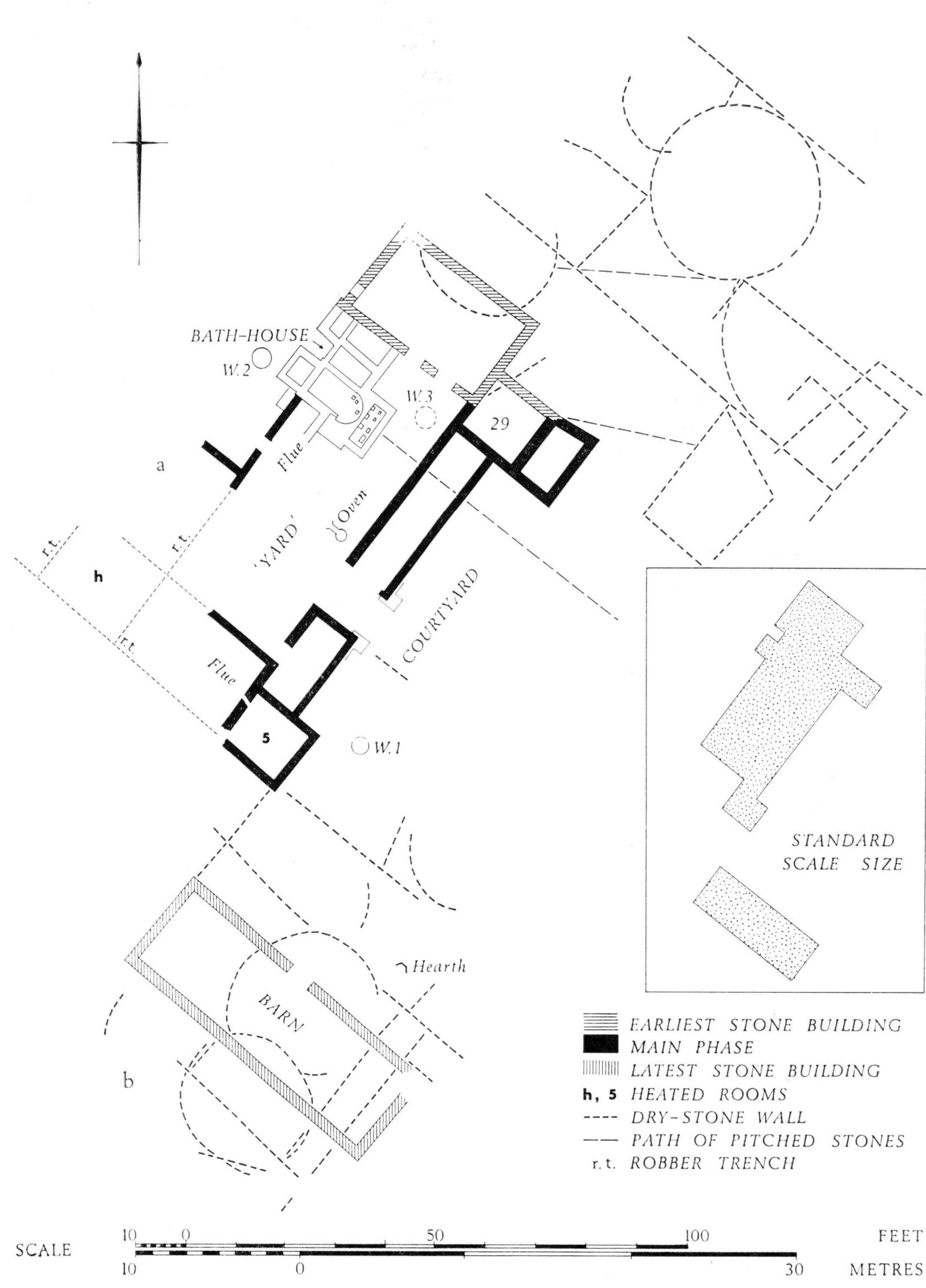

BARNSLEY. (1) Roman Villa, Barnsley Park.

(2) 'Celtic' Fields (sp 074064–sp 085058), Barnsley Park, disturbed in various ways, but a rare survival in their situation, cover some 120 acres and occupy most of the N. half of the park surrounding the buildings described in (1). They are linked to and, except at E. and S.E., follow the general alignment of 4 or more acres of dry-stone walled closes around the buildings. An area of pasture with an undated enclosure (c), adjacent to a pond, separates the domestic closes from the fields on the N.W. For the most part the land is almost flat, but it rises gently towards the W. where the remains of a substantial bank and ditch (d) stand at the limit of the more clearly defined fields; lesser traces of field banks extend further W. To the N. the ground drops gently to the natural bounds of a narrow valley, potentially marshy, where the headwaters of a stream in Cadmoor are flanked on the N. by Deadlands Copse. A lesser re-entrant bounds the fields on the S.W. A lateral gulley from Cadmoor lies outside the park wall, towards the E., beyond which the ground is ploughed. Ridge-and-furrow covers much of the S. half of the park and intrudes into the field area at sp 084059.

The remains have been surveyed and selectively excavated by Mr. P. J. Fowler. The soil is a rich red loam, about a foot deep above the broken surface of Forest Marble bedrock. Field boundaries examined consist of narrow earthen banks. Their position has been emphasised by ancient plough action on both sides, leaving either low baulks up to 40 ft. across, or lynchets up to 3½ ft. high. There is no sign of original fences or walls. Abraded pottery in the ploughsoil, thought to be the consequence of manuring with domestic refuse, includes grass-tempered ware probably of the 5th century and later than any finds from (1), as well as sherds which could match pottery from that building.

Original sizes of individual fields cannot in general be determined. The overall pattern is akin to that of prehistoric and Romano-British 'Celtic' fields. Earthwork (d) extends across the greater part of the field area in the W. At the N. it survives as an unploughed ditch, 30 ft. to 60 ft. across and 5 ft. deep below its W. lip; there is little sign of a bank. The ditch is interrupted by a narrow gap at the angle, facing the head of a gentle re-entrant. In its S. parts the earthwork appears as a much-ploughed low ditch, about 25 ft. or more across, with traces of a bank on one side or the other. Beyond this, almost levelled field lynchets extend N., one pair spaced 40 yds. apart. Other features may be contemporary with the fields. In the S.E. a flat-bottomed area (x), some 2 ft. deep, is approached by four linear hollows on alignments comparable with those of the fields; a small elongated mound about 2 ft. high lies centrally in the sunken area. About 1,000 ft. S.E. of (x), a low wide bank extending the line of the lane S.W. from Cadmoor is thought by Dr. Webster to be part of a Roman road which thereafter continues S.W., flanking The Grove plantation.

Some 200 yds. N.N.W. of (1) a small undated enclosure (c) is defined by a slight bank, up to 1½ ft. high above an external ditch; it lies in an area without field boundaries at the head of a shallow lateral re-entrant from Cadmoor. Other earth-works in the park are later, or probably later, than the fields. They include certain banks and ditches crossing the fields, and many roughly circular low mounds. These most probably have to do with trees and are omitted from the plan.

N.M.R., OAP SP 0706/2/476–98; 0806/9/386; 0806/16/461–75. Plan and details supplied by Mr. P. J. Fowler.

(3) ? Enclosure (sp 093053), undated, seen as a crop-mark near Poultmoor Farm, 1,500 yds. S.E. of (1), lies on the E. side of a stream flowing along a shallow bottom. There is an entrance in the S.E. side and a broad way appears to pass its N. side.

N.M.R., OAP SP 0905/3/390–2.

(4) Probable Settlement (sp 097052), undated, seen as a crop-mark ¼ mile S.E. of (3), lies around Furzey Furlong Barn covering perhaps 2 acres (Plate 55). An entrance occurs towards the N. end of the E. side. The earthwork is associated with other ditches of irregular pattern. The nearly level site falls gently westwards.

N.M.R., OAP SP 0905/1/395–6.

(5) Probable Settlement (sp 096049), undated, seen as crop-marks on flat ground 200 yds. S.E. of (4), lies just N. of the Welsh Way and has an entrance in the S.E. side. There are other ditches, one intersecting the enclosure.

N.M.R., OAP SP 0905/2/393–4.

BARRINGTON

(14 miles N.E. of Cirencester)

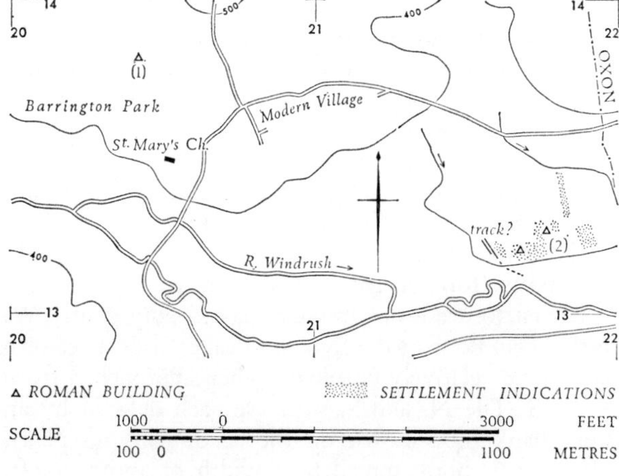

Monuments in BARRINGTON.

(1) ROMANO-BRITISH BUILDING (SP 204138), in Barrington Park approximately 330 yds. N. of St. Mary's Church, on a gentle S.-facing slope, was discovered by chance about 1867 and was partly dug in 1882. A well-built wall 4 ft. thick, a plunge bath, roof slates and tiles, 'grooved' tiles, pottery and bones were noted.

MS. Notebook III of Dr. John Moore, pp. 14–16 (9 Mar. 1882), in library of Brist. & Glos. Archaeol. Soc.
N.M.R., OAP SP 2013/1/16–23; 2013/2/24–30.

(2) ROMANO-BRITISH SETTLEMENT (SP 217132), $\frac{4}{5}$ mile E.S.E. of St. Mary's Church, extends over some 7 acres on the almost flat alluvial terrace immediately N. of the R. Windrush. Remains of buildings with stone footings and tessellated pavements are reported in parts of the area. Two channelled streams flow through the site. Disturbed earthworks survive at SP 217132, but the ground to the E. is flattened in arable. Air photographs (Plate 50) indicate a double ditched feature (t), probably a track, earlier than modern enclosure and drainage patterns, approaching the site from N.W. Roman tiles, tesserae and wall plaster, possibly found on this site in 1931, are now in Gloucester City Museum. Similar material was found *c.* 1935 together with a coin of Gratian.

Information, from letters and notebooks in private possession, supplied by Dr. J. Liversidge.
Air photographs: W. G. Allen OAP 585–7.

BATSFORD

(22 miles N.E. of Cirencester)

A small stone panel now in Chedworth Museum, inscribed *Dea Regina* below a low relief of a goddess, is allegedly from Lemington, E. of Dorn (*JRS*, XXXIX (1949), 114; Toynbee (1964), 175; *RIB*, I, No. 125).

(1) ROMANO-BRITISH SETTLEMENT (SP 207339), at Dorn (formerly in Worcestershire), is marked by an oblong enclosure of some 10 acres, extremely disturbed and mostly in ground which has long been ploughed. Its existence was already recognised in the 17th century (Bodleian Lib. MS., Ashmole 1817 A; data communicated by Mr. H. E. M. Icely). The enclosure butts on the Foss Way (3), 300 yds. N. of the point where the road changes course at its intersection with another ancient road line. The enclosure is massively ditched, unlike any civil site in this area. The name Dorn probably means 'fort' or 'gate' (*PNG*, I, 235).

The enclosure is on Boulder Clay sloping gently W. to the level floor of the Evenlode valley, but its eastern parts stand relatively dominant when approached from N. or S. The N. and S. sides are each defined by an inner bank (not shown on the accompanying plan), 1 ft. to 2 ft. high, spread to a width of about 100 ft. and standing some 3 ft. to 5 ft. above a ditch apparently

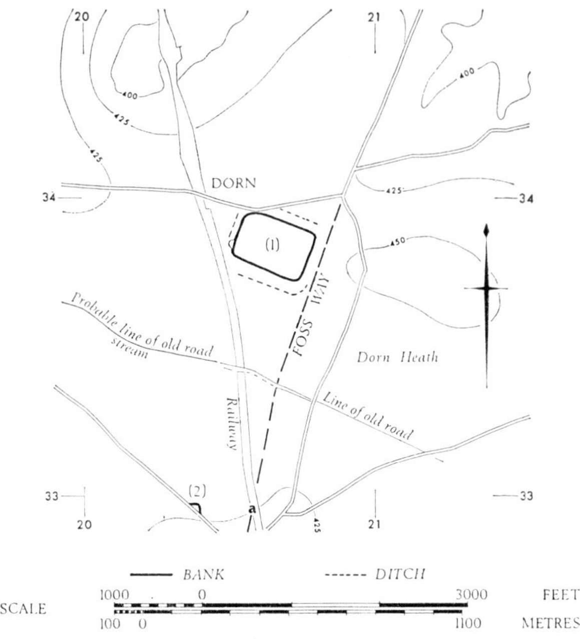

Monuments in BATSFORD.

150 ft. to 200 ft. across, with a counterscarp bank beyond. On the E., downhill from the *agger* of the Foss Way, the ditch line is filled. At 'r', on the S.W., the line of the ditch is corrugated by ridge-and-furrow. To the N. of the railway cutting, at the foot of the natural slope, feeble or disturbed scarps probably indicate its approximate position.

Inside the enclosure, crop-marks suggest a wall extending S.E. from 'b' and a rectangular pattern of paved roads (Plate 48); the latter seem to have been visible on the surface in 1731 (Cox, *Magna Britannia et Hibernia*, vi, 240). Excavation at 'e' in 1937 by Lieut.-Col. R. K. Morcom showed occupation from the 1st to the 5th century. A stone building with corridor, tiled roof, plastered walls and some tesserae belonged to the latest period. There were two wells. Finds in-

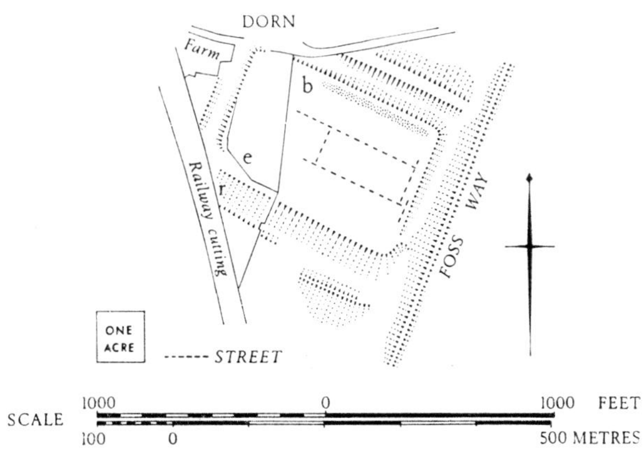

cluded: pottery of the 1st century including butt-beaker and samian; samian ware of the 2nd century with potters' stamps; much calcite-gritted ware, some with finger-pressed bands, and colour-coated ware; two steelyards and an ornamental spit (now in Birmingham Museum on loan from B.M.) from a late 2nd-century level, and other iron objects, mainly agricultural; also fragments of glass and of pewter.

Construction of the railway exposed a score of pits and two stone blocks with carved panels, both now lost; one panel was recognisable as depicting a *genius*. Finds recorded at other times include many coins, mostly of the 3rd and 4th centuries, limestone and other building stone, and part of a rotary quern. Pottery has been noted in the field W. of the railway cutting and can be found outside the enclosure on the south.

Some of the surviving finds are in private possession.

C.U.A.P., OAP ABV 31–41, ABW 78, AHU 7, AIJ 41–4. T. Nash, *Collections for the History of Worcestershire*, I (1781), 101. *Ibid.*, II (1782), postscript, 20. *VCH, Worcs.* I (1901), 221 (F. Haverfield). *JRS*, LI (1961), 119–35. *TBGAS*, 81 (1962), 194–5 (sculptures); 82 (1963), 18–24 (excavation of 1937).

(2) RECTANGULAR ENCLOSURE (SP 20383296), on the parish boundary, ½ mile S.S.W. of (1), undated, covers ½ acre. It lies on the flat valley floor and is partly destroyed by the road which crosses it and by buildings on the south. No original entrance survives. The N.E. angle, in pasture, is rounded. The bank, some 20 ft. across, stands 1½ ft. above the interior and 4 ft. above the ditch, which is about 20 ft. across with a bottom 9 ft. wide. The interior of the enclosure lies about 6 in. above the ground outside. The ditch is wet where it coincides with the parish boundary to the S.; the bank in this part is very spread and overgrown. Roman finds are reported, but without corroboration.

Playne (1876), 207. Witts (1883), 4, No. 7. *Arch J.* CIX (1952), 23.

(3) ROMAN ROAD, The Foss Way (N.N.E. from SP 205328), largely destroyed, but visible in places, continues its former alignment northwards from MORETON-IN-MARSH. An *agger* 25 ft. across and 1 ft. high with contiguous side ditches, deepest on the E. side, is preserved for some 75 yds. before destruction by the railway cutting at 20573297 (**a** on general plan). After some 500 yds. it crosses an ancient road line (marked further S.E. by the Warwickshire/Oxfordshire county boundary) which meets it at right angles; here the Foss Way veers about 12 degrees to the E. Some 300 yds. further N.E., where it adjoins (1), the road is seen as a low, spread ridge following a natural N. shoulder (Plate 48).

C.U.A.P., OAP ABV 31–41, ABW 78, AHU 7, AIJ 41–4, YT 47.

BAUNTON

(Adjacent to Cirencester on N.E.)

Crop-marks of rectangular enclosures, undated, are detectable on air photographs,[1] W. of Cirencester golf-course (SP 011048).

1. N.M.R., OAP SP 0104/3/342–4.

(1) PROBABLE SETTLEMENT (SP 025058), Romano-British, on Baunton Downs. Recent excavations, on a natural ledge in an exposed position just above the 500-ft. contour, produced a large amount of pottery including 2nd-century samian ware, also a copy of a coin of Claudius I and a coin of Trajan Decius; these were found in deep ploughsoil. There was no evidence of structures. Former surface finds in the same field include some fifteen 4th-century coins, two uninscribed altars and pottery of all Roman periods (data supplied by the excavator, Mr. R. Reece; the finds are in private possession). A light scatter of 1st to 4th-century pottery occurs over the modern flat arable field adjacent on the S.E., at SP 028057. In 1955 a collection of Roman sherds, including samian, a coin of Carus and a very small stone altar with an illegible inscription were passed to the Corinium Museum, as from 'Downs Farm'.

BEVERSTONE

(11 miles S.W. of Cirencester)

An uninscribed gold coin of 'British Q' type is recorded from the parish.[1]

On Nesley Farm (ST 854925), ploughing *c.* 1846 revealed an inscribed gabled tombstone.[2] Another tombstone of which no description survives is said to have been found near by.[3] An inscribed tombstone found on Bowldown Farm to the W. is noted under WESTONBIRT WITH LASBOROUGH. Other finds from the parish include two fibulae from Chavenage (about ST 870955), one of them with an enamelled bird figure.[4]

1. Now lost. D. F. Allen in *IASB*, 200.
2. In the Corinium Museum. *RIB*, I, No. 136.
3. *TBGAS*, XI (1886–7), 336.
4. In the Ashmolean Museum (Sir John Evans Collection).

BIBURY

(6 miles N.E. of Cirencester)

Romano-British pottery was reported[1] during ploughing in 1946 close to platforms, themselves unploughed and undated, at SP 12050672, 200 yds. N.W. of a Roman villa (2).

1. O.S. records.

(1) ABLINGTON CAMP (SP 105074), univallate hill-fort of Iron Age type, unexcavated, encloses 8 acres at 400 ft. above O.D. on the edge of the plateau above the

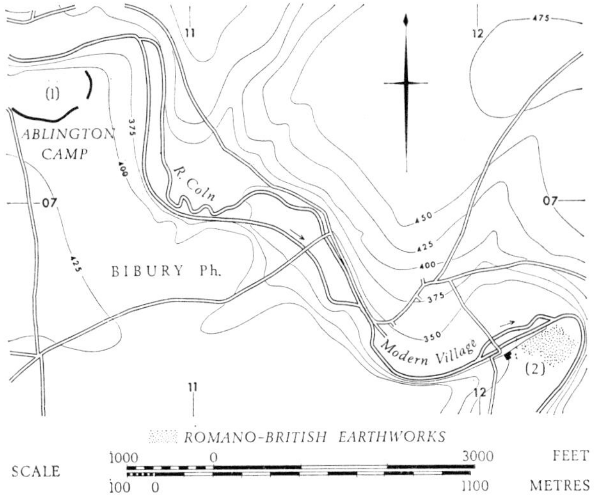

Monuments in BIBURY.

R. Coln. Most of the area has been ploughed. On the E. side, linear quarrying of unknown date lies inside the partly preserved bank; there is no other visible ditch at this point.

The N. side is marked only by the natural scarp, dropping steeply to the river. On W. and S. the bank is about 27 ft. wide and not more than 1 ft. high, being sliced by the modern road at S.W.; on the E. it is up to 5 ft. high, but N. and S. of the surviving bank there

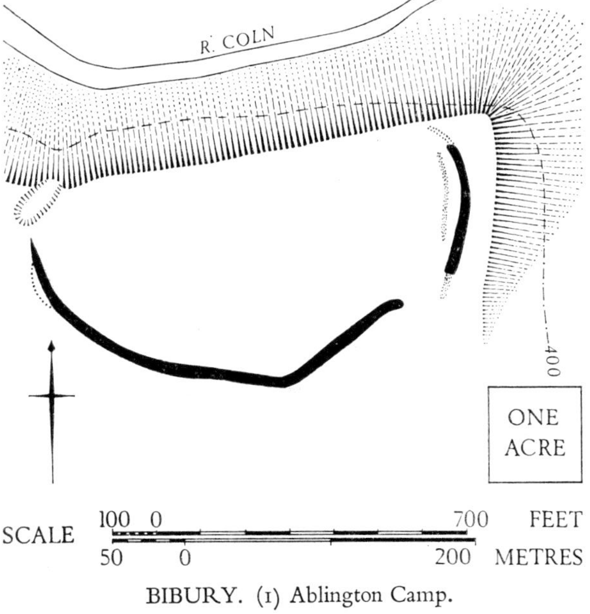

BIBURY. (1) Ablington Camp.

are only short stretches of low scarp. Signs of a 'wall' were noted after ploughing in 1881 (Witts (1883), 2). The entrance was apparently on the S.E. where there now is a gap 100 ft. wide. There is also a narrow gap in the N.E., between the bank and the natural scarp. On the N.W. the bank stops short of a broad gully at the upper end of a hollow-way leading to the river.

Witts (1883), No. 2, 'Ablington Camp'. Bryant's *Map of Gloucestershire* (1824), 'Rawbarrow Camp'.

(2) ROMAN VILLA (SP 122065), near Bibury Mill, is contained within a loop of the R. Coln and is sheltered, particularly from the E., by ground rising steeply from the river; it was first recorded *c.* 1670. The site, disturbed by a variety of diggings, is marked by earthworks which suggest the possibility of a range of buildings extending S. from 'b' for 300 ft., and of another range extending W. from 'a'. Small platforms, probably for individual buildings, are inset into the gentle N.W. slope between these two long platforms. A further small platform of uncertain date lies across the N.E. end of a terrace-way, otherwise rounded by ploughing, which approaches the earthworks from the S.W. This terrace-way is 12 ft. wide where it is undisturbed (to the S.W. of the area shown on the plan). Rectangular areas defined by very low scarps, E. of the main earthworks, are immediately above an area of low ground intersected by drainage channels. A ditch about 3 ft. deep and presumably of recent date has been cut through the earthworks W. of 'b'. Plan, p. 15.

Accounts refer generally to mosaic pavements, baths, pottery and coins. More recent casual discoveries include finds of glass and substantial masonry footings.

R.A.F., VAP 106G/UK 1721: 4273–4.

J. Pointer, *An Account of a Roman Pavement lately found at Stunsfield in Oxfordshire . . .* (1713), 37. Camden, *Britannia* (ed. Gough, 1789), I, 282. *TBGAS*, II (1877–8), 24 (coins exhibited, no details). Witts (1883), 55, No. 1, 'Bibury Villa'.

(3) 'CELTIC' FIELD TRACES (SP 097089–SP 099095), on Ablington Downs, are suggested by air photographs over some 30 acres of ground falling gently E. between 450 ft. and 400 ft. above O.D. Scarps visible in the area have been ploughed almost flat.

R.A.F., VAP 106G/UK 1721: 6276–7.

BISLEY WITH LYPIATT

(8 miles W.N.W. of Cirencester)

A Dobunnic gold coin inscribed COMVX is recorded from the parish.[1]

Roman altars and votive plaques have been found in such numbers as to suggest a religious centre or centres.[2] Finds have come from two sites about 1½ miles apart. In *c.* 1861 an altar of equestrian Mars and one of Silvanus or a native counterpart, and a plain fragment, were dug from under the S.W. corner of the tower of St. Mary's church, together with calcined stone; Roman pottery was later reported from the churchyard.[3] At Custom Scrubs (about SO 894081) quarrying of 'Roman Tump' *c.* 1800 revealed gabled reliefs of a *genius* and of Mars,

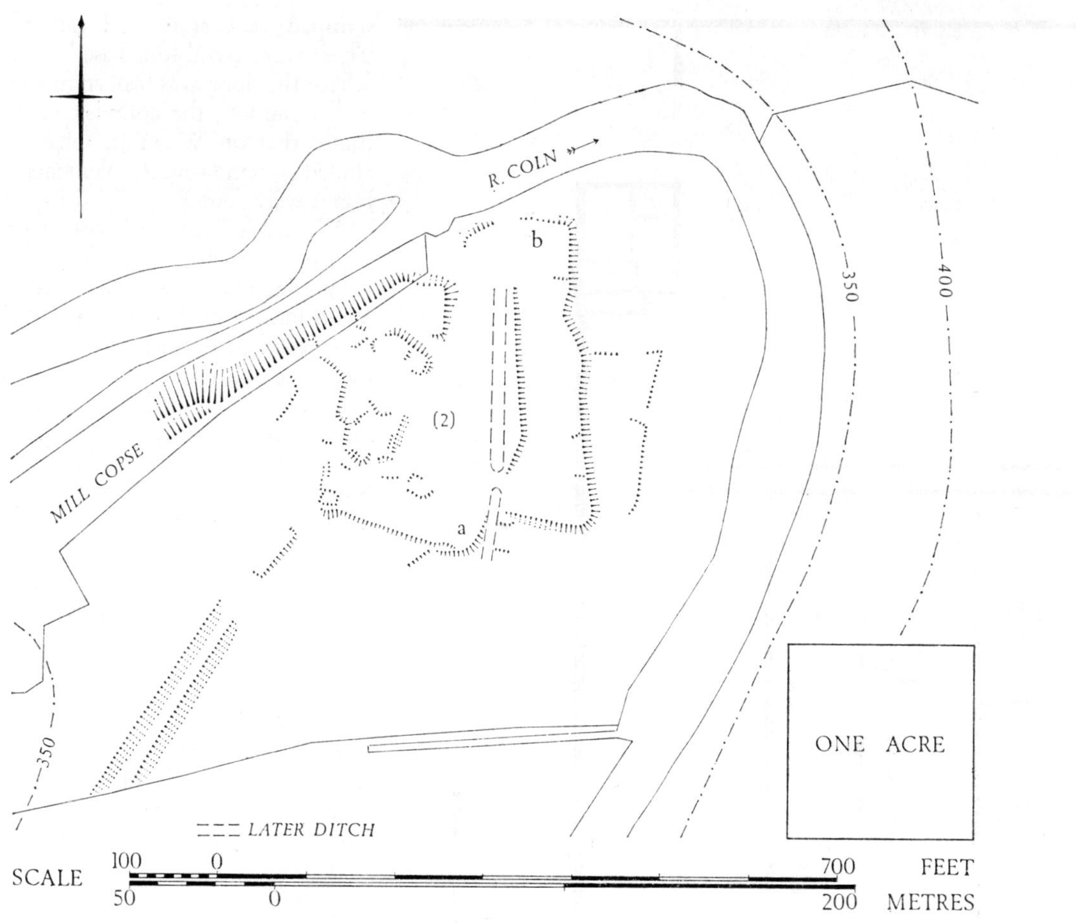

BIBURY. (2) Roman Villa near Bibury Mill.

both with cornucopiae and both inscribed, the first MARTI OLLVDIO.[4] An uninscribed relief of a warrior with a shield was found *c.* 1851.[5] Another altar, with a ram-headed serpent, is believed to have been found on the Lypiatt estate.[6] Six further altars, said to have been recovered from a mound on 'Bisley Common', are probably from CHALFORD (*q.v.*).

A Roman coin and a brooch have been found in a field about 500 yds. S.E. of villa (1), about SO 916040.[7]

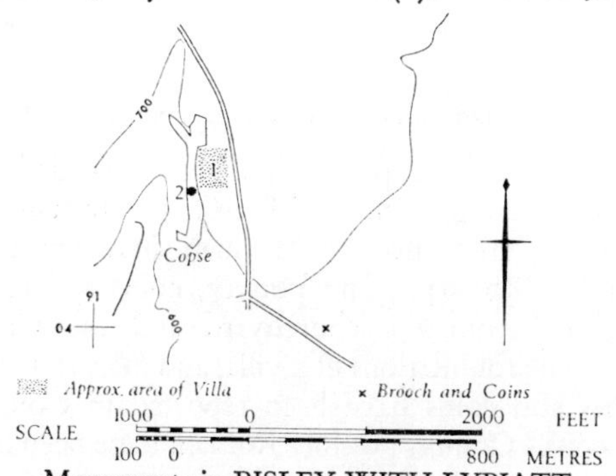

Monuments in BISLEY WITH LYPIATT.

'The Trench', SO 929046, extensively quarried, is basically a geological phenomenon.

1. Allen in *Bagendon*, 119.
2. Cf. Lewis (1966), 125–6.
3. *Arch J*, XX (1863), 186–7. *TBGAS*, V (1880–1), 39; 60 (1938), 299–300. Toynbee (1964), 154, 159. Altars in British Museum.
4. Both in Gloucester City Museum; 'Marti Ollvdio' now defaced. Lysons (1817), II, Pl. xxviii, Nos. 5 and 6. *RIB*, I, Nos. 131, 132. Toynbee, *Art in Roman Britain* (1962), Plates 65 and 66. *Ibid.* (1964), 154, 163. Ross, *Pagan Celtic Art* (1967), 185 and Plate 59 (a) and (b). *TBGAS*, XXIX (1906), 173–80.
5. Church, *Corinium Museum* (1905), 41. *TBGAS*, XLV (1923), 87–90. In Cirencester Museum.
6. *TBGAS*, 60 (1938), 298. Ross, *Pagan Celtic Art* (1967), 186, 344 and Plate 44 (b). In Stroud Museum.
7. Information from Curator, Stroud Museum.

(1) ROMAN VILLA (SO 91320438), Lillyhorn, Bournes Green, discovered and partly dug by T. Baker in 1841–5, lay in the N. half of an arable field called Church Piece, which slopes gently W. from the present Oakridge–Bisley road towards the steep scarp edge at 700 ft. above

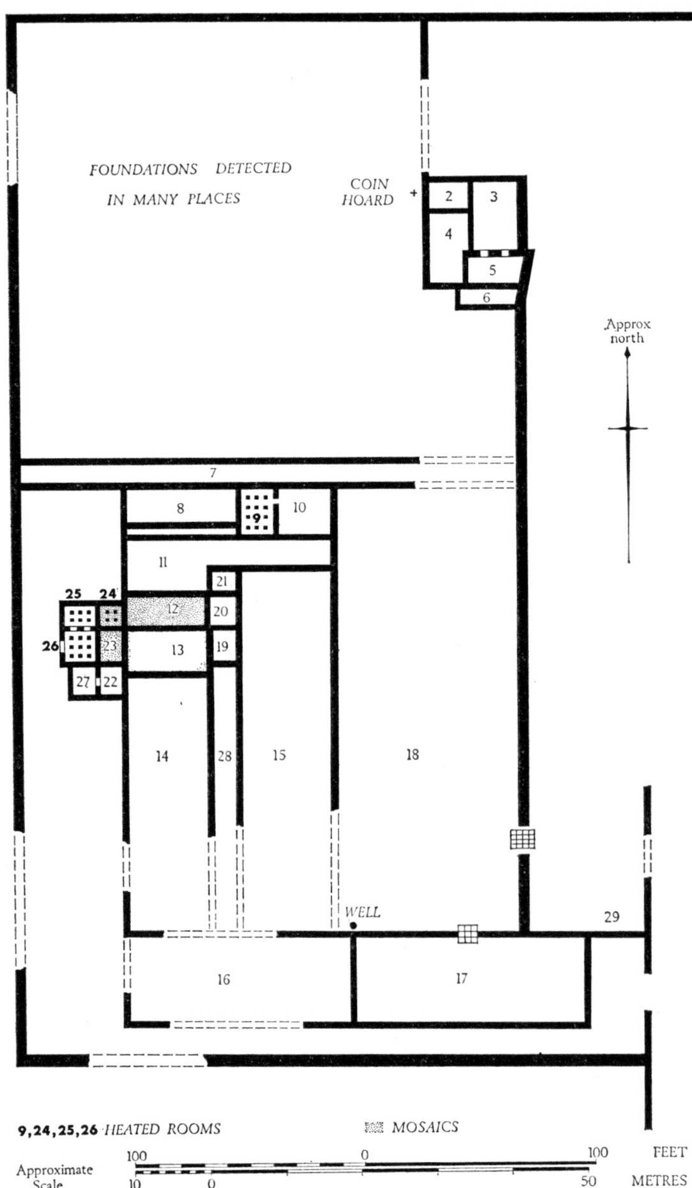

BISLEY WITH LYPIATT. (1) Roman Villa, Lillyhorn.

O.D.; it is now almost obliterated. The villa extended over the entire width of the field, covering about 3 acres. Some rooms were only partly cleared by Baker and large areas were investigated by random probing. The whole site has been very extensively robbed, much Roman building material being incorporated in the field walls. A mound (2) containing Roman debris and burials lies just W. of the villa site, below the scarp edge. The spring-line is 150 ft. below this, at the head of a steep combe.

No mosaic patterns survived. Wall plaster, window glass, large iron nails, hexagonal stone tiles and tiles stamped TPFA, TPFC and TPFP were noted. There were two 'stone bases', on natural soil where the floor was broken in room 12. The wall bounding the complex on S. was 5 ft. thick; that on W., 4 ft. thick. Pottery included samian ware. 'Implements' and animal bones were found.

A hoard of 1,223 3rd-century coins, found in a pot buried close to the N.E. cluster of rooms, included 629 of the Tetrici and 353 of Victorinus. About a third of the collection survives in Stroud Museum. An incomplete catalogue and notes on the dispersion of the coins are in the Baddeley Collection, loose paper 98, Gloucester City Library. Other finds are in Cirencester and Stroud Museums. Some tiles and other material are built into a summerhouse at Watercombe House (SO 925049).

Arch J, II (1845), 42–5. *JBAA*, I (1846), 44–5. *JBAA*, II (1847), 324–7. *TBGAS*, XXIX (1906), 173–80. *JRS*, XLIV (1955), 68–72 (stamped tiles).

(2) LONG MOUND OR RUBBISH-DUMP (SO 91250440), Roman, at Lillyhorn, in a plantation immediately W. of the villa (1), consists of rubble and occupation debris in which at least four burials had been made. The irregularly shaped mound lies N.–S., along the slope just below the scarp edge. One of the skeletons was female.

TBGAS, 60 (1938), 351–2. MS. notes in Stroud Museum.

(3) PROBABLE SETTLEMENT (SO 936049), Romano-British, N.W. of King's House, is suggested by samian and coarse pottery, sandstone and part of a glass bracelet found in ploughsoil. Finds in Stroud Museum.

Archaeol. Review, 4 (1969), 38.

BITTON

(29 miles S.W. of Cirencester)

Romano-British occupation has been recorded from imprecise locations in the parish. In 1850 'Roman brick' was found built into the Norman masonry of the church (ST 68206935), and pottery, coins and tesserae have come from the churchyard and the vicarage garden.[1] The foundations of a villa, and querns, pottery, brooches and coins have been reported in Congrove (ST 710698).[2] Coffins, possibly Roman, have been found in a field named Coffin Tyning, centred at ST 69807092, near Beach;[3] a large stone coffin has been ploughed up at Upton.[4] Numerous Roman coins have been found at Oldland Bottom (ST 672713).[5]

'Bitton Camp' has been shown by excavation to be mediaeval.[6]

1. H. T. Ellacombe, *History of the Parish of Bitton*, II (1883), 267. *TBGAS*, XXIII (1900), 60. Finds in Bristol City Museum include four tesserae found in 1843.
2. H. M. Scarth, *Aquae Solis* (1864), 125.
3. H. M. Scarth, *Somerset Procs.* (1854), 59. Tithe Map, 1843.
4. Rudder (1779), 294.
5. H. T. Ellacombe, *loc. cit.* Three 4th-century coins from the parish are in Gloucester City Museum.
6. *TBGAS*, 77 (1953), 45–8.

BLEDINGTON

No Iron Age or Romano-British monument is known in this parish.

BLOCKLEY

(22 miles N.E. of Cirencester)

(1) PROBABLE SETTLEMENT (SP 150345), Romano-British, at Upton, is indicated by finds at points spread over 4 acres in and near a deserted mediaeval village excavated by Birmingham University; some finds are in stratified levels, but as yet none is associated with any structure. The greatest diversity of finds comes from beneath a mediaeval house at 'a'. The site, on Inferior Oolite, is adjacent to springs.

Finds include 1st to 4th-century pottery, 3rd and 4th-century coins, stone and pottery roof tiles, quern fragments, and iron and bronze brooches.

TBGAS, 85 (1966), 70, 89, 99–100, 106, 109, 112, 125, 129, 134–6; 88 (1969), 77–80, 102, 104–8, 110.

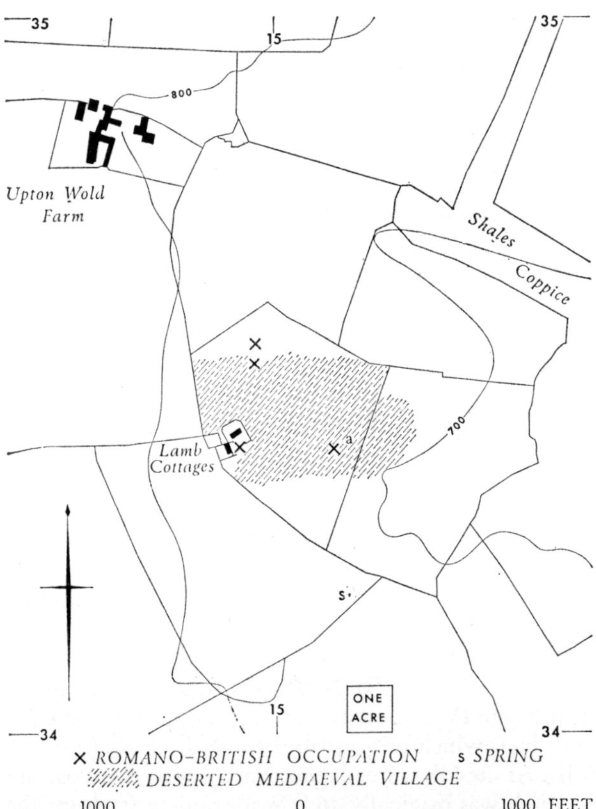

BOURTON-ON-THE-HILL

(21 miles N.N.E. of Cirencester)

(1) ROMAN ROAD, Ryknild Street (SP 139315–SP 132335), is traceable on air photographs in a continuous straight line for almost 1¼ miles in the W. of the parish; it extends N.N.W. across Bourton Downs and continues on the E. shoulder of Snowshill Hill (SNOWSHILL (1)). On the ground, faint traces of the road are visible along most of its length, the *agger* being spread and very low, but up to 1 ft. high on Bourton Downs (SP 13643218) and under walls on the parish boundary (SP 13363301). Suggestions of former side ditches are noted.

R.A.F., VAP F21 and F22, 543/RAF/1913: 0033–4.

BOURTON-ON-THE-WATER

(15½ miles N.E. of Cirencester)

The position of Bourton in the angle between the R. Dikler and the R. Windrush, mostly on gravel, on the line of the 'Jurassic Way', has favoured settlement since the Neolithic period.[1] Within Salmonsbury (1) there is evidence to suggest continuity of occupation through most of the Iron Age and Romano-British periods. In the latter period Bourton became a major settlement—a town without walls—and the Iron Age defences ceased to be significant. Attracted by the Foss Way, where a posting station probably stood near a paved ford and a footbridge, dense occupation developed in the area of Bourton Bridge and also along the Foss Way to S.W. A metalled road forked E. from the Foss Way. The area occupied by Roman settlement is at least 55 acres. Buckle Street, the road N. from Bourton Bridge, may be Roman in origin (see p. xlv and map, p. 18).

The accounts below owe much to information kindly given by Mrs. H. E. O'Neil and Dr. G. C. Dunning.

1. *V.C.H.*, Glos. VI (1965), 33–5.

(1) SALMONSBURY (SP 173208), an Iron Age fortified settlement of hill-fort proportions occupying a gravel platform between the R. Dikler and R. Windrush, about 425 ft. above O.D., covers 56 acres and is bounded by two close-set ramparts, each with an external ditch. Entrances are in the N.W. and N.E. sides and another gap probably occurred on the S.E.: little is known of

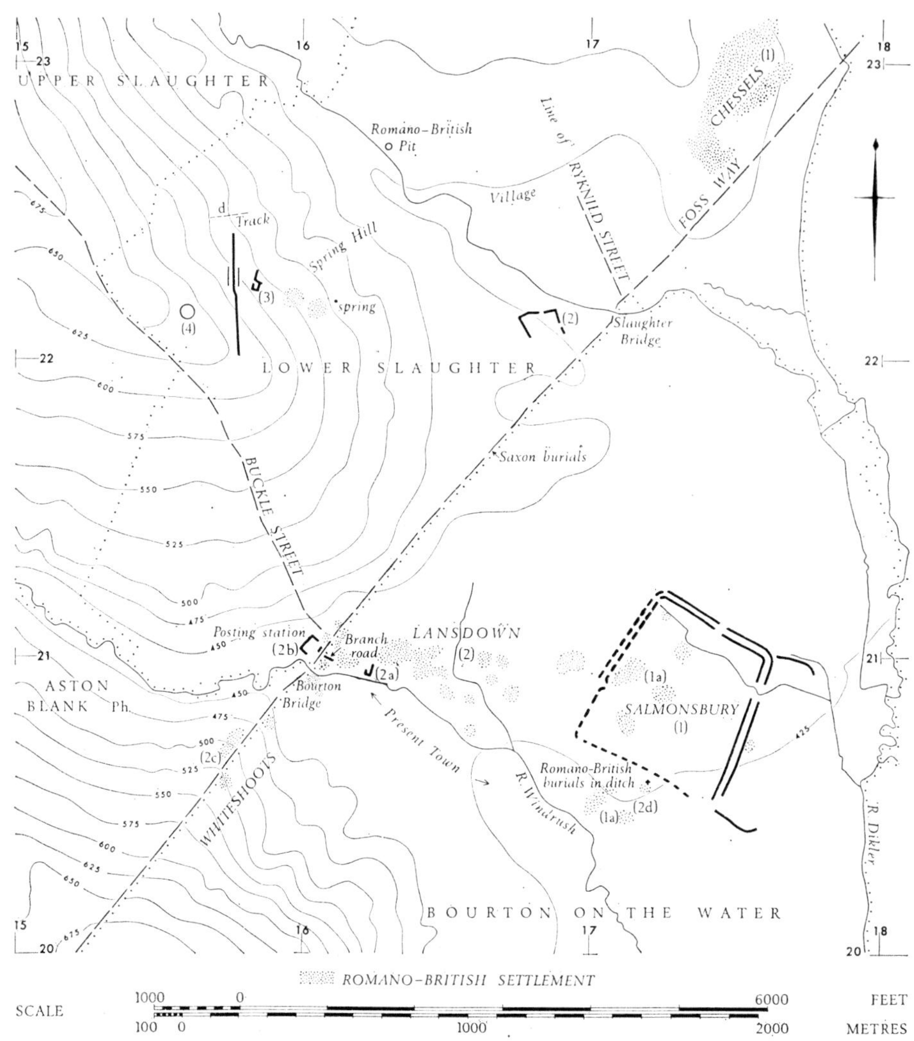

Monuments in BOURTON-ON-THE-WATER and LOWER SLAUGHTER.

the S.W. side. Banks, each with external ditch, extend the line of the outer rampart S.E. from the S. and E. angles, defining an annex of perhaps 15 acres flanking a naturally marshy area. An intermittent stream flows through the interior and out at the S.E. The defences survive clearly only in parts of the S.E. and N.E. sides; information about their position elsewhere derives from close surveillance of chance exposures and from air photographs. Excavation by G. C. Dunning in 1931–4 indicated that some Iron Age 'A' settlement preceded the building of the rampart. The enclosure and main occupation were of Iron Age 'B' culture with 'Belgic' elements appearing at the end of the period. Abundant finds include a large hoard of currency bars. The defences were disused in the Roman period, but much of the interior continued to be occupied (see (1a)). Saxon objects have been recovered from Romano-British building sites, and Saxon burials have been found in or near the ramparts (*TBGAS*, 56 (1934), 5). The name *Sulmonnes Burg*, 'ploughman's stead', is first recorded in 779 (*PNG*, I, 195). Courts of the Liberty or of the Hundred of Salmonsbury assembled traditionally by the entrance in the N.E. side. The present field pattern indicates that the interior was largely taken up by arable strip fields before modern enclosure (C.U.A.P., OAP AJL 48).

The banks where best preserved are up to 3 ft. high. Excavation in 1931–4 was concentrated on a section across the defences at S.E. (site I), entrance structures at N.E. (site V), occupied areas immediately behind the defences at S.E. (site I), N.W. (site III), and towards the centre (site IV). Sections were also dug across the bank and ditch which project from the N.E. angle (sites VI, VII). At site I the spread inner bank was 60 ft. across and its ditch was originally 36 ft. wide and 12 ft. deep; the almost levelled outer bank, immediately beyond, was

40 ft. across and its ditch was 18 ft. wide and 9 ft. deep, with a notably sharp V-shaped cross-section. The banks were of gravel and there were indications of a revetment of Oolite slabs near the crest of the inner rampart. Other slabs in the ditch fill suggested the possibility of Roman slighting. In 1881, when the entire circuit was still traceable, 'masonry' was noted in the main rampart, then said to be about 5 ft. high. Large worked stones were seen on its line in 1925. Subsequent observations by Mrs. H. E. O'Neil have demonstrated the position of an entrance in the N.W. side, S. of site III. The excavated entrance at N.E. (site V) was 28 ft. wide between curved terminal limestone revetments; spur walls narrowed the entrance on the inside. A storage pit to one side of the entrance, filled with stones, was crossed by an entrance track 16 ft. wide and worn to a depth of 2 ft. The entrance was subsequently blocked by a row of six large posts and by a stone wall.

Pre-rampart occupation discovered at site I included five apparently shallow pits sealed by the core, 24 ft. wide, of the inner bank. An iron hook, a bronze loop and Iron Age 'A' sherds lay in or on the old ground surface. Early Iron Age sherds were found in the ditch fill, and a relatively large number of Romano-British sherds low in the fill indicated that the defences had been made—or scoured—not long before the Roman conquest.

Two huts at site I, each 22 ft. in diameter, were defined by rings of post-holes and a central post; both huts lay immediately within a single curved ditch. Portions of similar curving ditches were found at site III, where they had been cut by a 'Belgic' ditch and a palisade trench, apparently forming part of an enclosure 60 ft. wide. The enclosure ditches had been backfilled and covered by rough paving on which were at least two stone-footed round huts, one only 11 ft. across. Such paving was characteristic of the 'Belgic' phase; it was found also in site IV where a pattern of successive curved ditches, and at least one round hut, 26 ft. across, were overlaid by paving.

Pits were found on all sites. The largest number of storage pits was at site I. There were two skeletons in pre-Belgic pits at site IV and three at site III.

The bank projecting E. from the N.E. angle was of clay and gravel, 32 ft. across and 3 ft. high; outside it was a ditch, presumably once wet, 18 ft. across and about 2 ft. deep, filled with black mud. The present stream lies 6 ft. beyond. Air photographs suggest that this ditch was continuous with the outer ditch of the main enclosure. A crouched burial, thought by the excavator to be probably of the Iron Age, was found in the bank.

Finds, apart from those mentioned, include Iron Age 'B' pottery, some with incised (not stamped) decoration, from huts and pits. 'Belgic' pottery at site III was associated with an unusual fluted pedestal vase (*TBGAS*, 56 (1934), 3–5; *Bagendon*, 20 and 30). Two stratified Dobunnic silver coins were found; one belongs to Allen's uninscribed class 'C', the other, inscribed ANTED, was associated with a Claudian coin and pottery, and perhaps with another uninscribed coin of class 'B' (D. Allen in *Bagendon*, 96–7 and 248). A gold quarter stater of Tasciovanus has now been lost (D. Allen in *IASB*, 221; *TBGAS*, 83 (1964), 15, n). A hoard of 147 currency bars, of which 40 survive, was found in 1860, buried as though in a chest in the area of site II. In more recent years a single currency bar was found at 'b' on the plan, in an area with Iron Age ditches, and two fragmentary bars were found in the make-up of 'Belgic' paving (*PPS*, XXXIII (1967), 328–9; R. F. Tylecote, *Metallurgy in Archaeology* (1962), 210–11; cf. *Antiquity*, XIV (1940), 427–33). Thirteen brooches of iron and bronze included three of 'Camulodunum' type III. Other finds were a carved limestone 'idol' (cf. *Ant J*, XIV (1934), 59–61), saddle querns, a gritstone 'beehive' quern of Hunsbury type (*Antiquity*, XV (1941), 20; *Trans. Leics. Arch. Soc.*, XXVI (1950), 77), iron bill-hooks, bone needles, ornaments and knife handles, stone spindle-whorls, and bones of ox, sheep, pig and goat.

Finds are in Gloucester City Museum, Corinium and Cheltenham Museums, Ashmolean Museum, B.M., Bristol City Museum, National Museum of Wales, and in private hands.

N.M.R., OAP SP 1720/3/325–6; 1721/2/319, 327–30. C.U.A.P., OAP AJL 48–9.

Camden, *Britannia* (ed. Gough, 1789), 279. Rudder (1779), 303. *JBAA*, XIX (1863), 104. Playne (1876), 209. Witts (1883), No. 88, 43–4. *TBGAS*, VII (1882–3), 16; XLVII (1925), 48–9. *PCNFC*, XXIV (1931–2), 145–8. *Antiquity*, V (1931), 489–91; VIII (1934), 351–2 (excavation). *TBGAS*, 56 (1934), 3–5; 57 (1935), 256–9; 83 (1964), 11.

(1a) ROMAN REMAINS INSIDE AND IMMEDIATELY OUTSIDE SALMONSBURY (SP 17022052), represented by abundant chance finds, include very large numbers of coins ranging in date from Claudian to late Roman. Structural remains include 'floors' and 'walls'.

A rectangular 'hut' in the centre of Salmonsbury was about 14 ft. wide and at least 38 ft. long; it lay over a circular Iron Age hut. Two rubbish pits and two drainage ditches yielded late 1st-century and early 2nd-century pottery. A floor had 3rd-century pottery beneath it and 4th-century pottery above.

When a drainage trench was cut in 1946 in the field S. of Salmonsbury, a series of rubbish pits was observed over 2 acres, reaching the road by the R. Windrush; they varied from 6 ft. to 11 ft. across and were $2\frac{3}{4}$ ft. to $3\frac{3}{4}$ ft. deep. In the field S. of this (about SP 172204) air photographs show a narrow ditch with a rounded angle, possibly part of an enclosure. Finds, including a gilt bronze buckle, were mostly of the 2nd century.

N.M.R., OAP SP 1719/6.

TBGAS, VII (1882–3), 16; 57 (1935), 234–59. *Ant J*, XXIX (1949), 85–6. *JRS*, XXIV (1934), 212.

(2) ROMANO-BRITISH SETTLEMENT, BOURTON TOWN AREA, S.E. from SP 161210 and W. of (2), is known mostly from chance finds. Settlement covers at least 30 acres along the R. Windrush and a tributary, includes one excavated house site (4) and connects with the settlement area around the probable posting station (5). Development along the Foss Way (8) extended S.W. of this, beyond the river, on Whiteshoots Hill (6). Burials have been noted only S.E. of the town (7).

A gap of about 250 yds. separates the main concentration of recorded remains, W. of a stream along the line of the present High Street, from those in Salmonsbury and on its fringes (2).

A branch road ran E.S.E. from the Foss Way in the area of (5), past the 'Leadenwell Villa' (4), towards Salmonsbury.

Structures include walls, wells, shallow pits, ovens and floors, but nothing is known of any town walls. Coins range from Republican issues to those of Honorius.

TBGAS, 57 (1935), 234–59; 87 (1968), 29–55. *Ant J*, XXIX (1949), 85–6.

(2a) ROMAN BUILDINGS, LANSDOWN ('Leadenwell Villa' and area) (SP 16212098). A courtyard 18 ft. wide with adjacent walls and other features, excavated in 1933–4, lay on gravel just N. of the R. Windrush and 216 yds. E. of Bourton Bridge, in an area that has yielded

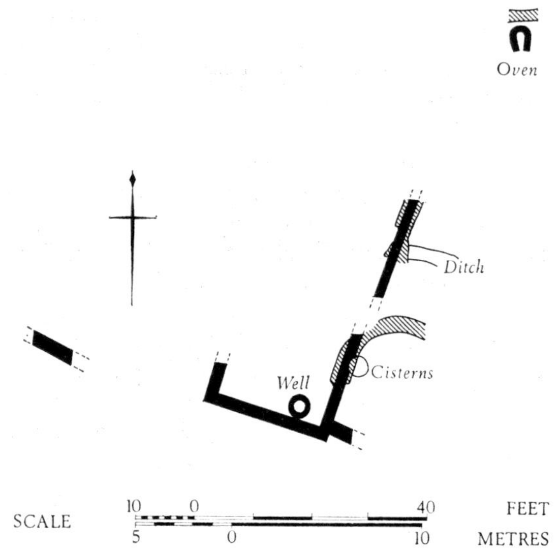

numerous Roman finds. Four phases were recognised, dating from the 2nd to the late 4th century. There was a well, 8 ft. deep, an ovoid oven and two tub-shaped lead tanks of 40 and 65 gallons capacity; the tanks are now in Cheltenham Museum.

TBGAS, LV (1933), 377–81; 56 (1934), 99–128; 57 (1935), 260–5 (oven). *JRS*, XXV (1935), 216. *Ant J*, XXIII (1943), 155–7 (cisterns).

(2b) ROMANO-BRITISH SETTLEMENT (SP 16102105), with probable posting station (*mansio* or *mutatio*), at Bourton Bridge, covered at least 4 acres immediately around the Foss Way, N.E. of the bridge. The remains were observed and diagrammatically planned by Witts in 1875–81, before the 'posting station' was largely destroyed. The adjacent settlement area was investigated by Mrs. H. E. O'Neil briefly in 1959 and during road widening in 1967. Occupation appears to have been continuous from the 1st to the early 5th century. The parish boundary follows the road and bisects the settlement.

Building foundations over 5 ft. high and perhaps 240 ft. long were noted during clearance for the railway, as also was the base of a column 9 in. across. The main part of the presumed posting station appears to have formed three sides of a rectangle, perhaps 240 ft. by 140 ft., facing S.E. Occupational layers (including samian as well as 4th-century pottery) together with a wall which probably bounded the fourth side of the courtyard, were found in 1967. Other buildings examined in 1967 were interpreted as providing public services for travellers; they extended along both sides of the road, from the bridge to a point 500 ft. N.E., where the Roman road changes course to S. by about 5°. Features included forges and ovens. There was one short length of very massive wall and near it was a stone column base.

Very large quantities of occupational material recovered in 1875–81 included several hundred coins ranging from M. Aurelius and L. Verus to Constans, samian ware with ten different potters' stamps, horseshoes and spurs. A group of 23 *minimissimi* probably came from the area.

TBGAS, 57 (1935), 247–59; 87 (1968), 29–55; 91 (1972), 92–116. *Num. Chron.*, 5th series, XV (1935), 275–81, 284–6. *Brit. Num. Journ.* XXVI (1949), 11, 25, 340–3 (*minimissimi*).

(2c) ROMANO-BRITISH SETTLEMENT (SP 157206–SP 16032092), on Whiteshoots Hill, has been observed on both sides of the Foss Way, extending into Aston Blank parish, over a length of some 500 yds. S.W. from Bourton Bridge (plan, p. 18). Structures include masonry walls. Pottery includes amphorae, samian and late Roman wares. Recorded coins are from Gallienus to Magnentius. Two large hoards of *folles*, datable to 307–18, were found (one as though formerly in a bag) under a deposit of stones. A 'deep trench' is said to run at right angles, E. from the Foss Way about SP 15732060, in front of Whiteshoots House.

TBGAS, 57 (1935), 239, 242–3; 87 (1968), 48–60; also forthcoming; *PCNFC*, XXVI (1936), 105.

(2d) ROMANO-BRITISH BURIALS (approx. SP 17102047 and SP 17202055), two, have been reported S.W. of Salmonsbury, one in a sarcophagus.

TBGAS, 57 (1935), 243.

(3) Foss Way, Roman Road (sp 137175–sp 172222), generally overlain by the modern road, follows a N.E. course for 3½ miles on the parish boundary, between 677 ft. and 440 ft. above O.D., on Inferior Oolite, Cotteswold Sand, Upper and Lower Lias, and river gravel. The road crosses two streams and the R. Windrush; at the latter (Bourton Bridge) there was a paved ford and a footbridge. Local deviations appear to be for topographical reasons. There is a slight deflection in, or at the E. entrance to, the Romano-British settlement (2b) at Bourton Bridge, the main alignment being rejoined a corresponding distance S.W. of the bridge. Excavations by Mrs. O'Neil have shown details of structure and of disturbance, relationships with structures of the settlement, a road diverging towards Salmonsbury (2), and a junction with Ryknild Street ('Condicote Lane') immediately E. of Slaughter Bridge (sp 171222). The road is followed by the parish boundary, which therefore divides the settlement area. Eight pagan Saxon burials (sp 166217) in the road ¾ mile N.E. of (5) indicate disuse of the *agger*.

The *agger* was built of gravel layers on pitched stones, but 260 yds. N.E. of the ford it was composed of small stones and yellow silt on a bed of rammed slag. A kerb was found in the area of settlement (2b), where also at least one building impinged on the road. The only observed width is 22 ft.

The Roman ford, under the present bridge over the R. Windrush, had a surface of large pebbles with, in places, two courses of rough stone blocks. The presence of a footbridge on the E. side of the ford was deduced from the discovery of small piers, possibly about 2¾ ft. square originally, built of cemented rough Oolite rubble.

Some 60 yds. N.E. of the ford a branch road led E.S.E., but the actual junction with the Foss Way was not observable. Its course was established by excavation 100 ft. from the junction, where buildings lay beside it on the S. The branch road was 18 ft. to 24 ft. wide, cambered, and built of pitched stone and gravel. Samian ware was found below the kerb of its first phase. It was apparently rebuilt early in the 3rd century.

TBGAS, 87 (1968), 29–55.

(4) Settlement (sp 174194), undated, shows as unclear crop-marks of interlocked enclosures over some 8 acres of the Santhill gravels immediately W. of the R. Windrush. The remains of a Roman building with heated rooms have been noted close to the confluence of the R. Windrush and the R. Dikler. Hut floors and a well have also been noted in the area.

N.M.R., OAP SP 1719/1–4 (Baker).
H. E. O'Neil in *Studies in Building History* (ed. Jope, 1961), 29.

BOXWELL WITH LEIGHTERTON

(13 miles s.w. of Cirencester)

There are references to imprecisely located Roman remains. Coins, human bones and burnt stones were found in the 'Warren', probably E. of the parish church.[1] Pottery and several late Roman coins were found at Boxwell Lodge[2] (st 82389245).

1. Bigland (1791), I, 229.
2. *TBGAS*, LII (1930), 162.

BRIMPSFIELD

A wide scatter of Romano-British pottery, a coin of Faustina II and evidence of infant burial have been found by Mrs. E. D. Gander in the area of 'Manless Town' (so 929115).

Mortaria sherds have been found among earthworks of uncertain date E. of the modern road (C.U.A.P., OAP, AWO 16), but other finds are mediaeval and later. Roman pottery has been found in arable fields W. of the road (so 927117–929114). The burial was discovered by excavation towards the S. of the area, in a Roman quarry (so 92871147).

The observations are too recent for inclusion in the distribution map (end pocket).

BROADWELL

(20 miles n.e. of Cirencester)

(1) Roman Building (sp 19922792), on a N.E.-facing slope, lies above the 500-ft. contour and 200 yds. E. of the present line of the Foss Way (2). It was partly excavated by D. Talbot Rice in 1923, when a well-preserved wall was traced for 30 ft. The building was of at least two periods, as in one place a tiled floor overlay fallen wall plaster. A surface scatter of pottery in arable is of 2nd to 4th-century date. Surface finds are in Gloucester City Museum.

JRS, XII (1922), 262.

(2) Roman Road, The Foss Way (sp 195276–sp 197282), follows a line N.N.E. from Stow-on-the-Wold and in places forms part of the W. boundary of the parish. The Roman road fabric, which consisted of pitched stones of local Oolite, was exposed in 1931 and 1936 immediately E. of the present road.

TBGAS, LIV (1932), 385–8; 57 (1935), 280–1.

BROCKWORTH

(11 miles n.e. of Cirencester)

There have been suggestions that a complex of Iron Age defences extended S. from Cooper's Hill to High

Brotheridge, Cranham,[1] covering a total of some 200 acres; these earthworks are described under CRANHAM, p. 41. Quarrying has destroyed any sign of fortifications on the N. tip of the hill (SO 892147), where a 'camp' is shown on O.S. 6 inch, but traditional maypole ceremonies[2] in the area could be taken to suggest the existence of an ancient site, as might the former name 'Castle Hill'.[3] The only clearly recognisable defensive or boundary earthwork, probably of Iron-Age origin, is the cross-ridge dyke (1) 500 yds. S. of this point.

1. *Bagendon* (1961), 157 and fig. 27. Witts (1883), 15–16, No. 32.
2. *Glos. Notes and Queries*, V (1891–3), 506–9.
3. *PNG*, IV, 191.

(1) CROSS-RIDGE DYKE (SO 89191416–SO 89341413), in Brockworth Wood on Cooper's Hill at about 900 ft. above O.D. (map, p. 41, *s.v.* CRANHAM), spans the narrow Great Oolite ridge which rises gently N. from this point; it ends on the shoulders of the ridge at E. and W.

The bank is 18 ft. wide and 2 ft. high; the ditch on the S. side is a further 2 ft. deep and from 12 ft. to 20 ft. wide. The dyke runs straight for a total length of 655 ft.; 475 ft. in the E. are on Oolite and 180 ft. in the W. are on Fuller's Earth.

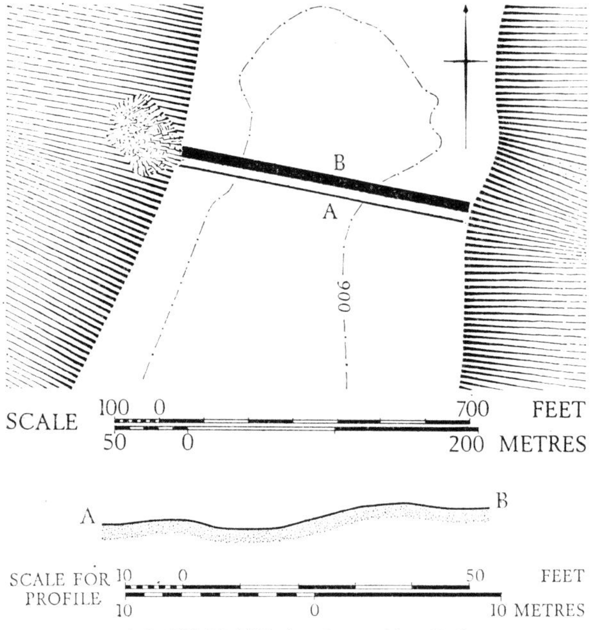

BROCKWORTH. (1) Cross-ridge Dyke.

(2) ROMANO-BRITISH BUILDING (SO 891168) is indicated by finds in allotments about 200 yds. S. of the church, close to Horsbere Brook, 150 ft. above O.D. The finds include 2nd to 4th-century pottery, and *tegulae*, in association with a hard gravel floor (*TBGAS*, 87 (1968), 203).

BROOKTHORPE WITH WHADDON

(14 miles N.W. of Cirencester)

A scatter of Romano-British pottery of the 2nd and 3rd centuries is recorded from Court Farm, Whaddon (SO 837136).[1]

1. *Archaeol. Review*, 6 (1971), 26.

(1) ROMANO-BRITISH VILLA (SO 833124), Brookthorpe Court, revealed during construction of the M5 motorway in 1969, lies in the vale on Lias clay about 140 ft. above O.D. A brook (channelled) flows 150 yds. to E.

Structures planned during 'rescue' excavation included limestone wall-footings with associated loose tesserae of blue Lias and sandstone roofing-tiles. Adjacent to the building was a possible paved courtyard; some 100 ft. distant were *pilae* lying between two walls.

Finds, in Gloucester City Museum, include samian and coarse wares, *tegula* fragments stamped ARVERI, box tiles and fragments of painted plaster.

TBGAS, 90 (1971), 50–3.

BUCKLAND

(22 miles N.N.E. of Cirencester)

(1) HILL-FORT (SP 085363), on Burhill, univallate, unexcavated, occupies a spur of the Cotswold escarpment ¼ mile N.E. of the village; parts of the bank have been levelled.

The surviving N.E. side is defined by a bank with an outer ditch, now extending less than half-way across the neck of the spur. The bank is 25 ft. wide and 5 ft. high, the ditch 30 ft. wide and 3 ft. deep. Plan, p. 23.

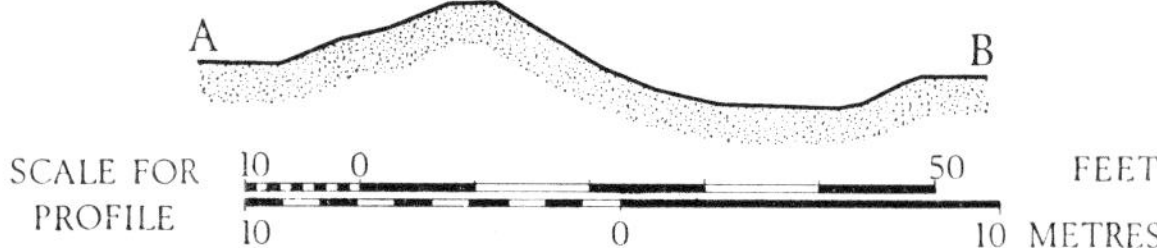

A dozen small sherds of undecorated hand-made pottery, including a simple rim, found in ploughsoil along the inner edge of the bank are in Gloucester City Museum.

The hill-fort, not shown on O.S. maps, was discovered by L. V. Grinsell in 1960 (cf. D. Verey, *Gloucestershire: The Cotswolds* (1970), 140).

CAM

(17 miles W. of Cirencester)

'Cam Long Down Camp' is mentioned by Witts.[1] The top of the hill has been quarried away and there are no recognisable defences.

1. Witts (1883), 10, No. 22. Playne (1876), 227, No. 51 ('earthwork').

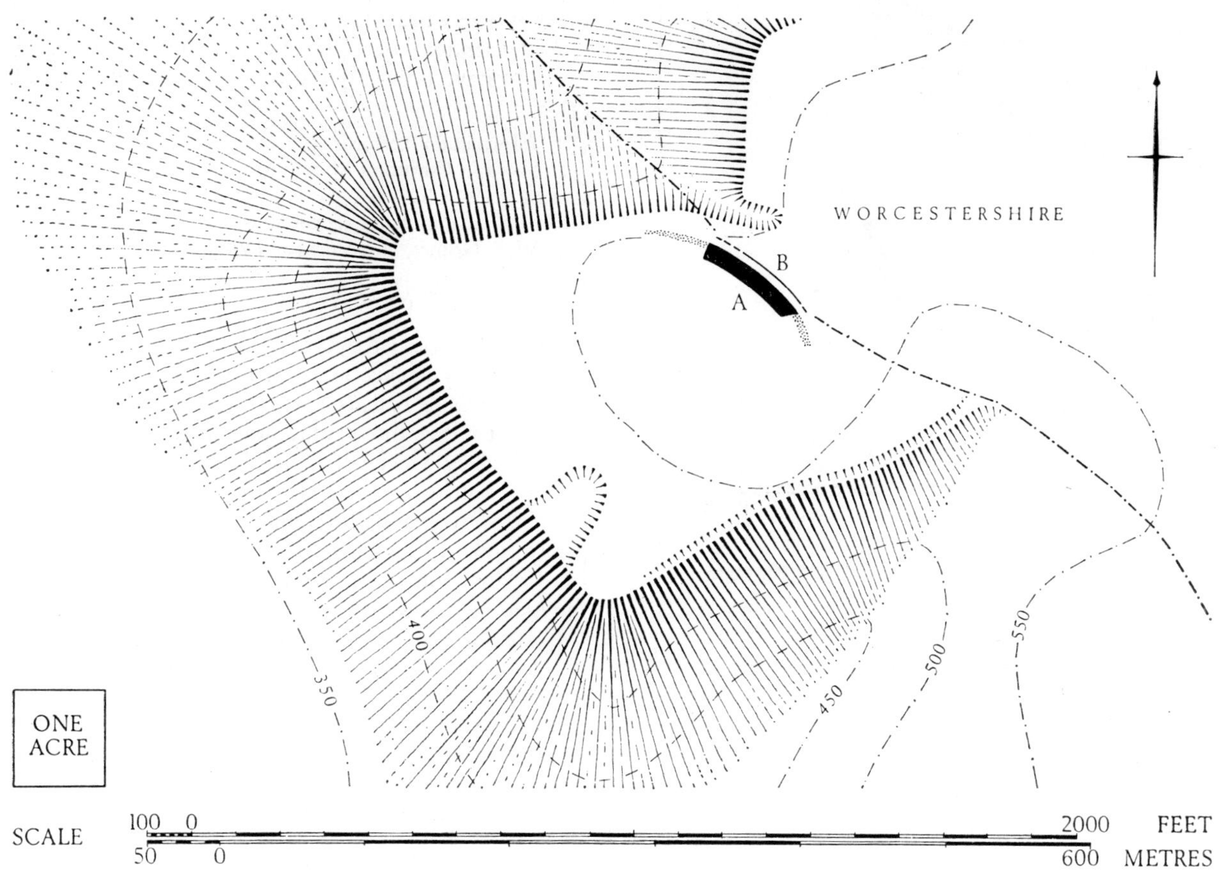

BUCKLAND. (1) Hill-fort on Burhill.

CHALFORD

(8 miles W. of Cirencester)

(1) Mound, possibly Roman (SO 89560384), N. of Middle Hill Farm, was totally carted away in 1866; original accounts refer to the find-place as 'Bisley Common'. Finds included: six Roman altars, four of them to Mars and two small ones uninscribed, a 2nd-century coin, Roman pottery, bones and 'unctuous animal matter'. Surviving objects are in Stroud Museum.

TBGAS, V (1880–1), 11, 39; 60 (1938), 297. Toynbee (1964), 154. Further information from Mr. L. J. Walrond.

CHARLTON KINGS

(12 miles N.N.W. of Cirencester)

'Battledown' or 'Hewletts Camp' (SO 970220),[1] on a hill capped with Middle Lias, seems best interpreted as a group of gullies, scarps and ridges, natural in origin.

A Romano-British inhumation discovered in 1939 during gravel-digging at Sandy Lane is not precisely located (map, p. 77, *s.v.* Leckhampton). Five iron nails lay beside the skeleton of an adult male unaccompanied by grave-goods; there was no trace of a coffin.[2]

1. Witts (1883), 26, No. 52. See p. xxxi.
2. *TBGAS*, 60 (1938), 350.

(1) Probable Settlement (about SO 95461972), Iron Age and Romano-British, lies W. of Sandy Lane (map, p. 77, *s.v.* Leckhampton). Material recovered from the face of a sand pit *c.* 1950 included some 70 sherds and numerous animal bones. Further investigation in 1971 showed that the Iron Age and Roman material is contained in a deposit of hill-wash. The Iron Age pottery found *c.* 1950 included fragments with incised geometric motifs, with some white inlay.

TBGAS, 69 (1950), 197–9. Other information supplied by the Committee for Research into the Iron Age in the N.W. Cotswolds.

(2) Linear Dyke (SO 99172195), 300 yds. N.W. of Arle Grove, unexcavated, extends for about 350 ft. on gently

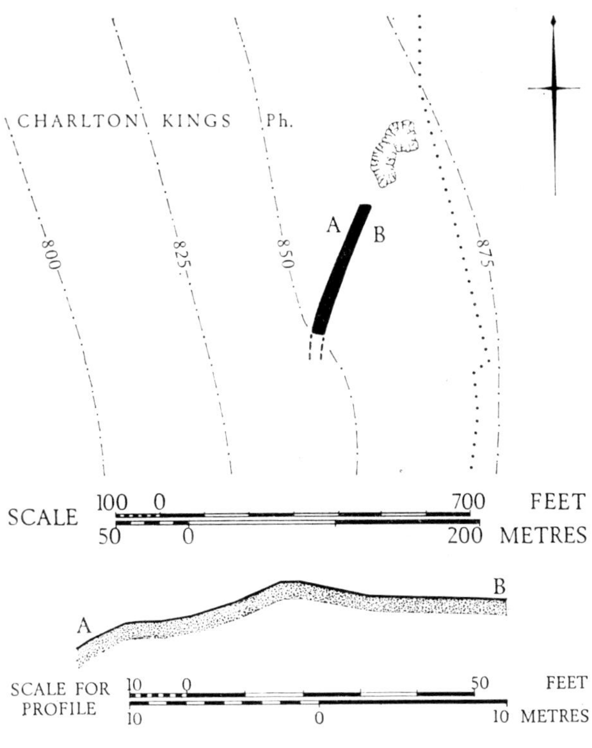

CHARLTON KINGS. (2) Linear Dyke.

sloping ground between 850 ft. and 875 ft. above O.D. It is 20 ft. wide and nearly 3 ft. high.

CHEDWORTH

(6 miles N.E. of Cirencester)

Roman finds from points imprecisely located in the area of the village include late Roman coins, bronze dividers, a plumb-bob (said to have been found at Manor Farm) and, allegedly, a stone bas-relief of Aesculapius. Tesserae have been reported in the gardens of Church Row Cottages, about 50 yds. S.E. of the church.[1] From the crest of a hill N.W. of the village come an inscribed potsherd, a 4th-century coin and samian and mortaria sherds.[2] An extension of the 'White Way' probably ran N.E. across the area now occupied by the airfield and Chedworth Woods (SP 0413), but no trace of it has been found.

Several Roman sites occur in the vicinity of the villa (1), some of them in adjacent parishes. About ½ mile N., at two points 300 yds. apart in WITHINGTON (SP 05321432, 05021429), pottery has been found by Mr. A. N. Irvine. Romano-British potsherds and an iron gouge, probably Roman, were noted during excavation on and near a round barrow ¾ mile S.W. of the villa, at SP 04081285.[3] A terraced track in Streetfold (YANWORTH (2)) aligns on the villa, and another track extends in its general direction S.W. from the settlement at YANWORTH (1).

A description[4] of eight alleged Roman 'cisterns' is likely to have been inspired by details of 'The Capitol' (3).

1. Information from Mr. J. Scotford.
2. Sherd in Corinium Museum; other finds in private possession. *JRS*, XXXVII (1947), 182; XXXVIII (1948), 104. Other information from private sources.
3. W. F. Grimes, *Excavations on Defence Sites 1939–45* (1958), 133.
4. *TBGAS*, LII (1930), 259, n. 6.

(1) ROMAN VILLA (SP 053135), Chedworth Woods, was discovered by chance in 1864. It stands, 100 ft. below the level where Fuller's Earth overlies Inferior Oolite, at a point where three gullies join to form the head of a single valley which falls gently E. towards the R. Coln, 250 yds. distant. Soon after discovery the extensive remains were exposed by James Farrer; later they were partly built up and roofed over by Farrer's nephew, Lord Eldon. Much patched, they are now in the care of the National Trust. Plan, p. 26.

Certain features shown on the plan are no longer visible on the ground. Some rebuilt walls differ slightly in position or structure from the original elements, and ground-levels, notably in the courtyard, are in places very different from those of Roman times. The 'fulling establishment' which once was thought to occupy the W. of the N. range is now interpreted as a much-altered bath house.

The N. and W. ranges of the villa stand on artificial terraces partly recessed into the hillside; the S. wing is set lower, near the valley floor. The complete form of the S. wing remains uncertain, as does the E. limit of the N. range, in an area of slumping. Debris and indications of further structures have been noted in pits dug for electricity poles at points up to 255 ft. E. of room 1a in the S. wing. There has been confirmation that much debris occurs around the villa, and dark earth, coins and pottery have been found on rough terraces above the steep artificial scarps which rise from the central part of the W. range and from the N. range. In the latter area copious finds and an alleged 'chamber' were noted in 1864, before there could be any possibility of confusion with excavators' spoil heaps. Occupational debris lies against the walls of the S. wing.

Small excavations carried out in recent years by Sir Ian Richmond and others have shown development from the early 2nd century to the late 4th century, with evidence of fire in early and late phases. Richmond's excavations in 1958–65 (upon which much of our information as to sequence and function depends) consisted of sections or selective clearance in the following areas: the corridor between rooms 1 and 2; in and near rooms 1b, 3, 6, 7, 8 and 12; the *nymphaeum* (17); rooms 19, 21, 21a, 22, 24, 25, and 25a; the corridor S.W. of

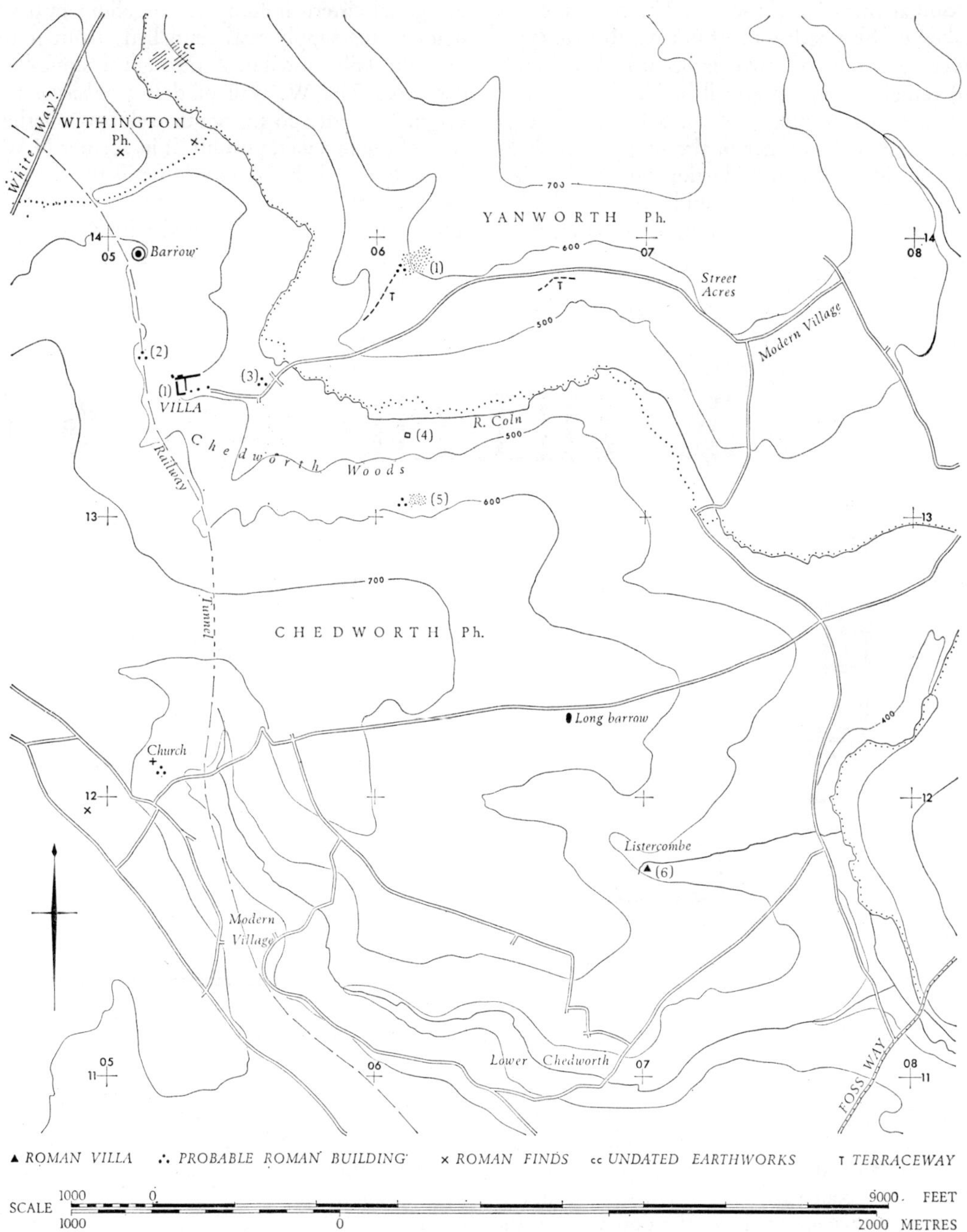

Monuments in CHEDWORTH and YANWORTH.

room 30 and S. of room 32; E. of room 33, and the terrace N. of room 30.

The early structures, three separate blocks, formed three sides of a rectangle open on the E. The W. end of the S. block, a timber-framed gable, suffered from fire before reconstruction and enlargement, as did much of the W. range. The S. wall of room 3 is built up from footings that are slightly offset. These could be part of an early precinct wall, otherwise traceable to an angle about 45 ft. W. of room 5a and thence in fragmentary exposures N. to a possible N.W. angle under the *nymphaeum*; its upper courses, when formerly exposed, partly revetting the W. scarp, were seen to be of herring-bone construction. The early details of the W. range are largely obscured by later development; an entrance 4½ ft. wide occurred in the W. wall of the narrow compartment N. of room 7. The N. range was largely taken up by a bath suite of normal Roman type. The lower portions of two lathe-turned columns (Plate 26) remain *in situ* on a wall beside the N. range (20). The main water supply to the villa was from a spring, S, at the N.W. corner of the site; it was channelled into a cistern just outside the suggested N.W. angle of the precinct wall. A roughly circular sinking 6 ft. across, possibly the site of a well, occurs at H, some 30 yds. E. of room 12.

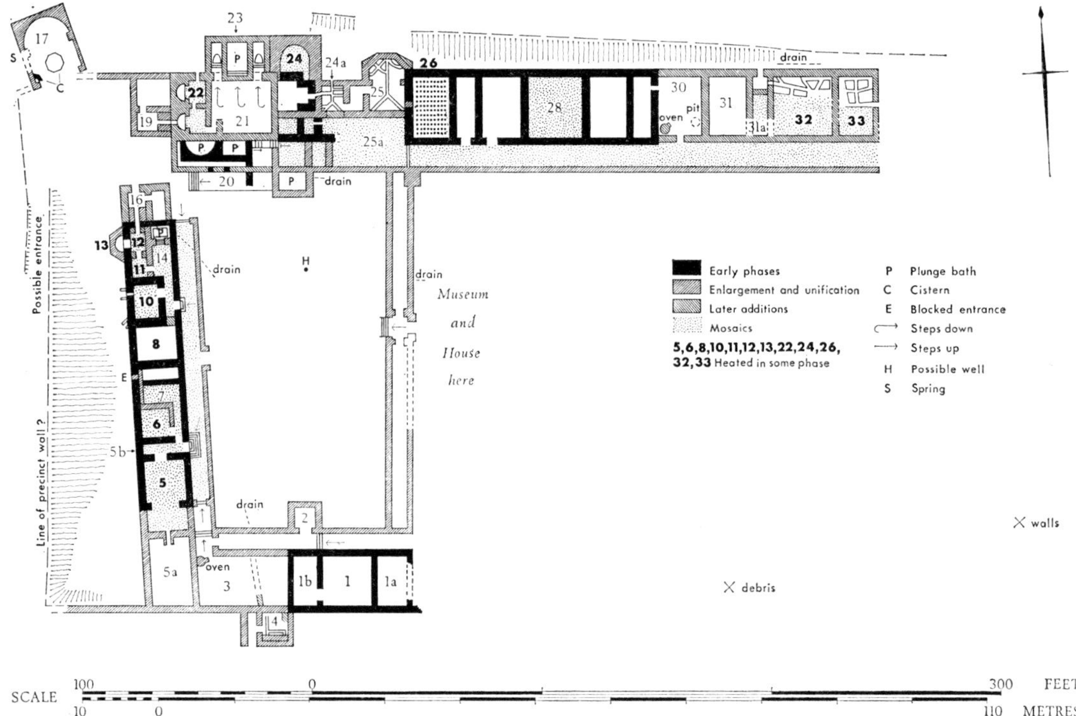

CHEDWORTH. (1) Roman Villa. Chedworth Woods.

Subsequently the villa was enlarged and the earlier buildings were integrated into a single complex. Corridors, interrupted on the E. side by a gateway, defined the inner courtyard and linked the N. and S. ranges. Room 7 was enlarged and the doorway on the W. was blocked. The bath suite in the W. wing (rooms 8–14) was established. The damp-heat baths in the N. wing (rooms 19–24) were converted by stages to a dry-heat establishment of sauna type (Plate 25). Lead pipes connect the immersion baths (23). An entrance $7\frac{1}{2}$ ft. wide into room 21 from the S., and another $4\frac{1}{4}$ ft. wide in the W. side of the western bath of 23 were blocked. A floor built over the stoke-hole S. of room 24 sealed a fill containing Oxfordshire red colour-coated ware, conventionally datable after 270. A porticoed *nymphaeum* (17) was constructed, having at its centre an octagonal cistern holding 1,100 gallons into which the main water supply was funnelled; from it the water was allegedly distributed through a stone-lined junction box. The W. wall of the *nymphaeum* crosses the original cistern and the south stylobate overlies the N. wall of the precinct, possibly at its former N.W. corner. A column $5\frac{1}{2}$ ft. high, now loose in the bath suite near room 23, probably comes from the *nymphaeum* portico. The *nymphaeum* was associated with Christianity when *chi-rho* inscriptions were carved on at least three of the trapezoidal stones edging the cistern. These stones, recognisable by their shape, were removed late in the Roman period and one was built into the footings of steps to room 10.

The wall which extends W. from the S.W. corner of the *nymphaeum* is probably an addition, designed to overlap rather than to join the surviving part of the presumed precinct wall on the W., thus providing a ramped approach.

In its final form the villa covered at least 2 acres, but the E. limits have not as yet been determined. It was arranged in tiers, with steps joining the different levels and leading to rooms with floors raised above ground-level hypocausts. The corridor beside the final E. extension of the N. range represents the widening of an earlier version; at the E. end it is built above earlier

Roman levels. The later masonry incorporates much reused stone; a baluster hypocaust pillar, for instance, is built into an apse of room 22. Drains led from the baths into the courtyard areas; one served the latrine (4); another is still visible N. of room 32. There were two dining rooms (5 and 32) and two kitchens (3 and 30) as well as bath suites in both W. and N. ranges. The piers of the channelled hypocaust in room 33 are about a foot higher than those surviving in room 32, suggesting the possibility that it was a dais at the E. end of dining room 32, rather than separate. The S. wing, as so far explored, had no heated living rooms or mosaic pavements. The latrine 4, S. of this wing, was finally altered for some different use. Outside it, in the angle with room 1b, an infant burial was found in a Blue Lias slab cist, inserted in rubbish spanning the 2nd to 4th centuries (dated by excavation in 1954).

Fire in the last Roman phase is indicated by the discovery of 67 lb. of melted lead in a room of the N. range. The villa has suffered from extensive stone robbing, and much stone, including calcined fragments of sculpture, has been found in and around a lime-kiln on the terrace 20 yds. N. of the N. range.

Tessellated floors of 4th-century date exist or existed in at least fifteen rooms and over most of the W. and N. corridors (Plates 2–7). All the mosaics except those of rooms 5 and 10, which are recognisably of the Corinian school of mosaicists (Plates 2–5), have geometric patterns. Two mosaics in the W. range were superseded: a pavement was crossed by the N. wall of room 6, and a pavement in room 14 (Plate 6) had a floor of Lias flags built over it. The 'hall' (25a) is said to have had tesserae over its entire length, some 56 ft. Repairs which resulted in changes of detail are seen in rooms 5 and 10. Patches of ancient burning in these rooms include one on the tessellated threshold of room 10, unlikely to be the result of scorching from a brazier. Tesserae vary in size from about ¼ in. in fine detail to 1½ in. for borders. Colours derive from the materials used: red from tile or Old Red Sandstone; blue from Lias; white and brown from limestones. Pennant flags, concrete and *opus signinum* were used for floors in all phases.

Heating was by means of hypocausts with pillars of tile (rooms 5, 11 and 12), of stone (rooms 24, 26 and the S. part of room 32), or channelled (rooms 6, 10, 24a, the N. of 25, and parts of rooms 32 and 33). The stone pillars, 108 originally in room 26, are of limestone, up to 2½ ft. high, square in section and expanded, baluster-like, at top and bottom to squares of 7 in. to 10 in. (Plate 25). Rearrangement involved the blocking or filling-in of hypocausts in rooms 6, 8, 21, 22, S.E. of 24 and 26. Fragments of stone pillars are built into the piers of the channelled system in the N. of room 32 and whole pillars into the S. apse of room 22.

Architectural details (Plate 26) and small finds contribute to the picture of a rich villa, with some poor objects possibly from the final phase. Painted plaster was extensively used inside, and there was also some marble facing; externally there was cement rendering. Room 21 had a quoin of tiles. The apses of room 22 were jacketed with flue tiles. Hollow baked clay voussoirs were noted from the roof of compartment 12. Other roofing materials include *tegulae*, hexagonal stone-slates and lead. Two stone bases with the surviving feet of two small figures probably once stood in a recess in the W. wall of room 5b. Fragments of fretted limestone balustrade embodying an 'S' motif probably derive from a corridor or a veranda. Other architectural stonework includes numerous column fragments, part of a cornice, and ridging stones. Huge iron beams weighing 256, 356 and 484 lbs., found in the corner of room 19, had probably been used to support a massive hot-water tank of copper or lead.

Inscribed stones include the three mentioned above, with *chi–rho* monograms, and one with ruled lines, all removed from the *nymphaeum*, and a building stone which had PRASINA carved on it.

Four altars were found. One, barbarously carved, is dedicated to Mars Lenus. One with a crude pilaster-like body and with scribed or drilled detail probably represents a Celtic god. The third, uninscribed, was found buried in the *nymphaeum*. The fourth, very crude and with saltires on the sides, was found just outside the S. wing.

The abundant finds include 360 coins, mostly from positions in or near room 2, suggesting that it was a steward's office. At least one-third of the coins belong to the period 364–78 and only 2 per cent. date from before 240; the three latest recognisable are of Gratian (issue of 378–83). Pottery includes samian ware of the early 2nd century (some with potters' stamps), an amphora with potter's stamp, a Rhenish beaker, large quantities of Oxfordshire late colour-coated and some painted ware, New Forest beakers, Nene Valley and a little Severn Valley ware and black-burnished ware of the 2nd to 4th century. A silver spoon inscribed CENSORINE GAUDEAS, now lost, was found in 'rubbish' on the W. of the W. range. Bronze finds include spoons, rings, a stylus, two prick-spurs of rivet type and the cast finger of a large effigy. Other metal finds include a pewter jug, iron saws, chisels, knives, shears, spade-irons, alleged hunting arrows, a pair of small shackles, horseshoes, hinges and locks. Glass was found from windows, bottles and bowls. Stone finds include a quern-stone 2½ ft. in diameter from room 30, a rectangular basin from room 4, and moulded and carved table-tops. There was a moulded disc of Kimmeridge shale, and bone pins, needles and handles. Other bones included two pieces of a human skull, and bones of pigs and sheep. There were antlers of red deer and oyster shells.

A late Roman zoomorphic buckle (Hawkes and Dunning type IIA) was found roughly 25 yds. E.N.E. of the museum, in the outer court of the villa. The museum contains at least two finds of uncertain origin. St. Clair Baddeley suggests that a unique brooch with seven human heads embossed on a bronze disc could have come from a quarry (perhaps that adjacent to the temple (4)) in the neighbourhood. A small limestone Christian cross is unprovenanced. Most surviving finds are in the museum, but some architectural fragments are dispersed in the rooms of the villa.

JBAA, XXIV (1868), 129–35; XXV (1869), 215–25; XXVI (1870), 251–2. *PSAS*, VI (1868), 278–83. *Arch*, LIX (1905), 210–14 (fulling theory). *TBGAS*, 76 (1957), 160–4 (room 4 and adjacent); 78 (1959), 5–23 (reinterpretation of *laconicum*), and 162–5 (coins); 86 (1967), 102–6 (mosaic). *Ant J*, XXXIX (1959), 66 (spurs). *Med. Archaeol.*, V (1961), 51, No. 5 (buckle). *Arch J*, XLIV (1887), 322–36; CXXII (1965), 203. Toynbee (1964), *passim*. *RIB*, Nos. 126–8. Rivet (ed.), *The Roman Villa in Britain* (1969), *passim*. *Britannia*, II (1971), 200–2 (iron beams).

G. E. Fox collection in Soc. Ants., London, Box I, sheets 8–17; Box III, sheets 25, 29–31. Site drawings and notes by Sir Ian Richmond in Ashmolean Museum. Information and personal observations from Mr. A. N. Irvine (warden) and Mr. R. Goodburn.

(2) Roman Building (SP 05121358) in Chedworth Woods, 170 yds. N.W. of (1), is probably the structure called 'The Capitol' by its 19th-century discoverers; it was destroyed in the construction of a railway. The building stood precisely at the head of the narrow gully taking 'Dark Lane' N.W. from (1). Several small rooms are said to have been partly cleared, and in 1869 H. M. Scarth refers to the building as a 'circular temple'. The area immediately W. of the railway is flat enough for buildings, but it shows no sign of disturbance.

Finds include coins, hexagonal tiles, fragments of pillars, part of a shell-headed niche, and glass tesserae. The stone relief of a 'hunter god' with hare, dog and stag, sometimes ascribed to (4), might have come from this site. Surviving finds are in the museum at (1).

PSAS, VI (1868), 283. *JBAA*, XXV (1869), 222. *Arch J*, XLIV (1887), 323. Toynbee (1964), 179.

(3) Roman Building (SP 05571346), about 230 yds. E. of (1), is now a low knoll, perhaps partly artificial; cf. Duntisbourne Rouse (4), (a). The knoll extends 50 ft. N. from the road and has a nearly level top, about 40 ft. wide. Building debris can be seen on it when it is under the plough.

(4) Roman Temple (SP 06111329) in Chedworth Woods, ½ mile E. of (1), is now a massive but much disturbed artificial platform some 35 yds. from, and 50 ft. above, the flood-plain of the R. Coln. Excavations in 1864–5 and in 1930 show that the platform is a relic of a stone temple (Lewis's Romano-Celtic type IA) about 50 ft. square, with a colonnaded portico and *cella* set on a podium of very large hewn limestone blocks. The downhill scarp of the platform is 12 ft. high and a scarp rises uphill from it to a height of about 8 ft. The orientation of the platform is roughly 10°. In 1931 it was suggested that there might be an extension or annex at the N.W. angle of the platform.

A round-bottomed stone-lined hole, 7 ft. across and 5 ft. deep, midway along the ambulatory on the E. side, contained bones of red deer. Other finds in the platform area included the drums of stone columns 1½ ft. in diameter, and a fragment of a capital; also pieces of moulded stone architrave, sandstone hexagonal slates, tiles, *opus signinum* and concrete. Similar debris just outside the platform included 'hypocaust tiles', stone troughs and blocks of tufa. Much stone debris is said to have been taken for the repair of buildings in the area. Undated fragments of human skull were found in the ambulatory. Coins ranged from the mid 2nd to the 4th century. Two slabs roughly scribed with armed figures are said to have come from the site. The relief of a 'hunter god' with animals (see (2)) is sometimes ascribed to this site. Surviving small finds are in the museum at (1).

PSAS, VI (1868), 262. *JRS*, XIV (1924), 231. *TBGAS*, LII (1931), 255–64. Lewis (1966), *passim*.

(5) Romano-British Settlement (SP 06121307) in Chedworth Woods, 250 yds. S. of (4), was noted by James Farrer in 1865. The site is a natural shelf on a steep hillside at the junction of Inferior Oolite and Fuller's Earth. Traces of walls occur at the head of a rise in the shelf (about 06101307). Black earth and Romano-British potsherds have been found in an area extending about 100 yds. E.

PSAS, VI (1868), 283. Information from Mr. A. N. Irvine.

(6) Roman Villa (SP 07011175) at Listercombe, discovered by chance *c.* 1760, stood almost on the valley bottom, near the junction of Inferior Oolite and Fuller's Earth, on ground sloping gently to an adjacent stream. Other remains occur a little uphill to the W., below the steep (perhaps scarped) valley-side. The site has been explored several times without publication of results. A mosaic pavement is said to have been seen in 1892 during the rebuilding of a field wall immediately W. of the remains shown on the plan (information from Mr. J. Scotford). In 1930 Mr. C. E. Key uncovered a hypocaust (at least 10 ft. by 5 ft., internally) with tile *pilae* on Oolite bases; traces of walls, possible floors and

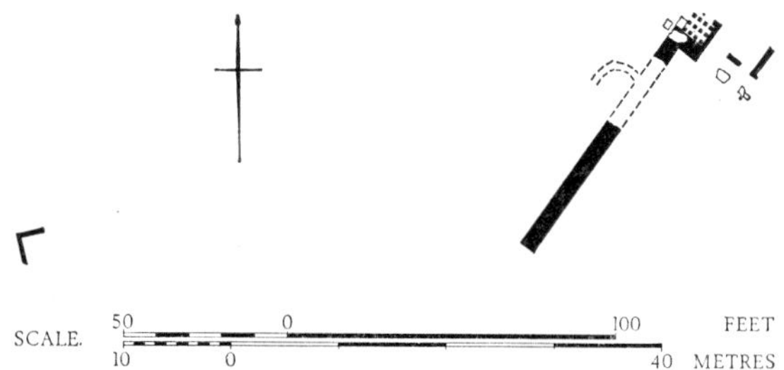

a paved 'corridor' lay to S.E. Wall footings 4½ ft. wide extended S.W. for at least 90 ft. from the side of the hypocaust. Fifty yards to the W., the corner of another Roman room was discovered in an area where earthen platforms survive.

Building material included *tegulae*, Cotswold stone roofing tiles, box-tiles and painted wall-plaster. Former reports note a bath or cistern, tiles stamped ARVERI from a hypocaust, and tesserae. It is likely, though not certain, that a hypocaust uncovered before 1865, and perhaps again by St. Clair Baddeley in 1926, was the same as that dug out by Mr. Key. Finds, in Cheltenham Museum, include six coins (untraced) one of them allegedly 'Constantinian'; also pottery including Oxfordshire colour-coated ware, a 4th-century mortarium and calcite-gritted wares, iron strapping and nails, a stone cosmetic palette, and bones and oyster shells.

Rudder (1779), 334. Bigland (1791), I, 305. *JBAA*, XXV (1889), 222–3. *Chedworth Villa Guide* (1926). *JRS*, XXI (1931), 239. *Cheltenham Echo*, 11 Apr., and *Cheltenham Chronicle and Gloucestershire Graphic*, 23 Aug. 1930. Information provided by Mr. C. E. Key, whose plan is in Cheltenham Museum. Plan by St. Clair Baddeley in Gloucester City Library.

R.A.F., VAP CPE/UK 1913: 4094–6.

CHERINGTON

(5 miles W.S.W. of Cirencester)

An altar[1] to Silvanus or a hunter god has been found in the parish.

1. *TBGAS*, 60 (1938), 305 and fig. 29. Toynbee (1964), 159. In private possession.

(1) ROMAN BUILDING (ST 9096), at Hailstone, is not closely located, but presumably was in the area of Hailstone Barn where the ground rises gently N. between 400 ft. and 500 ft. above O.D. Foundations and

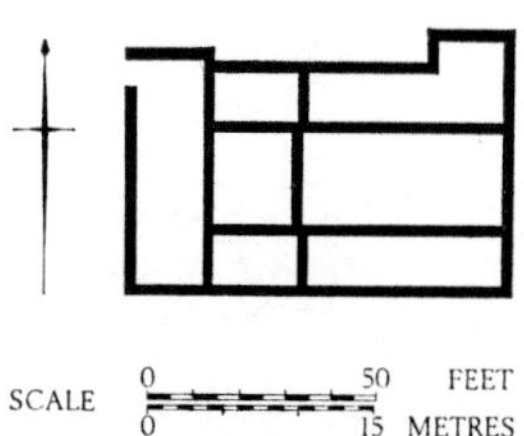

coins had been noted during ploughing, and Lysons excavated the complete building in 1795 finding some walls 2 ft. high (*Arch*, XVIII (1817), 117 and Pl. V, 2). There were no indications of heating or of tessellated floors. The structure may have been aisled (*Arch J*, CXX (1963), 28). Iron slag and coins of the 'lower Empire' were found.

CHIPPING CAMPDEN

(23 miles N.N.E. of Cirencester)

(1) ROMAN ROAD, Ryknild Street (extending N.N.W. from SP 13083376), forms the W. boundary of the parish and also the county boundary with Warwickshire. The alignment continues southwards in SNOWSHILL (1). In Hare Park Plantation the *agger* is generally 1½ ft. high and 30 ft. wide; at SP 13093376, where a track crosses it, it is about 2½ ft. high and there are indications of side ditches about 100 ft. apart.

Sections cut across the *agger* by G. B. Grundy at about SP 125356 and SP 127349 revealed small broken stones overlying a layer of stone slabs 6 in. thick; this layer was separated from bedrock by compacted earth.

PSA, 2nd ser., XXVI (1913–14), 204–8.

CIRENCESTER

A general description of *Corinium* is included in the preface (p. xxxv), but the formal catalogue of the Iron Age and Roman monuments of the town (many under excavation and study at the time of writing) is outside the scope of this Inventory.

A tessellated pavement is said to have been found at Haines Ash in Oakley Park (around SO 980035).[1]

At Stratton, 1 mile N.W. of the Roman town, a skeleton found E. of Ermin Street, near the mill (around SP 020034), was accompanied by a socketed iron hatchet.[2] A strap-tag and the pin of a fibula were found near one of two skeletons uncovered W. of Ermin Street when a cemetery (SP 011040) was laid out in 1886.[3]

A number of individual burials in the environs, some of them imprecisely located, may be related to the town rather than to rural settlement.

1. A. H. Church, *Corinium Museum* (1905), 11.
2. *PCNFC*, XXII (1926), 299–301. The hatchet is in Corinium Museum.
3. *TBGAS*, XII (1887–8), 1.

(1) ROMAN VILLA (SP 016022), The Barton, about 400 ft. above O.D., adjacent to a spring-line and some 70 yds. W. of the present course of the Daglingworth Stream, stood 400 yds. N.W. of the Roman town wall. Partial excavation in 1824, 1909 and again in 1937 revealed an Orpheus mosaic pavement of the Corinian school, 21 ft. wide (Plate 1). It was found at the E. edge of a levelled terrace, now largely occupied by The Barton House. Possibly the pavement was superimposed on another,

also tessellated, but of different shape and size. Associated finds include part of a column, fragments of coloured plaster, two fibulae, an unworn coin of Allectus and another coin, illegible; all these appear to have been stratified beneath the upper pavement. Two pagan Saxon burials had been inserted through the pavement.

Yorkshire Chronicle, 20 May 1824. *TBGAS*, XXXIII (1910), 67–77; 70 (1951), 51–3. Smith (1965), 95–116.

(2) Probable Settlement (SP 016025), Romano-British, N. of The Barton, is indicated by abundant pottery, fibulae, bracelets and 4th-century coins from a gravel pit. Loose coins ranged from Constantine to Magnentius. A hoard of 214 worn and damaged bronze coins, contained in a pot, included issues ranging from Valens to Arcadius. Some of the finds are in Corinium Museum.

TBGAS, XIX (1894–5), 394–8. *PSA*, 2nd ser., VI (1873–6), 538. *Num. Chron.*, 6th ser., XII (1952), 128–9.

(3) Romano-British Settlement (SU 015999), S.E. of Chesterton Farm, ploughed out on level ground at about 390 ft. above O.D., is indicated by occupation

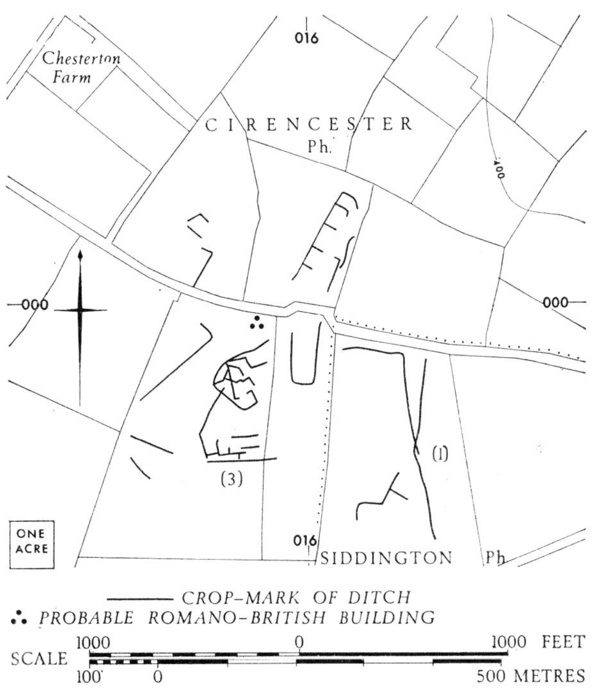

CIRENCESTER. (3) Romano-British Settlement.

debris and crop-marks. A building is indicated at SU 01549997 by large slabs of limestone, sandstone tiles and pottery, including Oxfordshire colour-coated ware. The adjacent crop-marks, covering about 40 acres, extend into the next parish (see Siddington (1)).

C.U.A.P., OAP AOO 45–6, AOS 10–11, ASM 47.

(4) Enclosure (SP 00150387), W. of Stratton, shows as a crop-mark on level ground at about 400 ft. above O.D. Its area is approximately $\frac{3}{5}$ acre (Plate 65).

C.U.A.P., OAP VM 30.

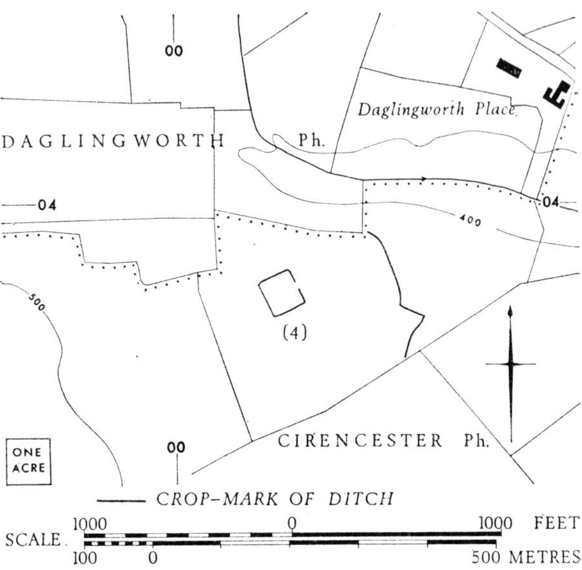

CIRENCESTER. (4) Enclosure.

(5) Enclosures (SP 037020), undated, E. of The Beeches, show as crop-marks over about 35 acres of level ground at 400 ft. above O.D.

C.U.A.P., OAP AOO 33–4. N.M.R., OAP SP 0302/2/265–72; 0302/4/338–41.

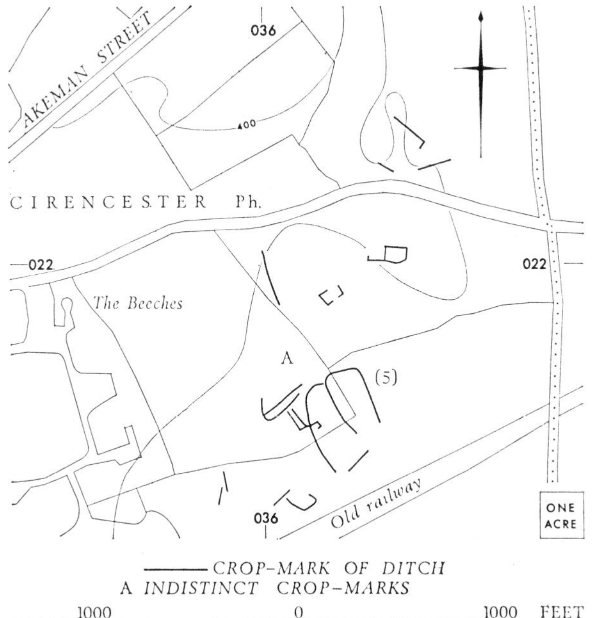

CIRENCESTER. (5) Enclosures.

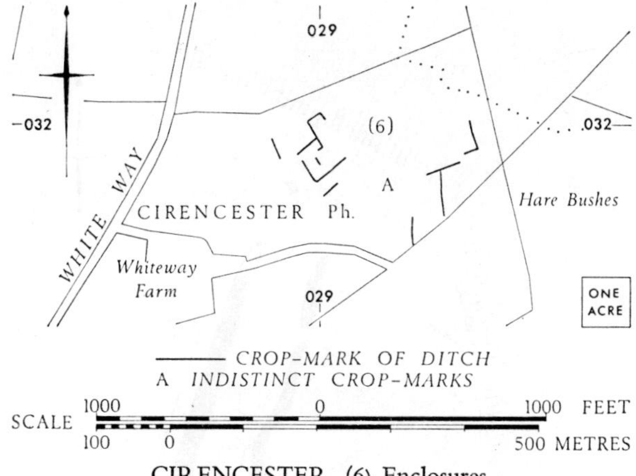

CIRENCESTER. (6) Enclosures.

(6) Enclosures (SP 029032), undated, E. of the White Way, show as crop-marks over some 8 acres at about 430 ft. above O.D.

N.M.R., OAP SP 0303/1/273–5; 0302/2/273.

(7) Roman Villa (SP 02200117), Somerford Road, Chesterton, is indicated by reported elements of a building, including fragments of a column.

JBAA, XXIII (1867), 291. *Arch*, 69 (1920), 178.

CLAPTON

No Iron Age or Romano-British monument is known in this parish.

COALEY

(16 miles w. of Cirencester)

The Roman road from Gloucester to Sea Mills (*Abonae*) passes through the N.W. part of the parish. Concentrations of Romano-British pottery have been recorded on Elmcote Farm, N. of the R. Cam, at SO 757032, 759035 and 760029.[1] A bearded head in Oolite, now in Gloucester City Museum, was found in the garden of Woodleigh House (SO 786004).

1. *Archaeol. Review*, 4 (1969), 16.

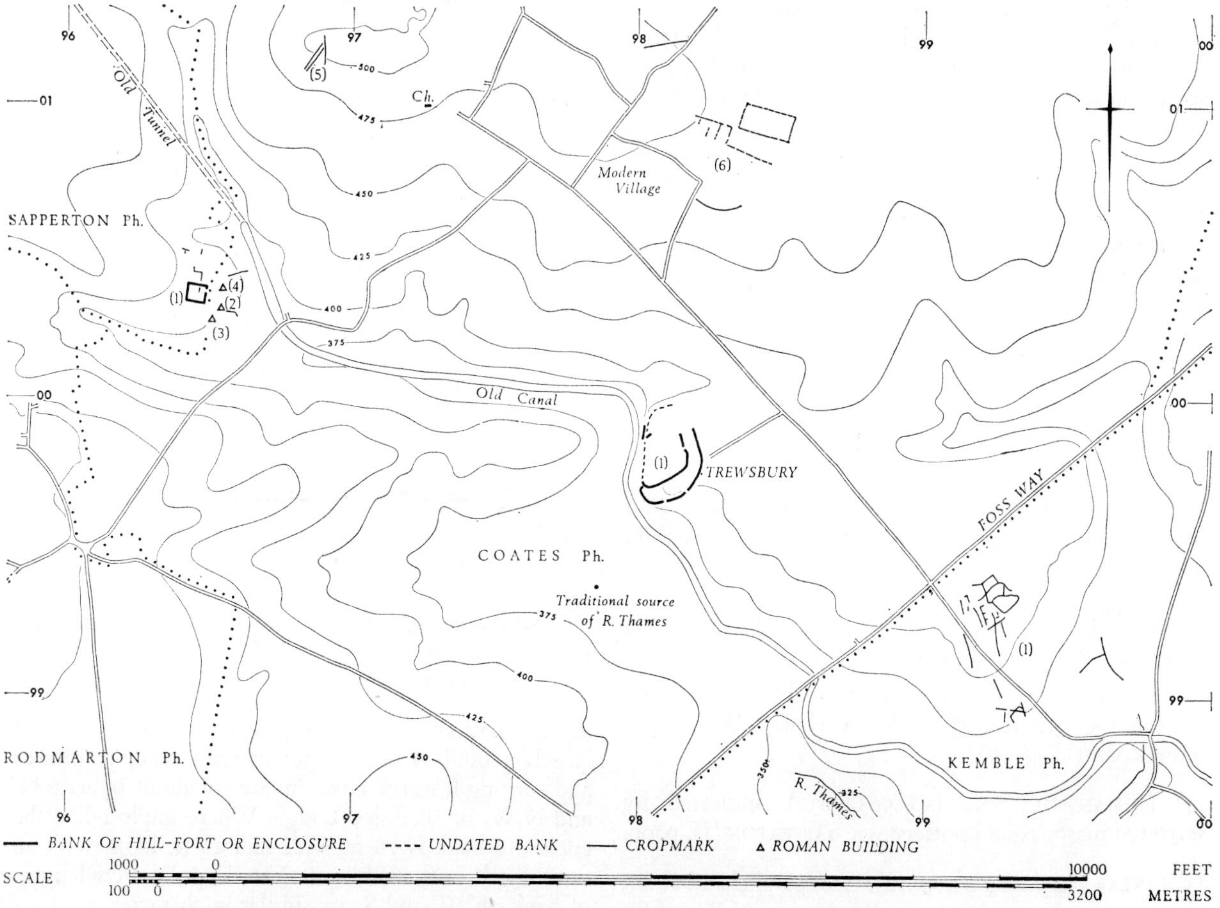

BANK OF HILL-FORT OR ENCLOSURE ---- UNDATED BANK —— CROPMARK ▲ ROMAN BUILDING

SCALE 1000 0 10000 FEET; 100 0 3200 METRES

Monuments in COATES, SAPPERTON and KEMBLE.

(1) ROMANO-BRITISH BUILDING (SO 782021), ½ mile N.E. of the village, lies on level ground less than 200 ft. above O.D., beside a stream.

Coarse pottery, building stone and sandstone roof tiles were recorded from a small area of dark soil. A ditch was exposed by an industrial trench.

TBGAS, 87 (1968), 203, No. 5.

(2) RECTANGULAR ENCLOSURE (SO 78890101), undated, on Coaley Peak, shows as a crop-mark on a terrace of the Cotswold escarpment, about 400 ft. above O.D. The sides are about 150 ft. by 120 ft. and there is a gap through the ditch on the E. side.

N.M.R., OAP SO 7801/1/210–11.

COATES

(3 miles W. of Cirencester. Map, p. 31)

(1) TREWSBURY HILL-FORT (ST 981998), partly bivallate, unexcavated, encloses about 12 acres on a spur at the edge of a shallow valley, 200 yds. N. of the source of the R. Thames and ¾ mile S. of the village.

The E. and S. sides are defined by two widely spaced banks, each with an outer ditch; the W. and N. sides are disturbed. The inner bank, 24 ft. wide and 2½ ft. high, has a ditch 30 ft. wide and 3 ft. deep. Traces of an exterior revetment wall were noted in pole-holes in 1966. The entrance, now obliterated, was in the N.E. The outer bank, 45 ft. wide and 6 ft. high, with a ditch 35 ft. wide and 4 ft. deep, turns sharply at its southernmost point and proceeds N.W. to join the inner bank. There is an entrance 200 ft. E. of the turn; another gap 240 ft. further E. is less certainly original.

Part of a low bank without a ditch in the N.W. of the fort is set between the steep westward fall of the spur and a secondary scarp; a slighter bank turns inward from its S. end.

In 1895 it was reported that Roman coins had been found within the hill-fort, and Roman pottery was found. In 1937 marks of a rectangular structure were noted in the turf between the ramparts at S.

Playne (1876), 215, No. 33. Witts (1883), 50, No. 103. *PCNFC*, III (1865), 124; VI (1877), 215. A. L. F. Rivet, in *IASB*, 34. Information from Mrs. H. E. O'Neil.

(2), (3) BUILDINGS (SO 965003), probably Roman, are indicated by crop-marks S.E. of Hailey Wood (see SAPPERTON (1), p. 99).

(4) ROMAN BUILDING (SO 96530036), indicated by scattered masonry and pottery; see SAPPERTON (1), p. 99.

(5) LINEAR DITCHES (SO 969012), two, parallel and about 20 ft. apart, show as crop-marks 450 yds. N.W. of St. Matthew's church (plan on parish map); possibly they represent a drove. Another ditch extends N.–S. immediately to the E.

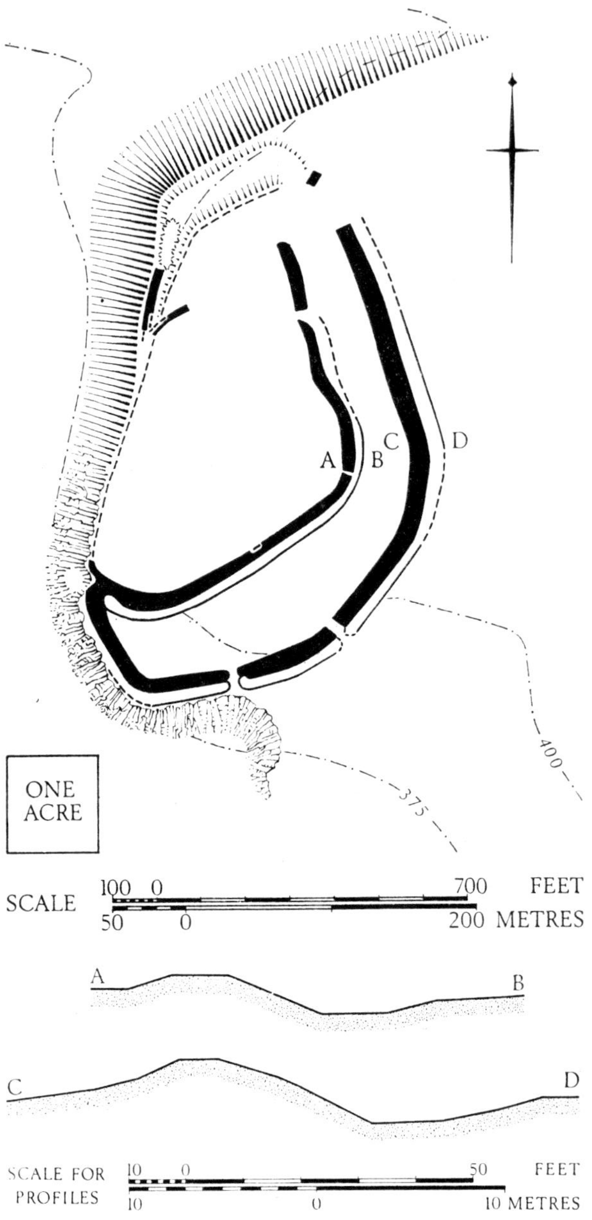

COATES. (1) Trewsbury Hill-fort.

C.U.A.P., OAP AXO 85.

(6) ENCLOSURE (SO 984009), (Plate 58) undated and largely ploughed over, together with other rectilinear and curving features, cover an area of about 16 acres N. and N.W. of Bledisloe Lodge. Where unploughed the enclosure bank is 10 ft. wide and 1½ ft. high, with an outer ditch 20 ft. wide and 1½ ft. deep. Discrete lengths of bank on W. and S. are similar in character.

O.S., VAP 65.17, 060. N.M.R., OAP SO 9800/5 (Baker).

COBERLEY

(9 miles N.W. of Cirencester)

(1) Hill-fort (SO 927161), Crickley Hill, is a promontory enclosure of some 9½ acres, contained by a single rampart and ditch with occasional traces of a further ditch beyond. Within it a Neolithic earthwork cuts off about 3 acres at the tip of the Inferior Oolite spur. Axially the interior is almost flat between the Iron Age and Neolithic earthworks, but it rises gently W. from the latter; on either side of the axis there is a gentle slope down to N. and S. The N. edge comprises a very steep natural slope, now partly quarried. The S. edge has a similar sharp shoulder towards the W., but quarrying over most of this side has resulted in sheer cliffs.

Excavations begun in 1969 by Mr. P. Dixon indicate that the hill-fort dates from the beginning of the Iron Age and that there was occupation and some use of the rampart area in Roman times.

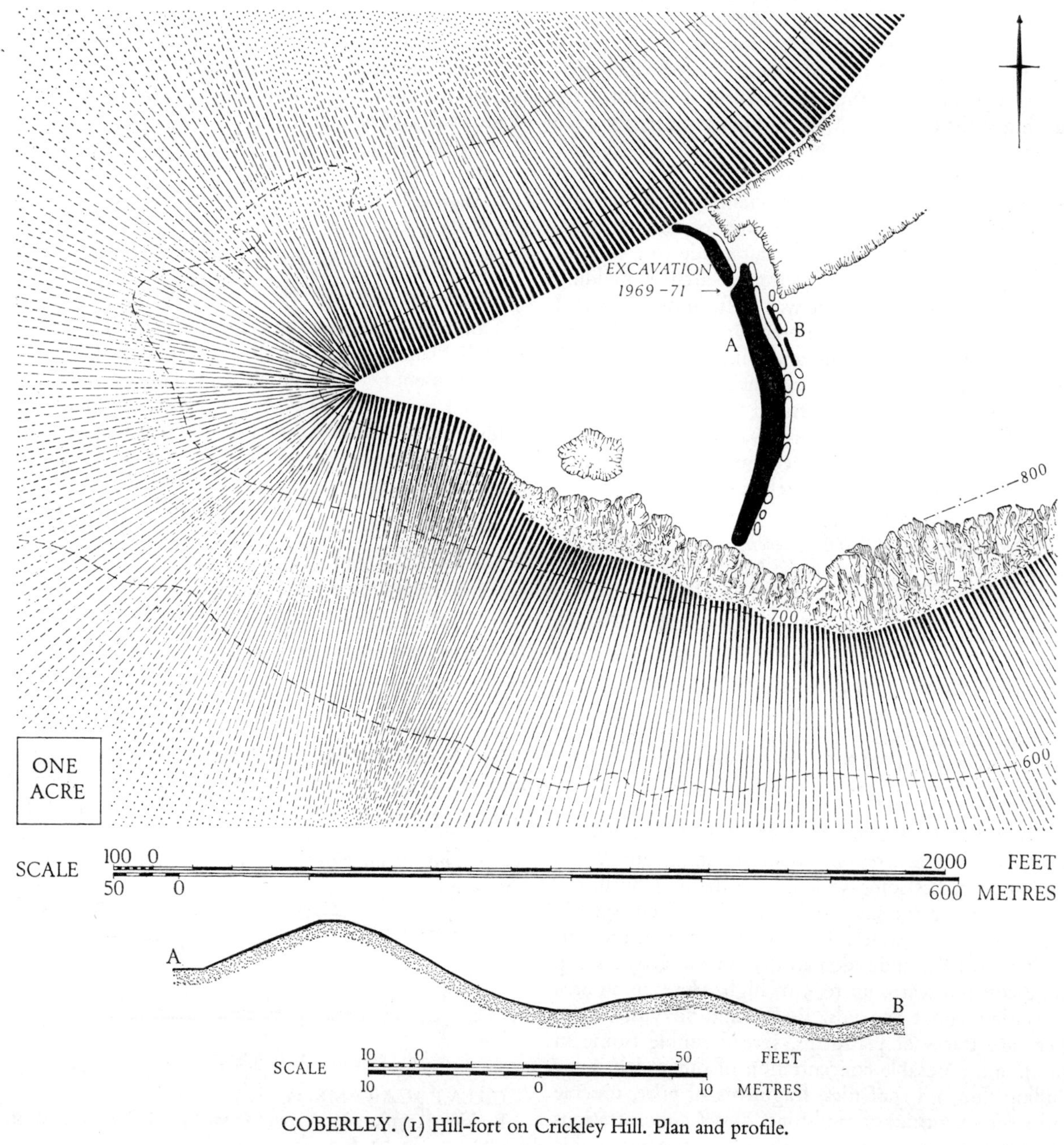

COBERLEY. (1) Hill-fort on Crickley Hill. Plan and profile.

The first phase is represented by post-holes and a rock-cut drain, which underlie the rampart. The phase-2 fortification took the form of a timber-laced rampart with facing walls about 23 ft. apart. A berm some 2 ft. to 5 ft. wide lay between the rampart and a flat-bottomed ditch, about 24 ft. across and originally 6 ft. deep. There was an entrance with front and rear gates. Aligned on either side of the road from the entrance were rectangular timber buildings in the form of aisled halls, each about 24 ft. wide and ranging in length from 28 ft. to 80 ft. Two had central hearths. Associated pottery was coarse and undecorated. The buildings and the rampart had been burnt. In phase 3 the defences were rebuilt, perhaps in two stages. Solid bastions with irregularly curved walls flanked the gate, which was further protected by an out-turned hornwork with similarly curving walls and with its own ditch built partly over the pre-existing ditch. The original ditch was further modified by the construction, on the floor near the inner side, of a revetment wall retaining a rubble core between itself and the former line of the rampart. The ditch was widened on the outer side to a total of 40 ft. (Plate 40). In the interior a circular building replaced those of phase 2; it was 48 ft. in diameter and had a central hearth and a porch facing west. Pottery associated with this building and with the reconstructed rampart includes sherds with incised chevrons and white inlay. This phase also ended with an intense fire; afterwards the rampart entrance was not reconstructed. Evidence for occupation in the Roman period includes metal-working in the silted ditch and gateway.

C.U.A.P., OAP AIN 52–8.

P. Dixon, *Crickley Hill: Third Report, 1971* (Committee for Research into the Iron Age in the North West Cotswolds, 1971). *Antiquity*, XLVI (1972), 49–52; XLVII (1973), 56–9.

(2) Probable Settlement, Romano-British, in Short Wood, is indicated by finds at two points. Two tesserae were found in a paved area (SO 93101642) beside the corner of a boundary dyke, itself probably post-Roman. Other finds, including samian ware, come from a point ¼ mile N.N.E. (SU 93351680).

TBGAS, 83 (1964), 40–8.

(3) Romano-British Settlement (SU 967152), extending over about 12 acres on ground sloping gently W. to a steep edge, lies some 50 ft. above the R. Churn, between two re-entrant gullies down which springs occasionally send water. The ground between the gullies is almost flat and is demarcated on the S. by a sharp stone-covered scarp, up to 5 ft. high. Here, in an area measuring about 200 yds. E.–W. and 70 yds. N.–S., there are traces of platforms, spread rubble (some in lines), and a notable concentration of other debris including flue and roof tiles, fragments of *pilae*, tesserae and large quantities of sandstone. Lesser concentrations occur over most of the remainder of the modern arable field; they extend as far as the road on the E., but end sharply along the S. re-entrant gully. Small finds include samian and mortaria fragments, and painted plaster.

Information from Mrs. E. Gander, who drew our attention to the site.

COLD ASHTON

(25 miles S.W. of Cirencester)

For a linear dyke probably of Iron Age date on Freezing Hill, see Doynton (1).

A burial in a stone coffin, possibly Roman, was found in a garden (ST 75007266) near the manor house in 1935.[1]

The 'ancient earthwork' on Tog Hill (about ST 730721), described by Playne[2] and noted by Witts,[3] appears to comprise a low boundary bank, probably mediaeval, and several tracks.

1. *UBSS*, 4 (No. 3), (1935), 267.
2. Playne (1876), 220, No. 45.
3. Witts (1883), 49, No. 100 ('Tog Hill Camp').

COLESBOURNE

(7 miles N.W. of Cirencester)

A Dobunnic silver coin inscribed BODVOC, found S. of Penhill Plantation (about SP 005117), is in Gloucester City Museum.[1] Romano-British pottery has been reported from an area near the 600-ft. contour, S. of Penhill Farm (about SO 992130, see area map, p. 54).[2] A Roman building is said to be in 'Penswell Field' on the line of Ermin Street, 3 miles N. of monument (1);[3] presumably it is in the area of Pinswell (SO 985153).

1. *PCNFC*, XXX (1949), 202. D. F. Allen in *Bagendon*, 121 (under Rendcomb), Pl. xxxix, No. 24.
2. Information from Mr. J. Partridge.
3. Lysons, *The Romans in Gloucestershire* (1860), 420.

(1) Norbury Hill-fort (SO 990150), univallate, unexcavated and mostly ploughed-out, lies on a hill-top 1 mile N. of the village; it probably enclosed about 8 acres (Plate 37).

The S. end is defined by a bank 18 ft. wide and 3 ft. high with an outer ditch 20 ft. wide and 3 ft. deep. A scarp 2½ ft. high marks the E. side; at the N.E. angle the ditch appears as a band of dark soil with a slight outer scarp. The entrance in the S.W. is between overlapping bank-ends.

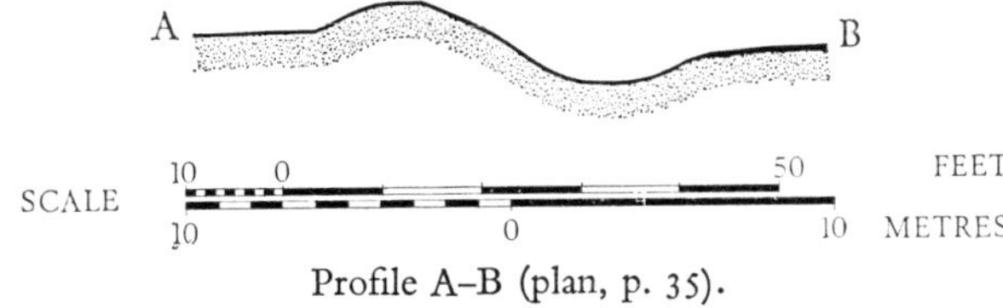

Profile A–B (plan, p. 35).

C.U.A.P., OAP AMK 59, 61.

Rudder (1779), 383. Playne (1876), 210, No. 16. Witts (1883), 37, No. 73. *Bagendon*, 25, n. 4.

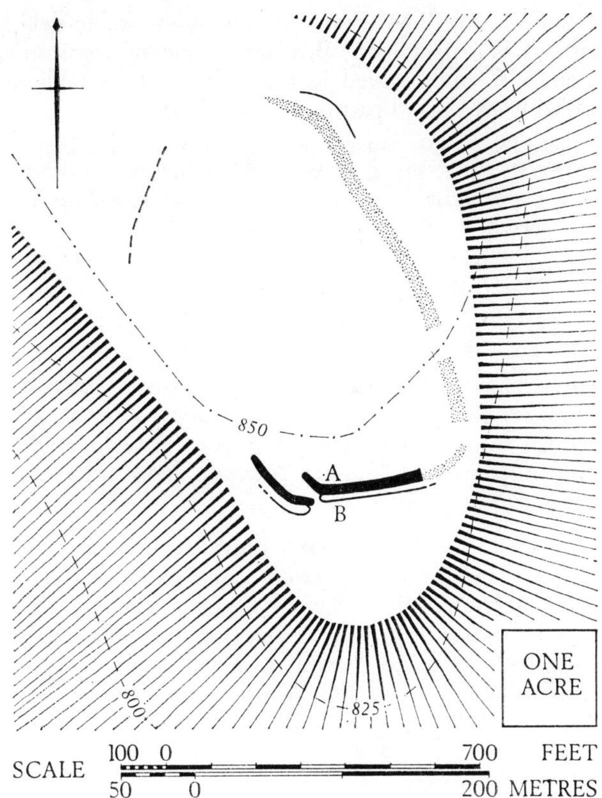

COLESBOURNE. (1) Norbury Hill-fort. Plan.

(2) ROMAN VILLA (SO 98461108), Stockwood(s), sometimes known as 'Combend' after adjacent land in ELKSTONE, appears to comprise five or more separate buildings. A and B were exposed by quarrying in 1779 and 1787 and are described by Lysons, who also dug into B and C in 1794. D seems to represent the footings of a building about 25 ft. long. All these are in rough pasture, with abundant water near by at the junction of the Fuller's Earth and the Inferior Oolite. In arable ground to the S., on the same narrow natural shelf as B, C and D, two dense concentrations of debris include sandstone tiles, *tegulae*, large irregular blocks of Oolite, and pottery including 4th-century types. The ground here is $3\frac{1}{2}$ ft. lower than the platform marking B and the 19th-century cottage which formerly stood over it. There are faint indications of a terrace, conceivably a corridor, along the S.W. edge of the western concentration. Site A lies on the broken slope which rises from the natural shelf and its corridor alone is recognisable.

Platforms further N. and N.W. lack the black earth apparent on the sites described. A long terrace on the N.E. of A, C and D is flat and about 12 yds. wide; bounded by scarps 10 ft. high above and 8 ft. below, it continues further E. than is shown on plan. Other scarps of uncertain origin occur to the N.E., uphill; some of them are broken by narrow gullies.

According to Lysons the corridor of building A, perhaps 7 ft. wide, had a patterned mosaic (Plate 7); it is said to have been 56 ft. long. Rhomboidal roof

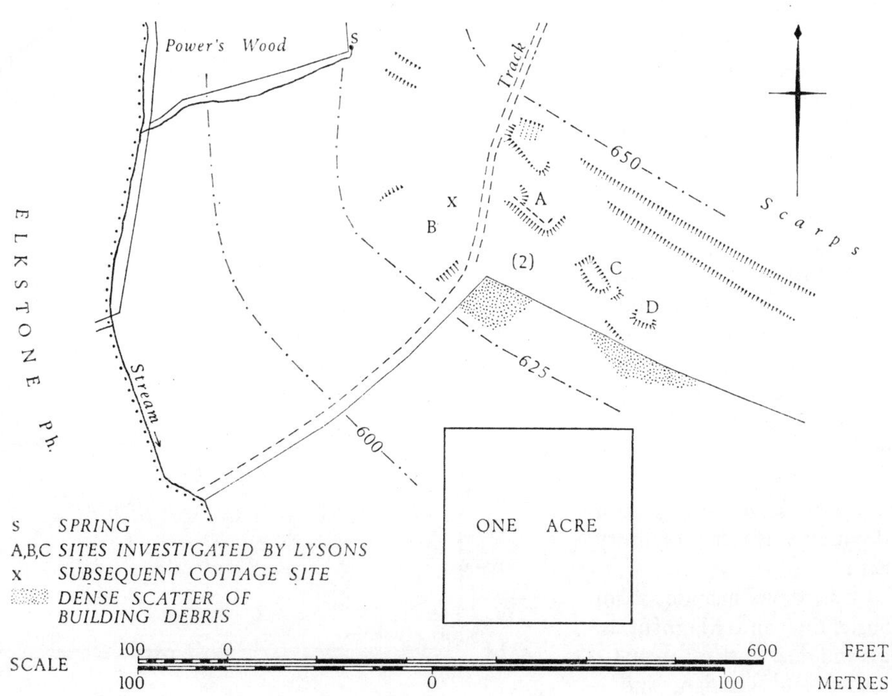

COLESBOURNE. (2) Roman Villa. Stockwood.

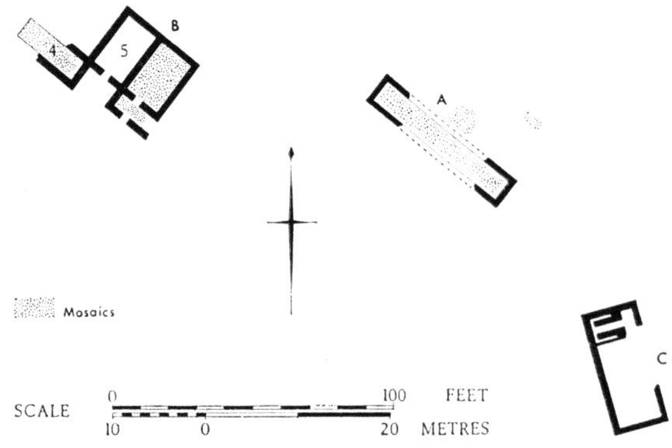

Buildings A, B and C as planned by Lysons.

slates were noted. The room behind the corridor retained traces of a red and white chequered mosaic pavement at a level 2 ft. higher. The 'large building' (B) was said to consist of a row of 6 rooms with (?) corridors; a hypocaust occurred at one end, unspecified. An estimated 200 cart-loads of building stone were removed. Three geometric mosaic pavements were partly drawn by Lysons. The most northerly (4) had a pattern which for some reason was reproduced as the mirror image of that indicated in his original plan of the building; it has been reversed in Plate 7 to accord with the plan. Two other rooms were said to have had pavements patterned with fishes and birds. Other floors were of stucco, and inside walls were plastered. Room 5 had an elaborate and rare plaster fresco on the S.E. wall, but only the lowest part remained; a drawing made before destruction shows part of a scene, probably mythological. Two moulded limestone columns about 4 ft. high and the capital of a smaller column were found near the hypocaust. Two column bases with torus mouldings like those illustrated by Lysons, the rectangular terminals of three columns conceivably of the form that inspired Lysons's reconstruction of a capital, and a strongly tapered stone shaft of unusual form, are now in the garden of Combend Manor, Elkstone (Plate 27). Lysons also noted a rectangular moulded stone base, 2 ft. 4 in. by 1 ft. 7½ in. Building C was 38 ft. by 15 ft., with stone walls 2 ft. thick. A feature at the N. end appears to have been a corn dryer; associated with it was a large quantity of charred 'wheat'.

Finds recorded by Lysons include: from B, coins of Constantine and Magnentius, also window glass and deer antlers; from C, coins of Valentinian and Gratian, and a pottery colander. An iron axe and spade iron are in the B.M. From an 'adjoining' arable field, perhaps W. of building B, came an incomplete stone about 1 ft. high carved in low relief with a soldier, probably Mars, and part of another figure.

Arch, IX (1789), 319–22; XVIII (1817), 112–13. Lysons (1817), II, Pt. 1, Pls. i, ii. Witts (1883), 58, No. 7. B.M., *Guide to the Antiquities of Roman Britain* (1951), 50 and fig. 24, No. 5 (axe). Toynbee (1964), 219–20 (fresco).

COLN ST. ALDWYNS

(8 miles E.N.E. of Cirencester)

The Roman Settlements on Akeman Street, Coln St. Aldwyns (2) and Quenington (3), 200 yds. apart, are divided by the now marshy floor of the Coln valley. Roman coins in Corinium Museum have been collected from both sites.

(1) Dean Camp (SP 165087), univallate hill-fort, unexcavated, encloses 12 acres on a spur of Great Oolite at the junction of the R. Leach and a tributary, 2¼ miles N.N.E. of the village. The E. and N.E. sides are defined by a bank up to 40 ft. wide and 6 ft. high, with no visible ditch; the N. and W. sides are defined by a

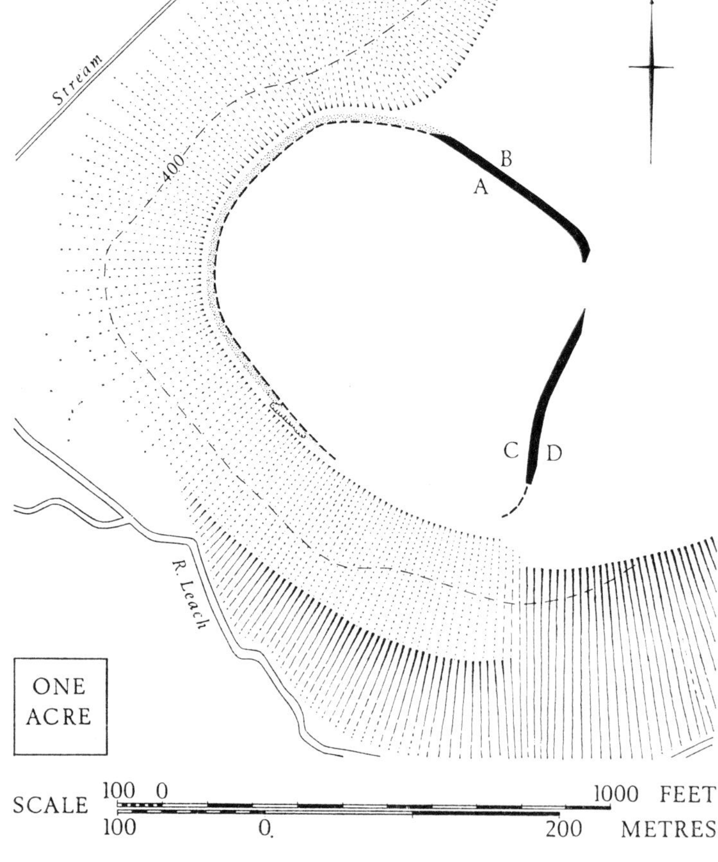

COLN ST. ALDWYNS. (1) Dean Camp.

short scarp which does not continue on the S. The entrance is probably marked by a gap in the bank on the E.

Playne (1876), 213, No. 26. Witts (1883), 30, No. 60 (Ladborough Camp). *Bagendon*, 25, n. 4.

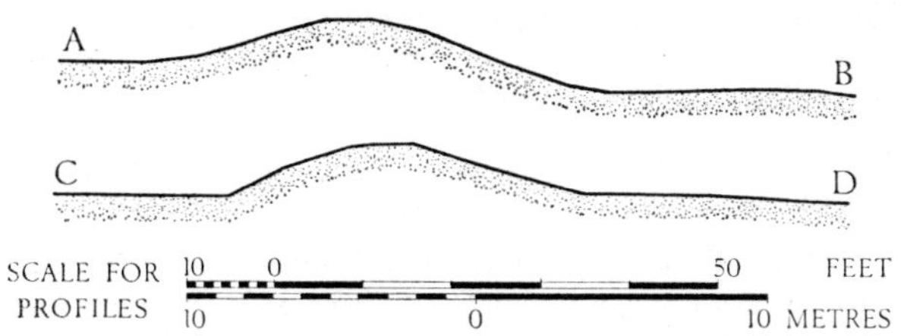

COLN ST. ALDWYNS. (1) Dean Camp. Profiles.

(2) Romano-British Settlement (sp 140055), The Chessels (*TBGAS*, 76 (1957), 35), lies at about 325 ft. above O.D., in arable, on an E.–W. terrace above the R. Coln (plan, p. 96, *s.v.* Quenington). It is marked by building debris in the form of large limestone blocks, pottery of the 2nd to 4th centuries, 3rd and 4th-century coins, and other small finds made along and immediately N. of Akeman Street, over a length of 300 yds. or more. Similar debris is scattered in a restricted area on the S. of the Roman road, at the W. limit of settlement (sp 13840540).

Small finds include a fragment of glass, a 4th-century tinned bronze spoon with ring-and-dot ornament, and 3rd and 4th-century coarse pottery; these are in the Ashmolean Museum. Part of the neck of a coarse-ware flagon in the form of a woman's head, and bronze coins of Constantine I and Constantine II are in Gloucester City Museum.

(3) Roman Road, Akeman Street (sp 141055), is traceable through The Chessels (2) as a crop-mark, and its line is further marked on the ground by a later hollow-way on the steep rise at sp 14280555. To the E., where ploughing has taken place in Williamstrip Park, the straight line of the road is confirmed by crop-marks. (Plan *s.v.* Quenington).

COLN ST. DENNIS

(7 miles N.N.E. of Cirencester)

The Foss Way forms the W. boundary of the parish. Lysons notes the discovery of Roman coins in the immediate vicinity of a barrow,[1] but the position of the barrow itself is not known.

1. Lysons, *The Romans in Gloucestershire* (1860), 56.

(1) Enclosures and Linear Ditches (sp 074088), undated, show as crop-marks extending over some 40 acres on the plain, ½ mile S.E. of Foss Cross. Enclosure 'a', covering about ⅔ acre, has gaps in the two rounded

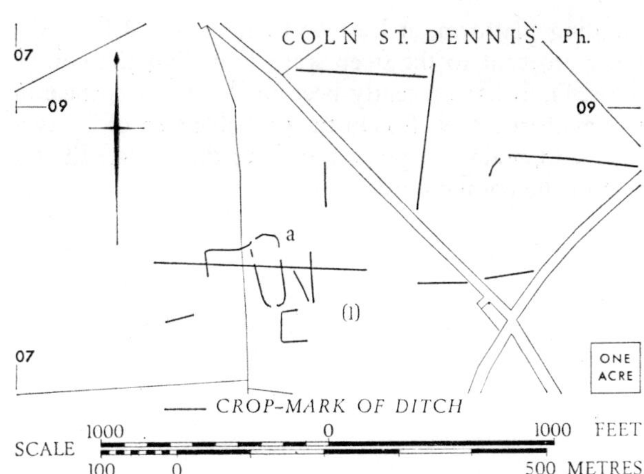

ends and in each side near the N. end. The other crop-marks are ill defined.

N.M.R., OAP SP 0708/1/382.

COMPTON ABDALE

(9 miles N.N.E. of Cirencester)

The well-defined, but undated earthworks of a settlement at Cassey Compton (sp 05201465) are excluded from the Inventory. It has been said that they represent a Roman villa,[1] but from their situation and form[2] a mediaeval origin is more likely. For position, see plan, p. 25, *s.v.* Chedworth.

1. *Arch J*, CXXII (1965), 178, fig. 2, No. 8.
2. Air photographs by Mr. H. Wingham, copies N.M.R.

Note: The Roman Villa (1), lying in a narrow combe, cannot be securely linked to monuments (2), (3) and (4), but it is likely that all four are contemporary. Tiles stamped with similar marks were found in the area of the villa and on a Neolithic long barrow (n on plan), ¼ mile to the S., on Sales Lot in Withington.

(1) Roman Villa (sp 04821624), Compton Grove, excavated by C. E. Key in 1931, is now marked by slight terraces and by abundant surface finds within an area covering ⅔ acre, on the level, narrow floor of a combe facing S.E. Uphill from the area a number of scarps cross the rising valley floor. Two streams flow from the junction of Great Oolite with the Fuller's Earth on which the villa was built. Between the two spring-heads, above a 9-ft. scarp, is a roughly circular depression (b), 18 ft. by 16 ft. and over 3 ft. deep. An irregular platform 10 ft. wide lies just W. of this. Scarps about 3 ft. high crossing the combe head further uphill, and others in arable ground to S., could be the remains of 'Celtic' fields.

The excavations of 1931 took place in the area on the S. side of the combe floor, mainly N.W. of a modern swimming-pool (s) and also, probably, S.E. of it, but not extending to feature (a). The latter appears to be a building platform, at least 60 ft. long by 18 ft. wide, lying adjacent to the steep scarp bounding the combe floor. Finds have recently been made on the surface of this platform, as well as in the probable area of excavation, and again at a point 100 ft. to the N., on the far side of the combe floor.

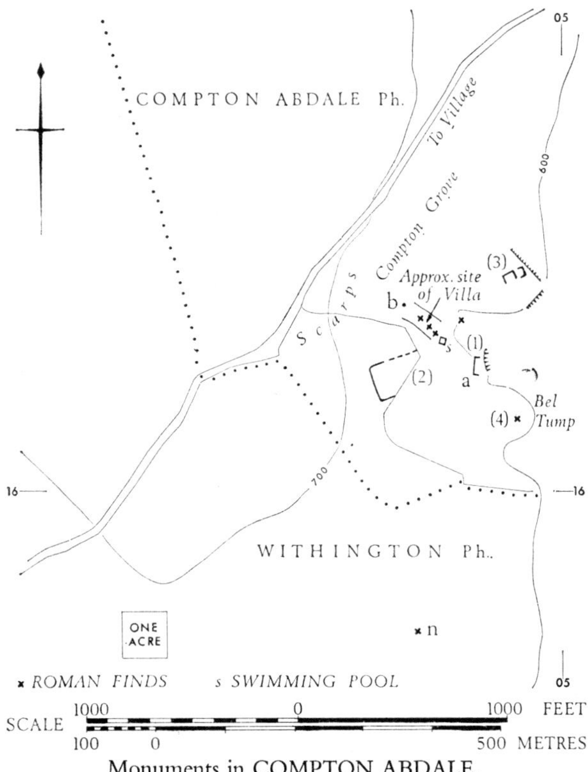

Monuments in COMPTON ABDALE.

Notes taken during the excavations indicate a building walled in Oolite, without a corridor. The building, 10 ft. wide and probably longer than the 74 ft. investigated had, according to the excavator, five or six rooms, not all shown on his plan; at least two of them were heated; one hypocaust had stone pillars, the other had tile *pilae*. Only concrete floors were found.

Finds, mostly in Cheltenham Museum, include 3rd-century coins, samian ware of the late 2nd century and pottery of the 3rd and 4th centuries including colour-coated wares, stone and earthenware roof tiles, much

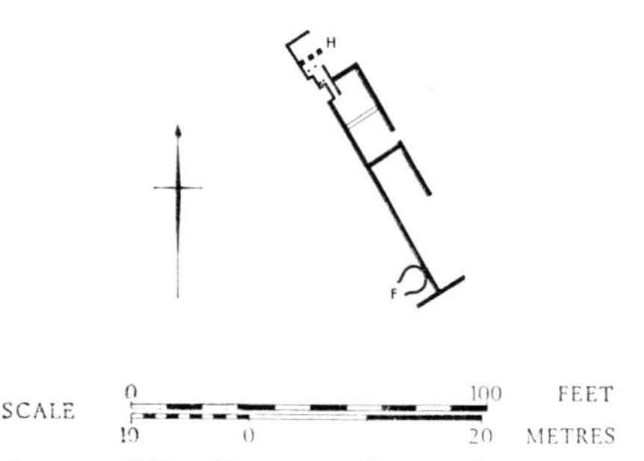

Roman Villa, Compton Grove. Plan, 1931.

coloured wall-plaster including fragments of designs in panels, flue tiles (one now in Chedworth Museum inscribed VL), a horseshoe, barrel lock and 'frying pan' all of iron, glass, a bronze tooth-pick, a quernstone, and coal.

JRS, XXII (1932), 214. MS. notes provided by Mr. C. E. Key and Dr. J. Liversidge, and plan by Cheltenham Museum; accounts in *Cheltenham Chronicle and Gloucester Gazette*, August 1931. *JRS*, XLV (1955), 72 (flue tile), No. 21.

(2) ENCLOSURE (SP 04741616), probably Romano-British, W. of Compton Grove and 50 yds. S.W. of (1) (see adjacent map), occupies ground rising above the narrow combe; only parts of three sides survive as a much-worn bank and ditch. The N.W. angle shows a return E., the area formerly enclosed therefore being not less than ⅓ acre. The boundary of Compton Grove cuts the S. side, and the E. end of the enclosure has been destroyed. Where best preserved, at the N. end of the W. side, the bank is 14 ft. wide and stands about 2 ft. above an external ditch of the same width. The interior slopes 7° E.

R.A.F., VAP CPE/UK 1846: 4067–8.

(3) BUILDING PLATFORM (SP 04921630), probably Romano-British, rectangular, about 51 ft. by 32 ft. (map with (1)), is cut diagonally into the brow of the hill, N.E. of (1). Another platform about 10 ft. across, poorly defined, lies immediately to the E. To the N.E. a substantial artificial scarp up to 5 ft. high and at least 50 yds. long approaches, at its S.E. end, a lesser scarp which follows the contour for 30 yds; the two scarps suggest the bounds of an enclosed area.

Oxfordshire colour-coated ware of the late 3rd or 4th century and fragments of *opus signinum* were found on the building platform.

(4) PROBABLE SETTLEMENT (SP 04951610), Bel Tump, Romano-British but of uncertain nature, lies 170 yds. S.S.E. of (1) and is marked by an irregular heap of large rough limestone blocks on the almost flat narrow tip of an E.-facing spur. The ground falls steeply to the E. and rises gently to the W.

Digging in 1931 yielded 15 coins, including one of Allectus and pottery including samian ware.

MS. notes by Mr. C. E. Key and Dr. J. Liversidge.

(5) CIST BURIAL (SP 05261746), unaccompanied, probably Romano-British, was found in 1938 immediately N.E. of the outbuildings of Springhill. The grave, about 1½ ft. deep, was completely stone-lined, its cover-stones lying some 2 ft. below the surface.

TBGAS, 61 (1939), 118–19.

(6) SCARPS (SP 053167), possibly the remains of 'Celtic' fields broken by strip and later ploughing, occur W. of Smallhope Cottages on a S.-facing slope of up to 12°.

CONDICOTE

(18 miles N.N.E. of Cirencester)

The pit-alignment (1) is one of only three examples in the Gloucestershire Cotswolds, rare in its situation (see p. xxvii). The Roman road, Ryknild Street, ran through the parish just E. of (1) and (2), but no sign of it is now seen.

Of four enclosures formerly noted in the parish only one, incomplete and much flattened, can be substantiated; it is a 3-acre circular earthwork, 200 yds. E. of the church (SP 154284), with a large causewayed ditch inside its single bank (X on map, p. xxxii). Although an Iron Age sherd has been found high in the main fill of the ditch, the earthwork is probably of Neolithic 'henge' type.[1] An undated enclosure of 1 acre on Staites Brake (SP 150302), called 'Hinchwick Camp' in *VCH*, was almost flattened in 1803 and the present enclosure is modern (p. xxxii). An 'oval British camp' reported W. of the village[2] cannot be confirmed; there are rings and semicircles of geological origin in this area and to the north. Immediately E. of these are the alleged remains of a hill-fort, *Eubury Camp*,[3] which cannot be accepted as such on present evidence (p. xxxi). In 1937 Romano-British pottery was found just W. of the 'hill-fort'.[4]

1. Playne (1876), 208, No. 6. Witts (1883), 15, No. 31. *TBGAS*, 76 (1957), 141–6.
2. *VCH* Glos. VI, 64.
3. Witts (1883), 21, No. 43.
4. Information from Mrs. H. E. O'Neil.

(1) PIT-ALIGNMENT, DITCH AND ENCLOSURE (SP 14562923–14312993) show as crop-marks above the indented W. side of a dry valley (Plate 56). The pit-alignment extends for 630 yds. across the head of two minor re-entrants W. of Old Hinchwick, thence N. across gently sloping ground to an almost level shelf; here it meets a ditch at least 300 yds. long above a steep drop to the east. A rectangular enclosure (a) of about $\frac{1}{5}$ acre projects from the E. side of the ditch near its N. end. Beyond the ditch the ground drops sharply into a narrow gully, N. of which was the Romano-British burial noted below.

N.M.R., OAP SP 1429/1/346–51.

(2) ROMANO-BRITISH INHUMATION (SP 14202999) (map with (1)), crouched, associated with an iron-hinged wooden container in a partly stone-lined grave dug into limestone bedrock, was exposed at the W. end of Lodge Ground Quarry in 1937. The ground drops sharply just N. of the now derelict quarry. A bronze pin probably from the grave is in Cheltenham Museum.

TBGAS, 61 (1939), 109.

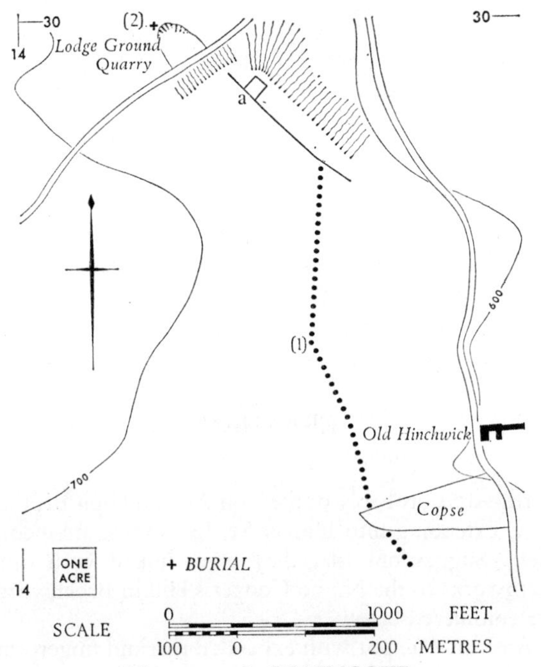

Monuments in CONDICOTE.

COWLEY

(9 miles N.N.W. of Cirencester)

'Birdlip Camp' (SO 925150) is an alleged hill-fort[1] whose existence is dubious (p. xxix). A Dobunnic gold coin inscribed BODVOC, found at Birdlip, is lost.[2] The late Iron Age inhumation cemetery at Barrow Wake (1) is unique in the Cotswolds.

Numerous Roman coins are said to have been found during the construction of houses along the course of Ermin Street in Birdlip.[3]

1. Playne (1876), 210, No. 15. Witts (1883), 5, No. 11.
2. D. F. Allen, in *Bagendon*, 119.
3. Witts (1883), 111.

(1) IRON AGE INHUMATION CEMETERY (SO 93191532), Barrow Wake, Birdlip, near the edge of the escarpment, came to light during quarrying in 1879. Imprecise and varying accounts refer to four burials. Three found together, possibly under a cairn, are said to have been in cists lined and covered with limestone flags. The group comprised a female wih an ornamented bronze mirror (the 'Birdlip mirror'), two bronze bowls, an iron knife-handle with a bronze bull's-head terminal, a silver-gilt fibula datable within the early 1st century A.D., a bracelet, rings, tweezers and other bronze objects, and beads from a necklace of amber, marble and shale; with her were two unaccompanied skeletons, thought to be male. The fourth skeleton, found near by in a shallow grave, was accompanied by the remains of a bronze-mounted wooden bucket and an iron weapon with a blade 13 in. long, perhaps a dagger. Apart from the iron weapon, these grave-goods are in Gloucester City Museum. Part of a gold torque, found in the area in 1947 and now lost, may have come from a fifth grave.

TBGAS, V (1880–1), 137–41. *PCNFC*, VIII (1881–2), 81–2. *PPS*, XV (1949), 188–90. Additional data from Mr. J. F. Rhodes, Gloucester City Museum. *Early Celtic Art* (Festival Exhibition Catalogue), Edinburgh Univ., 1970, pp. 28–9, Nos. 146–9. *Bedfordshire Archaeol. J*, 5 (1970), 13 (date of fibula).

(2) ROMAN ROAD, Ermin Street (SO 92921422). The *agger* probably survives E. of Birdlip (2a on map), where a mutilated flat-topped ridge 300 ft. long and up to 3 ft. high lies parallel to the S. side of the modern road. No ditch can be seen in the disturbed marshy ground to the south. Other denuded remains (2b) exist in gardens in the village (SO 92601433). A terrace-way (t) in Great Witcombe, possibly the original course of Ermin Street as it descended the escarpment, has gentler gradients than those of the modern road on Birdlip Hill.

R.A.F., VAP F21 58/RAF/1970: 0120–1 (Birdlip Hill). Witts (1883), 111.

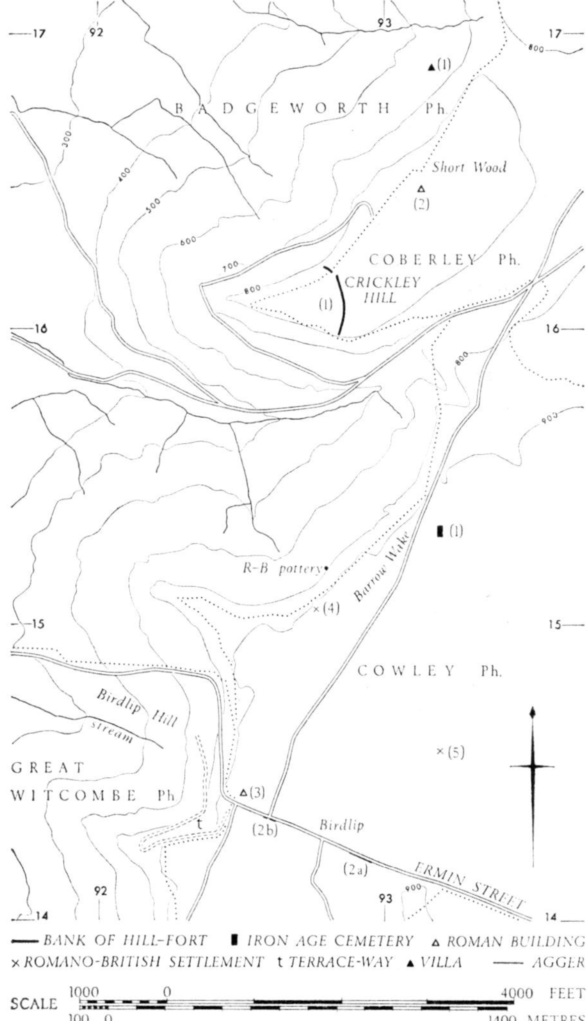

Monuments in COBERLEY and COWLEY.

(3) ROMAN VILLA (SO 92501443), near the Royal George Hotel, stood on level ground at the edge of the escarpment, N. of Ermin Street. There is a disturbed platform in gardens W. of the hotel.

A limited investigation *c.* 1918 revealed a wall with painted plaster, hypocaust flue-tiles, and pottery. Over 200 Roman coins are said to have been found here in 1890–1. Apart from fragments of masonry in the hotel grounds, possibly from this building, no finds survive.

TBGAS, XLV (1923), 294–5; LIV (1932), 387–8. *JRS*, XIV (1924), 231.

(4) ROMAN BUILDING (SO 92761506), at Barrow Wake, is denoted by a rectangular platform yielding pottery, reported in 1970. The finds are in Gloucester City Museum.

(5) PROBABLE SETTLEMENT (SO 93251463), Romano-British, ploughed out, is reported on level ground ½ mile N.E. of Birdlip. A hypocaust flue-tile and pottery are in a private collection.

Information from Mr. J. F. Rhodes.

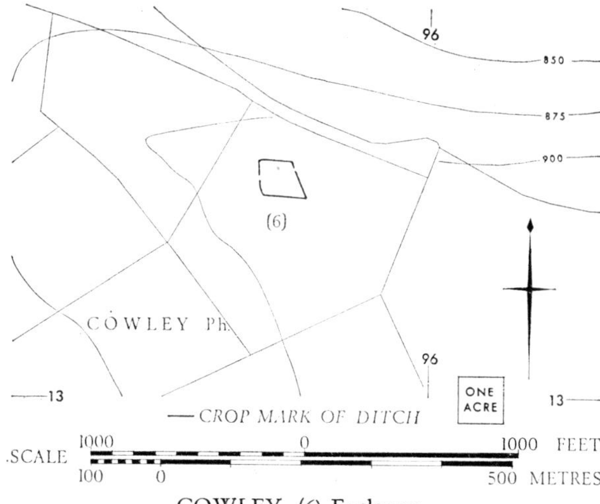

COWLEY. (6) Enclosure.

(6) ENCLOSURE (SO 958133), S. of Cowley Wood, undated, shows as a crop-mark on the flat top of an eminence in the plateau (Plate 57). The area enclosed is about ¾ acre.

C.U.A.P., OAP UM 35.

CRANHAM

(9 miles N.W. of Cirencester)

Earthworks probably of the Iron Age on High Brotheridge, extending into UPTON ST. LEONARDS, are incomplete. Suggestions that they were linked with other earthworks to the N., on Cooper's Hill in Brockworth, are considered below.

An Iron Age pot with expanded rim and fingerprints on the neck is alleged to have contained a cremation and to have been found in 'the round barrow at Ebworth' in 1882.[1] The mound, not precisely located, may not have been a barrow.[2]

1. W. St. Clair Baddeley, *A Cotswold Manor* (1929), 15. *Ant J*, XXII (1942), 216–18.
2. *TBGAS*, 79 (1960), 111 [Cranham 5].

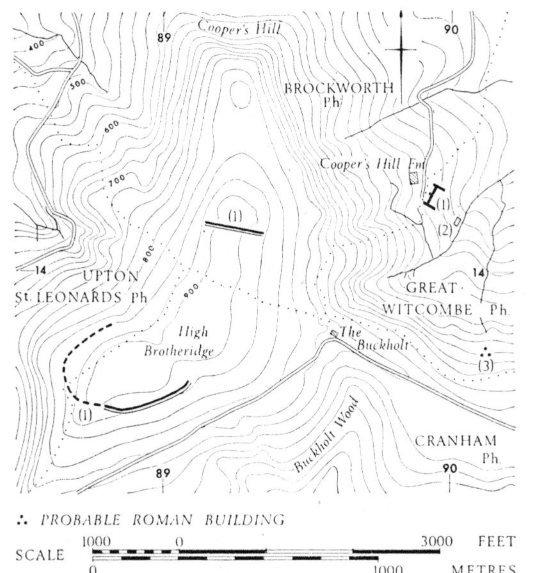

Monuments in BROCKWORTH, GREAT WITCOMBE and CRANHAM.

(1) DYKE (SO 888138), High Brotheridge, probably of the Iron Age and possibly part of a former or unfinished enclosure, comprises a degraded bank or scarp with an outer ditch, bounding the S.W. parts of High Brotheridge hill, between 850 and 900 ft. above O.D. The ground slopes gently downhill at first, and then steeply, except at the W. extremity where there is an immediate steep fall into Buckholt Wood and the adjoining Rough Park. Indications of another bank with an uphill ditch or hollow, shown on O.S. 6-inch maps just W. of this place, coincide with a track approaching an old quarry in Rough Park.

The bank first mentioned ends sharply to the E., where a gully crosses the hill-top. The bank is now 27 ft. across at most and 4 ft. high above a ditch of similar width. Witts (1883) suggests a former height of 15 ft., but his description is unusually difficult to reconcile with the existing remains. The main bank is arranged in a series of straight lines. Slight banks and scarps in Brockworth are either natural or undatable. A sinuous scarp line shown on O.S. maps, following the E. side of Cooper's Hill, N. of the transverse gully, is at most 3 ft. high and is crossed by the parish boundary bank. A small bank tops the scarp in places N. of this, and the dyke in BROCKWORTH (1) ends against this scarp line. Northwards from about SO 89371438 the line is continued by a slight bank with a ditch on its W. side.

C.U.A.P., OAP ACQ 54–7.

Arch, XIX (1821), 170. Witts (1883), 15, No. 32. Burrow (1924), 130. *Bagendon*, 157–8.

CUTSDEAN

(18 miles N. of Cirencester)

A burial (approx. SP 091305) of an adult male, probably in a wooden coffin, was found in 1955; two Romano-British sherds were in the grave fill.[1] The ploughed out *agger* of the Roman road, Ryknild Street, is clearly visible on air photographs[2] at SP 14213058, continuing the straight section across Bourton Downs (see BOURTON-ON-THE-HILL).

1. *TBGAS*, 74 (1955), 176.
2. N.M.R., OAP 352–3/129.

DAGLINGWORTH

(3 miles N.W. of Cirencester)

A linear dyke (1) may form part of the system of dykes at Bagendon.

A dedication slab mutilated by the cutting of window lights is built upside down into the outer N. wall of the vestry of the parish church.[1] Two fragmentary votive tablets bearing representations of *genii cucullati*, one retaining also the figure of a seated goddess and part of an inscription,[2] are recorded from a field in the vicinity of monument (2); two 4th-century bronze coins have been recovered from the same field.[3] It has been suggested that the inscribed and carved stones come from a temple.[4]

Ermin Street forms part of the E. boundary of the parish. Map, p. 42.

1. *RIB*, I, No. 130.
2. *RIB*, I, No. 129. Toynbee (1964), 177–8, Pl. XLIVb. Toynbee in O. M. Griffiths, *Daglingworth: the Story of a Cotswold Village* (1959), 4, Pls. I, II. Both tablets are in Corinium Museum.
3. Toynbee in Griffiths, *op. cit.*, 7.
4. Lewis (1966), 126.

(1) LINEAR DYKE. See BAGENDON (1), p. 8.

(2) ROMAN VILLA? (SO 99850443, according to O.S.), 'Cave Close', occupied the level top of a slight promontory above a stream, 800 yds. S.E. of the parish church. A tessellated pavement was reported here towards the end of the 17th century. Recent finds from the vicinity of the building are described above.

R. Atkyns, *The Ancient and Present State of Glostershire* (1712), 379. Rudder (1779), 400. Witts (1883), 61, No. 11.

(3) ENCLOSURE (SO 99400310), undated, is revealed by

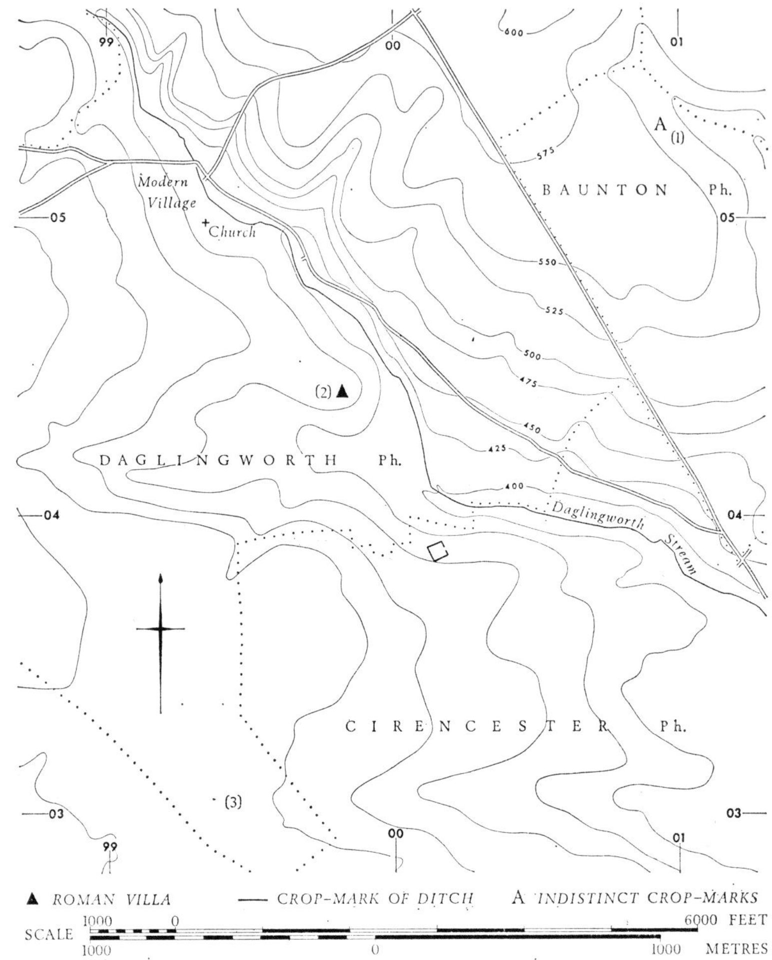

Monuments in DAGLINGWORTH.

crop-marks N.E. of Cirencester Park. It occupies nearly an acre, on level ground.

C.U.A.P., OAP AOR 94; N.M.R., OAP SO 9903/1/345–6.

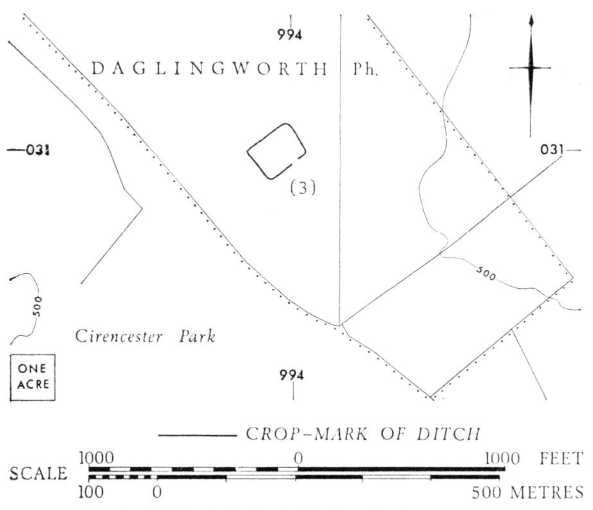

DAGLINGWORTH. (3) Enclosure.

DIDMARTON

(18 miles s.w. of Cirencester)

(1) Probable Settlement (ST 812875), undated, S.E. of Tump Barn, is revealed by crop-marks. The clearest

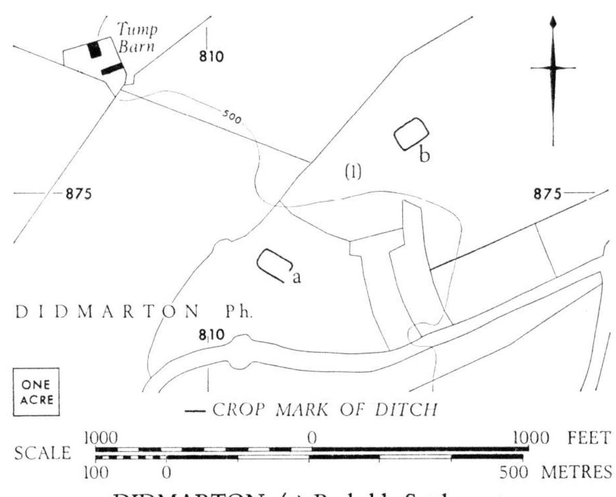

DIDMARTON. (1) Probable Settlement.

features are two enclosures, a and b, each about 140 ft. long. Ill-defined marks suggest other features in the vicinity of enclosure a.

C.U.A.P., OAP AYG 31–2.

DODINGTON

(23 miles S.W. of Cirencester)

Leland[1] records the discovery in the fields of a Roman coin hoard contained in a pot, and, in the road near the church (ST 75217989), of a cremation in a glass vessel, possibly Romano-British. Roman coins were found by St. Clair Baddeley;[2] a coin of Valens and one of Valentinian I are in Gloucester City Museum.

1. *Itin.*, ed. Toulmin Smith, IV, 130–1.
2. *TBGAS*, LII (1930), 163, n. 29.

DONNINGTON

No Iron Age or Romano-British monument is known in this parish.

DOWDESWELL

(11 miles N. of Cirencester)

Three 'camps' have been suggested in this parish, but only one of them can be accepted as a hill-fort of Iron Age date (see p. xxxiii).

(1) HILL-FORT (SO 999191), on Dowdeswell Hill, formerly called 'The Castles',* univallate, unexcavated, encloses 14½ acres of the E. side of a spur projecting N. from Dowdeswell Hill at about 700 ft. above O.D. The rampart has been extensively damaged on all sides except part of the S.W. The ditch has been filled on the S. and

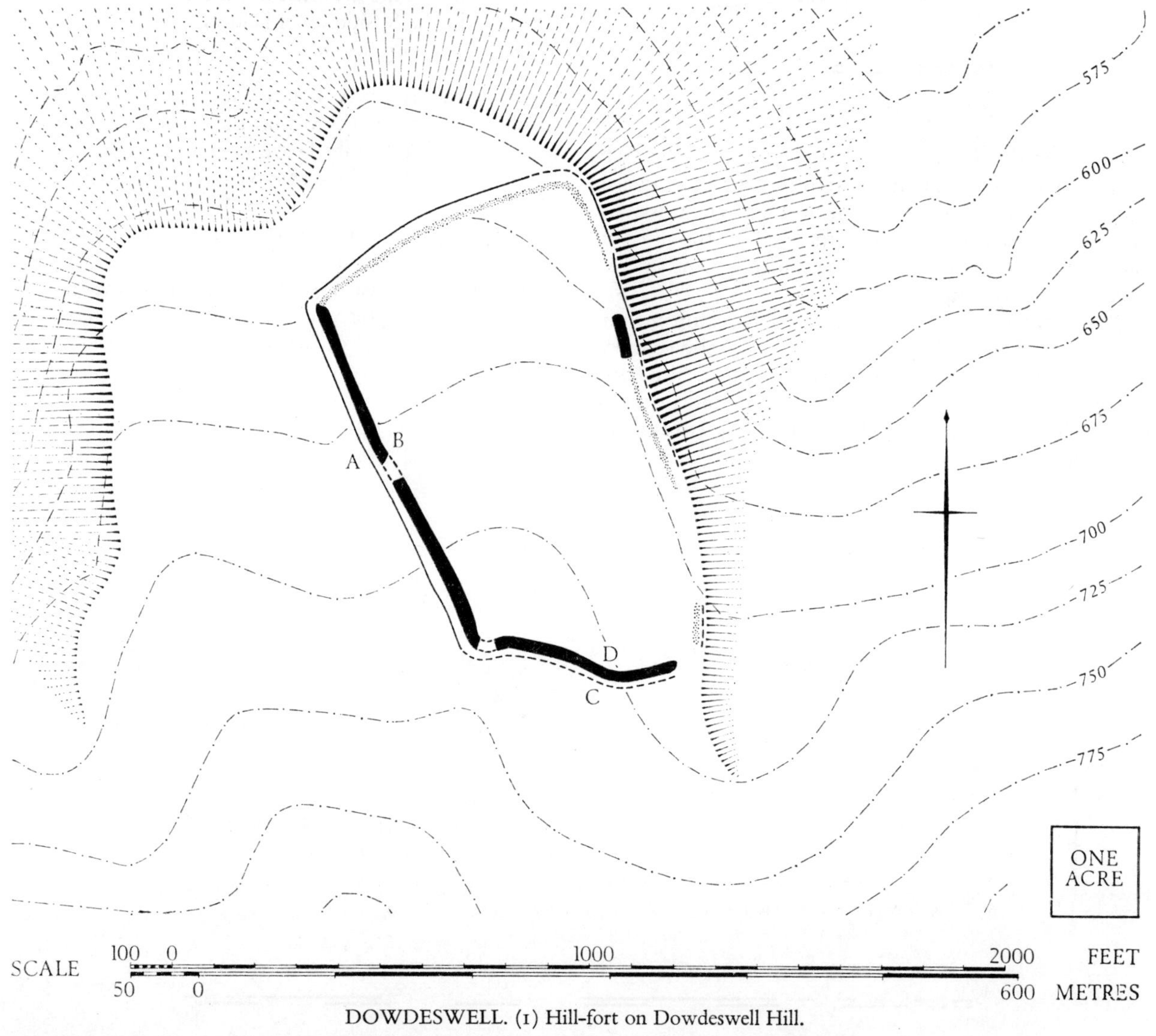

DOWDESWELL. (1) Hill-fort on Dowdeswell Hill.

* Dowdeswell Court Book, Jan. 1660/1 (G.C.R.O., D 269 A, T/46).

it appears to have slipped downhill on the steep E. side. The interior has been ploughed, perhaps since mediaeval times, accounting for the division of the area into two parts (Plate 38). A surface scatter of Romano-British potsherds is particularly noticeable in the N. half.

The rampart, where best preserved on the S.W., is 23 ft. across, 4 ft. above the interior and 8 ft. above the ditch fill. The ditch, 25 ft. across the top, has been disturbed by use as a track. On the N.W. side the ditch has been largely filled in, but there is a suggestion of a slight counterscarp bank. On the E. side the bank has been almost totally levelled, but a terrace marking the

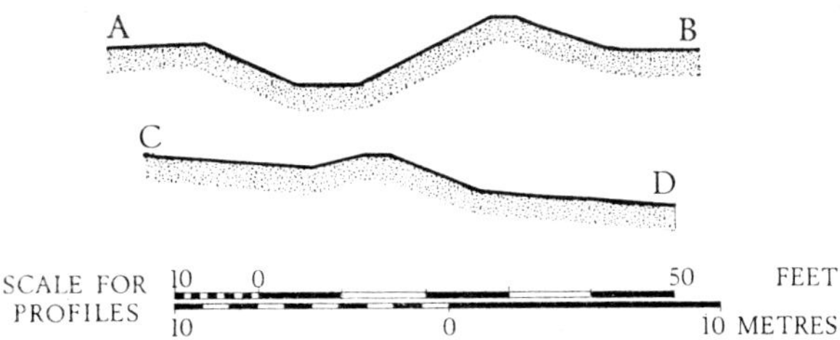

DOWDESWELL. (1) Hill-fort. Profiles (plan, p. 43).

line of the ditch extends S. for 450 ft. from the N.E. angle. Beyond this point the terrace extends outwards and downwards until, 700 ft. from the angle, it is 20 ft. below the scarp which marks the edge of the interior, and 50 ft. E. of it. The original entrance appears to have been at the S.E. angle.

Potsherds found in the N. half of the camp include fragments of samian ware, probably of the 2nd century, and of colour-coated mortaria from Oxfordshire kilns. Some mediaeval and later sherds were found in the S. half. The valley immediately on the E. is covered by strip fields.

Finds made in the course of investigation have been deposited in the Gloucester City Museum.

Witts (1883), No. 1.

DOWN AMPNEY

(5 miles S.E. of Cirencester)

(1) ENCLOSURES AND LINEAR DITCHES (SU 102960), undated, show as crop-marks E. of Bean Hay Copse, ⅜ mile S.S.E. of All Saints' Church and about 270 ft. above O.D. A sub-circular enclosure 300 ft. in diameter, defined by an interrupted ditch, is intersected by a straight ditch, possibly the S.E. side of a rectilinear enclosure with an entrance on the east. A small irregular oval enclosure in the E. corner of the rectilinear enclosure has a gap in the S. side (plan below).

N.M.R., OAP SU 1095/6/327–8.

(2) SETTLEMENT AND ROAD (SU 108959), undated, showing as crop-marks within the S. boundary of the airfield, N.W. of Gully Leaze Copse, lie about 260 ft. above O.D. The settlement covers about 4 acres and is indicated by traces of twelve or more sub-rectangular and D-shaped enclosures partly surrounded by a ditch (plan below). Adjacent on the N.E. are three or four rectangular plots, each 50 ft. wide and some 300 ft. long. The road, upon which the settlement abuts in the S.E., is defined by two pairs of side-ditches, each 40 ft. apart and of slightly differing widths, suggesting reconstruction.

N.M.R., OAP SU 1096/1/325–6; 1095/7–8; 1095/10 (infra-red).

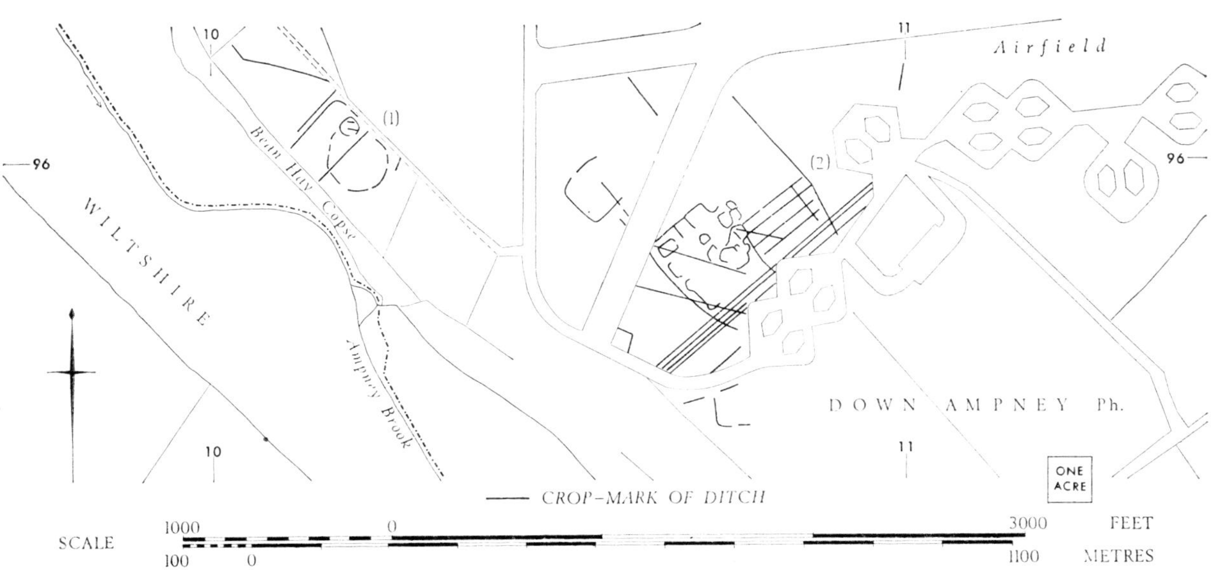

DOWN AMPNEY. (1) Enclosures and Linear Ditches. (2) Settlement and Road.

(3) Rectangular Enclosures (su 10809665), undated, show as crop-marks within the W. boundary of the airfield, E. of Poplar Wood. An enclosure about 200 ft. long and 170 ft. wide with two gaps in the N. side is intersected almost at right angles by ditches apparently belonging to another enclosure.

N.M.R., OAP SU 1096/3/305–7.

(4) Rectilinear Enclosure (su 124965), undated, seen with other ditches as crop-marks, 400 yds. W. of Wetstone Bridge, lies on flat ground at about 250 ft. above O.D. The E. side lies partly beneath the modern road; the N. side is not traceable. There are gaps in the E. and W. sides.

C.U.A.P., OAP BW 7.

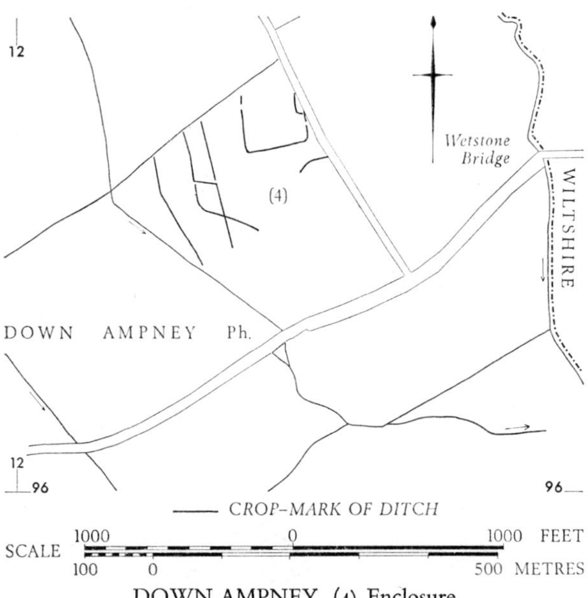

DOWN AMPNEY. (4) Enclosure.

DOYNTON

(28 miles s.s.w. of Cirencester)

Undated 'fortifications and intrenchments' are said to have existed in the 18th century on each bank of the R. Boyd (about st 704732);[1] by the late 19th century the earthworks on the E. bank, in this parish, were untraceable and remain unconfirmed.[2] An unpublished sketch of unknown date and origin purports to show them.[3]

1. Rudder (1779), 406. Bigland (1791), 469.
2. Playne (1876), 231, No. 61. Witts (1883), 18, No. 38.
3. Panoramic view from Tog Hill, in the Middleton Collection, Society of Antiquaries of London.

(1) 'Royal Camp',* (st 723713), possibly a linear dyke and probably of Iron Age date, unexcavated, extends, partly in Cold Ashton, for some 600 yds. along the

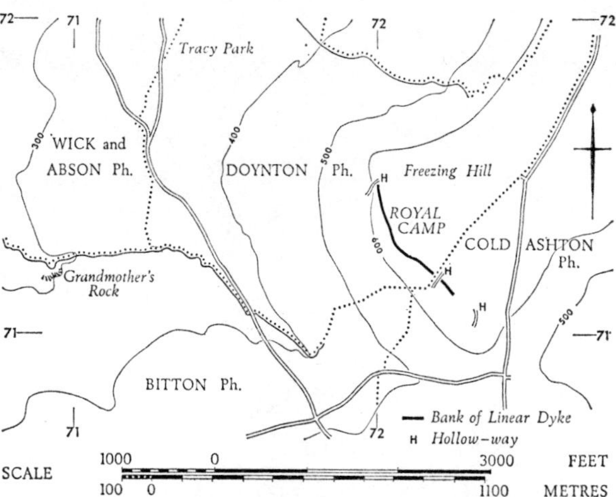

Monuments in DOYNTON and COLD ASHTON.

S.W. side of Freezing Hill on the forward edge of a spur of the Cotswold escarpment, 1½ miles S. of Doynton village. It is called 'eald dic' in Saxon charters (Grundy (1935–6), 93, 205; Sawyer, No. 414).

The bank, 24 ft. wide and 2 ft. high, stands on the edge of the escarpment; the ditch, also 24 ft. wide, lies 9 ft. below it. At either end the dyke terminates at hollow-ways leading down the slope. It is interrupted at the parish boundary, where bank and ditch are cut by a deep hollow-way and are over-ridden by an associated boundary bank. Playne and Witts refer to an internal ditch, and Witts shows a N.E. continuation of the dyke, but neither of these features can now be traced. Plan, p. 46.

Playne (1876), 220, No. 45a. Witts (1883), 22, No. 45, and map.

DRIFFIELD

(3 miles e.s.e. of Cirencester)

A Romano-British stone coffin containing bones, an iron axe-head, a flagon, a dish and other pottery, was found in 1861 beside the Ampney Brook, on or close to the boundary between this parish and Latton, Wiltshire.[1]

1. *PSA*, 2nd ser., III (1864–7), 203. A. H. Church, *Corinium Museum* (1905), 30, 47. On O.S. 2½-in. sheet SU 09, it appears on the boundary (su 08849803).

(1) Roman Villa and Enclosures (sp 082005), now ploughed out, lay ⅔ mile N.E. of the village on level ground W. of the Ampney Brook (Plate 49). The villa is marked by an ill-defined platform about 1½ ft. high, its surface and vicinity strewn with tiles, tesserae and limestone blocks. The platform lies inside a 1-acre enclosure, possibly walled, with an entrance on the east.

Crop-marks indicate that the enclosure was itself set within traces of other enclosures and surrounded by other ditches which covered an area of 12 acres or

* The name used in Isaac Taylor's Map of Gloucestershire, 1777.

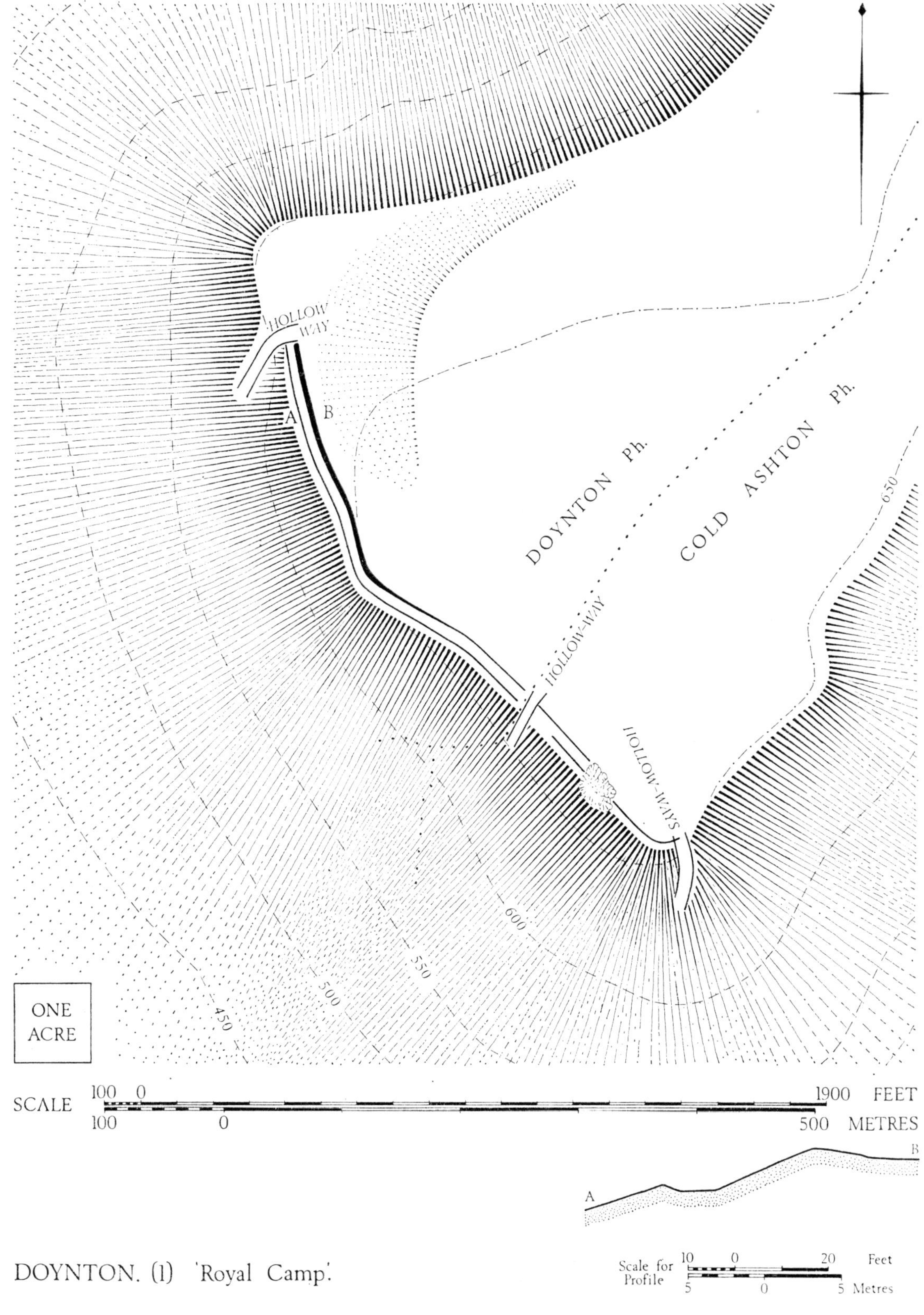

DOYNTON. (1) 'Royal Camp.'

more. Finds on the building site include coarse red, grey and white tesserae, fragments of imbrex, *tegula* and box-tiles, tiles with nail holes, dressed stone and sandstone, and a little pottery. An area of dark soil S.E. of the inner ditch yielded sherds of late 1st-century samian ware, coarse pottery of the 3rd–4th century, and part of a box tile. Finds are in Gloucester City Museum.

C.U.A.P., OAP AOO 30.

(2) Enclosures and Linear Ditches (su 059996), undated, show as faint crop-marks 600 yds. W.S.W. of Westhams Copse and 300 yds. N. of Ermin Street; a ring-ditch adjacent on the N.W. is presumably a barrow.

N.M.R., OAP SU 0599/1.

(3) Enclosures and Linear Ditches (su 072987), undated, show as crop-marks ½ mile S. of the village. Of two conjoined enclosures with entrances on the W., the larger, covering nearly an acre, retains traces of internal ditches semicircular on plan.

N.M.R., OAP SU 0798/1/259–60; 0798/2.

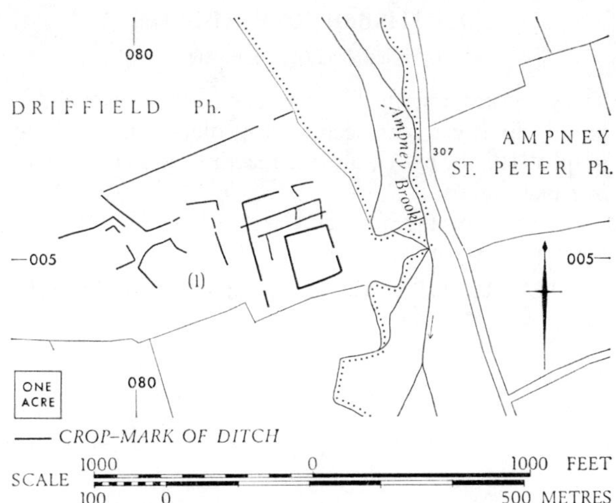

DRIFFIELD. (1) Roman Villa and Enclosures.

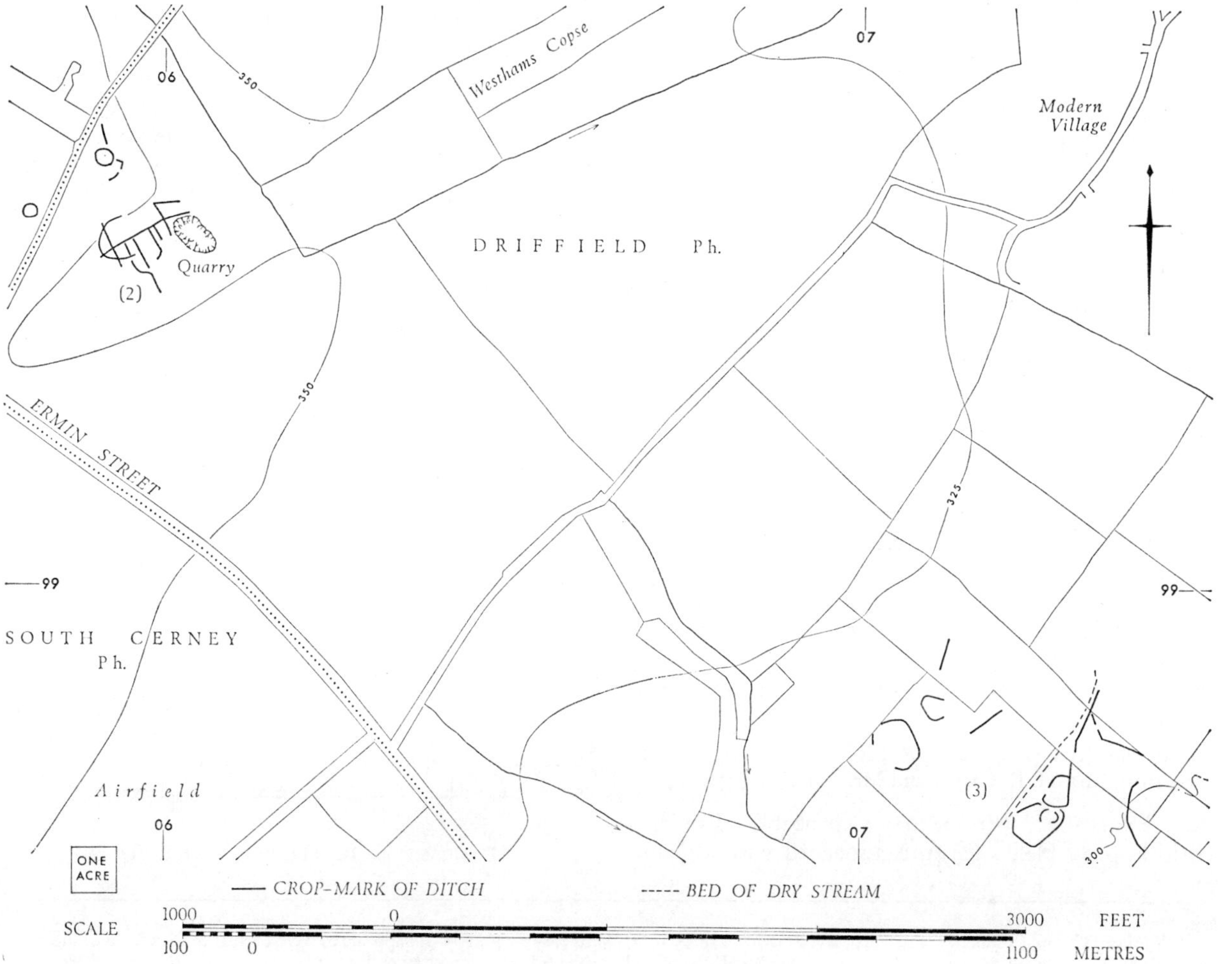

DRIFFIELD. (2), (3) Enclosures and Linear Ditches.

DUNTISBOURNE ABBOTS

(5 miles N.W. of Cirencester)

The two sites described below may have been linked by broad, ditched tracks, seen as crop-marks on air photographs[1] (Plates 62–3), almost meeting at Ermin Street (see plan below).

A native butt-beaker and a cooking-pot, found by workmen, are imprecisely located.[2]

1. N.M.R., OAP SO 9808/1/183–91; 9808/2/180–2; 9808/3/348–9; and 9808/4 (infra-red).
2. *TBGAS*, 83 (1964), 145–6.

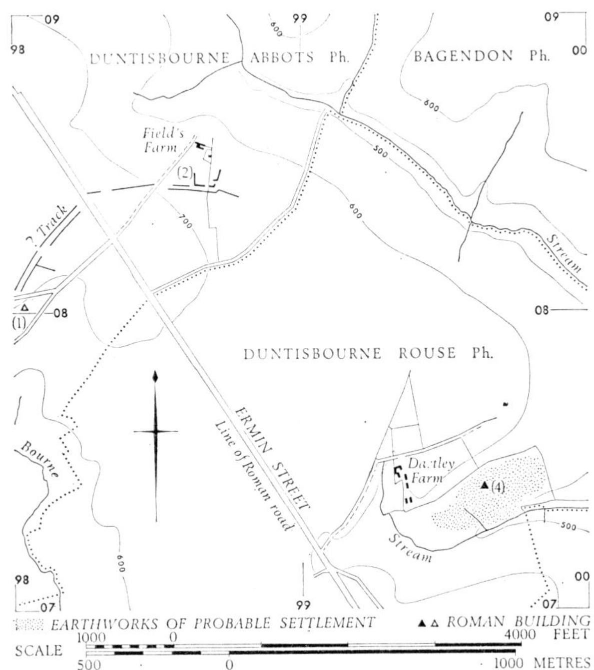

Monuments in DUNTISBOURNE ABBOTS and DUNTISBOURNE ROUSE.

(1) Romano-British Building (about SO 981081), situated on a nearly level shoulder of ground above the stream at Duntisbourne Leer, but no longer to be located precisely, was uncovered in 1924 in a single day's excavation. Walls and concrete floor lay in a field with Romano-British debris, including 3rd and 4th-century coins. A stone some 7 ft. long with a single long groove in it, from the same field, is now at Leer Farm.

TBGAS, XLV (1923), 295. *JRS*, XIV (1924), 231. Information from Mrs. H. R. Carver and Mr. P. D. C. Brown.

(2) Enclosure (SO 987085), probably Romano-British, S. of Field's Farm, is associated with a feature which appears to be a ditched track leading W. to Ermin Street (see above; also Plate 63). Only three sides of the enclosure are recognisable. On S. and E. faint traces of bank and external ditch survive; there was an entrance at the S.E. corner. Within the enclosure the land slopes down towards the N. at an inclination of up to 6°. Small abraded potsherds of Roman date, including samian, have been found on the surface.

DUNTISBOURNE ROUSE

(4 miles N.W. of Cirencester)

A poorly marked Dyke (SP 001075) in the E. of the parish is described *s.v.* Bagendon (1), p. 9.

(1) Pinbury Hill-fort* (SO 958053), univallate, unexcavated, encloses about 25 acres on a spur between the valleys of the R. Frome and a tributary, 2 miles S.W. of the village. The N. and E. sides are defined by a bank with an outer ditch almost levelled by ploughing; the relationship between the ends of the bank and the scarps to S. and W. is not clear. A degraded bank cuts across the S.W. tip of the spur. An entrance about 30 ft. wide occurs in the middle of the E. side.

A few featureless sherds of hand-made pottery from ploughsoil over the bank, and fragments of abraded Romano-British pottery from the interior of the hill-fort, are in Gloucester City Museum.

R.A.F., VAP 3G TUD/UK 102: 5025–6. C.U.A.P., OAP AMK 71, AMZ 61, ATZ 80.

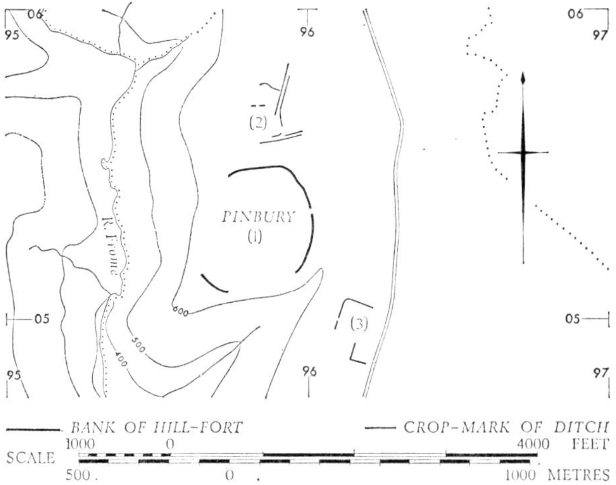

Monuments in DUNTISBOURNE ROUSE.

* 'Pinbury Camp' (Rudder (1779), 424; Playne (1876), 212, No. 22; Witts (1883), 40, No. 81) appears to have been at the S.W. tip of the spur. It was probably defined on the N.E. by the degraded S.W. bank and, on the S.E. at a lower level, by garden earthworks of Pinbury House.

(2) CROP-MARKS (SO 959056), centred 200 yds. N. of the main bank of (1), suggest the conjunction of wide tracks.

(3) CROP-MARKS (SO 962050), centred 300 yds. S.E. of the main bank of (1), appear to represent parts of two rectangular enclosures.

(4) ROMANO-BRITISH SETTLEMENT (SO 997074), Stancombe, S.E. of Dartley Farm (plan, p. 50), marked by some well-preserved platforms and by others greatly disturbed, covers some 10 acres of a sheltered valley-side, facing S.E. (Plate 50). Other traces of settlement or of associated fields extend W. over a further 5 acres. Water gushes profusely at the spring-line, high up the valley-side at the junction of the Great Oolite and the Fuller's Earth. On a natural shelf at this level a rectangular mound contains the footings of a Roman building (a), recently uncovered. A broken block of worked limestone, probably Roman, lies in the nearby spring-head (e). Romano-British building and occupation debris (b) occurs in soil which has slipped down from the brow of the steep slope above the building (a) and is exposed above a terraced farm track. At a lower level, trial cuts (c and d) in the narrow platforms which cover much of the site show that the forward edges of these platforms consist of earthy rubble; small potsherds were found in both cuts, also sandstone (c) and a single small tessera (d). Below the platforms, narrow terraced plots, sloping in cross-section, are an unusual feature. The E. part of the settlement area is greatly disturbed by quarrying. A small platform (f), probably for a building, has much dark matter in its surface soil. The stream in the S., flowing E. to the Briting Brook on the parish boundary with Bagendon about 300 yds. away, appears to be the boundary of the settlement.

The recently excavated building (a) occupies the E. end of a mound, 80 ft. long, 40 ft. wide and up to 6 ft. high. In the W. part of the excavated area (12 ft. by 10 ft.) is the angle of a room with walls of coarse Oolite masonry 2 ft. thick. The angle contains a flue, infilled and covered by a pavement of large earthenware tesserae (Plate 51). The remains of a later wall are built directly on the pavement. On the E., a wall of fine coursed Oolite abuts the external angle of the room, and in the space so defined is a stone-floored hearth. The building has foundations of clay and limestone rubble. Other building materials in the mound include *pila* tiles, box-tiles and sandstone 'slates'. Dating evidence as yet is sparse; a *minimus* was found above the tessellated floor.

Information from the excavators, Mr. M. K. Baker and Mr. J. Partridge.

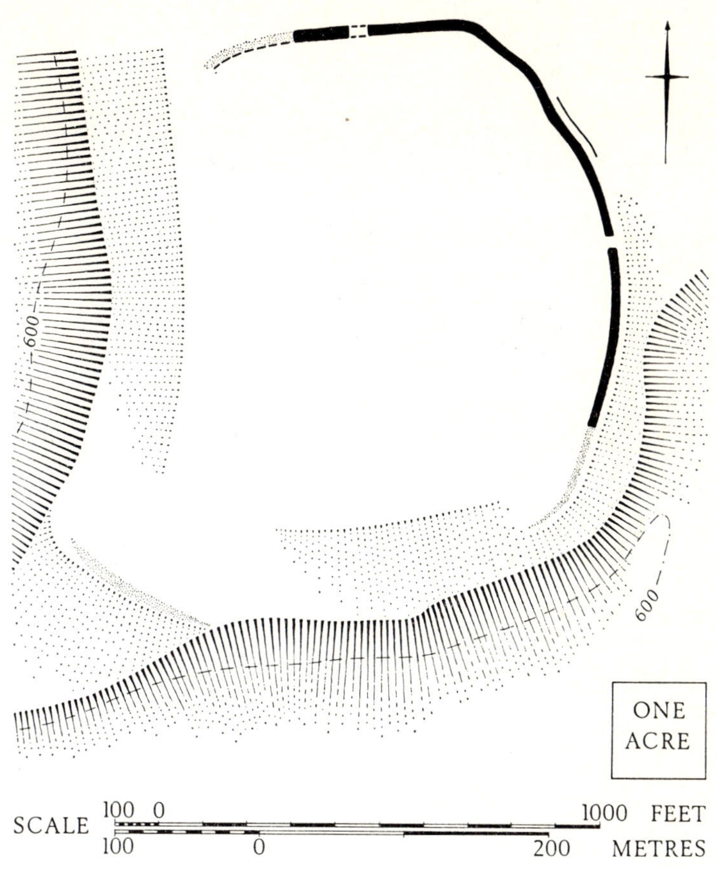

DUNTISBOURNE ROUSE. (1) Pinbury Hill-fort.

DURSLEY

(17 miles W. of Cirencester)

Romano-British pottery collected from a new playing field at Kingshill (ST 750993)[1] and a coin of Domitian are in Gloucester City Museum.

1. *Archaeol. Review*, 4 (1969), 39.

(1) ROMAN BUILDING (ST 761984), Chestals Farm, Woodmancote, was revealed when drains were cut in 1971. Walls and a concrete floor 9 in. thick were exposed. Finds included pottery, an imbrex, and sandstone tiles.

Information from Captain H. S. Gracie, R.N.

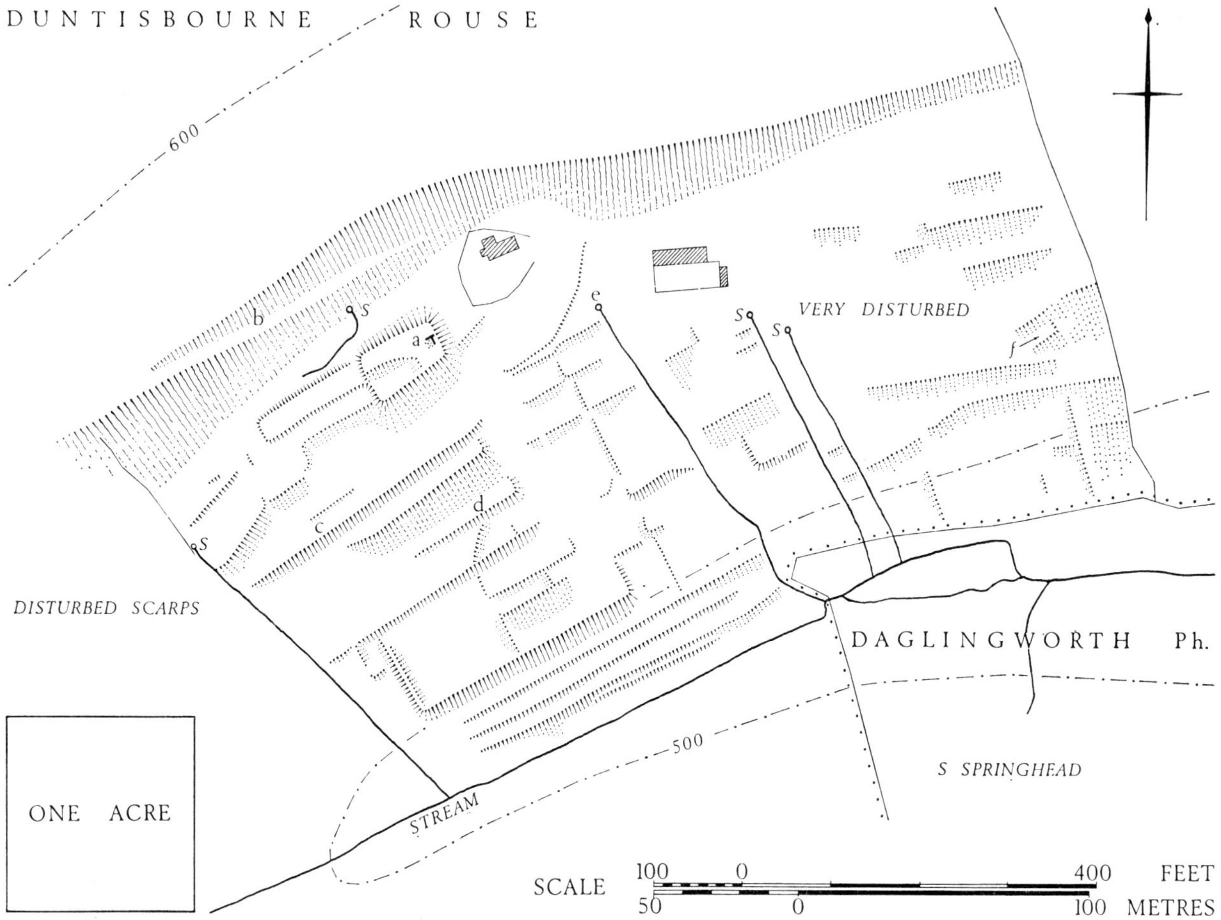

DUNTISBOURNE ROUSE
600
VERY DISTURBED
DISTURBED SCARPS
DAGLINGWORTH Ph.
S SPRINGHEAD
500
STREAM
ONE ACRE
SCALE 100 0 400 FEET
50 0 100 METRES

DUNTISBOURNE ROUSE. (4) Romano-British Settlement, Stancombe.

HINTON HILL
Hinton Village
R. Boyd
DYRHAM AND HINTON Ph.
DOYNTON Ph.
Dyrham Village
St. Peter's Ch.
Stream
BANK OF HILL-FORT
SCARP EDGE
CROP-MARK OF DITCH
SCALE 1000 0 11000 FEET
100 0 3500 METRES

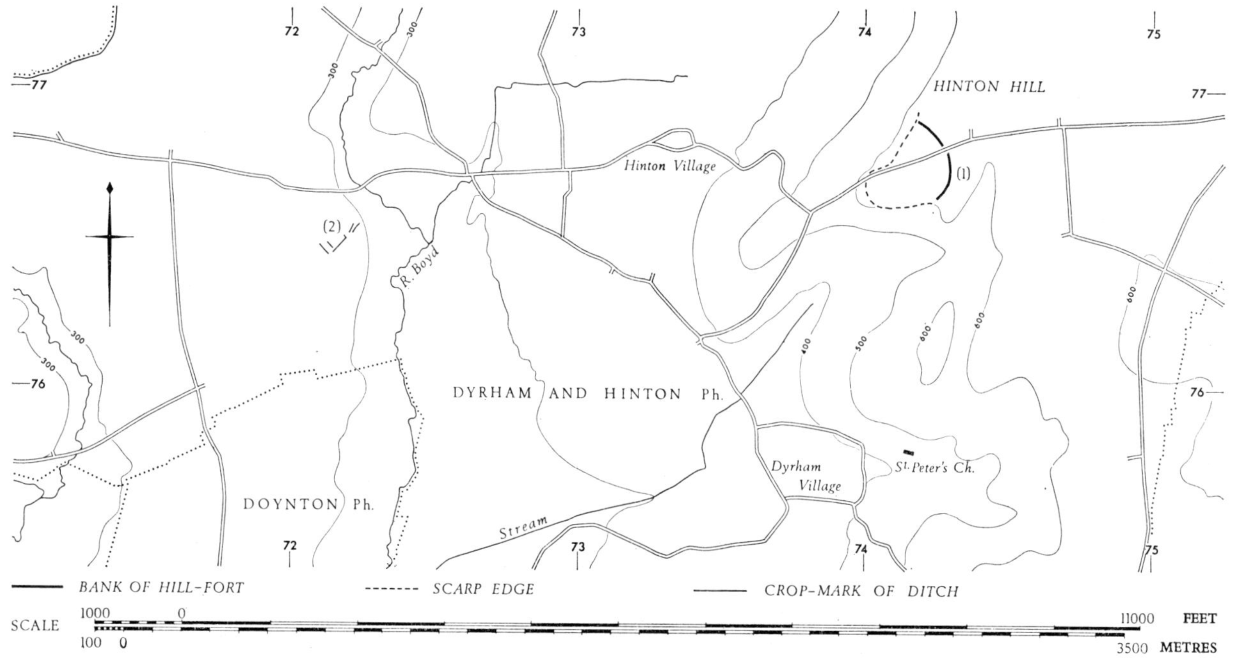

Monuments in DYRHAM AND HINTON.

DYRHAM AND HINTON

(25 miles S.W. of Cirencester)

(1) HILL-FORT (ST 741767), on Hinton Hill,* univallate, unexcavated, cuts off about 12 acres of a spur of the Cotswold escarpment, ½ mile E. of Hinton village.

The E. side is defined by a rampart with an outer ditch, the W. and S. by scarps. The unploughed S. half of the rampart, about 35 ft. wide, rises 8 ft. above the interior and 13 ft. above the surface of the ditch, which is 20 ft. wide. The entrance, occupied by a modern road, was in the centre of the E. side.

Lloyd Baker (1821), 165, No. 10. Playne (1876), 219, No. 42. Witts (1883), 19, No. 40.

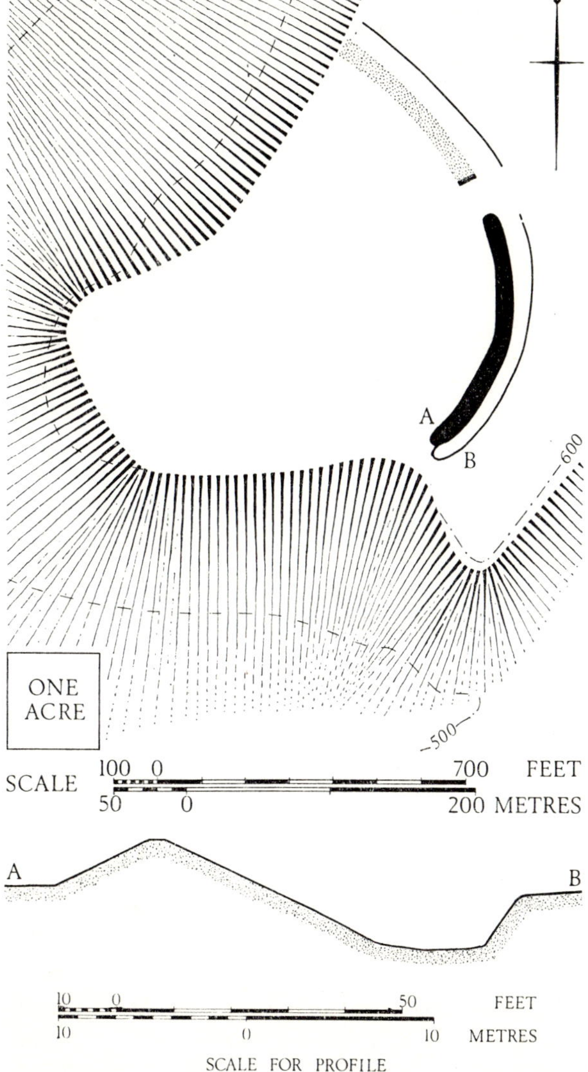

DYRHAM AND HINTON. (1) Hill-fort. Plan and profile.

(2) PROBABLE SETTLEMENT (ST 722765), indicated by crop-marks including rectilinear arrangements, and by a scatter of Romano-British occupation debris over them, lies on gently sloping ground about 300 ft. above O.D. and 200 yds. W. of the R. Boyd (Plate 64).

C.U.A.P., OAP ABI 31–4.

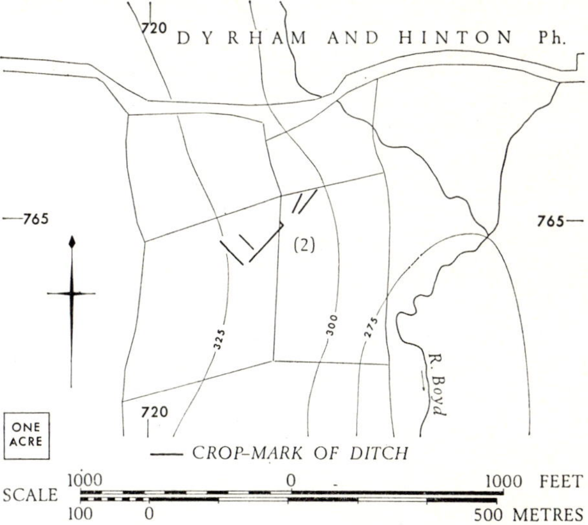

DYRHAM AND HINTON. (2) Probable Settlement.

(3) ROMANO-BRITISH BURIALS (about ST 742742), two, in stone coffins, one accompanied by potsherds, were found in a field on Sands Farm in 1932, while it was being ploughed.

UBSS, 4 (1933), 151–2. *TBGAS*, 61 (1939), 160–1.

EASTLEACH

(10 miles E. of Cirencester)

(1) 'CELTIC' FIELDS (SP 190070), disturbed by later ploughing and tracks, are visible over some 10 acres of pasture on the limestone spur W. of Sheepbridge Copse (Plate 43). The terrace-way of the Roman road (2) probably crosses over the former S. edge of this group. There are traces of other 'Celtic' fields to N. and S.

Lynchets are up to 3 ft. high on slopes of 13° at most. There are no complete fields, but individual sides are about 50 yds. long. There was probably at least one alteration from the original pattern during the 'Celtic' phase, when part of the S. boundary of field 'a' was ploughed over. Subsequent prolonged ploughing has destroyed the remains which formerly extended down to the Roman road. It is possible that a protuberance at 'y', 50 yds. S.W. of Sheepbridge Copse, represents the corner of a 'Celtic' field cut by the road, and that another field angle was cut 160 yds. further S.W.

* An early name was *Burrill* (Camden, *Britannia* (ed. Gough, 1789), I, 275), or *Burrell's Camp* (Grundy (1935–6)), 124; 19th-century writers call it *Dyrham Camp*.

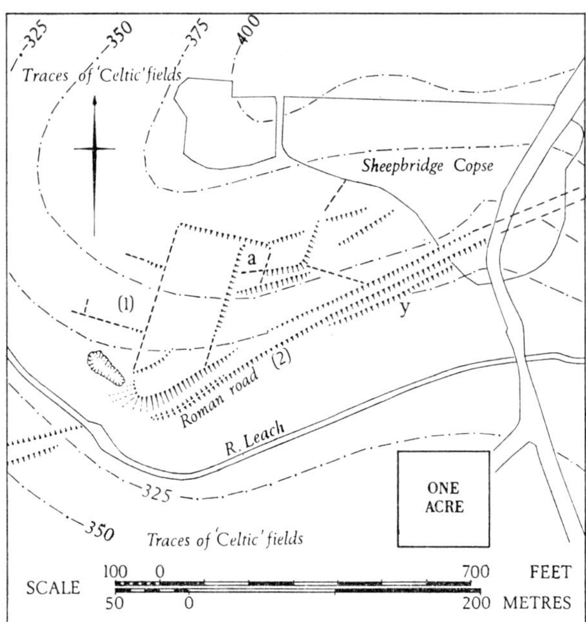

EASTLEACH. (1) 'Celtic' Fields. (2) Roman Road.

Other traces of lynchets, probably 'Celtic', occur as follows: (i) immediately S. of Hatherop Piece at SP 18750716, (ii) W. of Sidelands Grove SP 181086, (iii) S. of the R. Leach, between the river and the modern road, about SP 18870677 and SP 191068. At the last-named point, scarps are cut by a hollow-way which is older than the modern road.

R.A.F., VAP 106G/UK 1721: 4261–2. N.M.R., OAP SP 1806/1/438–55.

(2) Roman Road, Akeman Street (SP 18870687 to SP 19300702), (see plan above) is marked by a disturbed bank, up to 3 ft. high with a flat top 27 ft. across, immediately W. of the point of crossing of the R. Leach, here only a stream. The bank rises to a flat terrace-way and continues E.N.E. for 250 yds. to Sheepbridge Copse, where the remains are destroyed. A terrace-way, perhaps a continuation, emerges from Sheepbridge Copse 30 yds. further E., slightly S. of the former alignment, climbs E. for 30 yds., and then N.E. as if to rejoin the alignment. Profiles across the terrace-way W. and E. of Sheepbridge Copse indicate a road surface generally about 14 ft. wide, but occasionally a little wider or narrower (cf. I. D. Margary, *Roman Roads in Britain*, I (1957), Pl. X, lower). The slope of the road

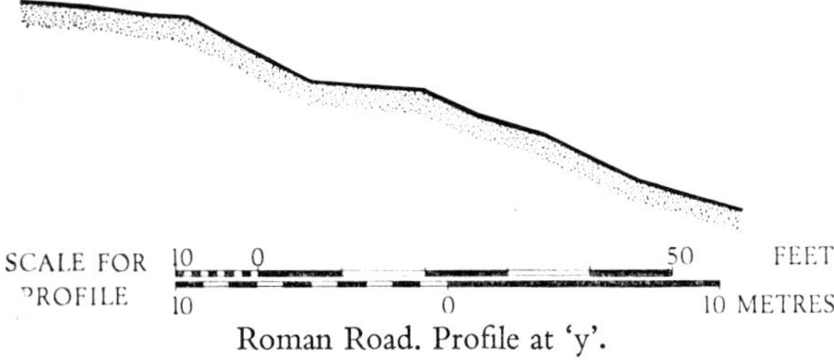

Roman Road. Profile at 'y'.

rising E. from the R. Leach, and that of the terrace-way E. of Sheepbridge Copse, does not exceed 9°.

Limestone blocks, some of them more than 1 ft. across, are exposed on both sides of the R. Leach. There is no sign of a bridge abutment. The surface has been partly hollowed by later traffic where the road rises from the river, and the further line of this traffic is marked by a hollow-way branching N.E. from the Roman road and crossing the 'Celtic' fields.

(3) 'Celtic' Fields (SP 188087), covering some 40 acres of Oolite, have been almost completely destroyed; they lay in the extreme N.W. of the parish, W. of No Man's Land Plantation, where ground falling gently S.W. is penetrated by shallow gullies. For plan, see Aldsworth (1). The pattern seen on air photographs shows that they extended in all directions beyond the area which could be plotted, possibly to link with those in Aldsworth. Unusually dense limestone rubble, visible on the modern arable ground, strongly supports other indications that the 'Celtic' fields were walled. Earthworks, probably a track bounded by spread walls, spanning more than 40 ft., ran N.N.E. through SP 18510866 in an alignment similar to that of a comparable feature in Aldsworth, 765 yds. to the east. The fields which are possibly complete have areas of 1 and 1½ acres. A lynchet joined a round barrow, now almost destroyed, at SP 18800858. Three other newly discovered round barrows, the biggest 50 ft. across and 3 ft. high, survive in a small copse just S. of this (SP 188085), where there are no signs of 'Celtic' fields.

R.A.F., VAP 106G/UK 1721: 6261–2; CPE/UK 2098: 4156–7. N.M.R., OAP SP 1709/4/314; SP 1708/1/434–7; SP 1808/1/372.

(4) Soil-marks (SP 194092–195089), N.E. of No Man's Land Plantation, suggest linked rectangular enclosures, possibly fields, on a different alignment from those of (3). No remains survive on the heavily ploughed flat ridge-top.

C.U.A.P., OAP AYG 67.

EBRINGTON

(26 miles N.N.E. of Cirencester)

According to O.S. records, Roman coins were found in 1850 at SP 18794007, where now a garden and buildings on the S. edge of a natural terrace overlook the Romano-British site (1), 200 yds. to the S.E.

(1) Roman Villa (SP 19013990), described by the excavator as a 'bathing establishment', lies between The Grove and an old mill-pond on a shelf of ground which slopes S.E.; it was partly excavated in 1958–9. An exceptionally copious spring just to the N. occurs at the foot of a steeper slope. The rooms were sumptuously appointed and very little domestic rubbish was found.

Monuments in EBRINGTON.

Room 1, with a tessellated floor of white Oolite and Blue Lias (Plate 8), lay next to a heated room (2), where the pavement had been almost entirely destroyed. The furnace of the heated room received its air supply through an arched vent with a tufa-block ceiling, running under corridors 3 and 4. A drain built of very large dressed stones led out of the cold plunge bath (p) and through room 'e' which is thought to have been a latrine.

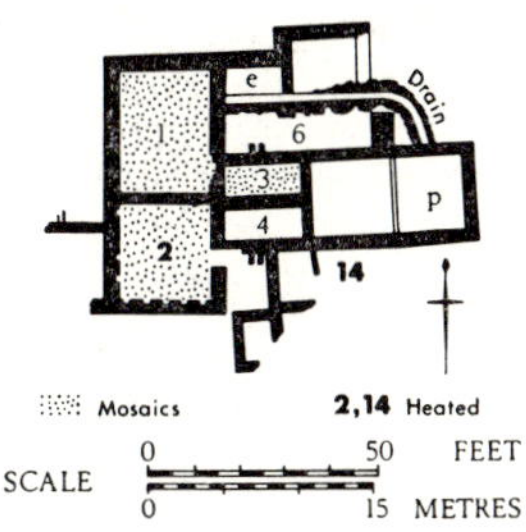

Local stone was generally used, but steps into the plunge bath were faced with imported white marble. Painted plaster from the bath area included a design with fishes; a doorway soffit had foliage pattern. *Pilae* under room 2 included a few constructed of upright box tiles packed with mortar. Some of the roof tiles were inscribed TCM. Cotswold stone tiles were also found.

There were remarkably few small finds. Among the little pottery was a sherd of 2nd-century samian ware and one rosette-stamped sherd.

JRS, XLIX (1959), 127; LI (1961), 186. *PCNFC*, XXXVI (1971–2), 87–93.

EDGEWORTH

(5 miles N.W. of Cirencester)

(1) CROSS-RIDGE DYKE (SO 93130639), on Juniper Hill, of Iron-Age type, excavated, lies across the neck of a sloping spur on the E. side of a valley drained by a tributary of the R. Frome, a mile N.W. of the village.

The bank, 230 ft. long and generally about 35 ft. wide and 7 ft. high, stops short of the scarp edges to N. and S. It runs straight, except for a slight change in direction away from the edge, about 30 ft. from the N.

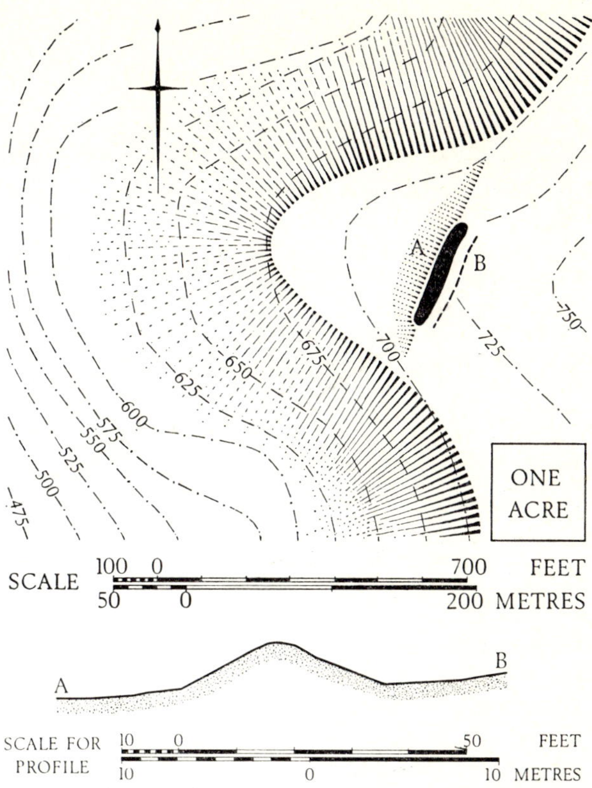

EDGEWORTH. (1) Cross-ridge Dyke. Plan and profile.

end. From this point and for the last 50 ft. on the S. it gradually diminishes in height and width.

A section cut by Mrs. E. M. Clifford showed the levelled ditch on the E. to be 5 ft. deep and about 25 ft. wide. The bank, mainly of rubble, was revetted on this side by a dry-stone wall to a height of 3 ft. No evidence of date was recovered.

Bagendon, 158–9, fig. 28. Interpreted as a long barrow: Witts (1883), No. 13; Crawford, *Long Barrows of the Cotswolds* (1925), 107, No. 33. Interpreted as a hill-fort: O.S., *Map of Southern Britain in the Iron Age* (1962).

ELKSTONE

(7 miles N.W. of Cirencester)

The remains of five Roman columns, probably from Stockwood Roman villa, COLESBOURNE (2), are in the garden of Combend Manor. A sixth column, of anomalous form with a very small rectangular capital, perhaps recut, is of uncertain attribution (Plate 27).

(1) PROBABLE ROMANO-BRITISH SETTLEMENT (SO 984127), Slutswell, extends over about 2 acres in arable on the N. shoulder of a Great Oolite ridge; a spring flows down a narrow re-entrant gully immediately to the N.W. Within 50 ft. of the N. side of the modern road there are at least three concentrations of building debris, mostly Oolite, but including sandstone, Roman

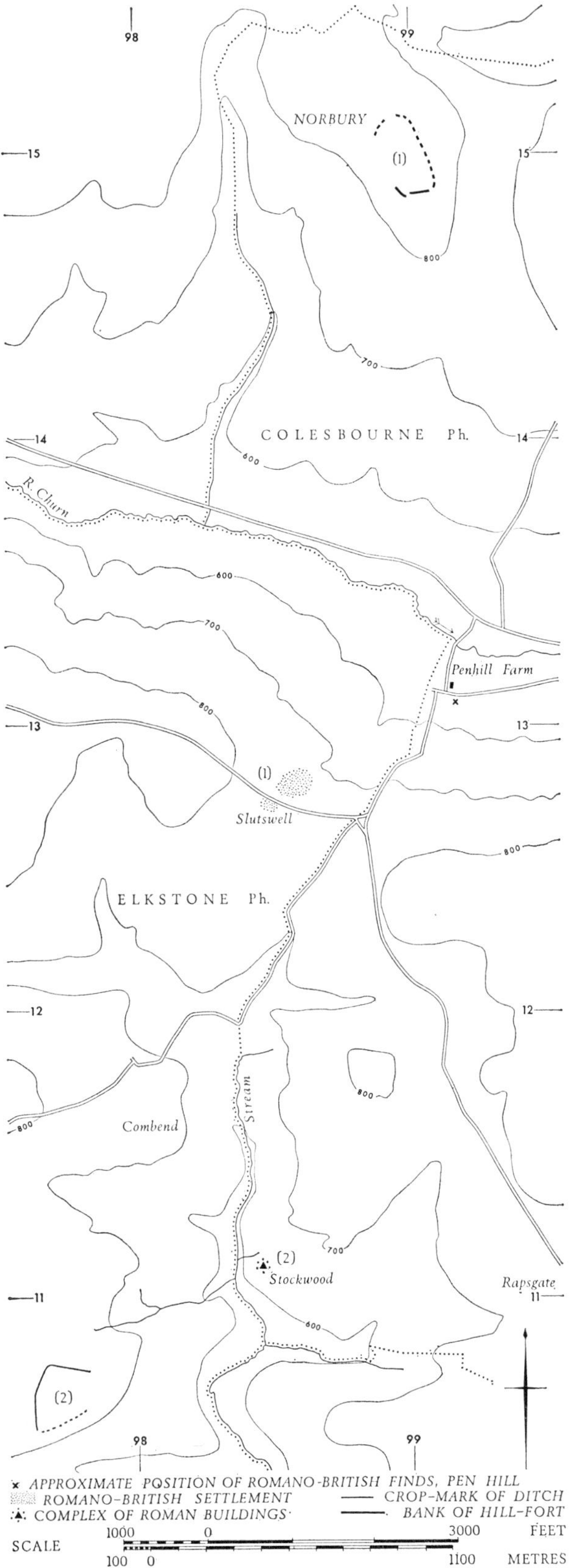

Monuments in ELKSTONE and COLESBOURNE.

tiles and a few Romano-British potsherds. Further N., air photographs indicate two or more building sites. One of them is about 50 ft. by 30 ft. and has an approach track some 25 ft. wide; building debris, including tile, is scattered over much of this area. Mediaeval pottery and one or two Romano-British sherds have been found.

Romano-British finds probably from the arable field S. of the road include a coin of Carausius, 5 clay 'kiln-supports', a stone grinder and a polisher; all these are in Gloucester City Museum.

R.A.F., VAP CPE/UK 1846: 1086.

(2) ENCLOSURE (SO 977106), undated, S. of Watercombe Farm, shows as a crop-mark straddling the E. end of a spur and covering at least 5 acres (Plate 59). The N. side is continued E. for about 150 ft. by a low scarp in rough pasture. The ground drops sharply from just outside the modern field boundary on the S.

N.M.R., OAP SO 9710/1/366.

EVENLODE

No Iron Age or Romano-British monument is known in this parish.

FAIRFORD

(8 miles E. of Cirencester)

An Iron Age terret has been recognised among finds from the area of a Saxon cemetery W. of the village.[1]

Fragments of five or six Iron Age pots were recovered in 1964 from a shallow ditch exposed in a gravel-pit (SP 171006); shoulder fragments exhibit fingertip impressions; closely spaced incised lines appear on other sherds.[2] Finds reported from an adjacent gravel-pit (SP 173006) include another Iron Age pot, much coarse Romano-British pottery, an inscribed sandstone weight[3] and a cross-bow brooch.[4]

Irregular enclosures and ditches seen in 1942, S.W. of the place where the former railway track ended,[5] cannot now be located.

1. I. M. Stead, *The La Tène Cultures of Eastern Yorkshire* (1965), 9. W. M. Wylie, *Fairford Graves* (1852), 15, Pl. V, 7.
2. Pottery in Gloucester City Museum.
3. These in Ashmolean Museum. *JRS*, XXXV (1945), 91 (weight).
4. In Gloucester City Museum.
5. *Oxon*, VIII–IX (1943–4), 95, No. 3.

(1) TRACK (SP 133003), notably wide, undated, N.W. of Lady Lamb's Copse, shows as crop-marks on level ground in the plain. There are indications of settlement to the N.E., and also at 'A' to the S.W., across the county boundary with Wiltshire.

N.M.R., OAP SP 1300/1/404–7.

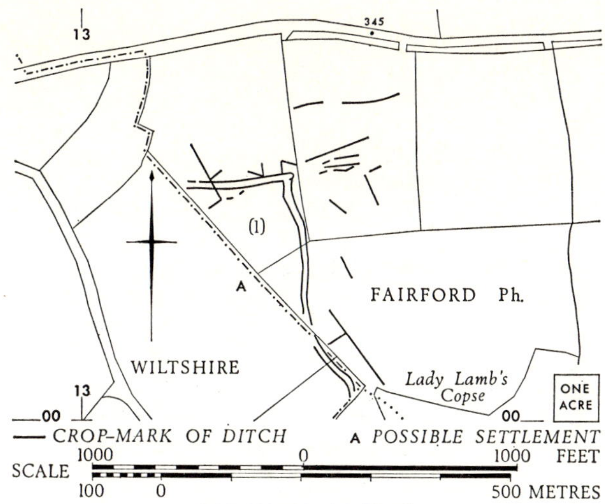

FAIRFORD. (1) Track.

(2) Enclosures and Linear Ditches (SP 154030), undated, N.E. of Obelisk Park, are revealed by crop-marks covering about 15 acres of level ground. Feature 'a', likely to be an enclosure of about 3 acres (Plate 66), has a ditch probably of defensive dimensions. Other enclosures are at 'b' and 'c'.

C.U.A.P., OAP ASM 61.

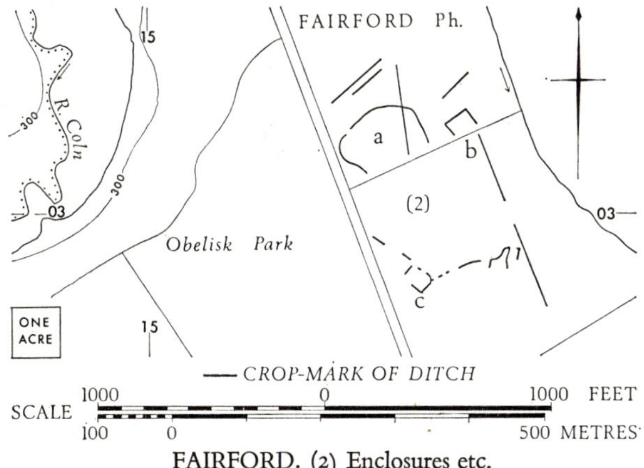

FAIRFORD. (2) Enclosures etc.

(3) Double-ditched Enclosure (SP 168004), undated, is partly disclosed by crop-marks on gravel N. of the R. Coln (Plate 58). The area enclosed is about ⅓ acre (map opposite).

C.U.A.P., OAP AM 32.

(4–6) Settlements, Enclosures and Tracks (SU 175999, 183998, 191996), N. of the R. Coln, undated, show as crop-marks extending over some 150 acres on gravel in the S.E. of the parish (map opposite). Monument (4) is illustrated on Plate 66; monument (6), Plate 61, is continuous with Lechlade (8).

C.U.A.P., VAP RC 8–M 272–5; OAP CD 051; AXP 61; AYI 6, 13.
Oxon, VIII–IX (1943–4), 95, No. 4.

FARMINGTON

(11 miles N.E. of Cirencester)

For general map, see p. 88, *s.v.* Northleach with Eastington. Monument (1) is in many respects similar to Barnsley (1).

(1) Roman Villa (SP 13231585), Clearcupboard, in land formerly arable, was excavated by Mr. P. E. Gascoigne in 1964–7. The site occupies a small spur top of Inferior Oolite projecting N. from the valley side, 150 ft. below Norbury Hill-fort (Northleach (1)), in which there is a Romano-British settlement (Northleach (2)). Abundant water flowing from the junction of Great Oolite and Fuller's Earth immediately below the hill-fort was apparently channelled towards Clearcupboard. Plan, p. 56.

The basic structure, a rectangle 92 ft. by 31½ ft., was divided into two areas numbered 1 and 2 on the plan. Area 2, with a bath-house later inserted in one corner and with numerous hearths, fire pits and various kinds of floor, may have been only partly roofed. To it was added a corridor with symmetrical end rooms, one of them heated. The heated room (6) was subsequently rebuilt and the W. end of the corridor was obliquely partitioned. Other rooms were added; that at E. (4) contained a corn-drying oven and a raised floor of pitched stones; the other two added rooms (5 and 10) yielded no significant finds. The building appears to have evolved during the first three quarters of the 4th century.

The masonry in the two earlier phases of construction was generally of high quality, with the wall-cores of mortar-bound rubble, but the E. wall of room 1 was inferior and butt-jointed at the ends. The added rooms (4, 5 and 10) had masonry of poorer quality. The roof of the bath-house had tufa voussoirs and some walls had painted plaster. There was some reused moulded stone. Roof and ridging tiles were of local Oolite. In room 1 the wall plaster was coved at its junction with the *opus signinum* floor. Room 7 had painted plaster walls and a concrete floor. The plunge bath (P) had a floor of patterned red tiles. Building rubble found 55 yds. S.E. of the villa included a stone column from a hypocaust.

Finds include 23 coins ranging from 320 to 350, a pottery scatter including 2nd-century samian ware, a box flue tile stamped VLA, scraps of glass, the bolt of a barrel padlock and a spindle whorl. There were also probable cressets of stone, many large nails and a few horse-shoe nails. Bones included some of pig, sheep and cow together with antlers of red deer and a worked antler tine.

TBGAS, 88 (1969), 34–67; 90 (1971), 224.

(2) Romano-British Settlement (SP 129166), Chestles, now ploughed out, was discovered in 1970 by Mr. P. E. Gascoigne who kindly supplied information; it covered

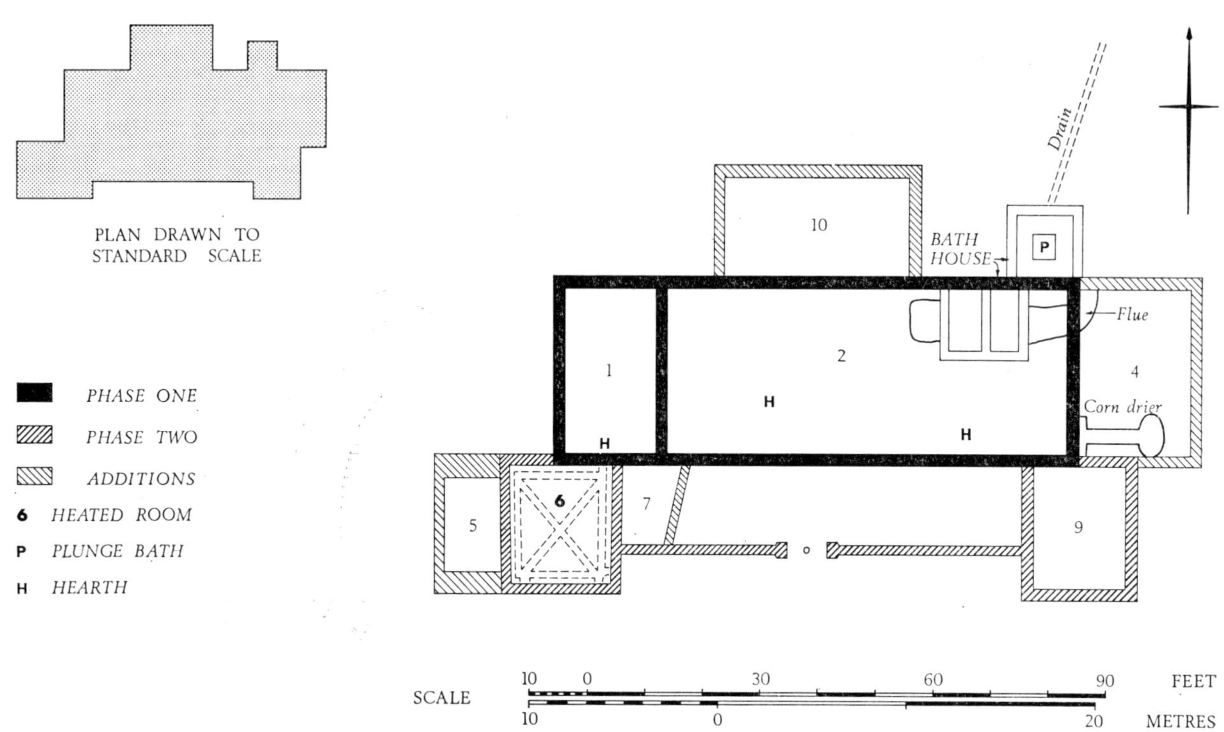

FARMINGTON. (1) Roman Villa, Clearcupboard.

at least 2¾ acres. The name Chestles is on the Enclosure Map of 1707. Finds include 2nd-century samian and black burnished wares, 3rd to 4th-century pottery, and building stone.

(3) Rectangular Enclosure (sp 134167), undated, shows as a crop-mark on gently sloping ground. The ditch defines an area about 160 ft. square with an entrance in the centre of the S. side.

N.M.R., OAP (Baker) SP 1316/1–5; OAP 1316/6/368–9. *TBGAS*, 82 (1963), 215 (where it is called 'a small building').

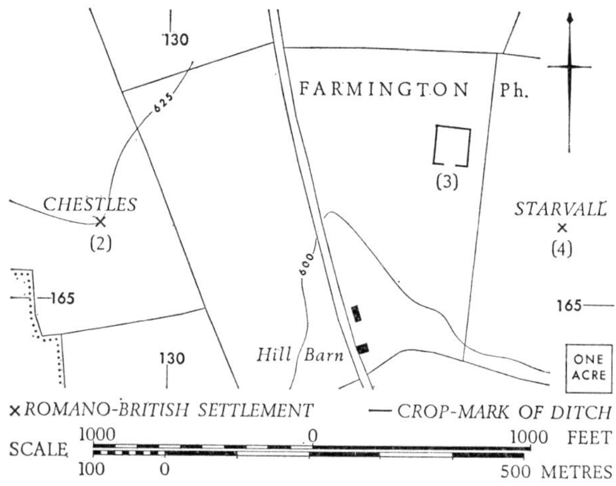

FARMINGTON. (3) Enclosure. (2), (4) Romano-British Settlements.

(4) Romano-British Settlement (sp 13551660), Starvall, 200 yds. S.E. of (3), is indicated by pottery and building stone scattered in ploughsoil around a clump of trees. Pottery collected by Mr. P. E. Gascoigne includes a shell-gritted fragment in Iron Age tradition, a flagon-neck perhaps of the 2nd century, and Oxfordshire mortaria and colour-coated wares of the late 3rd–4th century.

TBGAS, 82 (1963), 215.

FROCESTER

(14 miles w. of Cirencester)

There are lynchets up to 4 ft. high within some 5 acres on a N.-facing slope of Lias, about 1 mile S.S.E. of monument (1), (so 796018). Landslip and other disturbance make it impossible to see a clear pattern, but details suggest that it was an area containing 'Celtic' fields.

Romano-British pottery was noted in disturbed material during the excavation of Nympsfield long barrow (so 79390132).[1]

A length of metalling, thought to represent a Roman road, has been observed in a trench dug alongside the modern road which passes N. of the Frocester Court villa (2).[2]

1. *PPS*, IV (1938), 192.
2. Information from Mr. E. G. Price and Capt. H. S. Gracie, R.N.

(1) ROMAN VILLA (SO 771033), by St. Peter's Church (demolished), on a slight gravel ridge between two streams, was shown by excavation S. of the church to lie partly over ditches which had been back-filled with debris including 2nd and 3rd-century pottery, wall-plaster, tiles, window-glass and unused tesserae. Walls were of local Oolite. Roman remains have been found under the church and outside the churchyard on the N.

Finds include hexagonal roofing tiles, mostly of Old Red Sandstone, some having iron nails in position, a tile stamped ARVERI and fragments of mosaic floors.

TBGAS, 82 (1963), 148–67.

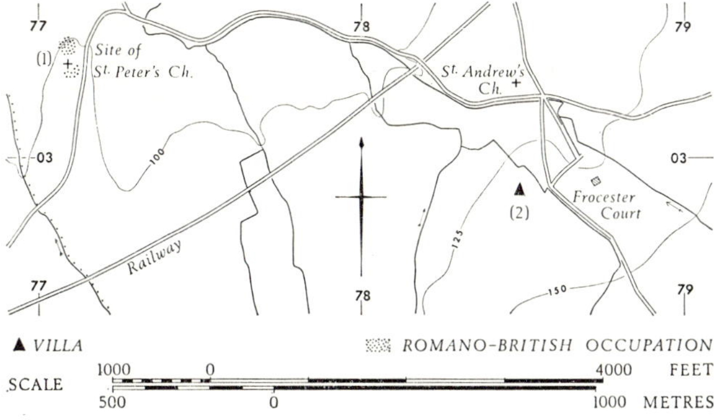

Monuments in FROCESTER.

(2) ROMAN VILLA (SO 785029), Frocester Court, is sited about ½ mile W. of the Cotswold escarpment, on level ground where calcareous gravel overlies Lias Clay (plan, p. 58). Excavations by Capt. H. S. Gracie, R.N., begun in 1961 and still in progress, show that the villa (building A) was occupied from late in the 3rd century until perhaps late in the 5th century; finds on the surface and from the excavations indicate that other Roman buildings in the immediate vicinity had been occupied from the 1st century. A double ditch, not yet completely traced, defines the S.W. and N.W. sides of a probable enclosure surrounding the villa; it cuts through a filled-in ditch which almost certainly is related to earlier buildings on the S.E. The field in which the remains are sited is called Big Stanborough. Stone robbing probably began early, became systematic in the 13th century and was followed by mediaeval and later ploughing, the furrows causing damage and the ridges giving protection. Deeper modern ploughing has destroyed the ridges and exposed the Roman remains afresh.

The excavations have indicated the sequence of construction and have disclosed details of building method. The first structure, erected *c.* 275, comprised a range with a large central area (2), a S.W. room (1) with a forge, a N.E. room (4) with an *opus signinum* floor, and a passage separating 2 from 4. Area 2 was partitioned into three parts with floors of gravel, concrete and earth; ovens and a soakaway in the S.W. part suggest its use as a kitchen. Massive foundations 8½ ft. deep suggest that there was an upper storey.

In 'period II', very soon after 275, a front corridor and wing rooms (5–7) and a row of back rooms (8–11) were added to the first structure; room 5 contained a corn-drier. In *c.* 340 the corn-drier was converted into an oven, a channelled hypocaust and probably a mosaic floor were inserted in room 7, and a mosaic of the Corinian School (Plate 8) replaced an earlier floor, probably of paving stones, in corridor 6; a small compartment (20) was added outside room 7. At this time a lean-to shed, subsequently succeeded by room 12, stood against the N.E. end of the house. Fuller's Earth in long soakaways close to the house wall suggested that cloth was processed here.

Room 12 and the bath suite N.W. of it were built *c.* 360, in 'period III'. The hot-room floor (13) was supported on *pilae*, later altered to channels, and tesserae were found here in quantity to suggest a mosaic floor. The *frigidarium* (17) had a paved plunge bath with plastered sides, and a latrine.

A walled courtyard S.E. of the villa contains traces of a formal garden. A cambered approach road 17 ft. wide, ultimately kerbed to 13 ft., ended in a cobbled 'turning space' outside the corridor (6).

In the last period crude repairs were carried out. Grass-tempered pottery, possibly of the late 5th century, came from the latest occupation levels. Finally the main block was burned down, but not the bath-suite. A shallow grave in an area outside room 16, possibly a garden, contained a male skeleton, probably of the latest period.

Structural details include: stone packed in 2 ft. strips into the surface immediately outside the walls; an unexplained honeycomb of narrow empty holes (4½ ft. deep) piercing the hard gravel of hypocaust floors; a lime-slaking pit with pot-boilers; a clay-lined pit 10 ft. deep linked to a water channel; a 4th-century timber-lined pit possibly associated with tanning; and the working sites of tilers, metal-workers and plasterers. Structural finds include potsherds used to repair a floor in area 2; some Old Red Sandstone roof tiles trimmed for eaves and ridges; a tile stamped (T)PLF, *tegula* stamped ARVERI and 'brick' stamped probably RPG; also quarter-round plaster mouldings edging the floor of room 4, coloured wall-plaster (including angled pieces from splays, pieces with protuberances and some pieces backed by wattle impressions), green window glass, and fragments of an oak door (in room 2). An iron-bound chest (B), sunk in the corner of room 11 where twenty-three coins were associated with the lowest floor, suggests that the room was an office before the structural alterations of phase III (cf. CHEDWORTH (1), room 2). Fragments of a probable wall mosaic were found in robber trenches around room 4.

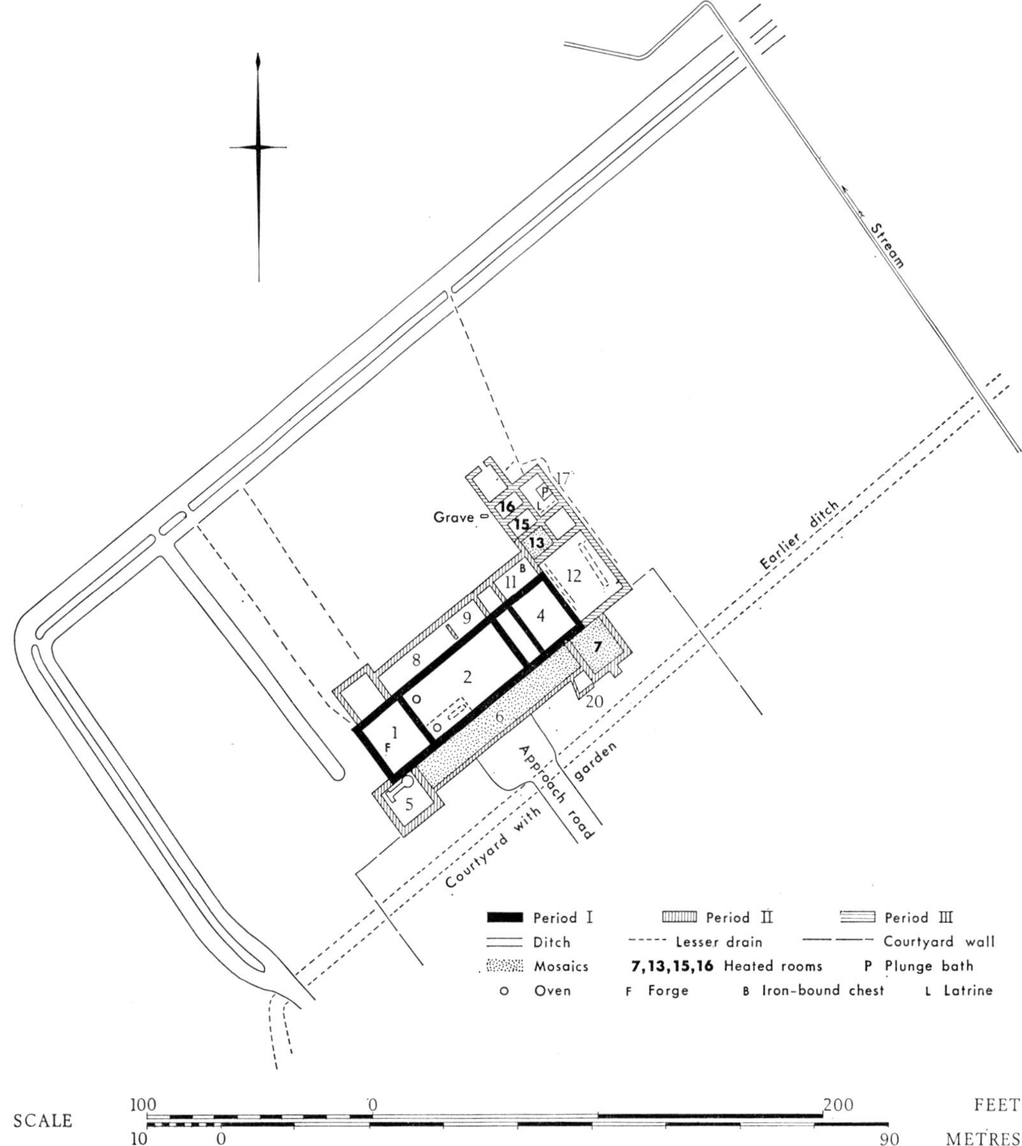

FROCESTER. (2) Roman Villa, Frocester Court.

Small finds antecedent to building A include an Aucissa brooch and a black samian jar with appliqué decoration. Finds associated with the building include some 365 coins, among them a hoard of barbarous radiate *minimi*, two silver coins of Constantius II and coins as late as Arcadius; the grass-tempered pottery indicates occupation continuing for perhaps a hundred years after this date. Many bronze bracelets were found, but very few bow brooches. Two bronze belt tags with Germanic analogies were also found. Other finds include cosmetic articles, a sheep bell, a clasp knife, a steelyard rod and miscellaneous iron pieces. Glass included pieces of *millefiori* and of a Rhineland goblet. There were 11 shale bracelets, a jet plaque, a moulded stone stand and a quern stone (room 5). Charred wheat and barley came from the latest period. Analysis of charcoal showed the presence of oak, ash, poplar, hawthorn, box and hazel. There was much scattered coal. Animal bones included ox, sheep, pig, goat, horse, dog, cat, hen, goose and duck. Shellfish included oysters, mussels and whelks.

TBGAS, 89 (1970), 15–89. *Archaeol. Review*, 6 (1971), 27.

(3) Romano-British Settlement (SO 794027), $\frac{3}{5}$ mile E. of (2), has been noted in arable ground. It is marked by a spread of building material and domestic refuse; one 4th-century coin has been found.

TBGAS, 87 (1968), 203–5.

GOTHERINGTON

(18 miles N.N.W. of Cirencester)

(1) NOTTINGHAM HILL CAMP (SO 987282), promontory fort, bivallate, unexcavated, cuts off some 120 acres on a spur of the main escarpment, 1½ miles S.E. of the village (plan opposite; see also map, p. 107, *s.v.* SOUTHAM). Its Saxon name was *Cocca burh* (*PNG*, II, 90).* Sinking across the line of the present entrance may result from a former ditch and show that it is not original; nevertheless an early charter (Sawyer No. 141) mentions a 'gate' where the parish boundary meets the rampart.

Two close-set banks, each with an outer ditch, 105 ft. across overall, cross the spur on the S.E.; the other sides are defined by the scarp edges. The inner bank is placed on rising ground and stands 5 ft. above the interior and 10 ft. above the inner ditch. The less massive outer bank, springing from the edge of the inner ditch, reaches a height of 7 ft. above the outer ditch. The earthworks on the S. are extremely disturbed. A hollow-way leads from lower ground into the N. end of the outer ditch.

According to *Norman's History of Cheltenham* (J. Goding ed., 1863), p. 12, a Dobunnic coin, a lancehead and part of a human skeleton were found in 1844 while quarrying was taking place in the 'lower mound' of the hill. British coffins and coins, and also Roman coins, are reported from the encampment (Allen, in *IASB*, 283). All these finds have been lost.

In 1972, two leaf-shaped bronze swords were ploughed up just inside the main rampart. A third sword, a socketed knife, a palstave and other objects including pottery were subsequently recovered by excavation (information from the Committee for Research into the Iron Age in the North-west Cotswolds).

Lloyd Baker (1821), 171, No. 24. Playne (1876), 209, No. 8. Witts (1883), 38, No. 75.

(2) RECTANGULAR ENCLOSURES (SO 95102920) show as crop-marks on flat ground at about 175 ft. above O.D., 1 mile S.W. of the village. The ditches, partly overlapping, cover approximately 1 acre. The pattern is confused by the furrows of former ridge-and-furrow cultivation and by numerous soil marks of natural origin.

N.M.R., OAP (Baker), SO 9429/2–5.

GREAT RISSINGTON

(15 miles N.E. of Cirencester)

A scatter of many Romano-British potsherds was noted during airfield construction.[1]

1. *TBGAS*, 59 (1937), 334.

(1) ROMAN VILLA (SP 189163), in a field named 'Chessels' which formerly was covered by broad plough-ridges, but now is almost levelled by modern ploughing, stands at the edge of the Middle Lias and some 8 ft. above the level of streams which flank it to N. and S.; these flow into the R. Windrush, 200 yds. to the west. The villa is partly marked by a roughly rectangular platform with rounded edges, approximately 240 ft. long by 80 ft. wide and up to 4 ft. high. Building stone lies scattered on it, and concentrations of nettles extend from it eastwards for some 450 ft. on a natural shelf, beyond which the ground rises gently.

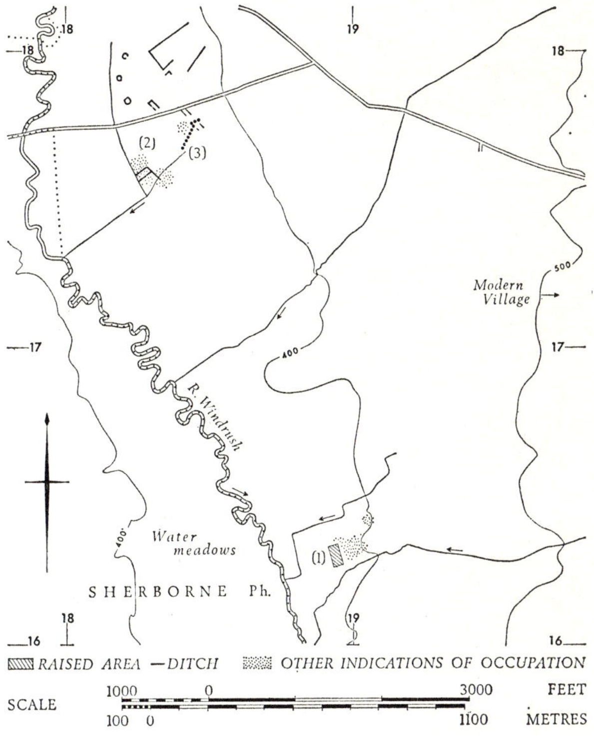

Monuments in GREAT RISSINGTON.

Surface finds, in private possession, include hypocaust and roofing tiles, sandstone roof-slates, fine and coarse tesserae (some in concentrations), *opus signinum*, and pottery ranging from late 1st-century and 2nd-century samian ware to 3rd and 4th-century types, including Oxfordshire rosette-stamped colour-coated ware. Iron slag was also found.

R.A.F., VAP CPE/UK 2013: 4179–80.
TBGAS, 82 (1968), 204.

Note: Monument (2) is a complex of many different features, some of them probably related to the adjacent pit-alignment (3). The latter is listed separately because of its rarity in the Cotswold area.

* The name survives as Stony Cockbury in Southam, Rushy Cockbury in Prescott and Cockbury Butts in Stanley Pontlarge.

(2) Probable Settlement (sp 183177), probably Iron Age and Romano-British, shows as crop-marks on almost flat low-lying ground, drained by canalised streams which flow S.W. past the crop-marks into the R. Windrush, some ¼ mile away. A group of at least four penannular features (18271762), from 30 ft. to 40 ft. across, with entrances on the E. and S.E., possibly hut-circles, lies immediately N. of a pattern of linked rectangular enclosures. To the S. are traces of parallel ditches, and possibly of trackways and pits. About 80 yds. N.E. of the area described, a pit-alignment (3) extends N.E. for at least 100 yds., intersecting other linear features. There are further suggestions of occupation in this area, as well as linear ditches. In the field N. of the modern road is an incomplete rectangular enclosure (a), about 40 ft. wide and perhaps 100 ft. long. Another enclosure (b) is irregular and about 70 ft. across, with two straight and possibly three curved sides. A circular ditch about 35 ft. across, 80 yds. N. of (b), could represent a barrow. Another circle about the same distance further N., some 45 ft. in diameter, has suggestions of an entrance in the S.E. Long straight ditches to the E. of these circles correspond approximately in alignment with the linear features around (3). There are faint indications of further linear ditches on these axes and of very small rectangular enclosures, all undated, some 300 yds. further N., centred at sp 18301833.

N.M.R., OAP (Baker), SP 1817/1–6; 1818/1.

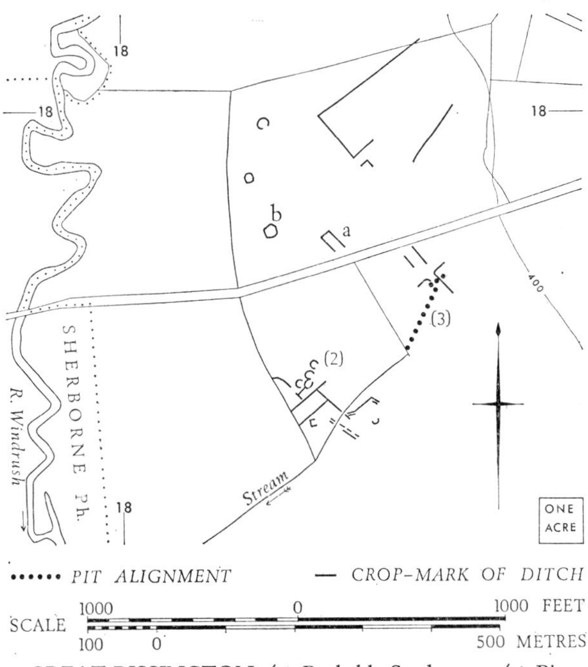

GREAT RISSINGTON. (2) Probable Settlement. (3) Pit-alignment.

(3) Pit-alignment (sp 18411768), extends N.N.E. for at least 100 yds. across almost flat ground, now arable (see (2)).

GREAT WITCOMBE

(10 miles n.w. of Cirencester)

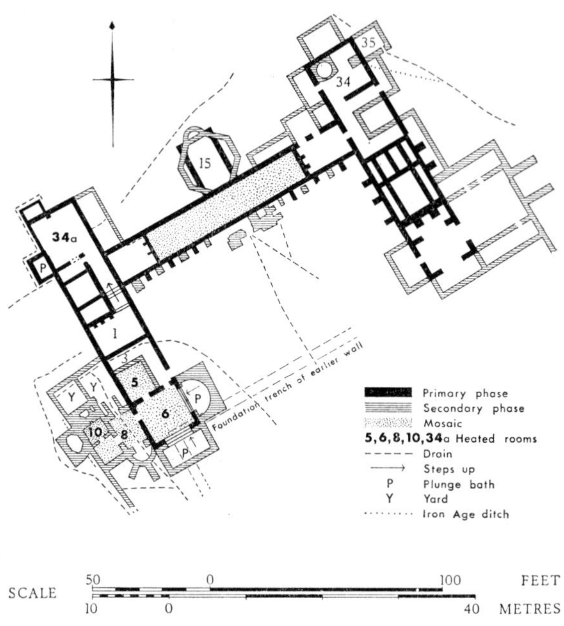

GREAT WITCOMBE. (1) Roman Villa.

(1) Roman Villa (so 899144), discovered in 1818 near Cooper's Hill Farm, was in the succeeding years largely uncovered by Samuel Lysons and Sir William Hicks. Modern excavations for the Inspectorate of Ancient Monuments were conducted by Mrs. E. M. Clifford in 1938–9 and, since 1961, by Mr. E. Greenfield. The situation is a moderate slope facing S.S.E., on Lias Clay, near the head of a broad re-entrant valley, with sand, then Oolite rising steeply above it. Springs emerging above the villa make the site naturally wet and unstable. There is a stream 100 yds. to S.E.; beside it was a small Roman building (2). Map, p. 41.

Slight indications of nearby Iron Age occupation include a ditch under the N.E. corner of the villa. Early Roman pottery and other finds point to occupation in the 1st and 2nd centuries. Foundation trenches show that a walled structure earlier than the villa lay immediately to the S., its N.W. angle under room 6. The villa is terraced. A ramp, formerly with steps, now an incline of 13°, joins rooms 1 and 34a. The main structure dates from *c.* 250 and occupation probably continued into the 5th century. The dominant feature is a room (15) at first rectangular (12 ft. by 21 ft.) with its N.W. corners rounded internally, later converted to an octagon of 21 ft. with an apsidal projection from the N.W. side (Plate 24). The room was fronted by a tessellated gallery, 12 ft. wide, with a 'portico' and buttresses on the downhill or courtyard side. The wing E. of the gallery contained a kitchen with an oven (34) and a latrine (35) adjacent. No mosaics have been reported in the E. wing; the S.E. rooms lay, partly at least, under post-Roman ridge-and-furrow (C.U.A.P., OAP ATZ 79). The W. wing was devoted largely to bath arrangements, with projecting plunge baths, hot and cold. There were seven tessellated floors and an elaborate threshold between rooms 6 and 8. The surviving mosaics are fragmentary; representations of fish and geometric patterns recorded by Lysons are illustrated on Plates 10–12. Materials included cut samian sherds. There are no recognisable heated 'living' rooms. Room 3 was a latrine.

The thick walls and buttresses (the latter otherwise found in this area only at Woodchester) to some extent reflect the natural difficulties of the site, as do the numerous drains, but the substantial nature of parts of the structure might also suggest that there was an upper storey over certain rooms. A possible reconstruction of the villa, made by Mr. D. S. Neal of the Department of the Environment and kindly communicated in advance of publication, shows the gallery as a dominant feature connecting with upper floors in the N. part of the W. wing and extending over most of the E. wing. Room 1 in the W. wing has interior projections integral with the N. wall; these are generally thought to have formed niches, though a buttressing function is also likely, the floor of the room on the N.W. being 5 ft. higher. A small cistern in the middle of room 1, projecting 6 in. above the Old Red Sandstone floor, was fed with water which drained into the system serving the adjacent latrine (3). Ritual usages were deduced from the niches, the water, and from a pottery model of a fir-cone found in the room.

Extensive additions and rebuilding included the conversion of room 5 from *apodyterium* to *caldarium* and the reuse of parts of Oolite columns in the structure of the hypocaust. A corner passage or 'slype' joined rooms 5 and 8. The door between rooms 5 and 6 was blocked; its doorstep, apparently reused, is grooved. Fragments of Oolite columns loose in room 6 display a variety of simple mouldings, including the common double torus base. Two sizes are represented. The smaller ones (Plate 29) have shafts about 6 in. across and are unweathered; the larger, with shafts over 9 in. across, are markedly weathered (Plate 28).

Materials include Oolite and tufa, the latter mostly from the W. wing. Most roof tiles found are earthenware, but some are of Old Red Sandstone. Imported white marble was used in some moulded cornices (a fragment is preserved in the Gloucester City Museum) and painted pieces of fine sandstone were also found. Window glass, both green and colourless, appeared in quantity in the rooms of the S.W. bath block. Painted plaster has been reported from the W. wing only, where it was extensive and notable; polychrome designs were reported up to 6 ft. high in room 1. In the plunge bath E. of room 6, *opus signinum* occurred as a cove between the floor and the sides. Around room 34a, inserted ovens and a spread of rubbish belong to the final phases. Fragments of fretted balustrade, 2⅓ ft. high, with S-motifs, have decoration on one face only, with keying on the reverse (Plate 28).

Early Roman finds include a coin of Domitian, much first-century *Glevum* ware, a *Hod Hill* brooch and 2nd-century samian ware. Coins are predominantly late Roman; of 26 found, about half are later than 367; one belongs to the House of Theodosius. There is much 4th-century pottery. A penannular bronze brooch (Fowler, type F) may attest activity in the 5th century. Other finds include an earthenware fir-cone from room 1, a bronze 'dog' box-handle, a bronze steelyard, a key and pins. An iron knife-coulter, now in the B.M. and once thought to provide secure evidence of a heavy plough, could have belonged to a ploughed ard, though doubt must remain because of the set of the blade. There are a number of querns, one made of puddingstone. Glass includes *millefiori*, snakethread, beaker fragments and an intaglio. Bones include ox, sheep, pig, hare, domestic fowl and other birds. Much wood includes cherry and other species new in the Roman period. A piece of coal was found. Paint pigments were noted and analysed in two pots; an oyster shell had served as a palette. Graffiti include unintelligible lettering on a tile and the scoring of a 'lyre' on two stones.

Arch, XIX (1821), 178–83. *JBAA*, I (1846), 56 (intaglio). Witts (1883), 66–7, No. 22. *Ant J*, XIX (1939), 194 (fir-cone). *Antiquity*, IX (1935), 339–41; cf. *JRS*, LIV (1964), 54–65 (coulter). *TBGAS*, XXX (1907), 246; 57 (1935), 275; 73 (1954), 5–69; 74 (1955), 171–2 (graffito). *JRS*, LI (1961), 186; LIII (1963), 41; LVI (1966), 212; LVII (1967), 194 (graffito). Toynbee (1964), 92, 271, 334. *RVB*, 143, 146–7 (plaster). Lysons's plan is in the library of the Society of Antiquaries (Red Portfolio).

(2) ROMAN VILLA (SO 90021417), on Lias Clay, lies on a gentle slope below and 100 yds. S.E. of (1). A stream flows N.E. about 10 yds. to the east. Excavations by Sir William Hicks uncovered the major part of a building with at least eight rooms. Floors of 'red plaster' were recorded in four rooms and 'some brown tiles for roofing' were found, together with coloured wall-plaster, white tesserae and further tiles. It seems that the entrance to room 1 was marked by a grooved doorstep. Although no scale accompanies the original plan, on the ground a slightly sunken platform approximately 100 ft. by 50 ft. suggests the maximum possible size of the building uncovered.

TBGAS, 73 (1954), 13–15.

(3) ROMANO-BRITISH SETTLEMENT (SO 90121372), is indicated by sherds and roofing tiles found over approximately ½ acre on a natural terrace in the Oolite, some 100 yds. above the spring-line marking the junction with Lias Clays.

TBGAS, 81 (1962), 214.

(4) ROMANO-BRITISH SETTLEMENT (SO 90751370), is suggested by sherds and tiles found in black soil, apparently slipped from terraces which may have been used as building platforms. Springs marking the junction between the Oolite and Lias are adjacent.

TBGAS, 81 (1962), 214–15.

GUITING POWER

(16 miles N.N.E. of Cirencester)

A water-pipe trench revealed a pit at Wood House[1] (SP 084261) containing Iron Age pottery, iron slag and the skeleton of a baby.

1. *Archaeol. Review*, 6 (1971), 22.

HAMPNETT

(10 miles N.N.E. of Cirencester)

A bronze statuette of Hercules, now in Cheltenham Museum, was found in the parish.

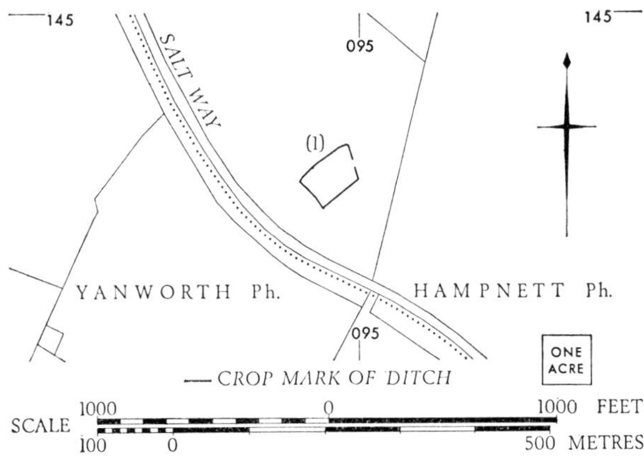

(1) ENCLOSURE (SP 09461428), undated, shows as a crop-mark adjacent to the Salt Way. The ditch, on nearly level ground at about 650 ft. above O.D., encloses ¾ acre; there is a gap in the N.E. side.

N.M.R., OAP SP 0815/2/3 (Baker).

HARESCOMBE

(13 miles N.W. of Cirencester)

(1) ROMAN VILLA (SO 84000914), Stockend, is situated on the Cotteswold Sands or Upper Lias Clay at about 450 ft. above O.D., near the head of a combe, one of several within a broad and deep N.-facing valley, surrounded by steep slopes which rise to 800 ft. on the W., S. and E. The source of Daniel's Brook is near by map *s.v.* HARESFIELD).

Before 1883, stone had been removed by the cartload and digging into the site had yielded roof and flue tiles, two columns, tesserae, coloured plaster, pottery and a silver coin of Theodosius. All of these are now lost.

Witts (1883), 62–3, No. 14 ('Haresfield Villa'). *TBGAS*, 83 (1964), 147.

(2) ENCLOSURE (SO 835086), Haresfield Dyke Camp, is undated. Air photographs show two sides as ploughed-down banks, S. of the parish boundary on Scotsquarr Hill.

Arch J, CIX (1952), 27, fig. 2.
R.A.F., VAP CPE/UK 2098: 3094–5. C.U.A.P., OAP AN 44–5.

HARESFIELD

(16 miles W.N.W. of Cirencester)

A Romano-British cemetery, reported from 'a spot in the Weald',[1] appears to be additional to that noted below (4). Skeletons lying N.–S., pottery and a quern fragment were observed.

1. *JBAA*, II (1847), 96.

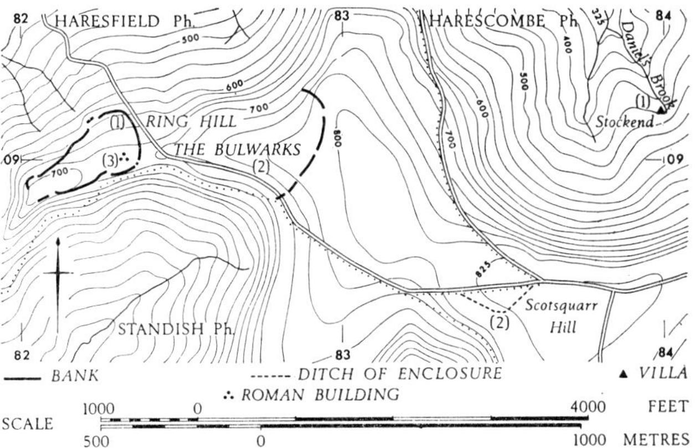

Monuments in HARESCOMBE and HARESFIELD.

(1) HILL-FORT ON RING HILL (SO 822090), univallate with traces of internal quarry pits but without external ditch, unexcavated, encloses nearly 10 acres at the end of a spur of the Cotswold escarpment, one mile S.E. of the village.

The N. and S. sides are defined by banks, set along the edges of the scarp, varying in size from very slight to 30 ft. wide and 4 ft. high (at N.W.); the E. bank, about 2½ ft. high, rises to follow the crest of a natural ridge above a gully. The W. end, at the tip of the spur and formerly the site of a beacon, is entirely broken by quarrying. Of the five gaps in the bank two on the N. are approached by terrace-ways, probably following original lines; a third gap is approached by a hollow-way. Two large gaps in the S. bank are at least partly due to quarrying.

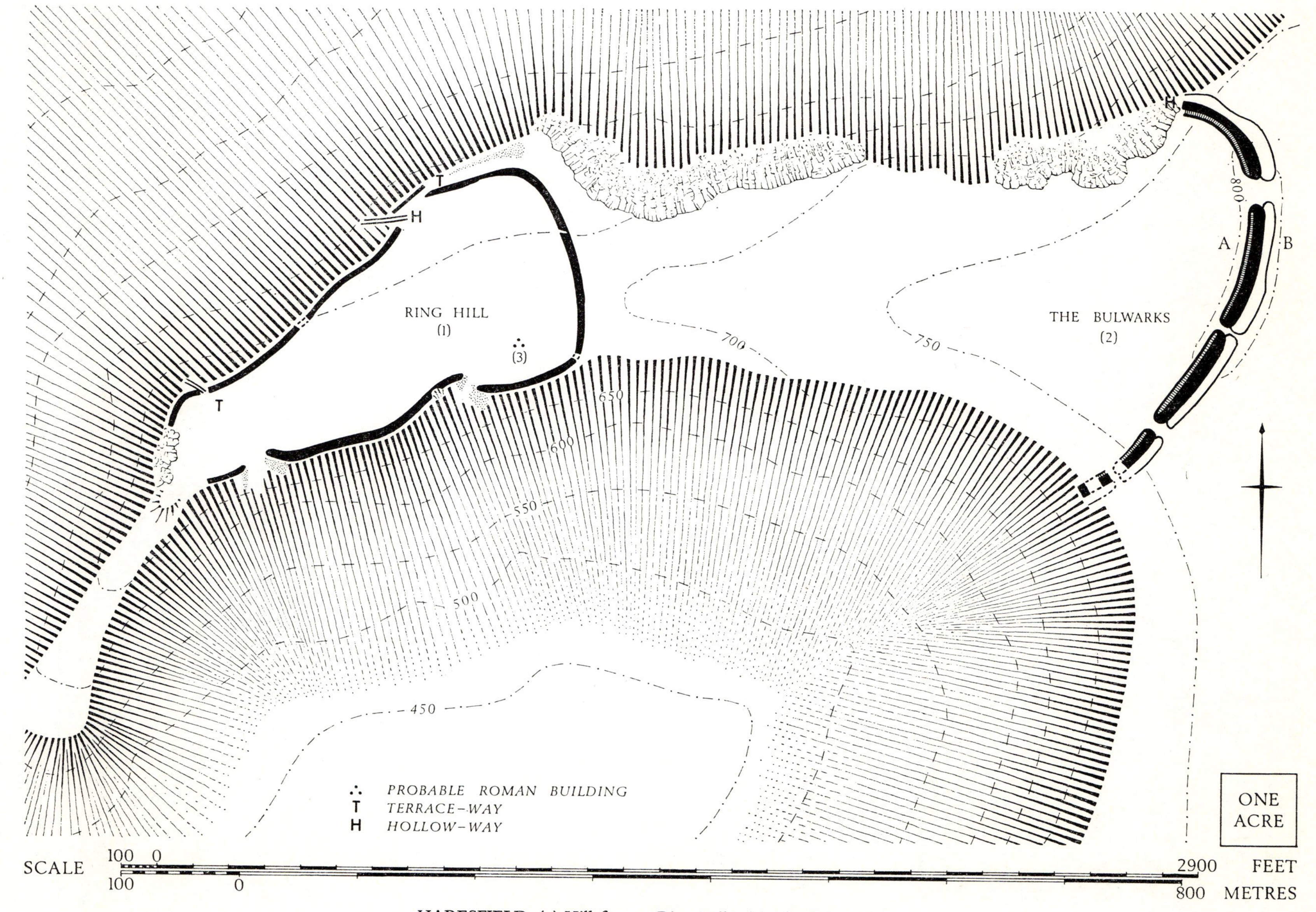

HARESFIELD. (1) Hill-fort on Ring Hill. (2) The Bulwarks.

Part of a saddle-quern found in the E. half of the interior is in Gloucester City Museum.

S. Lysons, *Woodchester* (1797), plan of 'Broadridge Green' inset in 'Map of the Roman Stations'. Lloyd-Baker (1821), 169, No. 16. Playne (1876), 211, No. 21 (Haresfield Beacon). Witts (1883), 23, No. 47 (Roman Camp).

(2) THE BULWARKS* HILL-FORT (SO 829091), unexcavated, consists of a single bank with an outer ditch crossing the neck of the spur, 630 yds. E. of Ring Hill (1). Plan, p. 63.

The bank, 45 ft. wide and 7 ft. high, is of glacis construction externally and has a ledge 2 ft. high and up to 10 ft. wide along the inner side; the ditch is 40 ft. wide and 7 ft. deep. The slope from bank to ditch is lengthened at the N. end, where the ditch runs into a gully and the

HARESFIELD. (2) The Bulwarks. Profile A–B (p. 63).

bank curves away along the edge of the scarp. Four gaps in the bank, 20 ft. to 80 ft. wide, have corresponding causeways in the ditch. A hollow-way enters the N. end of the ditch by way of the gully.

A few sherds of featureless hand-made pottery, found in ploughsoil in the field to the W. of the bank, are now in Gloucester City Museum.

Bibliography as in (1).

(3) ROMAN BUILDING (SO 82320900), on Ring Hill (see p. 63), occurs near the E. end of (1). A scatter of pottery, tile fragments and limestone slabs suggests occupation near the E. entrance in the S. side, where a pot was found in 1837 containing from 2,000 to 3,000 bronze coins. Pottery, part of a rotary quern and animal bones, exposed by landslips on the slope outside the hill-fort bank at N.E., may be refuse from this settlement.

The hoard is said to have consisted mainly of issues of the period A.D. 306–40; many coins were in mint condition. Two coins to survive from the hoard (Claudius Gothicus and Constantine) are in Gloucester City Museum. The same museum has records of two recent finds, one a bronze coin of Constantine II. An *Urbs Roma* in mint condition, now in Stroud Museum, is attributed to the hoard. Fragments of glass vessels and 3rd–4th-century pottery are in G.C.M.

J. D. T. and C. S. Niblett, MS. Commonplace Book (1834–8), 287–9 (in Gloucester Public Library). J. Buckman and C. H. Newmarch, *Illustrations of the Remains of Roman Art in Cirencester, the Site of Anticnt Corinium* (1850), 6. *PCNFC*, XXI (1922), 79, 141–50.

(4) ROMANO-BRITISH CEMETERY (SO 815120), on Long Hill, Colethrop, S. of the Shorn Brook, lies in the vale at about 90 ft. above O.D. Several skeletons were discovered when drains were laid, *c.* 1847, some of them in stone cists. Samian ware, coarse pottery, an illegible coin and a bronze figurine were also found.

JBAA, II (1847), 96. *TBGAS*, 90 (1971), 53.

(5) ROMANO-BRITISH SETTLEMENT (SO 819115), in 'The Lessons' at Colethrop near the S. bank of the Shorn Brook, ⅓ mile S.E. of (4), is indicated by pottery of the 2nd and 3rd centuries and building debris in an area of shallow banks and depressions, all ploughed over.

TBGAS, 90 (1971), 53.

HATHEROP

(8 miles N.E. of Cirencester)

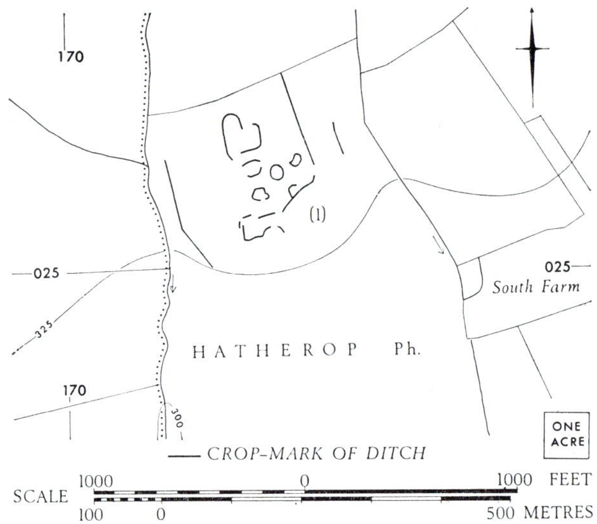

HATHEROP. (1) Probable Settlement.

(1) PROBABLE SETTLEMENT (SP 173027), undated, shows as crop-marks N.W. of South Farm. The area is defined by linear ditches on E. and W. and covers 6 acres or more.

C.U.A.P., OAP AYI 9–10.

HAWKESBURY

(21 miles S.W. of Cirencester)

A univallate hill-fort is reputed to exist on Hawkesbury Knoll (ST 768872), ¼ mile N. of the village, but no earthworks of Iron Age type are identifiable (see p. xxxiii).

For 'Celtic' Fields, see BADMINTON.

* Former names appear to have been Suberesburia, Ezimbury, Eresbury, Estbury and, more recently, Eastbury (*PNG*, II, 184).

HAWLING

(13 miles N.N.W. of Cirencester)

A Roman glass unguent bottle found at Hawling is in the Corinium Museum.

HAZLETON

(11 miles N. of Cirencester)

(1) PROBABLE ROMANO-BRITISH SETTLEMENT (around SP 075212), lies 2 miles N. of the village, on the plateau at about 860 ft. above O.D.

A silver Dobunnic coin inscribed ANTED was found with Romano-British pottery, including samian, iron slag and burnt stones. The finds are in a private collection.

Archaeol. Review, 4 (1969), 41.

HORSLEY

(12 miles W. of Cirencester)

An inscribed Roman gabled tombstone was found *c.* 1835 in Horsley Wood, about ½ mile S.W. of the village.[1] A collection of unprovenanced Roman coins in Stroud Museum is thought to come from Horsley or Kingscote. 'Enoch's Hill Camp' (ST 847975) consists of banks and enclosures, possibly mediaeval.[2]

1. *RIB*, I, 133. The stone is now on loan to Stroud Museum.
2. *TBGAS*, VIII (1883–4), 78. *UBSS*, III (1926), 44.

(1) ROMANO-BRITISH VILLA (ST 852972), about ½ mile E. of Tiltups End, in a broad and shallow depression at about 550 ft. above O.D., is identified by a scatter of tesserae, roof tiles, nails and pottery in arable. Two coins (3rd and 4th century) were found.

TBGAS, 87 (1968), 204.

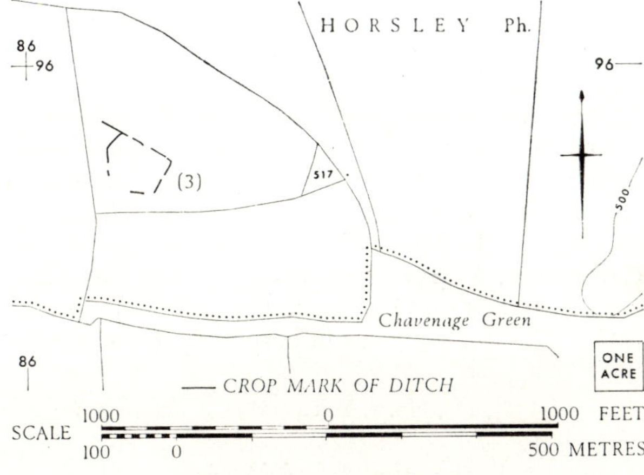

HORSLEY. (3) Enclosure.

(2) SETTLEMENT SITE (ST 85789733), Romano-British, on a gentle S.-facing slope, about 700 yds. E. of (1) and about 580 ft. above O.D., is indicated by an extensive scatter of sandstone tiles, large slabs of limestone and Romano-British pottery in arable.

Oral information, D. A. Mears.

(3) ENCLOSURE (ST 86159585), undated, about 1 acre, shows as a crop-mark at about 530 ft. above O.D., on land falling gently S.E.

N.M.R., OAP ST 8695/1/276–7.

HORTON

(19 miles S.W. of Cirencester)

(1) 'THE CASTLES'* HILL-FORT (ST 764844), univallate, unexcavated, encloses just under 5 acres on a spur of the main escarpment, ½ mile E. of Horton village and 1 mile N. of Sodbury. The N. and E. sides of the enclosure are defined by a rampart 40 ft. wide and 10 ft.

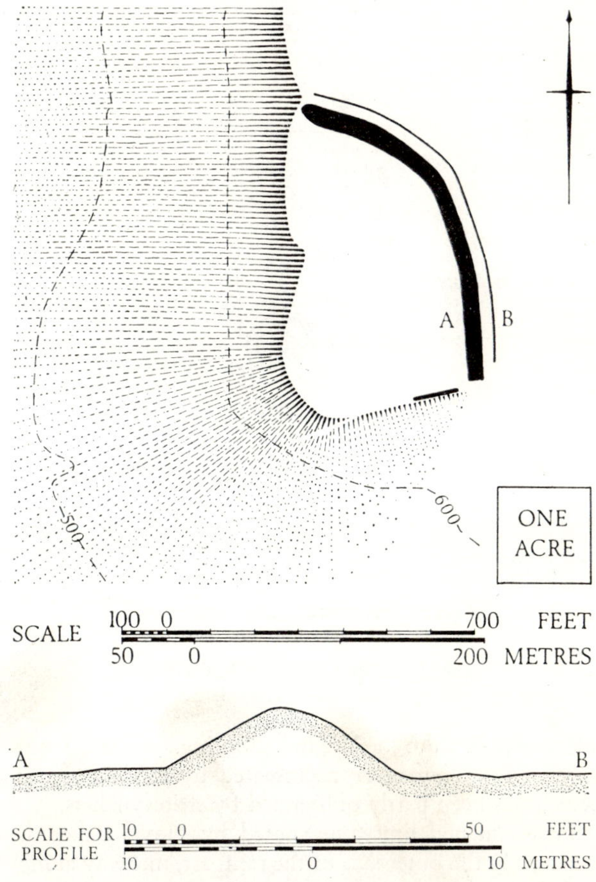

HORTON. (1) 'The Castles' hill-fort. Plan and profile.

* The name used by Rudder (1779), p. 503.

high (Plate 35); an outer ditch is traceable as a band of dark, stoneless ploughsoil about 25 ft. wide. To the W. of the S.E. corner a slight bank, 100 ft. long, is set upon the scarp edge; elsewhere the interior is delimited by natural scarps. The original entrance from the plateau was probably at the S.E. corner; a second

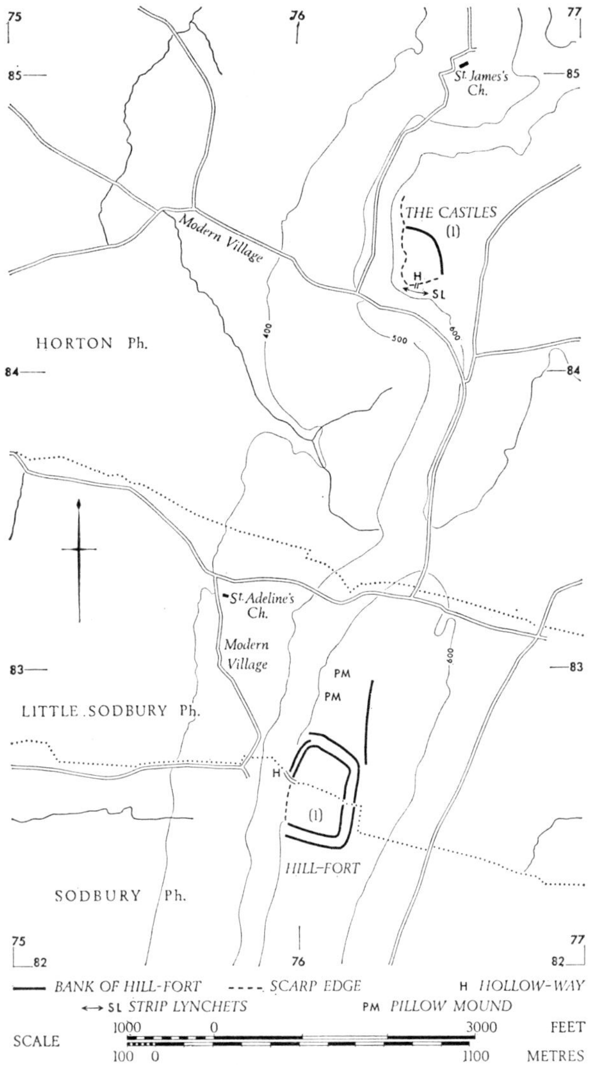

Monuments in HORTON and SODBURY.

entrance, 300 ft. to the W. and affording approach from lower ground, may be represented by a hollow-way which has been partly obliterated by strip lynchets.

Fire-reddened limestone, noted by Lloyd Baker, is exposed in the outer face of the rampart, midway along its length.

Lloyd Baker (1821), 165, No. 12. Playne (1876), 219, No. 40. Witts (1883), 27, No. 54.

C.U.A.P., OAP AIP 3.

ICOMB

(18 miles N.E. of Cirencester)

(1) **Probable Hill-fort** (SP 205230), unexcavated and almost completely destroyed, stands on Icomb Hill, $\frac{3}{4}$ mile N.W. of the village, its E. end dropping below the summit of the hill (Plate 36).

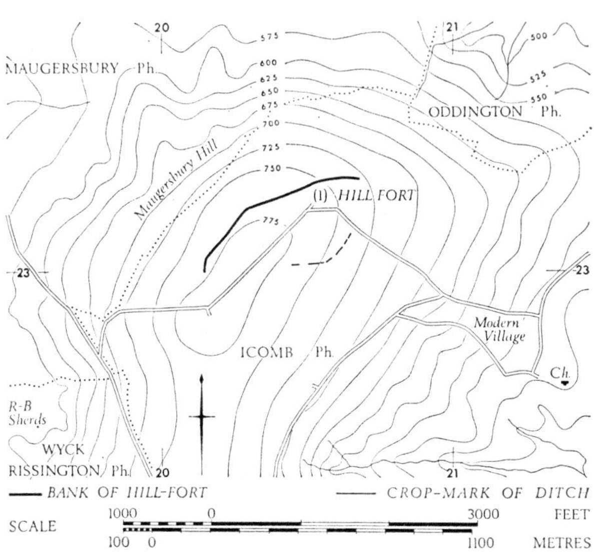

Monuments in ICOMB.

The surviving bank, 30 ft. wide and generally under 1 ft. high, with a ditch formerly on the N. side, can be traced for about 780 yds. in arable fields, along the N. and N.W. sides of the hill only. There are indications of discontinuous ditches on the S. slope of the hill, in a position that could suggest an unfinished part of the supposed hill-fort. Plan, p. 67.

During investigation three featureless sherds of coarse hand-made pottery (now in Gloucester City Museum) were recovered from ploughsoil over the E. end of the bank.

A late 18th-century map, made when the bank was already extensively ploughed, depicts an irregular oval enclosure in which the N.W.-S.E. diameter measured approximately 1,100 ft. (I. Taylor, *Map of Gloucestershire* (1777); T. Nash, *Collections for the History of Worcestershire*, II (1782), 2). In its N. half this plan conforms to that on O.S., 1816, which shows the bank continuing S. for some 700 ft. beyond the point where it now disappears.

Playne (1876), 208, No. 7. Witts (1883), 27, No. 55. *Bagendon*, 25, n. 4.

N.M.R., OAP SP 2023/4/199 to 2023/7/208.

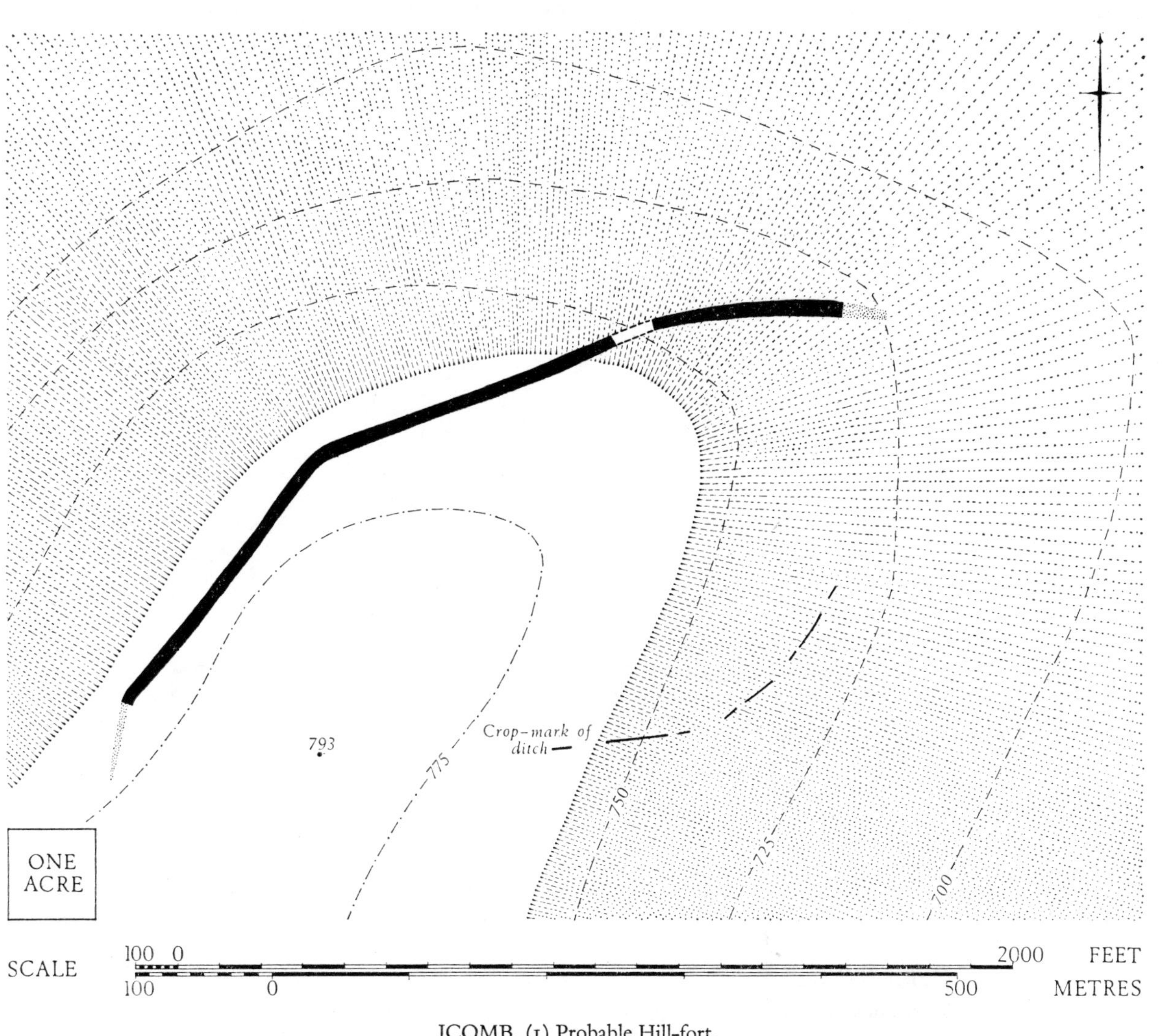

ICOMB. (1) Probable Hill-fort.

KEMBLE

(3 miles S.W. of Cirencester)

The Foss Way forms the N.W. boundary of the parish. 'Roman flue-tiles' are reported from Ewen (SU 00489721),[1] but field investigation has not confirmed the existence of a building.

1. O.S. records.

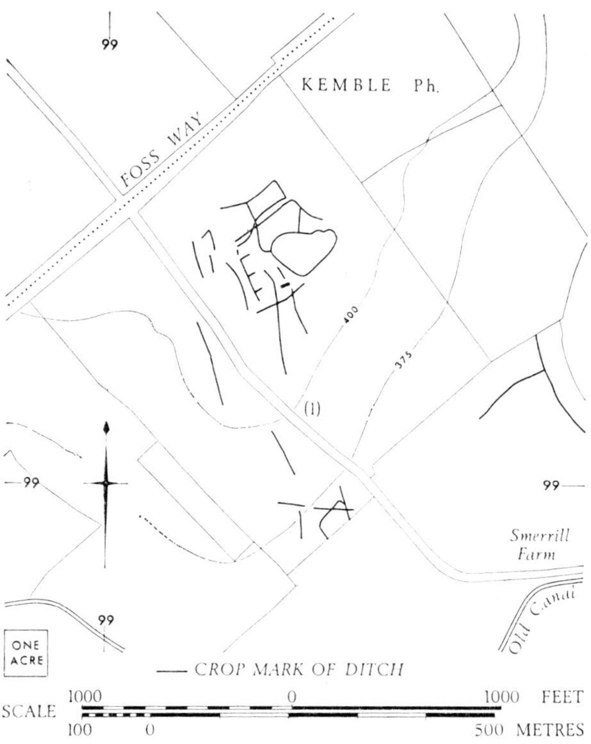

KEMBLE. (1) Probable Settlement.

(1) Probable Settlement (ST 993993), undated, is revealed by crop-marks 100 yds. S.E. of the Foss Way (Plate 63); the main area, about 6 acres, occupies generally level ground on a spur of the plateau.

C.U.A.P., OAP AOS 7–8.

KEMPSFORD

(9 miles S.E. of Cirencester)

An approximately circular enclosure about 70 yds. across (SU 19209715), E. of Dudgrove Ham Barn, survives as ploughed banks with interior ditches; it is undated and has been classed with circles of 'Highworth type'[1] (Plate 64).

A 2nd-century cooking-pot, now in the Ashmolean Museum, was found beside the R. Thames at Hannington Bridge (SU 174961).[2]

All monuments lie on gravel terraces of the R. Coln and R. Thames, between 250 ft. and 300 ft. above O.D. Some rings shown on the plans may relate to Bronze Age barrows (see p. lv).

1. *WAM*, XLVII (1935), 121, No. 40. N.M.R., OAP SU 1997/2.
2. *Oxon*, XXI (1956), 82.

(1) Roman Settlement (SP 150005). Two wells discovered in a gravel-pit at Horcott lay 30 yds. apart; both were lined with stone. Pottery recovered from the wells and from a nearby pit was attributed to the 3rd century. A block of Oolitic limestone with a circular perforation, found at the bottom of one of the wells, is in Cirencester Museum.

Gloucestershire Countryside, IX (1957), 154. H. E. O'Neil in *Studies in Building History* (ed. Jope, 1961), 36.

(2) Enclosures, Track and Linear Ditches (SU 141991), undated, are revealed by crop-marks covering some 18 acres N.W. of Rhymes Barn.

N.M.R., OAP SU 1499/2/409–11; 1499/3.

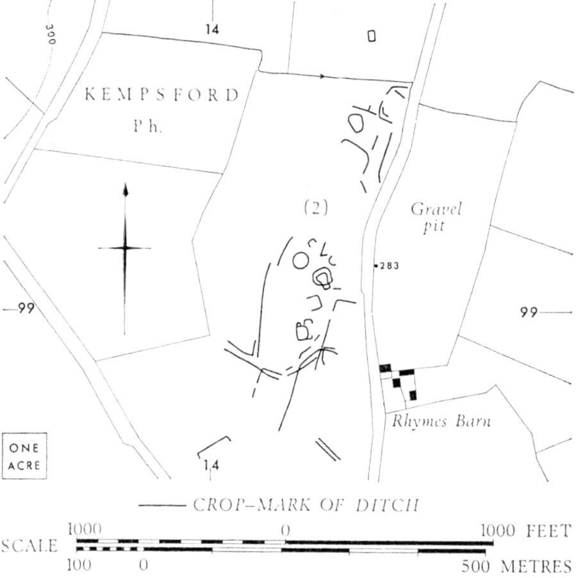

KEMPSFORD. (2) Enclosures etc.

(3) Enclosures and Linear Ditches (SU 161974), undated, show as crop-marks extending over about 30 acres N. of the village. A and B mark the position of further enclosures, less well defined. Plan, p. 69.

N.M.R., OAP SU 1597/1/418–21.

(4) Enclosures and Linear Ditches (SU 168995), undated, show as crop-marks covering about 5 acres on the W. bank of the R. Coln, N.W. of Whelford (plan opp. p. 55, *s.v.* Fairford).

Air photograph: Allen, OAP 1368.

(5) Enclosure (SU 180993), undated, shows as a crop-mark N.E. of Whelford (plan opp. p. 55).

C.U.A.P., OAP AYI 17.

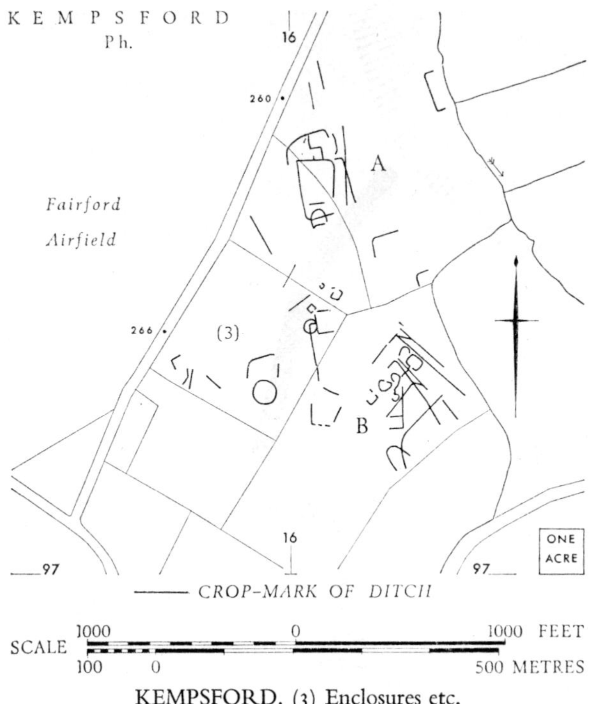

KEMPSFORD. (3) Enclosures etc.

(6) ENCLOSURES (SU 184978), undated, include small circular, penannular and D-shaped features, W.S.W. of Dudgrove Farm; they show as crop-marks over about 18 acres on a low hill (Plate 62).

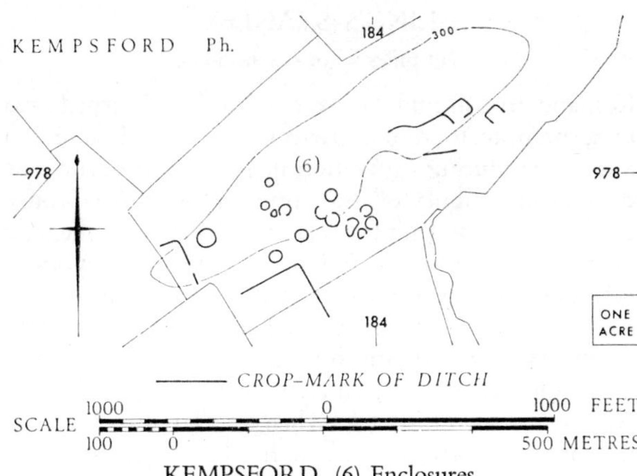

KEMPSFORD. (6) Enclosures.

C.U.A.P., OAP LY 86–7, AYI 2–3.
Arch J, CI (1944), 16, Pl. V, B. *Oxon*, VIII–IX (1943–4), 95, No. 2.

(7) ENCLOSURES, TRACKS AND LINEAR DITCHES (SU 180966), undated, are revealed by crop-marks extending over some 70 acres along the N. bank of the R. Thames around Manor Ham Barn. One of the focal points of the settlement complex appears to be an 'open space' around a ring-ditch (SU 18359672); there are only slight signs of other ditches encroaching on its S.W. side (Plate 60). See also p. lv.

C.U.A.P., OAP AYI 4. N.M.R., OAP SU 1896/8/422–32.

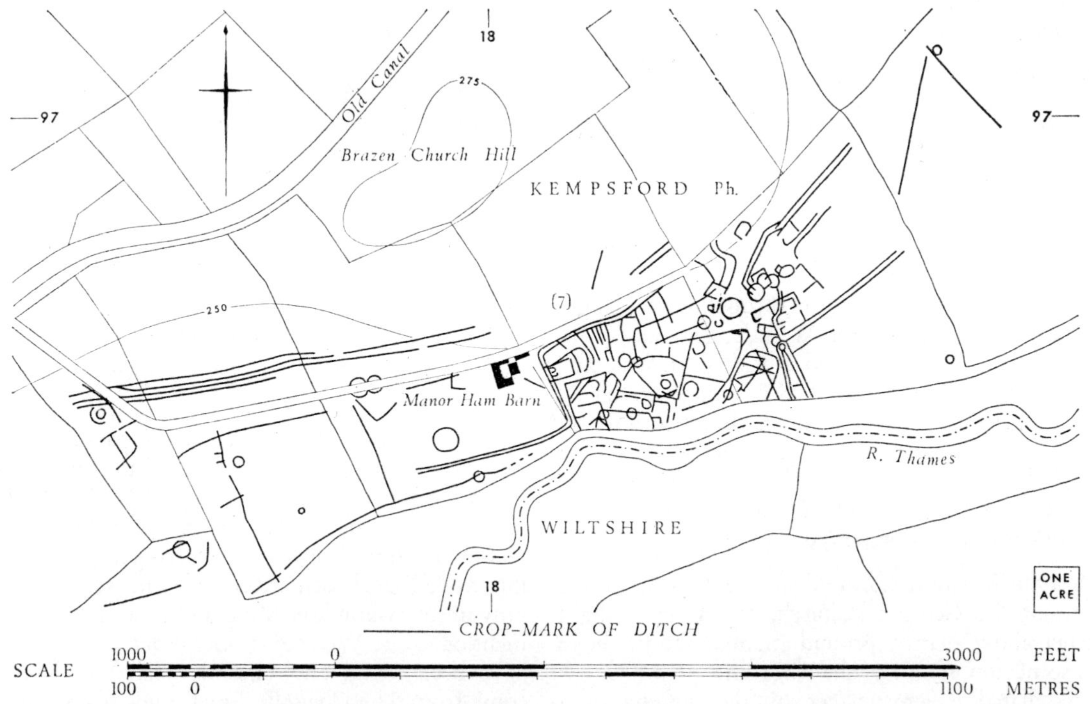

KEMPSFORD. (7) Enclosures, Tracks and Linear Ditches.

KING'S STANLEY

(13 miles W. of Cirencester)

Romano-British finds recovered from a disturbed area in a prehistoric round barrow near Ivy Lodge (SO 81100198), during excavation in 1948–9, comprise part of a bronze fibula of 1st-century type, three bronze coins—Constans (minted 341–5), Valens and illegible (3rd or 4th century)—and five fragments of pottery including samian of the early 3rd century. Four human skeletons accidentally discovered in 1929 may have been secondary Romano-British burials.[1]

Six uninscribed Roman altars and a coin of Severus Alexander, found in 1781 when a cellar was dug,[2] are not precisely provenanced. It has been suggested that they come from Stanley House, adjacent to St. George's Church[3] and to a former Roman building (2). The find has been thought to imply the existence of a temple.[4] Five of the altars are in the B.M.; three carry representations of Mars as god of agriculture, the fourth depicts a *genius* and the fifth portrays an armed deity, probably British.[5] Another altar with a figure of Mars in relief, attributed to King's Stanley, is in Stroud Museum.[6]

1. *TBGAS*, 69 (1950), 59–77; 79 (1960), King's Stanley 1.
2. S. Lysons, *Etchings of Views and Antiquities in the County of Gloucester* (1791), Pl. XXXIII.
3. *TBGAS*, XLIV (1922), 223.
4. Lewis (1966), 126.
5. Toynbee (1964), 154, 163, 178. *TBGAS*, 60 (1938), 299–300, Pls. I–III.
6. *TBGAS*, XLIV (1922), 222, Pl. I. (See also *TBGAS*, 60 (1938), pl. XVI, fig. 30, where it is said to have been found in Hazelwood.) It was in private possession in 1915.

(1) CROSS-RIDGE DYKE (SO 81850205), of Iron Age type, unexcavated, crosses a narrow neck of a long W.–E. ridge which here forms part of the main W. escarpment of the Cotswolds. The N. end of the earthwork lies in King's Stanley, the S. part in Woodchester.

The dyke crosses fairly level ground at about 675 ft. above O.D., but to the E. the ridge is crowned by Bown Hill with an altitude of 735 ft. The earthwork, 720 ft. long, is of regular form throughout its length and comprises a ditch on the W. side, generally 35 ft. across, a berm 15 ft. wide, and a bank 50 ft. wide and up to 3½ ft. high. The N.W.–S.E. course of the N. section changes after 315 ft. with an abrupt turn to W. There is no sign of an original entrance at this point although later traffic has caused the ditch to be filled and has cut through the bank. To the S. of the turn the earthwork is less well preserved.

(2) ROMAN BUILDING (around SO 81000410), in the vicinity of St. George's Church, stood on a slight eminence above marshy ground at about 130 ft. above O.D., some 200 yds. S. of the R. Frome.

A tessellated pavement, cut by the digging of a grave on the E. of the church, apparently extends into

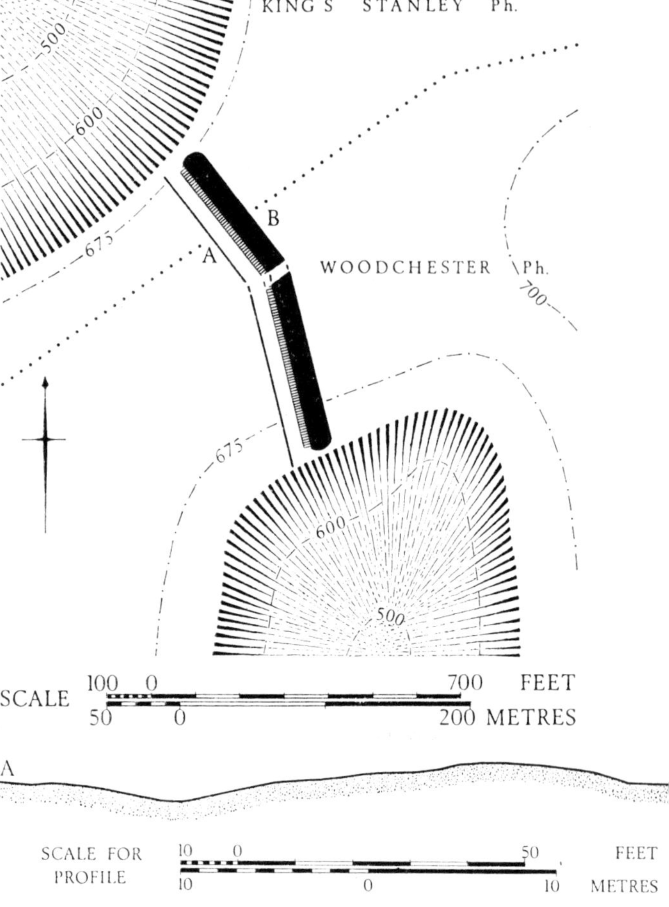

KING'S STANLEY. (1) Cross-ridge Dyke. Plan and profile.

the grounds of Stanley House; no details are known. A Romano-British ditch and some pottery have come to light during the excavation of a mediaeval moat on the W. and N.W. of the church. A tile stamped ARVERI is built into the inner wall of the church tower.

Information from Captain H. S. Gracie, R.N.

KINGSCOTE

(11 miles W.S.W. of Cirencester)

The Chessalls (1) is a very large unwalled Romano-British settlement, associated with paved roads (cf. WHITTINGTON (2)). The nature of the finds suggests an early Roman origin, possibly military. Until 1942 an inscribed semicircular Oolite relief, probably depicting an equestrian Mars with worshippers, was built into a mediaeval barn at Calcot Farm (ST 839949); it is now in the Ashmolean Museum.[1] A stone votive tablet mentioned *s.v.* WOTTON-UNDER-EDGE (p. 134), said to have been found on Symonds' Hall Hill, may have come from The Chessalls. Small finds from this parish and from HORSLEY, now in Stroud Museum and Bristol

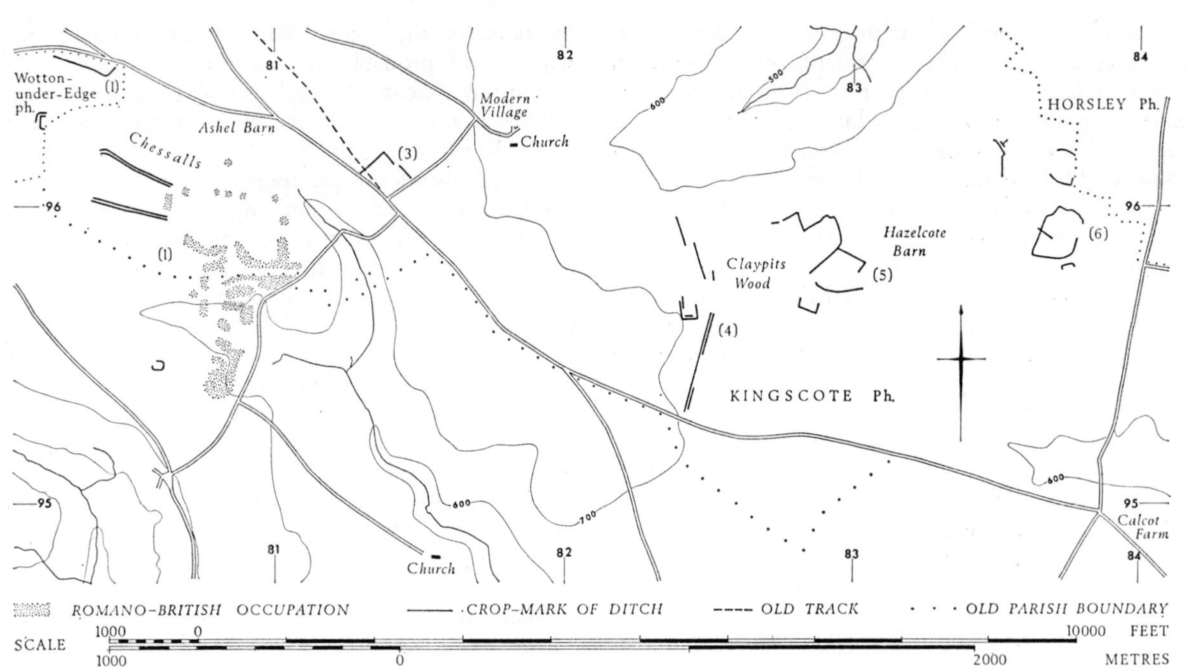

Monuments in KINGSCOTE.

City Museum, are not closely provenanced. Romano-British pottery found *c.* 1890 near Kingscote Wood (a large area in the N.E. of the parish) is in Stroud Museum.

1. *Gent. Mag.* LXV (1795), i, 385. *TBGAS*, 73 (1954), 230–2. Toynbee (1964), 154. *RIB*, No. 135. Ross (1967), 189.

(1) ROMANO-BRITISH SETTLEMENT (ST 808953–807963–810961), The Chessalls, covers at least 50 acres of arable ground S. of Ashel Barn; it is identified by numerous finds (plan in end pocket). The name 'Chesle' was associated with the site in 1772 (Camden, *Britannia* (ed. Gibson, 1772), I, 286); it is also used by Rudder. The site falls gently from about 725 ft. above O.D. and occupies both sides of an eastward-facing valley head, the southern of two depressions which join S.E. of the site and continue into the more steeply sided Hay Bottom. Gullies in the valley sides require in places a terraced setting for the former buildings. A spring (s) occurs on the N. side of the valley immediately above the 675-ft. contour. Beyond a gently domed plateau the N. part of the settlement occupies a broad and shallow depression which drains through withy beds into the northern valley head; N. of the withy beds only one building site is recorded. The field called Middle Chessalls probably marks the W. limit of occupation; on the E. side the limit appears to correspond roughly with the modern road since no significant remains have been found in gardens E. of the road; on the S., other building sites may await discovery. Today the S. edges of the two fields named Chessalls stand 4 ft. above those adjacent on the S.; this is the result of post-Roman lynchet formation along the old boundary with the former parish of Newington Bagpath. Similar lynchet formation has raised the E. side of Middle Chessalls almost 2 ft. above Lower Chessalls.

The sites of at least 75 buildings are identifiable on the ground, generally as concentrations of limestone slabs, sandstone tiles, mortar and associated dark soil containing pottery, quern fragments and other occupation debris. Near the middle of the W. side of Lower Chessalls field (around ST 80759610) there are slight traces of rectangular platforms. Some 80 yds. S.W. (ST 80619601), a long rectangular mound (a), 2 ft. high and aligned N.E.–S.W., with concentrations of building debris and potsherds, lies nearly at right angles to and S. of a probable track. A quarry on the N. of the same track is possibly Roman in origin. The outline of the building under the mound on the S. of the track is partly visible as a crop-mark on an air photograph (N.M.R., VAP ST 8096/1/102). A little further S., and approximately parallel with the first track, a paved road about 30 ft. across, with side ditches up to 3 ft. deep on the S. and less than 2 ft. deep on the N., approaches from the W., crossing Middle Chessalls field and narrowing sharply as it enters the settlement area.

In the S. of the settlement area, at (c) and (d), other air photographs show the crop-marks of two rectangular buildings. Further W., at (b), a sub-rectangular enclosure is similarly indicated.

Elsewhere in the settlement area some building sites

appear to be aligned one with another, and there are also long spreads of debris. Potsherds, tiles and mortar found in large quantities near ST 80899565 probably mark the position of a large building (22), situated some 50 yds. N.E. of the spring (s); a prominent knoll at this point is a likely setting for an important building.

The record of finds begins in 1691 with an enamelled brooch (Camden, ed. Gibson, *loc. cit.*). In the 18th century a mosaic pavement, numerous coins and the head of a statue of Minerva, perhaps from a temple, were recorded. A stone coffin now in Kingscote churchyard was found in the 'Middle Chestles' in 1872; it lay less than 3 in. below ground with the head pointing exactly north. Widespread occupation debris including brooches and coins dating from the 1st to the 4th century have also been recorded; they include a Dobunnic silver coin.

The central and southern parts of the site have yielded much Claudian and early Flavian material: two military copies of Claudian *asses*, a coin of Nero, twelve brooches, a 'baldric' loop and an ornamental bronze knob, perhaps military, and samian ware. Finds of the 4th century (particularly the second half of the century) occur widely and probably represent the settlement at its maximum extent. A single sherd of grass-tempered pottery is reported. Of 226 coins available for study, 60 are later than Constantine I and the latest are of the House of Theodosius (up to 402).

Other finds include building stone, mostly Oolite (some ashlar) and a variety of sandstones; also imbrices, tegulae, and hypocaust tiles. Of bronze were brooches, finger-rings, bracelets, a nail-cleaner and tweezers, two pins (one spiral-headed), a late Roman buckle (Hawkes type I (b)), fragments of jugs, and clippings. An axe, a chisel and two styli were of iron. There were glass beads and fragments of glass vessels. Parts of twelve stone querns include one of Niedermendig Lava; there were also whetstones. Pottery includes samian (some of it Claudio-Neronian), and Severn Valley, Rhenish, Nene Valley, Oxfordshire, New Forest and calcite-gritted wares. Oyster shells and a very few animal bones were also found.

Many of the finds are in Gloucester City and Stroud Museums; others are in private possession. The Minerva

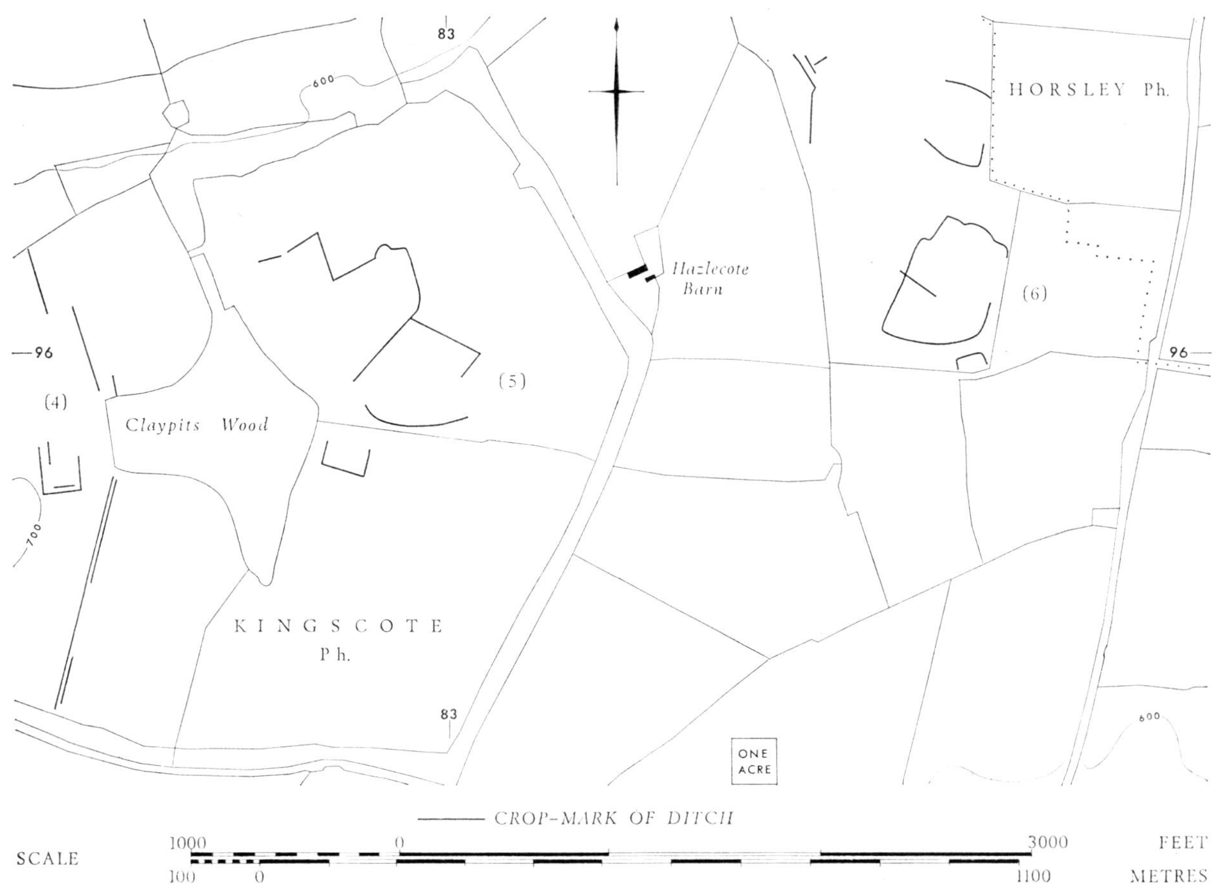

KINGSCOTE. (4)–(6) Enclosures, Tracks and Linear Ditches.

head is in Corinium Museum. A coin is in Liverpool Museum.

N.M.R., OAP ST 8095/1/225–31; 8096/1/102.
Rudder (1779), 512. Kingscote family archives (Gloucestershire Record Office, D 471/C16), 30 Aug., 1872 (coffin). *UBSS*, II, iii (1925), 294. *TBGAS*, 72 (1953), 154–8; 91 (1972), 60–91. Toynbee (1964), 79 (head of Minerva). Lewis (1966), 126. Additional data from Messrs. J. Rhodes, L. J. Walrond, D. A. Mears, D. F. Mackreth; Professor F. Rainey of Pennsylvania Univ. (geophysical survey); Mr. N. Spry (excavation of road ditches, Middle Chessalls, 1971).

(2) Romano-British Burial (approx. st 825972), S. of Kingscote Wood, comprised part of a skeleton with a 'Polden Hill' brooch, now in Stroud Museum; the grave was exposed in 1955 by soil-slip on a N.-facing slope near the stream.

TBGAS, 72 (1963), 205–7, and information from D. A. Mears.

(3) Enclosure (st 81409610), undated, is partly revealed by a crop-mark 500 yds. S.W. of the church.

N.M.R., OAP ST 8095/37/174.

(4) Enclosure, Track and Linear Ditches (st 825957), undated, show as crop-marks W. of Claypits Wood.

N.M.R., OAP ST 8295/1/245–50.

(5) Enclosures (st 829960), undated, are partly revealed by crop-marks E. of Claypits Wood.

N.M.R., OAP ST 8295/2/251–6.

(6) Enclosures and Linear Ditches (st 837962), undated, show as crop-marks E. of Hazlecote Barn.

C.U.A.P., OAP AXT 34–5.

LECHLADE

(12 miles E. of Cirencester)

A Roman building discovered 'in a meadow near Lechlade' before 1742 is not precisely located; it is reported that it measured about 50 ft. by 40 ft. and had a tessellated floor supported on brick pillars.[1] Early O.S. records site it at sp 21660061 (see (4), below), but the 'subterranean building' marked on the O.S. 6-inch edition of 1873–85 (Glos. LII, S.W.) is noted as having been found about the end of the 18th century; hence the early account may refer to the building at Great Lemhill Farm (7), or perhaps to another building now lost.

All but one of the monuments in the parish lie on gravel terraces of the rivers Thames, Coln and Leach, around 250 ft. above O.D.; the exception (9) is situated on limestone at 300 ft. above O.D.

Crop-marks in Fairford (6) are continuous with others in Lechlade (8).

1. D. Defoe, *A Tour thro' the Whole Island of Great Britain* (reprint of 1742 with additions by Samuel Richardson), II, 244.

(1) Iron Age Pit (su 212996), in 'The Loders', 400 yds. W.N.W. of the church, yielded pottery, including haematite ware, and sherds bearing incised decoration with white inlay. Plan, p. 74.

MPBW Excavations, 1965, 4. Oral information from Mrs. M. U. Jones.

(2) Enclosures and Tracks (sp 211002), undated, are revealed by crop-marks extending over some 50 acres N.W. of the parish church (Plate 60). The S.E. ditch of the track intersecting a ring-ditch at sp 209000 was almost certainly cut into a mound within the ring ditch (cf. Kempsford (7) and p. lv).

OAP Allen, 721–2. C.U.A.P., OAP AM 29–30, CD 46–9, DX 32–4, PV 38–9, VM 6–12, AFV 23, AYG 52, 54–7, 59, 61, AYI 20.
Oxon, VII (1942), 113, No. 7; VIII–IX (1943–4), 96, No. 6a.

(3) Enclosures, Linear Ditches and Track (su 223999), undated, show as crop-marks covering about 5 acres, 900 yds. N.E. of the church.

N.M.R., OAP SU 2299/3/383–4. C.U.A.P., OAP ZH 90. O.S., VAP 70 167, 080–1.
Oxon, VII (1942), 113, No. 9.

(4) Probable Roman Building (sp 21660061), $\frac{2}{3}$ mile N. of the church, has been obliterated, but the site is marked on O.S. maps (see introductory paragraph).

(5) Iron Age and Romano-British Settlement (sp 217008), by Roughground Farm, partly excavated before destruction by gravel-digging, extended over more than 20 acres W. of the R. Leach and N. of the village (Plate 52). Preliminary reports of excavations carried out by Mrs. M. U. Jones on behalf of the Ministry of Works from 1958 to 1965 suggest the following data. (Folding plan in end pocket.)

Of the Iron Age, traces of a circular house (a), 20 ft. in diameter and defined by post-holes and stake-holes, were found at sp 22000078. Finds from the post-holes include incised and carinated sherds. Two pits contained decorated Iron Age pottery.

Parts of three Romano-British buildings (b) were represented by the foundations of walls and floors; that on the E. had probably been rebuilt twice, but in its final form it was at least 80 ft. long and had two or three heated rooms. Tesserae and painted plaster were recovered. Finds antedating the building included two brooches of the 1st century A.D. and samian ware up to 150. Coins from the destruction levels ranged from about 270 to after 395. There were indications that at least two other buildings in the vicinity had been destroyed by the gravel-digging before investigation.

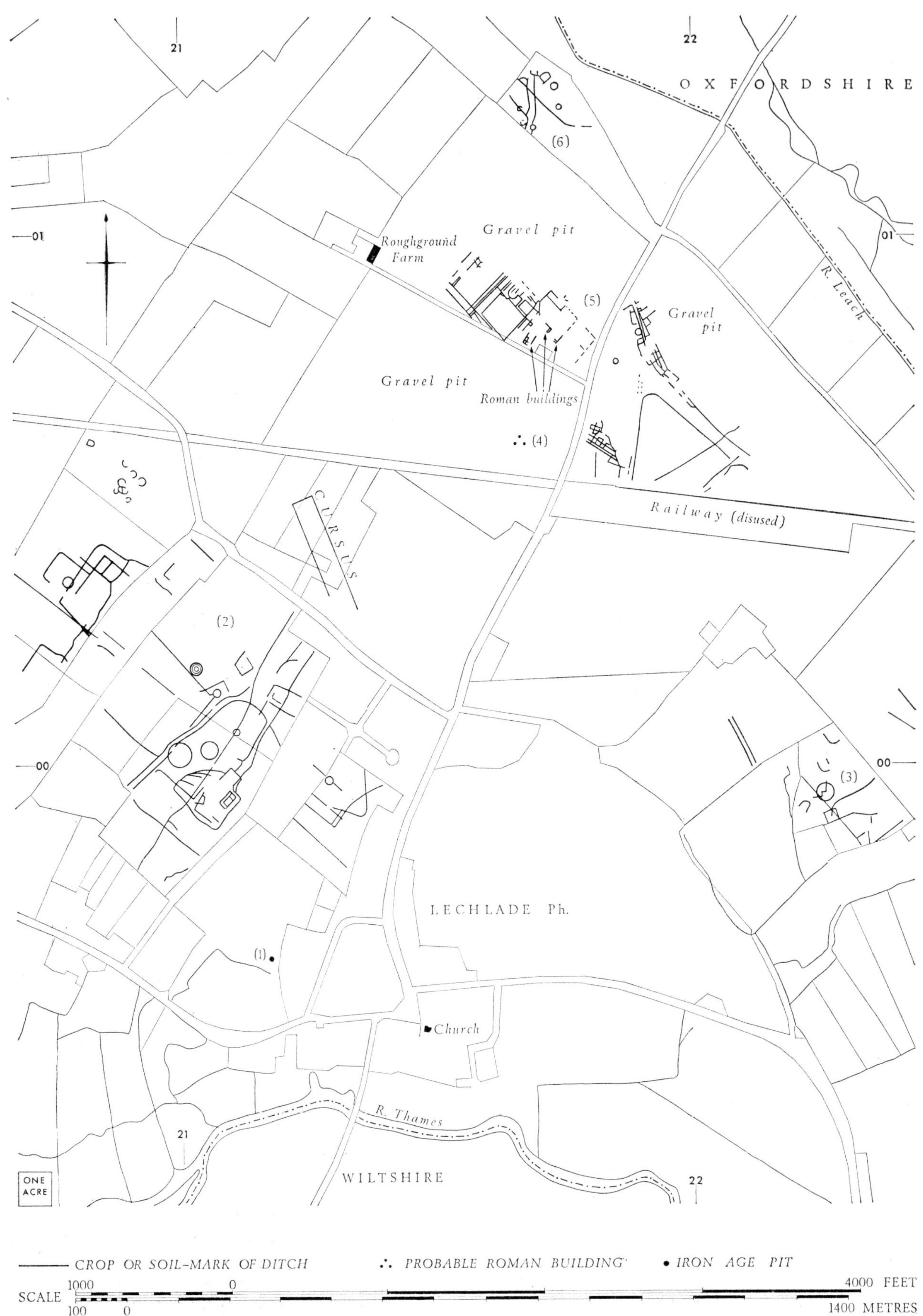

LECHLADE. (1)–(6) Iron Age Pit, undated Enclosures, Tracks etc., Roman Buildings and Settlement.

Pottery from pits in the complex of ditches on the N.W. of the buildings was of 2nd to 4th-century date.

Building and domestic debris was recovered from the complex of ditches and pits to the E., around SP 219008. The only stone-built structure to remain here was a T-shaped corn-drying oven enclosed by a circular ditch. Further S., shallow refilled scoops (c) containing abraded samian and coarse Romano-British pottery were interpreted as gravel-pits. At SP 21840075 a broad circular ditch (d), enlarged in the course of half a dozen recuttings to a diameter of 50 ft., surrounded a central area 10 ft. across, in which was a single post-hole. Scanty finds from the ditch comprised Romano-British pottery, animal bones and building debris. At SP 22010077 a shallow ditch (e), 19 ft. square, surrounded a roughly circular arrangement of post-holes, within which were four post-holes at the corners of a rectangle and two amorphous scoops. Part of a pot containing burnt bones and five small nails was recovered from one of the scoops. About 100 yds. to the S.W. was a rectangular enclosure in which were concentrated seven of the fifteen recorded inhumation graves. Most of the burials were unaccompanied, but one was accompanied by a bronze bracelet; hob-nails came from two other graves.

A Triton plaque in black samian ware was found in the course of excavation; a *genius* sculptured in limestone, with traces of paint, was previously recovered during gravel-digging; both are in the Ashmolean Museum. Objects found prior to 1958 are in Stroud Museum.

C.U.A.P., OAP VQ 21, 31, 39, 40. N.M.R., OAP (Baker) 1994, 1997, 1998, 2006, 2010.

Oxon, VIII–IX (1943–4), 96, No. 5; XXVIII (1963), 89–90. *MPBW Excavations, 1961*, 8; *1962*, 7; *1965*, 5. *JRS*, XLVIII (1958), 100, 144; LII (1962), 179–80. *Archaeological News Letter*, 7 (1961), 117. Toynbee (1964), 90; *Oxon*, XIII (1948), 76, pl. VIIA (*genius*). D. W. Harding, *The Iron Age in the Upper Thames Basin* (1972), 24 (Iron Age house). Oral information from Mrs. M. U. Jones.

(6) PROBABLE SETTLEMENT (SP 217013), undated, is revealed by crop-marks of small sub-circular and D-shaped enclosures, and of linear ditches, covering about 4 acres (map, p. 74).

C.U.A.P., OAP VQ 23.

(7) ROMAN VILLA (SP 21200250), 600 yds. N.N.E. of Great Lemhill Farm, lies partly in Southrop. A disturbed mound about 170 ft. long, 80 ft. across and up to 3 ft. high occupies a low hillock, 50 yds. W. of the R. Leach; it is bisected by the parish boundary. Pottery and building debris, including limestone, tufa, tiles and sandstone roof-tiles, are exposed in animal burrows. Part of the site was excavated in 1937, but the results have not been published.

Information from Inspectorate of Ancient Monuments, Department of Environment.

(8) ENCLOSURES, TRACKS AND LINEAR DITCHES (SU 195995), undated, show as crop-marks S. of Claydon House (map opp. p. 55, *s.v.* FAIRFORD).

C.U.A.P., OAP VM 13–15, AXP 61, AYI 68; VAP RC8–M 273.

(9) ENCLOSURE AND LINEAR DITCHES (SP 185018), are revealed by crop-marks N. of Lechlade Downs. The

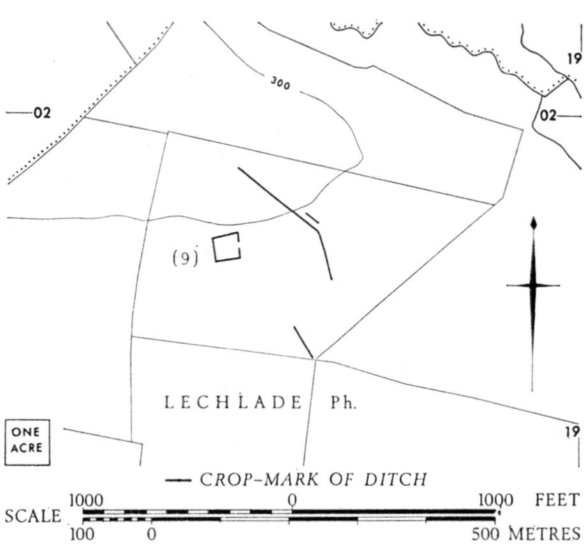

LECHLADE. (9) Enclosure and Ditches.

enclosure, on a gentle S.-facing slope, occupies about ⅓ acre.

C.U.A.P., OAP AYI 18.

Oxon, VIII–IX (1943–4), 87–8.

(10) ENCLOSURE AND TRACKS (SU 228989), undated, show as crop-marks E. of the R. Thames and S. of Leaze Farm (map, p. 76).

N.M.R., OAP SU 2298/1/385–6; 2298/3/438–9.

(11) ENCLOSURE, TRACKS AND LINEAR DITCHES (SU 231997), undated, show as crop-marks extending over some 25 acres, E. of the R. Leach at Lechlade Mill. The enclosure occupies about ⅔ acre (map, p. 76).

OAP, Allen, 724. D. N. Riley, OAP V 7–8. C.U.A.P., OAP ZH 91.

(12) ENCLOSURES, AND LINEAR DITCHES (SU 227998), undated, are revealed by crop-marks covering about 20 acres, W. of the R. Leach at Lechlade Mill.

OAP, Allen, 724. D. N. Riley, OAP V 7–8. C.U.A.P., OAP ZH 91–2.

(13) ROMANO-BRITISH SETTLEMENT (SU 238984) ploughed out, lies N. of the R. Thames and S.E. of Paradise Farm (map, p. 76). Enclosures, tracks and linear ditches show as crop-marks covering some 23 acres. Romano-British pottery and limestone slabs indicate the probable site of a building on slightly

LECHLADE. (10)–(12) Enclosures, Tracks and Linear Ditches. (13) Romano-British Settlement.

higher ground at the N. limit of the crop-marks (SU 23799861).

N.M.R., OAP SU 2398/2/480–2; 2398/3/477–9.

Oxon, VII (1942), 113, No. 10; VIII–IX (1943–4), 83. Information from Gloucester City Museum and Mrs. D. G. Stevens.

(14) LINEAR DITCHES (SP 198006), undated, show as indistinct crop-marks W. of Bryworth Farm.

C.U.A.P., OAP DX 31.

(15) LINEAR DITCHES (SP 206008), undated, show as indistinct crop-marks E. of Bryworth Farm.

O.S., VAP 70 167, 077–8.

LECKHAMPTON

(12 miles N.N.W. of Cirencester)

A Roman bronze crown found in 1844 on the skull of a 'doubled up' skeleton 'in a bank' on Leckhampton Hill (about SO 946186),[1] is paralleled in the British Isles by a single example from Hockwold-cum-Wilton, Norfolk.[2] Another skeleton, said to have had many

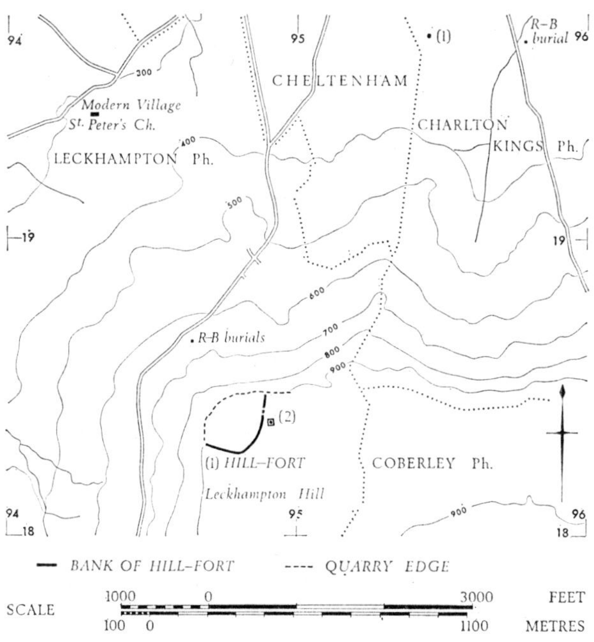

Monuments in LECKHAMPTON.

iron studs round the skull, was found near by, and Roman coins and pottery are reported from the vicinity.[3]

1. *Arch J*, I (1845), 386; III (1846), 352. The crown, formerly in the collection of Captain Henry Bell, is now lost.
2. Toynbee (1964), No. 128.
3. *Arch J*, III (1846), 353. *JBAA*, IV (1849), 58.

(1) HILL-FORT (SO 948183), on Leckhampton Hill, univallate, encloses about 7 acres on a spur of the Cotswold escarpment. The E. and S. sides are defined by a rampart with an outer ditch; the W. and N. sides by quarried scarp edges. Near its N. end the rampart crosses a gully, subsequently utilized by a quarry tramway. The entrance is in the E. An 'outer rampart' sometimes mentioned in connection with the hill-fort (*Bagendon*, 24) lies 350 yds. to the E., on the line of the parish boundary; it is undated.

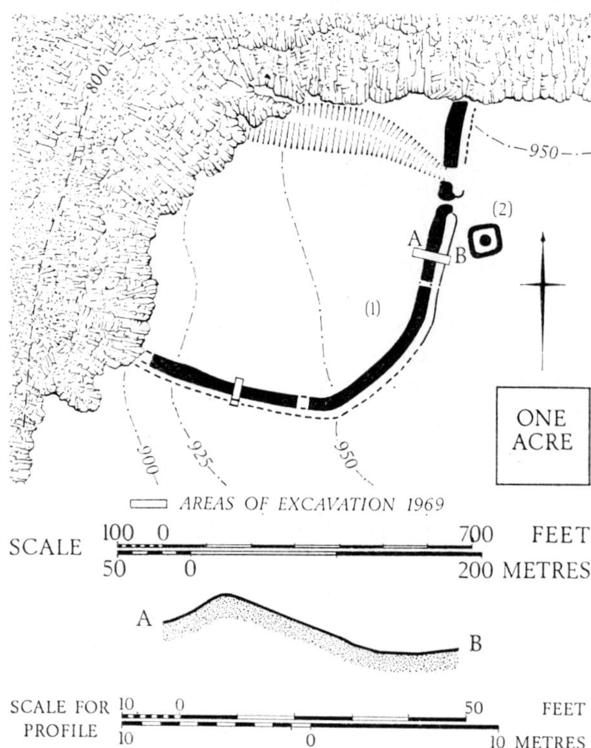

LECKHAMPTON. (1) Hill-fort. Plan and profile.

The results of excavation by Mr. E. J. Burrow and others in 1925 have been clarified by further investigations begun by Mrs. S. T. Champion in 1969. On the S. of the entrance, wherever it was examined, the rampart was found to be burnt; it was 20 ft. wide and up to 6 ft. high and consisted of a stone core revetted with dry-stone walls, tied together at the base by transverse timbers. The outer wall, better preserved than the inner, is 3 ft. thick and survives to a height of 1 ft. 8 in. A berm 3 ft. wide separates the rampart from the ditch, which is up to 14 ft. wide and 9 ft. deep, with the bottom locally flat or V-shaped. The filling of the ditch consists mainly of burnt stone from the collapsed outer revetment.

'Guard chambers' formerly thought to be rectangular in plan, on either side of the entrance, are now seen to be semicircular and inset into the ends of the rampart.

The few sherds of coarse Iron Age pottery recovered during the excavations of 1925 and 1969–71 are not closely datable. Romano-British pottery is recorded from superficial positions.

TBGAS, XLVII (1925), 81–113; 90 (1971), 5–21.

(2) Barrow ?, possibly Iron Age (SO 94921838), 30 yds. S.E. of the entrance of (1), previously disturbed, was excavated without material result in 1925. A surrounding bank 2 ft. high with sides of some 60 ft., forming an approximate square, suggests comparison with square-ditched barrows of Iron Age date.

TBGAS, XLVII (1925), 86–7, 101–2. *Ant J*, XLI (1961), 52.

LEONARD STANLEY

(14 miles W. of Cirencester)

A coin of Constans and a fragment of samian ware[1] have been recorded from the vicinity of (1).

1. *TBGAS*, 60 (1938), 182.

(1) Probable Settlement (SO 795038), undated, S. of Poplar Gate, shows on air photographs as indistinct crop-marks. They cover some 5 acres on a low eminence on the gravel terrace of the R. Frome, about 150 ft. above O.D. There are indications of enclosures amongst linear ditches.

C.U.A.P., OAP ABF 54–5.

LITTLE RISSINGTON

No Iron Age or Romano-British monument is known in this parish.

LITTLE SODBURY

(20 miles S.W. of Cirencester)

A linear bank of uncertain date, possibly contemporary with the hill-fort of Sodbury, together with other earthworks, are described under Sodbury (1).

LONG NEWNTON

(9 miles S.W. of Cirencester)

The Foss Way passes through the E. part of the parish. A section dug along the middle of the *agger* for a waterworks trench in 1961 revealed a layer of stones 3 ins. to 4 ins. thick, covered by 1 in. of small stone chips. The *agger* showed no signs of heavy wear or of repairs.[1]

1. O.S. records.

(1) Romano-British Settlement (ST 91639156), on Newnton Farm, lies in the plain, about 300 ft. above sea-level, ½ mile S.E. of the village. The site is 300 yds. W. of the Foss Way and 70 yds. W. of a brook. Occupation debris is spread over an area of about 1 acre in an arable field.

Finds (in a private collection) include two coins of the 3rd and 5th centuries, a 1st-century plate-brooch, pottery of 1st to 4th-century types, roof and flue tiles. Post-holes and a drain were revealed in a small excavation.

TBGAS, 87 (1968), 204, No. 10.

LONGBOROUGH

(20 miles N.E. of Cirencester)

The Foss Way passes through the parish.

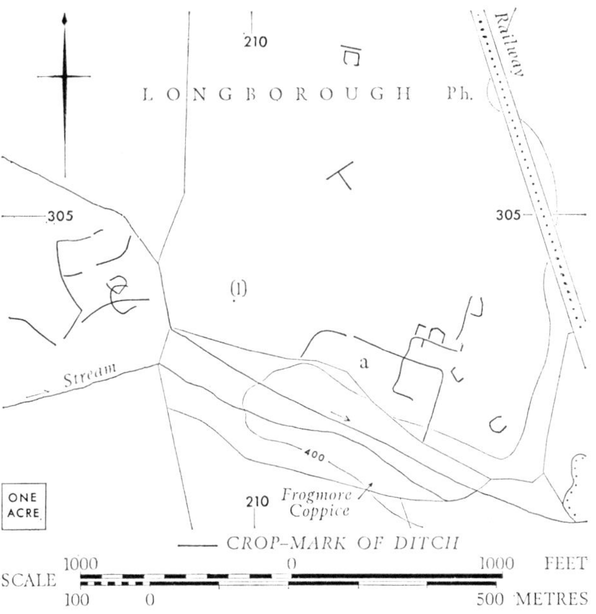

LONGBOROUGH. (1) Probable Settlement.

(1) Probable Settlement (SP 210305), undated, ½ mile E. of the Foss Way and in the vicinity of Frogmore Coppice, is revealed by crop-marks on glacial gravel among traces of frost-cracks and former ridge-and-furrow cultivation. The enclosure (a) occupies at least 3 acres.

N.M.R., OAP (Baker) SP 2030/1; 2130/1–5.

LOWER SLAUGHTER

(15 miles N.E. of Cirencester)

For general map, see p. 18, *s.v.* Bourton-on-the-Water.

The S. boundary of the parish follows the Foss Way. This stretch of Roman road, contemporary structures along it, and the junction with the now obliterated Ryknild Street are noted under Bourton-on-the Water (2b) and (3). Buckle Street, running N.N.W. from Bourton Bridge, is an ancient route possibly used in the Roman period (see p. xlv). During the war of

1914–18 an inhumed male skeleton with hob-nailed footwear was found in an Oolite coffin on a hill-slope close to Buckle Street, probably near (4).[1]

A pit containing two iron knives, red colour-coated rosette-stamped ware and other Romano-British pottery was found in a gravel pit just N. of the R. Dikler at Lower Slaughter village (about SP 163227);[2] adjacent was a short length of wall, possibly contemporary. The finds are in the Royce Collection in Bristol City Museum.

1. *Ant J*, I (1921), 340–1. Oral information from Miss M. Travell.

2. *TBGAS*, VII (1882–3), 80; 83 (1964), 12.

(1) ROMANO-BRITISH SETTLEMENT (SP 175231–SP 174226), Chessels, extending over more than 25 acres of alluvial gravels (plan opposite) and now largely destroyed by quarrying, lies N. of the Foss Way and overlies traces of earlier occupation. Ground observation, air photographs, and methodical examination and extensive excavation of the stripped gravel surface by Mrs. H. E. O'Neil since 1954 have revealed ditches, pits and the sites of structures in three contiguous fields: from N. to S., Great Chessels, Little Chessels (both referred to as the Farnworth gravel-pit) and the George Young gravel-pit. Ring-ditches (apparently including barrows) have been recorded in the last named area, together with Romano-British ditches, pits, post-holes, stone paving, and coins ranging from the early 2nd to the 4th century; a single cist burial was associated with a coin of Magnentius.

Indications, much disturbed, of Romano-British occupation occur over Great and Little Chessels. They include at least two rectangular buildings, round huts, a probable shrine or temple, eleven wells, and evidence for iron working, agriculture and possibly for the fashioning of stone. There were three burials, two being of infants. Pottery of Iron-Age form and a La Tène III brooch suggest that the settlement was pre-Roman in origin. Of three coin hoards found, one is of the 3rd and two are of the 4th century.

The recorded pattern of settlement in Great and Little Chessels is seen in the plan, where the notation used by Mrs. O'Neil is repeated. An air photograph (Plate 53) shows features additional to those marked on the plan, especially to S.E. where a broad way appears to be defined by ditches some 100 ft. apart, with further enclosures beyond; to N.E. a continuous bounding ditch seems to define the limits of the settlement.

Much of the site was formerly under ridge-and-furrow cultivation and this, together with earlier robbing and subsequent mechanical stripping of the surface, has caused much destruction or disturbance. Former buildings were indicated by ditches, occasional post-holes, and fragments of paving. Some were circular. One of these, apparently in use during the early 4th century, lay under a rectangular structure (47) with dressed and coursed stone footings 2 ft. wide enclosing an area 43 ft. by 23 ft., thought to have been divided into six rooms; it was built *c.* A.D. 350. Local stone slates, many nails, fragments of columns and traces of painted wall-plaster were found here. Pitched stone paving lay outside this and also outside another certainly rectangular building (67), identified by a line of 'veranda' post-holes and paved floors. Fragments of monumental masonry including pieces of column came from well 5, 36 yds. N. of structure 47, and from pit 20, 110 yds. S.S.E. Stone slates lay on paving E. of pit 20. Fragments of votive tablet were found at structure 47 and in pit 20, and eight votive objects came from well 5. A group of sub-rectangular ditch patterns S. of structures 47 and 67 are similarly aligned one with another, but a large complex of shallow ditches 180 yds. E. of 67 lies in a different orientation. Of the eleven wells noted, two were in the N. part of the last named complex, where also were found two burials. All wells were about 20 ft. deep and 2 ft. in diameter at the head, the latter usually stone-lined; well 8 was in an enclosure. Pits were generally shallow and irregular, but one was straight-sided and flat-bottomed; it contained rubbish. A corn-drier was of 4th-century date, and two probable forges occurred near structure 67 and pit 20.

Romano-British finds include coins from the mid 1st to the late 4th or early 5th century. There were three hoards. One found in a pot late in the 19th century is said to have numbered 1,500 coins, mostly *minimissimi*, together with a silver coin of Valens. A disturbed hoard of 134 coins, dating from 260–75, came from a bronze-studded chest buried in a hole covered by the courtyard paving of structure 67. The third hoard, also disturbed, was apparently buried in a bag in a deep ditch immediately W. of the floor in structure 83. It consisted of 1,170 coins dating from the middle to the end of the 4th century and included 482 *minimissimi*. Abundant pottery represents periods from the 1st to the 4th century. Votive objects, all damaged, comprise: from well 5 at varying depths, two small uninscribed portable altars, a similar altar with very crude sculpture, three votive plaques of Mars and of *genii cucullati*, and two small statuettes of seated headless figures; a fragment of votive tablet came from building 47 and another, as noted above, from pit 20. A small relief of Minerva found in 1769 (Camden's *Britannia* (ed. Gough, 1789), I, 279, Pl. xiv, fig. 8) probably came from this settlement. Nine late 4th-century glass vessels come from structure 47. Iron objects include bolts, a rake, a door-latch, chisels and, from the probable forge near building 67, an anvil and a 24-lb iron pig. Numerous nails and slag come from the area of the probable forge near pit 20, and coal was found near by. There were quern fragments (area 83), and a Kimmeridge shale bracelet. A miniature bronze bird, probably from a pin, was found on the surface. There were many animal bones and oyster shells. The bronze bird, the coins and some of the pottery are in Gloucester City Museum; the other finds are in private possession.

N.M.R., OAP SP 1722/4 and 1723/1–4 (Baker).

Ant J, XII (1932), 279–93. *Oxon*, XX (1955), 5–7. *TBGAS*, VII (1882–3), 71–2; 56 (1934), 133–9; 61 (1939), 114, 123 (finds in G. Young's gravel-pit); 89 (1960), 121 (barrows 1 a–c). *PPS*, XXVII (1961), 296 (Young's gravel-pit). *Num. Chron.* XX (1960), 275–7 (coins). *JRS*, XLVIII (1958), 49–55. Toynbee (1964), 161, 177, 178, 181. H. E. O'Neil in *Studies in Building History*, 1961 (ed. Jope), 27–38.

(2) Enclosure (sp 169221), undated, shows as crop-marks (Plate 55) immediately W. of the stream by Slaughter Bridge and 100 yds. from the Foss Way. Three sides are seen, containing an area of about 3 acres. Entrances in the N. and E. sides are respectively some 20 ft. and 30 ft. wide. The E. side ends sharply on the S. (cf. Southrop (1)). Air photographs show the W. side butting against extensive pitting where the S. side might have been. Map, p. 18.

N.M.R., OAP SP 1622/6–9 (Baker); 1622/5/355. C.U.A.P., OAP ABR 83, AZN 35.

(3) Romano-British Settlement (sp 16102216—sp 15832224), Spring Hill, is known from finds and excavation by Miss M. Travell and Mr. F. Gardiner. Crop-marks in the area include features almost certainly Romano-British; at sp 15832224 they show an enclosure about 100 ft. long from N. to S. and 60 ft. wide (map, p. 18, *s.v.* Bourton). Fourth-century Romano-British pottery as well as building debris have been found in the vicinity. About 250 ft. to W. crop-marks show a N.–S. linear boundary. A ditched track (d) about 20 ft. wide extends for at least 250 yds. W.S.W. from the modern road at sp 15842255. Scattered Romano-British pottery occurs in the modern field around it, and between it and the excavated area 500 yds. to S.E.

Excavation at sp 16042220, N.W. of a road and lane junction about 80 yds. W. from the present spring of Spring Hill, exposed stone floors, an oven and small pits, but no walls. Some pottery was found S.W. of the lane junction.

Finds include coins, mostly 4th century, but ranging from Hadrian to Arcadius and Honorius. Pottery was preponderantly late Roman and of a notably diverse range of fabrics including Oxfordshire, Nene Valley and New Forest products; there was a little 2nd-century samian ware and calcite-gritted ware presumably of late date. Bronze objects included spoons, a bow brooch, a ring-headed pin, a small decorated hook, fragments of bracelets and a finger ring. There were shears and a socketed spear-head, both of iron. Glass beads were found.

N.M.R., OAP SP 1522/1–4; 1622/3/350–2.

Archaeol. Review, 6 (1971), 28. Information from Miss M. Travell.

(4) Circular Enclosure (sp 157221), undated, appears as a crop-mark (Plate 65) on the ridge-top about 100 yds. W. of (3). About 180 ft. across, it is defined by two seemingly continuous narrow ditches set close together in uncertain relationship, but probably intersecting on the E. side. It probably lies over part of an irregular, broader ditch which curves N.E. from it.

N.M.R., OAP (Baker) SP 1522/1–4.

MAISEYHAMPTON

(6 miles E. of Cirencester)

(1) Probable Settlement (sp 119025), undated, S.E. of Sunhill, shows as indistinct crop-marks covering 1½ acres on Forest Marble about 350 ft. above O.D. Linear ditches appear to include those of a trapezoidal enclosure (11930247) of about ½ acre, with entrance at N.

N.M.R., OAP SP 1102/1/402–3.

MARSHFIELD

(23 miles s.w. of Cirencester)

(1) Probable Romano-British Settlement (st 754743), Blackies Field, is indicated by abraded 2nd to 4th-century sherds of samian ware and coarse pottery collected over many years, also by part of a bronze brooch and small pieces of sandstone tiles found in deep ploughsoil on a gentle S.E.-facing slope. Most of the finds have been made in an area covering less than an acre; they remain in private possession.

(2) Romano-British Building (st 78857340), The Hams, is situated on level ground at the shoulder of a valley side. Large numbers of flanged roofing tiles, fragments of sandstone tiles and 2nd to 4th-century sherds have been found in ploughsoil covering a marked platform, 100 ft. by 55 ft. by 1½ ft. high, lying approximately N.–S., athwart the slope. Pottery and tile fragments have also been found scattered along the valley shoulder to the E., up to 220 ft. from the building. In 1969, during ploughing above and to N.E. of this area, a short length of drain was uncovered, its sides and capping formed with limestone slabs; it is undated, but possibly Romano-British.

Some pottery in Bristol City Museum; other finds in private possession.

Information on (1) and (2) from Mr. R. Knight.

MAUGHERSBURY

No Iron Age or Romano-British monument is known in this parish.

MICKLETON

No Iron Age or Romano-British monument is known in this parish.

MINCHINHAMPTON

(8 miles W. of Cirencester)

A gold stater of BODVOC now in Stroud Museum came from Camp Field in 1925.[1] A Roman brooch was found in a barrow on a 'table-land' in Hyde, N.E. of Minchinhampton, about 1845.[2] Two urns, one said to be a 'Roman olla', with bones and charcoal, were found during quarrying at Burleigh, N.W. of Minchinhampton, in 1845.[3] Roman pottery and tiles, perhaps from a kiln, have been noted near Little Britain (SO 843021), near the valley bottom between Minchinhampton and Woodchester.[4]

1. *Bagendon*, 120.
2. *PCNFC*, V (1868), 51.
3. *JBAA*, I (1846), 149.
4. *TBGAS*, 61 (1939), 66.

MONUMENTS (1)–(8)

Complex, diverse and exceptionally well-preserved earthworks extend over the greater part of Minchinhampton Common, an almost flat-topped ridge capped by Great Oolite. North and east of Minchinhampton town there are more broken earthworks, and there has also been some levelling and creation of earthworks in later times. The gently sloping southern shoulder of the

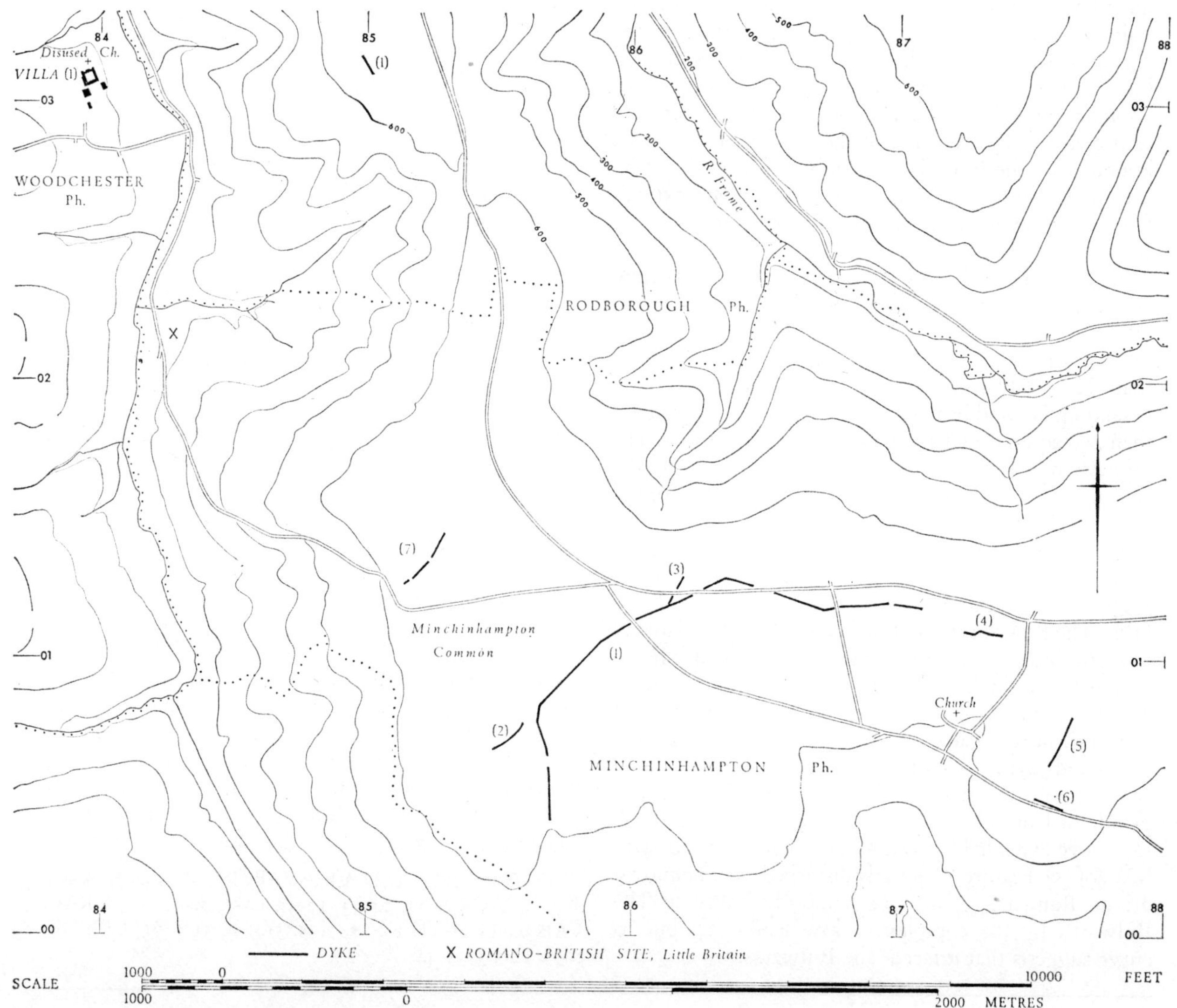

Monuments in MINCHINHAMPTON, RODBOROUGH and WOODCHESTER.

ridge is indented by re-entrant valleys in the area S. of monument (1). The earthworks include stretches of bank and ditch (1–7), various in form and size and probably if not certainly of the Iron Age, and a complex of long low banks (8) of uncertain but relatively early date, possibly Iron Age. Amberley Camp (so-called) is later;* its bank (a–a) touches an Iron Age rampart (7) which bisects the area, and also crosses elements of complex (8); it is known from excavation to lie over a pit which probably dates from historic times, one of many hundreds on Minchinhampton Common. It is matched by another large enclosure (b–b) immediately on the S., defined by a slight bank which crosses bank and ditch (2), itself probably of the Iron Age. Isaac Taylor noted 'wattle hedge' in this area on his map of 1777, but Bigland in 1792 could only guess at the origins of the earthworks. Fifty or more pillow mounds, including four or five round mounds, are probably relics of the rabbit farming which flourished in the region as late as the 18th century; one such mound is built on top of bank (2) and others lie on elements of complex (8). The pillow mounds and the pits are restricted to the S.W. half of the Common in an area bounded by the N.E. side of Amberley 'camp' and by a bank and ditch, 18 ft. across overall, which extends from the E. angle of the 'camp' to a break in The Bulwarks (1) at SO 85830102.

Neither The Bulwarks (1) nor the rampart (7) fully crosses the ridge-top, although the position of bank and ditch (2) suggests an unfinished attempt to prolong (1) to the scarp edge on the S.W. Present evidence suggests that The Bulwarks, probably continuous with and extending beyond bank (4), surrounded an area of more than 200 acres, now largely occupied by the town. The suggestion is strengthened by a reference in 1853 to 'the ancient earthwork which encloses the whole town' (*Arch*, XXXV (1853), 412–13).

Much disturbance, including at least two phases of enclosure and ploughing, and wartime construction (1939–45), conceal the probable link between (1) and (4) in The Park, an area defined on the N. by a relatively modern ditch. There are faint suggestions on air photographs that a ditch ran parallel with Butts Street, E. of The Park and S. of Blue Boys Farm. It is uncertain if bank (5), now isolated on the E., is of the same period as (1) and (4); if so, its relationship to the other earthworks is obscure since its ditch is on the E. side. The profile of bank (5) is akin to that of (1) at JK. A bank may have extended S. from SO 87460049, some 200 yds. S.W. of (5). Feature (6), greatly disturbed, is of unknown origin. Rampart (7) may be tenuously linked to The Bulwarks by the complex of low banks (8), but its curve suggests that it faced The Bulwarks.

The very large area of these remains, their diversity, their dissimilarity from hill-fort or cross-ridge dykes, and the large area left open to the S. of (1) and (4), all stress their divergence from the pattern of Iron Age works repeatedly found elsewhere in the Cotswolds. Despite notable differences of arrangement and situation, the Bagendon complex (p. 6) is the only other Cotswold site of which this can be said. As yet, however, no true Belgic material has been found in Minchinhampton.

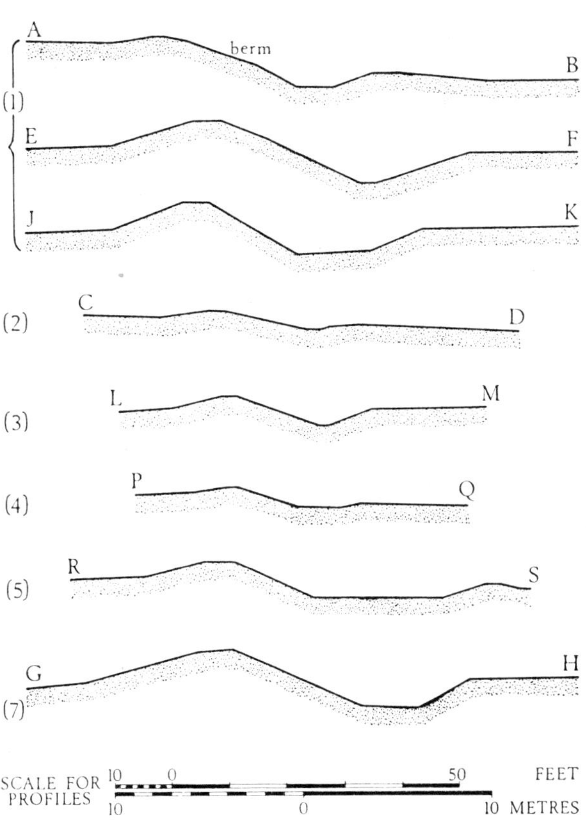

MINCHINHAMPTON. (1)–(8) Profiles. (Plan opposite.)

Occupation of Minchinhampton Common in the Romano-British period is shown by Roman tiles and pottery found during excavations in 1937 and also in the course of diggings among the widespread pits (e.g. *PCNFC*, V (1875), 288, 292; XIII (1898–9), 53–6). Similar material, now in Stroud Museum, came to light when wartime trenches were dug close to the reservoir.

Air Photographs: C.U.A.P., VAP RC8-L 152–7, V-CJ 81–100, V-CK 3–14, 24–33, 37–48, 60–7, 70–8, 85–98. RAF, VAP 3G/TUD/UK 102: 5071–5, 5103–8, 5156–61; CPE/UK 2098: F20, 3335–42.

* Features of later periods, sometimes impinging on the Iron Age and undated monuments described in the Inventory, are recorded in grey on the plan opposite.

C.U.A.P., OAP AIK 88–98, AIL 1–8, AIN 66–88, AJL 20–4, AMK 78–88, ARG 80–6.

Bibliography: Bigland (1791) II, 6. Playne (1872), 285–93. Witts (1883), 2–3. *TBGAS*, 59 (1937), 287–307 (excavation). *Antiquity*, XLII (1968), 312–14. *Bagendon*, 157. *TBGAS*, 80 (1961), 187.

(1) THE BULWARKS, IRON AGE BANK AND DITCH (Plates 44, 45), extend for at least 1⅛ miles from just N. of Halfway House Inn (SO 85700035) to a point in The Park (SO 87020120), beyond which they have been destroyed. Although the earthworks are continuous their form and scale of structure vary greatly: overall width from 47 ft. to 62 ft.; height of bank from 1½ ft. to 4½ ft. From the S.W. angle, N. of section AB, the ditch is relatively narrow and the bank is uneven and small; it is possible that the earthwork was once intended to continue S.W. on the line of (2). At section EF the ditch and bank are both some 8 ft. wider than at AB. As far as the N. angle (SO 86360130) there are surface indications of a berm on the E. side of the bank, and in 1937 Mrs. E. M. Clifford demonstrated its existence in her excavation some 400 yds. N.E. of section EF. Here the ditch, 9 ft. in front of a buried revetment wall, was 23 ft. across at the top and 7½ ft. deep; it had a flat bottom 5 ft. across. In the stretch E. of the northern angle (Plate 45 and profile JK) the character of the earthwork is entirely different from that hitherto described; there is no sign of a berm and the slope of the bank falling to the ditch bottom is particularly steep. Playne noted in 1872 that some part of the eastward continuation of the earthwork had been destroyed during the construction of The Park; he also averred that one of the two gaps near the N. angle, E. of (3), was an original entrance. It is probable that earthwork (4) represents a continuation of The Bulwarks. A roughly circular ditched platform in The Park (SO 870012), some 80 ft. in diameter and lying just N. of the line of the ditch, is of unknown origin.

The excavations of 1937 yielded Iron Age 'B' sherds from the bank as well as from the ditch, and Roman pottery from the ditch only. The finds are in Stroud Museum.

Bibliography: see above; also Rudder, 468; Witts (1883), No. 71; Playne (1876), 214, No. 31.

(2) BANK AND DITCH, probably Iron Age, extend for at least 520 ft. S.W. from SO 85600077 and are precisely sited at a slight change of slope on the W. side of a re-entrant valley. Near its N.E. end the earthwork is crossed by the small bank and ditch of an enclosure (b–b) and to the W. of this point two pillow mounds lie, end to end, on its crest.

Bank and ditch are each about 16 ft. across and the bank is up to 1½ ft. high (profile CD). The S. portion, exactly in alignment with The Bulwarks (1), has been flattened by ploughing and may formerly have continued further S.W. The well-preserved N. part of the earthwork is bowed towards the E.

It seems possible that this earthwork represents an abandoned scheme to extend The Bulwarks S.W., rather than S., from the region of the angle at SO 85670083.

(3) BANK AND DITCH, probably Iron Age, extend for 400 ft. N.E. from (1), against which they appear to butt at SO 86130117 (Plate 45). The natural slope drops gently from the N. end of the earthwork to the shoulder of the ridge about 190 yds. away. The earthwork is cut by the present road and the ditch is broken by quarries. At the N. end a low bank, probably cut by the ditch, lies approximately in line with the earthwork and extends N.E. for some 250 ft. Bank and ditch are each about 17 ft. across and the bank is about 2½ ft. high (profile LM).

(4) BANK AND DITCH, probably Iron Age, in the E. part of The Park, extend for 450 ft. E. from SO 87250110, some 800 ft. W. of the point where (1) is interrupted. Their continuation W. and E. has been destroyed. A sharp change in alignment near the W. end is unexplained. Generally the bank and ditch are each 12 ft. across, but at PQ they are respectively 21 ft. and 18 ft. across, and the ditch is 3 ft. below the bank (profile PQ).

(5) BANK AND DITCH (SO 876007), possibly Iron Age, E. of The Old Grange (Rectory), are 600 ft. long and formerly continued N. and S. The bank is about 22 ft. across and 3 ft. high; the very wide ditch is of similar depth (profile RS). A causeway appears to have been inserted opposite the avenue leading from The Old Grange. Some 30 yds. S. from the S. end of the monument a shallow flat-bottomed depression extends E., tapering slightly.

(6) BANK AND DITCH (?), possibly Iron Age, extend E. from a point 100 yds. S. of (5). The earthwork is greatly disturbed, and prominent only at the W. end; here the bank is 40 ft. broad and 2 ft. high above a poorly defined linear depression, 60 ft. across, possibly a ditch reused and widened as a track. The bank can be traced E. for 250 yds., eventually as a low scarp which turns towards the present road near the W. shoulder of the re-entrant from the south.

Bigland describes earthworks as extending to 'Woeful Dane Bottom', the re-entrant valley near by on the east. (Bigland (1791), II, 6).

(7) IRON AGE BANK AND DITCH, extend for 900 ft. N.E. from the escarpment edge at SO 85140124. The two main parts, on either side of the only entrance which is certainly original, some 300 ft. S. of the N. end, are slightly angled, with the concavity facing N.W. The bank, 32 ft. across, is now about 4 ft. high (profile GH).

The ditch is some 33 ft. across; Mrs. E. M. Clifford's excavation near the N. end in 1937 showed it to be 8 ft. deep, with a flat bottom 11 ft. across. Iron Age 'B' and so-called 'Belgic' pottery was found under the rampart and in low levels of the ditch. Finds are in Stroud Museum.

The work is now much disturbed, but there is no sign that the rampart ever continued further N. where an enclosure (a–a), 'Amberley Camp', appears to have been built against it. A low bank, part of complex (8), meets the ditch just S. of the entrance.

Bibliography: see above; also Rudder, 468; Playne (1876), 214, No. 30; Witts (1883), No. 4.

(8) LOW BANKS, undated, but possibly of the Iron Age, divide parts of Minchinhampton Common. The banks are mostly about 12 ft. across and 1 ft. high and there is no sign of accompanying ditches. They generally lie in straight runs or fluent curves and do not display the small, erratic changes of course apparent in parts of the enclosures (a–a), (b–b) mentioned above, and in the ditch S.E. of the reservoir. In places the ditchless banks run parallel, as if defining tracks up to 36 ft. across; three such 'tracks' converge on an 'open space' at SO 854010. One part of the earthworks almost spans the gap between (2) and (1); another part spans between (1) and (7). The banks extend N. of the area occupied by the enclosures (a–a), (b–b), the pillow mounds and the pits, and the bank of Amberley 'camp' crosses them at three points. Low banks, not shown on the plan facing p. 82, exist on the town side of The Bulwarks (1), extending E. from SO 857006. They are more prominent than most of the features embodied in monument (8).

C.U.A.P., VAP RC8-L 152–7.

MISERDEN

(7 miles N.W. of Cirencester)

A Roman coin of the 4th century, a flue tile and stone foundations have been found at Slad (SO 882081).[1]

St. Clair Baddeley claims that secondary interments found in 1920 in an unspecified barrow at Miserden were Romano-British.[2]

1. *TBGAS*, 87 (1968), 204. Finds in Stroud Museum.
2. *A History of Cirencester* (1924), 19, n. 5.

MORETON-IN-MARSH

(22 miles N.E. of Cirencester)

The Foss Way passes through the parish.

(1) PROBABLE SETTLEMENT (SP 210312), undated, E. of Stow Bridge, shows as crop-marks over some 15 acres on glacial gravel, about 415 ft. above O.D.

N.M.R., OAP (Baker), SP 2131/1–2.

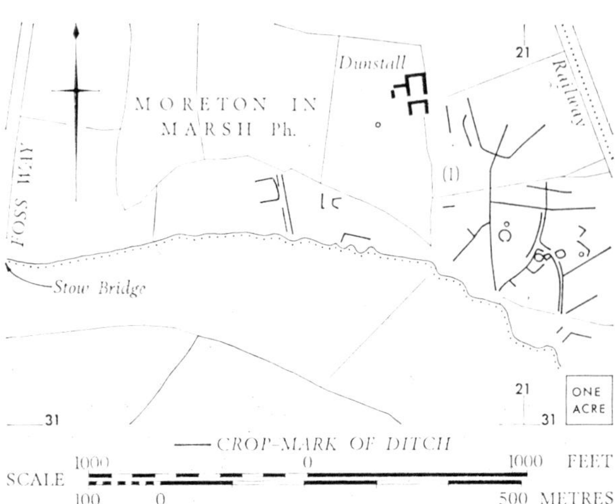

MORETON-IN-MARSH. (1) Probable Settlement.

NAILSWORTH

(11 miles W. of Cirencester)

A Dobunnic gold coin inscribed ANTED is recorded from the parish.[1]

1. D. F. Allen in *Bagendon*, 120; lost.

NAUNTON

(15 miles N.N.E. of Cirencester)

Stanborough Lane, partly followed by the S. boundary of the parish, is referred to as *straet* in a charter of 737–40 which survives in an 11th-century text.[1] During construction of the railway, in 1876, two Romano-British burials 'edged round with stones' were found at about SP 099215, some 300 yds. N. of Stanborough Lane and 2 miles S.W. of the village.[2] Much Roman pottery was noted in the area.

1. Grundy (1935–6), 178; B 165, K 90; Sawyer, No. 99, concerning grants of land at Aston Blank and Notgrove.
2. *TBGAS*, VII (1882–3), 71.

(1) PROBABLE ROMANO-BRITISH SETTLEMENT (SP 120245), at Summerhill, 1 mile N.E. of the village, ploughed out, lies on level ground at 750 ft. above O.D., above a slope which falls gently S. to the R. Windrush.

Dobunnic and Roman coins, pottery and tiles are recorded. The silver Dobunnic coins, uninscribed, include two (Allen's class A), now in Bristol City Museum; two more (classes B ii and E), probably from this site, are in a private collection. Roman coins recorded at Gloucester City Museum include two of 2nd and 3rd-century date.

In 1934 an undated burial with head to W. was

discovered at SP 12012461, in a grave paved and lined with limestone slabs.

E. F. Eales, *Naunton upon Cotswold* (1928). *TBGAS*, 56 (1934), 129–31; 86 (1967), 193–4. *Bagendon*, 89, 120–1.

(2) ENCLOSURE (SP 11042105), undated, shows as a crop-mark N. of Stanborough Lane. For plan, see p. 88, *s.v.* NOTGROVE.

N.M.R., OAP SP 1020/1/367.

NORTH CERNEY

(3 miles N. of Cirencester)

A small camp was said to lie close to the White Way (4); Rudder thought it of 'considerable extent', but Witts found it too flattened for interpretation. There are possible traces on air photographs of a circular ditched enclosure at SP 027075, 300 yds. W. of the White Way.[1] In Calmsden Field (? SP 0409) an 'outpost, with circumvallations' and a Roman 'lachrymatory' of blue glass were noted 'on the Downs'.[2] Finds from Downs Farm are described under BAUNTON (1), p. 13.

There are scarps, some possibly of 'Celtic' fields, on the spur N. of Old Park, about SP 009096 (cf. N.M.R., OAP SP 0009/1/338–9).

1. Bigland (1791), 285. Rudder (1779), 325. Witts (1883), 38, No. 74. N.M.R., OAP SP 0207/1/360–1.
2. Bigland (1791), 287. Rudder (1779), 325.

(1) SCRUBDITCH, see p. 8, *s.v.* BAGENDON.

(2) HILL-FORT (SO 996095), W. of the hamlet of Woodmancote, univallate and about 10 acres in area although largely destroyed, unexcavated, has recently been rediscovered from the air by W. A. Baker (Plate 36). It lies in part in an area called 'The Ditches' on drawings made for the first O.S., *c.* 1815, where the N. half is marked as a curving boundary. The bank and ditch around the S. half, not clearly seen on the ground, perhaps suffered destruction in Roman times when a

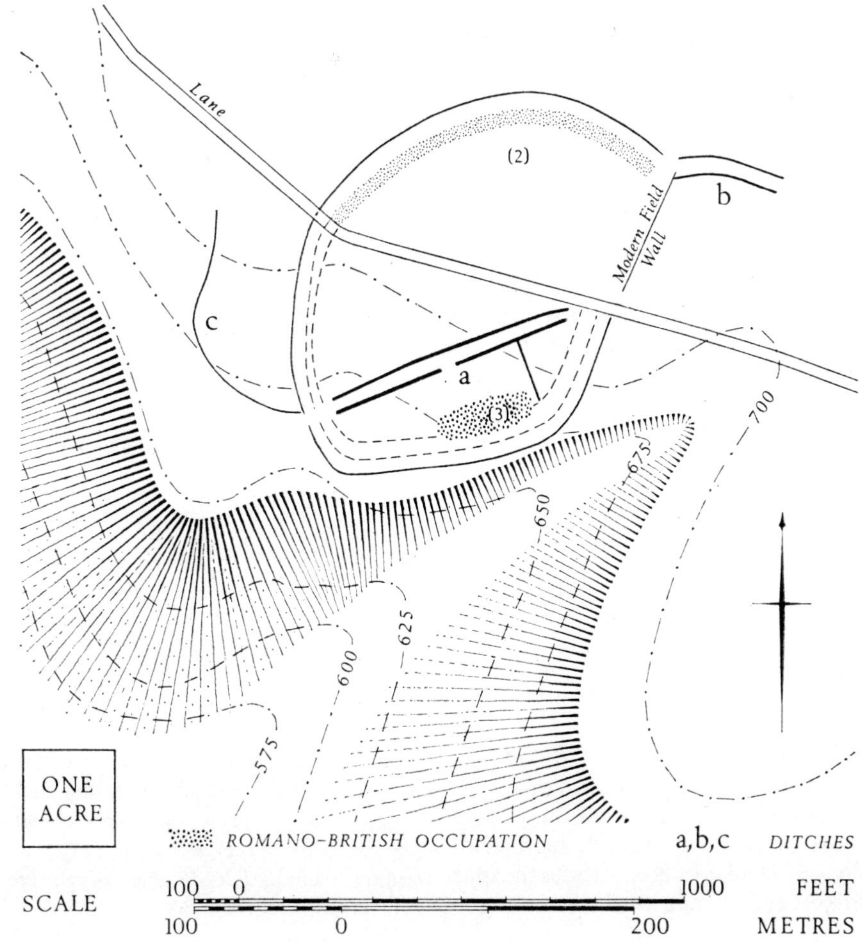

NORTH CERNEY. (2) Hill-fort near Woodmancote. (3) Romano-British Settlement.

settlement (3) was established in the S. part of the hill-fort.

The N. half of the hill-fort is on almost flat ground. Its E. side probably corresponds with a modern field wall. The ditch is still visible on the N. and W. sides as a depression about 40 ft. wide and up to 3 ft. deep, below a low spread bank. The S. half drops slightly to a small spur on the shoulder of the Great Oolite ridge. There are indications of a spread stone bank on the W. side, and air photographs taken in 1971 show a probable entrance at S.W. In the N. half of the hill-fort there are indications of one or two platforms, perhaps for structures.

N.M.R., OAP (Baker) SO 9909/2 and 3; 9909/7/291–3; 9909/8/362–5; 9909/13/80–2.

(3) ROMANO-BRITISH SETTLEMENT (SO 996093), under arable inside the hill-fort (2), is identified from patches of limestone blocks, some of them squared, associated with other building debris and pottery, mostly found in the S. of the hill-fort. Crop-marks of parallel ditches (a), defining a way about 30 ft. wide, extend across the area towards the hill-fort entrance; the northern ditch may be continued by ditch (c). A second pair of parallel ditches (b) meets the hill-fort at N.E.

Finds of pottery, mostly of the 3rd and 4th century, include Oxfordshire mortaria and colour-coated wares, with one or two pieces of samian.

Air photographs as for (1); also SO 9909/7/294–5 (N.E. ditches).

(4) WHITE WAY (*i*, SP 030068–SP 030076; *ii*, SP 02930825–SP 02970908), probable Roman road. The *agger* is suggested at (*i*) by a line of much-disturbed bank in Long Plantation, and at (*ii*) by the scattered stony remains of a wide, low bank, without a ditch, in the arable field S.W. of Nordown; a further wide, low bank continues in the field to the north. Both features are visible on a vertical air photograph. A hollow running close to (*i*) on the E. side might be explained as a worn track, but there is no sign of it beside (*ii*).

R.A.F., VAP CPE/UK 2098: 3006.

NORTH NIBLEY

(21 miles W.S.W. of Cirencester)

(1) BRACKENBURY* DITCHES HILL-FORT (ST 747949), partly bivallate, unexcavated, encloses 4 acres on a spur of the Cotswold escarpment, ¾ mile S.E. of the village.

The outer rampart, 25 ft. wide and 5 ft. high, with external ditch 20 ft. wide and 4 ft. deep, crosses the spur from N.W. to S.E., its ends resting on the scarp edges. The entrance from the plateau is through a gap 20 ft. wide near the S. end.

The inner defences surround the tip of the spur. The N.E. side is defined by a rampart, 50 ft. wide and 10 ft. high, separated by a berm 8 ft. wide from an external ditch, 45 ft. wide and 8 ft. deep, with a slight counterscarp bank. On the N.W. and S.E. sides the rampart, reduced in size, sits on the edges of the spur; it is 20 ft. above the ditch which, still with a counterscarp bank, drops from the N. corner to follow a ledge as far as

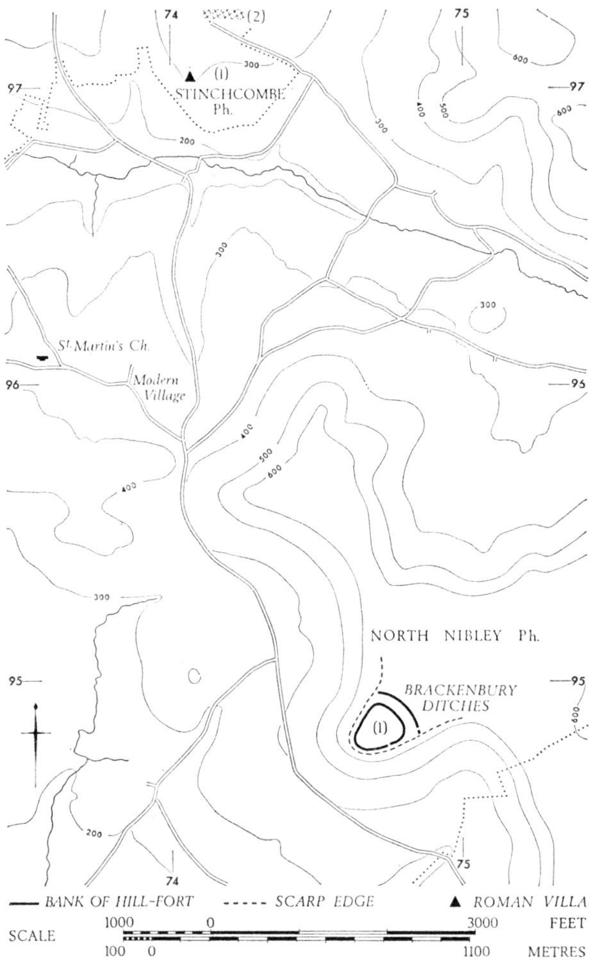

Monuments in NORTH NIBLEY and STINCHCOMBE.

the entrance in the middle of the S.E. side. This entrance, a 10 ft. gap between staggered bank ends, is approached from the vale by a hollow-way; access from the plateau is by way of the entrance through the outer rampart.

Lloyd Baker (1821), 166, No. 13. Playne (1876), 217, No. 37. Witts (1883), 6, No. 13 (Blackenbury Camp: 19th-century name). *TBGAS*, 74 (1957), 150–6 (Becketsbury: 17th–18th-century name).

* An earlier form is Blackenbury (*PNG*, II, 241).

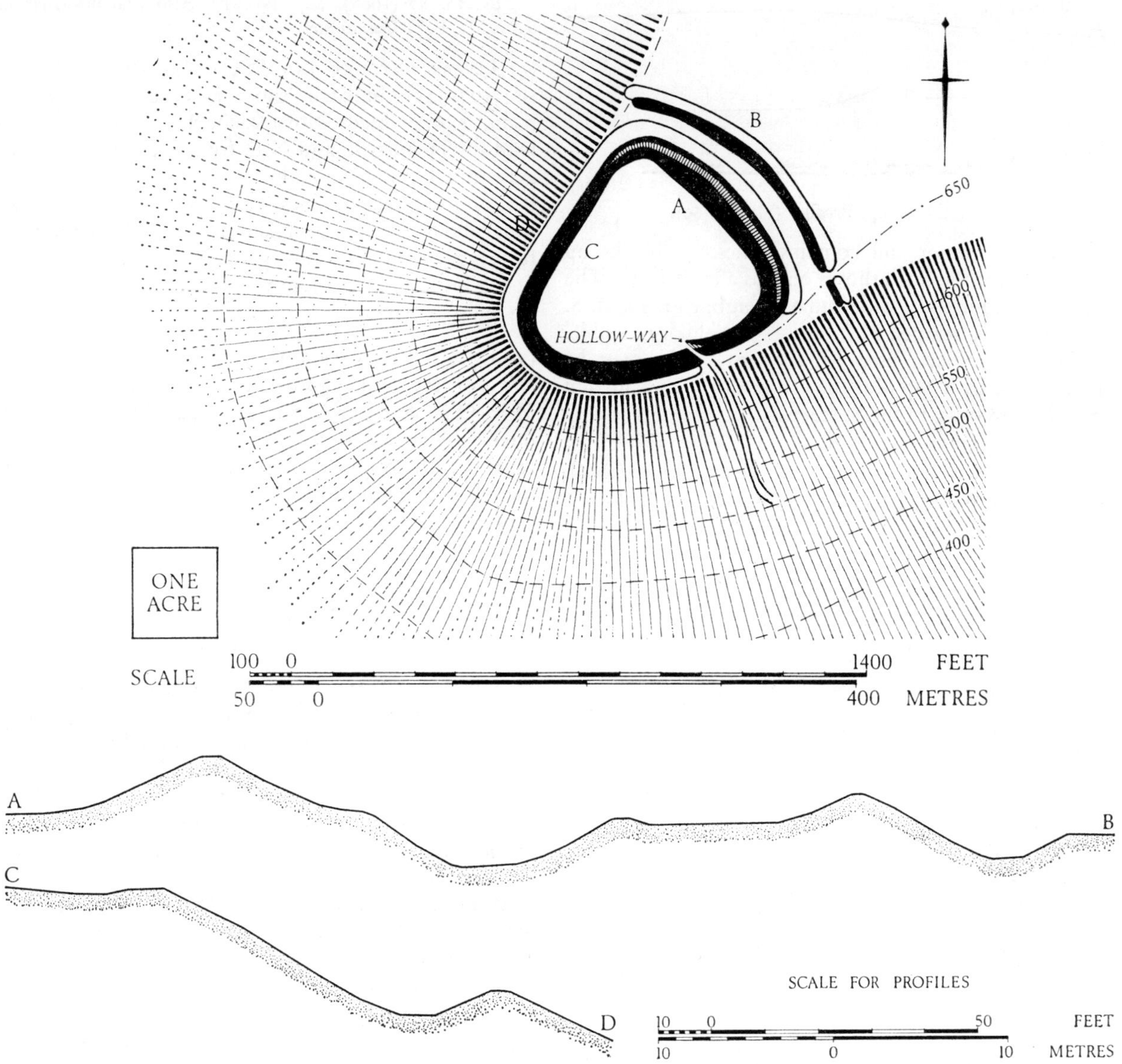

NORTH NIBLEY. (1) Brackenbury Ditches Hill-fort.

NORTHLEACH WITH EASTINGTON

(10 miles N.N.E. of Cirencester)

The notable series of linear ditches described under (3) is without close parallel in the area, although a comparable interrupted feature appears in BAGENDON (1) and YANWORTH (2). The Romano-British settlement (2) within Norbury Camp may represent the 'Farmington Villa' mentioned by Witts.[1] The Foss Way forms the N.W. boundary of the parish; its course on Leygore Hill is noted under (4).

1. Witts (1883), 37.

(1) NORBURY CAMP (SP 127155), univallate hill-fort, unexcavated, encloses 80 acres on a promontory between re-entrant valleys, 1 mile N.E. of Northleach. Plan, p. 89.

The W. and E. sides of the fort are defined by banks set along the extremities of a slight eminence; the N. and S. sides are defined by the edges of the promontory, accentuated in part at least by scarping. On the N., a low bank set on a terrace beneath the scarp edge and extending for about 220 ft. along the inner side of a track may be the northern 'mound' mentioned by Witts. The ploughed W. bank, 50 ft. wide, rises $1\frac{1}{2}$ ft.

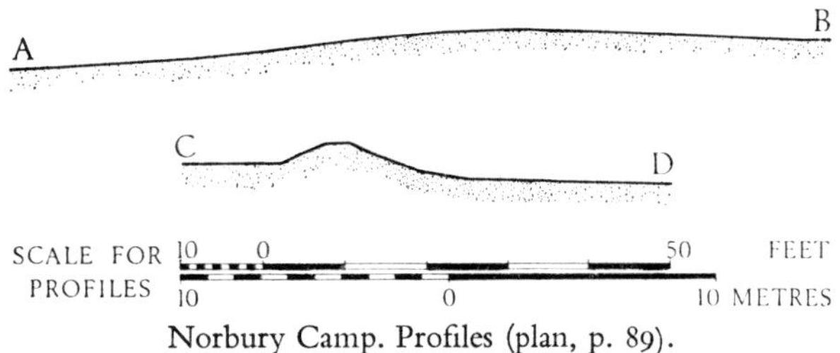

Norbury Camp. Profiles (plan, p. 89).

above the interior and contains limestone blocks up to 3 ft. long; the ditch shows only as a crop-mark. The E. bank, about 16 ft. wide and 2 ft. high, ends 200 ft. S. of the steeply scarped N.E. corner; no ditch is visible. Original entrances, used by modern roads, may be represented by a gap near the centre of the E. bank and by a hollow-way in the S. scarp.

N.M.R., OAP SP 1215/1/370–1.

Camden, *Britannia* (ed. Gough, 1789), I, 279. Playne (1876), 210, No. 17. Witts (1883), 37, No. 72. *Bagendon*, 25, n. 4.

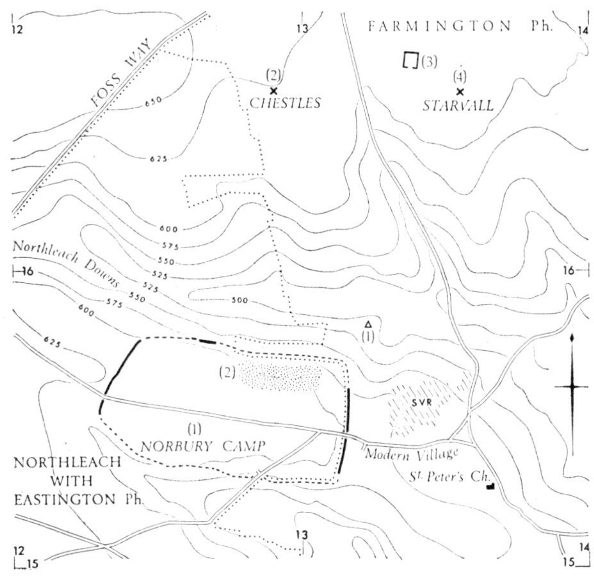

× ROMANO-BRITISH OCCUPATION ▵ ROMAN BUILDING
— BANK OF HILL-FORT ---- SCARP EDGE — CROP-MARK OF DITCH
AREA OF ROMANO-BRITISH SETTLEMENT SVR SHRUNKEN VILLAGE REMAINS

Monuments in FARMINGTON and NORTHLEACH WITH EASTINGTON.

(2) Romano-British Settlement (sp 129156), within Norbury Camp (1), ploughed out, covers at least 6 acres along the 600-ft. contour in the N.E. quarter of the hill-fort. It is 400 yds. S.W. of Clearcupboard Villa (Farmington (1)), and 100 ft. higher.

Pottery of 1st–4th-century date, roof and flue tiles, dressed stones and wall foundations are reported. The finds, including part of a stone trough, are in a private collection.

TBGAS, 87 (1968), 205, No. 17. Also oral information from Mr. P. E. Gascoigne.

(3) Linear Ditches and Enclosures (sp 10061261–sp 11971345), undated, show as crop-marks on the plain, 1 mile S. of Northleach. The earthworks extend for $1\frac{1}{4}$ miles E. and N.E. from the Salt Way over generally level ground, but crossing one dry valley. It is possible that the lines which cross the 600-ft. contour about sp 116129 relate to natural jointing or fissuring (an opinion kindly given by Dr. G. A. Kellaway of the Institute of Geological Sciences). Plan, p. 90.

N.M.R., OAP SP 1112/1/358–72.

(4) Roman Road (sp 118159). The *agger* of the Foss Way on top of Leygore Hill was excavated by Mrs. H. E. O'Neil and proved to be 20 ft. wide between the ditches. A terrace-way E. of the modern road (117161) represents the original course of the Roman road down the hill slope to the north.

PCNFC, XXXIV (1964), 133–7.

NOTGROVE

(12 miles N.N.E. of Cirencester)

'Stainbarrow Camp' is shown on Isaac Taylor's map of Gloucestershire (1777) as an oval enclosure, 1 mile N.W. of the village; it also appears on Bryant's map of 1824, where it is marked 'Scite of Stone Barrow or Turk's Hill Camp'. The site cannot now be identified.

A cinerary urn and other Roman pottery were found in the 19th century beneath St. Bartholomew's Church (sp 10931994).[1]

Monument (1) and Naunton (2) lie on either side of Stanborough Lane. In a charter reputedly of 8th-century date,[2] concerning grants of land at Aston Blank and Notgrove, this lane is called *straet*.

1. *TBGAS*, VII (1882–3), 32.
2. Grundy (1935–6), 178; B 165; K 90. Sawyer, No. 99.

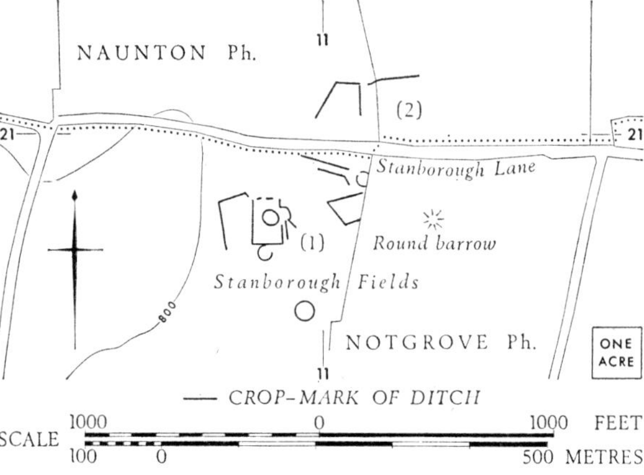

NOTGROVE. (1) Enclosures (p. 91).

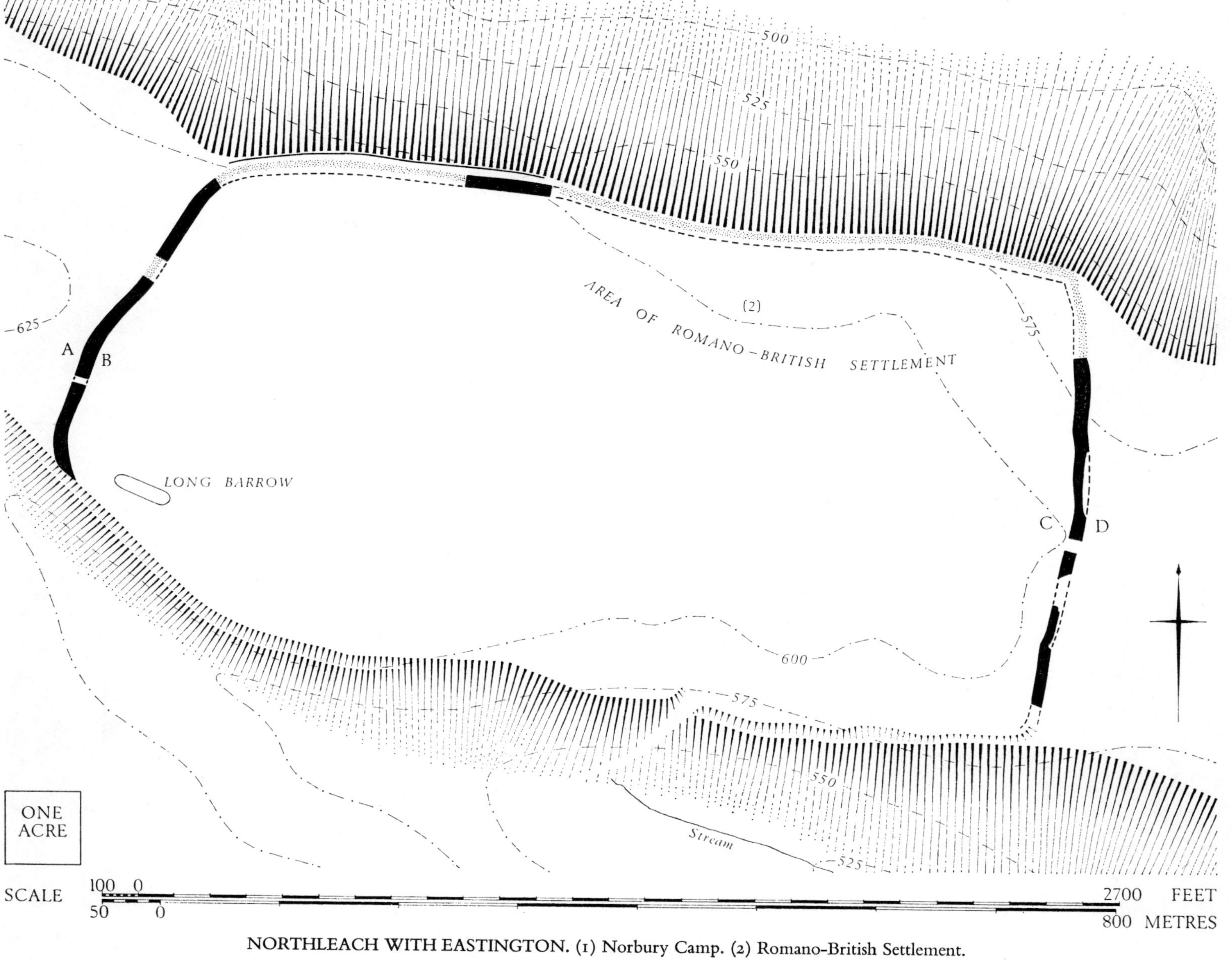

NORTHLEACH WITH EASTINGTON. (1) Norbury Camp. (2) Romano-British Settlement.

NORTHLEACH WITH EASTINGTON. (3) Linear Ditches and Enclosures.

(1) ENCLOSURES (SP 110209), undated, in Stanborough Fields, ½ mile N. of the village, show indistinctly as crop-marks over about 4½ acres of level ground between two low eminences. Each rectilinear enclosure appears to occupy about ½ acre. Other ditches, partly obscured by natural soil-marks, are visible as crop-marks 300 yds. to the south. Plan, p. 88.

N.M.R., OAP SP 1020/1/363–7.

NYMPSFIELD

(14 miles W. of Cirencester)

A multivallate hill-fort at one time supposed to exist at Owlpen (SO 800000) cannot be confirmed. A substantial bank of unknown date with slight ditches on either side, described in 1926,[1] still survives, but a slight bank which extended at right angles from the N.W. end of this feature to the edge of a steep scarp is no longer seen. Ridges and hollows immediately S.E. of the surviving bank are of natural origin. Romano-British pottery is said to have been found near Field Farm (ST 812994).[2] Pottery was also found in Nympsfield long barrow (see FROCESTER).

1. *UBSS*, 3, No. 1 (1926), 42.
2. *TBGAS*, LII (1930), 158, n. 15.

ODDINGTON

No Iron Age or Romano-British monument is known in this parish.

OWLPEN

(7 miles W.S.W. of Cirencester)

For discussion of possible hill-fort, see NYMPSFIELD.

OXENTON

(18 miles N.N.W. of Cirencester)

Iron Age pottery, including Iron Age 'A' forms and ware with incised decoration, worked and other bones, and flints from this parish are in Cheltenham Museum; some items are provenanced 'Woolston Camp' and 'Camp Openham', probably meaning Oxenton Knolls. Potsherds in Birmingham City Museum include three pieces probably from a production centre near the Malvern Hills (*PPS*, XXXIV (1968), 427).

(1) IRON AGE SETTLEMENT (SO 973313), on Oxenton Knolls, was excavated by T. G. E. Powell in 1931. An irregular mound of loose stones and clay about 22 ft. across contained Iron Age pottery, apparently of more than one period as shown by the reported presence of situlate vessels and duck-stamped ware. The mound (a on plan, p. 92) occupied the E. end of a long flat-topped natural knoll of the Marlstone Rock Bed of the Middle Lias, now almost entirely broken up and defaced by quarry-pits and dumps. Potsherds were also found in rabbit scrapes on the S.W. edge of the knoll. There are no clear signs of any defences on the hill-top, but steep scarps drop for 35 ft. or so on all sides, except in the extreme W. where the knoll attenuates into a long bank-like ridge, cut into by quarries. Near the foot of the S.E. and S.W. scarps are banks of uncertain origin, up to 80 ft. across and 10 ft. high, without ditches; they lie beside the line of a former parish boundary. Extensive areas of quarrying occur immediately downhill from the banks.

TBGAS, LV (1933), 383–4. *Arch J*, XCV (1938), 94. Witts (1883), 40, No. 80.

OZLEWORTH

No Iron Age or Romano-British monument is known in this parish.

PAINSWICK

(11 miles N.W. of Cirencester)

Roman finds not closely provenanced include coins[1] and an enamelled 'horse' brooch.[2]

'Entrenchments' on the N. end of Huddenknoll Hill (SO 848109) include a track and a V-shaped depression, 1½ ft. to 5 ft. deep, cut by quarrying at its N. end.[3] There is no good evidence for prehistoric earthworks formerly predicated on Longridge Hill, some 2 miles S.E. of (1).[4]

1. In Gloucester City Museum.
2. In Ashmolean Museum. *Arch J*, XII (1855), 279.
3. Witts (1883), 54. Burrows (1924), 131.
4. *TBGAS*, LI (1929), 253.

(1) KIMSBURY HILL-FORT (SO 869121), also called Painswick Beacon or Castle Godwyn, bivallate, unexcavated, encloses 7 acres on a spur of the Cotswold escarpment (Plate 37). The interior is almost entirely defaced by stone-quarrying and now contains part of a golf-course. Plan and profile, p. 93.

The defences on W., S.E. and N.E. are up to 180 ft. wide overall and comprise three ramparts with two medial ditches. The inner rampart, of glacis construction, rises 5 ft. above the interior and on the N. continues along the edge of a short steep scarp as a bank without a ditch. The middle rampart springs from the edge of the inner ditch and is separated from the outer ditch by a berm 15 ft. wide. The outer rampart turns W. at the N.E. corner to follow a sloping terrace for 350 ft.

At the main entrance, near the S.E. corner, the ramparts are offset from each other. The inner bank is inturned so that on the W. side it projects almost

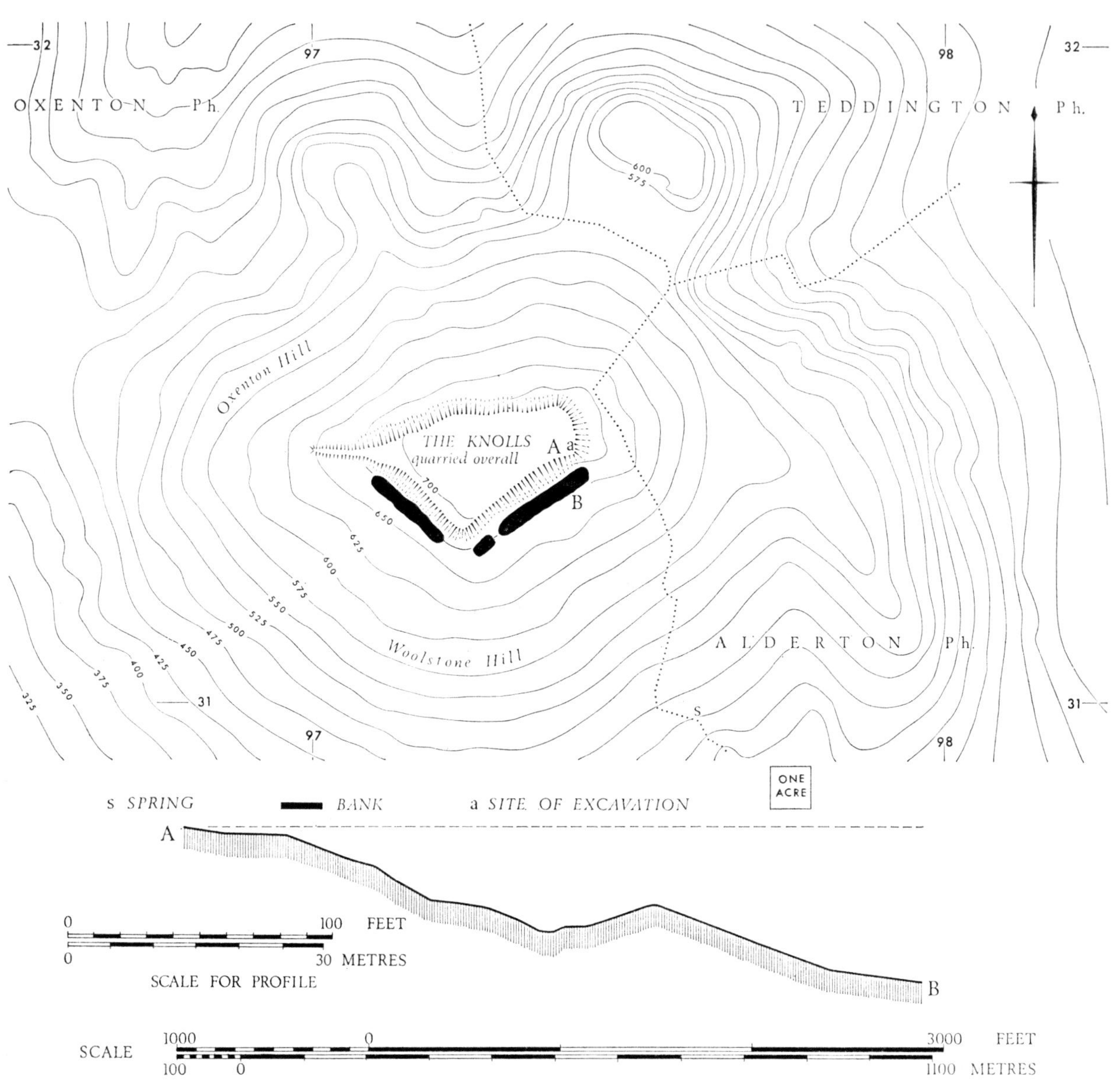

OXENTON. (1) Iron Age Settlement, Oxenton Knolls.

straight into the interior for 60 ft. The E. arm is markedly bowed for 80 ft. and its N. end has been much dug. Beyond this, a low and very irregular bank curves N.W. and W., to end 12 ft. N. of the top of the W. arm. The extent to which this represents the original arrangement cannot be determined by surface inspection alone (see p. xxvi). A second entrance may have existed at the N.W. corner, where the surviving end of the inner rampart turns inwards to flank a hollow-way.

Almost at the centre of the interior is a circular hollow (a), 20 ft. in diameter at the top, about 8 ft. deep and surrounded by a low bank; it is of unknown origin.

'Several Roman coins', 'a sword and some spearheads' (undated), said to be casual finds (Rudder (1779), 592), have not survived.

C.U.A.P., OAP AIK 76–81, AQM 83, 85.

Lysons, *Woodchester* (1797), Plate I. Camden, *Britannia* (ed. Gough, 1806), 398. Lloyd Baker (1821), 169, No. 17. Playne (1876), 211, No. 20. Witts (1883), 28, No. 57.

(2) Roman Villa (so 85781020), Ifold,* lies on Inferior Oolite sloping gently to S. and W., close to a spring-line. The site, first recorded in 1868, was excavated by W. St. Clair Baddeley in 1903–4. It has been extensively robbed for stone and disturbed by ploughing.

The plan is incomplete, but the excavator insists that room 1 was isolated. Lathe-turned columns 9½ in. in diameter lying N.E. of room 1, and a smaller column near the 'buttress' on the S., suggest a colonnade along the W. side of a corridor which was partly paved in black tesserae of three sizes. Lias slabs and cobbles were found in the N. half of the suggested corridor. Apsidal hypocausts, 26 and 27 (adjacent), with 2-ft.-high stone *pilae* of square section occasionally capped by single tiles, were heated from a furnace (29) on the N. The square plunge baths (P) were lined with *opus signinum*, and one was slate-floored with coved angles; a stone platform lay between the two baths. The mosaic floor of room 10 survives on the E. only (Plate 8); lias, tile

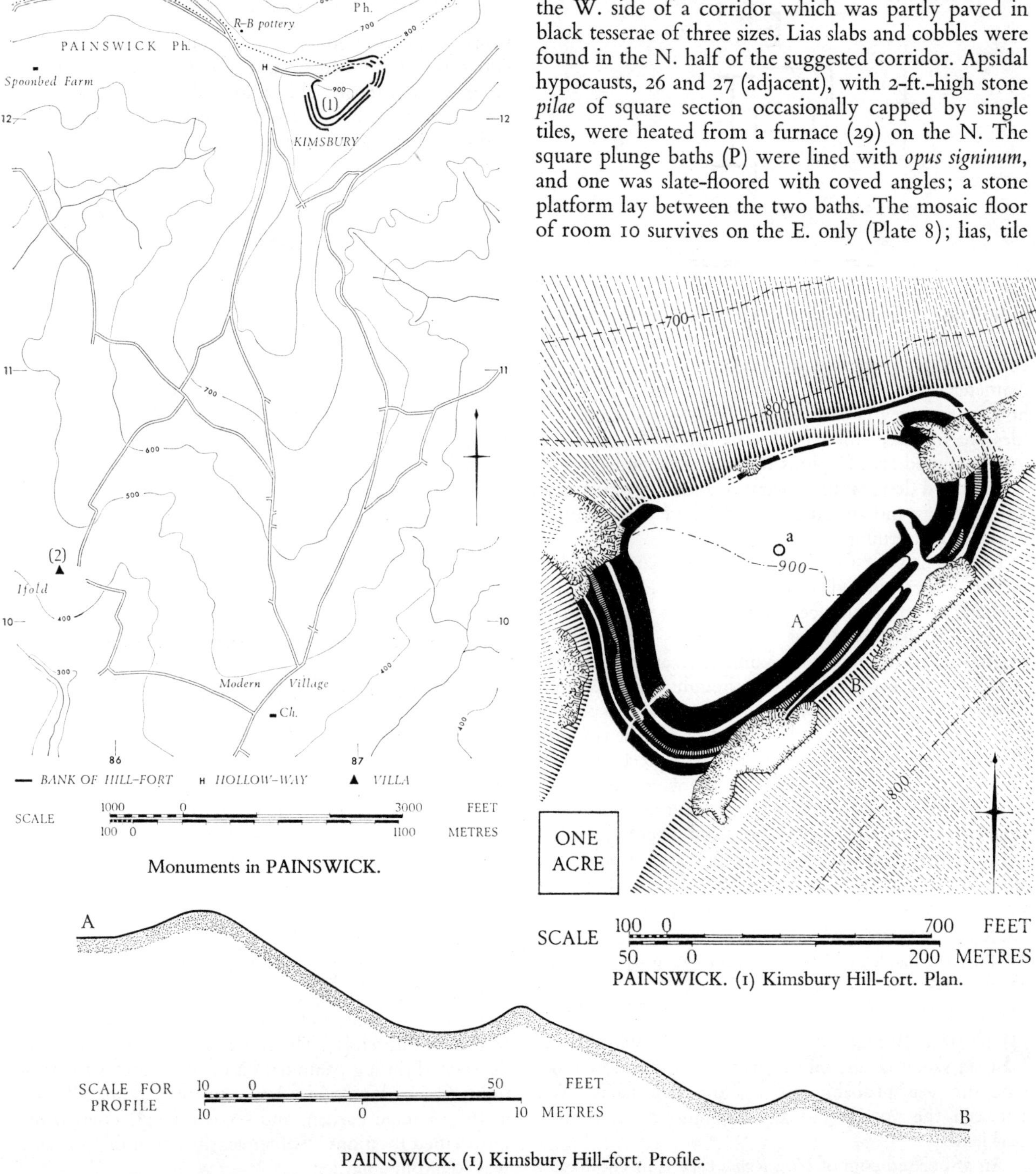

Monuments in PAINSWICK.

PAINSWICK. (1) Kimsbury Hill-fort. Plan.

PAINSWICK. (1) Kimsbury Hill-fort. Profile.

* Highfold on modern maps.

and Oolite were used for small and large tesserae. In the western part of the room cobbles were reported in place of the mosaic. In several places it seemed that the ruins of the villa had been reused as farm buildings.

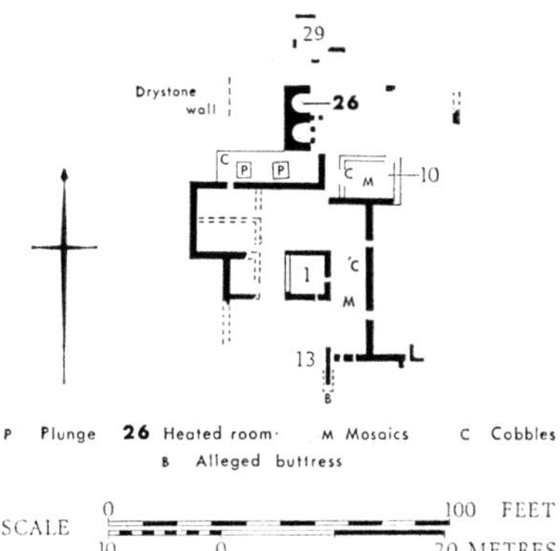

Building debris included large moulded rectangular stones, some possibly from cornices, a hexagonal stone column base integral with a column drum 9½ in. in diameter, pierced off-centre with a small octagonal hole, and a very large number of hexagonal sandstone tiles cut in three distinct sizes. Combed tiles included some stamped RPG. Copious wall plaster included much with striped designs; there were also small fragments of window glass and some melted lead. There was extensive evidence of burning.

Two coins were found, one Constantinian, the other earlier. Pottery included samian, amphorae, a jar with applied white scroll decoration, a 'red glazed' base stamped with a wheel of eight spokes (Oxfordshire rosette-stamped imitation samian?), and mortaria. A yellow-green glazed tile was thought to be Roman. Other finds were glass bottles and beads and a pewter pot; a sheath, cold chisels, hinges and a penannular shackle were of iron. There were also a piece of green porphyry and quernstones. There were numerous oyster shells and animal bones, including ox, horse, pig (one tile bore trotter marks), goat and sheep; also a red deer's antler, a boar's tusk and bones of small wild animals. Surviving finds are in Stroud and Gloucester City Museums.

TBGAS, XXVII (1904), 156–71; 73 (1954), 25 (porphyry). W. St. Clair Baddeley, *A Cotteswold Manor* (1929), 3, n. 1, 24 and illustrations opp. pp. 22–4. *JRS*, XLV (1955), 69 (stamped tile). *Archaeological News Letter*, 6 (1955), 47 (cornice stones).

(3) ROMAN BURIALS (SO 85500726), Brownshill. At least six skeletons are said to have been found in 1796. The site was probably on a slight shelf facing W., between the 300-ft. and 400-ft. contours; it is now parkland.

An associated coin of *Urbs Roma* type is in Gloucester City Museum.

TBGAS, 77 (1958), 155–6.

PITCHCOMBE

No Iron Age or Romano-British monument is known in this parish.

POOLE KEYNES

(4 miles S.S.W. of Cirencester)

Romano-British pottery and an iron axe-head, now in Gloucester City Museum, come from a gravel pit (approx. SU 010949) about 300 yds. N. of (1), at P. The pottery includes two rim sherds from mortaria and seventeen sherds of grey ware.

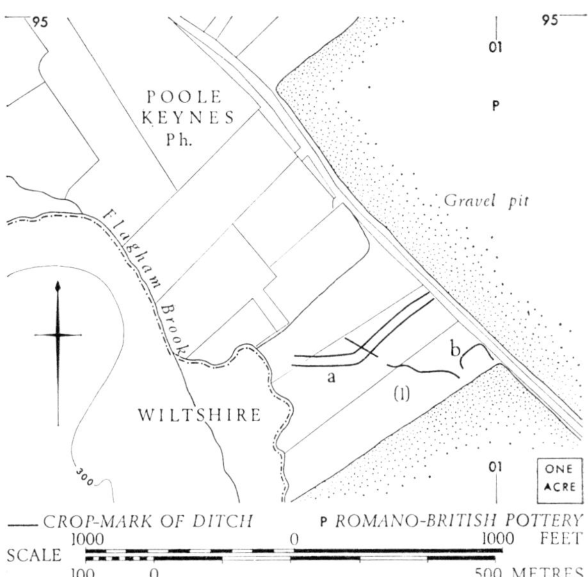

POOLE KEYNES. (1) Track and Enclosure.

(1) WIDE TRACK AND ENCLOSURE (SU 008945), seen as crop-marks on gravel, occur about 300 yds. E. of Flagham Brook. The track (a) is 40 ft. to 50 ft. wide; three visible sides of the enclosure (b) define an area of about ⅓ acre.

O.S., VAP 70 042, 132.

POULTON

(4½ miles E. of Cirencester)

Romano-British finds reported from the village in 1877 and 1958 probably relate to the settlement near St. Michael's Church (1). The earlier finds comprised sherds discovered during examination of the church's foundations, an oval piece of lead covering human bones in the vicarage garden, and six (Roman?) coins from unspecified locations.[1] Subsequently a coin of Constans was found in a garden.[2]

1. *TBGAS*, II (1877–8), 25. All lost.
2. In the Corinium Museum.

(1) ROMANO-BRITISH SETTLEMENT (SP 097006), 100 yds. W. of St. Michael's Church, ploughed out, covers at least 3 acres on level ground, about 170 yds. E. of a small stream (map, p. 3, *s.v.* AMPNEY ST. PETER).

Occupation debris is of 2nd to 4th-century date; concentrations of pottery, tile fragments and limestone slabs (many reddened) suggest three or four small buildings. The pottery is in Gloucester City Museum.

PRESCOTT

No Iron Age or Romano-British monument is known in this parish.

PRESTBURY

No Iron Age or Romano-British monument is known in this parish.

PRESTON

(1 mile E. of Cirencester)

Roman coins of the 3rd and 4th centuries and a fibula are reported[1] from a farm in the parish.

1. *TBGAS*, XIX (1894–5), 398.

(1) ENCLOSURES AND LINEAR DITCHES (SP 036012), undated, show as crop-marks covering about 13 acres on

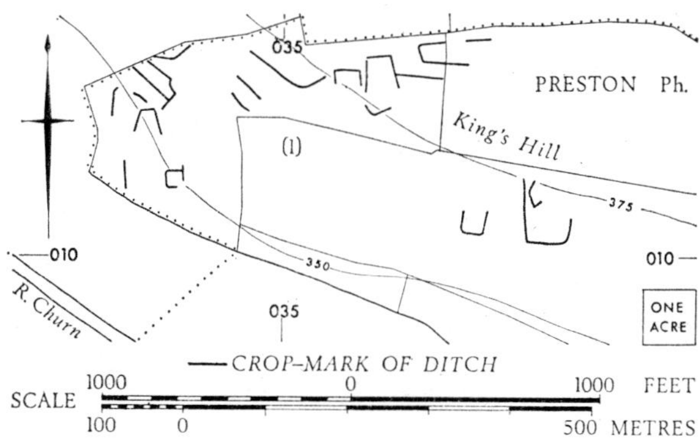

PRESTON. (1) Enclosures and Linear Ditches.

the gentle slopes of King's Hill, above the R. Churn. At N.W. the ditches appear to extend into allotment gardens in Cirencester parish.

N.M.R., OAP SP 0300/1/332–3; 0301/2/334–7.

(2) ENCLOSURES AND LINEAR DITCHES (SP 054006), undated, show as crop-marks on level ground around St. Augustine Farm. Faint indications in fields A and B suggest that the ditches extend over some 40 acres.

C.U.A.P., AOO 31–2. N.M.R., OAP SP 0500/3/263–4; 0500/5/177–8.

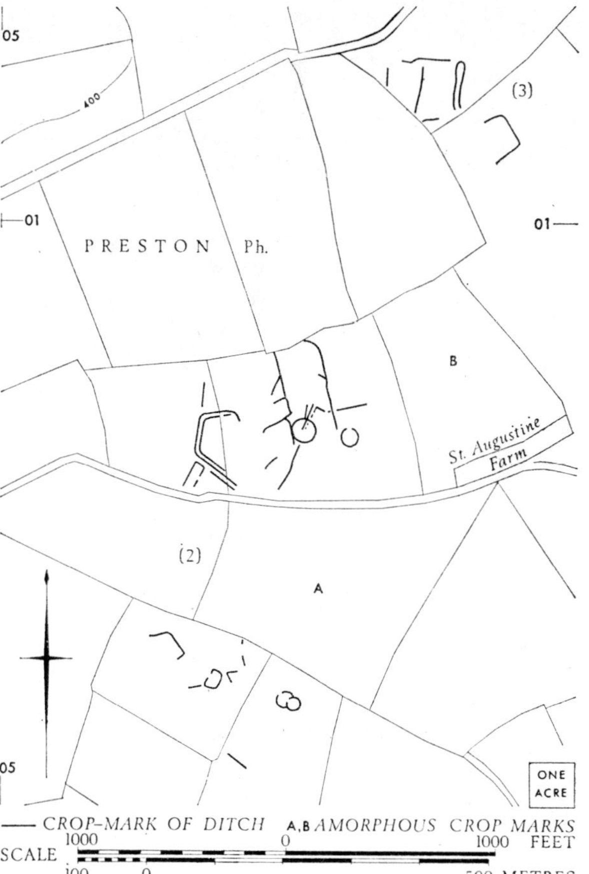

PRESTON. (2), (3) Enclosures etc.

(3) ENCLOSURES (SP 05700115), undated, are revealed by crop-marks N. of St. Augustine Farm.

C.U.A.P., OAP AOO 31, ASM 57.

QUENINGTON

(7 miles E. of Cirencester)

(1) PROBABLE SETTLEMENT AND LINEAR DITCHES (SP 121046), undated, exist as crop-marks over an area of at least 6 acres, extending N.–S., 600 ft. S. of the Roman road (2). Plan, p. 96.

N.M.R., OAP SP 1204/1/397–401.

(2) ROMAN ROAD, Akeman Street (SP 12400504, SP 13010520). The *agger* survives in pasture as an earthwork 1 ft. high and 24 ft. across, much disturbed by quarrying; it also forms the S. boundary of a copse. Plan, p. 96.

Excavations in 1952 at x (SP 13670538), across the line of the road where it sloped down to the R. Coln, revealed an *agger* of rammed gravel 31 ft. wide with a central channel. Kerbstones existed on the S. side, but on the N. the edge was obscured by Roman walling.

R.A.F., VAP 106G/UK/1721: 5271–3.

TBGAS, 76 (1957), 35–43.

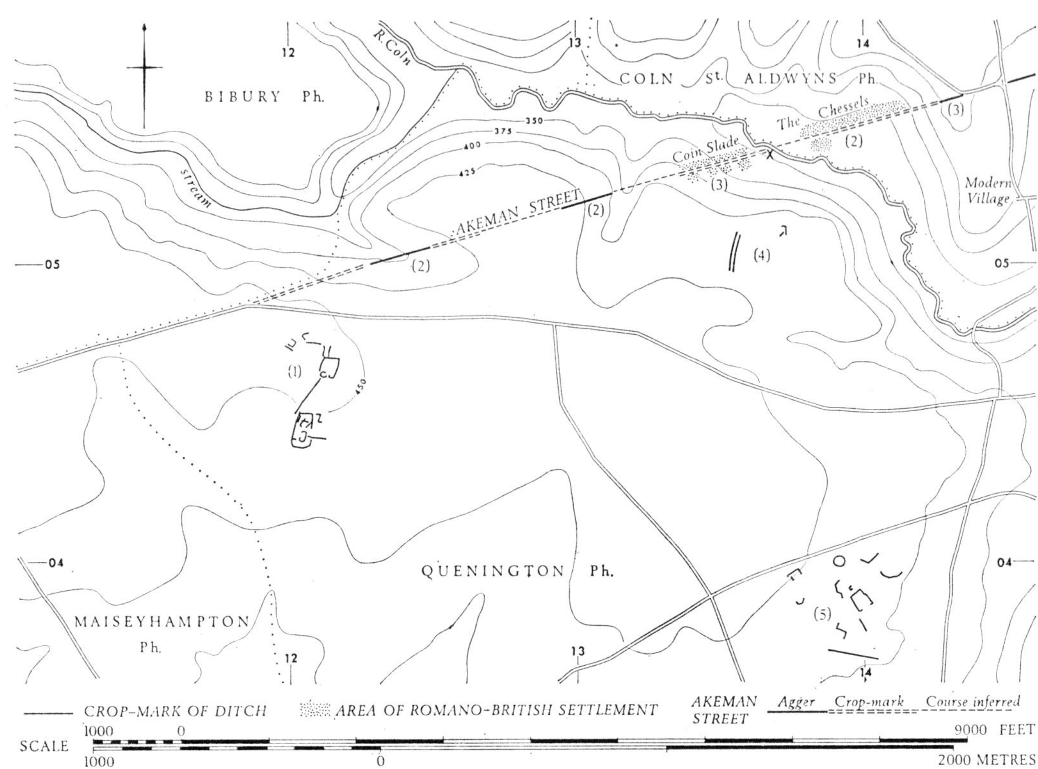

Monuments in QUENINGTON and COLN ST. ALDWYNS.

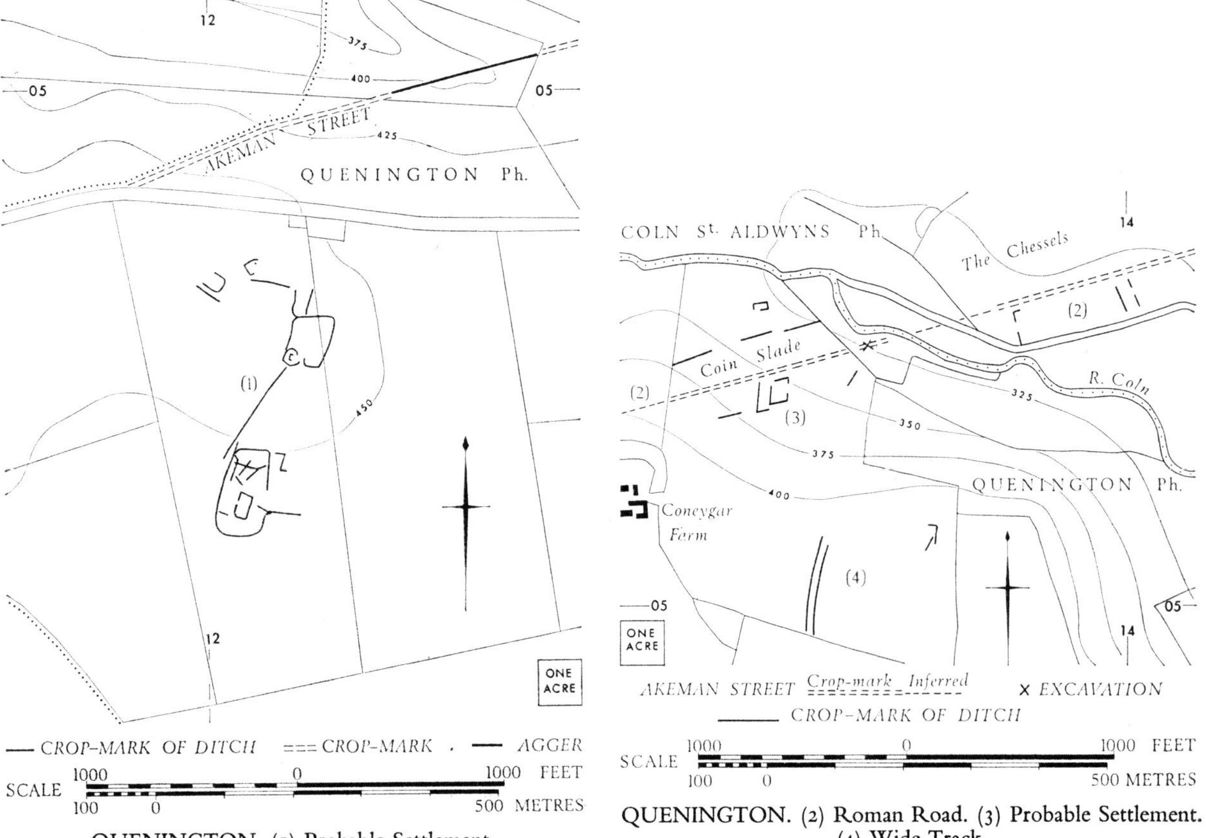

QUENINGTON. (1) Probable Settlement.

QUENINGTON. (2) Roman Road. (3) Probable Settlement. (4) Wide Track.

(3) PROBABLE SETTLEMENT (SP 135054), Romano-British, Coin Slade* (*TBGAS*, 76 (1957), 35–43), lies on both sides of Akeman Street as it descends to the R. Coln and is marked on the ground by a scatter of worked limestone blocks from buildings, and by samian ware and 3rd and 4th-century coarse pottery. A limited excavation in 1951–2 in the area around SP 13670538 (x) yielded a quantity of coarse pottery, largely of the 4th century and including a few stamped sherds; also 28 coins ranging from Gallienus to Valens and the gold bezel of a ring inscribed CONCORDIA. Roman coins in Corinium Museum from this site are not distinguished from others recovered at Coln St. Aldwyns.

A remarkable collection of almost complete samian vessels, at least ten of them with potters' stamps, was found near the settlement in 1958; this pottery is in Corinium Museum.

(4) WIDE TRACK (SP 135050), shows as a crop-mark about 300 yds. S. of Akeman Street.

N.M.R., OAP SP 1304/1/176–7.

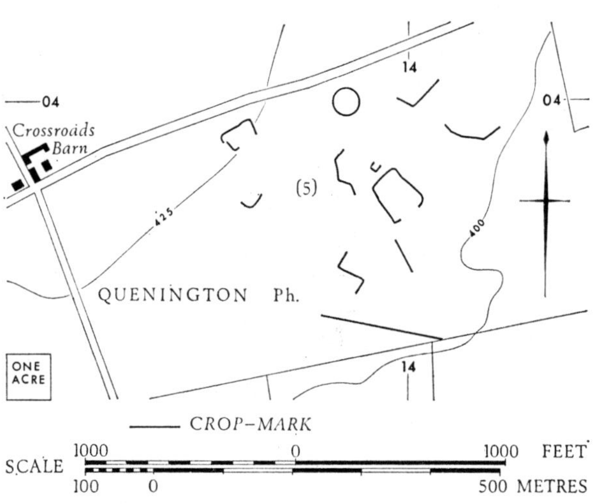

QUENINGTON. (5) Enclosures and Linear Ditches.

(5) ENCLOSURES AND LINEAR DITCHES (SP 140039), undated, show as crop-marks covering at least 20 acres, E. of Crossroads Barn.

N.M.R., OAP SP 1303/1/181–2.

RANDWICK

(12 miles W.N.W. of Cirencester)

Romano-British pottery from the chamber of the long barrow, Randwick I (SO 82500690),[1] is in Gloucester City Museum.

1. *PCNFC*, VIII (1883–4), 158. *TBGAS*, 79 (1960), 87.

(1) CROSS-RIDGE DYKE, in Randwick Wood, crossing the parish boundary into STANDISH (SO 82690710–82780693), 700 ft. above O.D., spans the top of a

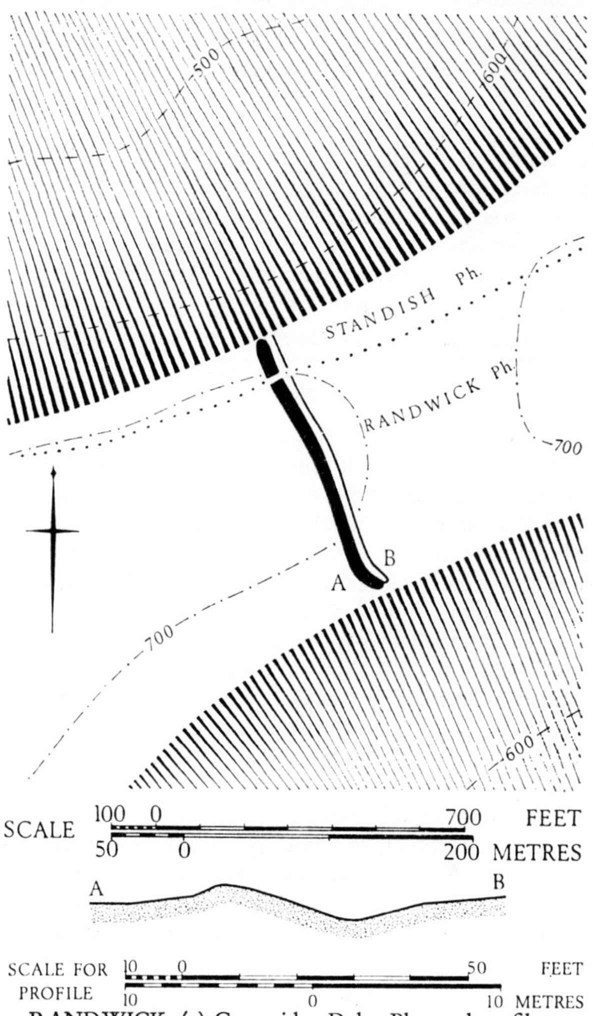

RANDWICK. (1) Cross-ridge Dyke. Plan and profile.

narrow ridge which projects S.W. from the main Cotswold escarpment. It is 600 ft. long with no original gap. The bank averages 12 ft. in width and $2\frac{1}{2}$ ft. in height; the ditch, uphill on the E., is 24 ft. wide and a further $2\frac{1}{2}$ ft. deep.

Witts (1883), 42, No. 85, 'Randwick Camp'.

RENDCOMB

(5 miles N. of Cirencester)

'Rendcomb Camp' (SP 020103) is not an archaeological monument, but the result of various human activities on and around prominent scarp lines of geological origin (see p. xxxiii).

* Alternative names are Quoin Slade and Cold Slad.

Low scarps, 650 yds. N. of the 'camp' (about SP 02101105 and further N.), can be seen crossing the road and just W. of it. These could be the remains of 'Celtic' fields.

RODBOROUGH

(10 miles W. of Cirencester)

Remains of a Belgic wooden bucket with embossed bronze hoops were found near an unlocated cottage on Rodborough Common.[1] Numerous small irregular pits and mounds on the common are similar to others widespread on Minchinhampton Common and are probably post-Roman in origin.[2]

1. B.M., *Guide to Early Iron Age Antiquities* (1925), 146. *PPS*, XV (1949), 189.
2. Cf. *PCNFC*, V (1870), 286–7.

(1) EARLY ROMAN SETTLEMENT (SO 850032), on Rodborough Common, with probable military associations, occurs near the W. end of a flat-topped ridge, on Inferior Oolite at over 600 ft. above O.D. (map, p. 81, *s.v.* MINCHINHAMPTON). Excavation, and observation of builders' trenches, has revealed mid 1st-century material associated with a ditch at least 250 ft. long, V-shaped in profile, about 14 ft. wide and 6½ ft. deep; the ditch lies inside and is truncated by an 8-acre enclosure, probably post-Roman. The W. bank of the enclosure, with an inner ditch, survives as a prominent earthwork. Similar finds were made to the south-east.

The material includes a Claudian *dupondius*, a bronze brooch of Camulodunum type IV, a bronze stud (possibly military), and pottery including Arretine or provincial Arretine, samian, mica-dusted ware, butt-beaker, and vessels in both local Iron Age tradition and with Belgic affinities, invariably associated with Savernake ware. The assemblage as a whole is strongly suggestive of a Roman military presence in the early years of the conquest. Most of the finds are in Stroud Museum.

R.A.F., VAP CPE/UK 2098: 4340–1; 3G TUD/UK 102 (Part I), 5072–3.

PCNFC, VI (1876), 214, No. 29. Witts (1882), 42, No. 86. *Arch J*, CIX (1952), 23–38. *TBGAS*, L (1928), 313–18; 59 (1937), 290–1; 78 (1959), 24–43; 83 (1964), 145–6.

RODMARTON

(5 miles S.W. of Cirencester)

A Dobunnic gold stater inscribed BODVOC has been found in the parish.[1]

Two Roman coins, one of Claudius Gothicus, the 'head of a Roman spear' and a clenched iron nail were recovered from 'depressions' in the Neolithic long barrow, Rodmarton I (ST 933973).[2] A coin of Severus Alexander was found by J. Y. Akerman in a barrow near Hare's Down Barn (ST 955974).[3]

The Foss Way Roman road extends along the parish boundary at S.E.; a section exposed at Culkerton Wood (ST 950956) showed alternating layers of limestone flags and gravelly sand; the basal layer of flags appears to have been laid in a foundation trench.[4]

Vague crop-marks, apparently in some ways similar to those at NORTHLEACH WITH EASTINGTON (3) appear on air photographs (Plate 66) at ST 928987.[5]

1. *Arch J*, I (1845), 388–9. D. F. Allen in *Bagendon*, 121. In Ashmolean Museum.
2. Lysons, *Our British Ancestors* . . . (1865), 144. *TBGAS*, 79 (1960), 88.
3. *PSA*, Ser. 1, IV (1856–9), 17.
4. *TBGAS*, 61 (1939), 132–4.
5. C.U.A.P., OAP AXP 50, 52–3; AXT 47 and 49.

(1) ROMAN VILLA (probably ST 94439843), 'Hocberry', excavated by Lysons in 1800, is part of a complex marked by debris covering about 4 acres in an arable field of this name, formerly in the open fields of the parish, about 450 ft. above O.D. A shallow combe with ponds near its head separates the site from Rodmarton village, ¼ mile to the S. Elsewhere the ground falls gently to S.E. and rises gently to N.W.

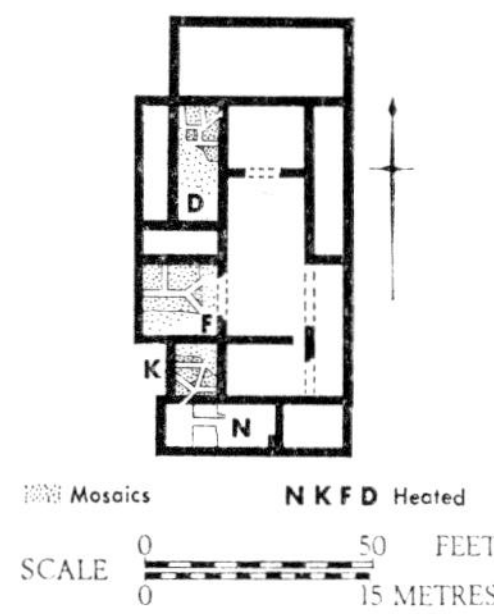

A slight 'shelf' about 100 ft. long, lying at the W. of an almost flat area of dark, discoloured soil, could be the site of Lysons' excavation. Building debris and tesserae, both coarse and fine, can be found on this shelf. Its axis falls a little west of north.

A tessellated pavement together with 2nd and 4th-century coins was found during ploughing, *c.* 1630. The excavations of 1800 suggested to Lysons that the rooms were constructed around a courtyard. Room N had *pilae* under the E. half. There were channelled hypocausts in K, F and D, with fragments of coarse tessellated pavement surviving above them. Tiles, one certainly flanged, were stamped TPFA, TPFC, and TPFP. A hoard of 200 4th-century 'copper' coins was found in a hypocaust, probably that of room N. Finds included an iron ring with an intaglio of Mars in blue paste. Some tiles are in the Corinium Museum; others, together with 'fragments of sculpture', are in the British Museum.

The site has been located by Mr. E. J. Swain. Copious surface finds include much limestone rubble marking the rough position of several buildings, sandstone, *tegulae* (but no stone-slates), and 2nd to 4th-century pottery with considerable quantities of samian. Records of all recent finds are in Gloucester City Museum; some finds are deposited in Stroud Museum.

Arch, XVIII (1817), 113–16. Lysons, *Reliquiae*, II (1817), Pt. i, Pl. VIII, No. 2, and Pl. IX. T. Morgan, *Romano-British Mosaic Pavements* (1886), 80.

SAINTBURY

(24 miles N.N.E. of Cirencester)

The earthworks known as Saintbury Camp or Castle Bank[1] on the hill S. of the village (SP 117393) appear to represent an extension of the system of mediaeval or later boundaries and settlement remains on lower ground W. of St. Nicholas's Church.

1. Rudder (1779), 635. Playne (1876), 207, No. 1. Witts (1883), 43, No. 87.

(1) PROBABLE SETTLEMENT (SP 11284169), Romano-British, with Roman coins and pottery, has been noted at Saintbury Grounds, ½ mile W. of Ryknild Street. The site is in a flat arable field in the valley, about 200 ft. above O.D.

Malkin MS., site No. 16.

SAPPERTON

(5 miles W. of Cirencester)

'Green Ditches',[1] possibly a hill-fort, is said to have been a small bivallate enclosure on the scarp edge S.E. of Frampton Mansell. It was levelled *c.* 1845 and the site has not been identified.

A Dobunnic gold coin inscribed BODVOC was found in the parish in 1901,[2] and an Armorican base silver coin (Coriosolitan, class II) is recorded from Frampton Mansell.[3]

Two hoards of 3rd-century Roman coins are recorded from the vicinity of Frampton Mansell: the Lark's Bush hoard, found buried in pots in 1759, was mostly dispersed at the time;[4] the other hoard, of 70 coins apparently associated with a skeleton, came to light in 1844 during construction of the Sapperton railway tunnel, probably near its S.E. end.[5]

Monument (1), an unusual Romano-British embanked enclosure with internal structures, lies partly in COATES. Adjacent buildings (COATES (2)–(4)), now separated from the enclosure by the parish boundary, are described here, as forming part of a complex, conceivably religious (see pp. l, li).

A villa in Hailey Wood (SO 9601) is indicated by reports of tesserae and pottery communicated by Mr. R. Reece.

1. Rudder (1779), 641. Playne (1876), 214, No. 32. Witts (1883), 21, No. 44 (Frampton Mansell Camp).
2. D. F. Allen, in *Bagendon*, 121.
3. D. F. Allen, in *IASB*, 272 (parish given as Chalford).
4. Rudder (1779), 641, with incomplete list. A list of those surviving is in Stroud Museum.
5. *Arch J*, II (1849), 45, incomplete list. *JBAA*, I (1846), 45, notes a distance of 1 mile from the find-spot of the Lark's Bush hoard.

(1) ROMAN SETTLEMENT (SO 96450036), 'Tunnel Mouth Camp', ploughed over, lies 230 yds. S.S.W. of the S. end of the Sapperton canal tunnel, on a slight knoll above a gentle slope to S.E. (Plate 49).

The sharply quadrangular enclosure, with entrance at E., is formed by three banks and two ditches measuring about 70 ft. across; the interior covers about ⅔ acre. The inner bank is still over 1 ft. high and contains large

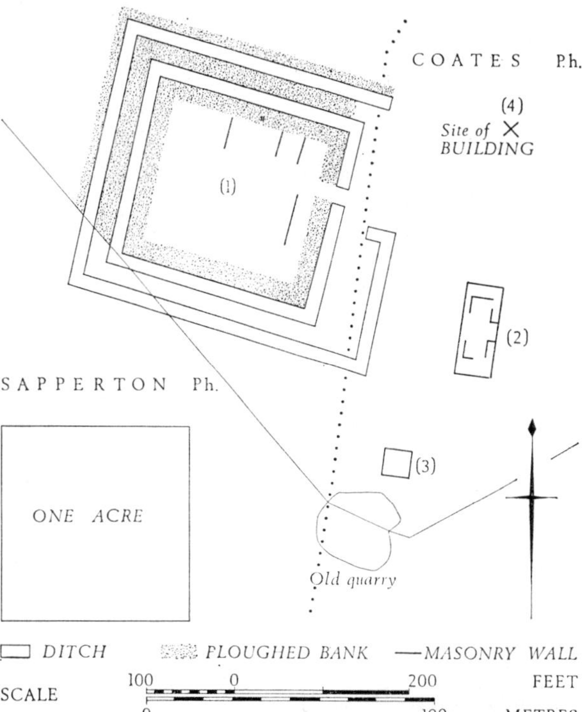

limestone slabs, possibly from the facing of a substantial wall. A building within the enclosure is defined by traces of a stone wall and a spread of pottery, tile, sandstone and reddened limestone fragments extending for about 60 ft. along the inner bank, S. of the entrance. Similar debris is associated with three walls offset from the N. bank. Finds are in Gloucester City Museum.

Some 30 yds. E. of the enclosure, crop-marks disclose a BUILDING, (COATES (2)), probably Roman; its foundations measure 100 ft. by 40 ft. and there are indications of internal walls.

Another BUILDING (COATES (3)), probably Roman, shows as a crop-mark 30 yds. S.W. of the foregoing. It is about 30 ft. square and is marked on the ground by scattered limestone slabs.

Some photographs (e.g. C.U.A.P., OAP FY 26, 29 and GX 0028) show a rectangular feature outside the S. wall of (1), but on the ground there is no confirmatory evidence of a building.

C.U.A.P., OAP ASM 40–3.
Arch J, CIX (1952), 24, fig. 1. *JRS*, LIX (1969), 128.

The site of a ROMAN BUILDING (COATES (4)) is indicated by large limestone slabs, sandstone tiles and pottery, about 60 yds. N. of COATES (2). Sherds collected there include samian ware of the late 1st or early 2nd century, and 4th-century Oxfordshire colour-coated ware.

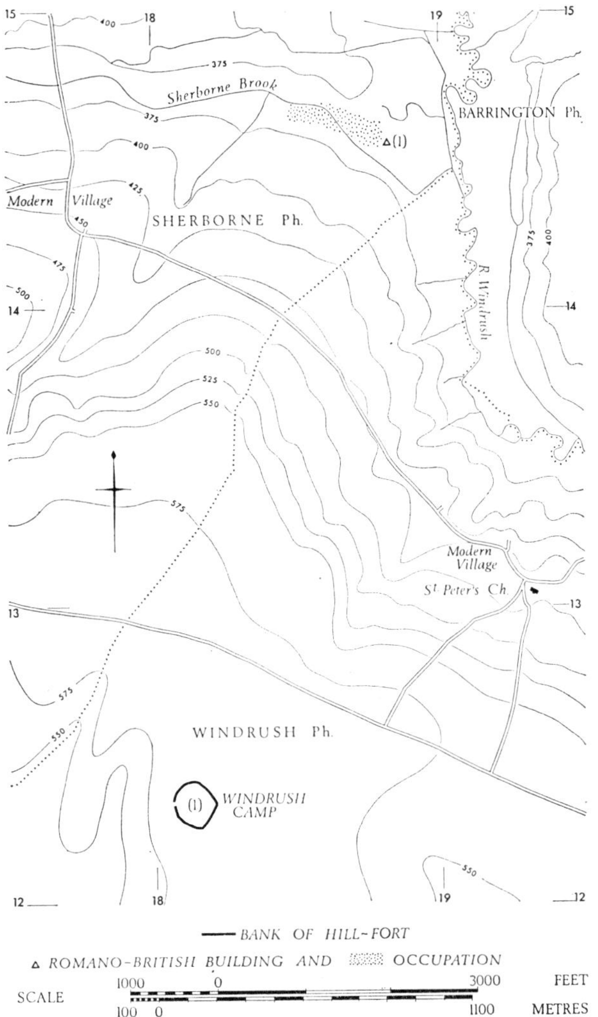

Monuments in SHERBORNE and WINDRUSH.

SEVENHAMPTON

(12 miles N. of Cirencester)

'Puckham Camp'[1] (SP 013228), no longer accepted as a hill-fort, probably originates in the remains of linear quarrying.

1. Witts (1883), 41, No. 83.

(1) ENCLOSURE (SP 05722065), 150 yds. E. of Hampen Cottages, shows as a crop-mark on an air photograph (Plate 54). The ditched perimeter is roughly square and encloses about ½ acre, above the 800-ft. contour. The entrance is on the east.

N.M.R., OAP SP 0520/1.

SEZINCOTE

No Iron Age or Romano-British monument is known in this parish.

SHERBORNE

(12 miles N.E. of Cirencester)

Nine Dobunnic gold coins (seven ANTED, one EISU and one CATTI) were found 'at or near Sherborne, Gloucestershire, about 1903'.[1]

1. MS. note by Sir J. Evans in Ashmolean Museum Library, on pp. 488 and 489 of his *Coins of the Ancient Britons*, supplement. Coins wrongly ascribed to Sherborne, Dorset in *IASB*, 293 (hoard 34). Correction by Mr. J. Robinson.

(1) ROMANO-BRITISH SETTLEMENT (SP 18821456), covering some 10 acres on an almost flat gravel terrace,

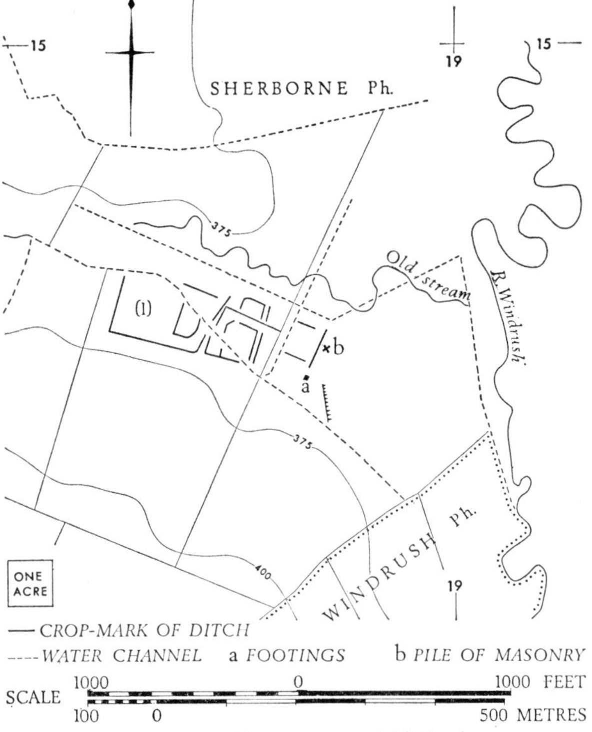

SHERBORNE. (1) Romano-British Settlement.

shows as crop-marks within which there is evidence of stone-footed buildings. The terrace lies immediately S. of the former line of the old Sherborne stream, now drained by water channels which partly traverse the settlement. Before modern ploughing, much of the area was under ridge-and-furrow.

A short length of wall-footing, ending against a stone base for a rectangular wooden shaft, has recently been uncovered immediately under the humus at 'a'. It lies within a slightly raised area defined on the E. by a spread scarp, 1½ ft. high, with remains of Oolite walling scattered along it for 230 ft. A pile of building stone stood some 60 yds. N.N.E., outside this area, at 'b'. A light scatter of Romano-British pottery has been noted over the whole area of the crop-marks, with occasional small concentrations of building debris towards the W. end. The settlement extended for some 30 yds. S. of the water channel on the S. of 'a', apparently ending at the foot of the gentle rise southwards.

N.M.R., OAP (Baker) SP 1814/1–5.

SHIPTON

(10 miles N. of Cirencester)

A potin ('speculum') coin of the Iron Age has been found in the parish (*Bagendon*, 133).

(1) Romano-British Settlement (SP 03171923), identified by Sgt. B. Beveridge 700 yds. S.E. of the major Roman settlement of Wycomb (Whittington (2)), lies in a shallow dry valley nearly 600 ft. above O.D. The site is crossed by a modern drystone wall incorporating reused stone and it is also marked by scattered blocks of Oolite, squared sandstone, much pottery and some animal bones; one clay slingstone was found. Large numbers of worked flints have been found here. Finds are in private possession.

A few Romano-British sherds and oyster shells are scattered near the N. shoulder of the valley, 200 yds. to the north-west.

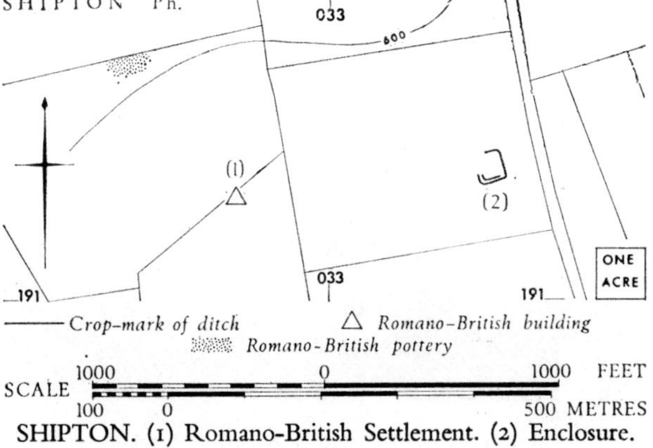

SHIPTON. (1) Romano-British Settlement. (2) Enclosure.

(2) Enclosure (SP 035193), undated, is suggested by crop-marks, 300 yds. E. of (1) on the N. slope of the same valley, bounding an area of perhaps $\frac{3}{5}$ acre. Three visible angles are rounded. The S. and W. sides are defined by parallel ditches.

C.U.A.P., OAP ASB 18, 23.

(3) Enclosure (SP 06661943), 'Salperton Camp' (1883) or 'Penhill Camp' (1952), undated, occupies the summit of a ridge above the 800-ft. contour and has been claimed as Roman. It was perhaps trapezoidal in shape, about 240 ft. by 175 ft. Only the N. side remains undisturbed. At N.W. it consists of a bank up to 4 ft. high above an external ditch, returning S. for some feet. Other remains on the W. are obscured by a copse in a ditched enclosure and elsewhere the earthwork has been degraded by ploughing. The S. side is continuous with a ditch to the W. and with a bank to the E., both extending its alignment.

Witts (1883), 44–5, No. 89. Burrow (1924), 132. *Arch J*, CIX (1952), 23–4.

SHIPTON MOYNE
and
SHURDINGTON

No Iron Age or Romano-British monument is known in these parishes.

SIDDINGTON

(adjacent to Cirencester on S.E.)

Ermin Street forms the N.E. boundary of the parish. An altar inscribed, but without a clear ascription, unprovenanced, was found in 1887.[1]

1. *RIB*, I, 101. In Cirencester Museum.

(1) Romano-British Settlement (SU 017997), mainly in the adjoining parish, is described *s.v.* Cirencester (3).

(2) Enclosures (SU 021993), undated, S.W. of Ewen Bridge, are partly visible as crop-marks on level ground. The S.E. side of the larger enclosure is about 180 ft. long.

C.U.A.P., OAP AOO 44, ASM 45.

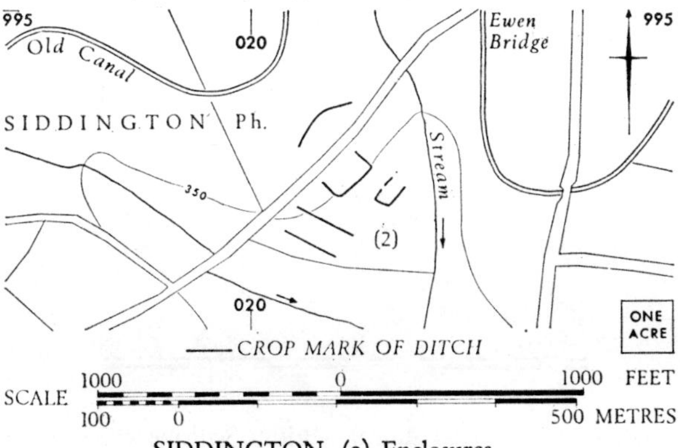

SIDDINGTON. (2) Enclosures.

(3) Romano-British Settlement (su 028988), ploughed out, S. of Clark's Lane, identified by Mr. R. Reece, is marked by concentrations of building debris and pottery covering an area of about 5½ acres on a low limestone ridge between two brooks. A well, discovered accidentally in 1966, remains unexcavated. Finds include a coin of Constantius II, pottery ranging from the late 1st to the 3rd or 4th century, and a white tessera.

SIDDINGTON. (3)–(5) Romano-British Settlement, Trackway and Enclosures.

(4) Enclosure and Trackway (su 031984), the latter of a width to suggest a drove, undated, W. of Dryleaze Farm, show as crop-marks along the bottom of a shallow valley beside a brook.

The enclosure (su 02899785) at the S. end of the trackway measures about 60 ft. by 110 ft. and has a gap in the W. side. The trackway is defined by ditches about 40 ft. apart and can be traced N.E., with one interruption, for 900 yds. A narrower spur forks E. near the N. end.

N.M.R., OAP SU 0398/2/372–6.

(5) Enclosure (su 028975), undated, is partly visible as a crop-mark 300 yds. S. of (4); the W. side is about 500 ft. long and there are internal subdivisions.

N.M.R., OAP SU 0297/7/381.

(6) Romano-British Settlement (su 047997), on Worm's Farm adjacent to Ermin Street, ploughed out, shows in the form of crop-marks over some 30 acres and as a spread of occupation debris on a more limited area. The N. part of the settlement is on level ground, the rest lies on a slope facing south.

Finds during investigation comprise a single sherd from a situlate vessel of Iron Age type and Romano-British pottery of 2nd–4th-century date, together with *tegula* and imbrex fragments. The finds are in Gloucester

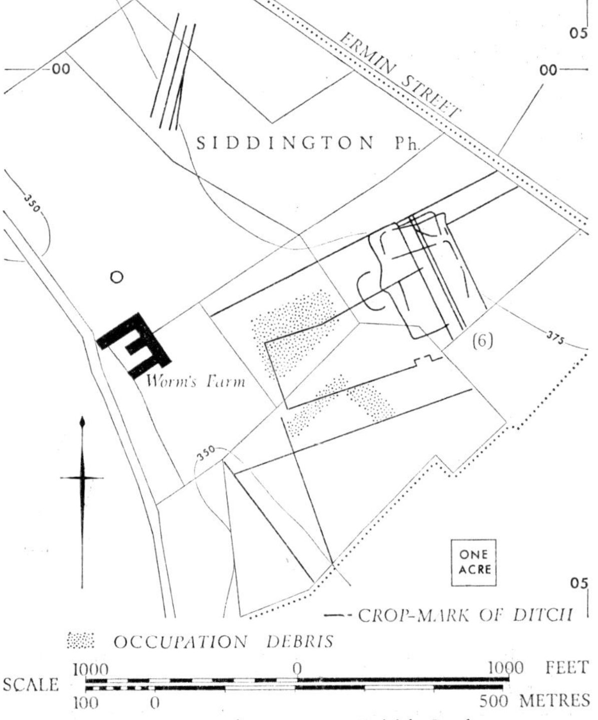

SIDDINGTON. (6) Romano-British Settlement.

City Museum. The crop-marks suggest reorganization of boundaries within the settlement. Linear ditches 300 yds. to the N. (SU 044000) are undated.

C.U.A.P., OAP AOR 98, ASM 51–2, 55, AXO 93.

(7) PROBABLE SETTLEMENT (SU 021984), undated, S.W. of Sandy Lane Farm, is faintly indicated by crop-marks over an area of about 3 acres.

C.U.A.P., OAP AZN 43.

(8) RECTILINEAR DITCHES (SU 02939932), undated, N.W. of The Quarries, defining three parallel strips each about 70 ft. across, are visible as crop-marks.

N.M.R., OAP SU 0299/1/377.

SNOWSHILL

(20 miles N.N.E. of Cirencester)

(1) ROMAN ROAD, Ryknild Street (SP 13363300–SP 13083376), is seen in the form of crop-marks extending N.N.W. in a straight line for $\frac{1}{3}$ mile across the indented E. shoulder of Snowshill Hill, above and below the 800-ft. contour. The alignment continues that noted in BOURTON-ON-THE HILL (1) to S.E., and it also continues to N.W., where it forms the county boundary with Worcestershire (CHIPPING CAMPDEN (1)). For 300 yds. S. of the county boundary all traces of the road have been obscured by modern tree-planting, but the *agger* appears in the same alignment under a wall on the boundary (SP 13083376).

R.A.F., VAP F21 543/RAF/1913: 0033, 34.

SODBURY

(23 miles S.W. of Cirencester)

An uninscribed early Gallo-Belgic gold coin[1] and a group of Romano-British finds[2] are recorded from the vicinity of Chipping Sodbury (ST 7282).

Crop-marks photographed in 1969 at ST 769805 (Plate 59) suggest a roughly rectangular ditched enclosure of about 3 acres, facing S.S.E. at 600 ft. above O.D. (C.U.A.P., OAP AYG 27).

1. D. F. Allen in *Bagendon*, 133. A second gold coin may have been attributed to Chipping Sodbury in error (Allen, *op. cit.*, 134).
2. *JRS*, XLIV (1954), 109.

(1) SODBURY CAMP (ST 760826), hill-fort, unexcavated, comprises two wide-spaced ramparts enclosing an inner area of 11 acres on the plateau edge, $\frac{1}{2}$ mile S.E. of Little Sodbury village, its N. half lying within that parish (area map *s.v.* HORTON, p. 66). All interior areas have been ploughed in the past (Plate 34). Plan and profiles, p. 104.

The inner rampart is set along the edges of a slight eminence on the N., E. and S., where it is about 35 ft. wide and rises 7 ft. above the interior; along the scarp edge on the N.W. it is lower. The ditch, 30 ft. wide and 7 ft. deep on the plateau, drops round the N. corner to follow, for some 400 ft., a natural terrace 25 ft. below the scarp edge. A low counterscarp bank accompanies the ditch from the point where it drops to the terrace. At the entrance, in the middle of the E. side, the slightly staggered ends of the rampart contain much fire-reddened limestone. The surface of the causeway across the ditch is somewhat sunken.

The outer rampart, set 50 ft. beyond the inner ditch, terminates to N. and S. at the escarpment edge. Irregularly constructed and apparently unfinished, it is 56 ft. wide and up to 11 ft. high, with a berm 12 ft. wide. The ditch, 45 ft. wide, is 6 ft. to 10 ft. deep in the middle of the E. side; elsewhere the depth is 3 ft. or less. The entrance is opposite that through the inner defences. A second causeway in the ditch, 170 ft. to N., corresponds with a reduction in rampart size.

There are other earthworks immediately adjacent to the hill-fort. A linear bank is possibly contemporary and for this reason is described here, although it lies within the parish of LITTLE SODBURY. The linear bank, 1,000 ft. long, 45 ft. wide and 2 ft. 6 in. high, with a ditch 28 ft. wide on its inner (W.) side, is possibly an addition to the hill-fort and continues the line of the E. defences northwards. At its S. end the bank runs for about 100 ft. along the outer edge of the ditch of the hill-fort. An embanked circle 22 ft. in diameter, possibly a tree-ring, stands on the bank 300 ft. from its N. end; about 145 ft. N. of the end is a second circle of similar character, 80 ft. in diameter. A plan by Witts (*TBGAS*, VIII (1883–4), 74–8, Pl. iii) shows the linear bank continuing beneath the second circle and thence, after a gap of 100 yds., W. to the escarpment edge. This continuation cannot now be traced. The alleged western end is a bank of mediaeval or later character with ditches on either side; it is one of a series which occurs N. of Little Sodbury Manor House. The long mounds described by Witts (ST 761829) are pillow mounds.

Banks within the hill-fort are as follows—(i) A low, flat-topped bank is built along the inner side of the inner rampart on the N.W., with a slight internal ditch. (ii) Two low parallel banks extend from the outer rampart towards the inner ditch on the N. (iii) Traces of a bank cross the interior, on the line of the parish boundary (map, p. 66).

Part of the rubber of a saddle-quern was found inside the hill-fort in 1958 (Gloucester City Museum records), and eight Roman coins ranging from Gallienus to Constantius II have been found within and in the

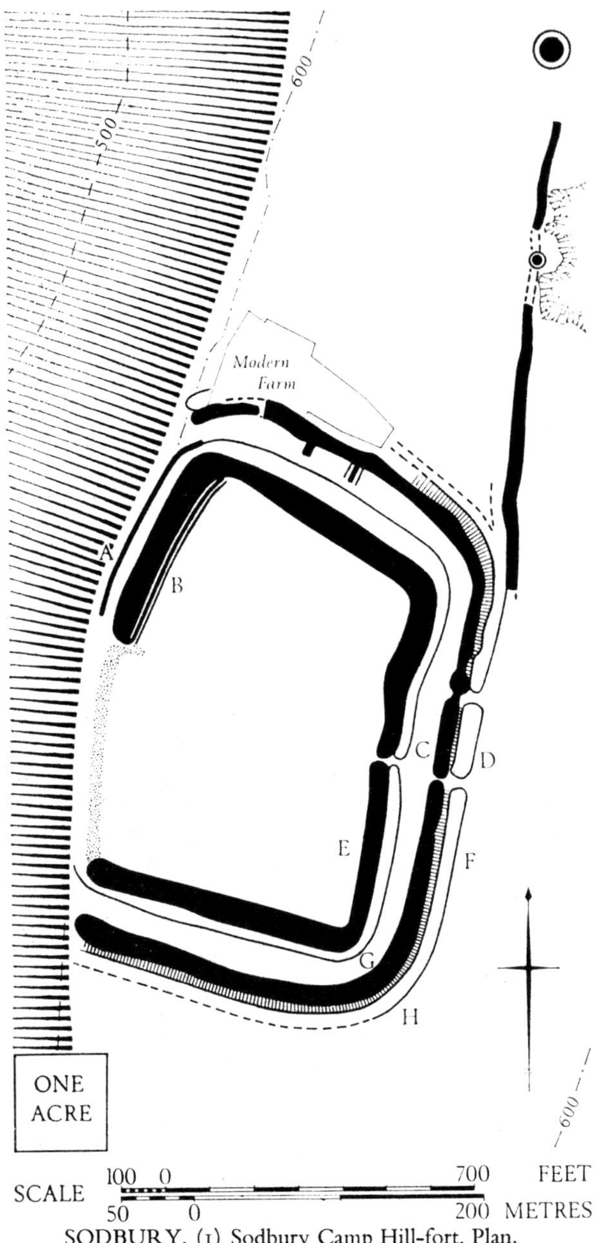

SODBURY. (1) Sodbury Camp Hill-fort. Plan.

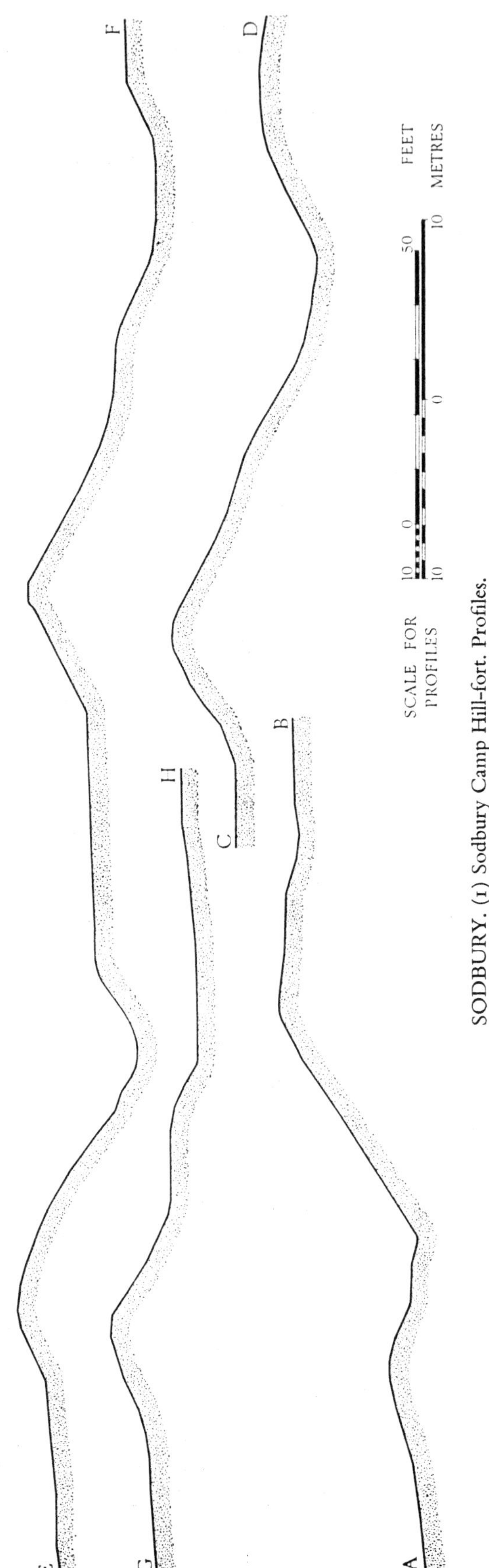

SODBURY. (1) Sodbury Camp Hill-fort. Profiles.

vicinity of the hill-fort (Gloucester City Museum); the find-spots of three are marked on a plan in *TBGAS*, LII (1930), facing p. 184.

Lloyd Baker (1821), 165, No. 11. Playne (1876), 219, No. 41. Witts (1883), 46, No. 92.

SOMERFORD KEYNES

(4 miles S. of Cirencester)

(1) Probable Settlement (SU 021936), between the Swill Brook and Flagham Brook, is revealed by crop-marks over an area of some 35 acres on a gravel terrace in the Thames Valley, about 280 ft. above O.D.

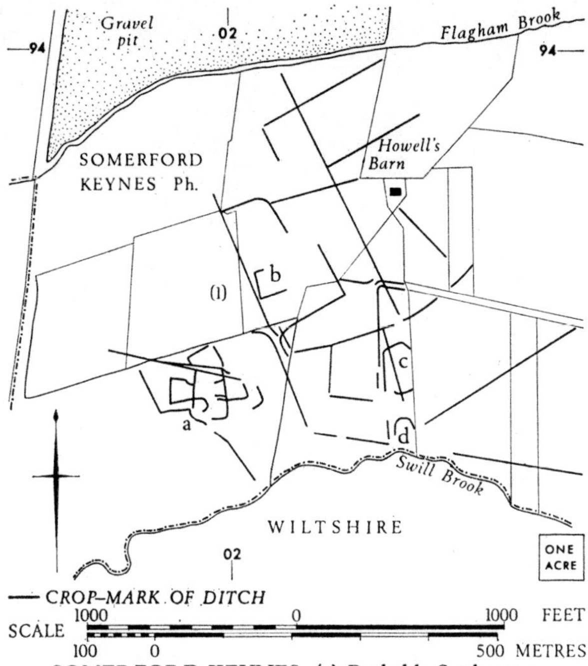

SOMERFORD KEYNES. (1) Probable Settlement.

Two fragments of samian ware, found near enclosure b, are in Gloucester City Museum.

N.M.R., OAP SP 0293/1/388–9; 0293/2/390–1.

(2) PROBABLE SETTLEMENT (SU 019945), undated, 200 yds. S. of the R. Thames at Neigh Bridge, shows indistinctly as a dense complex of crop-marks covering some 7 acres, on gravel at about 290 ft. above O.D. Multiple linear ditches divide the area into approximately rectangular figures, within which are indications of D-shaped and sub-circular enclosures.

O.S., VAP 70 030, 132.

(3) ENCLOSURES AND LINEAR DITCHES (SU 025957), undated, W. of Spratsgate Lane, show as indistinct crop-marks now partly destroyed by gravel-digging. They cover at least 15 acres, about 295 ft. above O.D. The complex includes a rectangular enclosure, probably beside a track (arrowed on Plate 59).

N.M.R., OAP (Baker) SU 0295/1.

(4) PROBABLE SETTLEMENT (SU 016968), undated, midway between the R. Thames and Shorncote, shows as crop-marks over some 17 acres of level ground, about 310 ft. above O.D.

The internal area of the double-ditched enclosure (a) is about ½ acre.

O.S., VAP 70 042, 158 (enclosures a and b). N.M.R., OAP SU 0196/1/383–5 (enclosures c–e).

(5) LINEAR DITCHES (SU 029967), undated, are revealed by indistinct crop-marks E. of Shorncote, at about 305 ft. above O.D.

O.S., VAP 70 042, 159. N.M.R., OAP SU 0396/1/110–11.

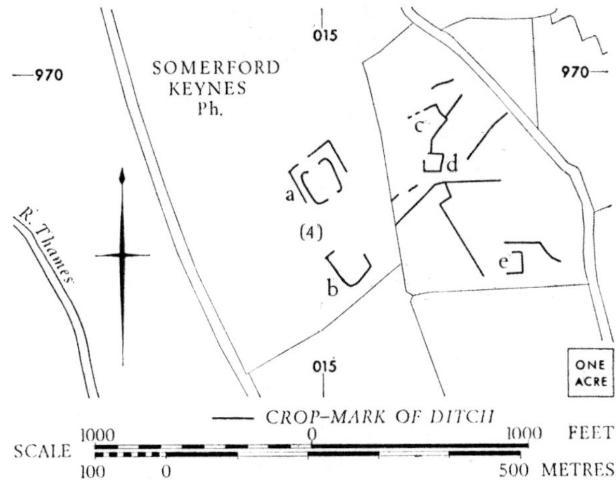

SOMERFORD KEYNES. (4) Probable Settlement.

(6) ROMANO-BRITISH SETTLEMENT (SU 030947), 1,000 yds. S.E. of the village and about 600 yds. N. of the R. Thames, on gravel, is disclosed by crop-marks which lie mainly in Ashton Keynes (Wiltshire). From the E. corner, adjacent to a Romano-British settlement, the N.E. and S.E. sides can each be traced for about 900 ft.; the S.E. side crosses the county boundary at SU 03049458 (approx.).

Romano-British pottery, said to be of 1st–2nd-century type, was recovered from the primary filling of the enclosure ditch during excavation of the settlement in 1971.

The ditch of another enclosure on a somewhat different alignment, undated, crosses the county boundary further N.W. (SU 02999471); it extends S.W. to SU 02659449 (approx.).

C.U.A.P., OAP AYG 38. N.M.R., OAP SU 0394/5/393–5. *MPBW Excavations, 1971* (1972), 23.

SOUTH CERNEY

(3 miles S.E. of Cirencester)

A Romano-British burial in a lead coffin, discovered in a gravel pit in 1941 (*TBGAS*, 76 (1957), 157–60), has no precise location. The coffin is lost.

(1) ENCLOSURE AND PARALLEL DITCHES (SU 053986), undated, on South Cerney airfield, show as crop-marks. The precise direction of the parallel ditches could not be plotted with certainty; they are irregular, about 90 ft. apart and 1,400 ft. long. The enclosure lies on the N. of the ditches. Some other ditches may be of recent origin. Plan, p. 106.

N.M.R., OAP SU 0598/1/169–72.

(2) RECTANGULAR ENCLOSURE (SU 05599830), undated, on the S. side of Northmoor Lane, shows as a crop-mark about 90 ft. by 40 ft., with a gap in the S. side.

C.U.A.P., OAP AYG 42.

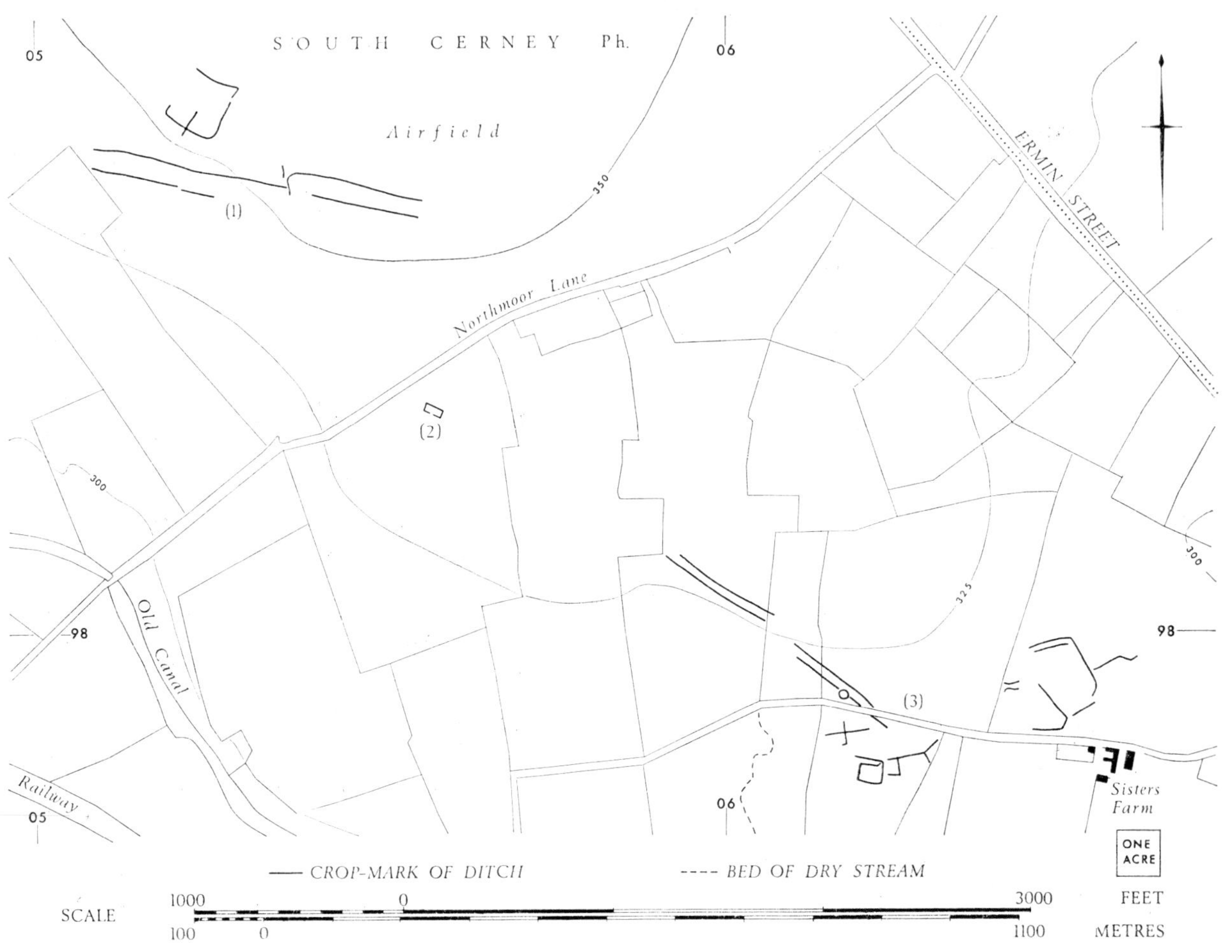

SOUTH CERNEY. (1–3) Enclosures etc. and possible Trackways.

(3) TRACKWAYS (?) AND ENCLOSURES (SU 063979), undated, W. of Sisters Farm, show as crop-marks at about 300 ft. above O.D.

C.U.A.P., OAP AYG 40–1. N.M.R., OAP SU 0697/5.

SOUTHAM

(14 miles N. of Cirencester)

Two slight banked circles some 50 ft. in diameter occur on Cleeve Hill. One of them is on the cliff edge inside the hill-fort (1) and the other is 50 yds. outside, to the north. They are shown on large scale O.S. maps and are clearly seen on Plate 40. They are probably of recent date, possibly tree-rings.[1]

Two pots with Roman coins of gold and silver are said to have been found at Cleeve, in or before 1811.[2] Bronze miniature models of a dagger and a socketed ploughshare from Cleeve Hill are in Cheltenham Museum.

1. Witts (1883, p. 13) refers to another and smaller ring outside the hill-fort; all three were assumed to represent buildings attached to the 'camp'. Burrow (1924), 63.

2. J. Goding (ed.), *Norman's History of Cheltenham* (1863), 18–19.

(1) HILL-FORT (SO 985255), Cleeve Cloud, unexcavated, bivallate with intermediate berm, now encloses about 3 acres of ground sloping gently W. to the partly quarried cliff edge of Inferior Oolite (Plate 40). No entrance survives. The banks and ditches have been disturbed in places by quarrying, and on the N. the outer defences have been cut through to make a golf-course. A rectangular platform abutting the inner bank, 100 ft. from its N. end, is probably recent.

Each bank and each ditch is about 30 ft. across, the banks standing $8\frac{1}{2}$ ft. to 11 ft. above the ditches. The

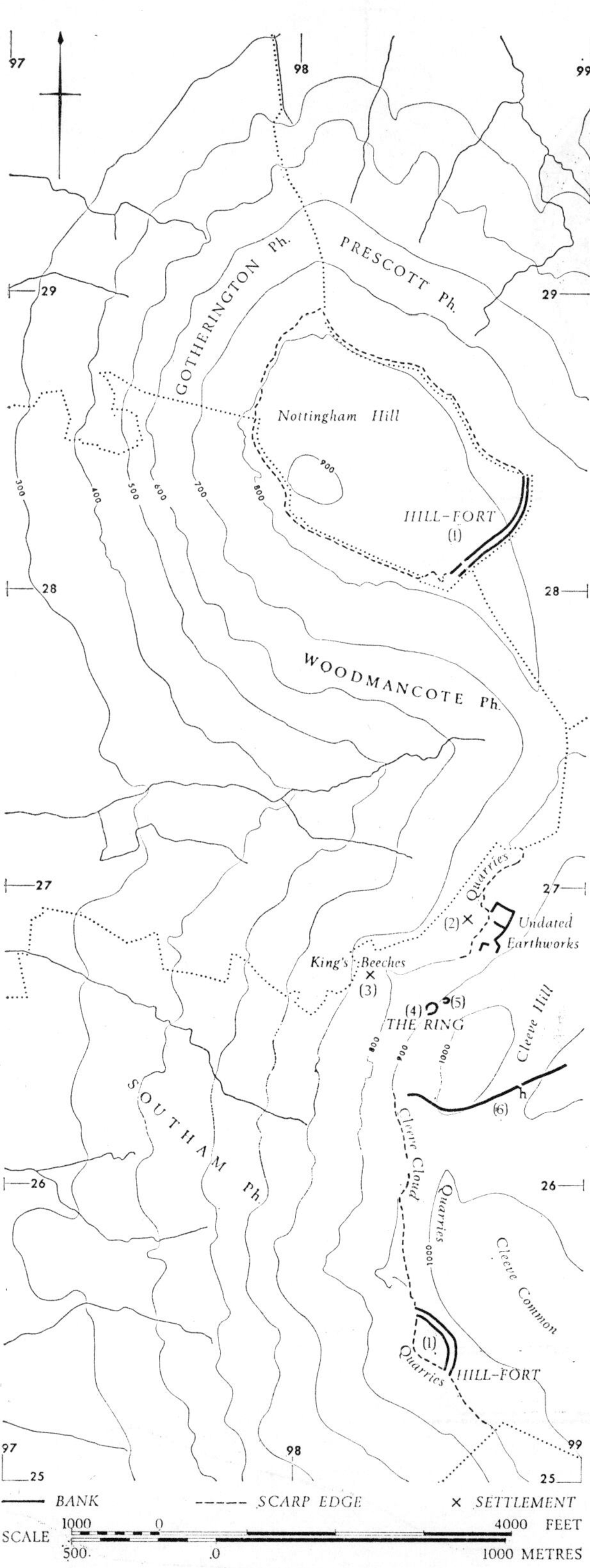

Monuments in SOUTHAM and GOTHERINGTON.

berm which separates the inner ditch from the outer bank is 30 ft. wide in a disturbed area S. of a golf-green; elsewhere it is half this width or less.

C.U.A.P., VAP RC8–N 97–8; OAP AIK 16.

Arch, XIX (1821), 171. *PCNFC*, VI (1876), 209, No. 9. Witts (1883), 13, No. 27. Burrow (1924), 61–3.

Note: The situation of monuments (2)–(6) can be seen in Plate 40.

(2) Iron Age Settlement (so 986269), near The Stables, S.E. of Cleeve Lodge, was identified *c.* 1903 in a quarry. Shallow pits and an assemblage of finds said to be similar to those described below (monument (3)) came to light. Pottery included stamped ware.

Uphill of the quarry on a moderate W.-facing slope the remains of undated ditched enclosures, roughly rectangular, cover some $1\frac{1}{2}$ acres. The ditches are up to 20 ft. across, below banks 4 ft. high.

C.U.A.P., VAP RC8–N, 94–5. R.A.F., VAP V58/RAF/8390: 0033.

PCNFC, XV (1904), 55. *Bagendon* (1961), 23. *TBGAS*, 58 (1936), 162.

(3) Settlement (so 98272670), King's Beeches, $\frac{1}{4}$ mile S.W. of (2), Iron Age and perhaps Romano-British, was noted in 1903 during quarrying into a platform, most of which still survives, some 90 yds. long by about 20 yds. wide. It is in a relatively exposed position near a spring. Of seven beech-trees planted about 1902, three have died. Some 5 ft. depth of soil and rubble, perhaps the result of quarrying, overlie soil containing occupation debris; below was the natural gravel into which a number of pits had been dug, some of them probably post-holes. Finds included pottery, most of it poorly fired, wattle-marked daub, bones including human and of fowls, sawn red deer antler, worked stones of various kinds and, still in the old soil, numbers of stone slabs. Three late 3rd-century Roman coins were found among these stones at a level above the old ground surface.

PCNFC, XV (1904), 49–67.

(4) The Ring (so 985266), undated, but possibly of the Iron Age, encloses about $\frac{1}{2}$ acre on a moderate west-facing slope (Plate 41). The S.W. entrance is original. Area (a) could be a hut-platform. The level area (g) in its present form is part of a golf-course.

R.A.F., VAP V58/RAF/8390: 0334–5.

(5) Platformed Ringwork, immediately N.E. of (4), undated, possibly Iron Age, has a flat interior about 30 ft. across, perhaps for a hut. The entrance, aligned as in (4), is original.

(6) Dyke (extending E. from so 98352630), undated, probably of the Iron Age, extends for over $\frac{1}{3}$ mile across the ridge of Cleeve Cloud, from a quarried area on the W. brow to a point scarcely 20 ft. above the floor of a

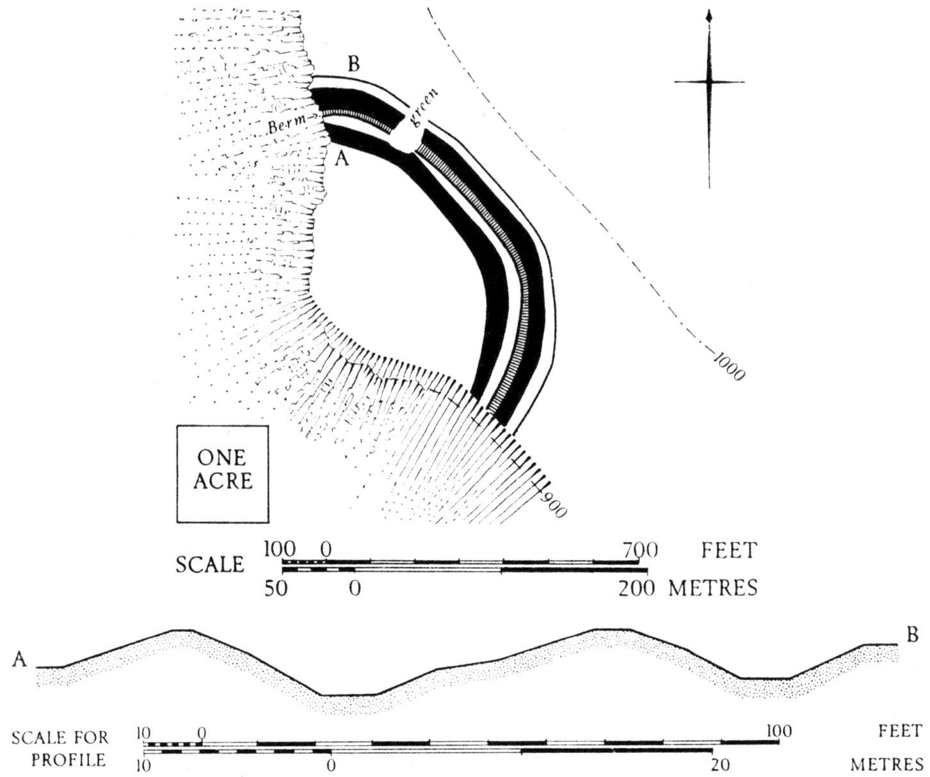

SOUTHAM. (1) Hill-fort, Cleeve Cloud. Plan and profile.

C
A
(5)
D
(4)
g
a
B
SCALE 100 0 100 FEET
10 0 50 METRES
FEET 10 0 100
METRES 5 0 30
SCALE FOR PROFILES
B
D
A
C

SOUTHAM. (4) The Ring. (5) Platformed Ringwork. Plan and profiles.

narrow re-entrant which penetrates the E. side of the ridge. Its course changes over short stretches towards the E. end.

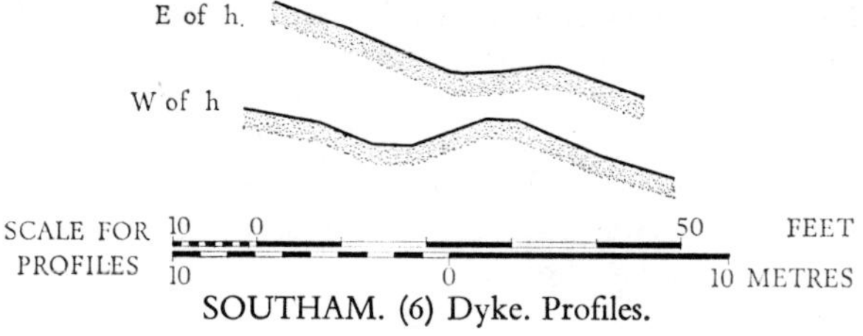

SOUTHAM. (6) Dyke. Profiles.

Much of the dyke comprises a bank some 15 ft. wide, standing up to 3 ft. high above a ditch of similar width. In general the bank is on the S. or downhill side, but at the W. end, where the N.–S. slope is insignificant and the dyke crosses a W.-falling slope of up to 18½°, it is on the north. A hollow-way about 7 ft. deep (h on the general map, p. 107) cuts the dyke at SO 98772634. To E. of h and for a short distance to W. the dyke appears as a terrace with a slightly hollowed surface; further W. it is more pronounced. No original entrance is seen.

R.A.F., VAP V58/RAF/8390: 0335.

SOUTHROP

(11 miles E. of Cirencester)

Part of a Roman villa (LECHLADE (7)) lies in this parish.

(1) ENCLOSURE (SP 174041), (Plate 54) undated, S.W. of Homeleaze Farm, shows as a crop-mark; adjacent indistinct crop-marks cover some 9 acres of level ground, about 350 ft. above O.D.

C.U.A.P., OAP AYG 47, 49–50.
Oxon, VII (1942), 111.

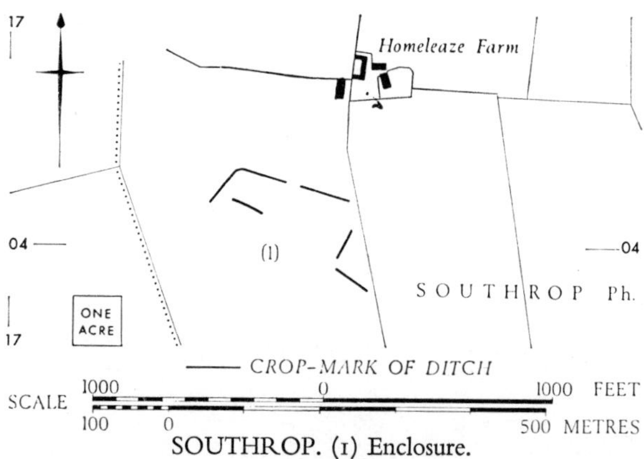

SOUTHROP. (1) Enclosure.

(2) ENCLOSURES AND TRACKS (SP 200018), undated, show indistinctly as crop-marks over an area of about 9 acres, W.S.W. of Great Lemhill Farm.

O.S., VAP 70 167, 072–4.

(3) LINEAR DITCHES (SP 204022), undated, show as faint crop-marks, W.N.W. of Great Lemhill Farm.

O.S., VAP 70 167, 072–4.

STANDISH

(14 miles W.N.W. of Cirencester)

For cross-ridge dyke partly in Standish Wood, see RANDWICK (1).

STANTON

(20 miles N. of Cirencester)

The hill-fort on Shenberrow Hill (1) is the smallest in the area covered by this volume of the Inventory.

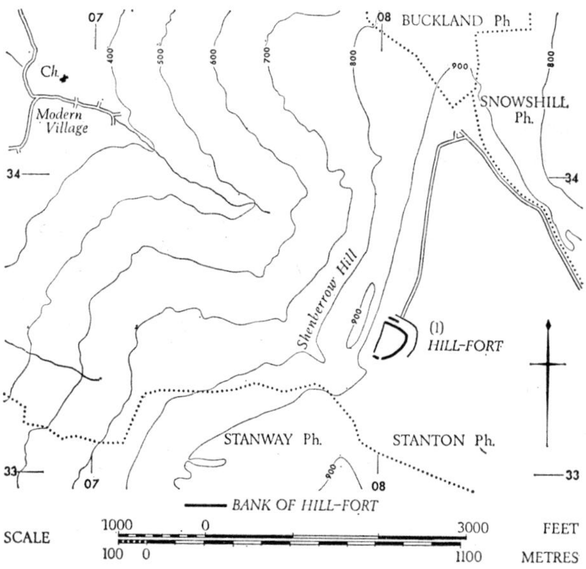

Monuments in STANTON.

(1) HILL-FORT (SP 080334), on Shenberrow Hill, bivallate, excavated, encloses 2½ acres on a sloping spur of the Cotswold escarpment, 1 mile E.S.E. of the village (Plate 39).

The inner defences consist of a rampart 30 ft. wide and 5 ft. high, and a ditch 25 ft. wide and 4 ft. deep, partly obscured by farm buildings on the S.E.; to N. and S. both features terminate at the scarp edge. A disturbed bank 20 ft. wide and 3 ft. high, set parallel with the scarp edge and linking the rampart ends, has no visible ditch. The entrance is through a gap in the rampart, 125 ft. E. of its S. end.

The outer defences are undisturbed on the N., where the rampart is 25 ft. wide and 2 ft. high and the ditch is 25 ft. wide and 3 ft. deep; elsewhere the rampart has been levelled and the ditch is traceable only as a crop-mark; farm buildings obscure its S. end.

A narrow bank defines the S. and E. sides of an enclosure, 60 ft. by 50 ft., in the N. corner of the interior. Excavation in 1935 showed that the inner rampart has a drystone revetment on its inner face at the point marked A on the plan, and the flat-bottomed ditch is nearly 11 ft. deep. Cuttings made across the scarp-edge bank disclosed a core of loose stones. Hand-made Iron Age pottery, including situlate jars with rounded shoulders and flat-topped rims, decorated predominantly with finger-nail or finger-tip impressions, was recovered from an occupation layer sealed beneath the scarp-edge bank. In cutting A similar pottery was recovered from the material of the inner rampart, from the primary silt of the ditch and from an occupation level overlying a prepared floor in the angle formed by the rampart and the scarp-edge bank. From the interior, similar pottery was recorded at B, where no structure was identified; also at C, in the fill of a rock-cut pit 10 ft. 2 in. in diameter and 9 ft. 6 in. deep, and at D, a cutting through the stone and earth bank of the enclosure in the north corner. Other finds included a bronze bracelet and fragments of iron objects, bones of domestic animals, bone tools and part of a saddle quern. Pieces of a rotary quern from cutting A were thought to be later than the main occupation. The finds are in Gloucester City Museum.

Romano-British pottery of the 2nd century or later was found in secondary positions during excavation of the hill-fort.

Playne (1876), 207, No. 3. (Witts) *TBGAS*, IV (1879–80), 207, 'Lidcomb'. Excavation report: *TBGAS*, 80 (1961), 16–41.

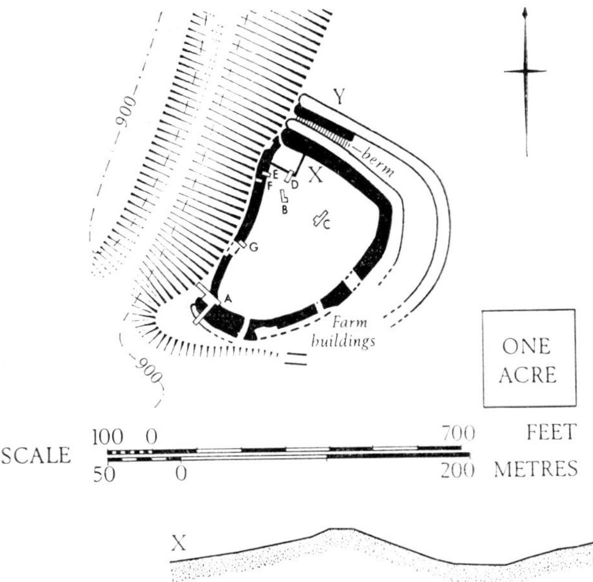

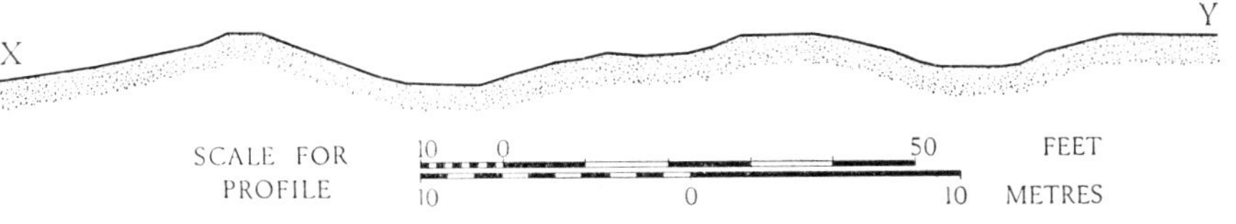

STANTON. (1) Hill-fort on Shenberrow Hill. Plan and profile.

STANWAY

(19 miles N. of Cirencester)

Supposed hill-forts at Upper Coscombe (SP 074295) and in Hailes Wood (SP 056301), the first certainly geological and the second probably so, are discussed in the preface (pp. xxxiii, xxxiv). Iron Age sherds and spreads of Romano-British pottery are recorded from arable fields N. of Ireley Farm and Hailes Farm.[1] Romano-British pottery is said to have been recovered from the vicinity of imprecisely recorded burials, 50 yds. S. of Millhampost farmhouse.[2]

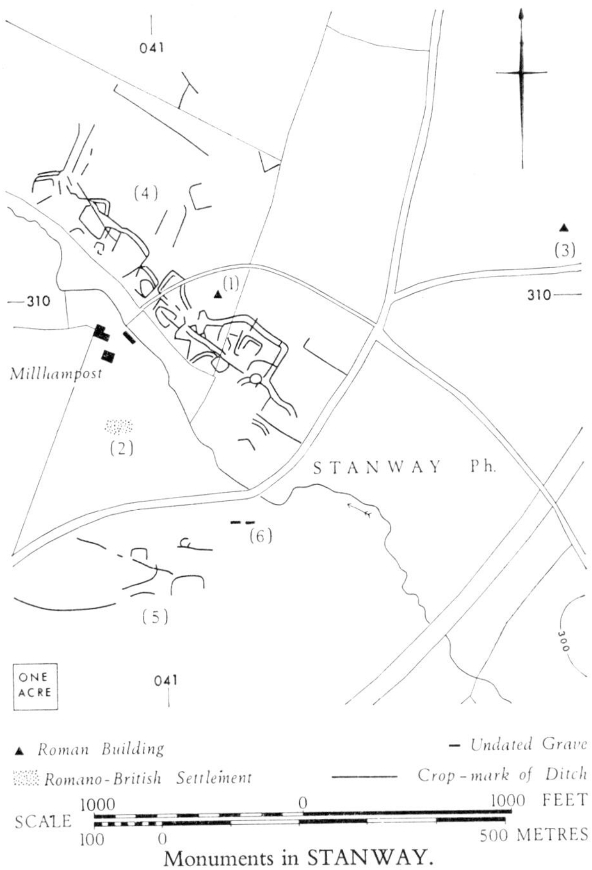

Monuments in STANWAY.

Monuments (1) to (6) lie about 270 ft. above O.D. on a gravel terrace of the R. Avon and are clustered on either side of a tributary of the R. Isbourne.

1. *PPS*, XXXIV (1968), 427. *TBGAS*, 65 (1944), 187–98. *Archaeol. Review*, 4 (1969), 42.

2. W. St. Clair Baddeley, *A Cotteswold Shrine* (1908), 6. The skeletons are in Gloucester City Museum.

(1) Roman Building (SP 04203101), Millhampost, ploughed out, stood near the N. bank of the brook close to (4). Records refer to large stones encountered in ploughing and to the finding of pottery and 2nd-century coins (Trajan to Antoninus) and 'later bronze issues'. The base of a pillar and a box-flue tile stamped LEG. XXII PR.P.F. are recorded from the immediate vicinity; the tile is probably a modern importation (Frere, *Britannia* (1966), 139 and note 2). Two *asses* of Claudius and some pottery are in Gloucester City Museum.

W. St. Clair Baddeley, *A Cotteswold Shrine* (1908), 6. *Ibid.*, letter to F. Haverfield, 26 Oct. 1900, in Haverfield Library, Ashmolean Museum. O.S. records.

(2) Romano-British Settlement (SP 04083082), S. of Millhampost. A trial excavation in 1965, 230 yds. S.W. of (1) and on the opposite side of the brook, yielded Romano-British pottery, shallow ditches and dark patches of occupation.

Information from Mrs. H. E. O'Neil and Mr. A. Marshall.

(3) Probable Roman Building (SP 047311), 560 yds. E.N.E. of (1), was revealed by the North Sea Gas pipe-trench in 1969. Stone foundations, roofing tiles and pottery of the 3rd and 4th centuries were recorded.

Archaeol. Review, 4 (1969), 39, 42 (two accounts appearing to refer to the same site).

(4) Enclosures and Tracks (SP 041310), undated, show as crop-marks covering about 20 acres along the bank of the brook, N. of Millhampost.

Arch J, CXXI (1964), 15 (site 32), fig. 9.
N.M.R., OAP (Baker) SP 0430/1, 2.

(5) Enclosures and Linear Ditches (SP 041306), undated, cover some 6 acres on Ireley Farm, about 200 yds. S. of (2).

N.M.R., OAP (Baker) SP 0430/6.

(6) Graves (SP 04233068), undated, two, situated N.E. of (5), were defined by limestone slabs. Fragments of Iron Age pottery and other occupation debris were found in the fill of the graves. Romano-British pottery occurred in the soil covering them.

TBGAS, 65 (1944), 187–98.

STINCHCOMBE

(18 miles W. of Cirencester)

On the evidence at present available the so-called hill-fort of Drakestone Point (ST 73639795) cannot be regarded as a prehistoric monument (see p. xxxiv).

(1) Roman Villa (ST 741971), Stancombe, is known from brief accounts of a limited examination by P. B. Purnell in 1845. It was probably large. Lynchets (2) adjacent on the N. are likely to represent 'Celtic' fields, (see map, p. 86, *s.v.* North Nibley).

The villa was sited near the edge of an extensive and almost flat terrace of Middle Lias, above a slope falling sharply S.E. into a valley with a stream. Accounts refer summarily to an extensive villa, a suite of heated rooms with two rows of stone columns, and a tessellated pavement. The plan made by P. B. Purnell is now lost. Fragments of pavement, probably from the villa, are in Gloucester City Museum; there are also two inscribed stones, one funerary. One was from the immediate area of the villa. A collection of other objects probably includes material from the same villa.

Many walls adjacent to Stancombe Park are built, wholly or in part, of reused stone which could come from the villa. A 200-yd. length of wall, N. of the road at ST 73859755, includes large squared blocks of Oolite and flags of sandstone, some burned.

JBAA, II (1847), 349; IV (1849), 320. *Sussex Arch. Colls.* II (1849), 313–15. Witts (1883), 208, No. 7. *The Antiquary*, XXVII (1893), 71. *RIB*, I, Nos. 123–4. *PNG*, II, 250–1.

(2) Lynchets (ST 742974), in a broken pattern, E. of Stancombe and about 300 yds. N. of (1), probably represent 'Celtic' fields. They are up to 3 ft. high, on a moderate slope of Cotteswold Sand, below the 400-ft. contour.

R.A.F., VAP CPE/UK 2098: 4385.

STONEHOUSE

No Iron Age or Romano-British monument is known in this parish.

STOW-ON-THE-WOLD

(18 miles N.E. of Cirencester)

It has been suggested[1] that an Iron Age hill-fort preceded the present hill-top town, the defences enclosing some 30 acres on the E. of the parish church. No certain remains have yet been found and the suggestion depends upon the oval pattern made by the old parish boundary on N. and E., where there is a steeply scarped edge to the spur, and by the line of streets on S. and W. The site may have been referred to as *Meilgaresbyri* in a charter of 714.[2]

1. *Antiquity*, VII (1933), 347–50. Test excavations were carried out by Mrs. H. E. O'Neil in 1972.
2. Sawyer, No. 1250. *PNG*, I, 222–5.

(1) Roman Road, The Foss Way (SP 18992543), is represented by the *agger*, 30 ft. wide, up to $1\frac{1}{2}$ ft. high and probably ditched on both sides, extending for 250 yds. in the cemetery S.W. of the town.

STROUD

(11 miles W. of Cirencester)

Roman pottery, including large unabraded pieces of samian and coarse wares, together with iron slag, was found in 1866 when West Grange House (SO 85000557) was being built;[1] the finds are in Stroud Museum. Ten Roman coins of the 3rd and 4th centuries, chance finds made in a wide area centred on Cashe's Green (SO 828056), are also in the museum. A coin of Allectus is in Gloucester City Museum.

1. *PCNFC*, IV (1868), 78; XXV, ii (1934), 205.

SUDELEY

(14 miles N. of Cirencester)

Romano-British activity about the Neolithic long barrow of Belas Knap is attested by finds including five coins of the 3rd and 4th centuries and samian and other pottery.[1] An enamelled harness mount, a La Tène I brooch and Romano-British finds have been reported from places not precisely located. Tesserae came from the garden of 'Sudeley Lanes Farm', possibly Lane's Barn (SP 038268), and from a field opposite 'Keeper's Lodge', probably that at SP 042275 about a mile N. of the Spoonley Wood villa (4).[2] A marble statuette of Bacchus comes from a grave in a field adjacent to Spoonley Wood and therefore near the same villa.[3] A scatter of diverse finds is reported from arable fields belonging to Spoonley Farm.[4] A collection of coins at Sudeley Castle includes examples, unspecified, excavated at Wadfield (2) and Spoonley Wood (4).[5] A late Roman bronze buckle (Hawkes and Dunning type I B) possibly of the 5th century, also in the Castle, may have come from Spoonley Wood.[6]

1. *PSA*, 2nd ser., III (1864–7), 277–9. *TBGAS*, LI (1929), 292; LII (1930), 137.
2. *Annals of Winchcombe and Sudeley* (1877), p. 15 and plate opp.
3. B.M. *Guide to the Antiquities of Roman Britain* (1951), 55, No. 10. Toynbee (1964), 69.
4. Information from Mr. F. G. Freeman.
5. *TBGAS*, 80 (1961), 75–80.
6. *Ant J*, XVII (1937), 446–8. *Med. Archaeol.*, V (1961), 49, No. 9.

(1) HILL-FORT? (SP 047243), probably Iron Age, on the ridge-top of Inferior Oolite, W. of Roel Gate, is bounded by a bank, some 20 ft. across, standing up to 3 ft. above the interior and up to 6 ft. above a disturbed ditch (Plate 32). The bank almost surrounds a slightly domed area of 2½ acres. The gap, 120 ft. wide, above the re-entrant on the N., shows no sign of former closure. Plan, p. 113.

C.U.A.P., OAP AIK 10, 11; ABR 85.

(2) ROMAN VILLA (SP 02312604), Wadfield, lies on a narrow natural shelf in a moderately steep E.-facing slope, near springs, just below the junction of Cotteswold Sand and Upper Lias. It was discovered during

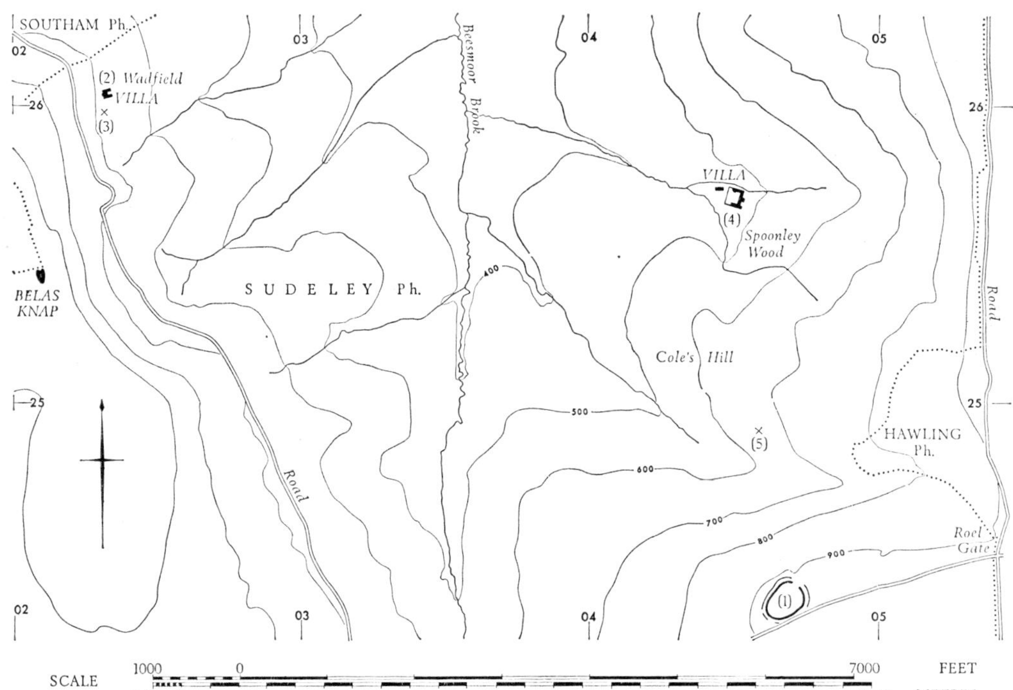

Monuments in SUDELEY.

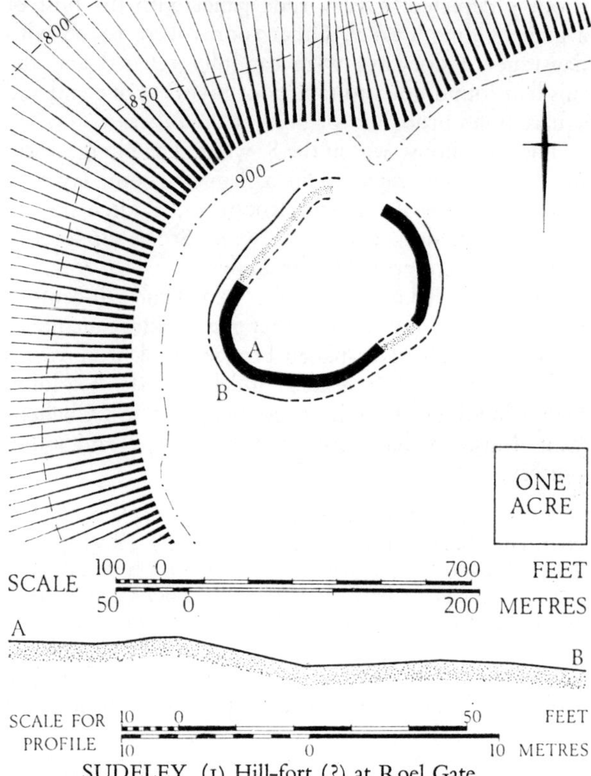

SUDELEY. (1) Hill-fort (?) at Roel Gate.

ploughing in 1863 and was excavated by P. Loftus Brock in 1894–5. Selected wall footings were left open and a protective building incorporating stones from the villa was put up over Room 1, with part of the mosaic pavement reconstructed. Some footings can still be traced. The building now stands in a wooded enclosure bounded by a wall largely composed of reused stones. Rubble, including burnt stone, lies spread on the arable ground outside the enclosure. Another Romano-British building (3) was recently discovered some 50 yds. to the S., and there are platforms of uncertain origin downhill from the villa, 50 yds. to the north.

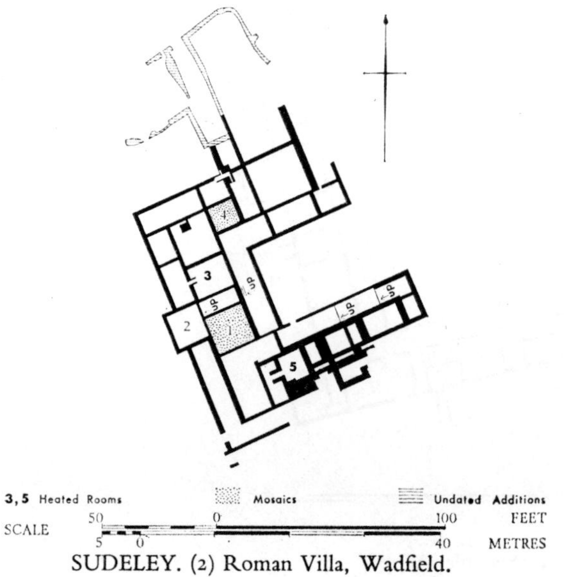

SUDELEY. (2) Roman Villa, Wadfield.

Loftus Brock noted that the villa was built in more than one phase. It seems certain that the irregular walls on the N. are additions or rebuilds and there seem to have been other walls and a paved courtyard not shown on the plan. The S. wing appears to have contained a bath-house. Confusing accounts show that the tessellated pavement from room 1 was removed to Sudeley Castle in 1863; but half of it, of small red, black and cream-coloured tesserae, was at some time reconstructed in the W. half of the room (Plate 13). A pavement of red tesserae was described, apparently in room 2, but one such, still visible in room 4, does not appear in the account. Internal walls were said to be covered with painted plaster. A half-octagonal moulded stone capital (?), formerly attached to a wall, now stands in the room on the W. of room 4. The block of masonry in that room was taken to be a table. The foot of a stone statuette had been found in 1863. Apart from *pilae* there were few tiles; some stone 'slates' were found. Small finds included a coin of Domitian, two of Hadrian and one of Arcadius, much coarse pottery and, possibly, small fragments of samian ware; also brooches, including one of fan-tail type, and a ring with an intaglio.

Annals of Winchcombe and Sudeley (1877), pp. 13, 15 and plates. Witts (1883), 66, No. 21. *JBAA*, 2nd ser. I, pt. iii (1895), 242–50.

(3) ROMANO-BRITISH BUILDING (SP 023260), 53 yds. S. of (2), was found in 1969 in the course of trenching for a major pipe-line to convey natural gas. It measured 28¾ ft. by about 39 ft. and had a gravel floor and walls of local stone rising ten courses high on the uphill side. A skeleton with Romano-British pottery lay in the line of the trench at SP 022260.

TBGAS, 90 (1971), 124–8.

(4) ROMAN VILLA (SP 045257), Spoonley Wood, lies on Middle Lias just above its junction with Lower Lias. The valley-bottom site occupies a spit of ground which slopes very gently westwards to the confluence of two streams, the northern of which runs past the villa at the foot of a scarp, now 12 ft. high. The rising ground immediately on the E. is intersected by wet ditches. Structural remains were clearly visible in the wood before 1877. Room 18 was uncovered by searchers for stone in 1882 and the site was subsequently excavated by Professor J. H. Middleton and the Rev. W. Bazeley. One of the mosaic pavements had been removed previously to Sudeley Castle. The walls were partly rebuilt, up to 6 ft. high in places on the E. and S., and reconstructed mosaic pavements were covered by wooden sheds over rooms 8 and 18. The sheds have now collapsed and the remains are suffering from weather and

from the encroaching wood (Plate 24). Traces of scarps up to 1 ft. high suggest the bounds of an inner court within the villa enclosure. Some 20 yds. W. of the N.W. parts of the enclosure are the footings of an aisled structure about 84 ft. by 35 ft.; a low earthen platform extending W. from the area excavated indicates its former length; at least one other wall continued S. from it. In recent years a track ran through the villa, across room 21 and along the roughly paved path which bisects the enclosure.

The N. wing of the villa has the plan of a winged corridor building, later incorporated into a courtyard form, but without direct access into the main range. The walls of the villa, averaging 2 ft. thick, are of local Oolite in small squared blocks. Stonesfield slates were used in the roof. Heated rooms had channelled or pillared hypocausts with *pilae* 12 in. to 16 in. square and with flues connecting certain rooms. Room 18 had a raised floor reached by 5 steps. A veranda, with a floor of coarse grey and white tesserae bounded by a dwarf wall surmounted by stone columns, fronted the E. range. Elsewhere the mosaic pavements (Plates 14, 15) were of small tesserae of brick and of various stones, for the most part comprising 'geometrical or conventional floral' patterns. A fragment from a destroyed floor in room 5 depicted 'a very rude panel with the bust of a man holding a rake'. Other rooms were paved with flagstones. Doorways were carefully rebated and the sills had round holes to take door pivots at one end and square holes probably for bolts at the other.

The bath-house was in the S. wing. The plunge-bath, lined with *opus signinum* in a flagged room, lay at a lower level on the north. Room 14, a kitchen, had a well 13 ft. deep and $2\frac{3}{4}$ ft. wide. Stone supports in this room were probably for a table.

Finds included a large number of 3rd and 4th-century bronze coins, window and other glass, pottery including samian, a small silver-plated bronze bowl, iron knives and tools; most of these are at Sudeley Castle. A column base is in Gloucester City Museum (Plate 30). Cheltenham Museum has three pottery lamps and other pottery.

Annals of Winchcombe and Sudeley (1877), 15. Witts (1883), 70–1, No. 26. *Arch*, LII (1890), 651–68. *Arch J*, XLVII (1890), 420–1. *Winchcombe and Sudeley Record*, 4 (1893) (with illustrations additional to those in *Arch*, LII). *TBGAS*, 71 (1952), 162–6. Middleton Collection MS. (Soc. Ants., Lond.).

(5) PROBABLE ROMANO-BRITISH SHRINE (SP 046249), Cole's Hill, in arable on a steep W.-facing slope at

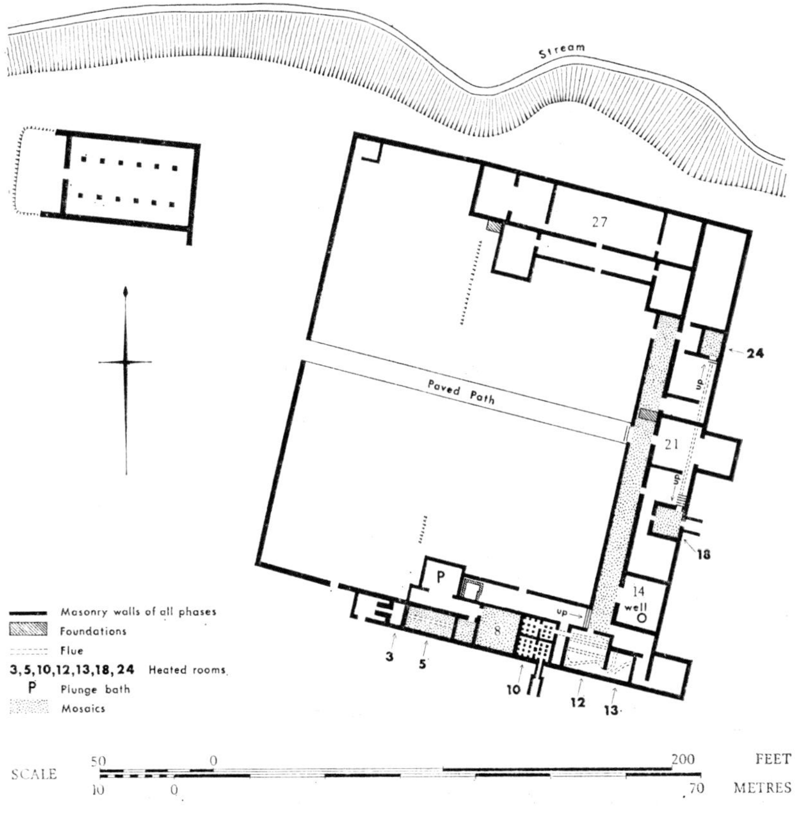

SUDELEY. (4) Roman Villa, Spoonley Wood.

about 650 ft. above O.D., near the junction of Upper and Middle Lias, is identified by finds made on the surface at various times. A few inhumations have been noted.

The finds include a carved limestone eagle, probably part of a large locally made monument, and an uninscribed altar, both now in Gloucester City Museum. Finds, in private possession, probably from the site, include 3rd and 4th-century coins, brooches, pins, rings and bracelets.

JRS, XLIX (1959), 127. Toynbee (1964), 129 (eagle mistakenly attributed to (4)).

SWELL

(18 miles N.E. of Cirencester)

The Roman 'Ryknild Street' is followed by the present road to Condicote over high ground in the W. of the parish. Its course is almost straight for about 2 miles, deflecting slightly in the locality of a barrow group (SP 159253). Roman coins and pottery have been noted at 'Swell Hill Homestead', probably Swell Hill Farm (SP 153262).[1] A 'Constantinian' coin came from the long barrow at (SP 13522627).[2]

1. *TBGAS*, VII (1882–3), 76.
2. *TBGAS*, 79 (1960), 90, Swell I.

(1) Romano-British Settlement (SP 174257), adjacent to and E. of St. Mary's Church, Lower Swell, lies on an almost level spur. The ground between the church and Lady's Well, 230 yds. to the E., is much disturbed. A now destroyed 'tumulus' inside the E. wall of the churchyard was of uncertain origin. The ground falls steeply S. from the church.

An ash-pit and a 'Constantinian' coin were found during 19th-century work on the nave. Abundant pottery and animal bones come from the churchyard; pottery has also been found around the 'village spring' (? Lady's Well). Finds, in the Royce Collection at Bristol, include 4th-century pottery, an iron hook-knife and a steelyard hook.

TBGAS, VII (1882–3), 69–80; 83 (1964), 13.

(2) Roman Villa (SP 18522627), Abbotswood, was noted in 1863 when dug into for building stone. Pottery recovered at the time was used as hard-core in a local farmyard. The site is in pasture. Part of a villa of unknown size is identifiable in a much disturbed platform, roughly corresponding with rooms A–D on the diagram published by D. Royce and adapted here (p. 116). With other low banks and scarps it is set above the shoulder of the valley, on ground sloping very gently S. and W. A circular structure (X), 30 ft. in diameter, is no longer clearly identifiable, but the long wall shown S. of X perhaps corresponds with an existing scarp above a rough track. Below this the ground falls unevenly to the valley bottom, the slope averaging 9°. A building (Y) described as an oblong room, 50 ft. by 30 ft., lay with its axis along the slope some 40 yds. S.S.W. of the

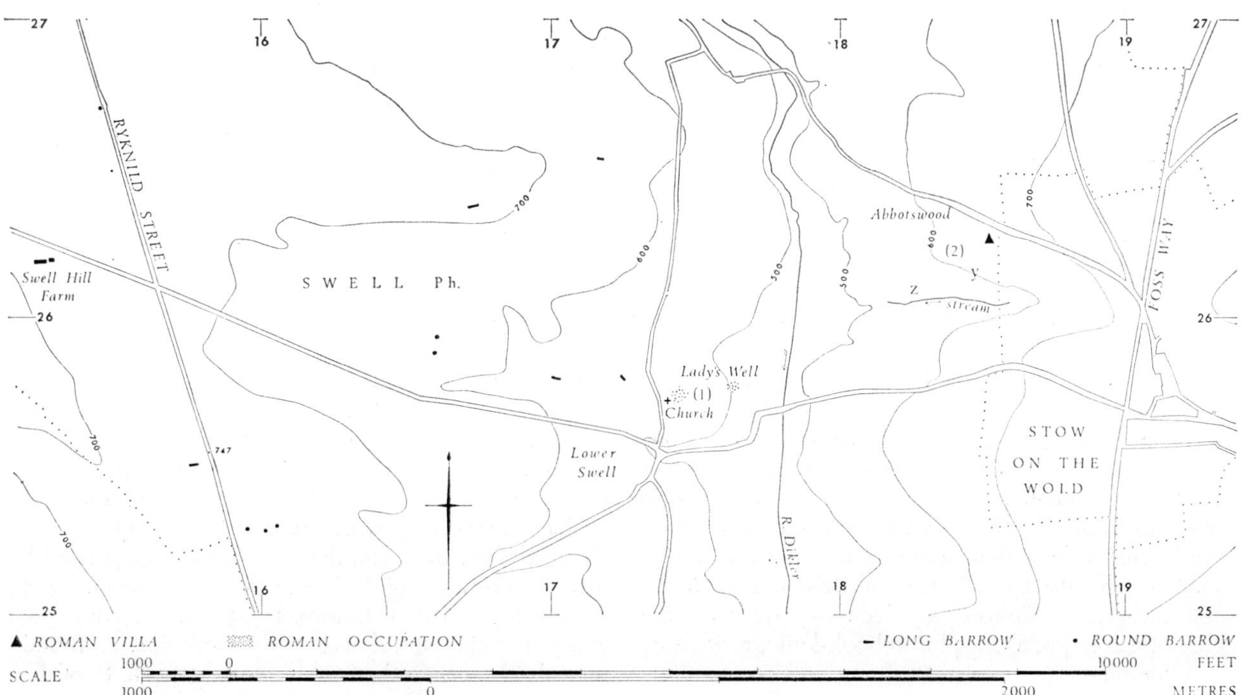

Monuments in SWELL.

long wall, near a spring. Another building (Z) lay some 250 yds. further W., nearer the valley bottom and stream. A pattern of low scarps W. of the villa recalls the arrangement of walled closes N. of the villa in Barnsley Park (BARNSLEY (1)). The most prominent of these scarps, parallel with the long axis of building A–D and some 100 yds. from it, is up to 3 ft. high; it meets the scarp (whether wall or not) which extends W. from below X and defines two sides of an enclosure measuring at least 300 ft. by 400 ft. Other slight parallel scarps to the W. of this are of uncertain origin.

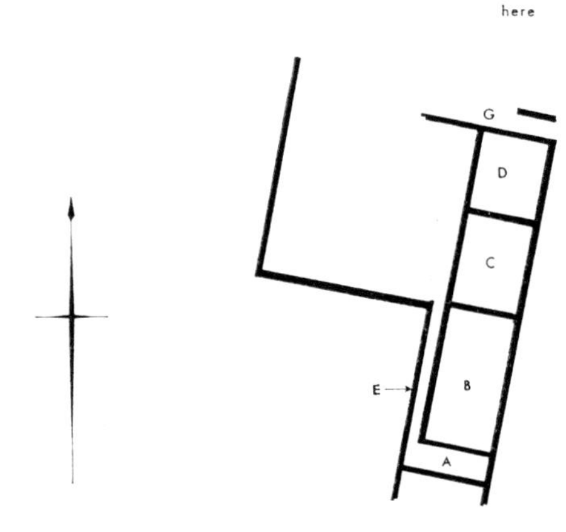

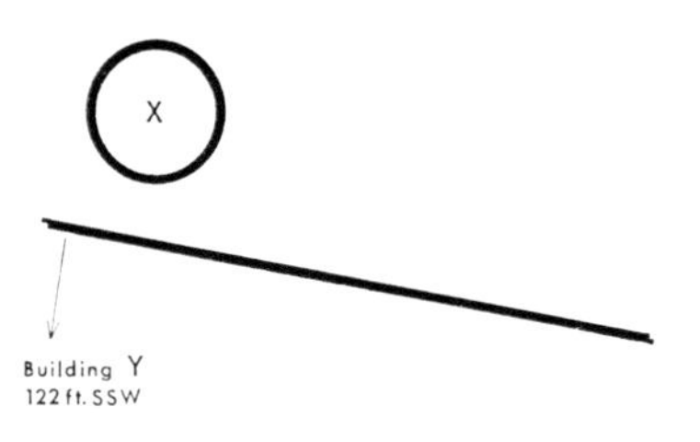

SWELL. (2) Roman Villa (after D. Royce).

Room B had a 'hole' with ashes set in a pitched stone floor, and the same was seen in room D. Passage G had very strong foundations. Extending N. of this as far as the road (some 30 yds.) was a copious scatter of building rubble. There is mention of a hypocaust. Finds, some in the Royce collection at Bristol, include 1st and 2nd-century samian ware, colour-coated wares, a coin of Carausius, a tanged iron hook-knife, roof slates, and flue tiles.

TBGAS, VII (1882–3), 69–80; 83 (1964), 13. Witts (1883), 65–6, No. 20.

SYDE

(7 miles N.W. of Cirencester)

(1) SETTLEMENT (SO 954116), Romano-British, at the W. edge of a plateau and immediately below the 900-ft. contour, lies 600 yds. W. of Ermin Street. A scatter of Romano-British pottery of the 1st to 4th centuries has been found by Mr. P. D. C. Brown. An inscribed lead ingot of A.D. 79 was recovered during ploughing in 1962.

JRS, LIII (1963), 162. Finds in Corinium Museum.

TEMPLE GUITING

(16 miles N.N.E. of Cirencester)

Seven monuments connected with prehistoric and Roman settlement are adjacent to roads which probably mark ancient ways. The road over Kineton Hill, passing monuments (2) and (3), is followed by the parish boundary. Monuments (4–6) lie by the ridgeway (Buckle Street) from Bourton-on-the-Water to Willersey. Monument (10) is close to the Salt Way.

The pit-alignment (4) is one of three examples known in the area of this volume and its high situation is very unusual (see p. xxvii).

Romano-British attention to Bronze Age round barrows is indicated by finds in two excavations. Pottery, including samian, together with a coin of Antoninus Pius was found in the ditch of a barrow (SP 08292910), ¼ mile S.W. of Ford and nearly 900 ft. above O.D.; the present whereabouts of the pottery is unknown.[1] At SP 108285, in a bell barrow 900 ft. above O.D. and 400 yds. W. of (6), (see plan, p. 118), six Romano-British sherds were found in topsoil and top fill of the ditch, and two 4th-century coins (Constantius II and Valens) were found in crevices between stones at the top of the barrow.[2]

1. M. Westerling, *Country Contentments* (1939), 197–8. *TBGAS*, 79 (1961), Temple Guiting (3).
2. *TBGAS*, 79 (1961), Temple Guiting (8); 86 (1967), 16–41.

(1) BECKBURY CAMP (SP 064299), univallate hill-fort, unexcavated, encloses 5½ acres on the edge of the plateau above Hailes Wood.

The N. and W. sides are defined by the steep slope of the escarpment; on the S. and E. the bank is about 25 ft. wide and rises 5 ft. above the interior. The entrance was probably in the S.W., where there is a 40-ft. gap between the end of the bank and the edge of the escarpment. A low scarp continuing the line of the bank across the gap is probably a natural feature. Fire-reddened stones are exposed in the outside face of the bank near A–B and may also be seen in the field wall on the bank, E. of the entrance. Except for a short length at the N. end, the outer ditch has been levelled.

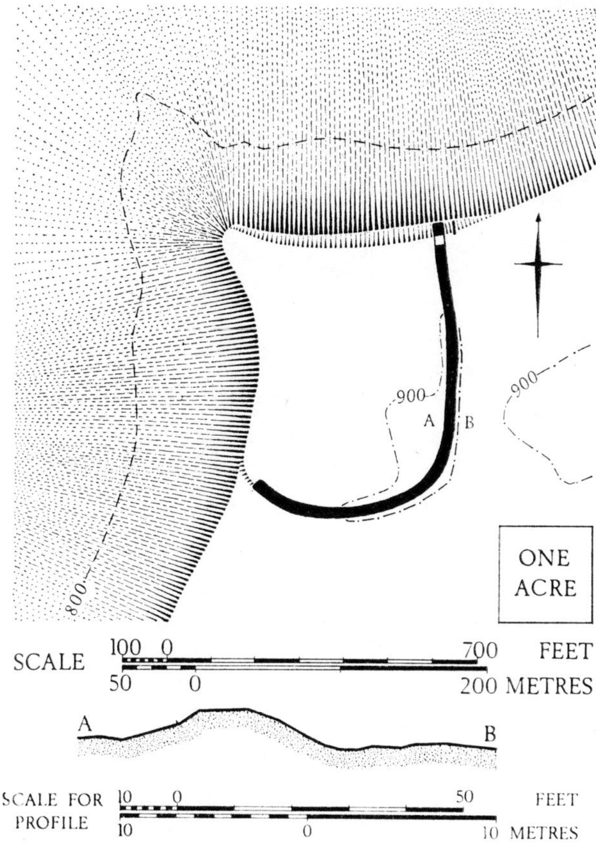

TEMPLE GUITING. (1) Beckbury Camp. Plan and profile.

A single Iron Age sherd with stamped decoration is a surface find (*PPS*, XXXIV (1968), 427, No. 19). Roman coins are said to have been found on the site.

W. St. Clair Baddeley, *A Cotteswold Shrine* . . . (1908), 7. *TBGAS*, LII (1930), 178, n. 44. Witts (1883), 4–5, No. 9.

(2) ROMANO-BRITISH SETTLEMENT (SP 13252830), at Rook Pool Piece, ploughed out, covers at least 3 acres, about 600 ft. above O.D., on gently rising ground immediately W. of the road from Bartonhill Farm to Hinchwick which here follows the shallow valley bottom. The settlement is 1¼ miles N. of (3), which lies close to the same road.

Occupation debris is of 2nd to 4th-century date; concentrations suggest at least twelve small buildings. The site probably extended into an area of plantation on the N., and possibly E. to the opposite slope, also rising gently from the road.

Finds, now in Gloucester City Museum, include three 4th-century coins (Constantius II and Gratian), abundant pottery with samian and Oxfordshire colour-coated vessels, a fragment of sandstone quern decorated with concentric incised lines, Stonesfield slate possibly from the area of (3), and a fragment of dressed limestone. Other dressed blocks have been reported.

TBGAS, 87 (1968), 203, No. 6.

(3) ROMANO-BRITISH CEMETERY and probable SETTLEMENT (SP 1226), on Kineton Hill, is known from accounts of finds made during quarrying. Burials, pottery and coins were reported; they are not closely located, but probably were near SP 128262. Fifteen recorded interments included inhumations in stone-lined graves, a wooden coffin, and cremations; the skull of one inhumation was at the feet, of another at the knees. Finds, in the Royce Collection in Bristol City Museum, include samian sherds, boot-nails, a bronze bracelet, an ornamented rectangular bronze stamp and a stone spindle-whorl.

A mediaeval building now recognised in the vicinity may be the structure thought in 1882 to be Roman.

TBGAS, VII (1882–3), 69–80; 83 (1964), 12–13; 77 (1958), 61–5 (mediaeval).

Note: The parallel alignments apparent in monuments (4), (5) and (6) suggest the possibility of an integral complex covering 80 acres or more. Intersections of ditched features indicate phases of development. The pit-alignment (4) is a type known elsewhere to be of the late Iron Age or of the early Romano-British period. No surface finds have been made, but two 4th-century coins came from the barrow W. of (6).

Markings of natural origin are widespread on air photographs of the area and obscure the nature of crop-marks ½ mile S. of (6), at Bembro (SP 107269). (N.M.R., OAP 1026/1/337–9; 1026/2/333–45.)

(4) PIT-ALIGNMENT (SP 10962798–SP 11052805), S.W. of Lots Barn (Plate 56 and plan on p. 118), extends for 130 yds. from S.W. to N.E. and is probably incomplete.

N.M.R., OAP SP 1127/9/325–30; 1128/4/322–3.

(5) ENCLOSURES AND DITCHES (SP 10962798–SP 114278), probably late Iron Age and Romano-British, show as crop-marks (Plate 57). Two clear ditched enclosures of irregular rectilinear form, each about 1 acre in area, have an entrance midway along the S.E. side (plan, p. 118). There are indications of an internal enclosure in the E. angle of the western of these enclosures, and there are very faint signs of a small rectangular enclosure attached to the N. side of pit-alignment (4).

N.M.R., OAP SP 1127/1, 3–6 (Baker); 1127/7/338–43. C.U.A.P., OAP AYF 65–8, AZN 24–8; VAP K17S 208–9. *Arch J*, LXXI (1964), 15, Nos. 35 and 36.

(6) ENCLOSURE AND DITCHES (SP 112285), probably late Iron Age and Romano-British, show as crop-marks extending S.E. from Charnal Plantation to beyond Lots Barn (plan, p. 118).

N.M.R., OAP SP 1128/1 (Baker). C.U.A.P., OAP AXT 55, 57, AYF 70–4.

(7) DITCH (SP 114287), undated, extends across a broad ridge, N. from Charnal Plantation for about ⅓ mile, as a narrow crop-mark in arable ground; it may have continued formerly to N. or S. (plan, p. 118).

N.M.R., OAP SP 1129/2/54–7.

TEMPLE GUITING. (4) Pit-alignment. (5)–(9) Enclosures, Ditches etc.

(8) Ditch (SP 11632900), undated, about 250 yds. E. of and roughly parallel with the N. part of (7), is visible on air photographs over a distance of some 450 yds. Near its N. end are faint traces of a small polygonal enclosure about 100 ft. across (plan, p. 118).

N.M.R., OAP SP 1129/1, 2 (Baker).

(9) Enclosure, Ditches and other Features (SP 121293), undated, N. of Keeper's Hill Wood and about ¼ mile N.E. of (8), comprise crop or soil-marks as follows: (a) *Ditch*, at least 300 ft. long, bowed out to the W. across a spur which falls gently S.E. (b) Traces of *rectangular platforms* on a gentle S.E. slope. (c) *Enclosure*, partly obliterated in the woodland, on a re-entrant valley floor. (d) Two almost parallel *banks*, possibly ditched, or ploughed-down lynchets, at least 130 yds. long, extending down the gentle slope to the valley floor. Plan, p. 118.

N.M.R., OAP SP 1229/4/50–3.

(10) Enclosure and Ditch (SP 05542684), undated, on Sudeley Hill, show as crop-marks on the flat ridge top, 150 yds. E. of the Salt Way. The enclosure has a narrow ditch with sides both straight and rounded enclosing at least an acre. Only one entrance is certain, near the S.E. angle; part of the W. side has been destroyed by quarries. N.N.W. of the enclosure a length of ditch extends for at least 80 yds., towards a point where O.S. records show that Roman coins were found in 1882. A gap near the N. end of the recorded stretch indicates that the ditch was probably part of an enclosure complex (cf. (6)).

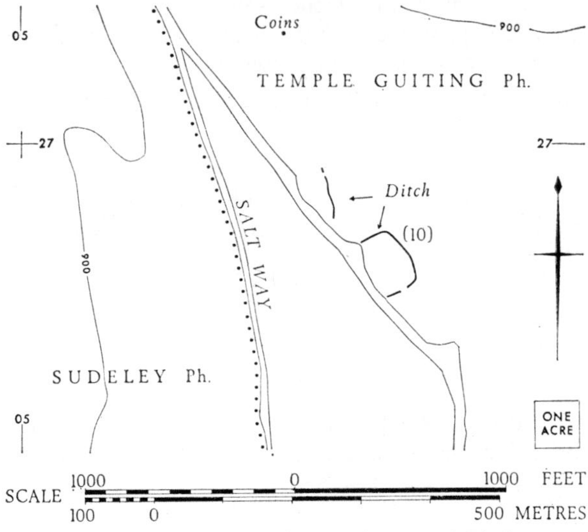

TEMPLE GUITING. (10) Enclosure and Ditch.

C.U.A.P., OAP ASM 25–6.

(11) Enclosure (SP 09172750), S. of St. Mary's Church, shows as a crop-mark (Plate 54) at the junction of Cotteswold Sand and Inferior Oolite, on ground which slopes gently E. to the R. Windrush, about 100 yds. away. The enclosure lies S. of the remains of deserted mediaeval or later settlement which lie between it and the church, and is differently aligned. It covers about ¾ acre and has a gap 30 ft. wide in the S.E. side.

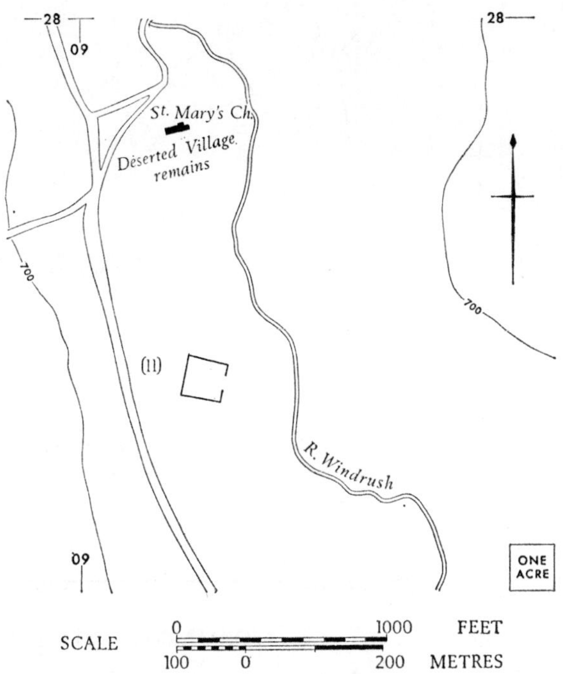

TEMPLE GUITING. (11) Enclosure.

C.U.A.P., OAP ABY 98.

TETBURY

(10 miles s.w. of Cirencester)

Two uninscribed gold coins are known from the parish; one is Allen type British B, the other is type British R A.[1] Roman coins have been found in and near the town.[2]

1. Both now lost; D. F. Allen in *IASB*, 176, 203.
2. Rudder (1779), 728. A coin of Diocletian is in Corinium Museum.

TETBURY UPTON

(9½ miles s.w. of Cirencester)

(1) Romano-British Villa? (ST 87829572), 600 yds. N.W. of Upton House, stands on level ground on the plain, about 530 ft. above O.D. There is no surface source of water in the vicinity. Walls, extensively disturbed by quarrying, occupy an area of at least 1 acre.

An exploratory excavation revealed at least three rooms and a probable hypocaust. Finds include numerous 3rd–4th-century coins. Three superimposed burials are reported, the middle one in a stone coffin, the other two in wooden coffins.

Archaeol. Review, 6 (1971), 28. Information kindly supplied by Captain H. S. Gracie, R.N.

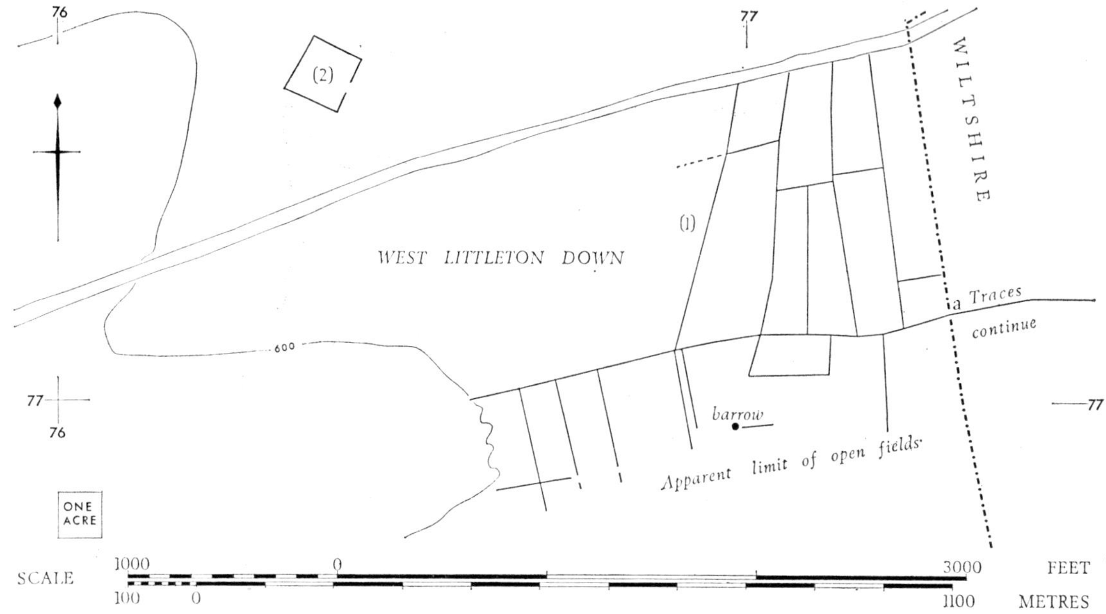

TORMARTON. (1) 'Celtic' Fields. (2) Rectangular Enclosure.

THRUPP

No Iron Age or Romano-British monument is known in this parish.

TODENHAM

No Iron Age or Romano-British monument is known in this parish.

TORMARTON

(10 miles s.w. of Cirencester)

Two Romano-British settlements and a burial in a stone coffin are reported on the line of road M4 in the S. of the parish.[1] Romano-British pottery of the 2nd–4th century has been noted on the surface and in a ditch cut by a pipe trench at ST 76467656, some 400 yds. S.W. of the surviving 'Celtic' fields (1).[2]

'Hebdown Camp' (ST 774766)[3] is a geological feature partly covered by strip lynchets.

1. *Archaeol. Review*, 4 (1969), 18.
2. Information from Mr. Charles Browne.
3. Witts (1883), 25, No. 50. *UBSS*, III (1926), 43.

(1) 'Celtic' Fields (ST 770771) on West Littleton Down, now destroyed, formerly covered at least 50 acres on the summit and gentle N.-facing slopes of a broad limestone ridge (Plate 43). Air photographs show an incomplete plan, with extensive ridge-and-furrow intermingled with and obscuring the 'Celtic' fields; these lie N. of the apparent edge of the open-field system of West Littleton. Very faint traces indicate that feature 'a', probably a major boundary line, continues into Wiltshire where, ½ mile further on, relatively well-preserved remains of 'Celtic' fields with broad banks suggesting substantial stone walls cover at least 200 acres. It is probable that the fields on West Littleton Down were also defined by stone walls.

R.A.F., VAP 106G/UK 1415: 4405–8; OAP Allen 1350 and 1351, 1 (Ashmolean Museum).

(2) Rectangular Enclosure (ST 76407745), covering 1¼ acres, undated, shows as a crop-mark 500 yds. N.E. of (1) (Plate 54); an entrance occurs half-way along the S.E. side. There is only a slight confirmatory scarp in arable ground, immediately above a moderate S.-facing slope.

R.A.F., VAP 106G/UK 1415: 4405–8. C.U.A.P., OAP AXT 23.

(3) Enclosure (ST 774798), S. of Brookman's Quarry, undated, covers about 1 acre of nearly level ground and

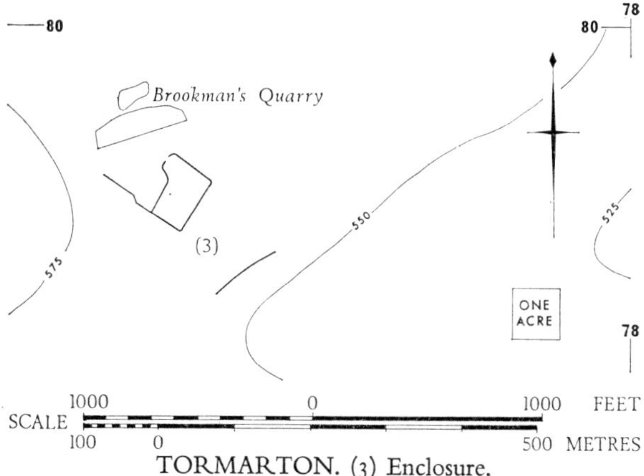

TORMARTON. (3) Enclosure.

has an entrance in the protuberant N.W. angle. A ditch extends N.W. from the W. angle and appears to return N.E. after 230 ft. A further line of ditch lies 300 yds. S.E. of the enclosure.

C.U.A.P., OAP AXT 26, 28–9.

TURKDEAN

No Iron Age or Romano-British monument is known in this parish.

ULEY

(15 miles W.S.W. of Cirencester)

An uninscribed Dobunnic gold stater (Allen's type British R A),[1] together with more than 150 Roman coins ranging from the 2nd to the 4th century,[2] and a bronze mask[3] were reported in the 19th century from

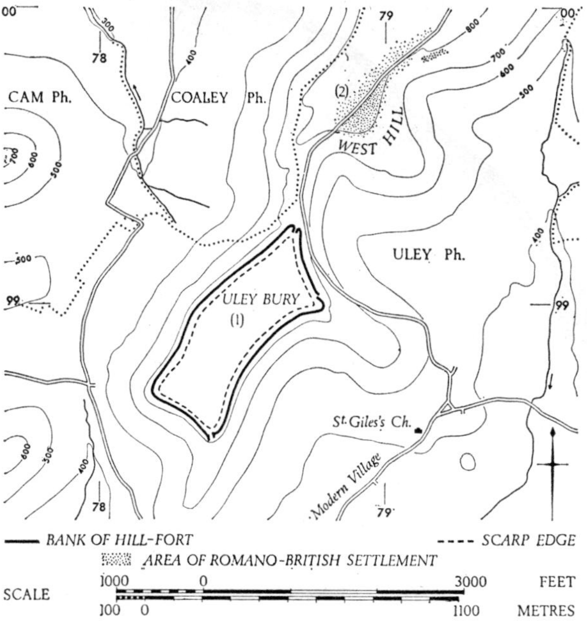

Monuments in ULEY.

the vicinity of monuments (1) and (2). Three coins, probably Constantinian, were noted with a secondary inhumation in the long barrow named Hetty Pegler's Tump (SO 78950004), 400 yds. N. of (2).[4]

1. In Gloucester City Museum. The Minute Book of the Gloucester Science and Art Society records (17 Sept. 1887) that it was found 'near Uley Bury'. D. F. Allen in *Bagendon*, 89, 120 and Pl. XXXIX, No. 19. *IASB*, 203.
2. *Arch J*, XI (1854), 325.
3. A. H. Church, *Corinium Museum* (1905), 16. The mask cannot now be identified in the collections.
4. *Antiquity*, XL (1966), 129. *TBGAS*, 79 (1961), Uley i.

(1) Uley Bury Hill-fort (ST 784989), univallate, unexcavated, is situated on a prominent spur of the Cotswold escarpment above the village (Plate 33). The bank encloses 38 acres, 6 acres of which are occupied by the terrace described below. Plan, p. 122.

The bank, up to 35 ft. wide and 4 ft. high, stands along the edges of a terrace, 30 ft. to 60 ft. wide overall, probably created by the digging out of material to make the bank. A scarp 3 ft. to 13 ft. high rises from the inner side of the terrace to the level interior, now arable. Externally, the scarp falls from the bank an average of 30 ft. to a greatly disturbed narrow ledge, apparently not a ditch, but probably associated with the defences. There are three entrances. Access from the N. is by way of a col, the inturned ends of the banks with a short hollow-way between them lying obliquely across it. Outside the N. entrance a series of banks and ditches across the col have been noted (*Arch*, XIX (1821), Pl. xi); most of them have gone and surviving features appear to be natural. At the E. corner overlapping bank-ends are associated with a hollow-way. At the damaged S. entrance another hollow-way is flanked on the W. by a down-slope extension of the bank and, at the edge of the terrace, by two partly artificial mounds. Roads shown on O.S. 1815 passed through the E. and S. entrances and traversed the eastern terrace.

Air photographs of crop-marks (N.M.R., OAP ST 7898/1/219–24) show ditched enclosures inside the hill-fort (Plate 32).

Recent finds, now in Gloucester City Museum, include small sherds of hand-made pottery and animal bones found beneath the eroded S. bank, also a saddle quern from the interior. 'Hand-mullers' were reported in 1876 (*PCNFC*, VI, 12). Finds now in Stroud Museum include an everted rim sherd of Iron Age type, found in the interior. A coin of Salonina is reported from the interior (*Glos. Notes & Queries*, I (1881), 320, n. cccxxvi), where also other 3rd-century coins are said to have been found (*TBGAS*, XXXV (1912), 151).

C.U.A.P., OAP AIO 11–15, AJL 16.
Lloyd Baker (1821), 167, No. 15. Playne (1876), 11, No. 28. Witts (1883), 50, No. 104. *Arch J*, CXXII (1965), 213.

(2) Romano-British Settlement (ST 790996), covering at least 7 acres on West Hill, lies about 500 yds. N.E. of (1) and immediately above the col which links Uley Bury with the main Cotswold escarpment.

A Dobunnic silver coin inscribed EISV has recently been found in the settlement area.

Occupation debris in arable fields on either side of the modern road includes worked limestone, sandstone tiles, tesserae, and animal bones. Over 60 coins found in 1966–70 extend from Trajan (issues of 101–2) to Theodosius. Numerous small finds include two almost identical and unusual intaglios, a bronze boss bearing a human face, a votive object, rings, a pin, a brooch

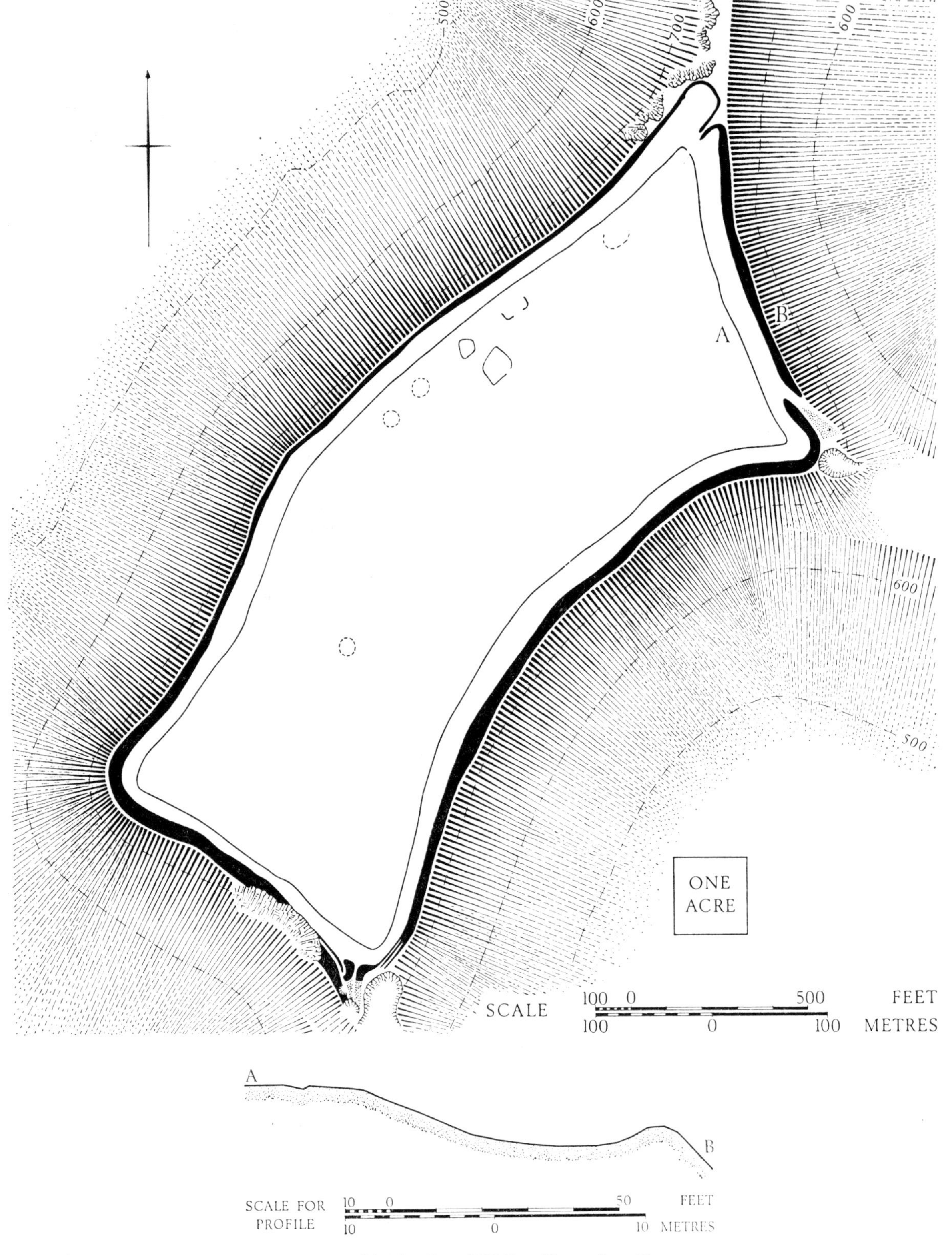

ULEY. (1) Uley Bury Hill-fort. Plan and profile.

and a bronze nail-cleaner. Pottery, including samian, ranges in date from the 1st to the 4th century, apart from one sherd of grass-tempered ware probably datable to the 5th century or later. Some of the recent finds are in private possession, others are in Stroud and Gloucester City Museums; one intaglio is in Stroud, the other in Gloucester.

Finds made *c.* 1873 and now lost are said to have included some 50 coins of the 3rd and 4th centuries, samian and coarse wares, mortaria, and animal and human bones.

Glos. Notes & Queries, I (1881), 319, n. cccxxvi. *TBGAS*, 87 (1968), 204, Nos. 13, 14.

UPPER SLAUGHTER

(16 miles N.E. of Cirencester)

Ryknild Street passed through the parish, but no remains have been found. Four Roman coins of 1st to 3rd-century date, now in the Royce Collection in Bristol City Museum, were found in the arable field W. of Granny's Bank, SP 162247;[1] as yet nothing else has been found in that place.

Numerous burials and a lead coffin have been noted W. of 'Beggy Hill Way', perhaps near SP 157228.[2]

Various finds have been made at imprecise points on Copse Hill. Iron Age pottery, a bone comb and bone 'points' from the area are in the Royce Collection.[3] Seven graves with associated Romano-British and possibly earlier pottery were found before 1875 during quarrying at about SP 164235. A contracted burial was found in a circular stone-cut pit S.W. of Copse Hill.[4]

1. *TBGAS*, 83 (1964), 12.
2. *Gent. Mag.* XVI (1864), 365. *TBGAS*, VII (1882/3), 79.
3. *TBGAS*, 83 (1964), 11.
4. *TBGAS*, VII (1822/3), 77–80.

(1) ROMANO-BRITISH BUILDING (SP 13262344), S.E. of New Buildings, is possibly that referred to as *caestello* in a Saxon charter (Sawyer, 1304). The site, identified by Mrs. H. E. O'Neil, has been ploughed out.

Grundy (1935–6), 172–5.

UPTON ST. LEONARDS

(11 miles W.N.W. of Cirencester)

For earthworks on High Brotheridge, see CRANHAM (1). Pottery, a bill-hook, a fibula of 2nd-century type and a human skull were discovered in 1921 in the garden of Castle End Bungalow, on the N. slope of Painswick Hill at SO 86511235 (see PAINSWICK (1)).[1]

A small quantity of abraded Romano-British pottery is recorded from St. Edmund's Hill at SO 85201405.[2]

1. W. St. Clair Baddeley, *A Cotteswold Manor* (1929), 20; pl. facing p. 45. Finds in Gloucester City Museum.
2. *TBGAS*, 90 (1971), 49–50.

(1) ROMANO-BRITISH SETTLEMENT (SO 86631588), ⅓ mile N. of Bondend, lies on a slight clay rise in the vale at about 170 ft. above O.D.

Features revealed during construction of road M5 include a T-shaped corn-drying oven partly built of reused limestone masonry, and small pits containing coarse pottery and animal bones. Finds, in Gloucester City Museum, range in date from the 2nd to the 4th centuries. Vegetable matter from the corn-drier included carbonised wheat (spelt and bread or club wheat) and 35 distinct weed species.

TBGAS, 90 (1971), 44–9.

WESTCOTE

(17 miles N.E. of Cirencester)

A fragmentary skeleton and a scatter of Romano-British pottery were recovered in 1937, while land was being levelled mechanically for the construction of Little Rissington airfield (SP 21781916).[1]

1. *TBGAS*, 59 (1937), 334.

WESTONBIRT WITH LASBOROUGH

(12 miles S.W. of Cirencester)

An inscribed gabled tombstone was found at Bowldown Farm (ST 839926) before 1779.[1] See BEVERSTONE for another inscribed tombstone from Nesley Farm, adjacent on the E. Roman coins are said to have been found at Bowldown,[2] and a Roman villa is believed to have existed at Lasborough (about ST 820940).[3]

1. Formerly at Kingscote House; now lost. *RIB*, I, No. 134.
2. *Arch*, XIX (1821), Pl. xii.
3. Lysons, *The Romans in Gloucestershire* (1860), 42.

WESTON SUBEDGE

(25 miles N.N.E. of Cirencester)

Roman finds including a bronze surgical instrument (*PSA*, 2nd ser., XXXII (1919–20), 94) have been recorded at 'The Lenches' (Lynches), probably some 300 yds. S.E. of monument (3).

(1) ROMAN BUILDING? (SP 123412), on Lower Lias, some 70 yds. E. of Ryknild Street, was noted in 1938 when flue-tiles, a whetstone, pottery including samian and a Kimmeridge shale ring were found. The site is now an orchard.

Malkin MS., site No. 17.

(2) ROMAN BUILDING? (SP 12554142), is indicated by pottery, coins and a stone roof-tile found where there is now an orchard. The site, on Lower Lias, occupies level ground adjacent to a stream.

Malkin MS., site No. 18.

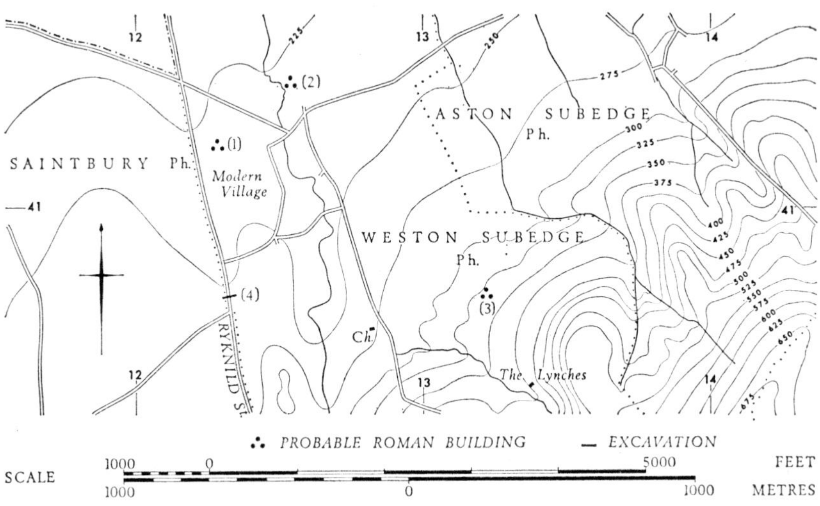

Monuments in WESTON SUBEDGE.

(3) ROMAN BUILDING? (SP 13294071), was identified in 1938 by building stone and pottery brought to the surface during ploughing. The site, on Lower Lias, occupies almost level ground in the lowest part of the main Cotswold escarpment, here generally falling N.W.

Malkin MS., site No. 19.

(4) ROMAN ROAD (SP 11684408–12403765), Ryknild Street, probably determines the entire W. boundary of the parish as well as marking the county boundary with Worcestershire for about $1\frac{3}{4}$ miles S. from Honeybourne Bridge.

A cross-section (SP 12334071) cut through the road in 1957, on gently rising ground, showed a cambered metalled structure of rounded pitched stones, $14\frac{1}{2}$ ft. wide, $1\frac{1}{2}$ ft. thick in the centre and 8 in. or 9 in. thick at the edges; in places the road was deeply rutted.

TBGAS, 76 (1957), 44–7. For the relationship between Buckle Street and Ryknild Street, see p. xlv.

WHITESHILL

No Iron Age or Romano-British monument is known in this parish.

WHITTINGTON

(12 miles N. of Cirencester)

The Romano-British major settlement at Wycomb (2), partly overlying an Iron Age occupation site, had paved streets and a temple, but no enclosing wall. The site of the Roman settlement was abandoned before the creation of the former parish boundary with Dowdeswell, which crossed it. The Roman villa (3), on the other hand, was succeeded by Saxon settlement in its immediate vicinity. A terrace-way just W. of the villa, is on a possible line of the White Way from Corinium; coffin burials to the S. in Sandywell Park[1] were close to this line.

Allegedly Roman metal objects were discovered *c.* 1865 during clearance of Whittington Wood, $1\frac{1}{4}$ miles

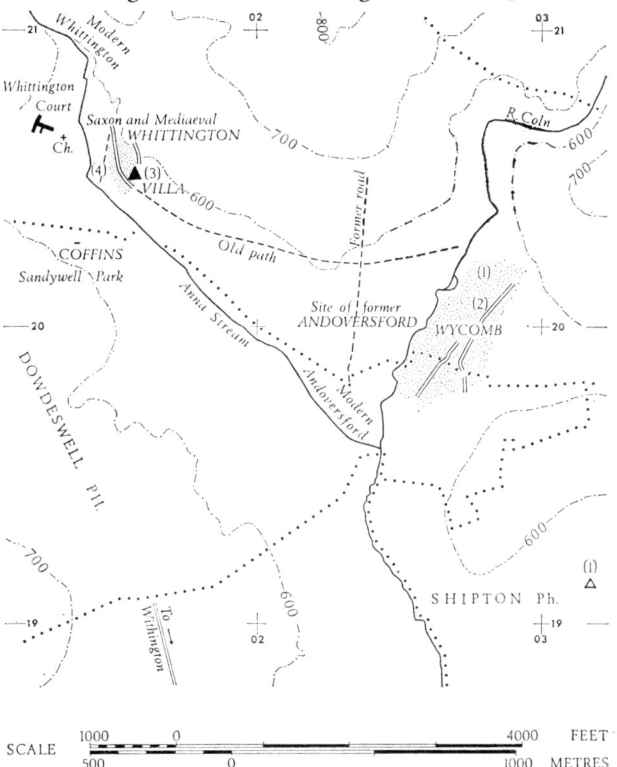

Monuments in WHITTINGTON.

N.W. of (3), probably near SO 997214. Traces of 'foundations and pavements' and two or three Constantinian coins were found 'at a little distance' from the wood.[2] Scattered Romano-British potsherds have been picked up on arable ground sloping gently E., just S. of Arle Grove (SO 994215), which appears to be a remnant of Whittington Wood.

The lower part of a Roman column, now at Whittington Court, but recovered from a cottage in the modern village, is of uncertain provenance, probably local (Plate 30).

1. Atkyns (1712), 401. Two coffins are noted on an Estate Map of 1839, one each side of a drain in Sandywell Park, and others may have been found during construction of the railway (*TBGAS*, 61 (1939), 168; 71 (1952), 13–18).

2. *PSA*, 2nd ser., III (1864–7), 129, 396.

(1) Iron Age Settlement (SP 027205), Syreford gravel pit and Wycomb; see (2).

(2) Romano-British Settlement (SP 028201), Wycomb, Syreford, covers about 28 acres of almost flat ground, just E. of the river Coln. At this point the Gravel is capped in places by a very thin layer of Clay. The settlement is known from extensive digging by W. L. Lawrence in 1863–4 prior to the construction of railway embankments across the site; also from more restricted excavation and observation of exposed structures in recent years, from air photographs (Plate 48) and from an abundance of surface debris when ploughed. The settlement extends into the modern parish of Andoversford as far as the railway embankment at S.W., and was thought by Lawrence to reach at least as far as the Andoversford Inn (SP 02391977). The accompanying plans show only part of the structures thought to exist. There are indications that the settlement was preceded by Iron Age, Bronze Age, Neolithic and Mesolithic occupation. Air photographs show traces of circular ditched enclosures adjacent to Lawrence's feature 5 and, possibly, also S. of the temple. Around the former area, now quite flat, there is a substantial scatter of worked flints, including microlithic cores and arrowheads both leaf-shaped and barbed-and-tanged. The Iron Age settlement is marked by finds at both N. and S., and other Iron Age finds under the heart of the Roman settlement may perhaps be inferred from early accounts. First-century Roman coins are known from S. and N. parts of the settlement, though most of the coins are of the 4th century. Samian pottery has been found in most parts.

Occupation debris of the pre-Roman Iron Age, including Iron Age 'A' pottery, burnished black ware with thin incised decoration and calcite-gritted pottery, has been found in recent disturbance within the area of Old Syreford gravel pit, in the N.W. corner of Wycomb field. Some of the debris came from a shallow pit immediately beside the surviving limits of Roman surface relics. Similar finds were made in the vicinity in 1934 and 1937 (*TBGAS*, 71 (1952), 16). At this point most of the surface levels have been totally removed. During the excavations of 1864 'rude British' pottery was noted beneath buildings 6 to 11 (Lawrence's plan). In 1936 Iron Age pottery was found near Roman coins and pottery (*PCNFC*, XXVI (1936), 105). 'British Roman' (unidentified British?) coins came from the original excavation, but they cannot now be traced. Three Dobunnic coins, one of them inscribed EISU, and two iron brooches of the Iron Age have recently been found by Mr. W. Cox in an excavation immediately S.W. of Black Close; another brooch of similar type has been found in the temple area. We are grateful to Mr. Cox for this and for much other information, some of it embodied in the accompanying plan.

The span of Roman coins is from Vespasian to Arcadius, the later coins predominating. A late Roman buckle has recently been found. The field-name Wycomb, formerly Wickham, may indicate that the site was recognised by Saxon immigrants as a Roman settlement, the *wic* possibly denoting a *vicus* (*Med. Archaeol.* XI (1967), 95–7; *PNG*, I, 185). There is no evidence of Saxon or later occupation.

The straight paved road running through the site from N.E. (its end corresponds with the limit of surface debris) to a point of apparent bifurcation was found by Lawrence to be 8 ft. to 10 ft. wide, and to embody large stones set vertically and smaller stones laid flat; it had been noted by him as a crop-mark in 1863. The plan published in 1864 after excavation is not sufficiently accurate in all its details to admit conflation with data from air photographs and recent ground observations, but in the accompanying illustration the full recoverable street system is shown on an adjoining diagram, together with the probable position of some of the early excavated features, and of others more recently noted. The transverse roads suggest buildings over a length of at least 600 yds., and accounts written in 1864 insist that foundations were discovered over all parts of the field, though no particulars were recorded. Black earth is still widespread. Recent excavation between Black Close and the railway embankment at S.W. has revealed a ditch with a rounded bottom, some 20 ft. across and over 4 ft. deep, roughly in line with the main axial road seen on air photographs. The ditch had been entirely filled with rubbish of late 4th-century date, including much burnt matter, and substantial quantities of large building stones had been thrown in from the S. side. Also in this area were at least three ovens and numerous other pits and ditches. Six unaccompanied skeletons lay sprawled on the Roman surface, immediately by the stream. A Romano-British urn with a cremation was recently found on the edge of the gravel pit in the N. of the settlement (*TBGAS*, 87 (1968), 202).

The road proceeding S.W. out of the settlement is aligned with the old parish boundary between Dowdeswell and Withington, suggesting that a roadway once extended S.W. to an intersection with the possible line of the White Way at about SP 017191 (see discussion on Roman roads, p. xlv), but there is no other indication of any road continuing beyond the bounds of the settlement, and recent excavation near the new by-pass at S.W. has disclosed no paved road on that line.

Recorded widths of foundations excavated in the 19th century varied generally between 1½ ft. and 2½ ft., but the wall at 9 on Lawrence's plan was about 3¼ ft. thick, with stone courses 10 in. high. All footings were of Oolite and there was little trace of tile. (Recently a limestone block with two pairs of shallow parallel grooves has been found near the temple.) Floors were 'mostly of stone, laid in cement and gravel concrete'. It is not clear if wall 5, 75 ft. long and thought to be part of a theatre, is an isolated fragment; it was said to be of 'strong rough masonry' although its recorded thickness was only 2⅓ ft. Buildings 6–9 and 11 were regarded as elements in a single arrangement, with a mass of pitched pavement between the component structures, the whole being built over a two-foot layer of black earth containing some pottery 'probably British'. The N. wall of 6 was described as 'heavy'. No. 13 was part of 'a large residential building destroyed by fire'; apsidal pitched stone foundations projected on its E. side; 'hypocausts', 'striated' tiles and tesserae were found in the area. Between 13 and 15 was a mass of foundations, including 18, and 'pavements, forges and fireplaces'. No. 15, measuring 41 ft. square internally and best regarded as a Romano-Celtic temple, was built over the remains of a smaller two-cell structure, No. 16; it apparently had a raised *cella*. Part of a pediment was reported and broken columns lay near. No. 29 was a stone-lined pit containing a 'rude fibula' and pottery with a cremation. Nos. 24, 26 and 28 were probably parts of a paved 'street'. Spread gravel has recently been found on some of the presumed spur tracks off the main street lines. 'Large' foundations at No. 30 were crossed by the old parish boundary, now removed, and continued into Black Close. Traces of building have since been found some 150 yds. S.W. of the parish boundary, but further S.W. on the line of the modern by-pass, neither buildings nor paved street were found.

Finds include the following—Votive Objects: two stone panels, each originally with three figures, the better-preserved showing a *genius cucullatus* and two hoodless deities; two small stone idols carved overall, one with a large figure (probably a local god) and two small figures on the main face, the other with a ?goddess outlined on one side; a bronze statuette of Mars, 3 in. high (a note by J. M. C. Toynbee on the hitherto unpublished figures will appear shortly in *TBGAS*); a bronze model axe, now lost. Coins: over half of some 1,100 coins found during the 1863–4 investigations came from the area of the temple; the earliest was a silver coin of Domitian, but most were 'late'; recently a coin of Vespasian was found in the extreme S.W., and one of Domitian was found just N. of the railway embankment which crosses the site; many other coins have been noted from time to time since 1799, including more than a hundred in the S.W., on and near the line of the new by-pass. Pottery: in abundance, including plain and figured samian ware, Oxfordshire red colour-coated ware, and mortaria. Brooches: several, including three of pre-Conquest type made of iron (one found near the temple), and one of Hod Hill type from the by-pass area. Iron Tools: including spoon-bit, cold chisel, mason's trowel, knives and pruning hook. Other small finds include a late Roman buckle (Hawkes, type I (b)); locks, keys and latch-lifters; small pieces of fine glass; styli; dividers; toilet articles; a bone chape. Querns: several, of Andernach grit. Animal bones: large numbers, including *Bos longifrons*.

Most of the stone objects and the statuette of Mars, as well as finds made in recent excavations, are in private possession. Some are in Stroud Museum. Apart from these the bulk of surviving finds is in Cheltenham Museum.

C.U.A.P., OAP ASB 13 15–17; ASM 31–6.

Gent. Mag. N.S., XV, pt. 2 (1863), 627; XVI, pt. 1 (1864), 86–8; XVII, pt. 2 (1864), 85–7 (with plan), 432–3. *PSA*, 2nd ser. II (1863–4), 302–7, 422–6. *Arch J*, XXI (1864), 96–7. Witts (1883), 70. *PCNFC*, XXVI (1936), 105; XXX (1949), 154. *TBGAS*, 78 (1959), 161–2. Toynbee (1964), 181. Lewis (1966), 3, 51. *Trans. Birmingham & War. Arch. Soc.*, 85 (1972), 147 (buckle).

The original excavation plan, scale 66 ft. = 1 inch, is in the Library of the Society of Antiquaries of London (Red Portfolio, Glos.).

(3) ROMAN VILLA (SP 01572051), in 'Cow Pasture', lies 300 yds. E.S.E. of Whittington Court at the S. end of the observable remains of the deserted Saxon and mediaeval settlement of Whittington, near the N. edge of the Vale of Andoversford (map, p. 124). The nearly level site, on Clay over the Upper Lias at 590 ft. above O.D., falls gently S. to the Anna Stream, about 100 yds. distant. It is near a natural springline. Excavation by Mrs. H. E. O'Neil (1948–51) exposed three structural periods from the 2nd to the early 5th century (plan, p. 128).

The first period, within the 2nd century, was represented by a small bath block, with *apodyterium*, *tepidarium*, *caldarium* and cold plunge, assumed to belong to another building which was undiscovered; walls possibly of Roman date were detected just S.W. of the villa under a mediaeval cottage (x on the plan on p. 127). Earthworks S.W. of the villa have an alignment which accords better with the villa as a whole than with the later settlement; the bank between x and y, where there probably was a structure, exemplifies this. In the second period, probably the second quarter of the 4th century, a small winged corridor house with an unusual apsidal room (1 on the plan), integrated with the old bath building, was constructed. In the third period, shortly after the second, the bath block was abandoned as such and was incorporated into enlarged rooms; at the same time the house was extended by the construction of a large hall (10); this was connected with the enlarged kitchen (8) by long corridors (I–III) around and outside the house. All the corridors and all the rooms except Nos. 7 and 8 had tessellated pavements, the surviving patterns being mainly geometric, with some foliate detail. Rooms 7 and 8 had gravel mortar floors. Two living-rooms (1 and 4) were heated. No bath block was found for the final period. Courtyards of rammed earth lay S.E. and N. of the house, with doorways giving access from corridor II.

The villa fell into decay in the 5th century, and a hearth in room 7 probably belongs to that period. Only two rooms, Nos. 3 and 10, suffered from fire and the collapse of timbers. Charred wheat on the floor of room 3 indicates that agriculture was being carried on in the last phase, after the abandonment of the villa as a fine house. There had been very extensive robbing of small objects and of building stone. Pottery and seven metal objects of the mid to late Saxon period were found. In the 13th century or thereabouts the W. wall of an enclosure, now represented by earthworks at 'a' on the site plan, was built across the remains, and shallow cultivation took place over the site. The E. wall of the enclosure formed one side of a track, 23 ft. wide, which bounded the villa site on the east. The street of the mediaeval village crossed the W. side of the villa.

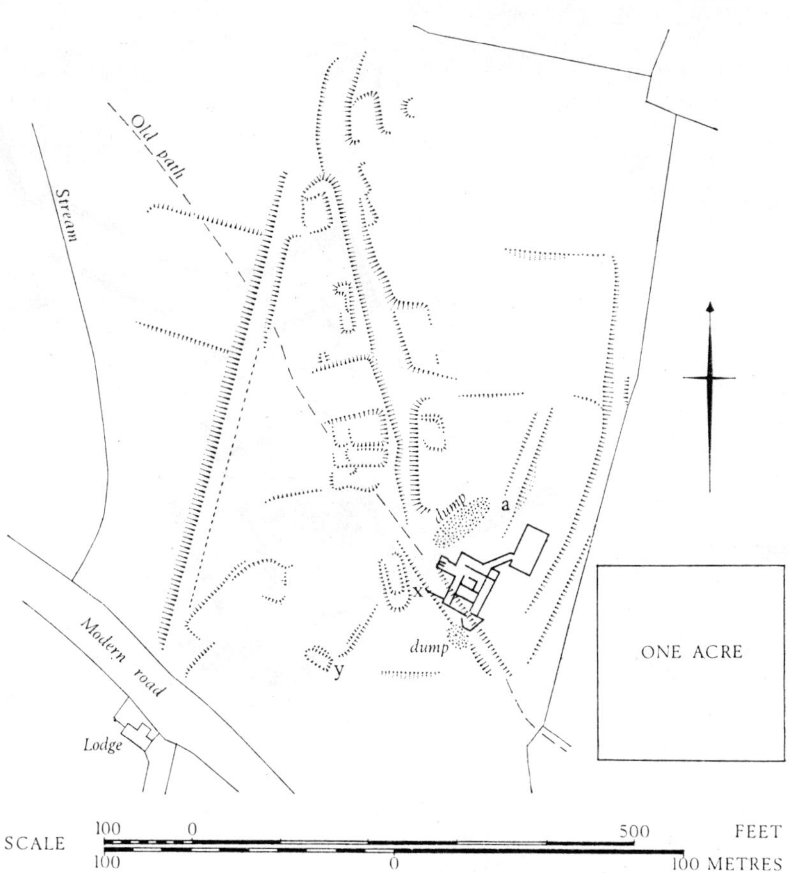

WHITTINGTON. (3) Roman Villa, 'Cow Pasture', and adjacent earthworks.

The villa walls, 1¾ ft. to 3 ft. thick, were of local Oolite in well-laid courses. In the first and second periods many of the footings were of pitched stones. Some Old Red Sandstone slabs were used as flue covers. Roofing was of local slate and Old Red Sandstone. Baked clay occurred only in tesserae, in certain pilae, in tiles of the plunge-bath floor and, copiously, as crushed brick in the mortar bedding for the tessellated floors. The first period was characterised by small axe-dressed blocks of white freestone on footings of larger undressed white freestone blocks; the two later periods had walls of larger, roughly dressed yellow Oolite.

Displaced sculptured fragments included the base of a small stone column, a broken impost with a rosette carved on one face (Plate 30), a block (1 ft. 6 in. by 1 ft. 4 in.) with a flat dressed face and with the opposite side cushion-shaped, and stone blocks (found E. of the house), probably voussoirs. An unprovenanced column base shown on Plate 30 possibly comes from this villa. In the third period a stone drain skirted the S.W. side of the house, passing the kitchen (room 8) which, in its final phase, was 33 ft. long by at least 22 ft. wide, possibly with a lean-to roof. In the second period the kitchen had had an oven 2 ft. across, but this was covered by the gravel mortar floor of the final phase.

The eight mosaics (Plate 9), all of 4th-century date, include in corridor II one of the most ambitious corridor pavements yet found in Britain (Toynbee (1964), 234). The mosaics of room 10 and of corridors II and III were made in the third period and are very similar in constructional detail and form of pattern. Tesserae are of white, grey and blue-grey local limestone, of Old Red Sandstone, and of red tile—some of the latter made from box-flue tiles. The cubes vary in size from ¾ in. to 2⅛ in., the average being 1¼ in. Room 3 was unusual in having both border and pattern made with large tesserae.

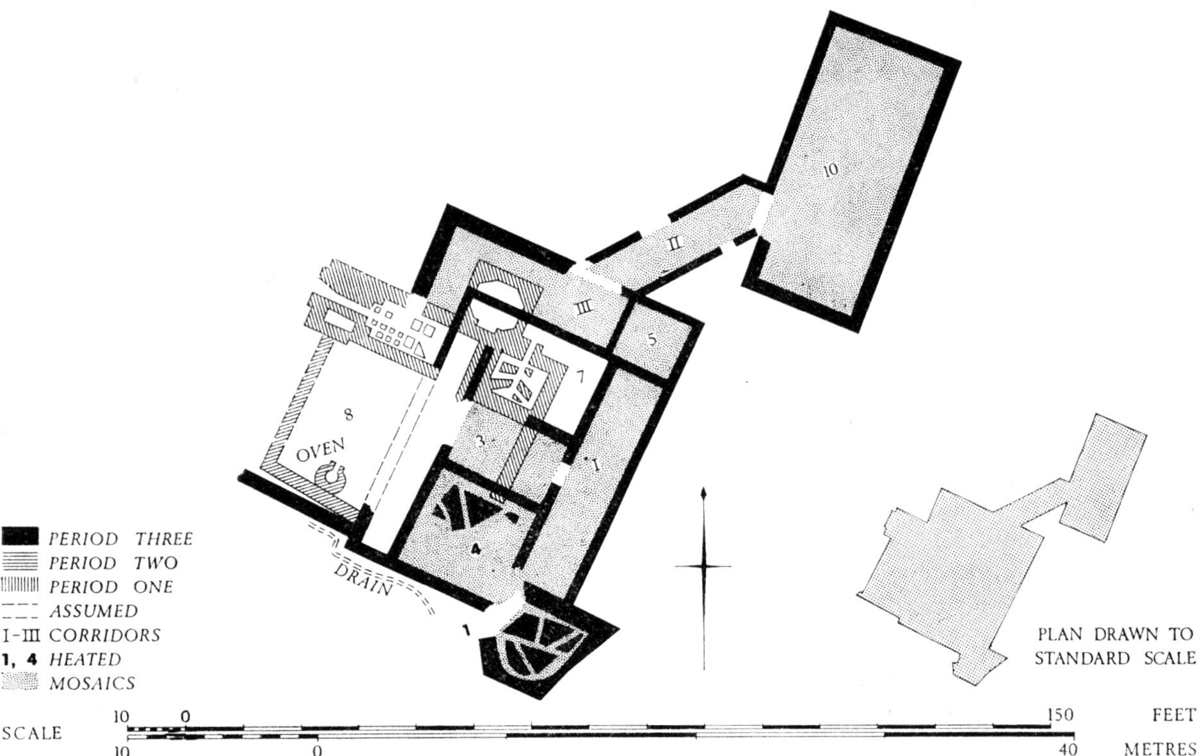

WHITTINGTON. (3) Roman Villa, 'Cow Pasture'.

Large quantities of wall plaster came from corridors II and III; dark crimson and pale blue were noted.

Dating evidence was meagre, but it was greatly helped by the distinctive building detail used in the different phases. Potsherds indirectly date the first period, and a coin of Constantine I embedded in the mortar underlying corridor III gives a secure date before which the third-period works cannot have started. Most of the 114 coins were later than 330, the range extending through the 4th century; 17 coins were Theodosian. Small finds included a turned Kimmeridge shale pot-lid, spindle whorls and coal.

TBGAS, 71 (1953), 13–87.

WILLERSEY

(24 miles N.N.E. of Cirencester)

For relationship between Buckle Street and Ryknild Street, see p. xlv.

(1) Hill-fort (SP 117379), Willersey Hill, probably bivallate, unexcavated and partly destroyed, lies on the summit and N. scarp of the hill, 1¼ miles S.E. of the village. A modern farm obliterates the relationship between banks on E. and S.W. There is no indication of banks defining a N. side.

The two close-set banks with a ditch between them are about 85 ft. wide overall. The inner bank, set along

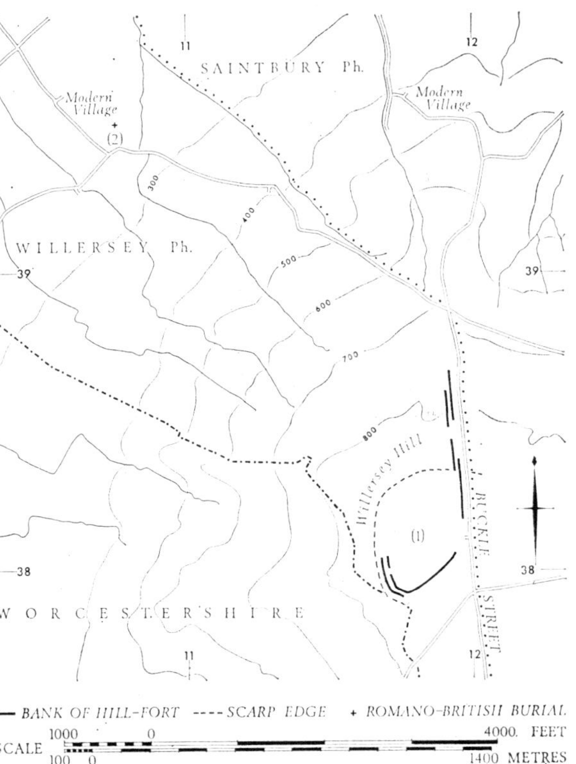

Monuments in WILLERSEY.

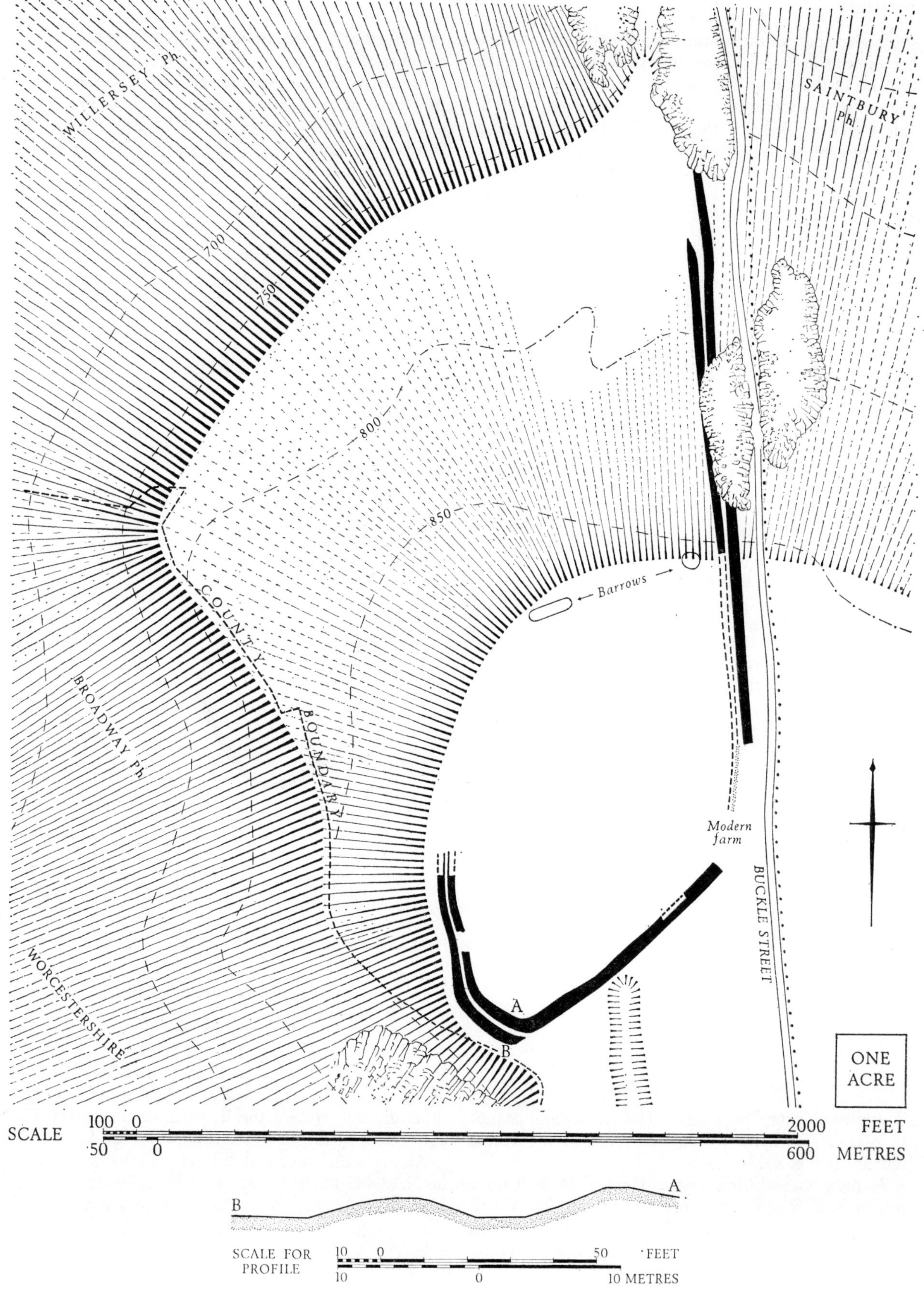

WILLERSEY. (1) Hill-fort, Willersey Hill. Plan and profile.

the highest part of the summit at S.W., rises 2 ft. above the interior and 8½ ft. above the present surface at the bottom of the ditch. The outer bank stands 4 ft. above the exterior; there is no sign of an outer ditch. The S. side is defined only by the inner bank, here standing 6 ft. high and skirting the head of a narrow combe. The double banks on the E. side drop northwards from the summit, down a slope of about 5°, steepening beyond the scarp edge to about 17°.

Isaac Taylor's map (1777) displays a complete sub-rectangular enclosure, some 40 acres in area. Bryant's map (1824) delineates the E., N. and N.W. sides of the enclosure, but it omits the extant S.W. and S. banks. Witts (1883) found no defences on the N. The area, formerly farm land and extensively disturbed by quarries, has undergone further alteration in the construction of a golf-course.

Rudder (1779), 823. Playne (1876), 207, No. 2. Witts (1883), 52, No. 107.

(2) Burials and Coin-hoard (SP 10743950), Romano-British, at Hill Farm, were found during construction work in 1968. Near a stone-lined grave containing two skeletons were 56 silver coins of the 4th century and a silver ring. The ring and two coins are in B.M.; the other coins are in Cheltenham Museum.

TBGAS, 90 (1971), 120–3.

(3) Probable Settlement (SP 09584165), Romano-British, near Willersey Barn, lies on a low ridge in the vale, less than 200 ft. above O.D.

A Dobunnic silver coin inscribed BODVOC, Roman coins, a fibula and pottery are recorded as having been found in an arable field. The Dobunnic coin is in a private collection; the Roman finds are in Worcester Museum.

D. F. Allen, in *Bagendon*, 121. Malkin MS., site No. 10.

(4) Romano-British Settlement (SP 09914023), Badsey Lane, lies on a slight ridge in the vale, about 200 ft. above O.D. Abundant pottery, fragments of flue and roof tiles and other building debris are recorded from ploughsoil.

Malkin MS., site No. 40.

WINCHCOMBE

(16 miles N. of Cirencester)

The alleged 'camp' on Langley Hill (SP 008290) cannot be accepted as a hill-fort on the basis of the visible remains (see p. xxxiv).

A monumental stone with a relief of a Roman soldier was found somewhere in Stancombe Wood (SP 039285).[1] A concentration of Romano-British pottery has been noted in a gas-pipe trench at SP 035279, with a further scatter extending N.N.E. past Stancombe Wood to SP 045305.[2]

Roman material of the 4th century has been found embodied in a Saxon rampart N. of the town (SP 024284),[3] and fragments of black urns 'of ancient British date' were reported from a nearby location N. of the church.[4]

1. *Annals of Winchcombe and Sudeley* (1877), p. 15 and plate opposite.
2. *Archaeol. Review*, 4 (1969), 42.
3. *MPBW Excavations, 1962*, 8; *1963*, 12.
4. *JBAA*, XXXII (1876), 454.

WINDRUSH

(12½ miles N.E. of Cirencester)

(1) Windrush Camp (SP 181123), univallate hill-fort, unexcavated, encloses just over 3 acres. Some ¾ mile S.W. of the village (map p. 100, *s.v.* Sherborne), it is sited on ground which slopes gently down from the summit of a very slight and narrow N.–S. ridge, close to it on the E.

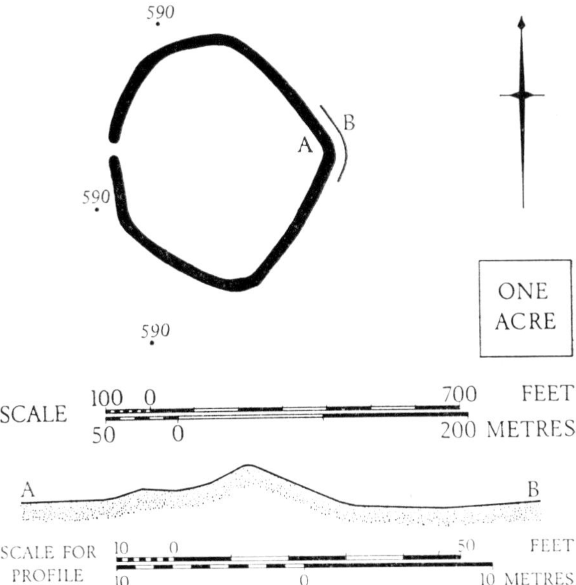

The bank, 25 ft. wide, rises 5½ ft. above the interior and 7½ ft. above the external ditch, generally levelled. The ditch, about 23 ft. wide, can be traced for only a short distance around the E. angle of the work. The entrance, a 25-ft. gap in the bank, is on the W.

Amorphous, broad and disjointed banks and mounds lie N. and E. of the Camp, in arable ground.

Bryant's Map of Gloucestershire (1824). Playne (1876), 210, No. 18. Witts (1883), 53, No. 108. *Bagendon*, 25, n. 4. *VCH, Glos.* VI (1965), 178.

WINSON

(5 miles N.E. of Cirencester)

(1) ROMANO-BRITISH SETTLEMENT (SP 076069), consisting of linked rectangular enclosures, is visible as soil-marks over at least 2 acres S.W. of Montreal House, on almost flat arable land (map, opp. p. 11). The W. part, crossed by the present field boundary at SP 07520687, stands as a platform about $1\frac{1}{4}$ ft. high and 90 ft. long. To the N., possibly bounding the settlement, a bank or wall 350 ft. long returns S. at the E. end. Romano-British pottery, including samian, with quern fragments and limestone debris are scattered in the ploughsoil.

C.U.A.P., OAP AMZ 49.

(2) PROBABLE ROMANO-BRITISH SETTLEMENT (SP 078074), $\frac{1}{4}$ mile N.N.E. of (1), is marked by a scatter of debris, including mid 4th-century pottery.

Information from Mr. P. E. Gascoigne.

WINSTONE

No Iron Age or Romano-British monument is known in this parish.

WITHINGTON

(8 miles N. of Cirencester)

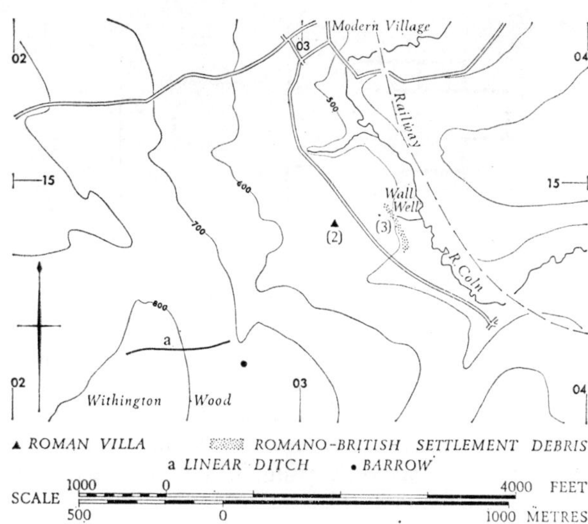

Monuments in WITHINGTON.

Excavation of the Neolithic long barrow on Sales Lot (SP 048158) yielded an Iron Age 'A' sherd from the outer edge of the barrow and two Romano-British tile fragments in the rubble of the barrow mound. A tile stamped VLA[1] is comparable with the broken VL stamp on a flue-tile from Compton Grove Villa, COMPTON ABDALE (1). Foxcote Tumulus (SP 011172), a large round barrow excavated in 1863, is said to have yielded more than 200 4th-century Roman coins; accounts differ as to whether they were contained in a jar. There were also Romano-British potsherds, a piece of iron and a skeleton, possibly in association.[2] Romano-British pottery has been found at SP 05021429 and 05321432 (see CHEDWORTH, p. 24).

The straight stretch of modern road which extends N. from Withington village may mark the line of a branch of the Roman 'White Way' (p. xlv).

A ditch (SP 02401440–02751447) in Withington Wood ('a' on the accompanying plan),[3] seen through dense vegetation, is of modest size and differs little from other ditches in the same wood which offer no evidence of ancient origin and are not mapped; in situation, however, it recalls the linear ditch at SOUTHAM (6).

1. *TBGAS*, 85 (1966), 11 and 28–9.
2. *PCNFC*, III (1865), 198–9; VI (1877), 335–6.
3. Cf. H. P. R. Finberg, *Lucerna* (1964), 28.

(1) IRON AGE SETTLEMENT (SP 01381803), cut by possibly late Romano-British pits, near Foxcote Manor, was noted in 1935 in the face of a small quarry, cutting into the Inferior Oolite. The site lies at 600 ft. above O.D. on the lower slopes of a wide valley, close to the Foxcote Brook. Three irregular pits contained Iron Age pottery including stamped ware; two of the pits also contained bone combs, perhaps late Romano-British rather than Saxon as originally reported, and human skeletons.

TBGAS, 58 (1936), 157–70.

(2) ROMAN VILLA (SO 03121487), N. of Withington Wood, was discovered by chance under part of the arable common field and was excavated by S. Lysons in 1811 (Plate 51).* The site, on the E. shoulder of a rounded spur above ground falling gently E. to a dry re-entrant valley, is now marked, when ploughed, by a thick scatter of building debris including tesserae and sandstone tiles.

Lysons emphasises that the incomplete structure which he planned was all that remained in the area, total destruction having occurred in the shallower soil to the east. The pavement of room A was several inches higher than that of room B, and those of D and B were similarly higher than room C.

* In 1811 the villa site is said to have been called 'the old town'; an alternative name was 'Withington upon Wall-Well'. Monument (3), not mentioned by Lysons, is close to Wall-Well and may account for the name. On the other hand, the debris at (3) could result from clearance and dumping from another part of the common field, perhaps nearer (2).

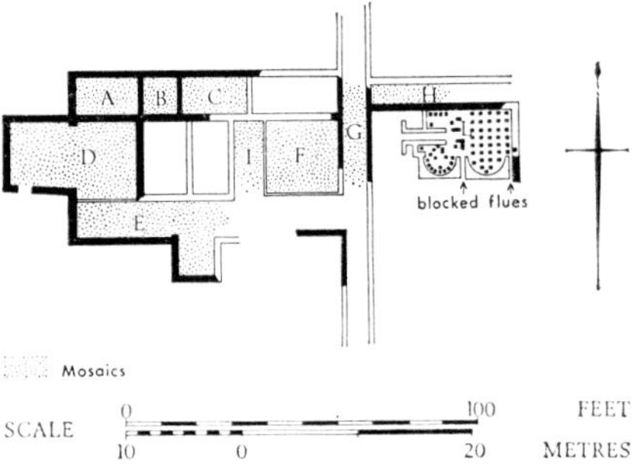

The plan suggests considerable structural alteration, including the blocking of the S. flues into the hypocaust (L) and the asymmetrical rebuilding of a wall in room D, to S.W. of an inserted asymmetrical mosaic panel. There was much evidence of burning, including melted lead.

The inserted mosaic (Plate 15), the only one to survive entire, depicts Oceanus with sea-creatures and is in Durotrigian style. The Orpheus pavement in the S. half of the same room (D), earlier in date and probably of the late 3rd century, together with the geometric panels (Plates 13, 14, 16), are of the Corinian School. Room I was paved with coarse white stone tesserae. The pieces of pavement recovered from room D are in the British Museum. Some tesserae are in Gloucester City Museum.

A hoard of over 1,200 late 3rd-century and 4th-century coins, from Valerian to Diocletian, was found in the area of the villa. The only other finds noted were a knife, a small 'lead' vessel, and unspecified pottery.

Arch, XVIII (1817), 118–21. Lysons (1817), II (1), Pls. xviii–xxi and head-piece to list of plates; III, 8–9. T. Morgan, *Romano-British Mosaic Pavements* (1886), 78–9. D. J. Smith, in Rivet (1969), *passim* (mosaics).

(3) PROBABLE SETTLEMENT (SP 03291493–03371478), Romano-British, Wall-Well, about 260 yds. E. of (1), extends along the edge of a modern arable field for some 200 yds., adjacent to a spring. The debris includes hypocaust and other tiles, and pottery.

WOODCHESTER

(11 miles W. of Cirencester)

A silver spoon in the Ashmolean Museum was recovered from West Park (SO 8101) in 1850.[1] A coin of Germanicus and Romano-British pottery found in 1863 in the long barrow on Bown Hill, at SO 82300180, was taken to Cheltenham College Museum.[2] The alleged site[3] of the 'Roman brickyard' serving the villa (1), about ¾ mile distant from it, is perhaps to be equated with the supposed kiln at Little Britain, noted on p. 81, *s.v.* MINCHINHAMPTON.

1. *JBAA*, VI (1851), 45.
2. *TBGAS*, 79 (1960), 95.
3. *TBGAS*, 61 (1939), 66 (note).

(1) ROMAN VILLA (SO 83970311), under and adjacent to a former church, now in ruins (map, p. 81, *s.v.* MINCHINHAMPTON), was excavated by Samuel Lysons in 1793–6 (Plate 31); it has been almost entirely reburied. A century before Lysons the graveyard was 'famous for its *tesseraick* work' (Gibson, *Camden's Britannia* (1695), col. 247). Evidence of sequence of construction is limited, but exploratory excavations conducted for the Department of the Environment by Mr. Giles Clarke in 1973 exposed successive room levels in the W. range of court A. The double W. wall of room 10 also probably represents succession. The villa had attained magnificence early in the 4th century, but considerable recent finds of samian pottery in the area of the outer court support previous indications of 2nd-century antecedents. Repairs indicate a period of decadence. A late Roman buckle has been found.

A sinking about 50 ft. square in the churchyard marks the site of room 1, with the most important of the known mosaic floors; it is uncovered from time to time for display to the public. Traces of platforms in the rough pasture field S. of the churchyard, known as The Parks, indicate the position of former structures around court B. Buildings have recently been found on the E. of the outer court. To S.E. of the rough scarp which marks the N. edge of the outer court, water, now uncontrolled, flowing from the pond (p in Plate 31), produces marshy conditions adjacent to the newly discovered walls.

Earthwork banks marking the Roman walls were noted by Lysons before he began his excavations. The site, limited to part of a natural shelf in the Great Oolite, is bounded on the E. by the river valley and on N. and S. by re-entrant gulleys; on the W. the rather broken ground of a former orchard rises gently to the foot of a steep N.–S. ridge. Springs just above the villa site feed the pond (p). Levels in the churchyard and in The Parks have been considerably altered and in places (*e.g.* in the range E. of court B) Lysons noted that floors had been entirely removed and that only the foundations of the walls were left.

The villa extended over at least 2 acres. Lysons excavated some 64 rooms in three courts, but he showed that the structure continued northwards, and also probably westwards. Substantial walls and part of a mosaic lay under the chancel of the old church, demolished in 1862, and a mosaic floor was reported to Lysons some 50 ft. N.W. of room 1, at the point marked 'a' on Plate 31; but it was not seen by him. A cement floor extended S.W. from the double wall flanking room 10. Court A was partly cemented and the rooms around it, mostly heated, had a remarkable series of mosaics (Plates 17–23); some of these are known only from fragments or loose tesserae. Room 22 has limestone pillars under its floor. Room 1, whose 'Orpheus and the Beasts' mosaic with an estimated

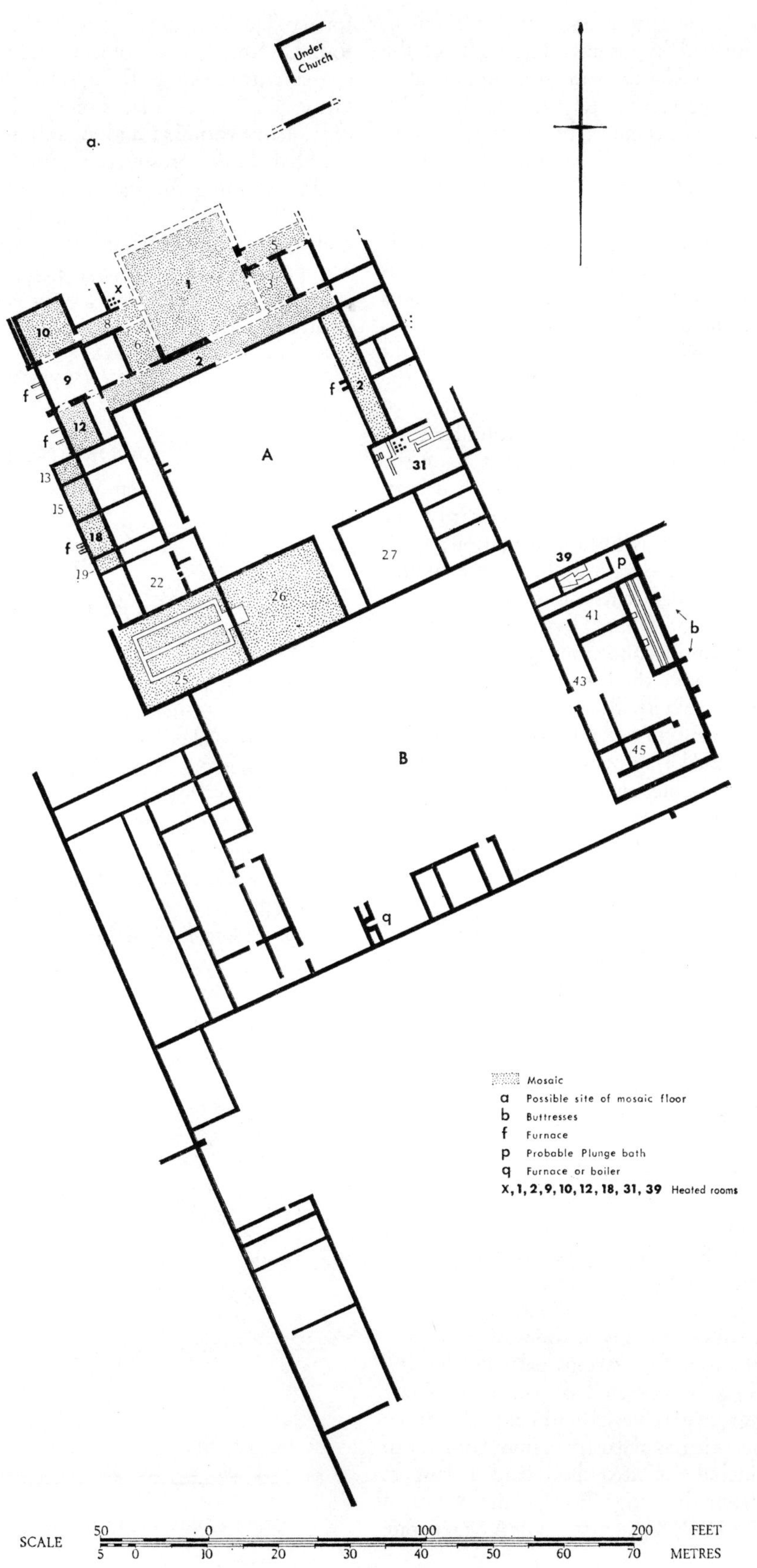

WOODCHESTER. (1) Roman Villa (after Lysons).

1½ million tesserae is the largest and finest known in Britain, has a channelled hypocaust. The walls of the room were over 3 ft. thick; the roof was supported in part by four shafts, the stone base for one of which remains *in situ*. Room 1 was entered from corridors on N.E. and S.W.; the evidence on the other two sides is lost. A corridor or gallery 10 ft. wide surrounded three sides of court A, and large rooms lay on the S.E. side; two at least had mosaic floors and contained marble statuary. Court B, said to be coarsely cemented, was flanked on the S.W. by a range without mosaic floors and on the N.E. by an aisled structure. The latter was buttressed above the slope on the E. and Lysons thought it had a bath block at the N. end, room 39 being the hot room; a recent suggestion, however, has made of it a brewery with adjacent granary. Lysons found marble statue fragments in this block. Foundations at q, on the S. of court B, were of a furnace where coal had been burned. Of the outermost court, not necessarily enclosed on its S. side, there is little information; walls and debris along the E. have recently been excavated.

Structural details include arches and bonding courses of tile in walls mainly of Oolite. Lysons often found that the walls were almost robbed away, but in places they stood 5 ft. high above the foundations. There was extensive use of plaster externally and internally, much of it painted; the recent investigations have revealed red, purple and marbled fragments in room 1. Other decorations include marble *opus sectile*. Some of the fine 'Corinian School' pavements were eventually patched, as in corridor 2, or they were abandoned and overlaid with cement, as was the pavement of room 10, inscribed BONUM EVENTUM (Plate 19). Mosaics varied in quality from those with very small and specially shaped tesserae to others with cubes larger than 1 inch. Small stone column bases and capitals were found in room 26. Pieces of larger columns were found near the building, possibly a gatehouse, on the S. of court B, but no footings for them were identified. The surviving stone base (one of four) in room 1 has a circular socket, probably to receive a wooden shaft (Plate 20). Hexagonal roof tiles were found.

Fragments of two small marble statues featuring 'Luna' and animals came from room 25. A marble group of Cupid and Psyche came from the 'gatehouse' at the centre of the S. wall of court B, and further remains of a marble statue came from corridor 43.

Finds include coins ranging from Hadrian to Valens, with numerous small brass coins of the 'lower empire' (Tetricus to Valens) found in various parts of the site. Among the pottery was decorated samian ware. There were fragments of green glass vessels and a blue glass tube; a small pedestal of 'oriental alabaster' came from room 25. Iron objects include an arrowhead and a dagger; two prick spurs from the range E. of court A are of mediaeval type (*Ant J*, XXXIX (1959), 69). A degenerate form of late Roman zoomorphic buckle has recently been found. Other bronze objects include a sword scabbard chape with a knob finial, brooches and a miniature votive axe. A circular stone weight of some 13½ lb. came from room 41 and an amphora came from room 45. Shale lathe cores were found. Most of the surviving finds, including the statuary, are in B.M.; other finds are in Stroud Museum, and a hypocaust tile with hobnail marks is in Gloucester City Museum.

S. Lysons, *Account of Roman Antiquities Discovered at Woodchester* (London, 1797). *TBGAS*, V (1880–1), 142–7; XLVII (1926), 75–96; 74 (1955), 172–5; 86 (1967), 102–6. Toynbee (1964) *passim*. Smith (1965), 105–11. *RVB*, *passim*. *Agrarian History of England*, I, pt. 2 (S. Applebaum), *passim*.

WOODMANCOTE

No Iron Age or Romano-British monument is known in this parish.

WOTTON-UNDER-EDGE

(18 miles S.W. of Cirencester)

Romano-British objects have been found in the vicinity of Symonds' Hall Farm (ST 790960). A fragment of a quern[1] was picked up immediately S. of the farm in 1969 (ST 790958). A metal spoon[2] was found below the farm in Tyley Bottom (ST 7794). A stone votive tablet[3] depicting three Celtic mother-goddesses may originate from this area, or from KINGSCOTE (1) further east. A brooch[4] was found in the parish in 1883.

1. In Gloucester City Museum.
2. *TBGAS*, 67 (1946–8), 398. The object is lost.

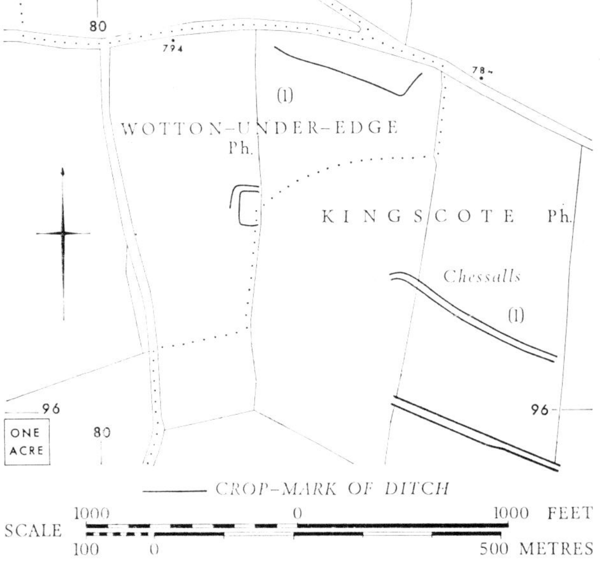

WOTTON-UNDER-EDGE. (1) Enclosures.

3. *PCNFC*, XVIII (1913), 123. Toynbee (1964), 173. In private possession.
4. In Sir John Evans's collection, Ashmolean Museum.

(1) ENCLOSURES (ST 802964), undated, are revealed by crop-marks in fields immediately W. of the Chessalls (KINGSCOTE (1), p. 71).

C.U.A.P., OAP AZN 51.

WYCK RISSINGTON

(16 miles N.E. of Cirencester)

As well as the evidence for Romano-British occupation noted below, isolated finds of Roman material are recorded at three points, none of them apparently associated with structures and only one of them (*b*) fairly closely located. They are as follows:

a. Several Roman coins[1] were found in the garden of Heath Hill House (SP 18472278), ½ mile E. of the Chessels settlement, LOWER SLAUGHTER (1).

b. Sherds of coarse Romano-British, mediaeval and later pottery[2] were found under a house extension at the N.W. end of the village (SP 18782181).

c. Fragments of samian and coarse ware[3] were found N. of Wyckhill House (around SP 196225); see map, p. 66, *s.v.* ICOMB.

1. *TBGAS*, VII (1882–3), 72.
2. Now in Gloucester City Museum.
3. *JRS*, XII (1922), 262.

(1) SETTLEMENT (SP 193208), Romano-British, is indicated by a spread of broken limestone slabs and of 2nd to 4th-century pottery, including samian, calcite-gritted ware and mortaria, in arable. The limestone slabs, which must denote former building as the site is on a flat spur of the Middle Lias, lie around the 600-ft. contour, on the E. side of the Dikler valley. On this side of the valley the spring-line breaks out along the 700-ft. contour, where the Upper Lias meets the Oolite.

TBGAS, 87 (1968), 205, No. 16.

YANWORTH

(8 miles N.E. of Cirencester)

Disjointed traces of a terrace-way in Streetfold lie along the N. side of copse banks between about SP 06651384 and 06741387, where the remains of a terrace 10 ft. wide are overlain by the E. bank of a wood. A modern field ¼ mile to the E. is known locally as Street Acres. Another terrace-way approaches Monument (1) from S.W. (map, p. 25, *s.v.* CHEDWORTH).

(1) ROMANO-BRITISH SETTLEMENT (SP 06051390–06151395) in Yanworth Wood lies on almost level ground. It is marked by a feature, probably a building platform, approximately 25 ft. by 17 ft., at SP 06051390, and by building stones (including a rectangular block 2 ft. 5 in. by 1 ft. 6 in., possibly *in situ*) which break the surface 65 yds. further N.E.

Finds, all now lost, said to have been scattered over the area between the two presumed buildings noted above and on arable ground immediately S. of the wood, include coins (one of Crispus), 4th-century pottery, and tile fragments.

A prominent terrace-way 10 ft. wide extends from a point in the wood about 25 yds. S.W. of the supposed building platform, for some 200 yds. S.W. of the site.

Arch J, LXXVIII (1921), 453; CXXII (1965), 178, fig. 2, No. 10, 'East Chedworth'. *TBGAS*, XLVII (1925), 77, note 14.

(2) DITCHES (SP 076149–084152), undated, show as crop-marks in two sections, following a S.W.–N.E. line on almost flat ground, interrupted by a shallow re-entrant around the 700-ft. contour. A narrow gap, apparently original, occurs in the S.W. section.

C.U.A.P., OAP AYB 65–6.

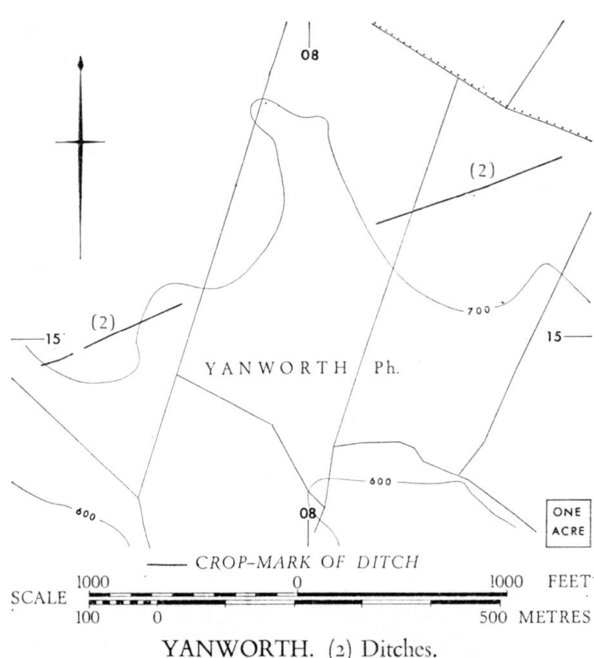

YANWORTH. (2) Ditches.

END OF INVENTORY

TABLES

CHRONOLOGY

RULERS NAMED ON COINAGE AND MENTIONED IN THE INVENTORY

Emperors and members of the Imperial families:

Germanicus (adopted son of Tiberius)	15 B.C.–A.D. 19
Claudius I	A.D. 41–54
Nero	54–68
Vespasian	69–79
Domitian	81–96
Trajan	98–117
Hadrian	117–138
Antoninus Pius	138–161
M. Aurelius	161–180
Faustina II (wife of M. Aurelius)	
L. Verus	161–169
Severus Alexander	222–235
Trajan Decius	249–251
Valerian	253–260
Gallienus	253–268
Salonina (wife of Gallienus)	
Claudius II (or Gothicus)	268–270
Victorinus	268–270
Tetricus	270–273
Carus	282–283
Diocletian	284–305
Carausius	287–293
Allectus	293–296
Constantine I	306–337
Crispus (son of Constantine)	317–326
Constantine II	317–340
Constans	333–350
Constantius II	323–361
Magnentius	350–353
Valentinian I	364–375
Valens	364–378
Gratian	367–383
Theodosius I	379–395
Arcadius	395–408
Honorius	395–423

Note: The Flavian dynasty is represented by Vespasian, Titus and Domitian (69–96). 'The Tetrici' means Tetricus and his son, who was Caesar in 271. 'House of Theodosius' means the dynasty founded by Theodosius I, but the latest references in the Inventory are to Arcadius and Honorius.

Native rulers:

Tasciovanus king of the Catuvellauni, *c.* 20 B.C.–*c.* A.D. 10.
Epaticcu son of Tasciovanus, *c.* A.D. 25–35.

Anted, Eisu, Catti — rulers of the Dobunni within the decade following *c.* A.D. 30.

Bodvoc, Corio — rulers of the Dobunni shortly after the foregoing.

Bibliography:

D. F. Allen in E. M. Clifford, *Bagendon* (1961), 68–149 (study of the uninscribed and inscribed coinage of the Dobunni); in *IASB*, 97–308 (study of the early Celtic coinage and gazetteer of the find-spots of all Celtic coins in Britain). J. R. Collis, *World Archaeology* (1971), 3–71; and in D. Hill and M. Jesson (ed.), *The Iron Age and its Hill-forts* (1971), 97–103 (nucleated settlements as market centres and use of coins in trade).

CONVERSION TABLES

IMPERIAL AND METRIC DIMENSIONS

1 metre = 3.281 feet 1 foot = 0.3048 metre

Metres		Feet
0.30	1	3.3
0.61	2	6.6
0.91	3	9.8
1.22	4	13.1
1.52	5	16.4
1.82	6	19.7
2.13	7	22.9
2.43	8	26.2
2.74	9	29.5
3.05	10	32.8

1 hectare (10,000 sq. metres) = 2.47 acres 1 acre = 0.4049 hectare

Hectares		Acres
0.40	1	2.5
0.80	2	4.9
1.21	3	7.4
1.61	4	9.9
2.02	5	12.3
2.42	6	14.8
2.83	7	17.3
3.23	8	19.8
3.64	9	22.2
4.04	10	24.7

GLOSSARY

AGGER – The consolidated artificial ridge carrying a Roman road.

AMPHORA – A large two-handled jar with narrow neck and pointed or rounded base, used for storage and carriage of wine, oil, etc.

ANDERNACH GRIT – See NIEDERMENDIG LAVA.

APODYTERIUM – The room in a Roman bath building set aside for dressing and undressing.

ARRETINE WARE – Red pottery of a kind commonly produced at *Arretium* in central Italy.

AS – Brass or copper coin worth $\frac{1}{16}$ of a *denarius*.

ASHLAR – Masonry wrought to an even face and square edges.

BARROW – A burial mound; in the Cotswolds usually a cairn composed of stone rubble. *Long Barrow*: an elongated burial mound of the Neolithic period; in the Cotswolds usually with one or more chambers. *Round Barrow*: a burial mound, circular in plan, usually of the Bronze Age.

BASTION – An outward projection from a defensive wall.

BERM – In earthworks, a ledge between a bank and its accompanying ditch or scarp, or a narrow space separating an inner bank and ditch from an outer bank.

BIVALLATE – With two banks, each with a ditch.

BOX TILE – A baked clay tile shaped like a rectangular box, open at both ends; often used for flues and occasionally for voussoirs.

BRONZE AGE – The period when bronze was the dominant metal; in Britain it is dated very roughly between 1800 and 600 B.C.

CAIRN – Mound composed of stone rubble.

CALCITE-GRITTED WARE – Pottery embodying crushed calcite.

CALDARIUM – Hot room in a Roman bath building.

CAUSEWAY – Length of ground interrupting the course of a ditch.

CELLA – The chamber at the centre of a temple.

'CELTIC' FIELDS – Small, rectangular fields usually bounded by lynchets, originating in the Bronze Age, but widespread in Romano-British times.

CHI-RHO – Emblem composed of Greek letters *chi* (*X*) and *rho* (*P*), common in early Christian art and epigraphy as abbreviation for *Χριστός*.

CIST – A grave or small burial chamber without an entrance, lined with stones.

COLOUR-COATED WARE – Pottery to which has been applied a thin coating of clay slip, usually red, brown, dark green or blackish in colour.

COUNTERSCARP – The outer face or slope of the ditch of a fortification. *Counterscarp bank*: a small bank immediately outside the counterscarp of a hill-fort or defensive work.

COVED – Provided with a concave moulding.

CROP-MARK – A trace of a buried feature revealed by differential growth of crops, best seen from the air.

CROSS-RIDGE DYKE – A bank and ditch, sometimes a ditch between two banks, crossing a ridge or spur of high ground. Such features are often of the Iron Age.

CURRENCY BAR – Iron bar, sword or spit-shaped, probably used as a form of currency before the introduction of coinage.

CURSUS – A Neolithic ritual monument comprising a pair of parallel banks with external ditches, often some 200 ft. apart and extending for distances of 500 ft. or more. The banks and ditches are usually returned at right angles to enclose the ends.

DENARIUS – Roman silver coin in standard use until A.D. 242.

DUPONDIUS – Coin worth $\frac{1}{8}$ of a *denarius*.

DYKE – A linear earthwork comprising a bank or ditch, or both.

FIBULA – A brooch with pin, guard and catch, comparable to a modern safety-pin.

FOLLES – Copper coins common at the beginning of the 4th century.

FREESTONE – Limestone of even, fine-grained texture.

FRIGIDARIUM – The cold room in a Roman bath building, equipped with cold plunge.

GENIUS – Guardian spirit or deity.

GENIUS CUCULLATUS – Hooded deity.

GLACIS – In earthworks, a bank and ditch so constructed as to present an unbroken slope from the crest of the bank to the bottom of the ditch.

GRASS-TEMPERED WARE – Pottery embodying chopped grasses, etc.

HEATED ROOM – In Roman or Romano-British buildings, a room heated by a hypocaust (*q.v.*)

HENGE – A round Neolithic or Bronze Age enclosure bounded by a bank, usually with an internal ditch, and having either a single entrance or two diametrically opposed entrances.

HILL-FORT – A defensive enclosure, usually of the Iron Age and on dominant ground, fortified with rampart and ditch, single or multiple.

HOLLOW-WAY – A sunken track caused either by wear or by the raising of the ground on each side.

HORNWORK – An outwork of an earthwork enclosure, such as a hill-fort, often consisting of a single bank thrown out to protect an entrance.

HYPOCAUST – Either a low basement chamber over which a fireproof floor is supported on small pillars (*pilae*), or a system of channels providing under-floor heating. Both systems were intended to allow the circulation of warm air from an external furnace, the air finally escaping through flues of box-tiles embedded in the walls.

IMBREX – A roof-ridge tile, semicircular in section.

IMPOST – A moulded stone at the top of a pilaster flanking an opening.

IRON AGE – The first period in which iron was the dominant metal; in Britain it dated from *c.* 600 B.C. to the Roman Conquest, A.D. 43.

KIMMERIDGE SHALE – A soft, fine-grained rock quarried in Dorset in the Iron Age and the Roman period. Manufactured articles include parts of furniture.

LYNCHET – A field scarp, usually produced by ploughing. See also STRIP LYNCHETS.

MILLEFIORI GLASS – Decorative glass formed by cutting slices from bundles of thin multicoloured glass rods, fused together.

MINIMI, MINIMISSIMI – Diminutive coins of low value.

MORTARIUM – In pottery, a stout bowl with a strong lip and a pouring spout, dusted on the inside with hard grit to strengthen it against wear during the pounding of foodstuffs.

NEOLITHIC – Of the later Stone Age; in Britain from about 3400 B.C. to 1800 B.C.

NIEDERMENDIG LAVA – Lava from the Niedermendig–Andernach–Eifel region of the Rhineland.

NYMPHAEUM – A place consecrated to nymphs, especially at a spring; commonly a monument placed over a water-source.

OPEN FIELDS – Unenclosed fields of mediaeval and later date, usually held in common and cultivated on a strip system.

OPUS SECTILE – Pieces of coloured stone cut to geometric shapes and set together to form a paved floor or wall covering.

OPUS SIGNINUM – Plaster for walls and floors made of broken pottery or tiles, and lime.

PILAE – Small pillars of stone or tile supporting the floor above a *hypocaust* (*q.v.*)

PILASTER – A pier of rectangular section attached to a wall.

PILLOW MOUND – A low mound, usually oblong on plan, but occasionally circular, of mediaeval or later date, probably connected with the rearing of rabbits.

PIT-ALIGNMENT – A line of pits, apparently forming a boundary, probably in conjunction with the spoil dug from them. See Preface, p. xxvii.

PITCHED STONE – Rubble foundations of floors or roads, with the stones packed on edge, or slightly inclined.

PLATFORM – In earthworks, a space artificially levelled, often to receive a building.

PLUNGE-BATH – see FRIGIDARIUM.

PORTICO – A porch with a colonnade.

POTIN COIN – British (or Gaulish) cast bronze coin with high tin content.

QUOIN – Dressed stones forming the angle of a building.

RIDGE-AND-FURROW – Remains of cultivation of mediaeval and later date forming a corrugated surface.

RING-DITCH – A ditch of circular or penannular plan. See Preface, p. lv.

SADDLE-QUERN – A prehistoric hand-mill operated by moving an upper stone backwards and forwards upon a lower.

SAMIAN WARE – Table pottery of the Roman period, mostly of Gaulish origin, with a glossy surface, generally red in colour; also known as *terra sigillata*.

SCARP – An abrupt slope, natural or artificial.

SECONDARY BURIALS – Burial made in a pre-existing barrow or grave.

SESTERTIUS – Coin worth ¼ of a *denarius*.

SETTLEMENT – An area of habitation, perhaps surrounded by associated closes, paddocks, approach ways and other features, which together constitute a complex of earthworks distinct from fields.

SITULATE – A term used to describe the form of vessels, chiefly of pottery, with wide mouths, short everted necks, high shoulders and straight sides tapering downwards. The form is characteristic of the earlier phases of the Iron Age in Britain.

SLATES – (In this volume) thin slabs of sandstone or limestone used for roofing.

SNAKE-THREAD GLASS – A well-defined series of glasses of Roman date decorated with serpent-like lines or threads of glass, sometimes the same colour as the body, sometimes not. They were made both in the East (probably in Syria) and in the West (Cologne and perhaps elsewhere).

SOFFIT – The underside of an architectural feature meant to be seen from below.

SOIL-MARK – A trace of a levelled or buried feature revealed by differences in colour or texture of the soil, usually in ploughed land.

STATER – Coin of gold, silver or bronze; the basic unit of currency in Britain from *c.* 100 B.C. until replaced by Roman coinage.

STONESFIELD SLATE – A sandy oolitic limestone, occurring in the Great Oolite series, which splits readily into thin slabs suitable for roofing.

STRIP FIELDS – Long, narrow fields, characteristic of mediaeval and later open-field agriculture.

STRIP LYNCHETS – Long, narrow strip fields (*q.v.*), set on hillsides and bounded by lynchets.

STYLOBATE – A continuous foundation supporting a row or rows of columns.

STYLUS – A writing implement consisting of a small rod with a pointed end for scratching letters on wax-covered tablets and with a blunt end for obliterating.

TEGULA – A flanged roofing tile.

TEPIDARIUM – Intermediate room of moderate temperature in a Roman bath.

TERRA NIGRA OF RUBRA – Table-ware, black or red, imported from Gaul.

TERRACE-WAY – Track cut into the side of a hill.

TERRET – Metal loop or ring, one of a set serving as rein guides.

TESSELLATED PAVEMENT – A floor surface of small cubes (*tesserae*) of stone, tile or glass, either plain or patterned in various colours, set in mortar to form mosaic.

TESSERA – A cube of stone, tile or glass, used in mosaic.

TIMBER-LACED RAMPART – A rampart reinforced by vertical and horizontal timbers tied together.

TORQUE – A neck-ring of twisted metal.

TORUS MOULDING – A bold convex moulding, generally a semicircle in section.

TUFA (CALCAREOUS) – Stony deposit of sponge-like texture formed as a result of evaporation of water heavily charged with lime.

UNIVALLATE – With a single bank and ditch.

VILLA – An independent rural establishment of consequence, marked by a building with heated rooms, baths, mosaic pavements or sophisticated architectural details such as columns.

VOUSSOIRS – Wedge-shaped stones or box-tiles forming an arch.

ABBREVIATIONS AND SHORTENED TITLES OF WORKS OF REFERENCE

Antiquity	Quarterly Review of Archaeology (1927–)
Ant J	*The Antiquaries Journal* (1921–)
Arch	*Archaeologia* (1770–)
Arch J	*The Archaeological Journal* (1845–)
Archaeol. Review	*The Archaeological Review* (1888–)
Atkyns (1712)	Sir Robert Atkyns, *The Ancient and Present State of Gloucestershire* (1712)
Bagendon	E. M. Clifford, *Bagendon, a Belgic Oppidum* (Heffer, Cambridge, 1961)
Bigland (1791)	*Historical, Monumental and Genealogical Collections relative to the County of Gloucester* (London, 1791–2)
B.M.	The British Museum
Burrow (1924)	E. J. Burrow, *The Ancient Entrenchments and Camps of Gloucestershire* (Cheltenham, 1924)
C.U.A.P.	Cambridge University Committee for Aerial Photography
G.C.R.O.	Gloucester County Record Office
Gent. Mag.	*The Gentleman's Magazine* (1731–1868)
Grundy (1935–6)	G. B. Grundy, *Saxon Charters and Field Names of Gloucestershire* (Bristol and Glos. Archaeol. Soc., 1935–6)
IASB	*Problems of the Iron Age in Southern Britain*, ed. S. S. Frere. (C.B.A. Conference, 1958; U.L.I.A. occasional paper No. 11)
JRS	*The Journal of Roman Studies* (1911–)
JBAA	*The Journal of the British Archaeological Association* (1845–)
Lewis (1966)	M. J. T. Lewis, *Temples in Roman Britain* (Cambridge, 1966)
Lloyd Baker (1821)	T. J. Lloyd Baker, 'An Account of a Chain of Ancient Fortresses . . .', *Arch*, XIX (1821), 161–75
Lysons (1817)	Samuel Lysons, *Reliquiae Britannico-Romanae* (1813, 1817)
Malkin MS.	Typescript by Dr. G. R. Malkin, *c.* 1935, in Worcester County Record Office
Med. Archaeol.	*Journal of the Society for Mediaeval Archaeology* (1957–)
MPBW Excavations	Ministry of Public Buildings and Works, *Excavations Annual Report/Archaeological Excavations* (H.M.S.O., 1961–)
N.M.R.	The National Monuments Record
OAP	Oblique air photograph
O.D.	Ordnance Datum; mean sea-level
O.S.	The Ordnance Survey
O.S. 1st ed.	Ordnance Survey, *Map of Gloucestershire*, scale 1 inch to 1 mile, edition of 1817–30
Oxon	*Oxoniensia* (Oxford Architectural and Historical Society, 1936–)
PCNFC	*Proceedings of the Cotteswold Naturalists' Field Club* (1846–)
Playne (1876)	G. F. Playne, *On the Ancient Camps of Gloucestershire* (*PCNFC*, vol. vi)
PNG	*The Place-Names of Gloucestershire* (English Place-Name Society, Vols. xxxviii–xli, 1960–4)
PPS	*Proceedings of the Prehistoric Society* (Cambridge, 1935–)
PSA	*Proceedings of the Society of Antiquaries of London* (1843–1920)
PSAS	*Proceedings of the Society of Antiquaries of Scotland* (1851–)
R.A.F.	Royal Air Force
R.C.H.M.	Royal Commission on Historical Monuments (England)
RIB	R. G. Collingwood and R. P. Wright, *The Roman Inscriptions of Britain*
Ross (1967)	Anne Ross, *Pagan Celtic Britain* (London and New York, 1967)
RVB	A. L. F. Rivet (ed.) *The Roman Villa in Britain* (1969)
Rudder (1779)	Samuel Rudder, *A New History of Gloucestershire* (Cirencester, 1779)
Sawyer	P. H. Sawyer, *Anglo-Saxon Charters: an annotated list and bibliography* (R. Hist. Soc., 1968)
Smith (1965)	D. J. Smith, 'Three 4th-century schools of Mosaic in Roman Britain', in Stern (ed.), *La Mosaïque Gréco-Romaine* (Paris, 1965), 95–116
TBGAS	*Transactions of the Bristol and Gloucestershire Archaeological Society* (1876–)
Toynbee (1964)	J. M. C. Toynbee, *Art in Britain Under the Romans* (Oxford, 1964)
UBSS	*Proceedings of the University of Bristol Speliological Society*
U.L.I.A.	University of London, Institute of Archaeology
VAP	Vertical Air Photograph
WAM	*Wiltshire Archaeological and Natural History Magazine* (Devizes, 1854–)
Witts (1883)	G. B. Witts, *Archaeological Handbook of the County of Gloucestershire* (Cheltenham, *c.* 1883)

INDEX

In compiling the index it has often been found necessary to adopt, for each monument, the terminology used in earlier reports. In consequence some duplication and a few inconsistencies occur.

The letters 'a' and 'b' denote the left-hand and right-hand columns of the page indicated.

Abbotswood, Roman villa, Swell (2), pp. xxxvii, xlii, liii, 115b.
Ablington Camp, Hill-fort, Bibury (1), pp. xxv, 13b.
,, **Downs,** 'Celtic' Field traces, Bibury (3), p. 14b.
Acton Turville, p. 1a.
Addy's Firs, Romano-British settlement, Ashley (1), p. 4a.
Adlestrop, p. 1b.
,, **Hill,** long barrow, Adlestrop, p. 1b.
Aesculapius, p. 24a; *see also* **Gods.**
Agriculture, *see* **'Celtic' Fields, Corn, Ploughs, Ovens, Querns, Ridge and Furrow, Strip Lynchets,** *and* **Tools.**
Akeman Street, *see* **Roman Roads.**
Akerman, J. Y., Ampney St. Peter, p. 3b; coins found, Rodmarton, p. 98b.
Alabaster, oriental, pedestal of, Woodchester (1), p. 134a.
Alderley, p. 2a.
Alderton, p. 2a.
Aldsworth, p. 2b.
Allectus, *see* **Coins: Roman**; *also* Chronology, p. 136.
Altars:
Preface, p. li.
Carved: Bisley with Lypiatt, p. 14b.
Dedicated:
to Mars: Bisley with Lypiatt, p. 14b; Chalford (1), p. 23a; King's Stanley, p. 70a.
to Mars Lenus: Chedworth (1), p. 27b.
to Silvanus: Bisley with Lypiatt, p. 14b; Cherington, p. 29a.
Inscribed: Siddington, p. 101b.
Uninscribed: Baunton (1), p. 13b; Bisley with Lypiatt, p. 15a; Chalford (1), p. 23a; Chedworth (1), p. 27b; Lower Slaughter (1), p. 79b; Sudeley (5), p. 115a.
Amber, p. 39b; *see also* **Beads.**
Amberley 'Camp', Minchinhampton, pp. xxix, xxx, 82a.
Amphitheatre, Preface, pp. xxxv, xxxvi.
Amphorae, *see* **Pottery: Roman.**
Ampney Brook, Romano-British finds, Driffield, p. 45b.
,, **Crucis,** p. 3a.
,, **St. Mary,** p. 3b.
,, ,, **Peter or Eastington,** p. 3b.
Andernach Grit, *see* **Querns.**
Andoversford, pp. 4a, 125.
Animal Bones:
Preface, p. xl.
Boar's Tusks: Painswick (2), p. 94a.
Bos Longifrons: Whittington (2), p. 126b.
Cat: Frocester (2), p. 58b.
Cow: Farmington (1), p. 55b.
Deer, Red: Chedworth (1), p. 27b; (4), p. 28b.
Dog: Bagendon (1), p. 8a; Frocester (2), p. 58b.
Duck: Frocester (2), p. 58b.
Goat: Bourton-on-the-Water (1), p. 19b; Frocester (2), p. 58b; Painswick (2), p. 94a.
Goose: Frocester (2), p. 58b.
Hen: Bagendon (1), p. 8a; Frocester (2), p. 58b; Great Witcombe (1), p. 61b.
Hare: Great Witcombe (1), p. 61b.
Horse: Bagendon (1), p. 8a; Frocester (2), p. 58b; Painswick (2), p. 94a.
Ox: Bagendon (1), p. 8a; Bourton-on-the-Water (1), p. 19b; Chedworth (1), p. 27b; Frocester (2), p. 58b; Great Witcombe (1), p. 61b; Painswick (2), p. 94a.
Animal Bones, *cont.*
Pig: Bagendon (1), p. 8a; Bourton-on-the-Water (1); p. 19b; Chedworth (1), p. 27b; Farmington (1), p. 55b; Frocester (2), p. 58b; Great Witcombe (1), p. 61b; Painswick (2), p. 94a.
Sheep: Bagendon (1), p. 8a; Bourton-on-the-Water (1), p. 19b; Chedworth (1), p. 27b; Farmington (1), p. 55b; Frocester (2), p. 58b; Great Witcombe (1), p. 61b; Painswick (2), p. 94a.
Unspecified: Barnsley (1), p. 9b; Chedworth (6), p. 29a; Lechlade (5), p. 75a; Lower Slaughter (1), p. 80a; Shipton (1), p. 101a; Southam (3), p. 107b; Stanton (1), p. 110a; Swell (1), p. 115b; Uley (1), p. 121b; (2), p. 122a; Upton St. Leonards (1), p. 123b; Whittington (2), p. 126b.
Anted, ruler of Dobunni, Preface, p. xxxiv; Chronology, p. 136; *see also* **Coins: Iron Age.**
Antlers, red deer, Chedworth (1), p. 27b; Colesbourne (2), p. 36a; Farmington (1), p. 55b; (worked tine)), p. 55b; Painswick (2) p. 94a; Southam (3), p. 107b.
Antoninus Pius, *see* **Coins: Roman;** *also* Chronology, p. 136.
Anvil, iron, Lower Slaughter (1), p. 79b.
Arcadius, *see* **Coins: Roman;** *also* Chronology, p. 136.
Architecture, *see* **Building Materials** *and* **Remains.**
Ard, *see* **Plough-coulter.**
Arle Grove, linear dyke, Charlton Kings (2), p. 23b; Romano-British potsherds found, Whittington, p. 125a.
Armorican silver, *see* **Coins: Iron Age.**
Arretine ware, *see* **Pottery: Roman.**
Arrows, iron, Chedworth (1), p. 27b; Woodchester (1), p. 134a.
Arveri, tiles stamped, Brookthorpe with Whaddon (1), p. 22b; Frocester (1), p. 57b; King's Stanley (2), p. 70b.
Ashel Barn, Romano-British settlement near, Kingscote (1), p. 71a.
Ashley, p. 4a.
,, **Marsh Covert,** Romano-British settlement N.E. of, Ashley (2), p. 4b.
Ashmolean Museum: Beverstone, p. 13b; Bourton-on-the-Water (1), p. 19b; Coln St. Aldwyns (2), p. 37b; Kempsford, p. 68a; Kingscote, p. 70b; Lechlade (5), p. 75a; Painswick, p. 91b; Woodchester, p. 132a; Wotton-under-Edge, p. 135a.
Ashton Keynes, Wiltshire, Romano-British settlement crosses into, Somerford Keynes (6), p. 105b.
Asses, Claudian, *see* **Coins: Roman.**
Aston Blank, p. 4b.
,, **Subedge,** p. 4b.
Aucissa, *see* **Brooches.**
Aulus Plautius, Preface, p. xxxiv.
Avening, p. 4b.
Awl, iron, Bagendon (1), p. 8a.
Axes:
Bronze (model): Whittington (2), p. 126a; Woodchester (1), p. 134a.
Iron: Colesbourne (2), p. 36a; Driffield, p. 45b; Kingscote (1), p. 72b; Poole Keynes, p. 94b.

Bacchus, p. 112a; *see also* **Gods.**
Baddeley, W. St. Clair, Chedworth (6), p. 29a; Painswick (2), p. 93b.
Badgeworth, p. 5b.
Badminton, p. 6a.
,, **Park,** 'Celtic' Fields, Badminton (1), p. 6a, Pl. 42; mosaics from, Badminton, pp. xli, 6a.
Badsey Lane, Romano-British settlement, Willersey (4), pp. xliii, 130a.

Bagendon, p. 6b.
Baker, Mr. T., Bisley with Lypiatt (1), p. 15b.
,, **Mr. W. A.,** Preface, p. xx.
'Baldric' loop, *see* **Military Equipment.**
Balustrades, Roman, fretted stone: Preface, p. xli; Chedworth (1), p. 27a, Pl. 26; Great Witcombe (1), p. 61a.
Banks and Ditches, *see* **Dykes.**
Barley, *see* **Corn.**
Barn, *see* **Building Remains.**
Barnsley, p. 9a.
,, **Park,** Roman villa, Barnsley (1), p. 9a; 'Celtic' Fields, Barnsley (2), pp. xxxviii, xlix, 11a.
Barrington, p. 11b.
,, **Park,** Romano-British building, Barrington (1), p. 12a.
Barrow, possibly Iron Age, Leckhampton (2), p. 78a.
Barrow Wake, Iron Age inhumation cemetery, Cowley (1), p. 39b; Roman building, Cowley (4), pp. xliii, 40b; Romano-British pottery found, Badgeworth, p. 5b.
Barrows containing Romano-British material:
Preface, pp. xlix, l; *also* Ring-Ditches, p. lv.
BELL: Temple Guiting, p. 116b.
LONG: Adlestrop, p. 1b; Aston Blank, p. 4b; Frocester, p. 56b; Randwick, p. 97a; Rodmarton, p. 98a; Sudeley, p. 112a; Swell, p. 115a; Uley, p. 121a; Withington, p. 131a; Woodchester, p. 132a.
ROUND: Coln St. Dennis, p. 37a; King's Stanley, p. 70a; Temple Guiting, p. 116b; Withington, p. 131a.
UNSPECIFIED: Minchinhampton, p. 81a; Miserden, p. 84a; Rodmarton, p. 98b.
Barton, The, Roman Villa, Cirencester (1), pp. xli, xlii, liii, 29b, Pl. 1.
Bartonhill Farm to Hinchwick, Romano-British settlement near road, Temple Guiting (2), p. 117a.
Basilica, Corinium, Preface, p. xxxv.
Basin, rectangular stone, Chedworth (1), p. 27b.
Bath-houses, *see* **Building Remains.**
Baths, Preface, p. xxxix.
Batsford, p. 12a.
Battledown, Charlton Kings, pp. xxix, xxxib, 23a.
Baunton, p. 13b.
,, **Downs,** probable Romano-British settlement, Baunton (1), p. 13b.
Bazeley, Rev. W., Sudeley (4), p. 113b.
Beach, coffins found, Bitton, p. 17a.
Beads:
AMBER: Cowley (1), p. 39b.
GLASS: Bagendon (1), p. 8a; Kingscote (1), p. 72b; Lower Slaughter (3), p. 80a; Painswick (2), p. 94a.
MARBLE: Cowley (1), p. 39b.
SHALE: Cowley (1), p. 39b.
Beaker fragments, glass, Great Witcombe (1), p. 61b.
Bean Hay Copse, undated enclosures and linear ditches, Down Ampney (1), p. 44b.
Beckbury Camp, Hill-fort, Temple Guiting (1), pp. xxiv, xxv, xxvi, xxxiva, 116b.
Beggy Hill Way, burials and coffin found near, Upper Slaughter, p. 123a.
Bel Tump, site of probable Romano-British settlement, Compton Abdale (4), p. 38b.
Belas Knap, long barrow, Sudeley, p. 112a.
'Belgic' occupation evidence, Bourton-on-the-Water (1), p. 18a.
Belgic wooden bucket, with embossed hoops, Rodborough, p. 98a.
Bembro, Temple Guiting, note on p. 117b.
Beveridge, Sgt. B., Preface, p. xx; Shipton (1), p. 101a.
Beverstone, p. 13b.
Bezel, gold, Quenington (3), p. 97a.
Bibury, p. 13b.
,, **Mill,** Roman villa, Bibury (2), pp. xxxvii, 14b.
,, **Old Racecourse,** 'Celtic' Fields overly, Aldsworth (1), p. 2b.
Big Stanborough, p. 57a; *see also* **Field Names.**
Bill-hooks:
IRON: Bourton-on-the-Water (1), p. 19b.
METAL: Upton St. Leonards, p. 123a.
Bird, enamel on fibulae, Beverstone, p. 13b.
,, miniature bronze, Lower Slaughter (1), p. 79b.
Birdlip, Cowley, p. 39b.
Birdlip Camp, alleged Hill-fort, Cowley, pp. xxix, xxxiib, 39b.
,, Iron Age inhumation cemetery, Cowley (1), p. 39b.
,, Roman Road E. of, Cowley (2), pp. xlv, 40a.
Birmingham Museum: Batsford (1), p. 13a; Oxenton, p. 91a.
Bisley Common, altars, Bisley with Lypiatt, p. 15a.
,, **with Lypiatt,** p. 14b.
Bitton, p. 16b.
,, **Camp,** Bitton, pp. xxix, 17a.
Black Close, Iron Age brooches found, Whittington (2), pp. xxxviii, 126a.
,, **Grove,** Bagendon (1), p. 6b.
Blackenbury, early name for North Nibley (1), note on p. 86.
Blackies Field, probable Romano-British settlement, Marshfield (1), p. 80b; *see also* **Field Names.**
Bledington, p. 17a.
Bledisloe Lodge, undated enclosure, Coates (6), p. 32b.
Blockley, p. 17a.
Boar's Tusks, p. 94a; *see also* **Animal Bones.**
Bodvoc, native ruler, Preface, p. xxxiv; Chronology, p. 136. *See also* **Coins: Iron Age.**
Bolts, iron, Lower Slaughter (1), p. 79b.
Bondend, Romano-British settlement, Upton St. Leonards (1), p. 123b.
Bone, *see* **Chape, Combs, Handles, Needles, Pins,** *and* **Points.**
'Bonum Eventum', inscription on mosaic, Woodchester (1), p. 134a, Pl. 19.
Boot nails, Temple Guiting (3), p. 117b.
Bos Longifrons, p. 126b; *see also* **Animal Bones.**
Boss, bronze, Uley (2), p. 121b.
Bottles, glass, Chedworth (1), p. 27b; Painswick (2), p. 94a.
Bournes Green, villa at, Bisley with Lypiatt (1), p. 15b.
Bourton Bridge, occupation area, Bourton-on-the-Water, p. 17b.
,, **Downs,** Bourton-on-the-Hill (1), p. 17b.
Bourton-on-the-Hill, p. 17b.
Bourton-on-the-Water, p. 17b.
Bowldown, Roman coins found, Westonbirt with Lasborough, p. 123b.
,, **Farm,** tombstones found, Beverstone, p. 13b; Westonbirt with Lasborough, p. 123b.
Bowls:
BRONZE: Cowley (1), p. 39b; Sudeley (4) (silver-plated), p. 114b.
GLASS: Chedworth (1), p. 27b.
Bown Hill, cross-ridge dyke on, King's Stanley (1), p. 70a; Romano-British finds, Woodchester, p. 132a.
Box tiles, *see* **Building Remains.**
Boxwell with Leighterton, p. 21b.
Bracelets:
BRONZE: Cowley (1), p. 39b; Kingscote (1), p. 72b; Lower Slaughter (3), p. 80a; Stanton (1), p. 110a; Temple Guiting (3), p. 117b.
GLASS: Bisley with Lypiatt (3), p. 16b.
IRON: Badgeworth, p. 5b.
METAL: Cirencester (2), p. 30a; Sudeley (5), p. 115a.
SHALE: Frocester (2), p. 58a; Lower Slaughter (1), p. 79b.
Brackenbury Ditches, Hill-fort, North Nibley (1), pp. xxv, xxvi, 86a.
Brad Straet, Preface, p. xlvii.
Bread Wheat, *see* **Corn.**
Brickbats, The, Lechlade, p. lii.
Brickyard, possible Roman, Woodchester, p. 132a.
Brimpsfield, p. 21b.
Bristol City Museum: Bitton, p. 17a; Bourton-on-the-Water (1), p. 19b; Kingscote, p. 70b; Lower Slaughter, p. 79a; Marshfield (2), p. 80b; Naunton (1), p. 84b; Swell (1), p. 115b; (2), p. 116a; Temple Guiting (3), p. 117b; Upper Slaughter, p. 123a.
Briting Broc, Saxon, Bagendon (1), p. 6b.
British coins, *see* **Coins: Iron Age.**
British Museum: Batsford (1), p. 13a; Bourton-on-the-Water (1), p. 19b; Colesbourne (2), p. 36b; Great Witcombe (1), p. 61b; King's Stanley, p. 70a; Rodmarton (1), p. 98b; Willersey (2), p. 130a; Withington (2), p. 130a; Woodchester (1), p. 134b.
Broadwell, p. 21b.
Brockworth, p. 21b.
,, **Wood,** cross-ridge dyke, Brockworth (1), p. 22a.
Bronze Age barrows, *see* **Barrows;** *also* **Ring-Ditches,** p. lv.
Bronze artefacts, *see* **Axe (model), Bird, Boss, Bowls, Bracelets, Brooches, Buckles, Crown, Dagger, Dividers, Finger-rings, Fish-hooks, Hoops, Key, Loop, Mask, Mirror,**

Bronze artefacts, *cont.*
Nail-cleaners, Necklace, Pins, Ploughshare (miniature), Prick-spurs, Rings, Scabbard Chape, Spoons, Stamp, Statuette, Styli, Steelyard, Stud, Surgical Instrument, Swords, Tooth-pick, *and* **Tweezers.**
Brooches:
BRONZE: Bagendon (1), p. 7b; Blockley (1), p. 17b; Bourton-on-the-Water (1), p. 19b; Frocester (2), p. 58a; King's Stanley, p. 70a; Kingscote (1), p. 72b; Lower Slaughter (3), p. 80a: Marshfield (1), p. 80b; Rodborough (1), p. 98a; Woodchester (1), p. 134b.
ENAMELLED: Painswick, p. 91b.
IRON: Bagendon (1), p. 7b; Blockley (1), p. 17b; Bourton-on-the-Water, p. 19b; Whittington (2), p. 126b.
LA TÈNE: Lower Slaughter (1), p. 79b; Sudeley, p. 112a.
METAL: Kingscote (1), p. 72a; Lechlade (5), p. 75a; Sudeley (2), p. 113b; (5), p. 115a; Uley (2), p. 121b.
COLCHESTER TYPE: Bagendon (1), p. 7b.
CROSS-BOW: Fairford, p. 54b.
FIBULAE: Cirencester, p. 29b; (1), p. 30a; (2), p. 30a; Preston p. 95a; Upton St. Leonards, p. 123a; Whittington (2), p. 126b; Willersey (3), p. 130b.
POLDEN HILL: Kingscote (2), p. 73a.
SILVER: Cowley (1), p. 39b.
Brookman's Quarry, undated enclosure, Tormarton (3), p. 120b.
Brookthorpe Court, Roman villa, Brookthorpe with Whaddon (1), p. 22b.
Brookthorpe with Whaddon, p. 22b.
Brown, Mr. P. D. C., Duntisbourne Abbots (1), p. 48a; Syde (1), p. 116b.
Browne, Mr. Charles, Tormarton, p. 120a.
Brownshill, Roman burials, Painswick (3), p. 94a.
Bryant's map, Notgrove, p. 88b.
Bryworth Farm, undated linear ditches, Lechlade (14) and (15), p. 77a.
Bucket, wooden, with bronze mountings, Cowley (1), p. 39b.
Buckholt Wood, probable Iron Age dyke, Cranham (1), p. 41a.
Buckland, p. 22b.
Buckle Street, *see* **Roman Roads.**
Buckles:
Preface, p. xxxviii.
BRONZE: Kingscote (1), p. 70a; Sudeley, p. 112b; Whittington (2), p. 126b; Woodchester (1), p. 134b.
GILT: Bourton-on-the-Water (1a), p. 19b.
ZOOMORPHIC: Chedworth (1), p. 27b; Woodchester (1), p. 134b.
Buggilde Street, Saxon, Preface, pp. xlv–xlvii.
Building Materials:
CEILINGS: (tufa-block) Ebrington (1), p. 53a.
FLOORING: Bourton-on-the-Water (1a), p. 19b.
CONCRETE: Barnsley (1), p. 9b; Chedworth (1), p. 27a; (4), p. 28b; Compton Abdale (1), p. 38a; Duntisbourne Abbots (1), p. 48a; Farmington (1), p. 55b; Frocester (2), p. 57a; Woodchester (1), p. 134a.
EARTH: Frocester (2), p. 57b.
GRAVEL: (hard) Brockworth (2), p. 22a; Frocester (2), p. 57a; Whittington (3), p. 127b.
OPUS SIGNINUM: Badgeworth (1), p. 6a; Chedworth (1), p. 27a; (4), p. 28b; Farmington (1), p. 55b; Frocester (2), p. 57a; Great Witcombe (1), p. 61a; Sudeley (4), p. 114b.
PATTERNED RED TILES: Farmington (1), p. 55b.
STONE:
COBBLED: Painswick (2), p. 94a.
FLAGGED: Badgeworth (1), p. 6a; Sudeley (4), p. 114b.
LIAS FLAGS: Chedworth (1), p. 27a; Painswick (2), p. 93b.
MARBLE: Ebrington (1), p. 53a.
PAVING: Frocester (2), p. 57b.
PENNANT FLAGS: Chedworth (1), p. 27a.
SANDSTONE: Badgeworth (1), p. 6a; Great Witcombe (1), p. 61a.
SLATE: Painswick (2), p. 93b.
STUCCO: Colesbourne (2), p. 36a.
TESSELLATED: Preface, p. xxxix, Pls. 1–23. Chedworth (1), p. 27a; Cirencester (1), p. 29b; Colesbourne (2), p. 35b; Daglingworth (2), p. 41b; Ebrington (1), p. 53a; Great Witcombe (1), p. 60b; 61a; King's Stanley (2), p. 70a; Kingscote (1), p. 72a; Lechlade, p. 73a; Painswick (2), p. 93b; Rodmarton (1), p. 98b; Stinchcombe (1), p. 111b; Sudeley (2), p. 113b; (4), p. 113b;
Building Materials, *cont.*
FLOORING, TESSELLATED, *cont.*
Whittington (3), p. 127b; Withington (2), p. 132a; Woodchester (1), p. 132b.
TESSERAE (LOOSE): Barrington (2), p. 12a; Batsford (1), p. 12b; Chedworth, p. 24a; Coberley (2), p. 34a; (3), p. 34a; Driffield (1), p. 47a; Frocester (1), p. 57a; Horsley (1), p. 65a; Lechlade (5), p. 73b; Painswick (2), p. 93b; Rodmarton (1), p. 98b; Siddington (3), p. 102b; Sudeley, p. 112a; (2), p. 113b; (4), p. 114a; Whittington (2), p. 126a.
ROOFING:
Preface, p. xl.
IMBREX: Driffield (1), p. 47a; Dursley (1), p. 49b; Kingscote (1), p. 72b; Siddington (6), p. 102b.
LEAD: Chedworth (1), p. 27b.
SLATE: Barrington (1), p. 12a; Swell (2), p. 116a.
STONE: Chedworth (1), p. 27b; Sudeley (2), p. 113b.
STONESFIELD: Sudeley (4), p. 114a; Temple Guiting (2), p. 117a.
TILES AND/OR TEGULAE: Ashley (1), p. 4b; Barrington (1), p. 12a; Batsford (1), p. 12b; Brockworth (2), p. 22a; Chedworth (1), p. 27b; (6), p. 29a; Coberley (3), p. 34a; Colesbourne (2), p. 36a; Ebrington (1), p. 53a; Kingscote (1), p. 72b; Lechlade (5), p. 73b; Northleach with Eastington (2), p. 88a; Rodmarton (1), p. 98b; Siddington (6), p. 102b; Stanway (3), p. 111a; Willersey (4), p. 130a; Yanworth (1), p. 135b.
POTTERY: Blockley (1), p. 17b; Compton Abdale (1), p. 38a.
SANDSTONE: Ashley (1), p. 4b; (2), p. 4b; Colesbourne (2), p. 36a; Dursley (1), p. 49b; Lechlade (5), p. 73b; (old red) Whittington (3), p. 127a.
STAMPED: Bisley with Lypiatt (1), p. 16b; Brookthorpe with Whaddon (1), p. 22b; Rodmarton (1), p. 98b.
STONE: Badgeworth (1), p. 6a; Bisley with Lypiatt (1), p. 15a; Blockley (1), p. 17b; Ebrington (1), p. 53a; Marshfield (1), p. 80b; (2), p. 80b; Weston Subedge (2), p. 123b.
WALLING:
HERRING-BONE MASONRY: Barnsley (1), p. 9b.
STONE: Ashley (2), p. 4b.
LIMESTONE (dressed): Avening (2), p. 5b; Batsford (1), p. 13a.
„ (fire-reddened): Ashley (1), p. 4b; Avening (1), p. 5a; Horton (1), p. 66a.
OOLITE: Badgeworth (1), p. 6a.
SANDSTONE (imported): Avening (1), p. 5a; (2), p. 5b.
WALL-LININGS:
OPUS SIGNINUM: Badgeworth (1), p. 6a; Painswick (2), p. 93b.
PLASTER: Barrington (2), p. 12a; Batsford (1), p. 12b; Bisley with Lypiatt (1), p. 16a; Broadwell (1), p. 21b; Colesbourne (2), p. 36a; Frocester (1), p. 57a; Painswick (2), p. 93b.
PAINTED: Preface, p. xl. Badgeworth (1), p. 6a; Brookthorpe with Whaddon (1), p. 22b; Chedworth (1), p. 24b; (6), p. 28b; Cirencester (1), p. 30a; Coberley (3), p. 34b; Colesbourne (2), p. 36a; Compton Abdale (1), p. 38b; Cowley (3), p. 40b; Ebrington (1), p. 53a; Farmington (1), p. 55b; Great Witcombe (1), p. 61a; (2), p. 61b; Lechlade (5), p. 73b; Painswick (2), p. 93b; Sudeley (2), p. 113b; Whittington (3), p. 127a.
STUCCO: Badgeworth (1), p. 6a.
Building Remains: *See also* **Buildings,** *and* **Earthworks.**
Preface, pp. xxxvii, xl, Plates 27–30.
ARCHITECTURAL DETAILS: *see* **Buildings** *and* **Building Materials.**
BARN: Barnsley (1), p. 9b.
HYPOCAUSTS:
Preface, pp. xxxix, xl.
BUILDINGS WITH: Barnsley (1), p. 9a; Brookthorpe with Whaddon (1), p. 22a; Chedworth (1), p. 24b; (6), p. 29a; Colesbourne (2), p. 36a; Compton Abdale (1), p. 38a; Cowley (3), p. 40b; (5), p. 40b; Ebrington (1), p. 53a; Farmington (1), p. 55b; Frocester (2), p. 57b; Great Rissington (1), p. 59b; Kingscote (1), p. 72b; Painswick (2), p. 93b; Rodmarton (1), p. 98b; Stanway (1), p. 111a; Sudeley (4), p. 114a; Swell (2), p. 116a; Tetbury Upton (1), p. 119b; Whittington (2), p. 126a; Withington (2), p. 132a; (3), p. 132a; Woodchester (1), p. 134a.
CHANNELLED: Barnsley (1), p. 9a; Chedworth (1), p. 24b; Frocester (2), p. 57b; Rodmarton (1), p. 98b; Sudeley (4), p. 114a; Woodchester (1), p. 134a.

Building Remains, *cont.*
Hypocausts, *cont.*
Materials:
Tiles: Brookthorpe with Whaddon (1), p. 22b; Chedworth (1), p. 24b; (6), p. 29a; Cowley (3), p. 40b; (5), p. 40b; Ebrington (1), p. 53a; Painswick (2), p. 93b; Stanway (1), p. 111a; Sudeley (4), p. 114a; Swell (2), p. 116a; Willersey (4), p. 130a; Woodchester (1), p. 134a.
Pilae: Brookthorpe with Whaddon (1), p. 22b; Frocester (2), p. 57b; Rodmarton (1), p. 98b.
Stone: Painswick (2), p. 93b; Sudeley (4), p. 114a.
Tile: Compton Abdale (1), p. 38a; Ebrington (1), p. 53a.
Bath-houses: Barnsley (1), p. 9b; Barrington (1), p. 12a; Chedworth (1), p. 26a; Ebrington (1), p. 52b; Farmington (1), p. 55b; Great Witcombe (1), p. 61a; Sudeley (4), p. 115b; Whittington (2), p. 126a.
Nymphaeum: Chedworth (1), p. 25b.
Wells: Barnsley (1), p. 9b; Batsford (1), p. 12b; Bourton-on-the-Water (2a), p. 20a; Kempsford (1), p. 68b; Lower Slaughter (1), p. 79a; Siddington (3), p. 102a.
Buildings: *See also* **Earthworks.**
Iron Age, list of, Preface, p. xxvi.
Roman, list of, Preface, pp. xlii–xliii.
Bull's head, terminal to iron knife (bronze), Cowley (1), p. 39b.
Bulwarks, The, Hill-fort, Haresfield (2), pp. xxvi, lii, 62b, plan 63.
Bulwarks, The, Iron age bank and ditch, Minchinhampton (1)–(8), pp. xxv, 83–4, Pls. 44–5.
Burhill, Hill-fort, Buckland (1), pp. xxv, lii, 22b.
Burials:
Preface, pp. xxvii–xxix, xliv.
Iron Age:
Inhumations:
Accompanied: Badgeworth, p. 5b; Cowley (1), p. 39b.
Cemetery: Cowley (1), p. 39b.
Cremations: Bagendon (1), p. 7b.
Crouched: Bourton-on-the-Water (1), p. 19b.
In Pits: Bourton-on-the-Water (1), p. 19b.
Romano-British:
Cremations: Dodington, p. 43a; Temple Guiting (3), p. 117b.
In Urns: Ampney Crucis, p. 3a; Lechlade (5), p. 75a; Minchinhampton, p. 81a; Notgrove, p. 88b; Whittington (2), p. 125b.
Inhumations:
Accompanied: Kingscote (2), p. 73a; Stanway, p. 110b; Temple Guiting (3), p. 117b.
Cemeteries: Haresfield (4), p. 64b; Temple Guiting (3), p. 117b; Upper Slaughter, p. 123a.
Cist: Chedworth (1), p. 27a; Compton Abdale (5), p. 38b; Lower Slaughter (1), p. 79b; Naunton (1), p. 84b; Stanway (6), p. 111a; Willersey (2), p. 130a.
Coffins:
Lead: South Cerney, p. 105b.
Stone: Bitton, p. 16b; Cold Ashton, p. 34b; Dyrham and Hinton (3), p. 51b; Kingscote (1), p. 72a; Lower Slaughter, p. 79a; Temple Guiting (3), p. 117b; Tetbury Upton (1), p. 119b; Tormarton, p. 120a.
Wood: Cutsdean, p. 41b; Temple Guiting (3), p. 117b; Tetbury Upton (1), p. 119b.
Contracted: Condicote (2), p. 39b; Leckhampton, p. 77a; Upper Slaughter, p. 123a; Withington (1), p. 131b.
Unspecified: Bourton-on-the-Water (2), p. 20a; Brimpsfield, p. 21b; Charlton Kings, p. 23b; Condicote (2), p. 39b; Painswick (3), p. 94a; Sudeley (5), p. 115a; Temple Guiting (3), p. 117b; Whittington (2), p. 125b; Willersey (2), p. 130a.
Saxon: Bourton-on-the-Water (1), p. 18a; (3), p. 21a; Cirencester (1), p. 30a.
Graves, undated: Stanway (6), p. 111a.
Burleigh, urns found, Minchinhampton, p. 81a.
Burrell Hill, early name for Buckland (1), p. lii.
Burrell's Camp, early name for Dyrham and Hinton (1), note on p. 51.
Burrill, Dyrham and Hinton (1), p. 51a.
Burrow, Mr. E. J., Leckhampton (1), p. 77b.
Butt-beaker, *see* **Pottery: Roman.**

Cadmoor, Barnsley (2), p. 11a.
Caestello, probable Romano-British building, Upper Slaughter (1), pp. lii, 123a.
Calcot Farm, relief of Mars built in to, Kingscote, p. 70b.
Calmsden Field, p. 85a, *see also* **Field Names.**
Cam, p. 22b.
,, **Long Down Camp,** Cam, pp. xxx, 22b.
Camp Farm, entrenchments, and long barrow E. of, Aston Blank, p. 4b.
,, **Field,** gold stater inscribed Bodvoc found, Minchinhampton, p. 81a.
'Camp Openham', probably Oxenton Knolls, p. 91a.
'Capitol', The, Roman building, Chedworth (2), pp. xli, xlii, 28a.
Carausius, p. 13b; *see also* **Coins: Roman;** *and* Chronology, p. 136.
Carus, *see* **Coins: Roman;** *also* Chronology, p. 136.
Carver, Mrs. H. R., Duntisbourne Abbots (1), p. 48a.
Cashe's Green, Roman coins found, Stroud, p. 112a.
Cassey Compton, undated settlement, Compton Abdale, p. 37b.
Castle Bank, earthworks, probably mediaeval, Saintbury, p. 99a.
,, **End Bungalow,** Roman objects found, Upton St. Leonards, p. 123a.
Castle Godwyn, another name for Painswick (2), p. 91b.
'Castle Hill', possible Iron Age defences, Brockworth, p. 22a.
Castles, The, Hill-fort, Dowdeswell (1), pp. xxv, 43b, Pl. 38.
,, ,, ,, , Horton (1), pp. xxv, xxvi, 65b, Pl. 35.
Cat, p. 58b; *see also* **Animal Bones.**
Catti, p. 100b; *see also* **Coins: Iron Age;** *and* Chronology, p. 136.
Cattle stalls, indicated at Sudeley (4), pp. xl, 114a.
Catuvellauni, *see* **Coins: Iron Age;** *also* Chronology, p. 136.
Cave, Dr. Richard, Preface, pp. xx, xxx, xxxiiia.
Cave Close, Roman villa, Daglingworth (2), p. 41b.
Ceastel, chessells, Preface, p. lii.
Ceiling, p. 51a; *see also* **Building Materials.**
'Celtic' Fields:
Preface, pp. xlviii–xlix.
Aldsworth (1), p. 2b; Badminton (1), p. 6a, Pl. 42; Bagendon (2), p. 9a; Barnsley (2), p. 11a; Eastleach (1), p. 51b, Pl. 43; (3), p. 52b; Tormarton (1), p. 120a, Pl. 43.
Probable: Bagendon (2), p. 9a; Bibury (3), p. 14b; Compton Abdale (1), p. 37b; (2), p. 38b; Duntisbourne Rouse (4), p. 49a; Frocester, p. 56b; North Cerney, p. 85b; Rendcomb, p. 98a; Stinchcombe (2), p. 111b; Tormarton (1), p. 120a, Pl. 43.
Cemeteries, *see* **Burials.**
Censorine Gaudeas, inscription on silver spoon, Chedworth (1), p. 27b.
Chalford, p. 23a.
Champion, Mrs. S. J., Leckhampton (1), p. 77b.
Chape, bone, Whittington (2), p. 126b.
Charcoal, Bagendon (1), p. 8a.
Charlton Kings, p. 23a.
Charnal Plantation, undated ditches, Temple Guiting (6), p. 117b; (7), p. 117b.
Chavenage, fibulae, Beverstone, p. 13b.
Chedworth, p. 24a.
,, **Museum:** Batsford, p. 12a; Chedworth, pp. 24–29; Compton Abdale (1), p. 38b.
,, **Woods,** Roman villa, Chedworth (1), pp. xxxix, xlii, 24b, Pls. 2–7, 25–6.
Cheltenham College Museum: Woodchester, p. 132a.
Cheltenham Museum: Bourton-on-the-Water (1), p. 19b; (2a), p. 20a; Compton Abdale (1), p. 38a; Condicote (2), p. 39b; Hampnett, p. 62a; Oxenton, p. 91a; Southam, p. 106b; Sudeley (4), p. 114b; Whittington (2), p. 126b; Willersey (2), p. 130a.
Cherry, wood, Great Witcombe (1), p. 61b.
Chessells, Chesle etc., Preface, p. lii; *see also* **Field Names.**
Chessalls, Romano-British settlement, Kingscote (1), pp. xliii, xlvii, liii, 71a.
Chessalls, The, undated enclosures, Wotton-under-Edge (1), p. 135a.
Chessells, Romano-British settlement, Preface, pp. xxiv, lii.
Chessels, Roman villa, Great Rissington (1), pp. xlii, liii, 59b.
Chessels, Romano-British settlement, Lower Slaughter (1), pp. xliii, xliv, xlvii, liii, 79a.
Chessels, The, Romano-British settlement, Coln St. Aldwyns (2), pp. xliii, liii, 37a.
Chestals Farm, Roman building, Dursley (1), pp. xliii, liii, 49b.
Chestels, Dyrham and Hinton, Preface, p. lii.
Chestles, Romano-British settlement, Farmington (2), pp. xliii, liii, 55b.
Chest, bronze studded, Lower Slaughter (1), p. 79b.

Chesterton Farm, Romano-British settlement, Cirencester (3), pp. xliii, 30a.
Cherington, p. 29a.
Chi-Rho, Chedworth (1), p. 26b.
Chipping Campden, p. 29b.
,, **Sodbury,** Romano-British finds, Sodbury, p. 103a.
Chisels, iron, Barnsley (1), p. 9b; Chedworth (1), p. 27b; Kingscote (1), p. 72b; Lower Slaughter (1), p. 79b; Painswick (2), p. 94a; Whittington (2), p. 126b.
Christianity, evidence of, Preface, pp. xxxvi, li; Barnsley (1), p. 9b; Chedworth (1), p. 26b.
Chronology, Preface, p. xxiv, *also* p. 136.
Church Row Cottages, tesserae found, Chedworth, p. 24a.
Churches, Romano-British material found in or near: Bisley with Lypiatt, p. 14b; Bitton, p. 16b; Boxwell with Leighterton, p. 21b; Brockworth (2), p. 22a; Daglingworth (2), p. 41b; Frocester (1), p. 57a; King's Stanley, p. 70a; Poulton, p. 94b; Swell (1), p. 115a; Whittington (3), p. 126 to 128; Winchcombe, p. 130b; Woodchester (1), p. 132b.
Cinerary Urn, *see* **Burials.**
Cirencester, p. 29b.
,, **Park,** enclosure, Daglingworth (3), p. 41b.
Cist burials, *see* **Burials.**
Cisterns, Chedworth (1), p. 27b.
Clapton, p. 31b.
Clark's Lane, Romano-British settlement, Siddington (3), p. 102a.
Clarke, Mr. Giles, Preface, p. xx; Woodchester (1), p. 132b.
Clasp Knife, Frocester (2), p. 58a.
Claudian finds, Kingscote (1), p. 72a; *see also* **Coins: Roman.**
Claudio-Neronian samian ware, Kingscote (1), p. 72b.
Claudius, *see* **Coins: Roman;** *also* Chronology, p. 136.
Claudius Gothicus, *see* **Coins: Roman;** *also* Chronology, p. 136.
Claydon House, undated enclosures, tracks and linear ditches, Lechlade (8), p. 75b.
Claypits Wood, enclosures, tracks and linear ditches, Kingscote (4), p. 73a.
Clearcupboard, Roman villa, Farmington (1), pp. xxiv, xlii, liii, 55b.
Cleeve, Roman finds, Southam, p. 106a.
,, **Cloud,** Hill-fort, Southam (1), pp. xxiii, xxv, xxvi, 106a, Pl. 40; dyke running across, Southam (6), p. 107b.
,, **Hill,** Roman finds, Southam, p. 106b.
,, **Lodge,** Iron Age settlement S.E. of, Southam (2), p. 107b.
Clifford, Mrs. E. M., Bagendon (1), p. 7a; Edgeworth (1), p. 53a; Great Witcombe (1), p. 60b; Minchinhampton (1), p. 83a; (7), p. 83b.
Club Wheat, *see* **Corn.**
Coal: Badgeworth (1), p. 6a; Bagendon (1), p. 8a; Compton Abdale (1), p. 38b; Frocester (2), p. 58b; Great Witcombe (1), p. 61b; Lower Slaughter (1), p. 79b; Whittington (3), p. 128a.
Coaley, p. 31b.
,, **Peak,** rectangular enclosure, Coaley (2), p. 32a.
Coates, p. 32a.
Coberley, p. 33a.
Cocca Burh, Gotherington (1), pp. lii, 59a.
Cockbury Butts, note on p. 59 and p. lii.
Coffin Tyning, p. 16b; *see also* **Field Names.**
Coffins, *see* **Burials.**
Coin dies, p. 7b; *see also* **Coins: Iron Age,** MOULDS FOR.
,, **Slade,** probable Romano-British settlement, Quenington (3), pp. xliii, 97a.
Coins: Iron Age: *See also* Chronology, p. 136.
ARMORICAN BASE SILVER: Sapperton, p. 99a.
BRITISH 'B': Tetbury, p. 119b.
BRITISH 'Q': Beverstone, p. 13b.
BRITISH RA: Tetbury, p. 119b; Uley, p. 121a.
CATUVELLAUNIAN: Bagendon (1), p. 7b; Bourton-on-the Water (1), p. 19b.
CLASS 'A': Naunton (1), p. 84b.
CLASS 'B': Bourton-on-the-Water (1), p. 19b; Naunton (1), p. 84b.
CLASS 'C': Bourton-on-the-Water (1), p. 19b.
CLASS 'E': Naunton (1), p. 84b.
DOBUNNIC: Bagendon (1), p. 7b; Bourton-on-the-Water (1), p. 19b; Gotherington (1), p. 59a; Whittington (2), p. 125b.
GOLD: Cowley, p. 39b; Minchinhampton, p. 81a; Nailsworth, p. 84b; Rodmarton, p. 98a; Sapperton, p. 99a; Sherborne, p. 100b; Uley, p. 121a; Willersey (3), p. 130a.

Coins: Iron Age, *cont.*
DOBUNNIC, *cont.*
INSCRIBED:
ANTED: Bagendon (1), p. 7b; Hazleton (1), p. 65a; Nailsworth p. 84b; Sherborne, p. 100b.
BODVOC: Colesbourne, p. 34b; Cowley, p. 39b; Minchinhampton, p. 81a; Rodmarton, p. 98a; Sapperton, p. 99a; Willersey (3), p. 130a.
CATTI: Sherborne, p. 100b.
COMVX: Bisley with Lypiatt, p. 14b.
CORIO: Preface, p. xxxiv.
EISU: Preface, p. xxxiv; Bagendon (1), p. 7b; Sherborne, p. 100b; Whittington (2), p. 125b.
EPATTICU: Bagendon (1), p. 7b.
SILVER: Bagendon (1), p. 7b; Colesbourne, p. 34b; Hazleton (1), p. 65a; Kingscote (1), p. 72a; Naunton (1), p. 84b.
DUROTRIGIAN: Bagendon (1), p. 7b.
GALLO-BELGIC (gold): Sodbury, p. 103a.
MOULDS FOR: Bagendon (1), p. 7b.
POTIN: Shipton, p. 101a.
TASCIOVANUS: Bourton-on-the-Water (1), p. 19b.
Coins: Roman: *See also* Chronology, p. 136.
ASSES: Kingscote (1), p. 72a; Stanway (1), p. 111a.
DUPONDIUS: Rodborough (1), p. 98a.
FOLLES: Bourton-on-the-Water (2c), p. 20b.
MINIMI: Frocester (2), p. 58a.
MINIMISSIMI: Bourton-on-the-Water (2b), p. 20b; Lower Slaughter (1), p. 79b.
URBS ROMA: Painswick (3), p. 94a.
OF THE 1ST CENTURY: Whittington (2), p. 126b.
CLAUDIUS I: Baunton (1), p. 13b; Bourton-on-the-Water (1a), p. 19b.
DOMITIAN: Dursley, p. 49b; Great Witcombe (1), p. 61b; Sudeley (2), p. 113b; Whittington (2), p. 126b.
GERMANICUS: Woodchester, p. 132a.
NERO: Kingscote (1), p. 72a.
VESPASIAN: Whittington (2), p. 126b.
OF THE 2ND CENTURY: Chalford (1), p. 23a; Naunton (1), p. 84b; Rodmarton (1), p. 98b; Stanway (1), p. 111a; Uley, p. 121a.
ANTONINUS PIUS: Stanway (1), p. 111a; Temple Guiting, p. 116b.
FAUSTINA II: Brimpsfield, p. 21b.
HADRIAN: Lower Slaughter (3), p. 80a; Sudeley (2), p. 113b; Woodchester (1), p. 134a.
L. VERUS: Bourton-on-the-Water (2b), p. 20b.
M. AURELIUS: Bourton-on-the-Water (2b), p. 20b.
SEVERUS ALEXANDER: King's Stanley, p. 70a; Rodmarton, p. 98a.
TRAJAN: Stanway (1), p. 111a; Uley (2), p. 121b.
OF THE 3RD CENTURY: Badgeworth, p. 5b; Bagendon (1), p. 7b; Barnsley (1), p. 9b; Batsford (1), p. 13a; Bisley with Lypiatt (1), p. 16b; Blockley (1), p. 17b; Coln St. Aldwyns (2), p. 37a; Duntisbourne Abbots (1), p. 48a; Horsley (1), p. 65a; Lechlade (5), p. 75a; Long Newnton (1), p. 78a; Naunton (1), p. 84b; Preston, p. 95a; Sapperton, p. 99a; Southam (3), p. 107b; Stroud, p. 112a; Sudeley, p. 112a; (4), p. 114b; (5), p. 115a; Tetbury Upton (1), p. 119b; Uley (1), p. 121b; (2), p. 123a; Withington (2), p. 132a.
ALLECTUS: Adlestrop, p. 1b; Cirencester (1), p. 30a; Compton Abdale (4), p. 38b; Stroud, p. 112a.
CARAUSIUS: Elkstone (1), p. 54b; Swell (2), p. 116a.
CARUS: Baunton (1), p. 13b.
CLAUDIUS GOTHICUS: Haresfield (3), p. 64a; Rodmarton, p. 98a.
GALLIENUS: Bourton-on-the-Water (2c), p. 20b; Quenington (3), p. 97a; Sodbury (1), p. 103b.
SALONINA: Uley (1), p. 121b.
TETRICUS AND THE TETRICI: Bisley with Lypiatt (1), p. 16b; Woodchester (1), p. 134a.
TRAJAN DECIUS: Baunton (1), p. 13b.
VALERIAN: Withington (2), p. 132a.
VICTORINUS: Bisley with Lypiatt, p. 15a.
OF THE 4TH CENTURY: Ashley (1), p. 4b; Badgeworth, p. 5b; Bagendon (1), p. 7b; Barnsley (1), p. 9b; Batsford (1), p. 13a; Baunton (1), p. 13b; Blockley (1), p. 17b; Chedworth, p. 24a; (1), p. 27b; Cirencester (2), p. 30a; Colin St. Aldwyns (2), p. 37a; Daglingworth, p. 41b; Duntisbourne Abbots (1), p. 48a; Farmington (1), p. 55b; Frocester (3), p. 58b; Horsley (1), p. 65a; Lechlade (5), p. 75a; Lower Slaughter (1), p. 79b; (3), p. 80a; Miserden, p. 84a; Poulton, p. 94b; Rodmarton (1), p. 98b;

Coins: Roman, *cont.*
OF THE 4TH CENTURY, *cont.*
Stroud, p. 112a; Sudeley, p. 112a; (4), p. 114b; (5), p. 115b; Temple Guiting, note, p. 117b; Tetbury Upton (1), p. 119b; Uley, p. 121a; (2), p. 123a; Whittington (2), p. 126b; (3), p. 128a; Willersey (2), p. 130a; Withington (2), p. 132a.
CONSTANS: King's Stanley, p. 70a; Leonard Stanley, p. 78a; Poulton, p. 94b.
CONSTANTINE: Chedworth (6), p. 29a; Cirencester (2), p. 30a; Colesbourne (2), p. 36a; Painswick (2), p. 94a; Swell, p. 115a; (1), p. 116a.
CONSTANTINE I: Coln St. Aldwyns (2), p. 37a; Haresfield (3), p. 64a; Kingscote (1), p. 72b; Uley, p. 121a; Whittington (3), p. 128a.
CONSTANTINE II: Coln St. Aldwyns (2), p. 37a; Haresfield (3), p. 64a.
CONSTANTIUS II: Frocester (2), p. 58a; Siddington (3), p. 102a; Sodbury (1), p. 103b; Temple Guiting, p. 116b; (2), p. 117a.
CRISPUS: Yanworth (1), p. 135b.
DIOCLETIAN: Withington (2), p. 132a.
GRATIAN: Barrington (2), p. 12a; Chedworth (1), p. 27b; Colesbourne (2), p. 36a; Temple Guiting (2), p. 117a.
MAGNENTIUS: Bourton-on-the-Water (2c), p. 20b; Cirencester (2), p. 30a; Colesbourne (2), p. 36a; Lower Slaughter (1), p. 79b.
THEODOSIUS: Harescombe (1), p. 62b; Uley (2), p. 123b; Whittington (3), p. 128a.
VALENS: Cirencester (2), p. 30a; Dodington, p. 43a; King's Stanley, p. 70a; Lower Slaughter (1), p. 79b; Quenington (3), p. 97a; Temple Guiting, p. 116b; Woodchester (1), p. 134a.
VALENTINIAN: Colesbourne (2), p. 36a; Dodington, p. 43a.
OF THE 5TH CENTURY: Long Newnton (1), p. 78b.
ARCADIUS: Cirencester (2), p. 30a; Frocester (2), p. 57b; Lower Slaughter (3), p. 80a; Sudeley (2), p. 113b; Whittington (2), p. 126b.
HONORIUS: Ampney Crucis, p. 3a; Lower Slaughter (3), p. 80a.
THEODOSIUS (HOUSE OF): Great Witcombe (1), p. 61b; Kingscote (1), p. 72b.
HOARDS: Ampney St. Peter, p. 3b; Bisley with Lypiatt (1), p. 16b; Cirencester (2), p. 30a; Dodington, p. 43a; Haresfield (2), p. 64a; Lower Slaughter (1), p. 79b; Rodmarton (1), p. 98b; Sapperton, p. 99a; Willersey (2), p. 130a.
UNSPECIFIED: Ampney Crucis, p. 3a; Aston Blank, p. 4b.
Colchester brooch, Bagendon (1), p. 7b.
Cold Ashton, p. 34b.
,, **Aston Camp,** Aston Blank, Preface, p. xxix.
,, **Slad,** Quenington (3), p. lii and note on p. 97.
Cole's Hill, probable Romano-British shrine, Sudeley (5), p. 114b.
Colesbourne, p. 34b.
Colethrop, Romano-British settlement, Haresfied (5), p. 64b.
Coln St. Aldwyns, p. 36b.
,, **Dennis,** p. 37a.
Colour-coated ware, *see* **Pottery: Roman.**
Column fragments, *see* **Building Remains.**
Combs, bone, Upper Slaughter, p. 123a; Withington (1), p. 131b.
Combend, Roman villa, Colesbourne (2), pp. liii, 35, Pl. 7.
Compton Abdale, p. 37b.
,, **Grove,** Roman villa, Compton Abdale (1), p. 37b; probable Romano-British enclosure, Compton Abdale (2), p. 38b.
Comvx, p. 14b; *see also* **Coins: Iron Age;** *and* Chronology, p. 136.
Concordia, inscription on gold bezel, Quenington (3), p. 97a.
Concrete, *see* **Building Materials.**
Condicote, p. 39a.
,, **Camp,** Condicote, pp. xxx, xxxiia, 39a.
,, **Lane,** Roman road near, Bourton-on-the-Water (3), pp. xlv, 21a.
Congrove, Roman objects found, Bitton, p. 16b.
Constans, *see* **Coins: Roman:** *also* Chronology, p. 136.
Constantine, *see* **Coins: Roman;** *also* Chronology, p. 136.
Constantius II, *see* **Coins: Roman;** *also* Chronology, p. 136.
Continuity, Iron Age to Roman, Preface, p. xxiv; Roman to Saxon, Preface, p. xliv.
Cooking pots, metal, Kempsford, p. 68a.
Cooper's Hill, possible Iron Age defences, Brockworth, pp. xxix, xxx, lii, 22a; cross-ridge dyke, (1), p. 22a.
Cooper's Hill Farm, villa near, Great Witcombe (1), p. 60b.
Copse Hill, Romano-British finds, Upper Slaughter, p. 123a; contracted burial, Upper Slaughter, p. 123a.
Corinian School of Mosaicists, *see* **Mosaicists.**
Corinion, probably Bagendon (1), p. 6b.
Corinium, Cirencester, p. 29b.
Corinium Dobunnorum:
Discussion, Preface, pp. xxxiv–xxxvi, xliii–xlv.
Map of environs, facing p. xxxvi.
Corinium Museum: Baunton (1), p. 13b; Beverstone, p. 13b; Bisley with Lypiatt (1), p. 16b; Bourton-on-the-Water (1), p. 19b; Chedworth, p. 24b; Cirencester, p. 29b; (2), p. 30a; Coln St. Aldwyns, p. 36b; Daglingworth, p. 41b; Hawling, p. 65a; Kingscote (1), pp. 68b; 73a; Poulton, p. 94b; Quenington (3), p. 97a; Rodmarton (1), p. 98b; Siddington, p. 101b; Tetbury, p. 119b; Uley, p. 121a.
Corio, *see* **Coins: Iron Age;** *also* Chronology, p. 136.
Corn:
WHEAT: Frocester (2), p. 58b; Upton St. Leonards (1), p. 123b; Whittington (3), p. 127b.
BARLEY: Frocester (2), p. 58b.
Corn-drying ovens, *see* **Ovens.**
Cosmetic palette, stone, Chedworth (6), p. 29a.
Cotteswold Sands, Harescombe (1), p. 62a; Sudeley (2), p. 112b; Temple Guiting (11), p. 119a.
Counters, glass, Bagendon (1), p. 8a.
Cow, p. 55b; *see also* **Animal Bones.**
Cow-byre, possible, Rodmarton (1), pp. xl, 98a.
'Cow Pasture', Roman villa, Whittington (3), pp. xlii, 126b, Pls. 9, 30.
Cowley, p. 39b.
Cowley Wood, undated enclosure S. of, Cowley (6), p. 40b.
Cox, Mr. W., Preface, p. xx; Whittington (2), p. 125b.
Cranham, p. 40b.
Cremations, *see* **Burials.**
Cresset lamp, stone, Farmington (1), p. 55b.
Crickley Hill, hill-fort, Coberley (1), pp. xxiv–xxvi, 33a, Pl. 40; probable Iron Age skeleton found, Badgeworth, p. 5b.
Crispus, p. 135b; *see also* **Coins: Roman,** *and* Chronology, p. 136.
Crockemede, Brockworth, p. lii.
Crop-Marks: Preface, pp. xxvii, xxx, xxxiii, xlii, xlviii, xlvix, l, lii–iii, Pls. 54–66; Ampney Crucis (1), p. 3b; Bagendon (1), p. 8a; Barnsley (3), p. 11b; (4), p. 11b; (5), p. 11b; Batsford (1), p. 12b; Baunton, p. 13b; Bourton-on-the-Water (4), p. 21a; Cirencester (3), p. 30a; (4), p. 30b; (5), p. 30b; (6), p. 31a; Coaley (2), p. 32a; Coates (2), (3), p. 32a; (4), p. 32a; Coln St. Aldwyns (3), p. 37a; Coln St. Dennis (1), p. 37; Condicote (1), p. 39; Cowley (6), p. 40b; Daglingworth (3), p. 41b; Didmarton (1), p. 42b; Down Ampney (1), p. 44b; (2), p. 44b; (3), p. 45a; (4), p. 45a; Driffield (1), p. 45; (2), p. 47a; (3), p. 47a; Duntisbourne Abbots, p. 48a; Duntisbourne Rouse (2), (3), p. 49a; Dyrham and Hinton (2), p. 51b; Elkstone (2), p. 54b; Fairford (1), p. 54b; (2), (3), (4) to (6), p. 55a; Farmington (3), p. 56a; Gotherington (2), p. 59a; Great Rissington (2), p. 60a; Hampnett (1), p. 62a; Hatherop (1), p. 64b; Horsley (3), p. 65b; Kemble (1), p. 68a; Kempsford (2)–(5), p. 68b; (6), (7), p. 69b; Kingscote (1), p. 71a; (3)–(6), p. 73a; Lechlade (2)–(3), p. 73b; (6), p. 75a; (8)–(13), p. 75b; (14)–(15), p. 76a; Leonard Stanley (1), p. 78a; Longborough (1), p. 78b; Lower Slaughter (2), (3), p. 80a; (4), p. 80b; Maiseyhampton (1), p. 80b; Moreton-in-Marsh (1), p. 84a; Naunton (2), p. 85a; North Cerney (3), p. 86a; Northleach with Eastington (1), p. 90a; (3), p. 90b; Notgrove (1), p. 91a; Poole Keyes (1), p. 94b; (4), (5), p. 97a; Rodmarton, p. 98b; Sapperton (1), p. 99b; 100a; Sevenhampton (1), p. 100b; Sherborne (1), p. 100b; Shipton (2), p. 101a; Siddington (2), p. 101b; (4)–(6), p. 102a; (7), (8), p. 103a; Snowshill (1), p. 103a; Somerford Keynes (1), p. 104a; (2)–(5), p. 105a; (6), p. 105b; South Cerney (1), (2), p. 105b; (3), p. 106a; Southrop (1), (2), p. 109a; (3), p. 109b; Stanway (4), p. 111a; Temple Guiting (5), (6), (7), p. 117b; (9)–(11), p. 119a; Tormarton (2), p. 120b; Uley (1), p. 121b; Whittington (2), p. 125b; Wotton-under-Edge (1), p. 135a; Yanworth (2), p. 135b.
Cross-ridge dykes, *see* **Dykes and Ditches.**
Crossroads Barn, undated enclosures and linear ditches, Quenington (5), p. 97a.
Crown, Roman, bronze, Leckhampton, p. 77a.
Cryptogram, probably Christian, Preface, p. xxxvi.
Culkerton Wood, Roman road passes through, Rodmarton, p. 98b.
Cupid, p. 134a; *see also* **Gods.**

Currency Bars, hoard, Bourton-on-the-Water (1), p. 19b; votive, miniature, Bagendon (1), p. 7b.
Custom Scrubs, Roman sculpture found, Bisley with Lypiatt, p. 14b.
Cutham Lane, dyke at Bagendon (1), p. 8a, Pl. 47.
Cutsdean, p. 41b.
Cynges Ferd-straet, Preface, p. xlvii.

Daggers:
IRON: Cowley (1), p. 39a; Woodchester (1), p. 134a.
BRONZE: (Miniature) Southam, p. 106a.
Daglingworth, p. 41b.
Dark Lane, Roman building, Chedworth (2), p. 28a.
Dartley Farm, Romano-British settlement, Duntisbourne Rouse (4), p. 49a.
Deadlands Copse, 'Celtic' Fields overlying, Barnsley (2), p. 11a.
Dean Camp, Hill-fort, Coln St. Aldwyns (1), pp. xxv, 36b.
Dea Regina, *see* **Gods.**
Deer, red, *see* **Animal Bones** *and* **Antlers.**
Defences of Hill-forts, discussion, Preface, p. xxvi.
Diana, p. xxxvi; *see also* **Gods.**
Didmarton, p. 42b.
Diocletian, p. 132a; *see also* **Coins: Roman.** Administration of, Preface, p. xxxv; Chronology, p. 136.
Discredited Hill-forts, *see* **'Hill-forts', discredited.**
Distribution, Preface, p. xxiii; map, end-pocket.
Ditches, *see* **Dykes and Linear Ditches.**
Ditches, The, North Cerney (2), pp. lii, 85b.
Dividers, Chedworth, p. 24a; Whittington (2), p. 126b.
Dixon, Mr. P., Coberley (1), p. 33b.
Dixton Hill, Alderton, Preface, pp. xxix, xxxia, lii, 2a.
Dobunni:
Capital of the, Preface, p. xxxv.
Chronology, p. 136.
Coins of, *see* **Coins: Iron Age.**
Kings, *see* **Anted, Eisu, Corio,** *and* **Bodvoc.**
Territory, Preface, p. xxxiv.
Dodington, p. 43a.
Dog, *see* **Animal Bones.**
Domitian, *see* **Coins: Roman**; *also* Chronology, p. 136.
Donnington, p. 43b.
Door-latch, iron, Lower Slaughter (1), p. 79b.
Dorn, settlement and possible Roman fort, Batsford (1), pp. xxxiv, xxxvii, xliii, xliv, lii, liii, 12a, Pl. 48.
Double-ditched enclosure, *see* **Enclosures.**
Dowdeswell, p. 43b.
,, **'Camp',** pp. xxix, xxx, xxxiia, 43b.
,, **Hill,** Hill-fort, Dowdeswell (1), p. 43b, Pl. 38.
Down Ampney, p. 44b.
Downs Farm, Baunton (1), p. 13b.
Doynton, p. 45a.
,, **Camps,** Doynton, pp. xxx, 45a.
Drakestone Point, Stinchcombe, pp. xxix, xxiva, 111a.
Driffield, p. 45b.
Drum, The, Icomb (1), pp. xxv, 66b.
Dryhill, Roman coins found, Badgeworth, p. 5b; Roman villa, Badgeworth (1), pp. xlii, liii, 5b.
Dryleaze Farm, undated enclosures and trackway W. of, Siddington (4), p. 102b.
Duck, p. 58b; *see also* **Animal Bones.**
Duck-stamped ware, *see* **Pottery: Iron Age.**
Dudgrove Farm, enclosures near, Kempsford (6), p. 69a, Pl. 62.
,, **Ham Barn,** enclosure of 'Highworth' type, Kempsford, p. 68a, Pl. 64.
Dunning, Dr. G. C., Preface, p. xx; Bourton-on-the-Water (1), p. 17a.
Duntisbourne Abbots, p. 48a.
Duntisbourne Leer, Romano-British building, Duntisbourne Abbots (1), pp. xliii, 48a.
Duntisbourne Rouse, p. 48b.
Dupondius, Claudian, p. 98a; *see also* **Coins: Roman.**
Durnovarian School of Mosaicists, *see* **Mosaicists.**
Durotrigian, p. 7b; *see also* **Coins: Iron Age.**
Dursley, p. 49b.
Dyke Hills, Dorchester, Oxon., cf. Bourton-on-the-Water (1), pp. xxvi, 17a.
Dykes and Linear Ditches:
DITCHES: Coates (5), p. 32a; Coln St. Dennis (1), p. 37a; Condicote (1), p. 39a; Down Ampney (1), p. 44b; Driffield (2), p. 47a; (3), p. 47a; Fairford (2), p. 55a; Kempsford (2)–(4), p. 68b; (7), p. 69b; Kingscote (4), (6), p. 73a; Lechlade (3), p. 73b; (8), (9), (11), (12), p. 75b; (14), (15), pp. 77a; Minchinhampton (1)–(8), pp. 83–4; Northleach with Eastington (3), p. 88b; Preston (1), (2), p. 95a; (5), p. 97a; Siddington (6), p. 102b; (8), p. 103a; Sodbury (1), p. 103b; Somerford Keynes (3), p. 105a; (5), p. 105a; South Cerney (1), p. 105b; Southrop (3), p. 109b; Stanway (5), p. 111a; Temple Guiting (5), (6), p. 117b; (8), (9), (10), p. 119a; Yanworth (2), p. 135b.
DYKES: Bagendon (1), pp. 6–9; Cranham (1), p. 41a; Southam (6), p. 107b.
CROSS-RIDGE: Brockworth (1), p. 22a; Edgeworth (1), p. 53a; King's Stanley (1), p. 70a; Randwick (1), p. 97b.
LINEAR: Bagendon (1), p. 8a; Charlton Kings (2), p. 23b; Daglingworth (1), p. 41b; Doynton (1), p. 45a.
Dyrham and Hinton, p. 51a.
Dyrham Camp, Dyrham and Hinton (1), pp. xxv, note on p. 51.

Eagle, carved limestone, Sudeley (5), p. 115a.
'Eald Dic', Saxon, Doynton (1), p. 45b.
Earthenware, *see* **Voussoirs** *and* **Tesserae.**
Earthworks (including faint vestiges):
AMPHITHEATRE: Preface, p. xxxv.
BARROW (IRON AGE): Leckhampton (2), p. 78a; *see also* **Barrows.**
'CELTIC' FIELDS: Aldsworth (1), p. 2b; Badminton (1), p. 6a; Barnsley (2), p. 11a; Compton Abdale (6), p. 38b; Eastleach (1), p. 51b; (3), p. 52b.
DISCREDITED HILL-FORTS: Alderton, pp. xxx, xxxi, 2a; Condicote, pp. xxx, xxxi, 39a; Cowley, pp. xxx, xxxii, 39b; King's Stanley, pp. xxx, xxxii; Nympsfield, pp. xxx, 91a; Oxenton (1), pp. xxx, 91a; Winchcombe, pp. xxx, xxxiv, 130a.
DYKES: (Preface, pp. xxvi–xxvii). Brockworth (1), p. 22a; Charlton Kings (2), p. 23b; Cranham (1), p. 41a; Doynton (1), p. 45a; Edgeworth (1), p. 53a; King's Stanley (1), p. 70a; Minchinhampton (1)–(8), pp. 83–4; Randwick (1), p. 97b; Southam (6), p. 107b.
ENCLOSURES WITH CAUSEWAYED DITCH: Condicote, p. 39a.
MOUNDS: Bisley with Lypiatt (2), p. 16b; Chalford, p. 23a.
RINGWORKS: Southam (4), (5), p. 107b.
ROADS, ROMAN: Batsford (3), p. 13a; Bourton-on-the-Hill (1), p. 17b; Chipping Camden (1), p. 29b; Cowley (2), p. 40a; Eastleach (2), p. 52a; North Cerney (4), p. 86a; Quenington (2), p. 95b; Stow-on-the-Wold (1), p. 111a.
SETTLEMENT, IRON AGE: Southam (3), p. 107b.
SETTLEMENTS, ROMANO-BRITISH: (Preface, p. xliii). Avening (2), p. 5a; Batsford (1), p. 12a; Duntisbourne Rouse (4), p. 49a; Sapperton (1), p. 99b.
SETTLEMENTS WITH DYKES, IRON AGE: Bagendon (1), p. 6b; Daglingworth (1), p. 41b; North Cerney (1), p. 85b.
TEMPLE, ROMAN: Chedworth (4), p. 28a.
TERRACES: Preface, p. xliv.
UNDATED: Avening, p. 4a; Bagendon (2), p. 9a; Batsford (2), p. 13a; Bibury, p. 13b; Coates (6), p. 32b; Cold Ashton, p. 34b; Compton Abdale (2), p. 38b; Dowdeswell, p. 43b; Rodborough (1), p. 98a; Siddington (3), p. 102a; Southam (3), p. 107b.
VILLAS, ROMAN: Barnsley (1), p. 9a; Bibury (2), p. 14b; Chedworth (1), p. 24b; Colesbourne (2), p. 35b; Compton Abdale (1), p.37b; Great Rissington (1), p. 59b; Great Witcombe (1), p. 60b; Sudeley (2), p. 112b; (4), p. 113b; Swell (2), p. 115b; Whittington (3), p. 126b.
See also:
DESERTED MEDIEVAL VILLAGES, SITE OF ROMANO-BRITISH SETTLEMENTS: Blockley (1), p. 17a; Whittington (3), p. 126b.
MEDIAEVAL: Bitton, p. 16b; Whittington (3), p. 126b.
PILLOW-MOUNDS: Minchinhampton, pp. 83–4.
RIDGE AND FURROW: Charlton Kings, p. 23a; Great Witcombe (1), p. 60b.
STRIP LYNCHETS: Preface, p. xlviii.
Eastbury, former name for Haresfield (2), note on p. lii and 64a.
Eastington, *see* **Ampney St. Peter,** p. 3b.
Eastleach, p. 51b.
Easton Grey, route of Foss Way, Preface, p. xlvii.
Ebrington, p. 52b.
Edgeworth, p. 53a.

Eisu, *see* **Coins: Iron Age;** *also* Chronology, p. 136.
Eldon, Lord, Chedworth (1), p. 24b.
Elkstone, p. 53b.
Elmcote Farm, Romano-British pottery found, Coaley, p. 31b.
Enamel decorated articles, *see* **Birds, Brooches,** *and* **Harness Mount.**
Enclosures:
Preface, p. xliii, Pls. 40, 41, 54–66.
CIRCULAR: Lower Slaughter (4), p. 80b.
'HIGHWORTH' TYPE: Kempsford, p. 68a.
RECTANGULAR AND RECTILINEAR: Batsford (2), p. 13a; Cirencester (4)–(6), p. 30b; Coaley (2), p. 32a; Coates (6), p. 32b; Coln St. Dennis (1), p. 37a; Compton Abdale (2), p. 38b; Condicote (1), p. 39a; Cowley (6), p. 40b; Daglingworth (3), p. 41b; Down Ampney (1), p. 44b; (3), (4), p. 45a; Driffield (2), p. 47a; Duntisbourne Abbots (2), p. 48a; Duntisbourne Rouse (4), p. 49a; Elkstone (2), p. 54b; Fairford (2), (4)–(6), p. 55a; Farmington (3), p. 56a; Gotherington (2), p. 59a; Hampnett (1), p. 62a; Harescombe (2), p. 62b; Horsley (3), p. 65b; Kempsford (2)–(5), p. 68b; (6), (7), p. 69a; Kingscote (3)–(6), p. 73a; Lechlade (2), (3), p. 73b; (8)–(12), p. 75b; Lower Slaughter (2), p. 80a; Naunton (2), p. 85a; Northleach with Eastington (3), p. 88b; Notgrove (1), p. 91a; Poole Keynes (1), p. 94b; Preston (1)–(3), p. 95; Quenington (5), p. 97a; Sevenhampton (1), p. 100a; Shipton (2)–(3), p. 101; Siddington (2), p. 101a ; (4), (5), p. 102b; Somerford Keynes (3), p. 105a; South Cerney (1), (2), p. 105a; (3), p. 106a; Southam (4), (5), p. 107b; Southrop (1), (2), p. 109a; Stanway (4), (5), p. 111a; Temple Guiting (5), (6), p.117b; (9)–(11), p. 119a; Tormarton (2), (3), p. 120b; Wotton-under Edge (1), p. 135a.
DOUBLE-DITCHED: Fairford (3), p. 55a; Somerford Keynes (4), p. 105a.
ROMAN: Duntisbourne Abbots (2), p. 48a.
Enoch's Hill Camp, probably mediaeval, Horsley, pp. xxx, 65a.
Epaticcu, p. 7b; *see also* **Coins: Iron Age;** *and* Chronology, p. 136.
Eresbury, Haresfield (1), p. 64.
Ermin Street, *see* **Roman Roads.**
Estbury, Haresfield (2), p. 64.
Eubury Camp, alleged hill-fort, Condicote, pp. xxix, xxx, xxxi, 39a, Pl. 68.
Evans-Lawrence, Miss S., Preface, p. xx.
Evenlode, p. 54b.
Ewen, flue-tiles, Kemble, p. 68a.
,, **Bridge,** undated enclosure S.W. of, Siddington (2), p. 101b.
Ezimbury, Haresfield (2), p. 64.

Fairford, p. 54b.
Farmington, p. 55b.
'Farmington Villa', possibly Norbury Camp, Northleach with Eastington (1), p. 87a.
Farrer, James, Chedworth (1), p. 24b; (5), p. 28b.
Faustina II, p. 21b; *see also* **Coins: Roman,** *and* Chronology, p. 136.
Fibulae, *see* **Brooches.**
Field Farm, Romano-British pottery, Nympsfield, p. 91a.
Field's Farm, probable Romano-British enclosure, Duntisbourne Abbots (2), p. 48a.
Field Names: *See also* Appendix A, p. lii.
BIG STANBOROUGH: Frocester (2), p. 57a.
BLACKIES FIELD: Marshfield, p. 80b.
CALMSDEN FIELD: North Cerney, p. 85a.
CHESSELS: Great Rissington (1), p. 59b.
CHURCH PIECE: Bisley with Lypiatt (1), p. 15b.
COFFIN TYNING: Bitton, p. 16b.
GREAT CHESSELS: Lower Slaughter (1), p. 79a; Sodbury, Preface, p. lii.
LITTLE CHESSELS: Lower Slaughter (1), p. 79a; Sodbury, Preface, p. lii.
LOWER CHESSALLS: Kingscote (1), p. 71b.
MIDDLE CHESSALLS: Kingscote (1), p. 71a.
PENSWELL FIELD: Colesbourne, p. 34b.
STANBOROUGH FIELDS: Notgrove (1), p. 91a.
STREET ACRES: Yanworth, pp. xlvii, 135b.
STREETFOLD: Yanworth, pp. xlvii, 135b.
WYCOMB:,Whittington (1), p. 125a; (2), p. 125a, Pl. 48.
Fields and Pastures, *see* **'Celtic' Fields, Ridge and Furrow,** *and* **Strip Lynchets.**
Finger-rings: *See also* **Rings.**
BRONZE: Kingscote (1), p. 72b; Lower Slaughter (3), p. 80a.
IRON: Rodmarton (1), p. 98b.
Firmini, inscription on wall-stone, Barnsley (1), p. 9b.
Fish-hooks, bronze, Bagendon (1), p. 8a.
Flagham Brook, wide track and enclosure E. of, Poole Keynes (1), p. 94b; probable undated settlement near, Somerford Keynes (1), p. 104a.
Flavian finds, Kingscote (1), p. 72a; period, Preface, p. xxxv.
Folles, p. 20b; *see also* **Coins: Roman.**
Ford, Romano-British finds, Temple Guiting, p. 116b.
Forest Marble, sites on, Acton Turville, p. 1a; Ampney Crucis (1), p. 3a; Barnsley, p. 9a; Maiseyhampton (1), p. 80b.
Forges, *see also* **Ovens,** Frocester (2), pp. xl, 57a; Lower Slaughter (1), p. 79a.
Forts, Corinium Dubunnorum, Preface, p. xxxv; Batsford (1), pp. xxxiv, xxxvii, 12a, Pl. 48.
Forum, Corinium, Preface, p. xxxv.
Foss Cross, enclosures and linear dykes S.E. of, Coln St. Dennis (1) p. 37a.
,, **Way,** *see* **Roman Roads.**
Fowler, Mr. P. J., Preface, p. xx; Barnsley (2), p. 11a.
Foxcote, Iron Age pit, Preface, p. xxiv.
,, **Manor,** Iron Age settlement near, Withington (1), p. 131b.
,, **Tumulus,** barrow yielding Romano-British finds, Withington, p. 131a.
Fragments of glass, Batsford (1), p. 13a; Coln St. Aldwyns; (2), p. 37a; Compton Abdale (1), p. 38b; Haresfield (3), p. 64; Kingscote (1), p. 72b; Whittington (2), p. 126b.
Frampton Mansell, Iron Age and Roman finds, Sapperton, p. 99a.
,, **on Severn,** Foss Way route, Preface, p. xlvii.
Freezing Hill, linear dyke, Iron Age, Doynton (1), p. 45a.
Frocester, p. 56b.
,, **Court,** Roman villa, Frocester (2), pp. xxxix, xlii, lii, 57a, Pl. 8.
Frogmore Coppice, undated probable settlement, Longborough (1), p. 78b.
'Frying Pan', of iron, Compton Abdale (1), p. 38b.
Fullers Earth: Preface, pp. xxxib, xxxiia, xxxvii, xxxviii; Bagendon (1), p. 7a; Chedworth (1), p. 24b; (5), p. 28b; (6), p. 28b; Colesbourne (2), p. 35b; Compton Abdale (1), p. 37b; Duntisbourne Rouse (4), p. 49a; Farmington (1), p. 55b.
Fulling, probable at Frocester (2), pp. xl, 57–8.
Furzey Furlong Barn, probable settlement, Barnsley (4), p. 11b, Pl. 55.

Gallienus, *see* **Coins: Roman;** *also* Chronology, p. 136.
Gallo-Belgic gold coins, p. 103a; *see also* **Coins: Iron Age.**
,, ,, pottery, *see* **Pottery: Roman.**
Gander, Mrs. E., Preface, p. xx; Brimpsfield, p. 21b; Coberley (3), p. 34b.
Gardiner, Mr. F., Lower Slaughter (3), p. 80a.
Gaulish samian ware, *see* **Pottery: Roman.**
Gascoigne, Mr. P. E., Preface, p. xx; Farmington (1), p. 55b; (2), p. 56a; (4), p. 56b; Northleach with Eastington (2), p. 88b; Winson (2), p. 131a.
Genii Cucullati, *see* **Gods.**
Genius, *see* **Gods.**
Geology, Preface, p. xxiii; *see also* **Cotteswold Sand, Forest Marble, Fullers Earth, Lias.**
Germanicus, p. 132a; *see also* **Coins: Roman;** *and* Chronology, p. 136.
Giant's Cave Long Barrow, Luckington, Wilts., Preface, p. xlix.
Gibbs, Capt. P., Preface, p. xx.
Glass, *see* **Beads, Beaker, Bottles, Bowls, Counters, Fragments, Goblet, Intaglio, Millefiori, Snakethread, Tesserae, Tubes, Unguent bottle, Vessels, Window.**
Glevum ware, *see* **Pottery: Roman.**
Gloucester City Museum: Avening (1), p. 5a; Badgeworth, p. 5b; Bitton, p. 17a; Bourton-on-the-Water (1), p. 19b; Broadwell (1), p. 21b; Brookthorpe with Whaddon (1), p. 22b; Buckland (1), p. 22b; Coaley, p. 32a; Colesbourne, p. 34b; Coln St. Aldwyns (2), p. 37b; Cowley (1), p. 39b; (4), p. 40b; Dodington, p. 43a; Dowdeswell (1), p. 44b; Driffield (1), p. 47a; Duntisbourne Rouse (1), p. 48b; Dursley, p. 49b; Elkstone (1), p. 54b; Fairford, p. 54b; Haresfield (1)–(3), p. 64a; Icomb (1), p. 66b; Kingscote (1), p. 72b; Lower Slaughter (1), p. 80a;

Gloucester City Museum, *cont.*
Naunton (1), p. 84b; Painswick, p. 91b; (2), p. 94a; Poole Keynes, p. 94b; Poulton (1), p. 95a; Randwick, p. 97a; Rodmarton (1), p. 99a; Sapperton (1), p. 99b; Siddington (6), p. 102b; Sodbury (1), p. 103b; Somerford Keynes (1), p. 105a; Stanton (1), p. 110a; Stanway, p. 110b; (1), p. 111a; Stroud, p. 112a; Sudeley (4), p. 114b; (5), p. 115a; Temple Guiting (2), p. 117a; Uley, p. 121a; (1), p. 121(b); (2), p. 123a; Upton St. Leonards, p. 123a; (1), p. 123b; Withington (2), p. 132a; Woodchester (1), p. 134b; Wyck Rissington, p. 135a.
Goat, *see* **Animal Bones.**
Goblet, Rhineland glass, Frocester (2), p. 58a.
Gods and Goddesses:
Preface, pp. xxxvi, xxxiv, xxxv.
AESCULAPIUS: Chedworth, p. 24a.
BACCHUS: Sudeley, p. 112a.
CUPID: Woodchester (1), p. 134a.
DEA REGINA: Batsford, p. 12a.
DIANA: Preface, p. xxxvi.
GENII: Batsford (1), p. 13a; Bisley with Lypiatt, p. 14b; Lechlade (5), p. 75a; King's Stanley, p. 70a.
GENII CUCULLATI: Daglingworth, p. 41b; Lower Slaughter (1), p. 79b; Whittington (2), p. 126a.
HERCULES: Hampnett, p. 62a.
JUPITER DOLICHENUS: Preface, p. xxxvi.
JUPITER OPTIMUS MAXIMUS: Preface, p. xxxvi.
LUNA: Woodchester (1), p. 134a.
MARS: Colesbourne (2), p. 36b; King's Stanley, p. 70a; Kingscote p. 70b; Lower Slaughter (1), p. 79b; Rodmarton (1), p. 98b; Whittington (2), p. 126a.
MARS LENUS: Chedworth (1), p. 27b.
MARTI OLLUDIO: Bisley with Lypiatt, p. 15a; Chalford, p. 23a.
MERCURY: Preface, p. xxxvi.
MINERVA: Kingscote (1), p. 72a; Lower Slaughter (1), p. 79b.
MOTHER GODDESSES: Wotton-under-Edge, p. 134b.
OCEANUS: Withington (2), p. 132a, Pl. 15.
PSYCHE: Woodchester (1), p. 134 a.
SILVANUS: Bisley with Lypiatt, p. 14b; Cherington, p. 29a.
Gold, *see* **Bezel, Coins: Iron Age,** *and* **Torque.**
Good Shepherd, Barnsley (1), p. 9b.
Goodburn, Mr. R., Preface, p. xx; Chedworth (1), p. 24b.
Goose, p. 58a; *see also* **Animal Bones.**
Gotherington, p. 59a.
Gouges, iron, Bagendon (1), p. 8a; Chedworth, p. 24a.
Gracie, Capt. H. S., Preface, p. xix; Frocester (2), p. 57a; Dursley (1), p. 49b; King's Stanley (2), p. 70b; Tetbury Upton (1), p. 119b.
Graffiti, Great Witcombe (1), p. 61b; *see also* **Cryptogram.**
Granny's Bank, Roman finds, Upper Slaughter, p. 123a.
Grass-tempered ware, *see* **Pottery: Grass-tempered.**
Gratian, *see* **Coins: Roman,** *also* Chronology, p. 136.
Gravel, *see* **Building Materials.**
Graves, *see* **Burials.**
Great Chessels, *see* **Field Names.**
,, **Chesterford,** scythe, Barnsley (1), p. 9b.
,, **Lemhill Farm,** Roman villa, Lechlade, p. 73a; (7), pp. liii, 75a; enclosures, tracks and linear ditches, undated, Southrop (2), p. 109a; (3), p. 109b.
,, **Rissington,** p. 59a.
,, **Witcombe,** p. 60b.
'Green Ditches', unidentified hill-fort, Sapperton, pp. xxx, 99a.
Greenfield, Mr. E., Great Witcombe (1), p. 60b.
Grey Ware, *see* **Pottery: Roman.**
Grim's Ditch, Oxfordshire, cf. Bagendon (1), p. 6b.
Grinder, stone, Elkstone (1), p. 54b.
Grinsell, L. V., Buckland (1), p. 22b.
Grove, The, Roman villa, Ebrington (1), p. 52b.
Grundy, G. B., Preface, p. xlvii; Chipping Campden (1), p. 29b.
Guard-chamber, Leckhampton (1), pp. xxvi, 77b.
Guiting Power, p. 62a.
Gully Leaze Copse, undated settlement and road, Down Ampney (2), p. 44b.

Hadrian, *see* **Coins: Roman,** *also* Chronology, p. 136.
Haematite ware, *see* **Pottery: Iron Age.**
Hailes Farm, Iron Age and Romano-British finds, Stanway, p. 110b.
,, **Wood,** possible hill-fort, Stanway, pp. xxix, xxxiva, 110b.
Hailey Wood, probable Roman building, Coates (2), p. 32a; probable Roman villa, Sapperton, p. 99b.
Haines Ash, tessellated pavement found, Cirencester, p. 29b.
Hampen Cottages, undated enclosure E. of, Sevenhampton (1), p. 110b, Pl. 54.
Hampnett, p. 62a.
Hams, The, Romano-British building, Marshfield (2), pp. xliii, 80b.
Hand-mullers, reported found at Uley (1), p. 121b.
Handles, bone, Chedworth (1), p. 27b.
Hannington Bridge, cooking pot found, Kempsford, p. 68a.
Hare, p. 61b; *see also* **Animal Bones.**
Hare Park Plantation, Roman road agger, Chipping Campden (1), p. 29b.
Hare's Down Barn, Roman finds from long barrow, Rodmarton, p. 98b.
Harescombe, p. 62a.
Haresfield, p. 62b.
,, **Beacon,** Haresfield (1), pp. xxv, 62b.
,, **Dyke Camp,** undated enclosure, Harescombe (2), p. 62b.
Harness mount, enamelled, Sudeley, p. 112a.
Hatherop, p. 64b.
,, **Piece,** 'Celtic' Fields, Eastleach (1), p. 52a.
Hawkesbury, p. 64b.
,, **Knoll,** Hawkesbury, pp. xxx, xxxiii, 64b, Pl. 68.
Hawling, p. 65a.
Hazel Wood, earthworks, Avening, p. 4b.
Hazlecot Barn, enclosures and linear ditches, Kingscote (6), p. 73a.
Hazleton, p. 65a.
Hazlewood Copse Camp, earthworks, Avening, pp. xxix, 4b.
Heath Hill House, Roman coins found, Wyck Rissington, p. 135a.
'Hebdown Camp', geological feature, Tormarton, pp. xxx, 120a.
Hen, *see* **Animal Bones.**
Henge, probable, Condicote, p. xxxii.
Hercules, p. 62a; *see also* **Gods.**
Hetty Pegler's Tump, long barrow, Roman coins and inhumation, Uley, p. 121a.
Hewletts, The, Charlton Kings, p. xxxib.
Hewletts Camp, natural feature, Charlton Kings, pp. xxxib, 23a.
Hicks, Sir William, Great Witcombe (1), p. 60b; (2), p. 61b.
High Brotheridge, possible Iron Age defences, Brockworth, p. 22a; Iron Age earthworks, Cranham, pp. xxix, xxx, 40b; Dyke, Cranham (1), p. 41a.
Highfold, Roman villa, Painswick (2), pp. liii, 93.
'Highworth', type enclosure, Kempsford, p. 68a; *see also* **Enclosures.**
Hill Farm, Romano-British burials and coin hoard, Willersey (2), p. 130a.
Hill-forts:
List of, Preface, p. xxv.
Comparative plans, Preface, facing p. xxvi.
Discussion, Preface, pp. xxv–xxvii, Pls. 32–40.
Hill-forts, discredited:
Discussion, pp. xxix–xxxi.
List of, p. xxix.
Selected sites, pp. xxxi–xxxiv.
Hinchwick Camp, undated, Condicote, pp. xxx, xxxiib, 30a.
Hinges, iron, Chedworth (1), p. 27b; Painswick (2), p. 94a.
Hinton Hill, Dyrham and Hinton (1), pp. xxv, 51a.
Hob-nails with burials, Preface, p. l; Lower Slaughter, p. 79a; Lechlade (5), p. 75a; mark on hypocaust tile, Woodchester (1), p. 134b.
'Hocberry', Roman villa, Rodmarton (1), pp. xlii, liii, 98b.
Hod Hill brooch, Great Witcombe (1), p. 61b.
Homeleaze Farm, undated enclosures S.W. of, Southrop (1), p. 109a, Pl. 54.
Honeybourne Bridge, Roman road S. of, Weston Subedge (4), p. 124a.
Honorius, *see* **Coins: Roman;** *also* Chronology, p. 136.
Hook, iron, Bourton-on-the-Water (1), p. 19b.
Hook-knives, iron, Swell (1), p. 115b; (2) (tanged), p. 116a.
Hoops, bronze, embossed for bucket, Rodborough, p. 98a.
Horcott, wells near, Kempsford (1), p. 68b.
Horse, *see* **Animal Bones.**
Horsebere Brook, Romano-British building near, Brockworth (2), p. 22a.
Horse-shoe nails, Farmington (1), p. 55b.
Horseshoes, Bourton-on-the-Water (2b), p. 20b; Chedworth (1), p. 27b; Compton Abdale (1), p. 38b.

Horsley, p. 65a.
,, **Wood,** Roman tombstone, Horsley, p. 65a.
Horton, p. 65b.
,, **Camp,** Horton (1), pp. xxv, 65b, Pl. 35.
Houses, Preface, p. xxxv; *see also* **Villas** *and* **Buildings.**
Huddenknoll Hill, possible earthworks, Painswick, p. 91b.
Hunsbury quern, *see* **Querns.**
Hyde, Roman brooch found, Minchinhampton, p. 81a.
Hypocausts, *see* **Building Materials.**

Icomb, p. 66b.
,, **Hill,** probable hill-fort, Icomb (1), pp. xxv, 66b, Pl. 36.
Idols, stone, Bourton-on-the-Water (1), p. 19b; Whittington (2), p. 126a; *see also* **Gods.**
Ifold, Roman villa, Painswick (2), pp. xlii, liii, 93a, Pl. 8.
Imbrex, *see* **Building Materials.**
Impost fragments, *see* **Building Materials.**
Ingot, lead, Syde (1), p. 116b.
Inhumations, *see* **Burials.**
Intaglios: (pottery) Barnsley (1), p. 9b; (glass) Great Witcombe (1), p. 61b; Uley (2), p. 121b.
Ireley Farm, Iron Age and Romano-British finds, Stanway, p. 110b; enclosures and linear ditches, undated, Stanway (5), pp. xxiv, 111a.
Iron Age, discussion, pp. xxiii–xxxiv.
,, ,, **Hill-forts,** *see* **Hill-forts.**
Iron Artefacts, *see* **Anvil, Arrows, Awl, Axe, Bill-hooks, Bolts, Bracelets, Brooches, Chisels, Clasp Knife, Daggers, Door-latch, Finger-rings, 'Frying pan', Gouge, Hatchet, Hinges, Hook, Hook-knife, Horsehoes, Knives, Locks, Nails, Plough-coulter, Pot-hook, Pruning-hook, Rake, Rods, Saws, Shackles, Sheath, Shears, Sheep-bells, Slag, Spade-irons, Spear-head, Spit, Spoon-bit, Spring-tongs, Steelyards, Strapping, Studs, Styli, Trowel** (masons), **Wire.**
Irvine, Mr. A. N., Preface, p. xx; Chedworth, p. 24a; (5), p. 28b.
Ivy Lodge, round barrow near, King's Stanley, p. 70a.

Jones, Mrs. M. U., Preface, p. xx; Lechlade (1), p. 73b; (5), p. 73b.
Jet, plaque, Frocester (2), p. 58a.
Juniper Hill, cross-ridge dyke, Edgeworth (1), pp. xxvii, xxix, xxx, 53a.
Jupiter Dolichenus, p. xxxvi; *see also* **Gods.**
,, **Optimus Maximus,** p. xxxvi; *see also* **Gods.**

Keeper's Hill Wood, undated enclosures and ditches, Temple Guiting (9), p. 119a.
'Keeper's Lodge', tesserae found near, Sudeley, p. 112a.
Kellaway, Dr. G. A., Preface, pp. xx, xxx; Northleach with Eastington (3), p. 88b.
Kemble, p. 68a.
Kempsford, p. 68a.
Key, Mr. C. E., Preface, p. xx; Chedworth (6), p. 28b; Compton Abdale (1), p. 37b.
Keys: (bronze) Great Witcombe (1), p. 61b; Whittington (2), p. 126b
Kilns, Preface, p. xxxvii; Chedworth (1), p. 24b; Minchinhampton, p. 81a; *see also* **Ovens.**
Kiln-supports, of clay, Elkstone (1), p. 54b.
Kimbsbury, Hill-fort, Painswick (1), pp. xxv, 91b, Pl. 37.
Kineton Hill, road traverses, Temple Guiting, p. 116b; Romano-British cemetery and probable settlement, Temple Guiting (3), p. 117b.
King's Beeches, Iron Age and possible Romano-British settlement, Southam (3), pp. xxiv, 107b.
King's Hill, undated crop-marks of enclosures and linear ditches, Preston (1), p. 95a.
King's Stanley, p. 70a.
Kingscote, p. 70b.
Kingshill, Romano-British pottery found, Dursley, p. 49b.
,, **Lane,** probably of Roman origin, Corinium, Preface, p. xxxv.
Knight, Mr. R., Preface, p. xx; Marshfield (1) and (2), p. 80b.
Knives:
IRON: Chedworth (1), p. 27b; Cowley (1), p. 39b; Frocester (2), p. 58a; Sudeley (4), p. 114b; Whittington (2), p. 126b.
METAL: Withington (2), p. 132a.

Lady's Well, Romano-British settlement, Swell (1), p. 115b.
Lamps, Sudeley (4), p. 114b.
Lane's Barn, tesserae found, Sudeley, p. 112a.
Langley Hill, 'camp', Winchcombe, pp. xxix, xxxi, xxxiva, 130a.
Lark's Bush, coin hoard, Sapperton, p. 99a.
Lasborough, possible villa at, Westonbirt with Lasborough, p. 123b.
La Tène, *see* **Brooches.**
Latch-lifters, Whittington (2), p. 126b.
Latrines, stone-built, Preface, p. xl; Chedworth (1), p. 27a; Ebrington (1), p. 53a; Great Witcombe (1), p. 61a.
Lawrence, W. L., Whittington (2), p. 125a, Pl. 48.
'Leadenwell Villa', Bourton-on-the-Water (2a), pp. xliii, liii, 20a.
Leaze Farm, undated enclosure and tracks, Lechlade (10), p. 75b.
Lechlade, p. 73a.
,, **Downs,** undated enclosure and linear ditches, Lechlade (9), p. 75b.
,, **Mill,** undated enclosures, tracks and linear ditches, Lechlade (11), (12), p. 75b.
Leckhampton, p. 77a.
,, **Hill,** burials, Roman, Leckhampton, p. 77a.
,, ,, hill-fort, Leckhampton (1), pp. xxv, xxvi, 77b.
Leer Farm, grooved stone at, Duntisbourne Abbots (1), p. 48a, Pl. 63.
Lemington, part of Dorn, Batsford, p. 12a.
'Lenches, The', Roman finds, Weston Subedge, p. 123b.
Leonard Stanley, p. 78a.
Lessons, The, Romano-British settlement, Haresfield (5), pp. xliii, 64b.
Leygore Hill, the Foss Way on, Northleach with Eastington, p. 87a; (4), p. 88b.
Lias, monuments on: Preface, pp. xxxia, xxxib; Brookthorpe with Whaddon, (1), p. 22b; Charlton Kings, p. 23a; Frocester, p. 56b; (2), p. 57a; Great Rissington (1), p. 59b; Great Witcombe (1), p. 60b; (2), (3), p. 61b; (4), p. 62a; Harescombe (1), p. 62a; Oxenton (1), p. 91b; Stinchcombe (1), p. 111b; Sudeley (2), p. 112a; (4), p. 113b; (5), p. 115a; Weston Subedge (1), (2), p. 123b; (3), p. 124a; Wyck Rissington (1), p. 135a.
Lias flags, *see* **Building Materials.**
,, **tesserae,** Preface, p. xli.
Lillyhorn, Roman villa, Bisley with Lypiatt (1), pp. xlii, liii, 15b.
Lime-slaking, evidence of, Frocester (2), pp. xl, 57b.
Limestone, dressed and reddened, *see* **Building Materials.**
Linear Bank or **Ditch,** *see* **Dykes and Ditches.**
Listercombe, Roman villa, Chedworth (6), pp. xlii, liii, 28b.
Little Britain, Roman pottery found, Minchinhampton, p. 81a.
,, **Chessels,** *see* **Field Names.**
,, **Rissington,** p. 78a.
,, ,, **airfield,** Romano-British pottery and skeleton found, Westcote, p. 123a.
,, **Sodbury,** *see* **Sodbury.**
,, ,, **Camp,** Sodbury (1), pp. xxv, 103a, Pl. 34.
,, ,, **Manor House,** mediaeval banks and mounds N. of Sodbury (1), p. 103b.
,, ,, **Village,** Hill-fort, Sodbury (1), p. 103b, Pl. 34.
Liverpool Museum, Kingscote (1), p. 73a.
Liversidge, Dr. J., Preface, p. xx; Compton Abdale (1), p. 38a; (4), p. 38b.
Locks, Chedworth (1), p. 27b; Compton Abdale (1), p. 38b; Whittington (2), p. 126b.
'Loders, The', Iron Age pit, Lechlade (1), p. 73b.
Lodge Ground Quarry, Romano-British inhumation, Condicote (2), p. 39b.
Loftus Brock, Mr. P., Sudeley (2), p. 113a.
Long Barrows, *see* **Barrows.**
,, **Hill,** Colethrop, Romano-British cemetery, Haresfield (4), p. 64b.
,, **Mound,** Bisley with Lypiatt (2), p. 16b.
,, **Newnton,** p. 78a.
,, **Plantation,** Roman road, North Cerney (4), p. 86a.
Longborough, p. 78b.
Longman's Barn Farm, Romano-British settlement near, Avening (2), p. 5a.
Longridge Hill, possible earthworks, Painswick, p. 91b.
Lots Barn, ditch, Temple Guiting (6), p. 117b; pit-alignment S.W. of, Temple Guiting (4), p. 117b, Pl. 56.

Lower Dowdeswell, Preface, p. xxxiiia.
,, **Slaughter,** p. 78b.
,, **Swell,** Romano-British settlement, Swell (1), p. 115a.
Luna, *see* **Gods.**
L. Verus, p. 20b; *see also* **Coins: Roman;** *and* Chronology, p. 136.
Lynchets, *see* **'Celtic' Fields;** *also* Kingscote (1), p. 71b.
Lysons, S., Preface, p. xxxix; Colesbourne (2), p. 35b; Rodmarton (1), p. 98b; Withington (2), p. 131b; Woodchester (1), p. 132b.

Mackreth, Mr. D. F., Kingscote (1), p. 73a.
Magnentius, *see* **Coins: Roman;** *also* Chronology, p. 136.
Maiseyhampton, p. 80b.
Malvern Hills, source of Iron Age pottery found in this area, Preface, p. xxiv; Oxenton, p. 91a.
'Manless Town', infant burial, Brimpsfield, p. 21b.
Manor Ham Barn, enclosures, tracks and linear ditches, Kempsford (7), p. 69b.
Marble, use of, Preface, p. xl; statues of, Woodchester (1), p. 134a; *see also* **Beads** *and* **Flooring.**
Marlstone Rock Bed, Alderton, Dixton Hill, Preface, p. xxxia.
Mars: *See also* **Gods.**
ALTARS TO: Bisley with Lypiatt, p. 14b; Chalford (1), p. 23a; Chedworth (1), p. 27b; King's Stanley, p. 70a.
GABLED RELIEF: Bisley with Lypiatt, p. 14b.
INTAGLIO: Rodmarton (1), p. 98b.
RELIEF: Colesbourne (2), p. 36b.
STATUETTE: Whittington (2), p. 126a.
VOTIVE PLAQUE: Lower Slaughter (1), p. 79b.
M. Aurelius, p. 20b; *see also* **Coins: Roman;** *and* Chronology, p. 136.
Marshall, Mr. A., Stanway (2), p. 111a.
Marshfield, p. 80b.
Mask, bronze, Uley, p. 121a.
Maughersbury, p. 80b.
Mears, Mr. D. A., Horsley (2), p. 65b; Kingscote (1), p. 73a; (2), p. 73a.
Mediaeval:
REMAINS: Preface, p. xxxvii.
BOUNDARIES: Saintbury, p. 99a.
'CAMP': Bitton, p. 17a.
VILLAGE: Blockley (1), p. 17a; Whittington (3), pp. xxxvii, 126b.
Meilgaresbyri, probable Saxon name for Stow-on-the-Wold, p. 111b.
Mercury, implied temple to, Preface, p. xxxvi; *see also* **Gods.**
Metal artefacts, *see* **Baldric Loop, Bill-hooks, Boot-nails, Bracelets, Bronze, Brooches, Cooking-pot, Dividers, Horseshoes, Intaglio, Iron, Keys, Knives, Latch-lifters, Locks, Nails, Pins, Plumb-bob, Rake, Rings, Scythes, Spearheads, Spoons, Spurs, Steelyard Hooks, Styli, Terret, Tools.**
Metal-working, evidence of, Bagendon (1), p. 7b.
Mica-dusted ware, *see* **Pottery: Roman.**
Mickleton, p. 81a.
Middle Hill Farm, Chalford, p. 23a.
Middleton, Prof. J. H., Sudeley (4), p. 113b.
Military dress, *see* **Buckles;** *see also* **Forts.**
,, **equipment:**
'BALDRIC' LOOP: Kingscote (1), p. 72a.
KNOBS: Kingscote (1), p. 72a.
STUD: Rodborough (1), p. 98a.
Millefiori glass, Frocester (2), p. 58a; Great Witcombe (1), p. 61b.
Millhampost, Roman building, Stanway (1), pp. xliii, 111a; Romano-British settlement S. of, Stanway (2), pp. liii, 111a; undated enclosures and tracks N. of, Stanway (4), p. 111a.
Millhampost Farmhouse, Romano-British burials near, Stanway, p. 110b.
Minchinhampton, p. 81a.
,, **Common,** possible Iron Age banks, Minchinhampton (8), p. 84a.
Minerva, *see* **Gods.**
Minimi, p. 58a; *see also* **Coins: Roman.**
Minimissimi, *see* **Coins: Roman.**
Mint, possible, Bagendon (1), p. 7b.
Mirror, bronze, Bagendon (1), p. 8a; Cowley, p. 39b.
Miserden, p. 84a.
Money Quarr, Uley (2), pp. lii, 121b.
Montreal House, Romano-British settlement near, Winson (1), p. 131a.
Morcom, Lt. Col. R. K., Batsford (1), p. 12b.
Mortaria, *see* **Pottery: Roman.**
Moreton-in-Marsh, p. 84a.
Mosaicists, Corinian School: Preface, pp. xxxv–xxxvi, xli–xlii, Pls. 1–5, 8, 15, 17–23; Chedworth (1), p. 27a; Cirencester (1), p. 29b; Frocester (2), p. 57b; Withington (2), p. 132a; Woodchester (1), p. 132b.
Mosaicists, Durnovarian School: Preface, p. xlii; Withington (2), p. 132a.
Mosaics, *see* **Building Materials.**
Mother-Goddesses, *see* **Gods.**
Museums, *see* **Ashmolean Museum, Birmingham Museum, Bristol City Museum, British Museum, Chedworth Museum, Cheltenham College Museum, Cheltenham Museum, Corinium Museum, Gloucester City Museum, Liverpool Museum, National Museum of Wales, Stroud Museum, Worcester Museum.**

Nail-cleaners, bronze, Kingscote (1), p. 72b; Uley (2), p. 123a.
Nails:
IRON: Bagendon (1), p. 7b; Bisley with Lypiatt (1), p. 16a; Charlton Kings, p. 23b; Chedworth (6), p. 29a; Frocester (1), p. 57a; Rodmarton, p. 98a.
METAL: Farmington (1), p. 55b; Horsley (1), p. 65a.
Nailsworth, p. 84b.
National Museum of Wales, Bourton-on-the-Water (1), p. 19b.
National Trust, custodians, Chedworth (1), p. 24b.
Naunton, p. 84b.
Neal, Mr. D. S., Great Witcombe (1), p. 61a.
Necklace, bronze, Bagendon (1), p. 8a. *See also* **Torque.**
Needles, bone, Bourton-on-the-Water (1), p. 19b; Chedworth (1), p. 27b.
Neigh Bridge, undated settlement, Somerford Keynes (2), p. 105a.
Nene Valley Ware, *see* **Pottery: Roman.**
Nero, p. 72a; *see also* **Coins: Roman;** *and* Chronology, p. 136.
Neronian timber buildings, Corinium, p. xxxv.
Nesley Farm, inscribed tombstone, Beverstone.
New Building, Romano-British building near, Upper Slaughter (1), p. 123a.
New Forest Ware, *see* **Pottery: Roman.**
Newington Bagpath, now Kingscote, p. 70b.
Newnton Farm, Romano-British settlement, Long Newnton (1), p. 78a.
Niedermendig Lava, *see* **Querns.**
No Man's Land plantation, 'Celtic' Fields, Eastleach (3), pp. xlix, liii, 52b; soil-marks of enclosures or possible fields, Eastleach (4), p. 52b.
Norbury Camp, Hill-fort, Northleach with Eastington (1), pp. xxv, 87b; Romano-British settlement within, Northleach with Eastington (2), pp. xliii, 88a.
Norbury Hill-fort, Colesbourne (1), pp. xxv, 34b, Pl. 37; adjacent Roman villa, Farmington (1), p. 55b.
Nordown, agger of Roman road near, North Cerney (4), p. 86a.
North Cerney, p. 85a.
,, **Nibley,** p. 86a.
Northfield Farm, Charlton Kings, p. xxxib.
Northleach with Eastington, p. 87a.
Northmoor Lane, undated rectangular enclosure, South Cerney (2), p. 105b.
Notgrove, p. 88b.
Nottingham Hill Camp, Hill-fort, Gotherington (1), pp. xxv, xxvi, lii, 59a.
Nymphaeum, Chedworth (1), p. 25b; *see also* **Building Remains.**
Nympsfield, p. 91a.
,, **long barrow,** Romano-British materials found, Frocester, p. 56b.

Oakley Park, tessellated pavement recorded, Cirencester, p. 29b.
Obelisk Park, undated enclosures and linear ditches, Fairford (2), p. 55a, Pl. 66.
Oceanus, mosaic depicts, Withington (2), p. 132a, Pl. 15; *see also* **Gods.**
Oddington, p. 91a.
Old Grange, possible Iron Age bank and ditch, Minchinhampton (5), p. 83b.

Old Park, 'Celtic' Field traces, North Cerney, p. 85b.
Oldland Bottom, Roman coins found, Bitton, p. 17a.
O'Neil, Mrs. H. E., Preface, p. xix: Bourton-on-the-Water, pp. 17–21; Coates (1), p. 32a; Condicote, pp. xxxi–ii; Lower Slaughter (1), p. 79a; Stanway (2), p. 111a; Upper Slaughter (1), p. 123a; Whittington (3), p. 126a.
Oolite, tesserae, Preface, p. xli; for monuments on, *see* Editorial Notes, p. lvi.
Open Settlements: *see also* **Earthworks** *and* **Settlements.**
Preface, p. xxvii; Bagendon (1), p. 6b; Bourton-on-the-Water (1), p. 17b; Charlton Kings (1), p. 23b; Duntisbourne Abbots (2), p. 48a; Fairford (4)–(6), p. 55a; Lechlade (1), p. 73b; (5), p. 73b; Oxenton (1), p. 91a; Rodborough (1), p. 98a; Southam (3)–(5), p. 107b; Upper Slaughter, p. 123a.
Opus Signinum, *see* **Building Materials.**
Orpheus, mosaics depict: Cirencester (1), p. 29b, Pl. 1; Withington (2), p. 132a, Pl. 15; Woodchester (1), p. 132b, Pl. 17.
Ovens, Roman:
Bourton-on-the-Water (2a), p. 20a; (2b), p. 20b.
CORN-DRIERS: Frocester (2), p. 57b; Lechlade (5), p. 73b; Lower Slaughter (1), p. 79b; Upton St. Leonards (1), p. 123b.
Owlpen, p. 91a.
,, discredited hill-fort, Nympsfield, pp. xxix, 91a.
Ox, *see* **Animal Bones.**
Oxenton, p. 91a.
,, **Knolls,** Iron Age settlement, Oxenton (1), pp. xxiii, xxiv, xxix, xxxi, 91a.
Oxfordshire ware, *see* **Pottery: Roman.**
Oysters, *see* **Shellfish.**
Oysterwell Grove, dyke 'g' at Bagendon (1), p. 8b.
Ozleworth, p. 91b.

Pagan Saxon Burials, *see* **Burials.**
Painswick, p. 91b.
,, **Beacon,** additional name for Painswick (1), pp. xxv, 91b, Pl. 37.
,, **Hill,** Roman objects found, Upton St. Leonards, p. 123a.
Paint pigments on pottery, Great Witcombe (1), p. 61b.
Parallel Ditches, *see* **Dykes and Linear Ditches.**
Park, The, Iron Age bank and ditch in, Minchinhampton (1), p. 83a, Pls. 44–5; (4), p. 83b.
Parks, The, possible villa footings, Woodchester (1), p. 132b.
Partridge, Mr. J., Colesbourne, p. 34b.
Patterned red tiles, *see* **Building Materials.**
Paving stones, *see* **Building Materials**
Pellets, lead, Bagendon (1), p. 8a.
'Penhill Camp', undated enclosure, Shipton (3), p. 101b.
Penhill Farm, Romano-British pottery found, Colesbourne, p. 34b.
,, **Plantation,** Dobunnic coin found, Colesbourne, p. 34a.
Pennant Flags, *see* **Building Materials.**
Penswell Field, p. 34b; *see also* **Field Names.**
Pewter, (fragments) Batsford (1), p. 13a; (jug) Chedworth (1), p. 27b; (pot) Painswick (2), p. 94a.
Pig, *see* **Animal Bones.**
Pilae, *see* **Building Materials.**
Pilasters, *see* **Building Materials.**
Pillow-mounds, Preface, p. xxxiiib; Minchinhampton (1), p.83a; Sodbury (1), p. 103b.
Pinbury, Hill-fort, Duntisbourne Rouse (1), pp. xxv, 48b.
Pins:
BONE: Chedworth (1), p. 27b.
BRONZE: Condicote (2), p. 39b; Great Witcombe (1), p. 61b; (spiral-headed) Kingscote (1), p. 72b.
METAL: Sudeley (5), p. 115a; Uley (2), p. 121b.
Pinswell, Colesbourne, p. 34b.
Pipes, lead, Chedworth (1), p. 27b.
Pit-alignments, Preface, pp. xxvii, xlix; Condicote (1), p. 39a, Pl. 56; Great Rissington (3), p. 60a; Temple Guiting (4), p. 117b, Pl. 56.
Pitchcombe, p, 95b.
Pits, Iron Age: Preface, p. xxvii; Guiting Power, p. 62a; Lechlade (1), p. 73b; (5), p. 75a.
Pits, Romano-British: Withington (1), p. 131b.
Plaster, painted, *see* **Building Materials.**
Place-Names, *see* Appendix A, p. lii.
Plough coulter, iron, Great Witcombe (1), pp. xlix, 61b.
Ploughshare, bronze (miniature, socketed), Southam, p. 106a.
Plumb-bob, Chedworth, p. 24a.
Plunge-bath, *see* **Building Remains.**
'Points', bone, Upper Slaughter, p. 123a.
Polisher, stone, Elkstone (1), p. 54b.
Poole Keynes, p. 94b.
Poplar Gate, probable settlement, Leonard Stanley (1), p. 78a.
,, **Wood,** undated rectangular enclosure, Down Ampney (3), p. 45a.
Porphyry, green, Painswick (2), p. 94a.
Portstraet, Saxon, Preface, p. xlvii.
Post-holes, Barnsley (1), p. 9b.
Posting station, Roman, Bourton-on-the-Water (2b), p. 20b.
Pot-hook, iron, Badgeworth, p. 5b.
Pot-lid, *see* **Shale.**
Potin ('speculum'), p. 101a; *see also* **Coins: Iron Age.**
Pottery: Grass Tempered, Preface, p. xxxvi; Barnsley (2), p. 11a; Frocester (2), p. 58a; Kingscote (1), p. 72b; Uley (2), p. 123a.
Pottery: Iron Age:
General discussion, Preface, p. xxiv.
'A' SHERDS: Bourton-on-the-Water (1), p. 19a; Oxenton, p. 91a; Whittington (2), p. 125a; Withington, p. 131a.
'B' SHERDS: Bourton-on-the-Water (1), p. 19a; Minchinhampton (1), p. 83a; (7), p. 84a.
BUTT-BEAKER, *see* **Pottery: Roman.**
DECORATED:
DUCK-STAMPED: Oxenton (1), p. 91a.
INCISED: Lechlade (1), p. 73b; (5), p. 73b; Oxenton, p. 91a.
INCISED CHEVRON: Coberley (1), p. 34a.
STAMPED: Southam (2), p. 107b; Temple Guiting (1), p. 117a; Withington (1), p. 131b.
WHITE INLAY: Coberley (1), p. 34a; Lechlade (1), p. 73b.
GENERAL:
BURNISHED BLACK WARE: Whittington (2), p. 125a.
CALCITE GRITTED: Whittington (2), p. 125a.
CARINATED: Lechlade (5), p. 73b.
SHELL-GRITTED: Farmington (4), p. 56b.
FUNERARY URNS: Bagendon (1), p. 7b.
HAEMATITE WARE: Lechlade (1), p. 73b.
SITULATE VESSELS: Oxenton (1), p. 91a; Siddington (6), p. 102b; Stanton (1), p. 110a.
Also: Coberley (1), p. 34a; Duntisbourne Abbots, p. 48a; Leckhampton (1), p. 77b; Uley (1), p. 121b.
Pottery: Roman:
AMPHORAE: Bourton-on-the-Water (2c), p. 20b; Chedworth (1), p. 27b (with potter's stamp); Painswick (2), p. 94a.
ARRETINE OR PROVINCIAL ARRETINE WARE: Bagendon (1), p. 7b; Rodborough (1), p. 98a.
BLACK-BURNISHED WARE: Chedworth (1), p. 27b; Farmington (2), p. 56a.
BUTT-BEAKER: Batsford (1), p. 13a; Duntisbourne Abbots, p. 48a; Rodborough (1), p. 98a.
CALCITE-GRITTED WARE: Batsford (1), p. 13a; Chedworth (6), p. 29a; Kingscote (1), p. 72b; Lower Slaughter (3), p. 80a; Wyck Rissington (1), p. 135a.
COLOUR-COATED WARE: Batsford (1), p. 13a; Compton Abdale (1), p. 38a; Farmington (4), p. 56b; Swell (2), p. 116a.
GLEVUM WARE: Great Witcombe (1), p. 61b; *see also* SEVERN VALLEY WARE.
MICA-DUSTED WARE: Rodborough (1), p. 98a.
MORTARIA: Brimpsfield, p. 21b; Chedworth, p. 24a; (6), p. 29a; Coberley (3), p. 34b; Painswick (2), p. 94a; Poole Keynes, p. 94b; Uley (2), p. 123a; Whittington (2), p. 126b; Wyck Rissington (1), p. 135a; *see also* OXFORDSHIRE LATE COLOUR-COATED WARE.
NENE VALLEY WARE: Chedworth (1), p. 27b; Kingscote (1), p. 72b; Lower Slaughter (3), p. 80a.
NEW FOREST WARE: Chedworth (1), p. 27b; Kingscote (1), p. 72b; Lower Slaughter (3), p. 80a.
OXFORDSHIRE LATE COLOUR-COATED WARE:
GENERAL: Chedworth (1), p. 27b; (6), p. 29a; Cirencester (3), p. 30a; Compton Abdale (3), p. 38b; Kingscote (1), p. 72b; Lower Slaughter (3), p. 80a; Sapperton, p. 100a; Temple Guiting (2), p. 117a; Whittington (2), p. 126b.
MORTARIA: Dowdeswell (1), p. 44a; Farmington (4), p. 56b; North Cerney (3), p. 86a.
ROSETTE-STAMPED: Ebrington (1), p. 53a; Great Rissington (1), p. 59b; Lower Slaughter, p. 79a.

Pottery: Roman, *cont.*
OXFORDSHIRE LATE PAINTED PARCHMENT WARE: Chedworth (1), p. 27b.
RHENISH WARE: Chedworth (1), p. 27b; Kingscote (1), p. 72b.
SAMIAN WARE: Preface, p. xxxviii; Avening (1), p. 5a; (2) (stamped), p. 5b; Bagendon (1) (South Gaulish), p. 7b; Barnsley (1), p. 9b; Batsford (1) (stamped and unstamped), p. 13a; Baunton (1), p. 13b; Bisley with Lypiatt (1), p. 16b; Bourton-on-the-Water (2b) (stamped), p. 20b; (2c), p. 20b; Brookthorpe with Whaddon (1), p. 22b; Chedworth, p. 24a; (1) (stamped and unstamped), p. 27b; Coberley (2), p. 34a; (3), p. 34b; Compton Abdale (1), p. 38a; (4), p. 38b; Dowdeswell (1), p. 44a; Driffield (1), p. 47a; Ebrington (1), p. 53a; Farmington (1), p. 55b; (2), p. 56a; Frocester (2), p. 58a; Great Witcombe (1), p. 61b; Hazleton (1), p. 65a; Kingscote (1), p. 72b; Lechlade (5), p. 75a; Lower Slaughter (3), p. 80a; Marshfield (1), p. 80b; North Cerney (3), p. 86a; Painswick (2), p. 94a; Quenington (3) (stamped and unstamped), p. 97a; Rodborough (1), p. 98a; Rodmarton (1), p. 99a; Sapperton, p. 100a; Somerford Keynes (1), p. 105a; Stroud, p. 112a; Sudeley, p. 112a; (2), p. 113b; (4), p. 114b; Swell (2), p. 116a; Temple Guiting, p. 116b; (2), p. 117a; (3), p. 117a; Uley (2), p. 123a; Weston Subedge (1), p. 123b; Whittington (2), p. 126b; Winson (1), p. 131a; Woodchester (1), p. 134a; Wyck Rissington (1), p. 135a.
SEVERN VALLEY WARE: Chedworth (1), p. 27b; Kingscote (1), p. 72b; *see also* GLEVUM WARE.
TERRA NIGRA: Bagendon (1), p. 7b.
TERRA RUBRA: Bagendon (1), p. 7b.
Poultmoor Farm, enclosure near, Barnsley (3), p. 11b.
Poulton, p. 94b.
Powell, Mr. T. G. E., Oxenton (1), p. 91a.
Prasina, carved on building stone, Chedworth (1), p. 27b.
Prescott, p. 95a.
Preservation, monuments most worthy, Preface, pp. xx–xxii.
Prestbury, p. 95a.
Preston, p. 95a.
Price, Mr. E. G., Frocester, p. 56b.
Prick-spurs, bronze, Chedworth (1), p. 27b.
Pruning-hook, iron, Whittington (2), p. 126b.
Psyche, p. 134a; *see also* **Gods.**
'Puckham Camp', discredited hill-fort. Sevenhampton, pp. xxx, 100b.
Pudding stone, *see* **Querns.**
Purnell, Mr. P. B., Stinchcombe (1), p. 111a.

Quenington, p. 95b.
Querns:
ANDERNACH GRIT/NIEDERMENDIG LAVA: Kingscote (1), p. 72b; Whittington (2), p. 126b.
BEEHIVE: Bourton-on-the-Water (1), p. 19b.
PUDDING STONE: Great Witcombe (1), p. 61b.
ROTARY: Batsford (1), p. 13a; Stanton (1), p. 110a.
SADDLE: Bourton-on-the-Water (1), p. 19b; Sodbury (1), p. 103b; Stanton (1), p. 110a; Uley (1), p. 121b.
UNSPECIFIED: Barnsley (1), p. 9b; Blockley (1), p. 17b; Chedworth (1), p. 27b; Compton Abdale (1), p. 38b; Frocester (2), p. 58b; Kingscote (1), p. 71b; Lower Slaughter (1), p. 79b; Painswick (2), p. 94a; Temple Guiting (2), p. 117a; Whittington (2), p. 126b; Winson (1), p. 131a; Wotton under Edge, p. 134b.
'Querns, The', burials near, Corinium, Preface, p. xxxvi.
Quoin Slade, alternative name for Quenington (3), p. lii and note on p. 97.

Rainey, Prof. E., Kingscote (1), p. 71a.
Rake: (iron) Lower Slaughter (1), p. 79b; (mosaic) Sudeley (4), p. 114b, Pl. 15.
Ramparts: *See also* **Hill-forts, Iron Age.**
IRON AGE: Preface, p. xxvi.
ROMAN: Preface, p. xxxv.
SAXON: Winchcombe, pp. xliv, 130b.
Ranbury Ring, Hill-fort, Ampney St. Peter (1), pp. xxv, 3b.
Randwick, p. 97a.
,, **'Camp',** cross-ridge dyke, Randwick (1), p. 97b.
Reconstructions, 'villa', Chedworth (1), p. 24b; Great Witcombe (1), p. 60b; Sudeley (2), p. 112b; (4), p. 113b.
Rectilinear ditches, *see* **Dykes and Linear Ditches.**
,, **enclosures,** *see* **Enclosures.**
Reece, Dr. R. M., Preface, p. xx; Baunton (1), p. 13b; Sapperton, p. 99a; Siddington (3), p. 102a.
Religious buildings and objects, *see* **Temples** *and* **Votive objects.**
Rendcomb, p. 97b.
,, **Camp,** Rendcomb, pp. xxix, xxxiiia, 97b.
Rhenish ware, *see* **Pottery: Roman.**
Rhodes, Mr. J. F., Preface, p. xx; Cowley (1), p. 39b; (5), p. 40b; Kingscote (1), p. 71a.
Rhymes Barn, enclosures, track and linear ditches near, Kempsford (2), p. 68b.
Richmond, Sir Ian, Chedworth (1), p. 24a.
Ridge and Furrow, Barnsley (2), p. 11a; Charlton Kings, p. xxxib; Gotherington (1), p. 59a; Great Rissington (1), pp. xxxvii, 59b; Longborough (1), p. 78b; Lower Slaughter (1), p. 79a; Sherborne (1), p. 100b; Tormarton (1), p. 120a; Withington (2), pp. xxxvii, 131b.
Ring, The, Southam (5), p. 107b, Pls. 40 and 41.
Ring Ditches, *see* Appendix B, p. lv.
,, **Hill,** Hill-fort, Haresfield (1), pp. xxv, xxvi, 62b; Roman building, Haresfield (3), pp. xliii, 64a.
Rings:
BRONZE: Chedworth (1), p. 27b; Cowley (1), p. 39b.
METAL: Sudeley (2), p. 113b; (5), p. 115a; Uley (2), p. 121b.
SHALE: Weston Subedge (1), p. 123b.
SILVER: Willersey (2), p. 130a.
Rodborough, p. 98a.
,, **Common,** Belgic bucket found, irregular pits, Rodborough, p. 98a; early Roman settlement, Rodborough (1), p. 98a.
Rodmarton, p. 98a.
Rods, iron, Badgeworth, p. 5b.
Roel Camp, Hill-fort, Sudeley (1), pp. xxv, 112b, Pl. 32.
Roman roads: *See also* **Tracks.**
Discussion, Preface, pp. xlv–xlviii.
List of, pp. xlvii–xlviii.
Map, p. xlvi.
AKEMAN STREET: Preface, p. xxxv; Coln St. Aldwyns, p. 36b; (2), p. 37a; (3), p. 37a; Eastleach (2), p. 52a; Quenington (1), p. 95b; (2), p. 95b; (3), p. 97a; (4), p. 97a.
BUCKLE STREET: Preface, p. xxiv; Lower Slaughter, p. 78b; Temple Guiting, p. 116b; Willersey, p. 128a.
ERMIN STREET: Preface, p. xxxv; Cirencester, p. 29b; Cowley (2), p. 40a; Daglingworth, p. 41b; Duntisbourne Abbots, p. 48a; (2), p. 48b, Pl. 63; Siddington, p. 101b; (6), p. 102b; Syde (1), p. 116b.
FOSS WAY: Preface, pp. xxiv, xxxiv. xxxv; Batsford (1), p. 12a; (3), p. 13a; Bourton-on-the-Water (2), p. 20a; (3), p. 21a; Broadwell (1), (2), p. 21b; Coln St. Dennis, p. 37a; Kemble, p. 68a; (1), p. 68a, Pl. 63; Long Newnton, p. 78a; (1), p. 78a; Longborough, p. 78b; (1), p. 78b; Lower Slaughter, p. 78b; (2), p. 80a; Moreton-in-Marsh, p. 84a; Northleach with Eastington, p. 87a; (4), p. 88b; Rodmarton, p. 98b; Stow-on-the-Wold (1), p. 111b.
RYKNILD STREET: Bourton-on-the-Hill (1), p. 17b; Chipping Campden (1), p. 29b; Condicote, p. 39a; Cutsdean, p. 41b; Lower Slaughter, p. 78b; Saintbury (1), p. 99a; Snowshill (1), p. 103a; Swell, p. 115a; Upper Slaughter, p. 123a; Weston Subedge (1), p. 123b; (4), p. 123 b; Willersey, p. 128a.
SALT WAY: Hampnett (1), p. 62a; Northleach with Eastington (3), p. 88b; Temple Guiting, p. 116b; (10), p. 119a.
WELSH WAY: Bagendon (1), p. 7a; Barnsley (5), p. 11b.
WHITE WAY: Preface, pp. xxxv, xlv; Chedworth, p. 24a; Cirencester (6), p. 31a; North Cerney, p. 85a; (4), p. 86a; Whittington, p. 124b.
Rook Pool Piece, Romano-British settlement, Temple Guiting (2), pp. xliii, 117a.
Rosette stamped ware, *see* **Pottery: Roman.**
Rotary Querns, *see* **Querns.**
Rough Park, probable Iron Age dyke in, Cranham (1), p. 41a.
Roughground Farm, Iron Age and Romano-British settlement, Lechlade (5), pp. xliii, xlvii, lii, liii, 73b, Pl. 52.
Round Barrows, *see* **Barrows.**
Royal Camp, Doynton (1), pp. xxix, xxx, 45a.
Royal George Hotel, Roman villa near, Cowley (3), p. 40b.
Royce, Rev. D., Swell (2), p. 115b.
Rubbish dump, Bisley with Lypiatt (2), p. 16b.
Rushy Cockbury, note on p. 59.
Ryknild Street, *see* **Roman Roads.**

St. Albans, gate at Corinium, Preface, p. xxxv.
St. Augustine Farm, crop-marks of undated enclosures and linear ditches, Preston (2), p. 95a; (3), p. 95b.
St. Bartholomew's Church, *see* **Churches.**
St. Edmund's Hill, Romano-British pottery found, Upton St. Leonards, p. 123a.
St. George's Church, King's Stanley, p. 70a.
St. Matthew's Church, linear ditches N.W. of, Coates (5), p. 32a.
St. Mary's Church, Romano-British settlement E. of, Swell (1), p. 115a; *see also* **Churches.**
St. Michael's Church, Dowdeswell 'Camp' near, Preface, p. xxxiiia; Romano-British settlement W. of, Poulton (1), p. 95a; *see also* **Churches.**
St. Nicholas's Church, settlement remains near, Saintbury, p. 99a.
St. Peter's Church, Roman villa near, Frocester (1), p. 57a.
Saddle Quern, *see* **Querns.**
Saintbury, p. 99a.
,, **Camp,** earthworks, probably mediaeval, Saintbury, pp. xxx, 99a.
,, **Grounds,** Romano-British settlement, Saintbury (1), p. 99a.
Sales Lot, Neolithic long barrow with Iron Age finds, Withington, pp. l, 131a.
Salmonsbury, Iron Age and Romano-British settlement, Bourton-on-the-Water (1), pp. xxiv, xxv, xxvi, xliii, 17b; Roman remains near, (1a), p. 19b.
Salt Way, *see* **Roman Roads.**
Salonina, p. 121b; *see also* **Coins: Roman;** *and* Chronology, p. 136.
'Salperton Camp', undated enclosure, Shipton (3), p. 101b.
Samian ware, *see* **Pottery: Roman.**
Sands Farm, Romano-British burials, Dyrham and Hinton (3), p. 51b.
Sandstone, *see* **Building Materials.**
,, **tesserae,** Preface, p. xli.
Sandy Lane, Preface, p. xxiv; Charlton Kings, p. 23a; probable settlement, (1), p. 23b.
Sandy Lane Farm, probable settlement N.W. of, Siddington (7), p. 103a.
Sandywell Park, burials, Andoversford, p. 4a; coffins found, Whittington, p. 124b; Roman road near, Whittington (3), pp. xlvi, 126b.
Sapperton, p. 99a.
,, **Railway Tunnel,** coin hoard, Sapperton, p. 99a.
Sarcophagus, burial in, Bourton-on-the-Water (2d), p. 20b.
Savage, Mr. R. D. A., Preface, p. xx.
Saws, iron, Chedworth (1), p. 27b.
Saxon: *See also* **Burials** *and* **Ramparts.**
Occupation of settlement sites, Preface, pp. xxxvii, xliv, Whittington (3), p. 126b.
Scabbard Chape, bronze, Woodchester (1), p. 134b.
Scarth, H. M., Chedworth (2), p. 28a.
Scotford, Mr. J., Chedworth (6), p. 28b.
Scotsquarr Hill, undated enclosure, Harescombe (2), p. 62b.
Scrubditch, part of Bagendon (1), p. 8b.
Sculptors, in Corinium, Preface, p. xxxv.
Scythes, Barnsley (1), pp. xl, 9b.
Sealt Straet, Preface, pp. xlv–xlvii.
Selsey Hill Camp, King's Stanley, Preface, pp. xxix, xxxiiia.
Settlements: *See also* **Open Settlements.**
Discussion, Preface, pp. xxvii (Iron Age); xxxvii, xliii–xliv (Roman).
Iron Age: Bourton-on-the-Water (1), p. 17b; Southam (2), p. 107b, Pl. 41; Whittington (1), but *see* (2), p. 125a; Withington (1), p. 131b.
Iron Age and Romano-British: Bagendon (1), p. 6b, Pl. 47 and frontispiece; Lechlade (5), p. 73b, Pl. 52; Southam (3), p. 107b, Pl. 41.
Probable Iron Age and Romano-British: Charlton Kings (1), p. 23b; Great Rissington (2), p. 60a.
Early Roman (possibly military): Rodborough (1), p. 98a.
Romano-British: Ashley (1), p. 4a; (2), p. 4b; Avening (1). p. 5a; (2), p. 5a; Barrington (2), p. 12a, Pl. 50; Batsford (1), p. 12a; Bourton-on-the-Water (2), p. 20a; (2c), p. 20b; Cirencester (3), p. 30a; Coberley (3), p. 34a; Coln St. Aldwyns (2), p. 37a; Duntisbourne Rouse (4), p. 49a, Pl. 50; Farmington (2), 55b; (4), p. 56b; Frocester (3), p. 58b; Great Witcombe (2), (3), p. 61b; Haresfield (5), p. 64b; Horsley (2), p. 65b; Kingscote (1), p. 71a; Lechlade (13), p. 75b; Long Newton (1), p. 78a;

Settlements, *cont.*
Romano-British, *cont.*
Lower Slaughter (1), p. 79a, Pl. 53; (3), p. 80a; North Cerney (3), p. 86a; Northleach with Eastington (2), p. 88a; Poulton (1), p. 95a; Sherborne (1), p. 100b; Shipton (1), p. 101a; Siddington (1), p. 101b; (3), p. 102a; (6), p. 102b; Somerford Keynes (6), p. 106b; Swell (1), p. 115a; Syde (1), p. 116b; Temple Guiting (2), p. 117a; Uley (2), p. 121b; Upton St. Leonards (1), p. 123b; Whittington (2), p. 125a, Pl. 48; Willersey (4), p. 130a; Winson (1), p. 131a; Wyck Rissington (1), p. 135a; Yanworth (1), p. 135b.
Probable, Romano-British: Baunton (1), p. 13b; Bisley with Lypiatt (3), p. 16b; Blockley (1), p. 17a; Cirencester (2), p. 30a; Coberley (2), p. 34a; Compton Abdale (4), p. 38b; Cowley (5), p. 40b; Dyrham and Hinton (2), p. 51b; Elkstone (1), p. 53b; Hazleton (1), p. 65a; Marshfield (1), p. 80b; Naunton (1), p. 88b; Quenington (3), p. 97a; Saintbury (1), p. 99a; Temple Guiting (3), p. 117b; Willersey (3), p. 130a; Winson (2), p. 131a; Withington (3), p. 132a.
Roman: Kempsford (1), p. 68b; Sapperton (1), p. 99b, Pl. 49.
Probable, undated: Barnsley (4), p. 11b, Pl. 55; (5), p. 11b; Didmarton (1), p. 42b; Hatherop (1), p. 64b; Kemble (1), p. 68a, Pl. 63; Lechlade (6), p. 75a; Leonard Stanley (1), p. 78a Longborough (1), p. 78b; Maiseyhampton (1), p. 80b; Moreton-in-Marsh (1), p. 84a; Quenington (1), p. 95b; Siddington (7), p. 103a; Somerford Keynes (1), p. 104a; (2), p. 105a; (4), p. 105a.
Uncertain: Ampney Crucis (1), p. 3b; Bourton-on-the-Water (4), p. 21a; Down Ampney (2), p. 44b; Fairford (4)–(6), p. 55a, Pls. 61 and 66.
Sevenhampton, p. 100b.
Severn Valley ware, *see* **Pottery: Roman.**
Severus Alexander, *see* **Coins: Roman;** *also* Chronology, p. 136.
Sezincote, p. 100b.
Shackles, iron, Chedworth (1), p. 27b (pair); Painswick (2), p. 94a (pennanular).
Shale, Kimmeridge, pot-lid, Whittington (3), p. 128a; *see also* **Beads. Bracelets,** *and* **Rings.**
Shears, iron, Chedworth (1), p. 27b; Lower Slaughter (3), p. 80a.
Sheath, iron, Painswick (2), p. 94a.
Sheep, *see* **Animal Bones;** bells, iron, Frocester (2), pp. xl, 58a.
Sheepbridge Copse, 'Celtic' Fields E. of, Eastleach (1), p. 51b, Pl. 43; Roman road at, Eastleach (2), p. 52a.
Shellfish:
Oysters: Bagendon (1), p. 8a; (2), p. 9a; Chedworth (1), p. 27b; (6), p. 29a; Frocester (2), p. 58b; Great Witcombe (1), p. 61b; Kingscote (1), p. 72b; Lower Slaughter (1), p. 80a; Painswick (2), p. 94a; Shipton (1), p. 101a.
Mussels: Frocester (2), p. 58b.
Whelks: Frocester (2), p. 58b.
Shell-gritted pottery, *see* **Pottery: Iron Age.**
Shenberrow Hill, Hill-fort, Stanton (1), pp. xxv, xxvi, 109b, Pl. 39.
Sherborne, p. 100b.
Shipton, p. 101a.
,, **Moyne,** p. 101b.
Shipton's Grave Lane, Romano-British settlement S. of, Avening (1), p. 5a.
Shorncote, undated probable settlement, Somerford Keynes (4), p. 105a; linear ditches, undated, Somerford Keynes (5), p. 105a.
Short Wood, probable Romano-British settlement, Coberley (2), p. 34a.
Shrine, probable Romano-British, Sudeley (5), p. 114b.
Shurdington, p. 101b.
Siddington, p. 101b.
Sidelands Grove, 'Celtic' Fields, Eastleach (1), p. 51b, Pl. 43.
Silvanus, *see* **Gods.**
Silver, *see* **Coins: Iron Age, Fibulae, Rings,** *and* **Spoons.**
Sisters Farm, undated trackway and enclosures W. of, South Cerney (3), p. 106a.
Slad, Roman coins and flue tile found, Miserden, p. 84a.
Slag, iron, Great Rissington (1), p. 59b; Guiting Power, p. 62a; Hazleton (1), p. 65a; Lower Slaughter (1), p. 79b; Stroud, p. 112a.
Slate, *see* **Building Materials.**
Slaughter Bridge, Roman road at, Bourton-on-the-Water (3), pp. xlv, 21a; undated enclosure, Lower Slaughter (2), p. 80a, Pl. 55.

Slingstone, clay, Shipton (1), p. 101a.
Slutswell, probable Romano-British settlement, Elkstone (1), pp. xxxvii, 53b.
Smallhope Cottages, 'Celtic' Fields, Compton Abdale (6), p. 38b.
Snakethread glass, Great Witcombe (1), p. 61b.
Snowshill, p. 103a.
,, **Hill,** Roman road runs over, Bourton-on-the-Hill (1), p. 17b; Snowshill (1), p. 103a.
Sodbury, p. 103a.
,, **Camp,** Hill-fort, Sodbury (1), pp. xxv, xxvi, 103a, Pl. 34.
Soil-Marks: Preface, p. xxxiii; Eastleach (4), p. 52b; Gotherington (2), p. 59a; Temple Guiting (9), p. 119a; Winson (1), p. 131a.
Somerford Keynes, p. 104a.
Somerford Road, Chesterton, indications of villa, Cirencester (7), p. 31b.
South Cerney, p. 105b.
,, **Farm,** probable undated settlement, Hatherop (1), p. 64b.
Southam, p. 106a.
Southrop, p. 109a.
Spade-irons, Chedworth (1), p. 27b; Colesbourne (2), p. 36a.
Spear-heads, Lower Slaughter (3), p. 80a; Rodmarton, p. 98a.
Spelt, *see* **Corn.**
Spindle whorls, Bourton-on-the-Water (1), p. 19b; Farmington (1), p. 55b; Temple Guiting (3), p. 117b; Whittington (3), p. 128a.
Spit, ornamental, iron, Batsford (1), p. 13a.
Spoon-bit, iron, Whittington (2), p. 126b.
Spoons:
BRONZE: Chedworth (1), p. 27b; Coln St. Aldwyns (tinned) (2), p. 27a; Lower Slaughter (3), p. 80a.
METAL: Wotton-under-Edge, p. 134b.
SILVER: Chedworth (1), p. 27b; Woodchester, p. 132a.
Spoonley Farm, Roman finds, Sudeley, p. 112b.
,, **Wood,** Roman villa, Sudeley (4), pp. xxxvii, xlii, 113b, Pls. 14, 15, 24 and 30.
Spratsgate Lane, undated enclosures and linear ditches, Somerford Keynes (3), p. 105a, Pl. 59.
Spring Hill, Romano-British settlement, Lower Slaughter (3), pp. xxiv, xliii, 80a.
Springhill, cist burial, Compton Abdale (5), p. 38b.
Spry, Mr. N., Preface, p. xx; Kingscote (1), p. 71a.
Spurs, metal, Bourton-on-the-Water (2b), p. 20b.
Stables, The, Iron Age settlement, Southam (2), pp. xxiv, 107b, Pl. 40.
'Stainbarrow Camp', Notgrove, pp. xxx, 88b.
Staites Brake or Hinchwick Camp, Condicote, pp. xxx, xxxiib, 39a.
Stamp, bronze, ornamental, Temple Guiting (3), p. 117b.
Stamped ware, *see* **Pottery: Iron Age.**
Stanborough Fields, undated enclosure, Notgrove (1), pp. lii, 91a; *see also* **Field Names.**
Stanborough Lane, probable *straet*, Naunton, pp. lii, 84b; undated enclosure, Naunton (2), p. 85a.
Stancombe, Romano-British settlement, Duntisbourne Rouse (4), pp. xxxvii, xliii, liii, 49a, Pl. 50.
Stancombe, Roman villa at, Stinchcombe (1), pp. liii, 111a.
,, **Park,** stone robbed from, Stinchcombe (1), p. 111b.
,, **Wood,** Sudeley, Preface, p. lii; relief of soldier, Winchcombe, p. 130a; scatter of pottery (Romano-British), Winchcombe, p. 130b.
Standish, p. 109b.
,, **Wood,** cross-ridge dyke, *see* Randwick (1), p. 97b.
Stanton, p. 109b.
Stanway, p. 110b.
Star Farm, possible Iron Age enclosures, Avening, p. 4b.
Starvall, Romano-British settlement, Farmington (4), pp. xliii, 56b.
Stater, *see* **Coins: Iron Age.**
Statuettes: (bronze) Jupiter Dolichenus, Preface, p. xxxvi; Mars, Whittington (2), p. 126a; (stone) Sudeley (2), p. 113b; (niche for) Chedworth (1), p. 27b.
Steelyards:
BRONZE: Great Witcombe (1), p. 61b.
IRON: Batsford (1), p. 13a; Frocester (2), p. 58a; Swell (1), p. 115b.
Stevens, Mr. D. G., Lechlade (13), p. 75b.
Stinchcombe, p. 111a.
Stockend, Roman villa, Harescombe (1), pp. liii, 62a.
Stockwood(s), Roman villa, Colesbourne (2), pp. liii, 35b, Pls. 7 and 27.
Stone, *see* **Basin, Building Materials, Cosmetic Pallet, Cresset Lamp, Eagle, Grinder, Idols, Polisher, Querns, Statuettes, Table Top, Troughs, Weight,** *and* **Whetstones.**
Stonehouse, p. 111b.
Stonesfield slates, *see* **Building Materials.**
Stony Cockbury, note on p. 59.
Storage Pits, Bourton-on-the-Water (1), p. 19a.
Stow Bridge, Moreton-in-Marsh (1), p. 84a.
Stow-on-the-Wold, p. 111b.
Strapping, iron, (Roman), Chedworth (6), p. 29a.
Stratton, skeleton found, Cirencester, p. 29b; enclosure W. of, Cirencester (4), p. 30b, Pl. 65.
Street (straet or stret), Saxon names, *see* Preface, pp. xlv–xlviii.
Street Acres, *see* **Field Names.**
Streetfold, *see* **Field Names;** terrace-way at, Yanworth, p. 135a.
Strip Lynchets, Dowdeswell, Preface, p. xxxiiia, Pl. 38; Hawkesbury, p. xxxiiia, Pl. 68.
Stroud, p. 112a.
Stroud Museum: Adlestrop, p. 1b; Avening (2), p. 5b; Bisley with Lypiatt (1)–(3), p. 16b; Chalford (1), p. 23a; Haresfield (3), p. 64a; Horsley, p. 65a; King's Stanley, p. 70a; Kingscote, p. 70b; (1), p. 72b; (2), p. 73a; Lechlade (5), p. 75a; Minchinhampton, p. 81a; 82b; (1), p. 83a; (7), p. 84a; Miserden, p. 84a; Painswick (2), p. 94a; Rodborough (1), p. 98a; Rodmarton (1), p. 99a; Sapperton, p. 99b; Stroud, p. 112a; Uley (1), p. 121b; (2), p. 123a; Whittington (2), p. 126b; Woodchester (1), p. 134b.
Stucco, *see* **Building Materials.**
Studs, iron, Leckhampton, p. 77a; *see also* **Military Equipment.**
Styli: Barnsley (1), p. 9b; (bronze) Chedworth (1), p. 27b; (iron) Kingscote (1), p. 72b; Whittington (2), p. 126b.
Subereburia, former name for Haresfield (2), note on p. 64.
Sudeley, p. 112a.
,, **Castle,** Roman finds, Sudeley, p. 112a.
,, **Hill,** undated enclosure and ditch, Temple Guiting (10), p. 119a.
,, **Lanes Farm,** tesserae found, Sudeley, p. 112a.
Sulmonnes Burg, Salmonsbury, Bourton-on-the-Water (1), p. 18b.
Summerhill, probable Romano-British settlement, Naunton (1), p. 84b.
Sunhill, undated probable settlement, Maiseyhampton (1), p. 80b.
Surgical instrument, bronze, Weston Subedge, p. 123b.
Swain, Mr. E. J., Rodmarton (1), p. 99a.
Swell, p. 115a.
,, **Hill Homestead,** Roman coins and pottery found, Swell, p. 115a.
Swill Brook, undated probable settlement, Somerford Keynes (1), p. 104a.
Swords, bronze, Gotherington (1), p. 59a.
Syde, p. 116b.
Symond's Hall Farm, Romano-British objects found, Wotton-under-Edge, p. 134b.
,, ,, **Hill,** votive objects found, Kingscote, p. 70b.
Syreford Gravel Pit, Iron Age settlement, Whittington (1) and (2), p. 125a, Pl. 48.

Table Top, stone, Chedworth (1), p. 27b.
Talbot Rice, D., Broadwell (1), p. 21b.
Tanks, lead, Bourton-on-the-Water (2a), p. 20a.
Tanning, evidence of, Frocester (2), pp. xl, 57b.
Tasciovanus, p. 19b; *see also* **Coins: Iron Age;** *and* Chronology, p. 136.
Tegulae, *see* **Building Materials.**
Temple Guiting, p. 116b.
Temples:
Preface, p. l.
Chedworth (4), p. 28a; Whittington (2), p. 126a.
POSSIBLE: Chedworth (2), p. 28a; Lower Slaughter (1), p. 79a.
Terra Nigra, *see* **Pottery: Roman.**
,, **Rubra,** *see* **Pottery: Roman.**
Terret, iron, Fairford, p. 54b.
Tessellated pavements, *see* **Building Materials.**
Tesserae, glass, Chedworth (2), pp. xli, 28a; *see also* **Building Materials.**
Tetbury, p. 119b.
,, **Upton,** p. 119b.
,, **Road,** probable barrow N. of, Corinium, Preface, p. xxxvi.
Tetrici, *see* **Coins: Roman;** *also* Chronology, p. 136.

Theodosius, *see* **Coins: Roman;** *also* Chronology, p. 136.
Thrupp, p. 120a.
Tiles, *see* **Building Materials.**
Tiltups End, Romano-British villa, Horsley (1), p. 65a.
Todenham, p. 120a.
Tog Hill, Mediaeval earthwork, Cold Ashton, p. xxix.
Tombstones, gabled and inscribed, Beverstone, p. 13b; Horsley, p. 65a.
Tongs, spring, iron, Bagendon (1), p. 7b.
Tools, general, Barnsley (1), p. 9b; *see also* **Bill-hooks, Chisels, Gouge, Hatchet, Hooks, Plough coulter, Plumb-bob, Pruning hook, Rake, Saws, Scythes, Shears, Spade-irons, Spoon-bit, Spring tongs, Steelyards,** *and* **Trowel.**
Tooth-pick, bronze, Compton Abdale (1), p. 38b.
Topography, Preface, p. xxiii.
Tormarton, p. 120a.
Torque, gold, Cowley (1), p. 39b.
Tracks, ditched:
List of, Preface, p. xlviii.
Discussion, Preface, pp. xlv–xlviii.
Trajan, *see* **Coins: Roman;** *also* Chronology, p. 136.
,, **Decius,** p. 13b; *see also* **Coins: Roman;** *and* Chronology, p. 136.
Trajanic ware, *see* **Pottery: Roman.**
Travell, Miss M., Preface, p. xx; Lower Slaughter, p. 79a; (3), p. 80a.
Trench, The, geological phenomenon, Bisley with Lypiatt, p. 15b.
Trewsbury Hill-fort, Coates (1), pp. xxv, 32a.
Triton plaque, in black samian ware, Lechlade (5), p. 75a.
Troughs, stone, Barnsley (1), p. 9b; Northleach with Eastington (2), p. 88a.
Trowel, mason's, iron, Whittington (2), p. 126b.
Tubes, blue glass, Woodchester (1), p. 134a.
Tufa: *See also* **Voussoirs.**
Preface, p. xl; Great Witcombe (1), p. 61a.
Tump Barn, probable undated settlement, Didmarton (1), p. 42b.
'Tunnel Mouth Camp', Roman settlement, Sapperton (1), pp. xliii, 99b, Pl. 49.
Turkdean, p. 121a.
Turk's Hill Camp, Notgrove, p. 88b.
Tweezers, bronze, Cowley (1), p. 39b; Kingscote (1), p. 72b.
Tyley Bottom, Wotton-under-Edge, p. 134b.

Uley, p. 121a.
,, **Bury,** Hill-fort, Uley (1), pp. xxv, xxvi, 121b, Pls. 32–3.
Unguent bottle, glass, Roman, Hawling, p. 65a.
Upper Coscombe, Stanway, pp. xxix, xxx, xxxiiib, 110b, Pl. 67.
,, **Slaughter,** p. 123a.
Upton, coffin found, Bitton, p. 17a; probable Romano-British settlement, Blockley (1), pp. xxxvii, xliii, 17a.
,, **House,** Romano-British villa?, Tetbury Upton (1), p. 119b.
,, **St. Leonards,** p. 123a.
Urbs Roma, p. 94a; *see also* **Coins: Roman.**
Urns, *see* **Burials.**

Valens, *see* **Coins: Roman;** *also* Chronology, p. 136.
Valentinian, *see* **Coins: Roman;** *also* Chronology, p. 136.
Valerian, p. 132a; *see also* **Coins: Roman;** *and* Chronology, p. 136.
Vase, fluted pedestal, Bourton-on-the-Water (1), p. 19a.
Verulamium, gate at Corinium, Preface, p. xxxv.
Vespasian, p. 126b; *see also* **Coins: Roman;** *and* Chronology, p. 136.
Vessels, (green glass) Lower Slaughter (1), p. 79v; Woodchester (1), p. 134a; (lead) Withington (2), p. 132a.
Victorinus, p. 15a; *see also* **Coins: Roman;** *and* Chronology, p. 136.
Village, *see* **Mediaeval.**
Villas:
Preface, pp. xxxviii–xlii.
List of, p. xlii.
Viner, Mr. D. J., Preface, p. xx.
Votive objects: *see also* **Gods.**
Preface, pp. l–li; Batsford, p. 12a; Baunton (1), p. 13b; Bisley with Lypiatt, p. 15a; Chalford (1), p. 23a; Chedworth (1), p. 27b; (2), p. 28a; Colesbourne (2), p. 36b; Daglingworth, p. 41b; Hampnett, p. 62a; Kingscote, p. 70b; King's Stanley, p. 70a; Lechlade (5), p. 75a; Lower Slaughter, p. 79b; Sudeley, p. 112a; Uley (2),

Votive objects, *cont.*
p. 121b; Whittington (2), p. 126b; Woodchester (1), p. 134a; Wotton-under-Edge, p. 134b.
Voussoirs:
TUFA: Barnsley (1), p. 9b; Farmington (1), p. 55b.
EARTHENWARE: Chedworth (1), pp. xl, 27b.

Wadfield, Roman villa at, Sudeley (2), pp. xlii, liii, 112b, Pl. 13.
Wall-Well, probable Romano-British settlement, Withington (3), pp. xliii, 132a, *see also* note on p. 131.
Walrond, Mr. L. J., Kingscote (1), p. 70b.
Wapley Hill-fort, Herefordshire, cf. Kimsbury, Painswick (1), pp. xxvi, 91b, Pl. 37.
'Warren, The', Roman material found, Boxwell with Leighterton, p. 21b.
Watch-tower, stone, Preface, p. xxxv.
Watercombe Farm, undated enclosure, Elkstone (2), p. 54b, Pl. 59.
,, **House,** material from, Bisley with Lypiatt (1), p. 16b.
Webster, Dr. Graham, Preface, p. xx; Barnsley (1), p. 16b.
Weeds, Upton St. Leonards (1), p. 123b.
Weight, stone, Fairford, p. 54b.
Wells, *see* **Building Remains.**
'Welsh Way', *see* **Roman Roads;** settlement near, Barnsley (5), p. 11b.
West Grange House, Roman finds, Stroud, p. 112a.
,, **Hill,** Romano-British settlement, Uley (2), pp. lii, 121b.
,, **Littleton Down,** 'Celtic' Fields, Tormarton (1), p. 120, Pl. 43.
,, **Park,** Roman finds, Woodchester, p. 132a.
Westchestle, Aldsworth, Preface, p. lii.
Westcote, p. 123b.
Westhams Copse, undated enclosures and linear ditches, Driffield (2), p. 47a.
Westonbirt with Lasborough, p. 123b.
Weston Subedge, p. 123b.
Wet Chessells, Driffield, Preface, p. lii, and p. 45b.
Wetstone Bridge, undated rectilinear enclosure, Down Ampney (4), p. 45a.
Wheat, *see* **Corn.**
Whelford, enclosures and linear ditches, Kempsford (4), p. 68b.
Whelks, p. 58b; *see also* **Shellfish.**
Whetstone, Kingscote (1), p. 72b.
White Way, *see* **Roman Roads.**
Whiteshill, p. 124a.
Whiteshoots Hill, Romano-British settlement on, Bourton-on-the-Water (2), p. 20a; (2c), pp. xliii, liii, 20b.
Whittington, p. 124a.
,, **Court,** Roman villa, Whittington (3), pp. xxxix, 126b, Pls. 9 and 30.
,, **Wood,** Roman and Romano-British objects found, Whittington, p. 124a.
'Wickham', former name for Whittington (2), p. 125b, Pl. 48.
Willersey, p. 128a.
,, **Barn,** probable Romano-British settlement near, Willersey (3), p. 130a.
,, **Hill,** Hill-fort, Willersey (1), pp. xxv, xxvii, 128a.
Williamstrip Park, Coln St. Aldwyns (3), p. 37a.
Winchcombe, p. 130a.
Window Glass, Preface, p. xl; Bisley with Lypiatt (1), p. 16a; Chedworth (1), p. 27b; Colesbourne (2), p. 36a; Frocester (1), p. 57a; Great Witcombe (1), p. 61b; Painswick (2), p. 94a; Sudeley (4), p. 114b.
Windrush, p. 130b.
,, **Camp,** Hill-fort, Windrush (1), pp. xxv, xxvi, 130b.
Winson, p. 131a.
Winstone, p. 131a.
Withington, p. 131a.
,, **Wood,** p. 131a; Roman villa N. of, Withington (2), p. 131b, Pls. 13–16 and 51.
Wire, steel, Bagendon (1), p. 8a.
Woeful Dane Bottom, possible bank and ditch near, Minchinhampton (6), p. 83b.
Wood, cherry, Great Witcombe (1), p. 61b.
,, **House,** Iron Age finds, Guiting Power, p. 62a.
Woodchester, p. 132a.
Woodleigh House, carved bearded head, Coaley, p. 31b.

Woodmancote, p. 134b.
Woodmancote, Hill-fort, North Cerney (2), pp. xxv, lii, 85b, Pl. 36; Roman building, North Cerney (3), pp. xliii, 86a.
'Woolston Camp', probable name for Oxenton Knolls, Oxenton (1), p. 91a.
Worcester Museum: Willersey (3), p. 130a.
Worm's Farm, Romano-British settlement, Siddington (6), pp. xliii, 102b.
Wotton-under-Edge, p. 134b.
Wyck Rissington, p. 135a.
Wyckhill House, pottery fragments found, Wyck Rissington, p. 135a.
Wycomb, Romano-British settlement, Whittington (2), pp. xxxviii, xliv, xlvii, l, lii, liii, 125a, Pl. 48.
Wylye Down, Wiltshire, cf. Preface, p. xlix.

Yanworth, p. 135a.
,, **Wood,** Romano-British settlement, Yanworth (1), p. 135b.
Young, George, gravel-pit, Lower Slaughter (1), p. 79a.

Printed in England for Her Majesty's Stationery Office by University Press, Oxford
Dd 505950 K12 3/76